W9-AFB-340

Historical Statistics of the States of the United States

Historical Statistics of the States of the United States

TWO CENTURIES OF THE CENSUS, 1790–1990

Compiled by
Donald B. Dodd

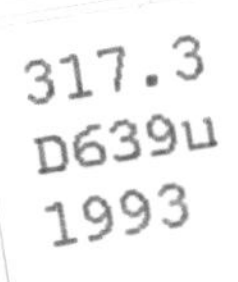

Greenwood Press
Westport, Connecticut • London

Library of Congress Cataloging-in-Publication Data

Historical statistics of the states of the United States : two
centuries of the census, 1790-1990 / compiled by Donald B. Dodd.
p. cm.
Includes bibliographical references and index.
ISBN 0-313-28309-5 (alk. paper)
1. United States—Statistics—History. 2. United States—
Population—Statistics—History. 3. United States—Census—
History. I. Dodd, Donald B.
HA214.H57 1993
317.3—dc20 93-25014

British Library Cataloguing in Publication Data is available.

Library of Congress Catalog Card Number: 93-25014
ISBN: 0-313-28309-5

First published in 1993

Greenwood Press, 88 Post Road West, Westport, CT 06881
An imprint of Greenwood Publishing Group, Inc.

Printed in the United States of America

The paper used in this book complies with the
Permanent Paper Standard issued by the National
Information Standards Organization (Z39.48-1984).

10 9 8 7 6 5 4 3 2

Contents

Preface

Historical Statistics of the States of the United States (HSSUS 93) is a census-focused compilation of state-level population, agriculture, and manufacturing data for the fifty states and the District of Columbia. Populations of the largest 1990 cities, 1790-1990, also included, do not fit the title but do match the basic purpose of the book--to fill the gap in historical statistics between United States data in Historical Statistics of the United States: Colonial Times to 1970 (Washington, D.C.: GPO, 1975) and the county-level data compiled by the Interuniversity Consortium for Political and Social Research (ICPSR) at the University of Michigan.

HSSUS 93 was prepared from the original statistics noted in the endnotes, but much of the organization is patterned after (although improved upon) two out-of-print regional volumes by the University of Alabama Press--Historical Statistics of the South (1973) and Historical Statistics of the Midwest (1976). As the endnotes document, the primary source of information is the United States Bureau of the Census. Agricultural Statistics, 1992, a Department of Agriculture publication, and Statistical Abstracts of the United States, 1991, a census publication that reprints statistics from census and non-census sources, were used for 1989-1990 data.

HSSUS 93 takes an historical approach by proceeding chronologically from then to now, i.e. 1790 to the present for population and 1850 to the present for agriculture and manufacturing. The basic method was to examine the 1850-1860 censuses to see what was available that could be compiled from the 1850-1860s to the present. In general, the historical method expedited selecting items for inclusion which were comparable for a number of consecutive enumerations because of the practicality of using the traditional definitions for as long as possible. Finding workable statistics for comparison for several censuses, however, was a major difficulty due to changed definitions. In some cases items were included despite changing definitions because they were too basic to a major category of information to exclude--number of farms to the agriculture section; number of manufacturing establishments to the manufacturing section; and the urban/rural population to the population section. Different definitions of a farm, a manufacturing establishment, and the urban/rural population occupies considerable space in the Glossary of Terms.

The Glossary reprints census explanations and the Census Bureau's analysis of the impact of the different definitions on the comparability of the data. In all cases the statistics are useful to the user interested in that specific year. Almost all data can be safely compared for several years. Not all of the items are comparable from 1850 to 1990.

A basic problem of 19th century census work is that for the 1790-1900 years--more than one-half the census's 200-year existence--there was not a Census Bureau. The census organization was assembled before each 10-year census and disbanded after the work was done. Long-range planning obviously suffered and apparently thoroughness of work too. Many errors appeared in the 1790-1840 population schedule. The revised figures appeared in 1870. The 1870 population census was judged seriously incomplete for the southern states and was revised upward in 1890. Due to errors in the original volumes and the census policy of correcting errors in subsequent censuses, the latest possible census reports were sought for the data herein. As a result the Census of 1890 figures for 1840 were preferred to the 1840 figures. As the source chronologically closer to information used is normally considered best in historical method, the point should be emphasized. HSSUS 93 deliberately uses the census source farthest from the original census. The data herein was taken from the specific census report indicated in the endnote and is represented as being only as accurate as the source cited. The information may not match information in sources not cited, e.g. earlier census reports.

HSSUS does not replace any census publication. Historical Statistics of the United States: Colonial Times to 1970 (HSUS 70 [1200 pages in two parts]) is the source to use for national historical statistics. HSUS 70 collects data from hundreds of sources and makes it available in a single source. It also includes text annotations that guide the user to sources of greater detail. Further the annotations define terms used in the tables and include essential qualifying statements. See the Glossary of Terms herein for examples. The annual volumes of Statistical Abstracts of the United States (986 pp. in 1991) bring Historical Statistics of the United States up to date. Historical Statistics of the United States and other more in-depth census reports contain explanations of terms often not adequately explained in Statistical Abstracts (or HSSUS 93). HSUS 70 does the best job of "standing on its own," but the specialist must dig deeper, especially ones who seek to compare data over long periods of time. Check the Glossary of Terms for reprints of Census Bureau qualifying statements on this type of use. Statistical Abstracts is also the best single source for contemporary data. The annual Agricultural Statistics volumes by the Department of Agriculture provide a similar service for that topic. HSSUS 93 supplements these three publications by presenting state-level population, agriculture, and manufacturing data and city population data on a historical basis.

Explanations of terms are in the Glossary of Terms. Some of the more important are definitions of race, urban population, farms, improved land in farms, cropland harvested, farm owners, livestock, value of livestock, manufacturing establishments, capital, and value added by manufacture. Endnotes document the source of information. Footnotes are explanatory notes. An asterisk is in front of alphabetically-lettered footnotes to clearly distinguish them from the numbered endnotes.

Items which refer to percent of a total mean the individual state's percentage of the national total. National totals in the United States tables were taken from the sources noted in the endnotes. Although from the same source the state totals were derived, the cumulative state totals do not always add up to the United States totals, e.g. the 1967 U.S. totals for manufacturing were based on industry rather than state detail and this basic difference was compounded by independent corrections to the industry and state tabulations. Another reason the U.S. totals do not match the cumulative state totals on all the tables is independent rounding.

No attempt to draw inferences from the data has been made. However, the data have potential for correlative and inferential statistics.

In collecting the raw data for HSSUS, Auburn University at Montgomery (AUM) librarians Betty Thames, Ricky Best, Jean Filson, Rita Mitchell, and Debbie West were of particular assistance. As AUM is a Federal Depository for government documents, most of the sources were available there. The librarian of the Office of the Air Force Historian at Bolling AFB, Washington D.C., Yvonne Kinkaid, helped obtain 1990 data. Brenda Powers of the Department of Agriculture was especially helpful.

Several individuals helped prepare the data for publication. Suzanne Clemens began the word processing and inputted much of the population data. Linda Smith ably completed most of the remaining word processing in the first draft and the initial revisions. Pamela Tyler assisted Linda in the latter stages and made major revisions responding to critiques by independent proofers and Greenwood editors. Participants in transcribing data and computing calculations include: Barbara and Micke Arant, Diane Farrior, Gayle and Christy Fulmer, Judy Hall, Frank Parquette, Jr., Ada Richardson, Pamela Tyler, and Elaine Wiggins. Proofreading was done at all stages of the project by all participants but independent proofing of several drafts was done by Vicki Adair, Lloyd Cornett, Judy Hall, Julie Haynes, Meredith Maddox, and Pamela Tyler. Amy Bartlett-Dodd helped coordinate the above work and participated in all phases except word processing. The project was assisted by a grant from AUM Faculty Research Council. I am particularly grateful for the patience and guidance throughout the project by Cynthia Harris, General Editor of Reference Books, Greenwood Press; and in the later stages, for the technical thoroughness of the Production Editor, Margaret Hogan.

Due to the complexity of the changes in the census enumerations during the past 200 years, as well as the bulk of statistical materials, there probably will be errors. Subsequent editions will correct errors noted by readers and incorporate helpful suggestions. Recommendations and comments should be sent to the author in care of: Greenwood Publishing Group; 88 Post Road West; Westport, Connecticut 06881-5007.

Donald B. Dodd

Historical Statistics of the States of the United States

General Population Statistics, 1790–1990

GENERAL POPULATION STATISTICS, 1790-1990										
ALABAMA										
Item No.		1790 (or 1789)	1800	1810	1820	1830	1840	1850	1860	1870
1.	Population[1]	---	1,250[*e]	9,046[*e]	127,901	309,527	590,756	771,623	964,201	996,992
2.	Decennial rates of increase in population over preceding census[2]	---	---	623.7	1,314.0	142.0	90.9	30.6	25.0	3.4
3.	Increase in population over previous census[1,3]	---	---	7,796	118,855[*b]	181,626	281,229	180,867	192,578	32,791
4.	Percent distribution of population[4]	---	---	0.1	1.3	2.4	3.5	3.3	3.1	2.6
5.	Population per square mile of land area[5,6]	---	---	---	---	---	---	15.0	18.8	19.4
6.	Membership of House of Representatives at each apportionment[7]	---	---	1	3	5	7	7	6	8
7.	White population[8,9,10]	---	---	---	85,451	190,406	335,185	426,514	526,271	521,384
8.	Percentage increase in white population over preceding census[9,10,11]	---	---	---	---	122.8	76.0	27.2	23.4	-0.9
9.	Black population[8,9,10]	---	---	---	42,450	119,121	255,571	345,109	437,770	475,510
10.	Percentage increase in Black population over preceding census[9,10,11,12,13,14]	---	---	---	---	180.6	114.5	35.0	26.8	8.6
11.	Percent Black in total population[1,8,9,10,14,15]	---	---	---	33.2[*a]	38.5[*a]	43.3[*a]	44.7	45.4	47.7
12.	Number of slaves in the area enumerated in 1790 and in the added area[16]	---	494[*f]	2,565[*g]	41,879	117,549	253,532	342,844	435,080	---
13.	Urban population[17]	---	---	---	---	3,194	12,672	35,179	48,901	62,700
14.	Percent urban increase over preceding census[17]	---	---	---	---	---	296.7	177.6	39.0	28.2
15.	Rural population[17]	---	1,250	9,046	127,901	306,333	578,084	736,444	915,300	934,292
16.	Percent rural increase over preceding census[17]	---	---	623.7	1,313.9	139.5	88.7	27.4	24.3	2.1
17.	Percent of urban to total population[17]	---	---	---	---	1.0	2.1	4.6	5.1	6.3
18.	Percent of rural to total population[17]	---	100.0	100.0	100.0	99.0	97.9	95.4	94.9	93.7

GENERAL POPULATION STATISTICS, 1790-1990 (Cont.)												
ALABAMA												
Item No.	1880	1890	1900	1910	1920	1930	1940	1950	1960	1970	1980	1990
1.	1,262,505	1,513,401	1,828,697	2,138,093	2,348,174	2,646,248	2,832,961	3,061,743	3,266,740	3,444,165	3,893,888	4,040,587
2.	26.6	19.9	20.8	16.9	9.8	12.7	7.1	8.1	6.7	5.4	13.1	3.8
3.	265,513	250,896[*b]	315,296[*b]	309,396[*a]	210,081[*a]	298,074[*a]	186,713[*a]	228,782[*a]	204,997	177,425	449,723[*a]	146,699
4.	2.5	2.4	2.4	2.3	2.2	2.1	2.1	2.0	1.8	1.7	---	1.6
5.	24.6	29.5	35.7	41.7	45.8	51.8	55.5	59.9	64.2	67.9	76.7	79.6
6.	8	9	9	10	10	9	9	9	8	7	7	---
7.	662,185	833,718	1,001,152	1,228,832	1,447,032	1,700,844	1,849,097	2,079,591	2,283,609	2,533,831	2,869,688	2,975,797
8.	27.0	25.9	20.1	22.7[*a]	17.8	17.5[*a]	8.7[*a]	12.5[*a]	9.8[*a]	11.0[*a]	13.3[*a]	3.7[*b]
9.	600,103	678,489	827,307	908,282	900,652	944,834	983,290	979,617	980,271	903,467	995,623	1,020,705
10.	26.2	13.1	21.9	9.8[*a]	-0.8	4.9	4.1[*a]	-0.4[*a]	0.1[*a]	-7.8[*a]	10.2	2.5[*b]
11.	47.53	44.8	45.2[*a]	42.5[*a]	38.4[*a]	35.7[*a]	34.7[*a]	32.0[*a]	30.0[*a]	26.2	25.6	25.3
12.	---	---	---	---	---	---	---	---	---	---	---	---
13.	68,518	152,235	216,714	370,431	509,317	744,273	855,941	1,228,209[*c] 1,340,937[*d]	1,689,417[*c] 1,791,721[*d]	2,011,941	2,337,713	---
14.	9.3	122.2	42.4	70.9	37.5	46.1	15.0	43.5[*c] ---[*d]	37.6[*c] 33.6[*d]	12.3	15.9	---
15.	1,193,987	1,361,166	1,611,983	1,767,622	1,838,857	1,901,975	1,977,020	1,833,534[*c] 1,720,806[*d]	1,577,323[*c] 1,475,019[*d]	1,432,224	1,556,175	---
16.	27.8	14.0	18.4	9.7	4.0	3.4	3.9	-7.3[*c] ---[*d]	-14.0[*c] -14.3[*d]	-2.9	9.1	---
17.	5.4	10.1	11.9	17.3	21.7	28.1	30.2	40.1[*c] 43.8[*d]	51.7[*c] 54.8[*d]	58.4	60.0	---
18.	94.6	89.9	88.1	82.7	78.3	71.9	69.8	59.9[*c] 56.2[*d]	48.3[*c] 45.2[*d]	41.6	40.0	---

[a] Percentage computed by compiler from data herein. See endnotes for source of data.
[b] Percentage computed by compiler from data herein is different from percentage given in source. The above percentage is the percentage computed by compiler.
[c] Previous urban definition (pre-1950).
[d] Current urban definition (1950 and after; see Glossary of Terms).
[e] Population of those parts of Mississippi Territory now in present state.
[f] Reported as for Washington County, Mississippi Territory.
[g] Reported as for Baldwin, Madison and Washington counties, Mississippi Territory.

GENERAL POPULATION STATISTICS, 1790-1990										
ALASKA										
Item No.		1790 (or 1789)	1800	1810	1820	1830	1840	1850	1860	1870
1.	Population[1]	---	---	---	---	---	---	---	---	---
2.	Decennial rates of increase in population over preceding census[2]	---	---	---	---	---	---	---	---	---
3.	Increase in population over previous census[1,3]	---	---	---	---	---	---	---	---	---
4.	Percent distribution of population[4]	---	---	---	---	---	---	---	---	---
5.	Population per square mile of land area[5,6]	---	---	---	---	---	---	---	---	---
6.	Membership of House of Representatives at each apportionment[7]	---	---	---	---	---	---	---	---	---
7.	White population[8,9,10]	---	---	---	---	---	---	---	---	---
8.	Percentage increase in white population over preceding census[9,10,11]	---	---	---	---	---	---	---	---	---
9.	Black population[8,9,10]	---	---	---	---	---	---	---	---	---
10.	Percentage increase in Black population over preceding census[9,10,11,12,13,14]	---	---	---	---	---	---	---	---	---
11.	Percent Black in total population[1,8,9,10,14,15]	---	---	---	---	---	---	---	---	---
12.	Number of slaves in the area enumerated in 1790 and in the added area[16]	---	---	---	---	---	---	---	---	---
13.	Urban population[17]	---	---	---	---	---	---	---	---	---
14.	Percent urban increase over preceding census[17]	---	---	---	---	---	---	---	---	---
15.	Rural population[17]	---	---	---	---	---	---	---	---	---
16.	Percent rural increase over preceding census[17]	---	---	---	---	---	---	---	---	---
17.	Percent of urban to total population[17]	---	---	---	---	---	---	---	---	---
18.	Percent of rural to total population[17]	---	---	---	---	---	---	---	---	---

GENERAL POPULATION STATISTICS, 1790-1990 (Cont.)

ALASKA

Item No.	1880	1890	1900	1910	1920	1930	1940	1950	1960	1970	1980	1990
1.	33,426	32,052	63,592	64,356	55,036	59,278[*e]	72,524[*e]	128,643	226,167	300,000	402,000	550,043
2.	---	-4.1	98.4	1.2	-14.5	7.7	22.3[*f]	77.4[*g]	75.8	32.8	32.8	36.9
3.	---	1,374	31,540	764[*a]	-9,320[*a]	4,242[*a]	13,246[*a]	56,119[*a]	97,524	73,833[*b]	102,000[*a]	148,043[*b]
4.	0.1	0.1	0.1	0.1	0.1	0.1	0.1	0.1	0.1	0.1	---	0.2
5.	---	---	---	---	0.1	0.1	0.1	0.2	0.4	0.5	0.7	1.0
6.	---	---	---	---	---	---	---	1	1	1	1	---
7.	---	---	---	---	---	---	---	92,808	174,546	236,767	308,455	415,492
8.	---	---	---	---	---	---	---	---	88.1[*a]	35.6[*a]	30.3[*a]	34.7[*b]
9.	---	---	---	---	---	---	---	[*h]	6,771	8,911	13,619	22,451
10.	---	---	---	---	---	---	---	---	---	31.6[*a]	52.8	64.9[*b]
11.	---	---	---	---	---	---	---	---	3.0[*a]	3.0	3.4	4.1
12.	---	---	---	---	---	---	---	---	---	---	---	---
13.	---	---	15,605	6,141	3,058	7,839	17,374	34,262	85,767	145,512	258,567	---
14.	---	---	---	-60.6	-50.2	156.3	121.6	97.2	150.3	69.7	51.2	---
15.	33,426	32,052	47,987	58,215	51,978	51,439	55,150	94,381	140,400	154,870	143,284	---
16.	---	-4.1	49.7	21.3	-10.7	-1.0	7.2	71.1	48.8	10.3	10.8	---
17.	---	---	24.5	9.5	5.6	13.2	24.0	26.6	37.9	48.4	64.3	---
18.	100.0	100.0	75.5	90.5	94.4	86.8	76.0	73.4	62.1	51.6	35.7	---

[a] Percentage computed by compiler from data herein. See endnotes for source of data.
[b] Percentage computed by compiler from data herein is different from percentage given in source. The above percentage is the percentage computed by compiler.
[c] Previous urban definition (pre-1950).
[d] Current urban definition (1950 and after; see Glossary of Terms).
[e] 1940 Census taken as of Oct. 1, 1939; 1930 Census, as of Oct. 1, 1929.
[f] Rate for period from Oct. 1, 1929, to Oct. 1, 1939.
[g] Rate for period from Oct. 1, 1939, to Apr. 1, 1950.
[h] Not identified separately.

GENERAL POPULATION STATISTICS, 1790-1990										
ARIZONA										
Item No.		1790 (or 1789)	1800	1810	1820	1830	1840	1850	1860	1870
1.	Population[1]	---	---	---	---	---	---	---	---	9,658
2.	Decennial rates of increase in population over preceding census[2]	---	---	---	---	---	---	---	---	---
3.	Increase in population over previous census[1,3]	---	---	---	---	---	---	---	---	9,658
4.	Percent distribution of population[4]	---	---	---	---	---	---	---	---	---
5.	Population per square mile of land area[5,6]	---	---	---	---	---	---	---	---	.1
6.	Membership of House of Representatives at each apportionment[7]	---	---	---	---	---	---	---	---	---
7.	White population[8,9,10]	---	---	---	---	---	---	---	---	9,581
8.	Percentage increase in white population over preceding census[9,10,11]	---	---	---	---	---	---	---	---	---
9.	Black population[8,9,10]	---	---	---	---	---	---	---	---	26
10.	Percentage increase in Black population over preceding census[9,10,11,12,13,14]	---	---	---	---	---	---	---	---	---
11.	Percent Black in total population[1,8,9,10,14,15]	---	---	---	---	---	---	---	---	0.3
12.	Number of slaves in the area enumerated in 1790 and in the added area[16]	---	---	---	---	---	---	---	---	---
13.	Urban population[17]	---	---	---	---	---	---	---	---	3,224
14.	Percent urban increase over preceding census[17]	---	---	---	---	---	---	---	---	---
15.	Rural population[17]	---	---	---	---	---	---	---	---	6,434
16.	Percent rural increase over preceding census[17]	---	---	---	---	---	---	---	---	---
17.	Percent of urban to total population[17]	---	---	---	---	---	---	---	---	33.4
18.	Percent of rural to total population[17]	---	---	---	---	---	---	---	---	66.6

GENERAL POPULATION STATISTICS, 1790-1990 (Cont.)

ARIZONA

Item No.	1880	1890	1900	1910	1920	1930	1940	1950	1960	1970	1980	1990
1.	40,440	88,243	122,931	204,354	334,162	435,573	499,261	749,587	1,302,161	1,770,900	2,717,866	3,665,228
2.	318.7	118.2	39.3	66.2	63.5	30.3	14.6	50.1	73.7	36.0	53.1	34.8
3.	30,782	47,803[*b]	34,688[*b]	81,423[*a]	129,808[*a]	101,411[*a]	63,688[*a]	250,326[*a]	552,574	468,739	946,966[*a]	947,362[*b]
4.	0.1	0.1	0.2	0.2	0.3	0.4	0.4	0.5	0.7	0.9	---	1.5
5.	.4	.8	1.1	1.8	2.9	3.8	4.4	6.6	11.5	15.6	23.9	32.3
6.	---	---	---	1	1	1	2	2	3	4	5	---
7.	35,460	55,734	92,903	171,468	291,449	378,551	426,792	654,511	1,169,517	1,604,948	2,240,033	2,963,186
8.	267.0	58.5	66.7	84.6[*a]	70.0	22.9[*a]	12.7[*a]	53.4[*a]	78.7[*a]	37.2[*a]	39.6[*a]	32.3[*b]
9.	155	1,357	1,848	2,009	8,005	10,749	14,993	25,974	43,403	53,344	75,034	110,524
10.	496.2	775.5	36.2	8.7[*a]	298.5	34.3	39.5[*a]	73.2[*a]	67.1[*a]	22.9[*a]	40.7	47.31[*b]
11.	0.4	1.5[*b]	1.5[*a]	1.0[*a]	2.4[*a]	2.5[*a]	3.0[*a]	3.5[*a]	3.3[*a]	3.0	2.8	3.0
12.	---	---	---	---	---	---	---	---	---	---	---	---
13.	7,007	8,302	19,495	63,260	120,788	149,856	173,981	273,794[*c] 416,000[*d]	909,903[*c] 970,616[*d]	1,408,864	2,278,728	---
14.	117.3	18.5	134.8	224.5	90.9	24.1	16.1	57.4[*c] ---[*d]	232.3[*c] 133.3[*d]	45.2	61.7	---
15.	33,433	79,941	103,436	141,094	213,374	285,717	325,280	475,793[*c] 333,587[*d]	392,258[*c] 331,545[*d]	362,036	439,487	---
16.	419.6	139.1	29.4	36.4	51.2	33.9	13.8	46.3[*c] ---[*d]	-17.6[*c] -0.6[*d]	9.2	21.4	---
17.	17.3	9.4	15.9	31.0	36.1	34.4	34.8	36.5[*c] 55.5[*d]	69.9[*c] 74.5[*d]	79.6	83.8	---
18.	82.7	90.6	84.1	69.0	63.9	65.6	65.2	63.5[*c] 44.5[*d]	30.1[*c] 25.5[*d]	20.4	16.2	---

[a] Percentage computed by compiler from data herein. See endnotes for source of data.
[b] Percentage computed by compiler from data herein is different from percentage given in source. The above percentage is the percentage computed by compiler.
[c] Previous urban definition (pre-1950).
[d] Current urban definition (1950 and after; see Glossary of Terms).

GENERAL POPULATION STATISTICS, 1790-1990										
ARKANSAS										
Item No.		1790 (or 1789)	1800	1810	1820	1830	1840	1850	1860	1870
1.	Population[1]	---	---	1,062	14,273	30,388	97,574	209,897	435,450	484,471
2.	Decennial rates of increase in population over preceding census[2]	---	---	---	1,244.0	112.9	221.1	115.1	107.5	11.3
3.	Increase in population over previous census[1,3]	---	---	---	13,211[*b]	16,115	67,186	112,323	225,553	49,021
4.	Percent distribution of population[4]	---	---	---	0.1	0.2	0.6	0.9	1.4	1.3
5.	Population per square mile of land area[5,6]	---	---	---	---	---	---	4.0	8.3	9.2
6.	Membership of House of Representatives at each apportionment[7]	---	---	---	---	1	1	2	3	4
7.	White population[8,9,10]	---	---	---	12,597	25,671	77,174	162,189	324,143	362,115
8.	Percentage increase in white population over preceding census[9,10,11]	---	---	---	1263.3	103.8	200.6	110.2	99.9	11.7
9.	Black population[8,9,10]	---	---	---	1,676	4,717	20,400	47,708	111,259	122,169
10.	Percentage increase in Black population over preceding census[9,10,11,12,13,14]	---	---	---	1,114.5	181.4	332.5	133.9	133.2	9.8
11.	Percent Black in total population[1,8,9,10,14,15]	---	---	---	11.7[*a]	15.5[*a]	20.9[*a]	22.7	25.6	25.2
12.	Number of slaves in the area enumerated in 1790 and in the added area[16]	---	---	136[*e]	1,617	4,576	19,935	47,100	111,115	---
13.	Urban population[17]	---	---	---	---	---	---	---	3,727	12,380
14.	Percent urban increase over preceding census[17]	---	---	---	---	---	---	---	---	232.2
15.	Rural population[17]	---	---	1,062	14,273	30,388	97,574	209,897	431,723	472,091
16.	Percent rural increase over preceding census[17]	---	---	---	1,244.0	112.9	221.1	115.1	105.7	9.4
17.	Percent of urban to total population[17]	---	---	---	---	---	---	---	0.9	2.6
18.	Percent of rural to total population[17]	---	---	100.0	100.0	100.0	100.0	100.0	99.1	97.4

GENERAL POPULATION STATISTICS, 1790-1990 (Cont.)												
ARKANSAS												
Item No.	1880	1890	1900	1910	1920	1930	1940	1950	1960	1970	1980	1990
1.	802,525	1,128,211	1,311,564	1,574,449	1,752,204	1,854,482	1,929,387	1,909,511	1,786,272	1,923,295	2,286,435	2,350,725
2.	65.6	40.6	16.3	20.0	11.3	5.8	5.1	-2.0	-6.5	7.7	18.9	2.8
3.	318,054	325,686[*b]	183,353[*b]	262,885[*a]	177,755[*a]	102,278[*a]	74,905[*a]	-19,8761[*a]	-123,239	137,023	363,140[*a]	64,290
4.	1.6	1.8	1.7	1.7	1.7	1.5	1.5	1.3	1.0	0.9	---	0.9
5.	15.3	21.5	25.0	30.0	33.4	35.3	37.0	36.3	34.2	37.0	43.9	45.1
6.	5	6	7	7	7	7	7	6	4	4	4	---
7.	591,531	818,752	944,580	1,131,026	1,279,757	1,375,315	1,466,084	1,481,507	1,395,703	1,565,915	1,890,002	1,944,744
8.	63.4	38.4	15.4	19.7[*a]	13.2	7.5[*a]	6.6[*a]	1.1[*a]	-5.8[*a]	12.2[*a]	20.7[*a]	2.9
9.	210,666	309,117	366,856	442,891	472,220	478,463	482,578	426,639	388,787	352,445	373,192	373,912
10.	72.4	46.7	18.7	20.7[*a]	6.6	1.3	0.9[*a]	-11.6[*a]	-8.9[*a]	-9.3[*a]	5.9	0.2
11.	26.3	27.4	28.0[*a]	28.1[*a]	27.0[*a]	25.8[*a]	25.0[*a]	22.3[*a]	21.8[*a]	18.3	16.3	15.9
12.	---	---	---	---	---	---	---	---	---	---	---	---
13.	32,020	73,159	111,733	202,681	290,497	382,878	431,910	617,153[*c] 630,591[*d]	742,869[*c] 765,303[*d]	960,865	1,179,556	---
14.	158.6	128.5	52.7	81.4	43.3	31.8	12.8	42.9[*c] ---[*d]	20.4[*c] 21.4[*d]	25.6	22.8	---
15.	770,505	1,055,052	1,199,831	1,371,768	1,461,707	1,471,604	1,517,477	1,292,358[*c] 1,278,920[*d]	1,043,403[*c] 1,020,969[*d]	962,430	1,106,879	---
16.	63.2	36.9	13.7	14.3	6.6	0.7	3.1	-14.8[*c] ---[*d]	-19.3[*c] -20.2[*d]	-5.7	15.0	---
17.	4.0	6.5	8.5	12.9	16.6	20.6	22.2	32.3[*c] 33.0[*d]	41.6[*c] 42.8[*d]	50.	51.6	---
18.	96.0	93.5	91.5	87.1	83.4	79.4	77.8	67.7[*c] 67.0[*d]	58.4[*c] 57.2[*d]	50.0	48.4	---

[a] Percentage computed by compiler from data herein. See endnotes for source of data.
[b] Percentage computed by compiler from data herein is different from percentage given in source. The above percentage is the percentage computed by compiler.
[c] Previous urban definition (pre-1950).
[d] Current urban definition (1950 and after; see Glossary of Terms).
[*] Reported as for "settlements of Hope Field and St. Francis" and for "settlements on the Arkansas" in the unorganized territory then called "Louisiana Territory." Compare with note for Louisiana.

GENERAL POPULATION STATISTICS, 1790-1990										
CALIFORNIA										
Item No.		1790 (or 1789)	1800	1810	1820	1830	1840	1850	1860	1870
1.	Population[1]	---	---	---	---	---	---	92,597	379,994	560,247
2.	Decennial rates of increase in population over preceding census[2]	---	---	---	---	---	---	---	310.4	47.4
3.	Increase in population over previous census[1,3]	---	---	---	---	---	---	92,597	287,397	180,253
4.	Percent distribution of population[4]	---	---	---	---	---	---	0.4	1.2	1.5
5.	Population per square mile of land area[5,6]	---	---	---	---	---	---	[(1)].6	2.4	3.6
6.	Membership of House of Representatives at each apportionment[7]	---	---	---	---	---	2	2	3	4
7.	White population[8,9,10]	---	---	---	---	---	---	91,635	323,177	499,424
8.	Percentage increase in white population over preceding census[9,10,11]	---	---	---	---	---	---	---	252.7	54.5
9.	Black population[8,9,10]	---	---	---	---	---	---	962	4,086	4,272
10.	Percentage increase in Black population over preceding census[9,10,11,12,13,14]	---	---	---	---	---	---	---	324.7	4.6
11.	Percent Black in total population[1,8,9,10,14,15]	---	---	---	---	---	---	1.0	1.1	0.8
12.	Number of slaves in the area enumerated in 1790 and in the added area[16]	---	---	---	---	---	---	---	---	---
13.	Urban population[17]	---	---	---	---	---	---	6,820	78,651	208,438
14.	Percent urban increase over preceding census[17]	---	---	---	---	---	---	---	1,053.2	165.0
15.	Rural population[17]	---	---	---	---	---	---	85,777	301,343	351,809
16.	Percent rural increase over preceding census[17]	---	---	---	---	---	---	---	251.3	16.7
17.	Percent of urban to total population[17]	---	---	---	---	---	---	7.4	20.7	37.2
18.	Percent of rural to total population[17]	---	---	---	---	---	---	92.6	79.3	62.8

GENERAL POPULATION STATISTICS, 1790-1990 (Cont.)

CALIFORNIA

Item No.	1880	1890	1900	1910	1920	1930	1940	1950	1960	1970	1980	1990
1.	864,694	1,213,398	1,485,053	2,377,549	3,426,861	5,677,251	6,907,387	10,586,223	15,717,204	19,953,134	23,668,562	29,760,021
2.	54.3	40.3	22.4	60.1	44.1	65.7	21.7	53.3	48.5	27.0	18.5	25.7
3.	304,447	348,704[*b]	271,655[*b]	892,496[*a]	1,049,312[*a]	2,250,390[*a]	1,230,136[*a]	3,678,836[*a]	5,130,981	4,235,930	3,715,428[*a]	6,091,459[*b]
4.	1.7	1.9	1.9	2.6	3.2	4.6	5.2	7.0	8.8	9.8	---	12.0
5.	5.5	7.8	9.5	15.3	22.0	36.5	44.1	67.5	100.4	127.6	151.4	190.8
6.	6	7	8	11	11	20	23	30	38	43	45	---
7.	767,181	1,111,833	1,402,727	2,259,672	3,264,711	5,408,260	6,596,763	9,915,173	14,455,230	17,761,032	18,031,689	20,524,327
8.	53.6	44.9	26.2	61.1[*a]	44.5	65.7[*a]	22.0[*a]	50.3[*a]	45.8[*a]	22.9[*a]	1.5[*a]	13.8
9.	6,018	11,322	11,045	21,645	38,763	81,048	124,306	462,172	883,861	1,400,143	1,819,282	2,208,801
10.	40.9	88.1	2.4	96.0[*a]	79.1	109.1	53.4[*a]	271.8[*a]	91.2[*a]	58.4[*a]	29.9	21.4
11.	0.7	0.9[*b]	0.7[*a]	0.9[*a]	1.1[*a]	1.4[*a]	1.8[*a]	4.4[*a]	5.6[*a]	7.0	7.7	7.4
12.	---	---	---	---	---	---	---	---	---	---	---	---
13.	370,611	589,464	776,820	1,468,419	2,326,959	4,160,596	4,902,265	7,208,825[*c] 8,539,420[*d]	11,274,401[*c] 13,573,155[*d]	18,136,045	21,607,606	---
14.	77.8	59.1	31.8	89.0	58.5	78.8	17.8	47.1[*c] ---[*d]	56.4[*c] 58.9[*d]	33.6	19.1	---
15.	494,083	623,934	708,233	909,130	1,099,902	1,516,655	2,005,122	3,377,398[*c] 2,046,803[*d]	4,442,803[*c] 2,144,049[*d]	1,817,089	2,060,296	---
16.	40.4	26.3	13.5	28.4	21.0	37.9	32.2	68.4[*c] ---[*d]	31.5[*c] 4.8[*d]	-15.3	13.9	---
17.	42.9	48.6	52.3	61.8	67.9	73.3	71.0	68.1[*c] 80.7[*d]	71.7[*c] 86.4[*d]	90.9	91.3	---
18.	57.1	51.4	47.7	38.2	32.1	26.7	29.0	31.9[*c] 19.3[*d]	28.3[*c] 13.6[*d]	9.1	8.7	---

[a] Percentage computed by compiler from data herein. See endnotes for source of data.
[b] Percentage computed by compiler from data herein is different from percentage given in source. The above percentage is the percentage computed by compiler.
[c] Previous urban definition (pre-1950).
[d] Current urban definition (1950 and after; see Glossary of Terms).

GENERAL POPULATION STATISTICS, 1790-1990										
COLORADO										
Item No.		1790 (or 1789)	1800	1810	1820	1830	1840	1850	1860	1870
1.	Population[1]	---	---	---	---	---	---	---	34,277	39,864
2.	Decennial rates of increase in population over preceding census[2]	---	---	---	---	---	---	---	---	16.3
3.	Increase in population over previous census[1,3]	---	---	---	---	---	---	---	34,277	5,587
4.	Percent distribution of population[4]	---	---	---	---	---	---	---	0.1	0.1
5.	Population per square mile of land area[5,6]	---	---	---	---	---	---	---	.3	.4
6.	Membership of House of Representatives at each apportionment[7]	---	---	---	---	---	---	---	---	1
7.	White population[8,9,10]	---	---	---	---	---	---	---	34,231	39,221
8.	Percentage increase in white population over preceding census[9,10,11]	---	---	---	---	---	---	---	---	14.6
9.	Black population[8,9,10]	---	---	---	---	---	---	---	46	456
10.	Percentage increase in Black population over preceding census[9,10,11,12,13,14]	---	---	---	---	---	---	---	---	891.3
11.	Percent Black in total population[1,8,9,10,14,15]	---	---	---	---	---	---	---	0.1	1.1
12.	Number of slaves in the area enumerated in 1790 and in the added area[16]	---	---	---	---	---	---	---	---	---
13.	Urban population[17]	---	---	---	---	---	---	---	4,749	4,759
14.	Percent urban increase over preceding census[17]	---	---	---	---	---	---	---	----	0.2
15.	Rural population[17]	---	---	---	---	---	---	---	29,528	35,105
16.	Percent rural increase over preceding census[17]	---	---	---	---	---	---	---	---	18.9
17.	Percent of urban to total population[17]	---	---	---	---	---	---	---	13.9	11.9
18.	Percent of rural to total population[17]	---	---	---	---	---	---	---	86.1	88.1

GENERAL POPULATION STATISTICS, 1790-1990 (Cont.)

COLORADO

Item No.	1880	1890	1900	1910	1920	1930	1940	1950	1960	1970	1980	1990
1.	194,327	413,249	539,700	799,024	939,629	1,035,791	1,123,296	1,325,089	1,753,947	2,207,000	2,890,000	3,294,394
2.	387.5	112.7	30.6	48.0	17.6	10.2	8.4	18.0	32.4	25.8	30.8	14.0
3.	154,463	218,922[*b]	126,451[*b]	259,324[*a]	140,605[*a]	96,162[*a]	87,505[*a]	201,793[*a]	428,858	453,053[*b]	683,000[*a]	404,394[*b]
4.	0.4	0.7	0.7	0.9	0.9	0.8	0.8	0.9	1.0	1.1	---	1.3
5.	1.9	4.0	5.2	7.7	9.1	10.0	10.8	12.8	16.9	21.3	27.9	31.8
6.	1	2	3	4	4	4	4	4	4	5	6	---
7.	191,126	404,534	529,046	783,415	924,163	1,018,793	1,406,502	1,296,653	1,700,700	2,112,352	2,570,615	2,905,474
8.	387.3	111.7	30.8	48.1[*a]	18.0	10.2[*a]	38.1[*a]	-7.8[*a]	31.2[*a]	24.2[*a]	21.7[*a]	13.0
9.	2,435	6,215	8,570	11,453	11,318	11,828	12,176	20,177	39,992	66,411	101,702	133,146
10.	434.0	155.2	37.9	33.6[*a]	-1.2	4.5	2.9[*a]	65.7[*a]	98.2[*a]	66.1[*a]	53.1	30.9
11.	1.3	1.5[*b]	1.6[*a]	1.4[*a]	1.2[*a]	1.1[*a]	1.1[*a]	1.5[*a]	2.3[*a]	3.0	3.5	4.0
12.	---	---	---	---	---	---	---	---	---	---	---	---
13.	60,961	185,905	260,651	402,192	453,259	519,882	590,756	759,939[*c] 831,318[*d]	1,090,012[*c] 1,292,790[*d]	1,733,311	2,329,869	---
14.	1,181.0	205.0	40.2	54.3	12.7	14.7	13.6	28.6[*c] ---[*d]	43.4[*c] 55.5[*d]	34.1	34.4	---
15.	133,366	227,344	279,049	396,832	486,370	515,909	532,540	565,150[*c] 493,771[*d]	663,935[*c] 461,157[*d]	473,948	560,095	---
16.	279.9	70.5	22.7	42.2	22.6	6.1	3.2	6.1[*c] ---[*d]	17.5[*c] -6.6[*d]	2.8	18.2	---
17.	31.4	45.0	48.3	50.3	48.2	50.2	52.6	57.4[*c] 62.7[*d]	62.1[*c] 73.7[*d]	78.5	80.6	---
18.	68.6	55.0	51.7	49.7	51.8	49.8	47.4	42.6[*c] 37.3[*d]	37.9[*c] 26.3[*d]	21.5	19.4	---

[a] Percentage computed by compiler from data herein. See endnotes for source of data.
[b] Percentage computed by compiler from data herein is different from percentage given in source. The above percentage is the percentage computed by compiler.
[c] Previous urban definition (pre-1950).
[d] Current urban definition (1950 and after; see Glossary of Terms).

Item No.	GENERAL POPULATION STATISTICS, 1790-1990 CONNECTICUT	1790 (or 1789)	1800	1810	1820	1830	1840	1850	1860	1870
1.	Population[1]	237,946	251,002	261,942	275,248	297,675	309,978	370,792	460,147	537,454
2.	Decennial rates of increase in population over preceding census[2]	---	5.5	4.4	5.1	8.1	4.1	19.6	24.1	16.8
3.	Increase in population over previous census[1,3]		13,056	10,940	13,306	22,427	12,303	60,814	89,355	77,307
4.	Percent distribution of population[4]	6.1	4.7	3.6	2.9	2.3	1.8	1.6	1.5	1.4
5.	Population per square mile of land area[5,6]	---	52.1	---	---	---	---	76.9	95.5	111.5
6.	Membership of House of Representatives at each apportionment[7]	7[*f]	7	7	6	6	4	4	4	4
7.	White population[8,9,10]	232,374	244,721	255,179	267,281	289,603	301,856	363,099	451,504	527,549
8.	Percentage increase in white population over preceding census[9,10,11]	---	5.3	4.3	4.7	8.4	4.2	20.3	24.3	16.8
9.	Black population[8,9,10]	5,572	6,281	6,763	7,967	8,072	8,122	7,693	8,627	9,668
10.	Percentage increase in Black population over preceding census[9,10,11,12,13,14]	---	12.7	7.7	17.8	1.3	0.6	-5.3	12.1	12.1
11.	Percent Black in total population[1,8,9,10,14,15]	2.3[*a]	2.5[*a]	2.6[*a]	2.9[*a]	2.7[*a]	2.6[*a]	2.1	1.9	1.8
12.	Number of slaves in the area enumerated in 1790 and in the added area[16*e]	2,648	951	310	97	25	17[1]	---	---	---
13.	Urban population[17]	7,170	12,722	15,941	20,804	27,847	38,952	59,321	122,121	177,153
14.	Percent urban increase over preceding census[17]	---	77.4	25.3	30.5	33.9	39.9	52.3	105.9	45.1
15.	Rural population[17]	230,776	238,280	246,001	254,444	269,828	271,026	311,471	338,026	360,301
16.	Percent rural increase over preceding census[17]	---	3.3	3.2	3.4	6.0	0.4	14.9	8.5	6.6
17.	Percent of urban to total population[17]	3.0	5.1	6.1	7.6	9.4	12.6	16.0	26.5	33.0
18.	Percent of rural to total population[17]	97.0	94.9	93.9	92.4	90.6	87.4	84.0	73.5	67.0

GENERAL POPULATION STATISTICS, 1790-1990 (Cont.)												
CONNECTICUT												
Item No.	1880	1890	1900	1910	1920	1930	1940	1950	1960	1970	1980	1990
1.	622,700	746,258	908,420	1,114,756	1,380,631	1,606,903	1,709,242	2,007,280	2,535,234	3,031,709	3,107,576	3,287,116
2.	15.9	19.8	21.7	22.7	23.9	16.4	6.4	17.4	26.3	19.6	2.5	5.8
3.	85,246	123,558	162,162	206,336[*a]	265,875[*a]	226,272[*a]	102,339[*a]	298,038[*a]	527,954	496,475	75,867[*a]	179,540
4.	1.2	1.2	1.2	1.2	1.3	1.3	1.3	1.3	1.4	1.5	---	1.3
5.	129.2	154.8	188.5	231.3	286.4	333.4	348.9	409.7	520.6	623.6	637.8	678.4
6.	4	4	5	5	5	6	6	6	6	6	6	---
7.	610,769	733,438	892,424	1,098,897	1,358,732	1,576,700	1,675,407	1,952,329	2,423,816	2,835,458	2,799,420	2,859,353
8.	15.8	20.1	21.7	23.1[*a]	23.6	16.0[*a]	6.3[*a]	16.5[*a]	24.1[*a]	17.0[*a]	-1.3[*a]	2.1
9.	11,547	12,302	15,226	15,474	24,046	29,354	32,992	53,472	107,449	181,177	217,433	274,269
10.	19.4	6.5	23.8	1.6[*a]	55.4[*b]	22.1[*b]	12.4[*a]	62.1[*a]	100.9[*a]	68.6[*a]	20.0	26.1
11.	1.9	1.7	1.7[*a]	1.4[*a]	1.7[*a]	1.8[*a]	1.9[*a]	2.7[*a]	4.2[*a]	6.0	7.0	8.3
12.	---	---	---	---	---	---	---	---	---	---	---	---
13.	260,718	379,853	543,755	731,797	936,339	1,131,770	1,158,162	1,390,504[*c] 1,558,642[*d]	1,749,569[*c] 1,985,567[*d]	2,345,052	2,449,774	---
14.	47.2	45.7	43.1	34.6	28.0	20.9	2.3	20.1[*c] ---[*d]	25.8[*c] 27.4[*d]	18.1	3.1	---
15.	361,982	366,405	364,665	382,959	444,292	475,133	551,080	616,776[*c] 448,638[*d]	785,665[*c] 549,667[*d]	686,657	657,802	---
16.	0.5	1.2	-0.5	50.	16.0	6.9	16.0	11.9[*c] ---[*d]	27.4[*c] 22.5[*d]	24.9	0.3	---
17.	41.9	50.9	59.9	65.6	67.8	70.4	67.8	69.3[*c] 77.6[*d]	69.0[*c] 78.3[*d]	77.4	78.8	---
18.	58.1	49.1	40.1	34.4	32.2	29.6	32.2	30.7[*c] 22.4[*d]	31.0[*c] 21.7[*d]	22.6	21.2	---

[a] Percentage computed by compiler from data herein. See endnotes for source of data.
[b] Percentage computed by compiler from data herein is different from percentage given in source. The above percentage is the percentage computed by compiler.
[c] Previous urban definition (pre-1950).
[d] Current urban definition (1950 and after; see Glossary of Terms).
[e] Exclusive of 37 slaves captured in the slaver Amistad.
[f] Membership in the House of Representatives in 1789: 5.

GENERAL POPULATION STATISTICS, 1790-1990										
DELAWARE										
Item No.		1790 (or 1789)	1800	1810	1820	1830	1840	1850	1860	1870
1.	Population[1]	59,096	64,273	72,674	72,749	76,748	78,085	91,532	112,216	125,015
2.	Decennial rates of increase in population over preceding census[2]	---	8.8	13.1	0.1	5.5	1.7	17.2	22.6	11.4
3.	Increase in population over previous census[1,3]	---	5,177	8,401	75	3,999	1,337	13,447	20,684	12,799
4.	Percent distribution of population[4]	1.5	1.2	1.0	0.8	0.6	0.5	0.4	0.4	0.3
5.	Population per square mile of land area[5,6]	---	32.7	---	---	---	---	46.6	57.1	63.6
6.	Membership of House of Representatives at each apportionment[7]	1[*e]	1	2	1	1	1	1	1	1
7.	White population[8,9,10]	46,310	49,852	55,361	55,282	57,601	58,561	71,169	90,589	102,221
8.	Percentage increase in white population over preceding census[9,10,11]	---	7.6	11.1	-0.1	4.2	1.7	21.5	27.3	12.8
9.	Black population[8,9,10]	12,786	14,421	17,313	17,467	19,147	19,524	20,363	21,627	22,794
10.	Percentage increase in Black population over preceding census[9,10,11,12,13,14]	---	12.8	20.1	0.9	9.6	2.0	4.3	6.2	5.4
11.	Percent Black in total population[1,8,9,10,14,15]	21.6[*a]	22.4[*a]	23.8[*a]	24.0[*a]	24.9[*a]	25.0[*a]	22.3	19.3	18.2
12.	Number of slaves in the area enumerated in 1790 and in the added area[16]	8,887	6,153	4,177	4,509	3,292	2,605	2,290	1,798	---
13.	Urban population[17]	---	---	---	---	---	8,367	13,979	21,258	30,841
14.	Percent urban increase over preceding census[17]	---	---	---	---	---	---	67.1	52.1	45.1
15.	Rural population[17]	59,096	64,273	72,674	72,749	76,748	69,718	77,553	90,958	94,174
16.	Percent rural increase over preceding census[17]	---	8.8	13.1	0.1	5.5	-9.2	11.2	17.3	3.5
17.	Percent of urban to total population[17]	---	---	---	---	---	10.7	15.3	18.9	24.7
18.	Percent of rural to total population[17]	100.0	100.0	100.0	100.0	100.0	89.3	84.7	81.1	75.3

GENERAL POPULATION STATISTICS, 1790-1990 (Cont.)

DELAWARE

Item No.	1880	1890	1900	1910	1920	1930	1940	1950	1960	1970	1980	1990
1.	146,608	168,493	184,735	202,322	223,003	228,380	266,505	318,085	446,292	548,104	594,338	666,168
2.	17.3	14.9	9.6	9.5	10.2	6.9	11.8	19.4	40.3	22.8	8.4	12.1
3.	21,593	21,885	16,242	17,587[*a]	20,681[*a]	15,377[*a]	38,125[*a]	51,580[*a]	128,207	101,812	46,234[*a]	71,830
4.	0.3	0.3	0.2	0.2	0.2	0.2	0.2	0.2	0.2	0.3	--	0.3
5.	74.6	85.7	94.0	103.0	113.5	124.3	134.7	160.8	225.2	276.5	307.6	340.8
6.	1	1	1	1	1	1	1	1	1	1	1	---
7.	120,160	140,066	153,977	171,102	192,615	205,718	230,528	273,878	384,327	466,459	488,543	535,094
8.	17.5	16.6	9.9	11.1[*a]	12.6	6.8[*a]	12.1[*a]	18.8[*a]	40.3[*a]	21.4[*a]	4.7[*a]	9.5[*b]
9.	26,442	28,386	30,697	31,181	30,335	32,602	35,876	43,598	60,688	78,276	95,971	112,460
10.	16.0	7.4	8.1	1.6[*a]	-2.7	7.5	10.0[*a]	21.5[*a]	39.2[*a]	29.0[*a]	22.6	17.2[*b]
11.	18.0	16.9	16.6[*a]	15.4[*a]	13.6[*a]	14.3[*a]	13.5[*a]	13.7[*a]	13.6[*a]	14.3	16.1	16.9
12.	---	---	---	---	---	---	---	---	---	---	---	---
13.	48,989	71,067	85,717	97,085	120,767	123,146	139,432	147,890[*c] 199,122[*d]	145,469[*c] 292,788[*d]	395,569	419,819	---
14.	58.8	45.1	20.6	13.3	24.4	2.0	13.2	6.1[*c] ---[*d]	-1.6 47.0	35.1	6.1	---
15.	97,619	97,426	99,018	105,237	102,236	115,234	127,073	170,195[*c] 118,963[*d]	300,823[*c] 153,504[*d]	152,555	174,519	---
16.	3.7	-0.2	1.6	6.3	-2.9	12.7	10.3	33.9[*c] ---[*d]	76.8[*c] 29.0[*d]	-0.6	14.4	---
17.	33.4	42.2	46.4	48.0	54.2	51.7	52.3	46.5[*c] 62.6[*d]	32.6[*c] 65.6[*d]	72.2	70.6	---
18.	66.6	57.8	53.6	52.0	45.8	48.3	47.7	53.5[*c] 37.4[*d]	67.4[*c] 34.4[*d]	27.8	29.4	---

[a] Percentage computed by compiler from data herein. See endnotes for source of data.
[b] Percentage computed by compiler from data herein is different from percentage given in source. The above percentage is the percentage computed by compiler.
[c] Previous urban definition (pre-1950).
[d] Current urban definition (1950 and after; see Glossary of Terms).
[*] Membership in the House of Representatives in 1789: 1.

GENERAL POPULATION STATISTICS, 1790-1990										
DISTRICT OF COLUMBIA										
Item No.		1790 (or 1789)	1800	1810	1820	1830	1840	1850	1860	1870
1.	Population[1]	---	8,144	15,471	23,336	30,261	33,745	51,687	75,080	131,700
2.	Decennial rates of increase in population over preceding census[2]	---	8,144	90.0	50.8	29.7	11.5	53.2	45.3	75.4
3.	Increase in population over previous census[1,3]	---	8,144[*b]	7,327[*b]	7,865[*b]	6,925[*b]	3,484[*b]	17,942[*b]	23,393	56,620
4.	Percent distribution of population[4]	---	0.2	0.2	0.2	0.2	0.2	0.2	0.2	0.3
5.	Population per square mile of land area[5,6]	---	156.6	---	---	---	---	891.2	1,294.5	2,270.7
6.	Membership of House of Representatives at each apportionment[7]	---	---	---	---	---	---	---	---	---
7.	White population[8,9,10]	---	10,066	16,079	22,614	27,563	30,657	37,941	60,763	88,278
8.	Percentage increase in white population over preceding census[9,10,11]	---	---	59.7	40.6	21.9	11.2	23.8	60.2	45.3
9.	Black population[8,9,10]	---	4,027	7,914	10,425	12,271	13,055	13,746	14,316	43,404
10.	Percentage increase in Black population over preceding census[9,10,11,12,13,14]	---	---	97.3	31.2	17.7	6.4	5.3	4.1	203.2
11.	Percent Black in total population[1,8,9,10,14,15]	---	49.5[*a]	51.2[*a]	44.7[*a]	40.6[*a]	38.7[*a]	26.6	19.1	33.0
12.	Number of slaves in the area enumerated in 1790 and in the added area[16*e]	---	---	---	---	---	---	---	---	---
13.	Urban population[17]	---	6,203	13,156	20,607	27,267	30,676	48,367	69,855	120,583
14.	Percent urban increase over preceding census[17]	---	---	112.1	56.6	32.3	12.5	57.7	44.4	72.6
15.	Rural population[17]	---	1,941	2,315	2,729	2,994	3,069	3,320	5,225	11,117
16.	Percent rural increase over preceding census[17]	---	---	19.3	17.9	9.7	2.5	8.2	57.4	112.8
17.	Percent of urban to total population[17]	---	76.2	85.0	88.3	90.1	90.9	93.6	93.0	91.6
18.	Percent of rural to total population[17]	---	23.8	15.0	11.7	9.9	9.1	6.4	7.0	8.4

GENERAL POPULATION STATISTICS, 1790-1990 (Cont.)												
DISTRICT OF COLUMBIA												
Item No.	1880	1890	1900	1910	1920	1930	1940	1950	1960	1970	1980	1990
1.	177,624	230,392	278,718	331,069	437,571	486,869	663,091	802,178	763,956	756,510	638,333	606,900
2.	34.9	29.7	21.0	18.8	32.2	11.3	36.2	21.0	-4.8	-1.0	-15.6	-4.9
3.	45,924	52,768	48,326	52,351[*a]	106,502[*a]	49,298[*a]	176,222[*a]	139,087[*a]	-38,222	-7,446	-118,177[*a]	-31,433
4.	0.4	0.4	0.4	0.4	0.4	0.4	0.5	0.5	0.4	0.4	---	0.2
5.	3,062.5	3972.3	4645.3	5,517.8	7,292.9	7,852.7	10,870.3	13,150.5	12,523.9	12,401.8	10,132	9,884.4
6.	---	---	---	---	---	---	---	---	---	---	---	---
7.	118,006	154,695	191,532	236,428	326,800	353,981	474,328	517,865	345,263	209,272	171,796	179,667
8.	33.7	31.1	23.8	23.4[*a]	38.2	8.3[*a]	34.0[*a]	9.2[*a]	-33.3[*a]	-39.4[*a]	-17.9[*a]	4.6
9.	59,596	75,572	86,702	94,440	109,966	132,068	187,266	280,803	411,737	537,712	448,229	399,604
10.	37.3	26.8	14.7	8.9[*a]	16.4	20.1	41.8[*a]	49.9[*a]	46.6[*a]	30.6[*a]	-16.6	-10.8[*b]
11.	33.6	32.8	31.1[*a]	28.5[*a]	25.1[*a]	27.1[*a]	28.2[*a]	35.0[*a]	53.9[*a]	71.1	70.2[*b]	65.8
12.	---	---	---	---	---	---	---	---	---	---	---	---
13.	159,871	230,392	278,718	331,069	437,571	486,869	663,091	802,178	763,956	756,510	638,333	---
14.	32.6	44.1	21.0	18.8	32.2	11.3	36.2	21.0	-4.8	-1.0	-15.6	---
15.	17,753	---	---	---	---	---	---	---	---	---	---	---
16.	59.7	---	---	---	---	---	---	---	---	---	---	---
17.	90.0	100.0	100.0	100.0	100.0	100.0	100.0	100.0	100.0	100.0	100.0	---
18.	10.0	---	---	---	---	---	---	---	---	---	---	---

[a] Percentage computed by compiler from data herein. See endnotes for source of data.
[b] Percentage computed by compiler from data herein is different from percentage given in source. The above percentage is the percentage computed by compiler.
[c] Previous urban definition (pre-1950).
[d] Current urban definition (1950 and after; see Glossary of Terms).
[*] Included in the total for Maryland.

GENERAL POPULATION STATISTICS, 1790-1990										
FLORIDA										
Item No.		1790 (or 1789)	1800	1810	1820	1830	1840	1850	1860	1870
1.	Population[1]	---	---	---	---	34,730	54,477	87,445	140,424	187,748
2.	Decennial rates of increase in population over preceding census[2]	---	---	---	---	---	56.9	60.5	60.6	33.7
3.	Increase in population over previous census[1,3]	---	---	---	---	34,730	19,747	32,968	52,979	47,324
4.	Percent distribution of population[4]	---	---	---	---	0.3	0.3	0.4	0.4	0.5
5.	Population per square mile of land area[5,6]	---	---	---	---	---	---	1.6	2.6	3.4
6.	Membership of House of Representatives at each apportionment[7]	---	---	---	---	---	1	1	1	2
7.	White population[8,9,10]	---	---	---	---	18,385	27,943	47,203	77,746	96,057
8.	Percentage increase in white population over preceding census[9,10,11]	---	---	---	---	---	52.0	68.9	64.7	23.6
9.	Black population[8,9,10]	---	---	---	---	16,345	26,534	40,242	62,677	91,689
10.	Percentage increase in Black population over preceding census[9,10,11,12,13,14]	---	---	---	---	---	62.3	51.7	55.8	46.3
11.	Percent Black in total population[1,8,9,10,14,15]	---	---	---	---	47.1[*a]	48.7[*a]	46.0	44.6	48.8
12.	Number of slaves in the area enumerated in 1790 and in the added area[16]	---	---	---	---	15,501	25,717	39,310	61,745	---
13.	Urban population[17]	---	---	---	---	---	---	---	5,708	15,275
14.	Percent urban increase over preceding census[17]	---	---	---	---	---	---	---	---	167.6
15.	Rural population[17]	---	---	---	---	34,730	54,477	87,445	134,716	172,473
16.	Percent rural increase over preceding census[17]	---	---	---	---	---	56.9	60.5	54.1	28.0
17.	Percent of urban to total population[17]	---	---	---	---	---	---	---	4.1	8.1
18.	Percent of rural to total population[17]	---	---	---	---	100.0	100.0	100.0	95.9	91.9

GENERAL POPULATION STATISTICS, 1790-1990 (Cont.)												
FLORIDA												
Item No.	1880	1890	1900	1910	1920	1930	1940	1950	1960	1970	1980	1990
1.	269,493	391,422	528,542	752,619	968,470	1,468,211	1,897,414	2,771,305	4,951,560	6,789,443	9,746,324	12,937,926
2.	43.5	45.2	35.0	42.4	28.7	51.6	29.2	46.1	78.7	37.1	43.5	32.7
3.	81,745	121,929	137,120	224,077[*a]	215,851[*a]	499,741[*a]	429,203[*a]	873,891[*a]	2,180,255	1,837,883	2,956,881[*a]	3,190,702[*b]
4.	0.5	0.6	0.7	0.8	0.9	1.2	1.4	1.8	2.8	---	---	5.2
5.	4.9	7.1	9.6	13.7	17.7	27.1	35.0	51.1	91.5	125.5	180.0	239.6
6.	2	2	3	4	4	5	6	8	12	15	19	---
7.	142,605	224,949	297,333	443,634	638,153	1,035,390	1,381,986	2,166,051	4,063,881	5,719,343	8,178,387	10,749,285
8.	48.5	57.7	32.2	49.2[*a]	43.8	62.2[*a]	33.5[*a]	56.7[*a]	87.6[*a]	40.7[*a]	43.0[*a]	31.4[*b]
9.	126,690	166,180	230,730	308,669	329,487	431,828	514,198	603,101	880,186	1,041,651	1,342,478	1,759,534
10.	38.2	31.2	38.8	33.8[*a]	6.7	31.1	19.1[*a]	17.3[*a]	45.9[*a]	18.3[*a]	28.9	31.1[*b]
11.	47.0	42.5	43.7[*a]	41.0[*a]	34.0[*a]	29.4[*a]	27.1[*a]	21.8[*a]	17.8[*a]	15.3	13.8	13.6
12.	---	---	---	---	---	---	---	---	---	---	---	---
13.	26,947	77,358	107,031	219,080	353,515	759,778	1,045,791	1,566,788[*c] 1,813,890[*d]	3,077,989[*c] 3,611,383[*d]	5,468,137	8,212,385	---
14.	76.4	187.1	38.4	104.7	61.4	114.9	37.6	49.8[*c] ---[*d]	96.5[*c] 101.9[*d]	49.3	48.1	---
15.	242,546	314,064	421,511	533,539	614,955	708,433	851,623	1,204,517[*c] 957,415[*d]	1,873,571[*c] 1,290,177[*d]	1,321,306	1,533,939	---
16.	40.6	29.5	34.2	26.6	15.3	15.2	20.2	41.4[*c] ---[*d]	55.5[*c] 34.8[*d]	2.4	23.2	---
17.	10.0	19.8	20.3	29.1	36.5	51.7	55.1	56.5[*c] 65.5[*d]	62.2[*c] 73.9[*d]	80.5	84.3	---
18.	90.0	80.2	79.7	70.9	63.5	48.3	44.9	43.5[*c] 34.5[*d]	37.8[*c] 26.1[*d]	19.5	15.7	---

[a] Percentage computed by compiler from data herein. See endnotes for source of data.
[b] Percentage computed by compiler from data herein is different from percentage given in source. The above percentage is the percentage computed by compiler.
[c] Previous urban definition (pre-1950).
[d] Current urban definition (1950 and after; see Glossary of Terms).

GENERAL POPULATION STATISTICS, 1790-1990										
GEORGIA										
Item No.		1790 (or 1789)	1800	1810	1820	1830	1840	1850	1860	1870
1.	Population[1]	82,548	162,686	252,433	340,989	516,823	691,392	906,185	1,057,286	1,184,109
2.	Decennial rates of increase in population over preceding census[2]	---	97.1	55.2	35.1	51.6	33.8	31.1	16.7	12.0
3.	Increase in population over previous census[1,3]	---	80,138	89,747	88,556	175,834	174,569	214,793	151,101	126,823
4.	Percent distribution of population[4]	2.1	3.1	3.5	3.5	4.0	4.1	3.9	3.4	3.1
5.	Population per square mile of land area[5,6]	---	1.5	---	---	---	---	15.4	18.0	20.2
6.	Membership of House of Representatives at each apportionment[7]	2[*e]	4	6	7	9	8	8	7	9
7.	White population[8,9,10]	52,886	102,261	145,414	189,570	296,806	407,695	521,572	591,550	638,926
8.	Percentage increase in white population over preceding census[9,10,11]	---	93.4	42.2	30.4	56.6	37.4	27.9	13.4	8.0
9.	Black population[8,9,10]	29,662	60,425	107,019	151,419	220,017	283,697	384,613	465,698	545,142
10.	Percentage increase in Black population over preceding census[9,10,11,12,13,14]	---	10.4	77.1	41.5	45.3	28.9	35.6	21.1	17.1
11.	Percent Black in total population[1,8,9,10,14,15]	35.9[*a]	37.1[*a]	42.4[*a]	44.4[*a]	42.6[*a]	41.0[*a]	42.4	44.1	46.0
12.	Number of slaves in the area enumerated in 1790 and in the added area[16]	29,264	59,406	105,218	149,656	217,531	280,944	381,682	462,198	---
13.	Urban population[17]	---	5,146	5,215	7,523	14,013	24,658	38,994	75,466	100,053
14.	Percent urban increase over preceding census[17]	---	---	1.3	44.3	86.3	76.0	58.1	93.5	32.6
15.	Rural population[17]	82,548	157,540	247,218	333,466	502,810	666,734	867,191	981,820	1,084,056
16.	Percent rural increase over preceding census[17]	---	90.8	56.9	34.9	50.8	32.6	30.1	13.2	10.4
17.	Percent of urban to total population[17]	---	3.2	2.1	2.2	2.7	3.6	4.3	7.1	8.4
18.	Percent of rural to total population[17]	100.0	96.8	97.9	97.8	97.3	96.4	95.7	92.9	91.6

GENERAL POPULATION STATISTICS, 1790-1990 (Cont.)												
GEORGIA												
Item No.	1880	1890	1900	1910	1920	1930	1940	1950	1960	1970	1980	1990
1.	1,542,180	1,837,353	2,216,331	2,609,121	2,895,832	2,908,506	3,123,723	3,444,578	3,943,116	4,590,000	5,464,265	6,478,216
2.	30.2	19.1	20.6	17.7	11.0	0.4	7.4	10.3	14.5	16.4	19.1	18.6
3.	358,071	295,173	378,978	392,790[*a]	286,711[*a]	12,674[*a]	215,217[*a]	320,855[*a]	498,538	646,884[*b]	874,265[*a]	1,013,951[*a]
4.	3.1	2.9	2.9	2.8	2.7	2.4	2.4	2.3	2.2	2.3	---	2.6
5.	26.3	31.3	37.7	44.4	49.3	49.5	53.4	58.9	67.8	79.0	94.1	111.9
6.	10	11	11	12	12	10	10	10	10	10	10	---
7.	816,906	978,357	1,181,294	1,431,802	1,689,114	1,837,021	2,038,278	2,380,577	2,817,223	3,391,242	3,948,007	4,600,148
8.	27.9	19.8	20.7	21.2[*a]	18.0	8.8[*a]	11.0[*a]	16.8[*a]	18.3[*a]	20.4[*a]	16.4[*a]	16.5
9.	725,133	858,815	1,034,813	1,176,987	1,206,365	1,071,125	1,084,927	1,062,762	1,122,596	1,187,149	1,465,457	1,746,565
10.	33.0	18.4	20.5	13.7[*a]	2.5	-11.2	1.3[*a]	-2.0[*a]	5.6[*a]	5.8[*a]	23.4	19.2
11.	47.0	46.7	46.7[*a]	45.1[*a]	41.7[*a]	36.8[*a]	34.7[*a]	30.9[*a]	28.5[*a]	25.9	26.8	27.0
12.	---	---	---	---	---	---	---	---	---	---	---	---
13.	145,090	257,472	346,382	538,650	727,859	895,492	1,073,808	1,426,206[*c] 1,559,447[*d]	1,963,012[*c] 2,180,236[*d]	2,768,074	3,409,081	---
14.	45.0	77.5	34.5	55.5	35.1	23.0	19.9	32.8[*c] ---[*d]	37.6[*c] 39.8[*d]	27.0	23.2	---
15.	1,397,090	1,579,881	1,869,949	2,070,471	2,167,973	2,013,014	2,049,915	2,018,372[*c] 1,885,131[*d]	1,980,104[*c] 1,762,880[*d]	1,821,501	2,054,024	---
16.	28.9	13.1	18.4	10.7	4.7	-7.1	1.8	-1.5[*c] ---[*d]	-1.9[*c] -6.5[*d]	3.3	12.8	---
17.	9.4	14.0	15.6	20.6	25.1	30.8	34.4	41.4[*c] 45.3[*d]	49.8[*c] 55.3[*d]	60.3	62.4	---
18.	90.6	86.0	84.4	79.4	74.9	69.2	65.6	58.6[*c] 54.7[*d]	50.2[*c] 44.7[*d]	39.7	37.6	---

[a] Percentage computed by compiler from data herein. See endnotes for source of data.
[b] Percentage computed by compiler from data herein is different from percentage given in source. The above percentage is the percentage computed by compiler.
[c] Previous urban definition (pre-1950).
[d] Current urban definition (1950 and after; see Glossary of Terms).
[e] Membership in the House of Representatives in 1789: 3.

GENERAL POPULATION STATISTICS, 1790-1990												
HAWAII												
Item No.	1880	1890	1900	1910	1920	1930	1940	1950	1960	1970	1980	1990
1.	---	---	154,001	191,874	255,881	368,300	422,770	499,794	632,772	769,000	965,000	1,108,229
2.	---	---	---	24.6	33.4	43.9	14.9	14.8	26.6	21.5	25.3	14.9
3.	---	---	---	37,873[*a]	64,007[*a]	112,419[*a]	54,470[*a]	77,024[*a]	132,978	136,228[*b]	196,000[*a]	143,229[*b]
4.	---	---	0.2	0.2	0.2	0.3	0.3	0.3	0.4	0.4	---	0.4
5.	---	---	---	---	39.9	57.0	66.0	78.0	98.5	119.6	150.1	172.5
6.	---	---	---	---	---	---	---	1	2	2	2	---
7.	---	---	---	---	---	---	---	114,793	202,230	298,160	318,608	369,616
8.	---	---	---	---	---	---	---	---	76.2[*a]	47.4[*a]	6.9[*a]	16.0
9.	---	---	---	---	---	---	---	2,651	4,943	7,573	17,352	27,195
10.	---	---	---	---	---	---	---	---	86.5[*a]	53.2[*a]	129.1	56.7[*b]
11.	---	---	---	---	---	---	---	0.5[*a]	0.8[*a]	1.0	1.8	2.5
12.	---	---	---	---	---	---	---	---	---	---	---	---
13.	---	---	39,306[*e]	58,928[*e]	92,251[*e]	197,937[*e]	264,262	344,869	438,645[*c] 483,961[*d]	638,683	834,592	---
14.	---	---	---	49.9[*e]	56.5[*e]	114.6[*e]	33.5	30.5	27.2[*c] 40.3[*d]	32.0	30.7	---
15.	---	---	114,695[*e]	132,946[*e]	163,630[*e]	170,363[*e]	158,508	154,925	194,127[*c] 148,811[*d]	129,878	130,099	---
16.	---	---	---	15.9[*e]	23.1[*e]	4.1[*e]	-7.0	-2.3	25.3[*c] -3.9[*d]	-12.7	0.2	---
17.	---	---	25.5[*e]	30.7[*e]	36.1[*e]	53.7[*e]	62.5	69.0	69.3[*c] 76.5[*d]	83.1	86.5	---
18.	---	---	74.5[*e]	69.3[*e]	63.9[*e]	46.3[*e]	37.5	31.0	30.7[*c] 23.5[*d]	16.9	13.5	---

[a] Percentage computed by compiler from data herein. See endnotes for source of data.
[b] Percentage computed by compiler from data herein is different from percentage given in source. The above percentage is the percentage computed by compiler.
[c] Previous urban definition (pre-1950).
[d] Current urban definition (1950 and after; see Glossary of Terms).
[e] The population reported in 1900 as urban is the population of Honolulu, and in 1910, 1920, and 1930, is the population of Hilo and Honolulu. Other places of this size were not reported separately in censuses prior to 1920.

GENERAL POPULATION STATISTICS, 1790-1990

IDAHO

Item No.		1790 (or 1789)	1800	1810	1820	1830	1840	1850	1860	1870
1.	Population[1]	---	---	---	---	---	---	---	---	14,999
2.	Decennial rates of increase in population over preceding census[2]	---	---	---	---	---	---	---	---	---
3.	Increase in population over previous census[1,3]	---	---	---	---	---	---	---	---	14,999
4.	Percent distribution of population[4]	---	---	---	---	---	---	---	---	---
5.	Population per square mile of land area[5,6]	---	---	---	---	---	---	---	---	.2
6.	Membership of House of Representatives at each apportionment[7]	---	---	---	---	---	---	---	---	---
7.	White population[8,9,10]	---	---	---	---	---	---	---	---	10,618
8.	Percentage increase in white population over preceding census[9,10,11]	---	---	---	---	---	---	---	---	---
9.	Black population[8,9,10]	---	---	---	---	---	---	---	---	60
10.	Percentage increase in Black population over preceding census[9,10,11,12,13,14]	---	---	---	---	---	---	---	---	---
11.	Percent Black in total population[1,8,9,10,14,15]	---	---	---	---	---	---	---	---	0.4
12.	Number of slaves in the area enumerated in 1790 and in the added area[16]	---	---	---	---	---	---	---	---	---
13.	Urban population[17]	---	---	---	---	---	---	---	---	---
14.	Percent urban increase over preceding census[17]	---	---	---	---	---	---	---	---	---
15.	Rural population[17]	---	---	---	---	---	---	---	---	14,999
16.	Percent rural increase over preceding census[17]	---	---	---	---	---	---	---	---	---
17.	Percent of urban to total population[17]	---	---	---	---	---	---	---	---	---
18.	Percent of rural to total population[17]	---	---	---	---	---	---	---	---	100.0

GENERAL POPULATION STATISTICS, 1790-1990 (Cont.)

IDAHO

Item No.	1880	1890	1900	1910	1920	1930	1940	1950	1960	1970	1980	1990
1.	32,610	88,548	161,772	325,594	431,866	445,032	524,873	588,637	667,191	712,567	943,935	1,006,749
2.	117.4	171.5	82.7	101.3	32.6	3.0	17.9	12.1	13.3	6.8	32.4	6.7
3.	17,611	55,938[*b]	73,224[*b]	163,822[*a]	106,272[*a]	13,166[*a]	79,841[*a]	63,764[*a]	78,554	45,376	231,368[*a]	62,814
4.	0.1	0.1	0.2	0.4	0.4	0.4	0.4	0.4	0.4	0.4	---	0.4
5.	.4	1.1	1.9	3.9	5.2	5.3	6.3	7.1	8.1	8.6	11.5	12.2
6.	1	1	1	2	2	2	2	2	2	2	2	---
7.	29,013	82,117	154,495	319,221	425,668	438,840	549,292	581,395	657,383	698,802	901,641	950,451
8.	173.2	183.0	88.1	106.6[*a]	33.3	3.1[*a]	25.2[*a]	5.8[*a]	13.1[*a]	6.3[*a]	29.0[*a]	5.4
9.	53	201	293	651	920	668	595	1,050	1,502	2,130	2,716	3,370
10.	-11.7	279.2	45.8	122.2[*a]	41.3	-27.4	-10.9[*a]	76.5[*a]	43.0[*a]	41.8[*a]	27.5	24.1
11.	.2	.2	0.2[*a]	0.2[*a]	0.2[*a]	0.2[*a]	0.1[*a]	0.2[*a]	0.2[*a]	0.3	0.3	0.3
12.	---	---	---	---	---	---	---	---	---	---	---	---
13.	---	---	10,003	69,898	119,037	129,507	176,708	234,138[*c] 252,549[*d]	276,258[*c] 317,097[*d]	385,434	509,702	---
14.	---	---	---	598.8	70.3	8.8	36.4	32.5[*c] ---[*d]	18.0[*c] 25.6[*d]	21.6	32.2	---
15.	32,610	88,548	151,769	255,696	312,829	315,525	348,165	354,499[*c] 336,088[*d]	390,933[*c] 350,094[*d]	327,133	434,233	---
16.	117.4	171.5	71.4	68.5	22.3	0.9	10.3	1.8[*c] ---[*d]	10.3[*c] 4.2[*d]	-6.6	32.7	---
17.	---	---	6.2	21.5	27.6	29.1	33.7	39.8[*c] 42.9[*d]	41.4[*c] 47.5[*d]	54.1	54.0	---
18.	100.0	100.0	93.8	78.5	72.4	70.9	66.3	60.2[*c] 57.1[*d]	58.6[*c] 52.5[*d]	45.9	46.0	---

[a] Percentage computed by compiler from data herein. See endnotes for source of data.
[b] Percentage computed by compiler from data herein is different from percentage given in source. The above percentage is the percentage computed by compiler.
[c] Previous urban definition (pre-1950).
[d] Current urban definition (1950 and after; see Glossary of Terms).

GENERAL POPULATION STATISTICS, 1790-1990										
ILLINOIS										
Item No.		1790 (or 1789)	1800	1810	1820	1830	1840	1850	1860	1870
1.	Population[1]	---	---	12,282[*f]	55,211	157,445	476,183	851,470	1,711,951	2,539,891
2.	Decennial rates of increase in population over preceding census[2]	---	---	---	349.5	185.2	202.4	78.8	101.1	48.4
3.	Increase in population over previous census[1,3]	---	---	12,282	42,929	102,234	318,738	375,287	860,481	827,940
4.	Percent distribution of population[4]	---	---	0.2	0.6	1.2	2.8	3.7	5.4	6.6
5.	Population per square mile of land area[5,6]	---	---	---	---	---	---	15.2	30.6	45.4
6.	Membership of House of Representatives at each apportionment[7]	---	---	1	1	3	7	9	14	19
7.	White population[8,9,10]	---	---	11,501	53,837	155,061	472,254	846,034	1,704,291	2,511,096
8.	Percentage increase in white population over preceding census[9,10,11]	---	---	---	368.1	188.0	204.6	79.1	101.4	47.3
9.	Black population[8,9,10]	---	---	781	1,374	2,384	3,929	5,436	7,628	28,762
10.	Percentage increase in Black population over preceding census[9,10,11,12,13,14]	---	---	---	75.9	73.5	64.8	38.4	40.3	277.1
11.	Percent Black in total population[1,8,9,10,14,15]	---	---	6.4[*a]	2.5[*a]	1.5[*a]	0.8[*a]	0.6	0.5	1.1
12.	Number of slaves in the area enumerated in 1790 and in the added area[16]	---	107[*e]	168	917	747	331	---	---	---
13.	Urban population[17]	---	---	---	---	---	9,607	64,427	245,545	596,042
14.	Percent urban increase over preceding census[17]	---	---	---	---	---	---	570.6	281.1	142.7
15.	Rural population[17]	---	---	12,282	55,211	157,445	466,576	787,043	1,466,406	1,943,849
16.	Percent rural increase over preceding census[17]	---	---	---	349.5	185.2	196.3	68.7	86.3	32.6
17.	Percent of urban to total population[17]	---	---	---	---	---	2.0	7.6	14.3	23.5
18.	Percent of rural to total population[17]	---	---	100.0	100.0	100.0	98.0	92.4	85.7	76.5

GENERAL POPULATION STATISTICS, 1790-1990 (Cont.)												
ILLINOIS												
Item No.	1880	1890	1900	1910	1920	1930	1940	1950	1960	1970	1980	1990
1.	3,077,871	3,826,352	4,821,550	5,638,591	6,485,280	7,630,654	7,897,241	8,712,176	10,081,158	11,113,976	11,426,518	11,430,602
2.	21.2	24.3	26.0	16.9	15.0	17.7	3.5	10.3	15.7	10.2	2.8	0.0
3.	537,980	748,481[*b]	995,198[*b]	817,041[*a]	846,689[*a]	1,145,374[*a]	266,587[*a]	814,935[*a]	1,368,982	1,032,818	312,542[*a]	4,084
4.	6.1	6.1	6.3	6.1	6.1	6.2	6.0	5.8	5.6	5.5	---	4.6
5.	55.0	68.3	86.1	100.6	115.7	136.4	141.2	155.8	180.4	199.4	205.3	205.6
6.	20	22	25	27	27	27	26	25	24	24	22	---
7.	3,031,151	3,768,472	4,734,873	5,526,962	6,299,333	7,295,267	7,504,202	8,046,058	9,010,252	9,600,381	9,225,575	8,952,978
8.	20.7	24.3	25.6	16.7[*a]	14.0	15.8[*a]	2.9[*a]	7.2[*a]	12.0[*a]	6.5[*a]	-5.0[*a]	-3.0
9.	46,368	57,028	85,078	109,049	182,274	328,972	387,446	645,980	1,037,470	1,425,674	1,675,229	1,694,273
10.	61.2	23.0	49.2	28.2[*a]	67.1	80.5	17.8[*a]	66.7[*a]	60.6[*a]	37.4[*a]	17.5	1.1
11.	1.5	1.5	1.8[*a]	1.9[*a]	2.8[*a]	4.3[*a]	4.9[*a]	7.4[*a]	10.3[*a]	12.8	14.7	14.8
12.	---	---	---	---	---	---	---	---	---	---	---	---
13.	940,504	1,719,172	2,616,368	3,479,935	4,403,677	5,635,727	5,809,650	6,486,673[*c] 6,759,271[*d]	7,650,582[*c] 8,140,315[*d]	9,229,821	9,518,039	---
14.	57.8	82.8	52.2	33.0	26.5	28.0	3.1	11.7[*c] ---[*d]	17.9[*c] 20.4[*d]	13.4	2.9	---
15.	2,137,367	2,107,180	2,205,182	2,158,656	2,081,603	1,994,927	2,087,591	2,225,503[*c] 1,952,905[*d]	2,430,576[*c] 1,940,843[*d]	1,884,155	1,908,479	---
16.	10.0	-1.4	4.7	-2.1	-3.6	-4.2	4.6	6.6[*c] ---[*d]	9.2[*c] -0.6[*d]	-2.9	2.5	---
17.	30.6	44.9	54.3	61.7	67.9	73.9	73.6	74.5[*c] 77.6[*d]	75.9[*c] 80.7[*d]	83.0	83.3	---
18.	69.4	55.1	45.7	38.3	32.1	26.1	26.4	25.5[*c] 22.4[*d]	24.1[*c] 19.3[*d]	17.0	16.7	---

[a] Percentage computed by compiler from data herein. See endnotes for source of data.
[b] Percentage computed by compiler from data herein is different from percentage given in source. The above percentage is the percentage computed by compiler.
[c] Previous urban definition (pre-1950).
[d] Current urban definition (1950 and after; see Glossary of Terms).
[e] Reported as for Randolph County, Indiana Territory.
[f] Population of Illinois Territory, which comprised area constituting state of Illinois, almost all of Wisconsin, the western part of the upper peninsula of Michigan, and the northeastern part of Minnesota.

GENERAL POPULATION STATISTICS, 1790-1990										
INDIANA										
Item No.		1790 (or 1789)	1800	1810	1820	1830	1840	1850	1860	1870
1.	Population[1]	---	5,641[*e]	24,520[*e]	147,178	343,031	685,866	988,416	1,350,428	1,680,637
2.	Decennial rates of increase in population over preceding census[2]	---	---	500.2	133.1	99.9	44.1	36.6	24.5	17.7
3.	Increase in population over previous census[1,3]	---	5,641	18,879	122,658	195,853	342,835	302,550	362,012	330,209
4.	Percent distribution of population[4]	---	0.1	0.3	1.5	2.7	4.0	4.3	4.3	4.4
5.	Population per square mile of land area[5,6]	---	---	---	---	---	---	27.5	37.6	46.8
6.	Membership of House of Representatives at each apportionment[7]	---	---	1	3	7	10	11	11	13
7.	White population[8,9,10]	---	5,343	23,890	145,758	339,399	678,698	977,154	1,338,710	1,655,837
8.	Percentage increase in white population over preceding census[9,10,11]	---	---	347.1	510.1	132.9	100.0	44.0	37.0	23.7
9.	Black population[8,9,10]	---	298	630	1,420	3,632	7,168	11,262	11,428	24,560
10.	Percentage increase in Black population over preceding census[9,10,11,12,13,14]	---	---	111.4	125.4	155.8	97.4	57.1	1.5	114.9
11.	Percent Black in total population[1,8,9,10,14,15]	---	5.3[*a]	2.6[*a]	1.0[*a]	1.1[*a]	1.0[*a]	1.1	0.9	1.5
12.	Number of slaves in the area enumerated in 1790 and in the added area[16]	---	28	237	190	3	3	---	---	---
13.	Urban population[17]	---	---	---	---	---	10,716	44,632	115,904	247,657
14.	Percent urban increase over preceding census[17]	---	---	---	---	---	---	316.5	159.7	113.7
15.	Rural population[17]	---	5,641	24,520	147,178	343,031	675,150	943,784	1,234,524	1,432,980
16.	Percent rural increase over preceding census[17]	---	---	334.7	500.2	133.1	96.8	39.8	30.8	16.1
17.	Percent of urban to total population[17]	---	---	---	---	---	1.6	4.5	8.6	14.7
18.	Percent of rural to total population[17]	---	100.0	100.0	100.0	100.0	98.4	95.5	91.4	85.3

GENERAL POPULATION STATISTICS, 1790-1990 (Cont.)												
INDIANA												
Item No.	1880	1890	1900	1910	1920	1930	1940	1950	1960	1970	1980	1990
1.	1,978,301	2,192,404	2,516,462	2,700,876	2,930,390	3,238,503	3,427,796	3,934,224	4,662,498	5,193,669	5,490,179	5,544,159
2.	17.7	10.8	14.8	7.3	8.5	10.5	5.8	14.8	18.5	11.4	5.7	1.0
3.	297,664	214,103	324,058	184,414*[a]	229,514*[a]	308,113*[a]	189,293*[a]	506,428*[a]	728,274	531,171	296,510*[a]	53,980*[b]
4.	3.9	3.5	3.3	2.9	2.8	2.6	2.6	2.6	2.6	2.6	---	2.2
5.	55.1	61.1	70.1	74.9	81.3	80.8	94.7	108.7	128.8	143.9	152.8	154.6
6.	13	13	13	13	13	12	11	11	11	11	10	---
7.	1,938,798	2,146,736	2,458,502	2,639,961	2,849,071	3,125,778	3,305,323	3,758,512	4,388,554	4,820,324	5,004,567	5,020,700
8.	17.1	10.7	14.5	7.4*[a]	7.9	9.7*[a]	5.7*[a]	13.7*[a]	16.8*[a]	9.8*[a]	3.8*[a]	0.3
9.	39,228	45,215	57,505	60,320	80,810	111,982	121,916	174,168	269,275	357,464	414,732	432,092
10.	59.7	15.3	27.2	4.9*[a]	34.0	38.6	8.9*[a]	42.9*[a]	54.6*[a]	32.8*[a]	16.0	4.2
11.	2.0	2.1	2.3*[a]	2.2*[a]	2.8*[a]	3.5*[a]	3.6*[a]	4.4*[a]	5.8*[a]	6.9	7.6	7.8
12.	---	---	---	---	---	---	---	---	---	---	---	---
13.	386,211	590,039	862,689	1,143,835	1,482,855	1,795,892	1,887,712	2,217,468*[c] 2,357,196[d]*	2,650,378*[c] 2,910,149*[d]	3,372,060*[d]	3,525,298	---
14.	55.9	52.8	46.2	32.6	29.6	21.1	5.1	17.5*[c] ---*[d]	19.5*[c] 23.5*[d]	15.9*[d]	4.5	---
15.	1,592,090	1,602,365	1,653,773	1,557,041	1,447,535	1,442,611	1,540,084	1,716,756*[c] 1,577,028*[d]	2,012,120*[c] 1,752,349*[d]	1,821,609*[d]	1,964,926	---
16.	11.1	0.6	3.2	-5.8	-7.0	-0.3	6.8	11.5*[c] ---*[d]	17.2*[c] 11.1*[d]	4.0*[d]	7.9	---
17.	19.5	26.9	34.3	42.4	50.6	55.5	55.1	56.4*[c] 59.9*[d]	56.8*[c] 62.4*[d]	64.9*[d]	64.2	---
18.	80.5	73.1	65.7	57.6	49.4	44.5	44.9	43.6*[c] 40.1*[d]	43.2*[c] 37.6*[d]	35.1*[d]	35.8	---

[a] Percentage computed by compiler from data herein. See endnotes for source of data.

[b] Percentage computed by compiler from data herein is different from percentage given in source. The above percentage is the percentage computed by compiler.

[c] Previous urban definition (pre-1950).

[d] Current urban definition (1950 and after; see Glossary of Terms).

[e] 1810 figure includes population of area separated in 1816; 1800 figure includes population (3,124) of those portions of Indiana Territory which were taken to form Michigan and Illinois Territories in 1805 and 1809, respectively, and that portion which was separated in 1816.

GENERAL POPULATION STATISTICS, 1790-1990										
IOWA										
Item No.		1790 (or 1789)	1800	1810	1820	1830	1840	1850	1860	1870
1.	Population[1]	---	---	---	---	---	43,112[*e]	192,214	674,913	1,194,020
2.	Decennial rates of increase in population over preceding census[2]	---	---	---	---	---	---	345.8	251.1	76.9
3.	Increase in population over previous census[1,3]	---	---	---	---	---	43,112	149,102	482,699	519,107
4.	Percent distribution of population[4]	---	---	---	---	---	0.3	0.8	2.1	3.1
5.	Population per square mile of land area[5,6]	---	---	---	---	---	---	3.5	12.1	21.5
6.	Membership of House of Representatives at each apportionment[7]	---	---	---	---	---	2	2	6	9
7.	White population[8,9,10]	---	---	---	---	---	42,924	191,881	673,779	1,188,207
8.	Percentage increase in white population over preceding census[9,10,11]	---	---	---	---	---	---	347.0	2,51.1	76.3
9.	Black population[8,9,10]	---	---	---	---	---	188	333	1,069	5,762
10.	Percentage increase in Black population over preceding census[9,10,11,12,13,14]	---	---	---	---	---	---	77.1	221.0	439.0
11.	Percent Black in total population[1,8,9,10,14,15]	---	---	---	---	---	0.4[*a]	0.2	0.2	0.5
12.	Number of slaves in the area enumerated in 1790 and in the added area[16]	---	---	---	---	---	16	---	---	---
13.	Urban population[17]	---	---	---	---	---	---	9,730	60,028	156,327
14.	Percent urban increase over preceding census[17]	---	---	---	---	---	---	---	516.9	160.4
15.	Rural population[17]	---	---	---	---	---	43,112	182,484	614,885	1,037,693
16.	Percent rural increase over preceding census[17]	---	---	---	---	---	---	323.3	237.0	68.8
17.	Percent of urban to total population[17]	---	---	---	---	---	---	5.1	8.9	13.1
18.	Percent of rural to total population[17]	---	---	---	---	---	100.0	94.9	91.1	86.9

GENERAL POPULATION STATISTICS, 1790-1990 (Cont.)												
IOWA												
Item No.	1880	1890	1900	1910	1920	1930	1940	1950	1960	1970	1980	1990
1.	1,624,615	1,912,297	2,231,853	2,224,771	2,404,021	2,470,939	2,538,268	2,621,073	2,757,537	2,824,376	2,913,808	2,776,755
2.	36.1	17.7	16.7	-0.3	8.1	2.8	2.7	3.3	5.2	2.4	3.1	-4.7
3.	430,595	287,682[*b]	319,556[*b]	-7,082[*a]	179,250[*a]	66,918[*a]	67,329[*a]	82,805[*a]	136,464	66,839	89,432[*a]	-137,053
4.	3.2	3.0	2.9	2.4	2.3	2.0	1.9	1.7	1.5	1.4	---	1.1
5.	29.2	34.4	40.2	40.0	43.2	44.5	45.3	46.8	49.2	50.5	52.1	49.1
6.	11	11	11	11	11	9	8	8	7	6	6	---
7.	1,614,600	1,901,090	2,218,667	2,209,191	2,384,181	2,452,677	2,520,691	2,599,546	2,728,709	2,782,762	2,838,805	2,683,090
8.	35.9	17.7	16.7	-0.4[*a]	7.9	2.9[*a]	2.8[*a]	3.1[*a]	5.0[*a]	2.0[*a]	2.0[*a]	-5.5
9.	9,516	10,685	12,693	14,973	19,005	17,380	16,694	19,692	25,354	32,596	41,700	48,090
10.	65.2	12.3	18.8	18.0[*a]	26.9	-8.6	-3.9[*a]	18.0[*a]	28.8[*a]	28.6[*a]	27.9	15.3
11.	0.6	0.6	0.6[*a]	0.7[*a]	0.8[*a]	0.7[*a]	0.7[*a]	0.8[*a]	0.9[*a]	1.2	1.4	1.7
12.	---	---	---	---	---	---	---	---	---	---	---	---
13.	247,427	405,764	572,386	680,054	875,495	979,292	1,084,231	1,229,433[*c] 1,250,938[*d]	1,439,525[*c] 1,462,512[*d]	1,616,405	1,708,232	---
14.	58.3	64.0	41.1	18.8	28.7	11.9	10.7	13.4[*c]	17.1[*c] 16.9[*d]	10.5	5.7	---
15.	1,377,188	1,506,533	1,659,467	1,544,717	1,528,526	1,491,647	1,454,037	1,391,640[*c] 1,370,135[*d]	1,318,012[*c] 1,295,025[*d]	1,207,971	1,205,576	---
16.	32.7	9.4	10.2	-6.9	-1.0	-2.4	-2.5	-4.3	-5.3[*c] -5.5[*d]	-6.7	-0.2	---
17.	15.2	21.2	25.6	30.6	36.4	39.6	42.7	46.9[*c] 47.7[*d]	52.2[*c] 53.0[*d]	57.2	58.6	---
18.	84.8	78.8	74.4	69.4	63.6	60.4	57.3	53.1[*c] 52.3[*d]	47.8[*c] 47.0[*d]	42.8	41.4	---

[a] Percentage computed by compiler from data herein. See endnotes for source of data.
[b] Percentage computed by compiler from data herein is different from percentage given in source. The above percentage is the percentage computed by compiler.
[c] Previous urban definition (pre-1950).
[d] Current urban definition (1950 and after; see Glossary of Terms).
[*] Includes population of area constituting that part of Minnesota lying west of the Mississippi River and a line drawn from its source northwards to the Canadian Boundary.

GENERAL POPULATION STATISTICS, 1790-1990										
KANSAS										
Item No.		1790 (or 1789)	1800	1810	1820	1830	1840	1850	1860	1870
1.	Population[1]	---	---	---	---	---	---	---	107,206	364,399
2.	Decennial rates of increase in population over preceding census[2]	---	---	---	---	---	---	---	---	239.9
3.	Increase in population over previous census[1,3]	---	---	---	---	---	---	---	107,206	257,193
4.	Percent distribution of population[4]	---	---	---	---	---	---	---	0.3	0.9
5.	Population per square mile of land area[5,6]	---	---	---	---	---	---	---	1.3	4.5
6.	Membership of House of Representatives at each apportionment[7]	---	---	---	---	---	---	---	1	3
7.	White population[8,9,10]	---	---	---	---	---	---	---	106,390	346,377
8.	Percentage increase in white population over preceding census[9,10,11]	---	---	---	---	---	---	---	---	225.6
9.	Black population[8,9,10]	---	---	---	---	---	---	---	627	17,108
10.	Percentage increase in Black population over preceding census[9,10,11,12,13,14]	---	---	---	---	---	---	---	---	2,628.5
11.	Percent Black in total population[1,8,9,10,14,15]	---	---	---	---	---	---	---	0.58	4.69
12.	Number of slaves in the area enumerated in 1790 and in the added area[16]	---	---	---	---	---	---	---	2	---
13.	Urban population[17]	---	---	---	---	---	---	---	10,045	51,870
14.	Percent urban increase over preceding census[17]	---	---	---	---	---	---	---	---	416.4
15.	Rural population[17]	---	---	---	---	---	---	---	97,161	312,529
16.	Percent rural increase over preceding census[17]	---	---	---	---	---	---	---	---	221.7
17.	Percent of urban to total population[17]	---	---	---	---	---	---	---	9.4	14.2
18.	Percent of rural to total population[17]	---	---	---	---	---	---	---	90.6	85.8

GENERAL POPULATION STATISTICS, 1790-1990 (Cont.)												
KANSAS												
Item No.	1880	1890	1900	1910	1920	1930	1940	1950	1960	1970	1980	1990
1.	996,096	1,428,108	1,470,495	1,690,949	1,769,257	1,880,999	1,801,028	1,905,299	2,178,611	2,246,578	2,363,679	2,477,574
2.	173.4	43.4	3.0	15.0	4.6	6.3	-4.3	5.8	14.3	3.1	5.1	4.8
3.	631,697	432,000[*b]	42,387	220,454[*a]	78,308[*a]	111,742[*a]	-79,971[*a]	104,271[*a]	273,312	67,967	117,101[*a]	113,895
4.	2.0	2.3	1.9	1.8	1.7	1.5	1.4	1.3	1.2	1.1	---	1.0
5.	12.2	17.5	18.0	20.7	21.6	22.9	21.9	23.2	26.6	27.5	28.9	30.3
6.	7	8	8	8	8	7	6	6	5	5	5	---
7.	952,155	1,376,619	1,416,319	1,634,352	1,708,906	1,811,997	1,734,496	1,828,961	2,078,666	2,122,068	2,167,752	2,231,986
8.	174.9	44.6	2.9	15.4[*a]	4.6	6.0[*a]	-4.3[*a]	5.4[*a]	13.7[*a]	2.1[*a]	2.2[*a]	3.0[*b]
9.	43,107	49,710	52,003	54,030	57,925	66,344	65,138	73,158	91,445	106,977	126,127	143,076
10.	152.0	15.3	4.6	3.9[*a]	7.2	14.5	-1.8[*a]	12.3[*a]	25.0[*a]	17.0[*a]	17.9	13.4
11.	4.3	3.5	3.5[*a]	3.2[*a]	3.3[*a]	3.5[*a]	3.6[*a]	3.8[*a]	4.2[*a]	4.8	5.3	5.8
12.	---	---	---	---	---	---	---	---	---	---	---	---
13.	104,956	269,539	329,696	492,312	616,485	729,834	753,941	903,468[*c] 993,220[*d]	1,228,646[*c] 1,328,741[*d]	1,484,870	1,575,899	---
14.	102.3	156.8	22.3	49.3	25.2	18.4	3.3	19.8[*c] ---[*d]	36.0[*c] 33.8[*d]	11.8	6.1	---
15.	891,140	1,158,569	1,140,799	1,198,637	1,152,772	1,151,165	1,047,087	1,001,831[*c] 912,079[*d]	949,965[*c] 849,870[*d]	761,708	787,780	---
16.	185.1	30.0	-1.5	5.1	-3.8	-0.1	-9.0	-4.3[*c] ---[*d]	-5.2[*c] -6.8[*d]	-10.4	3.4	---
17.	10.5	18.9	22.4	29.1	34.8	38.8	41.9	47.4[*c] 52.1[*d]	56.4[*c] 61.0[*d]	66.1	66.7	---
18.	89.5	81.1	77.6	70.9	65.2	61.2	58.1	52.6[*c] 47.9[*d]	43.6[*c] 39.0[*d]	33.9	33.3	---

[a] Percentage computed by compiler from data herein. See endnotes for source of data.
[b] Percentage computed by compiler from data herein is different from percentage given in source. The above percentage is the percentage computed by compiler.
[c] Previous urban definition (pre-1950).
[d] Current urban definition (1950 and after; see Glossary of Terms).

GENERAL POPULATION STATISTICS, 1790-1990										
KENTUCKY										
Item No.		1790 (or 1789)	1800	1810	1820	1830	1840	1850	1860	1870
1.	Population[1]	73,677	220,955	406,511	564,317	687,917	779,828	982,405	1,155,684	1,321,011
2.	Decennial rates of increase in population over preceding census[2]	---	199.9	84.0	38.8	21.9	13.4	26.0	17.6	14.3
3.	Increase in population over previous census[1,3]	---	147,278	185,556	157,806	123,600	91,911	202,577	173,279	165,327
4.	Percent distribution of population[4]	1.9	4.2	5.6	5.9	5.3	4.6	4.2	3.7	3.4
5.	Population per square mile of land area[5,6]	---	5.5	---	---	---	---	24.4	28.8	32.9
6.	Membership of House of Representatives at each apportionment[7]	2	6	10	12	13	10	10	9	10
7.	White population[8,9,10]	61,133	179,873	324,237	434,826	517,787	590,253	761,413	919,484	1,098,692
8.	Percentage increase in white population over preceding census[9,10,11]	---	194.2	80.3	34.1	19.1	14.0	29.0	20.8	19.5
9.	Black population[8,9,10]	12,544	41,082	82,274	129,491	170,130	189,575	220,992	236,167	222,210
10.	Percentage increase in Black population over preceding census[9,10,11,12,13,14]	---	227.5	100.3	57.4	31.4	11.4	16.6	6.9	-5.9
11.	Percent Black in total population[1,8,9,10,14,15]	17.0[*a]	18.6[*a]	20.2[*a]	22.9[*a]	24.7[*a]	24.3[*a]	22.5	20.4	16.8
12.	Number of slaves in the area enumerated in 1790 and in the added area[16]	12,430	40,343	80,561	126,732	165,213	182,258	210,981	225,483	---
13.	Urban population[17]	---	---	4,326	9,291	16,367	30,948	73,804	120,624	195,896
14.	Percent urban increase over preceding census[17]	---	---	---	114.8	76.2	89.1	138.5	63.4	62.4
15.	Rural population[17]	73,677	220,955	402,185	555,026	671,550	748,880	908,601	1,035,060	1,125,115
16.	Percent rural increase over preceding census[17]	---	199.9	82.0	38.0	21.0	11.5	21.3	13.9	8.7
17.	Percent of urban to total population[17]	---	---	1.1	1.6	2.4	4.0	7.5	10.4	14.8
18.	Percent of rural to total population[17]	100.0	100.0	98.9	98.4	97.6	96.0	92.5	89.6	85.2

GENERAL POPULATION STATISTICS, 1790-1990 (Cont.)												
KENTUCKY												
Item No.	1880	1890	1900	1910	1920	1930	1940	1950	1960	1970	1980	1990
1.	1,648,690	1,858,635	2,147,174	2,289,905	2,416,630	2,614,589	2,845,627	2,944,806	3,038,156	3,218,706	3,660,777	3,685,296
2.	24.8	12.7	15.5	6.6	5.5	8.2	8.8	3.5	3.2	5.9	13.7	0.7
3.	327,679	209,945	288,539	142,731[*a]	126,725[*a]	197,959[*a]	231,038[*a]	99,179[*a]	93,350	180,550	442,071[*a]	24,519
4.	3.3	3.0	2.8	2.5	2.3	2.1	2.2	1.9	1.7	1.6	---	1.5
5.	41.0	46.3	53.4	57.0	60.1	65.2	70.9	73.9	76.2	81.2	92.3	92.8
6.	11	11	11	11	11	9	9	8	7	7	7	---
7.	1,377,179	1,590,462	1,862,309	2,027,951	2,180,560	2,388,452	2,631,425	2,742,090	2,820,083	2,981,766	3,379,648	3,391,832
8.	25.3	15.5	17.1	8.9[*a]	7.5	9.5[*a]	10.2[*a]	4.2[*a]	2.8[*a]	5.7[*a]	13.3[*a]	0.4
9.	271,451	268,071	284,706	261,656	235,938	226,040	214,031	201,921	215,949	230,793	259,490	262,907
10.	22.2	-1.2	6.2	-8.1[*a]	-9.8	-4.2	-5.3[*a]	-5.7[*a]	6.9[*a]	6.9[*a]	12.4	1.3
11.	16.5	14.4	13.3[*a]	11.4[*a]	9.8[*a]	8.6[*a]	7.5[*a]	6.9[*a]	7.1[*a]	7.2	7.1	7.1
12.	---	---	---	---	---	---	---	---	---	---	---	---
13.	249,923	356,713	467,668	555,442	633,543	799,026	849,327	985,739[*c] 1,084,070[*d]	1,144,583[*c] 1,353,215[*d]	1,684,053	1,862,183	---
14.	27.6	42.7	31.1	18.8	14.1	26.1	6.3	16.11[*c] ---[*d]	16.1[*c] 24.8[*d]	24.4	10.6	---
15.	1,398,767	1,501,922	1,679,506	1,734,463	1,783,087	1,815,563	1,996,300	1,959,067[*c] 1,860,736[*d]	1,893,573[*c] 1,684,941[*d]	1,534,653	1,798,594	---
16.	24.3	7.4	11.8	3.3	2.8	1.8	10.0	-1.9[c] ---[*d]	-3.3[*c] -9.4[*d]	-8.9	17.2	---
17.	15.2	19.2	21.8	24.3	26.2	30.6	29.8	33.5[*c] 36.8[*d]	37.7[*c] 44.5[*d]	52.3	50.9	---
18.	84.8	80.8	78.2	75.7	73.8	69.4	70.2	66.5[*c] 63.2[*d]	62.3[*c] 55.5[*d]	47.7	49.1	---

[a] Percentage computed by compiler from data herein. See endnotes for source of data.
[b] Percentage computed by compiler from data herein is different from percentage given in source. The above percentage is the percentage computed by compiler.
[c] Previous urban definition (pre-1950).
[d] Current urban definition (1950 and after; see Glossary of Terms).

GENERAL POPULATION STATISTICS, 1790-1990										
LOUISIANA										
Item No.		1790 (or 1789)	1800	1810	1820	1830	1840	1850	1860	1870
1.	Population[1]	---	---	76,556	153,407	215,739	352,411	517,762	708,002	726,915
2.	Decennial rates of increase in population over preceding census[2]	---	---	---	100.4	40.6	63.4	46.9	36.7	2.7
3.	Increase in population over previous census[1,3]	---	---	76,556	76,851	62,332	136,672	165,351	190,240	18,913
4.	Percent distribution of population[4]	---	---	1.1	1.6	1.7	2.1	2.2	2.3	1.9
5.	Population per square mile of land area[5,6]	---	---	---	---	---	---	11.4	15.6	16.0
6.	Membership of House of Representatives at each apportionment[7]	---	---	1	3	3	4	4	5	6
7.	White population[8,9,10]	---	---	34,311	73,867	89,441	158,457	255,491	357,456	362,065
8.	Percentage increase in white population over preceding census[9,10,11]	---	---	---	115.3	21.1	77.2	61.2	39.9	1.3
9.	Black population[8,9,10]	---	---	42,245	79,540	126,298	193,954	262,271	350,373	364,210
10.	Percentage increase in Black population over preceding census[9,10,11,12,13,14]	---	---	---	88.3	58.8	53.6	35.2	33.6	3.9
11.	Percent Black in total population[1,8,9,10,14,15]	---	---	55.2[*a]	51.8[*a]	58.5[*a]	55.0[*a]	50.7	49.5	50.1
12.	Number of slaves in the area enumerated in 1790 and in the added area[16]	---	---	34,660[*e]	69,064	109,588	168,452	244,809	331,726	---
13.	Urban population[17]	---	---	17,242	27,176	46,082	105,400	134,470	185,026	202,523
14.	Percent urban increase over preceding census[17]	---	---	---	57.6	69.6	128.7	27.6	37.6	9.5
15.	Rural population[17]	---	---	59,314	126,231	169,657	247,011	383,292	522,976	524,392
16.	Percent rural increase over preceding census[17]	---	---	---	112.8	34.4	45.6	55.2	36.4	0.3
17.	Percent of urban to total population[17]	---	---	22.5	17.7	21.4	29.9	26.0	26.1	27.9
18.	Percent of rural to total population[17]	---	---	77.5	82.3	78.6	70.1	74.0	73.9	72.1

GENERAL POPULATION STATISTICS, 1790-1990 (Cont.)

LOUISIANA

Item No.	1880	1890	1900	1910	1920	1930	1940	1950	1960	1970	1980	1990
1.	939,946	1,118,588	1,381,625	1,656,388	1,798,509	2,101,593	2,363,880	2,683,516	3,257,022	3,641,306	4,205,900	4,219,973
2.	29.3	19.0	23.5	19.9	8.6	16.9	12.5	13.5	21.4	11.8	15.4	0.3
3.	213,031	178,642*b	263,037*b	274,763*a	142,121*a	303,084*a	262,287*a	319,636*a	573,506	384,284	564,594*a	14,073
4.	1.9	1.8	1.8	1.8	1.7	1.7	1.8	1.8	1.8	1.8	---	1.7
5.	20.7	24.6	30.4	36.5	39.6	46.5	52.3	59.4	72.2	81.0	94.5	96.9
6.	6	6	7	8	8	8	8	8	8	8	8	---
7.	454,954	558,395	729,612	941,086	1,096,611	1,322,712	1,511,739	1,796,683	2,211,715	2,541,498	2,911,243	2,839,138
8.	25.7	22.7	30.7	29.0*a	16.5	20.6*a	14.3*a	18.8*a	23.1*a	14.9*a	14.5*a	-2.5
9.	483,655	559,193	650,804	713,874	700,257	776,326	849,303	882,428	1,039,207	1,086,832	1,237,263	1,299,281
10.	32.8	15.6	16.4	9.7*a	-1.9	10.9	9.4*a	3.9*a	17.8*a	4.6*a	13.8	5.0*b
11.	51.5	50.0	47.1*a	43.1*a	38.9*a	36.9*a	35.9*a	32.9*a	31.9*a	29.8	29.4	30.8
12.	---	---	---	---	---	---	---	---	---	---	---	---
13.	239,390	283,845	366,288	496,516	628,163	833,532	980,439	1,379,998*c 1,471,696*d	1,831,812*c 2,060,606*d	2,406,150	2,887,309	---
14.	18.2	18.6	29.0	35.6	26.5	32.7	17.6	40.8*c ---*d	32.7*c 40.0*d	16.8	19.2	---
15.	700,556	834,743	1,015,337	1,159,872	1,170,346	1,268,061	1,383,441	1,303,518*c 1,211,820*d	1,425,210*c 1,196,416*d	1,235,156	1,318,591	---
16.	33.6	19.2	21.6	14.2	0.9	8.3	9.1	-5.8*c ---*d	9.3*c -1.3*d	3.2	8.2	---
17.	25.5	25.4	26.5	30.0	34.9	39.7	41.5	51.4*c 54.8*d	56.2*c 63.3*d	66.1	68.6	---
18.	74.5	74.6	73.5	70.0	65.1	60.3	58.5	48.6*c 45.2*d	43.8*c 36.7*d	33.9	31.4	---

[a] Percentage computed by compiler from data herein. See endnotes for source of data.
[b] Percentage computed by compiler from data herein is different from percentage given in source. The above percentage is the percentage computed by compiler.
[c] Previous urban definition (pre-1950).
[d] Current urban definition (1950 and after; see Glossary of Terms).
[e] In 1810 Louisiana was called "Orleans Territory," and the name "Louisiana Territory" was applied to the remainder of the Louisiana Purchase, which was unorganized.

GENERAL POPULATION STATISTICS, 1790-1990										
MAINE										
Item No.		1790 (or 1789)	1800	1810	1820	1830	1840	1850	1860	1870
1.	Population[1]	96,540	151,719	228,705	298,335	399,455	501,793	583,169	628,279	626,915
2.	Decennial rates of increase in population over preceding census[2]	---	57.2	50.7	30.4	33.9	25.6	16.2	7.7	-0.2
3.	Increase in population over previous census[1,3]	---	55,179	76,986	69,630	101,120	102,338	81,376	45,110	-1,364
4.	Percent distribution of population[4]	2.5	2.9	3.2	3.1	3.1	2.9	2.5	2.0	1.6
5.	Population per square mile of land area[5,6]	---	5.1	---	---	---	---	19.5	21.0	21.0
6.	Membership of House of Representatives at each apportionment[7]	---	---	---	7	8	7	6	5	5
7.	White population[8,9,10]	96,002	150,901	227,736	297,406	398,263	500,438	581,813	626,947	624,809
8.	Percentage increase in white population over preceding census[9,10,11]	---	57.2	50.9	30.6	33.9	25.7	16.3	7.8	-0.3
9.	Black population[8,9,10]	538	818	969	929	1,192	1,355	1,356	1,327	1,606
10.	Percentage increase in Black population over preceding census[9,10,11,12,13,14]	---	52.0	18.5	-4.1	28.3	13.7	0.1	-2.1	21.0
11.	Percent Black in total population[1,8,9,10,14,15]	0.6[*a]	0.5[*a]	0.4[*a]	0.3[*a]	0.3[*a]	0.3[*a]	0.2	0.2	0.3
12.	Number of slaves in the area enumerated in 1790 and in the added area[16]	---	---	---	---	2	---	---	---	---
13.	Urban population[17]	---	3,704	7,169	8,581	12,598	39,342	78,925	104,373	131,744
14.	Percent urban increase over preceding census[17]	---	---	93.5	19.7	46.8	212.3	100.6	32.2	26.2
15.	Rural population[17]	96,540	148,015	221,536	289,754	386,857	462,451	504,244	523,906	495,171
16.	Percent rural increase over preceding census[17]	---	53.3	49.7	30.8	33.5	19.5	9.0	3.9	-5.5
17.	Percent of urban to total population[17]	---	2.4	3.1	2.9	3.2	7.8	13.5	16.6	21.0
18.	Percent of rural to total population[17]	100.0	97.6	96.9	97.1	96.8	92.2	86.5	83.4	79.0

GENERAL POPULATION STATISTICS, 1790-1990 (Cont.)

MAINE

Item No.	1880	1890	1900	1910	1920	1930	1940	1950	1960	1970	1980	1990
1.	648,936	661,086	694,466	742,371	768,014	797,423	847,226	913,774	969,265	992,048	1,124,660	1,227,928
2.	3.5	1.9	5.0	6.9	3.5	3.8	6.2	7.9	6.1	2.6	13.2	9.2
3.	22,021	12,150	33,380	47,905[*a]	25,643[*a]	29,409[*a]	49,409[*a]	49,803[*a]	66,548	55,491	22,783[*a]	132,612
4.	1.3	1.0	0.9	0.8	0.7	0.6	0.6	0.6	0.5	0.5	---	0.5
5.	21.7	22.1	23.2	24.8	25.7	25.7	27.3	29.4	31.3	32.1	36.3	39.8
6.	4	4	4	4	4	3	3	3	2	2	2	---
7.	646,852	659,263	692,226	739,995	765,695	705,185	844,543	910,846	963,291	925,276	1,190,850	1,208,360
8.	3.5	1.9	5.0	6.9[*a]	3.5	-7.9[*a]	19.8[*a]	7.9[*a]	5.8[*a]	2.3[*a]	12.6[*a]	8.9
9.	1,451	1,190	1,319	1,363	1,310	1,096	1,304	1,221	3,318	2,800	3,128	5,138
10.	-9.7	-18.0	10.8	3.3[*a]	-3.9	-16.3	19.0[*a]	-6.4[*a]	171.7[*a]	-15.6[*a]	11.7	64.3
11.	0.2	0.2	0.2[*a]	0.2[*a]	0.2[*a]	0.1[*a]	0.2[*a]	0.1[*a]	0.3[*a]	0.3	0.3	0.3
12.	---	---	---	---	---	---	---	---	---	---	---	---
13.	146,608	185,725	232,827	262,248	299,569	321,506	343,057	374,507[*c] 472,000[*d]	387,187[*c] 497,114[*d]	504,157	534,072	---
14.	11.3	26.7	25.4	12.6	14.2	7.3	6.7	9.2[*c] ---[*d]	3.4[*c] 5.3[*d]	1.4	5.9	---
15.	502,328	475,361	461,639	480,123	468,445	475,917	504,169	539,267[*c] 441,774[*d]	582,078[*c] 472,151[*d]	487,891	590,588	---
16.	1.4	-5.4	-2.9	4.0	-2.4	1.6	5.9	7.0[*c] ---[*d]	7.9[*c] 6.9[*d]	3.3	21.0	---
17.	22.6	28.1	33.5	35.3	39.0	40.3	40.5	41.0[*c] 51.7[*d]	39.9[*c] 51.3[*d]	50.8	47.5	---
18.	77.4	71.9	66.5	64.7	61.0	59.7	59.5	59.0[*c] 48.3[*d]	60.1[*c] 48.7[*d]	49.2	52.5	---

[a] Percentage computed by compiler from data herein. See endnotes for source of data.
[b] Percentage computed by compiler from data herein is different from percentage given in source. The above percentage is the percentage computed by compiler.
[c] Previous urban definition (pre-1950).
[d] Current urban definition (1950 and after; see Glossary of Terms).

GENERAL POPULATION STATISTICS, 1790-1990										
MARYLAND										
Item No.		1790 (or 1789)	1800	1810	1820	1830	1840	1850	1860	1870
1.	Population[1]	319,728	341,548	380,546	407,350	447,040	470,019	583,034	687,049	780,894
2.	Decennial rates of increase in population over preceding census[2]	---	6.8	11.4	7.0	9.7	5.1	24.0	17.8	13.7
3.	Increase in population over previous census[1,3]	---	21,820	38,998	26,804	39,690	22,979	113,015	104,015	93,845
4.	Percent distribution of population[4]	8.1	6.4	5.3	4.2	3.5	2.8	2.5	2.2	2.0
5.	Population per square mile of land area[5,6]	---	34.4	---	---	---	---	58.6	69.1	78.6
6.	Membership of House of Representatives at each apportionment[7]	8[*e]	9	9	9	8	6	6	5	6
7.	White population[8,9,10]	208,649	216,326	235,117	260,223	291,108	318,204	417,943	515,918	605,497
8.	Percentage increase in white population over preceding census[9,10,11]	---	3.7	8.7	10.7	11.9	9.3	31.3	23.4	17.4
9.	Black population[8,9,10]	111,079	125,222	145,429	147,427	155,932	151,815	165,091	171,434	175,391
10.	Percentage increase in Black population over preceding census[9,10,11,12,13,14]	---	12.7	16.1	1.2	6.0	-2.6	8.7	3.7	2.5
11.	Percent Black in total population[1,8,9,10,14,15]	34.7[*a]	36.7[*a]	38.2[*a]	36.2[*a]	34.9[*a]	32.3[*a]	28.3	24.9	22.5
12.	Number of slaves in the area enumerated in 1790 and in the added area[16,*g]	103,036	107,707[*f]	115,056[*f]	111,917[*f]	107,499[*f]	93,057[*f]	94,055	90,374	---
13.	Urban population[17]	13,503	26,514	46,555	66,378	91,041	113,912	188,045	233,300	295,459
14.	Percent urban increase over preceding census[17]	---	96.4	75.6	42.6	37.2	25.1	65.1	24.1	26.6
15.	Rural population[17]	306,225	315,034	333,991	340,972	355,999	356,107	394,989	453,749	485,435
16.	Percent rural increase over preceding census[17]	---	2.9	6.0	2.1	4.4	---	10.9	14.9	7.0
17.	Percent of urban to total population[17]	4.2	7.8	12.2	16.3	20.4	24.2	32.3	34.0	37.8
18.	Percent of rural to total population[17]	95.8	92.2	87.8	83.7	79.6	75.8	67.7	66.0	62.2

GENERAL POPULATION STATISTICS, 1790-1990 (Cont.)

MARYLAND

Item No.	1880	1890	1900	1910	1920	1930	1940	1950	1960	1970	1980	1990
1.	934,943	1,042,390	1,188,044	1,295,346	1,449,661	1,631,526	1,821,244	2,343,001	3,100,689	3,922,399	4,216,975	4,781,468
2.	19.7	11.5	14.0	9.0	11.9	12.5	11.6	28.6	32.3	26.5	7.5	13.4
3.	154,049	107,447	145,654	107,302[*a]	154,315[*a]	181,865[*a]	189,718[*a]	521,757[*a]	757,688	821,710	294,576[*a]	564,493
4.	1.9	1.7	1.6	1.4	1.4	1.3	1.4	1.5	1.7	1.9	---	1.9
5.	94.0	104.9	119.5	130.3	145.8	165.0	184.2	237.1	313.5	396.6	428.7	489.2
6.	6	6	6	6	6	6	6	7	8	8	8	---
7.	724,693	826,493	952,424	1,062,639	1,204,737	1,354,226	1,518,481	1,954,975	2,573,919	3,194,888	3,158,412	3,393,964
8.	19.7	14.0	15.2	11.6[*a]	13.4	12.4[*a]	12.1[*a]	28.7[*a]	31.7[*a]	24.1[*a]	-1.1[*a]	7.5[*b]
9.	210,230	215,657	235,064	232,250	244,479	276,379	301,931	385,972	518,410	699,479	958,050	1,189,899
10.	19.9	2.6	9.0	-1.2[*a]	5.3	13.0	9.2[*a]	27.8[*a]	34.3[*a]	34.9[*a]	37.0	24.2
11.	22.5	20.7	19.8[*a]	17.9[*a]	16.9[*a]	16.9[*a]	16.6[*a]	16.5[*a]	16.7[*a]	17.8	22.7	24.9
12.	---	---	---	---	---	---	---	---	---	---	---	---
13.	375,843	495,702	591,206	658,192	869,422	974,869	1,080,351	1,425,707[*c] 1,615,902[*d]	1,742,138[*c] 2,253,832[*d]	3,003,935	3,386,555	---
14.	27.2	31.9	19.3	11.3	32.1	12.1	10.8	32.0[*c] ---[*d]	22.2[*c] 39.5[*d]	33.3	12.7	---
15.	559,100	546,688	596,838	637,154	580,239	656,657	740,893	917,294[*c] 727,099[*d]	1,358,551[*c] 846,857[*d]	918,464	830,420	---
16.	15.2	-2.2	9.2	6.8	-8.9	13.2	12.8	23.8[*c] ---[*d]	48.1[*c] 16.5[*d]	8.5	-9.6	---
17.	40.2	47.6	49.8	50.8	60.0	59.8	59.3	60.8[*c] 69.0[*d]	56.2[*c] 72.7[*d]	76.6	80.3	---
18.	59.8	52.4	50.2	49.2	40.0	40.2	40.7	39.2[*c] 31.0[*d]	43.8[*c] 27.3[*d]	23.4	19.7	---

[a] Percentage computed by compiler from data herein. See endnotes for source of data.
[b] Percentage computed by compiler from data herein is different from percentage given in source. The above percentage is the percentage computed by compiler.
[c] Previous urban definition (pre-1950).
[d] Current urban definition (1950 and after; see Glossary of Terms).
[e] Membership in the House of Representatives in 1789: 6.
[f] Alexandria County, which from 1800 to 1840, inclusive, formed a part of the District of Columbia, is here included with Virginia, for comparative purposes.
[g] Includes District of Columbia.

GENERAL POPULATION STATISTICS, 1790-1990

MASSACHUSETTS

Item No.		1790 (or 1789)	1800	1810	1820	1830	1840	1850	1860	1870
1.	Population[1]	378,787	422,845	472,040	472,040	610,408	737,699	994,514	1,231,066	1,457,351
2.	Decennial rates of increase in population over preceding census[2]	---	11.6	11.6	10.9	16.6	20.9	34.8	23.8	18.4
3.	Increase in population over previous census[1,3]	---	44,058	49,195	51,247	87,121	127,291	256,815	236,552	226,285
4.	Percent distribution of population[4]	9.6	8.0	6.5	5.4	4.7	4.3	4.3	3.9	3.8
5.	Population per square mile of land area[5,6]	---	52.6	---	---	---	---	123.7	153.1	181.3
6.	Membership of House of Representatives at each apportionment[7]	14[*e]	17	20	13	12	10	11	10	11
7.	White population[8,9,10]	373,324	416,393	465,303	516,547	603,359	729,030	985,450	1,221,432	1,443,156
8.	Percentage increase in white population over preceding census[9,10,11]	---	11.5	11.7	11.0	16.8	20.8	35.2	23.9	18.2
9.	Black population[8,9,10]	5,463	6,452	6,737	6,740	7,049	8,669	9,064	9,602	13,947
10.	Percentage increase in Black population over preceding census[9,10,11,12,13,14]	---	18.1	4.4	[*f]	4.6	23.0	4.6	5.9	45.3
11.	Percent Black in total population[1,8,9,10,14,15]	1.4[*a]	1.5[*a]	1.4[*a]	1.3[*a]	1.2[*a]	1.2[*a]	0.9	0.8	1.0
12.	Number of slaves in the area enumerated in 1790 and in the added area[16]	---	---	---	---	1	---	---	---	---
13.	Urban population[17]	51,202	65,300	100,617	119,187	189,657	279,454	503,861	733,209	972,081
14.	Percent urban increase over preceding census[17]	---	27.5	54.1	18.5	59.1	47.3	80.3	45.5	32.6
15.	Rural population[17]	327,585	357,545	371,423	404,100	420,751	458,245	490,653	497,857	485,270
16.	Percent rural increase over preceding census[17]	---	9.1	3.9	8.8	4.1	8.9	7.1	1.5	-2.5
17.	Percent of urban to total population[17]	13.5	15.4	21.3	22.8	31.1	37.9	50.7	59.6	66.7
18.	Percent of rural to total population[17]	86.5	84.6	78.7	77.2	68.9	62.1	49.3	40.4	33.3

GENERAL POPULATION STATISTICS, 1790-1990 (Cont.)												
MASSACHUSETTS												
Item No.	1880	1890	1900	1910	1920	1930	1940	1950	1960	1970	1980	1990
1.	1,783,085	2,238,947	2,805,346	3,366,416	3,852,356	4,249,614	4,316,721	4,690,514	5,148,578	5,689,170	5,737,037	6,016,425
2.	22.4	25.6	25.3	20.0	14.4	10.3	1.6	8.7	9.8	10.5	.8	4.9
3.	325,734	455,862[*b]	566,399[*b]	561,070[*a]	485,940[*a]	397,258[*a]	67,107[*a]	373,793[*a]	458,064	540,592	47,867[*a]	279,388
4.	3.6	3.6	3.7	3.7	3.6	3.4	3.3	3.1	2.9	2.8	---	2.4
5.	221.8	278.5	349.0	418.8	479.2	528.6	545.9	396.2	657.3	727.0	733.3	767.6
6.	12	13	14	16	16	15	14	14	12	12	11	---
7.	1,763,782	2,215,373	2,769,764	3,324,926	3,803,524	4,492,992	4,257,596	4,611,503	5,023,444	5,477,624	5,362,836	5,405,374
8.	22.2	25.6	25.0	20.0[*a]	14.4	18.1[*a]	-5.2[*a]	8.3[*a]	8.9[*a]	9.0[*a]	-2.1[*a]	0.8
9.	18,697	22,144	31,974	38,055	45,466	52,365	55,391	73,171	111,842	175,817	221,279	300,130
10.	34.4	18.4	44.4	19.0[*a]	19.5	15.2	5.8[*a]	32.1[*a]	52.9[*a]	57.2[*a]	25.9	35.6
11.	1.1	1.0	1.1[*a]	1.1[*a]	1.2[*a]	1.2[*a]	1.3[*a]	1.6[*a]	2.2[*a]	3.1	3.9	5.0
12.	---	---	---	---	---	---	---	---	---	---	---	---
13.	1,331,580	1,834,888	2,411,877	2,995,739	3,468,916	3,831,426	3,859,476	4,065,801[*c] 3,959,239[*d]	4,471,215[*c] 4,302,530[*d]	4,810,449	4,808,339	---
14.	37.0	37.8	31.4	24.2	15.8	10.5	0.7	5.3[*c] ---[*d]	10.0[*c] 8.7[*d]	11.8	---	---
15.	451,505	404,059	393,469	370,677	383,440	418,188	457,245	624,713[*c] 731,275[*d]	677,363[*c] 846,048[*d]	878,721	928,698	---
16.	-7.0	-10.5	-2.6	-5.8	3.4	9.1	9.3	36.6[*c] ---[*d]	8.4[*c] 15.7[*d]	3.9	5.7	---
17.	74.7	82.0	86.0	89.0	90.0	90.2	89.4	86.7[*c] 84.4[*d]	86.8[*c] 83.6[*d]	84.6	83.8	---
18.	25.3	18.0	14.0	11.0	10.0	9.8	10.6	13.3[*c] 15.6[*d]	13.2[*c] 16.4[*d]	15.4	16.2	---

[a] Percentage computed by compiler from data herein. See endnotes for source of data.
[b] Percentage computed by compiler from data herein is different from percentage given in source. The above percentage is the percentage computed by compiler.
[c] Previous urban definition (pre-1950).
[d] Current urban definition (1950 and after; see Glossary of Terms).
[e] Membership in the House of Representatives in 1789: 8.
[f] Less than one-tenth of one percent.

GENERAL POPULATION STATISTICS, 1790-1990										
MICHIGAN										
Item No.		1790 (or 1789)	1800	1810	1820	1830	1840	1850	1860	1870
1.	Population[1]	---	---	4,762[*e]	8,896[*e]	31,639[*e]	212,267	397,654	749,113	1,184,059
2.	Decennial rates of increase in population over preceding census[2]	---	---	---	86.8	255.7	570.9	87.3	88.4	58.1
3.	Increase in population over previous census[1,3]	---	---	4,762	4,134	22,743	180,628	185,387	351,459	434,946
4.	Percent distribution of population[4]	---	---	0.1	0.1	0.2	1.2	1.7	2.4	3.1
5.	Population per square mile of land area[5,6]	---	---	---	---	---	---	6.9	13.0	20.6
6.	Membership of House of Representatives at each apportionment[7]	---	---	---	---	1	3	4	6	9
7.	White population[8,9,10]	---	---	4,618	8,722	31,346	211,560	395,071	736,142	1,167,282
8.	Percentage increase in white population over preceding census[9,10,11]	---	---	---	88.9	259.4	574.9	86.7	86.3	58.6
9.	Black population[8,9,10]	---	---	144	174	293	707	2,583	6,799	11,849
10.	Percentage increase in Black population over preceding census[9,10,11,12,13,14]	---	---	---	20.8	68.4	141.3	265.3	163.2	74.3
11.	Percent Black in total population[1,8,9,10,14,15]	---	---	3.0[*a]	2.0[*a]	0.9[*a]	0.3[*a]	0.7	0.9	1.0
12.	Number of slaves in the area enumerated in 1790 and in the added area[16]	---	---	24	---	1	---	---	---	---
13.	Urban population[17]	---	---	---	---	---	9,102	29,025	99,701	237,985
14.	Percent urban increase over preceding census[17]	---	---	---	---	---	---	218.9	243.5	138.7
15.	Rural population[17]	---	---	4,762	8,896	31,639	203,165	368,629	649,412	946,074
16.	Percent rural increase over preceding census[17]	---	---	---	86.8	255.7	542.1	81.4	76.2	45.7
17.	Percent of urban to total population[17]	---	---	---	---	---	4.3	7.3	13.3	20.1
18.	Percent of rural to total population[17]	---	---	100.0	100.0	100.0	95.7	92.7	86.7	79.9

GENERAL POPULATION STATISTICS, 1790-1990 (Cont.)												
MICHIGAN												
Item No.	1880	1890	1900	1910	1920	1930	1940	1950	1960	1970	1980	1990
1.	1,636,937	2,093,890	2,420,982	2,810,173	3,668,412	4,842,325	5,256,106	6,371,766	7,823,194	8,875,083	9,262,078	9,295,297
2.	38.2	27.9	15.6	16.1	30.5	32.0	8.5	21.2	22.8	13.4	4.3	0.4
3.	452,878	456,953[*b]	327,092[*b]	389,191[*a]	858,239[*a]	1,173,913[*a]	413,781[*a]	1,115,660[*a]	1,451,428	1,051,889	386,995[*a]	33,219
4.	3.3	3.3	3.2	3.0	3.5	3.9	4.0	4.2	4.4	4.4	---	3.7
5.	28.5	36.4	42.1	48.9	63.8	84.9	92.2	111.7	137.7	156.2	162.6	163.6
6.	11	12	12	13	13	17	17	18	19	19	18	---
7.	1,614,560	2,072,884	2,398,563	2,785,247	3,601,627	4,663,507	5,039,643	5,917,825	7,085,865	7,833,474	7,868,956	7,756,086
8.	38.3	28.4	15.7	16.1[*a]	29.3	29.5[*a]	8.1[*a]	17.4[*a]	19.7[*a]	10.6[*a]	0.5[*a]	1.4[*b]
9.	15,100	15,223	15,816	17,115	60,082	169,453	208,345	442,296	717,581	991,066	1,198,710	1,291,706
10.	27.4	0.8	3.9	8.2[*a]	251.0	182.0	23.0[*a]	112.3[*a]	62.2[*a]	38.1[*a]	21.0	7.7
11.	0.9	0.7	0.7[*a]	0.6[*a]	1.6[*a]	3.5[*a]	4.0[*a]	6.9[*a]	9.2[*a]	11.2	12.9	13.9
12.	---	---	---	---	---	---	---	---	---	---	---	---
13.	405,412	730,294	952,323	1,327,044	2,241,560	3,302,075	3,454,867	4,166,165[*c] 4,503,084[*d]	5,085,882[*c] 5,739,132[*d]	6,553,773	6,551,551	---
14.	70.4	80.1	30.4	39.3	68.9	47.3	4.6	20.6[*c] ---[*d]	22.1[*c] 27.4[*d]	14.2	0.2	---
15.	1,231,525	1,363,596	1,468,659	1,483,129	1,426,852	1,540,250	1,801,239	2,205,601[*c] 1,868,682[*d]	2,737,312[*c] 2,084,062[*d]	2,321,310	2,710,527	---
16.	30.2	10.7	7.7	1.0	-3.8	7.9	16.9	22.4[*c] ---[*d]	24.1[*c] 11.5[*d]	11.4	17.4	---
17.	24.8	34.9	39.3	47.2	61.1	68.2	65.7	65.4[*c] 70.7[*d]	65.0[*c] 73.4[*d]	73.8	70.7	---
18.	75.2	65.1	60.7	52.8	38.9	31.8	34.3	34.6[*c] 29.3[*d]	35.0[*c] 26.6[*d]	26.2	29.3	---

[a] Percentage computed by compiler from data herein. See endnotes for source of data.

[b] Percentage computed by compiler from data herein is different from percentage given in source. The above percentage is the percentage computed by compiler.

[c] Previous urban definition (pre-1950).

[d] Current urban definition (1950 and after; see Glossary of Terms).

[e] Population of Michigan Territory as then constituted; boundaries changed in 1816, 1818, 1834, and 1836.

GENERAL POPULATION STATISTICS, 1790-1990										
MINNESOTA										
Item No.		1790 (or 1789)	1800	1810	1820	1830	1840	1850	1860	1870
1.	Population[1]	---	---	---	---	---	---	6,077	172,023	439,706
2.	Decennial rates of increase in population over preceding census[2]	---	---	---	---	---	---	---	1,000+	155.6
3.	Increase in population over previous census[1,3]	---	---	---	---	---	---	6,077	165,946	267,683
4.	Percent distribution of population[4]	---	---	---	---	---	---	---	0.5	1.1
5.	Population per square mile of land area[5,6]	---	---	---	---	---	---	*e	2.1	5.4
6.	Membership of House of Representatives at each apportionment[7]	---	---	---	---	---	---	2	2	3
7.	White population[8,9,10]	---	---	---	---	---	---	6,038	169,395	438,257
8.	Percentage increase in white population over preceding census[9,10,11]	---	---	---	---	---	---	---	2,705.5	158.7
9.	Black population[8,9,10]	---	---	---	---	---	---	39	259	759
10.	Percentage increase in Black population over preceding census[9,10,11,12,13,14]	---	---	---	---	---	---	---	564.1	193.1
11.	Percent Black in total population[1,8,9,10,14,15]	---	---	---	---	---	---	.64	0.15	0.17
12.	Number of slaves in the area enumerated in 1790 and in the added area[16]	---	---	---	---	---	---	---	---	---
13.	Urban population[17]	---	---	---	---	---	---	---	16,223	70,754
14.	Percent urban increase over preceding census[17]	---	---	---	---	---	---	---	---	336.1
15.	Rural population[17]	---	---	---	---	---	---	6,077	155,800	368,952
16.	Percent rural increase over preceding census[17]	---	---	---	---	---	---	---	2,463.8	136.8
17.	Percent of urban to total population[17]	---	---	---	---	---	---	---	9.4	16.1
18.	Percent of rural to total population[17]	---	---	---	---	---	---	100.0	90.6	83.9

GENERAL POPULATION STATISTICS, 1790-1990 (Cont.)

MINNESOTA

Item No.	1880	1890	1900	1910	1920	1930	1940	1950	1960	1970	1980	1990
1.	780,773	1,310,283	1,751,394	2,075,708	2,387,125	2,563,953	2,792,300	2,982,483	3,413,864	3,804,971	4,075,970	4,375,099
2.	77.6	67.8	33.7	18.5	15.0	7.4	8.9	6.8	14.5	11.5	7.1	7.3
3.	341,067	529,510[*b]	441,111[*b]	324,314[*a]	311,417[*a]	176,828[*a]	228,347[*a]	190,183[*a]	431,381	391,107	270,999[*a]	299,129
4.	1.6	2.1	2.3	2.3	2.3	2.1	2.1	2.0	1.9	1.9	---	1.8
5.	9.7	16.2	21.7	25.7	29.5	32.0	34.9	37.3	43.1	48.0	51.2	55.0
6.	5	7	9	10	10	9	9	9	8	8	8	---
7.	776,884	1,296,408	1,737,036	2,059,227	2,368,936	2,542,599	2,768,982	2,953,697	3,371,603	3,736,038	3,936,948	4,130,395
8.	77.3	66.9	34.0	18.5[*a]	15.0	7.3[*a]	8.9[*a]	6.7[*a]	14.1[*a]	10.8[*a]	5.4[*a]	4.9
9.	1,564	3,683	4,959	7,084	8,809	9,445	9,928	14,022	22,263	34,868	53,342	94,944
10.	106.1	135.5	34.6	42.9[*a]	24.4	7.2	5.1[*a]	41.2[*a]	58.8[*a]	56.6[*a]	53.0	78.0
11.	0.2	0.3	0.3[*a]	0.3[*a]	0.4[*a]	0.4[*a]	0.4[*a]	0.5[*a]	0.6[*a]	0.9	1.3	2.2
12.	---	---	---	---	---	---	---	---	---	---	---	---
13.	148,758	443,049	598,100	850,294	1,051,593	1,257,616	1,390,098	1,607,446[*c] 1,624,914[*d]	2,081,140[*c] 2,122,566[*d]	2,527,308	2,725,202	---
14.	110.2	197.8	35.0	42.2	23.7	19.6	10.5	15.6[*c] ---[*d]	29.5[*c] 30.6[*d]	19.1	7.6	---
15.	632,015	867,234	1,153,294	1,225,414	1,335,532	1,306,337	1,402,202	1,375,037[*c] 1,357,569[*d]	1,332,724[*c] 1,291,298[*d]	1,277,663	1,350,768	---
16.	71.3	37.2	33.0	6.3	9.0	-2.2	7.3	-1.9[*c] ---[*d]	-3.1[*c] -4.9[*d]	-1.1	6.1	---
17.	19.1	33.8	34.1	41.0	44.1	49.0	49.8	53.9[*c] 54.5[*d]	61.0[*c] 62.2[*d]	66.4	66.9	---
18.	80.9	66.2	65.9	59.0	55.9	51.0	50.2	46.1[*c] 45.5[*d]	39.0[*c] 37.8[*d]	33.6	33.1	---

[a] Percentage computed by compiler from data herein. See endnotes for source of data.
[b] Percentage computed by compiler from data herein is different from percentage given in source. The above percentage is the percentage computed by compiler.
[c] Previous urban definition (pre-1950).
[d] Current urban definition (1950 and after; see Glossary of Terms).
[e] Less than one-tenth of one percent.

GENERAL POPULATION STATISTICS, 1790-1990										
MISSISSIPPI										
Item No.		1790 (or 1789)	1800	1810	1820	1830	1840	1850	1860	1870
1.	Population[1]	---	7,600[*e]	31,306[*e]	75,448	136,621	375,651	606,526	791,305	827,922
2.	Decennial rates of increase in population over preceding census[2]	---	---	311.9	141.0	81.1	175.0	61.5	30.5	4.6
3.	Increase in population over previous census[1,3]	---	7,600[*b]	23,706[*b]	44,142[*b]	61,173	239,030	230,875	184,779	36,617
4.	Percent distribution of population[4]	---	0.1	0.4	0.8	1.1	2.2	2.6	2.5	2.1
5.	Population per square mile of land area[5,6]	---	.3	---	---	---	---	13.1	17.1	17.9
6.	Membership of House of Representatives at each apportionment[7]	---	---	1	1	2	4	5	5	6
7.	White population[8,9,10]	---	5,179	23,024	42,176	70,443	179,074	295,718	353,899	382,896
8.	Percentage increase in white population over preceding census[9,10,11]	---	---	344.6	83.2	67.0	154.2	65.1	19.7	8.2
9.	Black population[8,9,10]	---	3,671	17,328	33,272	66,178	196,577	310,808	437,404	444,201
10.	Percentage increase in Black population over preceding census[9,10,11,12,13,14]	---	---	372.0	92.0	98.9	197.0	58.1	40.7	1.6
11.	Percent Black in total population[1,8,9,10,14,15]	---	48.3[*a]	55.4[*a]	44.1[*a]	58.4[*a]	52.3[*a]	51.2	55.3	53.7
12.	Number of slaves in the area enumerated in 1790 and in the added area[16]	---	2,995	14,523	32,814	65,659	195,211	309,878	436,631	---
13.	Urban population[17]	---	---	---	---	2,789	3,612	10,723	20,689	33,255
14.	Percent urban increase over preceding census[17]	---	---	---	---	---	29.5	196.9	92.9	60.7
15.	Rural population[17]	---	7,600	31,306	75,448	133,832	372,039	595,803	770,616	794,667
16.	Percent rural increase over preceding census[17]	---	---	311.9	141.0	77.4	178.0	60.1	29.3	3.1
17.	Percent of urban to total population[17]	---	---	---	---	2.0	1.0	1.8	2.6	4.0
18.	Percent of rural to total population[17]	---	100.0	100.0	100.0	98.0	99.0	98.2	97.4	96.0

GENERAL POPULATION STATISTICS, 1790-1990 (Cont.)												
MISSISSIPPI												
Item No.	**1880**	**1890**	**1900**	**1910**	**1920**	**1930**	**1940**	**1950**	**1960**	**1970**	**1980**	**1990**
1.	1,131,597	1,289,600	1,551,270	1,797,114	1,790,618	2,009,821	2,183,796	2,178,914	2,178,141	2,216,912	2,520,638	2,573,216
2.	36.7	14.0	20.3	15.8	-0.4	12.2	8.7	-0.2	---	1.8	13.7	2.1
3.	303,675	158,003	261,670	245,844[*a]	-6,496[*a]	219,203[*a]	173,975[*a]	-4,882[*a]	-773	38,771	303,726[*a]	52,578
4.	2.3	2.0	2.0	1.9	1.7	1.6	1.7	1.4	1.2	1.1	---	1.0
5.	24.4	27.8	33.5	38.8	38.6	43.4	46.1	46.1	46.0	46.9	53.4	54.8
6.	7	7	8	8	8	7	7	6	5	5	5	---
7.	479,398	544,851	641,200	786,111	853,962	998,077	1,106,327	1,188,632	1,257,546	1,393,283	1,615,190	1,633,461
8.	25.2	13.7	17.7	22.6[*a]	8.6	16.9[*a]	10.8[*a]	7.4[*a]	5.8[*a]	10.8[*a]	15.9[*a]	1.1
9.	650,291	742,559	907,630	1,009,487	935,184	1,009,718	1,074,578	986,494	915,743	815,770	887,206	915,057
10.	46.4	14.2	22.2	11.2[*a]	-7.4	8.0	6.4[*a]	-8.2[*a]	-7.2[*a]	-10.9[*a]	8.8	3.1
11.	57.5	57.6	58.5[*a]	56.2[*a]	52.2[*a]	50.2[*a]	49.2[*a]	45.3[*a]	42.0[*a]	36.8	35.2	35.6
12.	---	---	---	---	---	---	---	---	---	---	---	---
13.	34,581	69,966	120,035	207,311	240,121	338,850	432,882	601,772[*c] 607,162[*d]	787,731[*c] 820,805[*d]	986,642	1,192,805	---
14.	4.0	102.3	71.6	72.7	15.8	41.1	27.8	39.0[*c] ---[*d]	30.9[*c] 35.2[*d]	20.2	20.9	---
15.	1,097,016	1,219,634	1,431,235	1,589,803	1,550,497	1,670,971	1,750,914	1,577,142[*c] 1,571,752[*d]	1,390,410[*c] 1,357,336[*d]	1,230,270	1,327,833	---
16.	38.0	11.2	17.3	11.1	-2.5	7.8	4.8	-9.9[*c] ---[*d]	-11.8[*c] -13.6[*d]	-9.4	7.9	---
17.	3.1	5.4	7.7	11.5	13.4	16.9	19.8	27.6[*c] 27.9[*d]	36.2[*c] 37.7[*d]	44.5	47.3	---
18.	96.9	94.6	92.3	88.5	86.6	83.1	80.2	72.4[*c] 72.1[*d]	63.8[*c] 62.3[*d]	55.5	52.7	---

[a] Percentage computed by compiler from data herein. See endnotes for source of data.
[b] Percentage computed by compiler from data herein is different from percentage given in source. The above percentage is the percentage computed by compiler.
[c] Previous urban definition (pre-1950).
[d] Current urban definition (1950 and after; see Glossary of Terms).
[e] Population of those parts of present state included in Mississippi Territory as then constituted.

GENERAL POPULATION STATISTICS, 1790-1990										
MISSOURI										
Item No.		1790 (or 1789)	1800	1810	1820	1830	1840	1850	1860	1870
1.	Population[1]	---	---	19,783	66,586	140,455	383,702	682,044	1,182,012	1,721,295
2.	Decennial rates of increase in population over preceding census[2]	---	---	---	236.6	110.9	173.2	77.8	73.3	45.6
3.	Increase in population over previous census[1,3]	---	---	19,783[*b]	46,803[*b]	73,869	243,247	298,342	499,968	539,283
4.	Percent distribution of population[4]	---	---	0.3	0.7	1.1	2.2	2.9	3.8	4.5
5.	Population per square mile of land area[5,6]	---	---	---	---	---	---	9.9	17.2	25.0
6.	Membership of House of Representatives at each apportionment[7]	---	---	---	1	2	5	7	9	13
7.	White population[8,9,10]	---	---	17,227	56,017	114,795	323,888	592,004	1,063,489	1,603,146
8.	Percentage increase in white population over preceding census[9,10,11]	---	---	---	225.2	104.9	182.1	82.8	79.6	50.7
9.	Black population[8,9,10]	---	---	3,618	10,569	25,660	59,814	90,040	118,503	118,071
10.	Percentage increase in Black population over preceding census[9,10,11,12,13,14]	---	---	---	192.1	142.8	133.1	50.5	31.6	-0.4
11.	Percent Black in total population[1,8,9,10,14,15]	---	---	18.3[*a]	15.9[*a]	18.3[*a]	15.6[*a]	13.2	10.0	6.86
12.	Number of slaves in the area enumerated in 1790 and in the added area[16]	---	---	2,875[*c]	10,222	25,091	58,240	87,422	114,931	---
13.	Urban population[17]	---	---	---	---	4,977	16,469	80,558	203,487	429,578
14.	Percent urban increase over preceding census[17]	---	---	---	---	---	230.9	389.1	152.6	111.1
15.	Rural population[17]	---	---	19,783	66,586	135,478	367,233	601,486	978,525	1,291,717
16.	Percent rural increase over preceding census[17]	---	---	---	236.6	103.5	171.1	63.8	62.7	32.0
17.	Percent of urban to total population[17]	---	---	---	---	3.5	4.3	11.8	17.2	25.0
18.	Percent of rural to total population[17]	---	---	100	100	96.5	95.7	88.2	82.8	75.0

GENERAL POPULATION STATISTICS, 1790-1990 (Cont.)												
MISSOURI												
Item No.	1880	1890	1900	1910	1920	1930	1940	1950	1960	1970	1980	1990
1.	2,168,380	2,679,185	3,106,665	3,293,335	3,404,055	3,629,367	3,784,664	3,954,653	4,319,813	4,676,501	4,916,686	5,117,073
2.	26.0	23.6	16.0	6.0	3.4	6.6	4.3	4.5	9.2	8.3	5.1	4.1
3.	447,065[*b]	510,825[*b]	427,480[*b]	186,670[*a]	110,720[*a]	225,312[*a]	155,297[*a]	169,989[*a]	365,160	356,688	240,185[*a]	200,387
4.	4.3	4.3	4.1	3.6	3.2	2.9	2.9	2.6	2.4	2.3	---	2.1
5.	31.6	39.0	45.2	47.9	49.5	52.8	54.6	57.1	62.6	67.8	71.3	74.3
6.	14	15	16	16	16	13	13	11	10	10	9	---
7.	2,022,826	2,528,458	2,944,843	3,134,932	3,225,044	3,403,876	3,539,187	3,655,593	3,922,967	4,177,495	4,346,267	4,486,228
8.	26.2	25.0	16.5	6.5[*a]	2.9	5.5[*a]	4.0[*a]	3.3[*a]	7.3[*a]	6.5[*a]	4.0[*a]	3.2
9.	145,350	150,184	161,234	157,452	178,241	223,840	224,386	297,088	390,853	480,172	514,274	548,208
10.	23.1	3.3	7.4	-2.3[*a]	13.2	25.6	0.2[*a]	32.4[*a]	31.6[*a]	22.9[*a]	7.1	6.6
11.	6.7	5.6	5.2[*a]	4.8[*a]	5.2[*a]	6.2[*a]	5.9[*a]	7.5[*a]	9.0[*a]	10.3	10.5	10.7
12.	---	---	---	---	---	---	---	---	---	---	---	---
13.	545,993	856,966	1,128,104	1,393,705	1,586,903	1,859,119	1,960,696	2,290,149[*c] 2,432,715[*d]	2,647,003[*c] 2,876,557[*d]	3,277,662	3,349,588	---
14.	27.1	57.0	31.6	23.5	13.9	17.2	5.5	16.8[*c] ---[*d]	15.6[*c] 18.2[*d]	13.9	2.2	---
15.	1,622,387	1,822,219	1,978,561	1,899,630	1,817,152	1,770,248	1,823,968	1,664,504[*c] 521,938[*d]	1,672,810[*c] 1,443,256[*d]	1,398,839	1,567,098	---
16.	25.6	12.3	8.6	-4.0	-4.3	-2.6	3.0	-8.7[*c] ---[*d]	0.5[*c] -5.2[*d]	-3.1	12.0	---
17.	25.2	32.0	36.3	42.3	46.6	51.2	51.8	57.9[*c] 61.5[*d]	61.3[*c] 66.6[*d]	70.1	68.1	---
18.	74.8	68.0	63.7	57.7	53.4	48.8	48.2	42.1[*c] 38.5[*d]	38.7[*c] 33.4[*d]	29.9	31.9	---

[a] Percentage computed by compiler from data herein. See endnotes for source of data.
[b] Percentage computed by compiler from data herein is different from percentage given in source. The above percentage is the percentage computed by compiler.
[c] Previous urban definition (pre-1950).
[d] Current urban definition (1950 and after; see Glossary of Terms).
[e] Reported as for Cape Girardeau, New Madrid, St. Charles, St. Louis, and St. Genevieve districts in the unorganized territory then called "Louisiana Territory." Compare with note for Louisiana.

GENERAL POPULATION STATISTICS, 1790-1990										
MONTANA										
Item No.		1790 (or 1789)	1800	1810	1820	1830	1840	1850	1860	1870
1.	Population[1]	---	---	---	---	---	---	---	---	20,595
2.	Decennial rates of increase in population over preceding census[2]	---	---	---	---	---	---	---	---	---
3.	Increase in population over previous census[1,3]	---	---	---	---	---	---	---	---	---
4.	Percent distribution of population[4]	---	---	---	---	---	---	---	---	0.1
5.	Population per square mile of land area[5,6]	---	---	---	---	---	---	---	---	0.1
6.	Membership of House of Representatives at each apportionment[7]	---	---	---	---	---	---	---	---	---
7.	White population[8,9,10]	---	---	---	---	---	---	---	---	18,306
8.	Percentage increase in white population over preceding census[9,10,11]	---	---	---	---	---	---	---	---	---
9.	Black population[8,9,10]	---	---	---	---	---	---	---	---	183
10.	Percentage increase in Black population over preceding census[9,10,11,12,13,14]	---	---	---	---	---	---	---	---	---
11.	Percent Black in total population[1,8,9,10,14,15]	---	---	---	---	---	---	---	---	0.9
12.	Number of slaves in the area enumerated in 1790 and in the added area[16]	---	---	---	---	---	---	---	---	---
13.	Urban population[17]	---	---	---	---	---	---	---	---	3,106
14.	Percent urban increase over preceding census[17]	---	---	---	---	---	---	---	---	---
15.	Rural population[17]	---	---	---	---	---	---	---	---	17,489
16.	Percent rural increase over preceding census[17]	---	---	---	---	---	---	---	---	---
17.	Percent of urban to total population[17]	---	---	---	---	---	---	---	---	15.1
18.	Percent of rural to total population[17]	---	---	---	---	---	---	---	---	84.9

GENERAL POPULATION STATISTICS, 1790-1990 (Cont.)												
MONTANA												
Item No.	1880	1890	1900	1910	1920	1930	1940	1950	1960	1970	1980	1990
1.	39,159	142,924	243,329	376,053	548,889	537,606	559,456	591,024	674,767	694,409	786,690	799,065
2.	90.1	265.0	70.3	54.5	46.0	-2.1	4.1	5.6	14.2	2.9	13.3	1.6
3.	18,564	103,765[*b]	100,405[*b]	132,724[*a]	172,836[*a]	-11,283[*a]	21,850[*a]	31,568[*a]	83,743	19,642	92,281[*a]	12,375
4.	0.1	0.2	0.3	0.4	0.5	0.4	0.4	0.4	0.4	0.3	---	0.3
5.	.3	1.0	1.7	2.6	3.8	3.7	3.8	4.1	4.6	4.8	5.4	5.5
6.	---	1	1	1	2	2	2	2	2	2	2	---
7.	35,385	127,690	226,283	360,580	534,260	519,808	540,468	572,038	650,738	663,043	740,148	741,111
8.	93.3	260.9	77.2	59.3[*a]	48.2	-2.7[*a]	4.0[*a]	5.8[*a]	13.8[*a]	1.9[*a]	11.6[*a]	0.1
9.	346	1,490	1,523	1,834	1,658	1,256	1,420	1,232	1,467	1,995	1,786	2,381
10.	89.4	330.6	2.2	20.4[*a]	-9.6	-24.2	13.1[*a]	13.2[*a]	19.1[*a]	36.0[*a]	-10.5	33.3
11.	0.9	1.1	0.6[*a]	0.5[*a]	0.3[*a]	0.2[*a]	0.3[*a]	0.2[*a]	0.2[*a]	0.3	0.2	0.3
12.	---	---	---	---	---	---	---	---	---	---	---	---
13.	6,987	38,787	84,554	133,420	172,011	181,036	211,535	252,906[*c] 258,034[*d]	312,232[*c] 338,457[*d]	370,676	416,402	---
14.	125.0	455.1	118.0	57.8	28.9	5.2	16.8	19.6[*c] ---[*d]	23.5[*c] 31.2[*d]	9.5	12.3	---
15.	32,172	104,137	158,775	242,633	376,878	356,570	347,921	338,118[*c] 332,990[*d]	362,535[*c] 336,310[*d]	323,733	370,288	---
16.	84.0	223.7	52.5	52.8	55.3	-5.4	-2.4	-2.8[*c] ---[*d]	7.2[*c] 1.0[*d]	-3.7	14.4	---
17.	17.8	27.1	34.7	35.5	31.3	33.7	37.8	42.8[*c] 43.7[*d]	46.3[*c] 50.2[*d]	53.4	52.9	---
18.	82.2	72.9	65.3	64.5	68.7	66.3	62.2	57.2[*c] 56.3[*d]	53.7[*c] 49.8[*d]	46.6	47.1	---

[a] Percentage computed by compiler from data herein. See endnotes for source of data.
[b] Percentage computed by compiler from data herein is different from percentage given in source. The above percentage is the percentage computed by compiler.
[c] Previous urban definition (pre-1950).
[d] Current urban definition (1950 and after; see Glossary of Terms).

GENERAL POPULATION STATISTICS, 1790-1990

NEBRASKA

Item No.		1790 (or 1789)	1800	1810	1820	1830	1840	1850	1860	1870
1.	Population[1]	---	---	---	---	---	---	---	28,841	122,993
2.	Decennial rates of increase in population over preceding census[2]	---	---	---	---	---	---	---	---	326.5
3.	Increase in population over previous census[1,3]	---	---	---	---	---	---	---	28,841	94,152
4.	Percent distribution of population[4]	---	---	---	---	---	---	---	0.1	0.3
5.	Population per square mile of land area[5,6]	---	---	---	---	---	---	---	0.2	1.6
6.	Membership of House of Representatives at each apportionment[7]	---	---	---	---	---	---	---	1	1
7.	White population[8,9,10]	---	---	---	---	---	---	---	28,696	122,117
8.	Percentage increase in white population over preceding census[9,10,11]	---	---	---	---	---	---	---	---	325.6
9.	Black population[8,9,10]	---	---	---	---	---	---	---	82	789
10.	Percentage increase in Black population over preceding census[9,10,11,12,13,14]	---	---	---	---	---	---	---	---	862.2
11.	Percent Black in total population[1,8,9,10,14,15]	---	---	---	---	---	---	---	0.28	0.64
12.	Number of slaves in the area enumerated in 1790 and in the added area[16]	---	---	---	---	---	---	---	15	---
13.	Urban population[17]	---	---	---	---	---	---	---	---	22,133
14.	Percent urban increase over preceding census[17]	---	---	---	---	---	---	---	---	---
15.	Rural population[17]	---	---	---	---	---	---	---	28,841	100,860
16.	Percent rural increase over preceding census[17]	---	---	---	---	---	---	---	---	249.7
17.	Percent of urban to total population[17]	---	---	---	---	---	---	---	---	18.0
18.	Percent of rural to total population[17]	---	---	---	---	---	---	---	100.0	82.0

GENERAL POPULATION STATISTICS, 1790-1990 (Cont.)												
NEBRASKA												
Item No.	1880	1890	1900	1910	1920	1930	1940	1950	1960	1970	1980	1990
1.	452,402	1,062,656	1,066,300	1,192,214	1,296,372	1,377,963	1,315,834	1,325,510	1,411,330	1,483,493	1,570,006	1,578,385
2.	267.8	134.9	0.3	11.8	8.7	6.3	-4.5	0.7	6.5	5.1	5.7	0.5
3.	329,409	610,254*[b]	3,644*[b]	125,914*[a]	104,158*[a]	81,591*[a]	-62,129*[a]	9,676*[a]	85,820	72,163	86,513*[a]	8,379*[b]
4.	0.9	1.7	1.4	1.3	1.2	1.1	1.0	0.9	0.8	0.7	---	0.6
5.	5.9	13.8	13.9	15.5	16.9	18.0	17.2	17.3	18.4	19.4	20.5	20.5
6.	3	6	6	6	6	5	4	4	3	3	3	---
7.	449,764	1,047,096	1,056,526	1,180,293	1,279,219	1,360,023	1,297,624	1,301,328	1,374,764	1,432,867	1,490,569	1,480,558
8.	268.3	132.8	0.9	11.7*[a]	8.4	6.3*[a]	-4.6*[a]	0.3*[a]	5.6*[a]	4.2*[a]	4.0*[a]	-0.7
9.	2,385	8,913	6,269	7,689	13,242	13,752	14,171	19,234	29,262	39,911	48,389	57,404
10.	202.3	273.7	-29.7	22.7*[a]	72.2	3.9	3.0*[a]	35.7*[a]	52.1*[a]	36.4*[a]	21.2	18.6
11.	0.5	0.8	0.6*[a]	0.6*[a]	1.0*[a]	1.0*[a]	1.1*[a]	1.5*[a]	2.1*[a]	2.7	3.1	3.6
12.	---	---	---	---	---	---	---	---	---	---	---	---
13.	61,307	291,641	252,702	310,852	405,293	486,107	514,148	606,530*[c] 621,905*[d]	733,595*[c] 766,053*[d]	912,598	987,859	---
14.	177.0	375.7	-13.4	23.0	30.4	19.9	5.8	18.0*[c] ---*[d]	20.9*[c] 23.2*[d]	19.1	8.2	---
15.	391,095	771,015	813,598	881,362	891,079	891,856	801,686	718,980*[c] 703,605*[d]	677,735*[c] 645,277*[d]	570,895	581,966	---
16.	287.8	97.1	5.5	8.3	1.1	0.1	-10.1	-10.3*[c] ---*[d]	-5.7*[c] -8.3*[d]	-11.5	1.9	---
17.	13.6	27.4	23.7	26.1	31.3	35.3	39.1	45.8*[c] 46.9*[d]	52.0*[c] 54.3*[d]	61.5	62.9	---
18.	86.4	72.6	76.3	73.9	68.7	64.7	60.9	54.2*[c] 53.1*[d]	48.0*[c] 45.7*[d]	38.5	37.1	---

[a] Percentage computed by compiler from data herein. See endnotes for source of data.
[b] Percentage computed by compiler from data herein is different from percentage given in source. The above percentage is the percentage computed by compiler.
[c] Previous urban definition (pre-1950).
[d] Current urban definition (1950 and after; see Glossary of Terms).

GENERAL POPULATION STATISTICS, 1790-1990										
NEVADA										
Item No.		1790 (or 1789)	1800	1810	1820	1830	1840	1850	1860	1870
1.	Population[1]	---	---	---	---	---	---	---	6,857[*e]	42,491
2.	Decennial rates of increase in population over preceding census[2]	---	---	---	---	---	---	---	---	519.7
3.	Increase in population over previous census[1,3]	---	---	---	---	---	---	---	6,857	35,634
4.	Percent distribution of population[4]	---	---	---	---	---	---	---	---	0.1
5.	Population per square mile of land area[5,6]	---	---	---	---	---	---	---	.1	.4
6.	Membership of House of Representatives at each apportionment[7]	---	---	---	---	---	---	---	1	1
7.	White population[8,9,10]	---	---	---	---	---	---	---	6,812	38,959
8.	Percentage increase in white population over preceding census[9,10,11]	---	---	---	---	---	---	---	---	471.9
9.	Black population[8,9,10]	---	---	---	---	---	---	---	45	357
10.	Percentage increase in Black population over preceding census[9,10,11,12,13,14]	---	---	---	---	---	---	---	---	693.3
11.	Percent Black in total population[1,8,9,10,14,15]	---	---	---	---	---	---	---	0.7	0.8
12.	Number of slaves in the area enumerated in 1790 and in the added area[16]	---	---	---	---	---	---	---	---	---
13.	Urban population[17]	---	---	---	---	---	---	---	---	7,048
14.	Percent urban increase over preceding census[17]	---	---	---	---	---	---	---	---	---
15.	Rural population[17]	---	---	---	---	---	---	---	6,857	35,443
16.	Percent rural increase over preceding census[17]	---	---	---	---	---	---	---	---	416.9
17.	Percent of urban to total population[17]	---	---	---	---	---	---	---	---	16.6
18.	Percent of rural to total population[17]	---	---	---	---	---	---	---	100.0	83.4

GENERAL POPULATION STATISTICS, 1790-1990 (Cont.)

NEVADA

Item No.	1880	1890	1900	1910	1920	1930	1940	1950	1960	1970	1980	1990
1.	62,266	47,355	42,335	81,875	77,407	91,058	110,247	160,083	285,278	488,738	799,184	1,201,833
2.	46.5	-23.9	-10.6	93.4	-5.5	17.6	21.1	45.2	78.2	71.3	31.7	50.1
3.	19,775	-14,911[*b]	5,020[*b]	39,540[*a]	-4,468[*a]	13,651[*a]	19,189[*a]	49,836[*a]	125,195	203,460	310,446[*a]	402,649[*b]
4.	0.1	0.1	0.1	0.1	0.1	0.1	0.1	0.1	0.2	0.2	---	0.5
5.	.6	.4	.4	.7	.7	.8	1.0	1.5	2.6	4.4	7.3	10.9
6.	1	1	1	1	1	1	1	1	1	1	2	---
7.	53,556	39,121	35,405	74,276	70,699	84,515	104,030	149,908	263,443	443,177	699,377	1,012,695
8.	37.5	-27.0	-9.5	109.8[*a]	-4.8	19.5[*a]	23.1[*a]	44.1[*a]	75.7[*a]	70.1[*a]	56.0[*a]	44.8[*b]
9.	488	242	434	513	346	516	664	4,302	13,484	27,762	50,791	78,771
10.	36.7	-50.4	-44.6	18.2[*a]	-32.6	49.1	28.7[*a]	547.9[*a]	213.4[*a]	105.9[*a]	83.0	55.1[*b]
11.	0.8	0.5	1.0[*a]	0.6[*a]	0.4[*a]	0.6[*a]	0.6[*a]	2.7[*a]	4.7[*a]	5.7	6.4	6.6
12.	---	---	---	---	---	---	---	---	---	---	---	---
13.	19,353	16,024	7,195	13,367	15,254	34,464	43,291	84,079[*c] 91,625[*d]	189,165[*c] 200,704[*d]	395,336	682,947	---
14.	174.6	-17.2	-55.1	85.8	14.1	125.9	25.6	94.2[*c] ---[*d]	125.0[*c] 119.0[*d]	97.0	72.8	---
15.	42,913	31,331	35,140	68,508	62,153	56,594	66,956	76,004[*c] 68,458[*d]	96,113[*c] 84,574[*d]	93,402	117,546	---
16.	21.1	-27.0	12.2	95.0	-9.3	-8.9	18.3	13.5[*c] ---[*d]	26.5[*c] 23.5[*d]	10.4	25.8	---
17.	31.1	33.8	17.0	16.3	19.7	37.8	39.3	52.5[*c] 57.2[*d]	66.3[*c] 70.4[*d]	80.9	85.3	---
18.	68.9	66.2	83.0	83.7	80.3	62.2	60.7	47.5[*c] 42.8[*d]	33.7[*c] 29.6[*d]	19.1	14.7	---

[a] Percentage computed by compiler from data herein. See endnotes for source of data.
[b] Percentage computed by compiler from data herein is different from percentage given in source. The above percentage is the percentage computed by compiler.
[c] Previous urban definition (pre-1950).
[d] Current urban definition (1950 and after; see Glossary of Terms).
[e] Population of Nevada Territory as organized in 1861.

GENERAL POPULATION STATISTICS, 1790-1990										
NEW HAMPSHIRE										
Item No.		1790 (or 1789)	1800	1810	1820	1830	1840	1850	1860	1870
1.	Population[1]	141,885	183,858	214,460	244,161	269,328	284,574	317,976	326,073	318,300
2.	Decennial rates of increase in population over preceding census[2]	---	29.6	16.6	13.8	10.3	5.7	11.7	2.5	-2.4
3.	Increase in population over previous census[1,3]	---	41,973	30,602	29,701	25,167	15,246	33,402	8,097	-7,773
4.	Percent distribution of population[4]	3.6	3.5	3.0	2.5	2.1	1.7	1.4	1.0	0.8
5.	Population per square mile of land area[5,6]	---	20.4	---	---	---	---	35.2	36.1	35.2
6.	Membership of House of Representatives at each apportionment[7]	4[*e]	5	6	6	5	4	3	3	3
7.	White population[8,9,10]	141,097	182,998	213,490	243,375	268,721	284,036	317,456	325,579	317,697
8.	Percentage increase in white population over preceding census[9,10,11]	---	29.7	16.7	14.0	10.4	5.7	11.8	2.6	-2.4
9.	Black population[8,9,10]	788	860	970	786	607	538	520	494	580
10.	Percentage increase in Black population over preceding census[9,10,11,12,13,14]	---	9.1	12.8	-19.0	-22.8	-11.4	-3.3	-5.0	17.4
11.	Percent Black in total population[1,8,9,10,14,15]	0.6[*a]	0.5[*a]	0.5[*a]	0.3[*a]	0.2[*a]	0.2[*a]	0.2	0.2	0.2
12.	Number of slaves in the area enumerated in 1790 and in the added area[16]	157	8	---	---	3	1	---	---	---
13.	Urban population[17]	4,720	5,339	6,934	7,327	13,475	28,531	54,327	72,038	83,456
14.	Percent urban increase over preceding census[17]	---	13.1	29.9	5.7	83.9	111.7	90.4	32.6	15.8
15.	Rural population[17]	137,165	178,519	207,526	236,834	255,853	256,043	263,649	254,035	234,844
16.	Percent rural increase over preceding census[17]	---	30.1	16.2	14.1	8.0	0.1	3.0	-3.6	-7.6
17.	Percent of urban to total population[17]	3.3	2.9	3.2	3.0	5.0	10.0	17.1	22.1	26.2
18.	Percent of rural to total population[17]	96.7	97.1	96.8	97.0	95.0	90.0	82.9	77.9	73.8

GENERAL POPULATION STATISTICS, 1790-1990 (Cont.)												
NEW HAMPSHIRE												
Item No.	1880	1890	1900	1910	1920	1930	1940	1950	1960	1970	1980	1990
1.	346,991	376,530	411,588	430,572	443,083	465,293	491,524	533,242	606,921	737,681	921,000	1,109,252
2.	9.0	8.5	9.3	4.6	2.9	5.0	5.6	8.5	13.8	21.5	24.8	20.5
3.	28,691	29,539	35,058	18,984[*a]	12,511[*a]	22,210[*a]	26,231[*a]	41,718[*a]	73,679	130,760	183,319[*a]	188,252[*b]
4.	0.7	0.6	0.5	0.5	0.4	0.4	0.4	0.4	0.3	0.4	---	0.4
5.	38.4	41.7	45.6	47.7	49.1	51.5	54.5	59.1	67.2	81.7	102.4	123.7
6.	2	2	2	2	2	2	2	2	2	2	2	---
7.	346,229	375,840	410,791	429,906	442,331	464,351	490,980	532,275	604,334	733,106	910,099	1,087,433
8.	9.0	8.6	9.3	4.7[*a]	2.9	5.0[*a]	5.7[*a]	8.4[*a]	13.5[*a]	21.3[*a]	24.1[*a]	19.5
9.	685	614	662	564	621	790	414	731	1,903	2,505	3,990	7,198
10.	18.1	-10.4	7.8	-14.8[*a]	10.1	27.2	-47.6[*a]	76.6[*a]	160.3[*a]	31.6[*a]	59.3	80.4
11.	0.2	0.2	0.2[*a]	0.1[*a]	0.1[*a]	0.2[*a]	0.1[*a]	0.1[*a]	0.3[*a]	0.3	0.4	0.6
12.	---	---	---	---	---	---	---	---	---	---	---	---
13.	104,105	147,913	192,240	223,152	250,438	273,079	283,225	312,278[*c] 306,806[*d]	362,859[*c] 353,766[*d]	416,040	480,325	---
14.	24.7	42.1	30.0	16.1	12.2	9.0	3.7	10.3[*c] ---[*d]	16.2[*c] 15.3[*d]	17.6	15.5	---
15.	242,886	228,617	219,348	207,420	192,645	192,214	208,299	220,964[*c] 226,436[*d]	244,062[*c] 253,155[*d]	321,641	440,285	---
16.	3.4	-5.9	-4.1	-5.4	-7.1	-0.2	8.4	6.1[*c] ---[*d]	10.5[*c] 11.8[*d]	27.1	36.9	---
17.	30.0	39.3	46.7	51.8	56.5	58.7	57.6	58.6[*c] 57.5[*d]	59.8[*c] 58.3[*d]	56.4	52.2	---
18.	70.0	60.7	53.3	48.2	43.5	41.3	42.4	41.4[*c] 42.5[*d]	40.2[*c] 41.7[*d]	43.6	47.8	---

[a] Percentage computed by compiler from data herein. See endnotes for source of data.
[b] Percentage computed by compiler from data herein is different from percentage given in source. The above percentage is the percentage computed by compiler.
[c] Previous urban definition (pre-1950).
[d] Current urban definition (1950 and after; see Glossary of Terms).
[e] Membership in the House of Representatives in 1789: 3.

GENERAL POPULATION STATISTICS, 1790-1990

NEW JERSEY

Item No.		1790 (or 1789)	1800	1810	1820	1830	1840	1850	1860	1870
1.	Population[1]	184,139	211,149	245,562	277,575	320,823	373,306	489,555	672,035	906,096
2.	Decennial rates of increase in population over preceding census[2]	---	14.7	16.3	13.0	15.6	16.4	31.1	37.3	34.8
3.	Increase in population over previous census[1,3]	---	27,010	34,413	32,013	43,248	52,483	116,249	182,480	234,061
4.	Percent distribution of population[4]	4.7	4.0	3.4	2.9	2.5	2.2	2.1	2.1	2.3
5.	Population per square mile of land area[5,6]	---	28.1	---	---	----	----	65.2	89.4	120.6
6.	Membership of House of Representatives at each apportionment[7]	5[*e]	6	6	6	6	5	5	5	7
7.	White population[8,9,10]	169,954	194,325	226,868	257,558	300,266	354,588	465,509	646,699	875,407
8.	Percentage increase in white population over preceding census[9,10,11]	---	14.3	16.7	13.5	16.6	17.1	32.4	38.9	35.4
9.	Black population[8,9,10]	14,185	16,824	18,694	20,017	20,557	21,718	24,046	25,336	30,658
10.	Percentage increase in Black population overpreceding census[1,10,11,12,13,14]	---	18.6	11.1	7.1	2.7	5.6	10.7	5.4	21.0
11.	Percent Black in total population[1,8,9,10,14,15]	7.7[*a]	8.0[*a]	7.6[*a]	7.2[*a]	6.4[*a]	5.8[*a]	4.9	3.8	3.4
12.	Number of slaves in the area enumerated in 1790 and in the added area[16]	11,423	12,422	10,851	7,557	2,254	674	236	18[*f]	---
13.	Urban population[17]	---	----	5,979	7,457	18,333	39,548	86,195	219,798	396,012
14.	Percent urban increase over preceding census[17]	---	----	----	24.7	145.8	115.7	118.0	155.0	80.2
15.	Rural population[17]	184,139	211,149	239,583	270,118	302,490	333,758	403,360	452,237	510,084
16.	Percent rural increase over preceding census[17]	---	14.7	13.5	12.7	12.0	10.3	20.9	12.1	12.8
17.	Percent of urban to total population[17]	---	---	2.4	2.7	5.7	10.6	17.6	32.7	43.7
18.	Percent of rural to total population[17]	100.0	100.0	97.6	97.3	94.3	89.4	82.4	67.3	56.3

GENERAL POPULATION STATISTICS, 1790-1990 (Cont.)												
NEW JERSEY												
Item No.	1880	1890	1900	1910	1920	1930	1940	1950	1960	1970	1980	1990
1.	1,131,116	1,444,933	1,883,669	2,537,167	3,155,900	4,041,334	4,160,165	4,835,329	6,066,782	7,168,164	7,364,823	7,730,188
2.	24.8	27.7	30.4	34.7	24.4	28.1	2.9	16.2	25.5	18.2	2.7	5.0
3.	225,020	313,817	438,736	653,498[*a]	618,733[*a]	885,434[*a]	118,831[*a]	675,164[*a]	1,231,453	1,101,382	196,659[*a]	365,365
4.	2.3	2.3	2.5	2.8	3.0	3.3	3.1	3.2	3.4	3.5	---	3.1
5.	150.5	192.3	250.7	337.7	420.0	537.8	553.1	642.8	805.5	953.1	986.2	1,042.0
6.	7	8	10	12	12	14	14	14	15	15	14	---
7.	1,092,017	1,396,581	1,812,317	2,445,894	3,037,087	---	3,931,087	4,511,585	5,539,003	6,349,908	6,127,090	6,130,465
8.	24.7	27.9	29.8	35.0[*a]	24.2	---	---	14.8[*a]	22.8[*a]	14.6[*a]	-3.5[*a]	0.1[*b]
9.	38,853	47,638	69,844	---	117,432	---	226,973	318,565	514,875	770,292	924,786	1,036,825
10.	26.7	22.6	46.6	---	30.5	78.3	---	40.4[*a]	61.6[*a]	49.6[*a]	20.1	12.1
11.	3.4	3.3	3.7[*a]	---	3.7[*a]	---	5.5[*a]	6.6[*a]	8.5[*a]	10.7	12.6	13.4
12.	----	----	----	----	----	----	----	----	----	----	---	----
13.	615,311	904,543	1,329,162	1,938,612	2,522,435	3,339,244	3,394,773	3,918,146[*c] 4,186,207[*d]	5,013,472[*c] 5,374,369[*d]	6,373,405	6,557,377	---
14.	55.4	47.0	46.9	45.9	30.1	32.4	1.7	15.4[*c] ---[*d]	28.0[*c] 28.4[*d]	18.6	2.9	---
15.	515,805	540,390	554,507	598,555	633,465	702,090	765,392	917,183[*c] 692,413[*d]	1,053,310[*c] 692.413[*d]	794,759	807,446	---
16.	1.1	4.8	2.6	7.9	5.8	10.8	9.0	19.8[*c] ---[*d]	14.8[*c] 6.7[*d]	14.8	1.6	---
17.	54.4	62.6	70.6	76.4	79.9	82.6	81.6	81.0[*c] 86.6[*d]	82.6[*c] 88.6[*d]	88.9	89.0	---
18.	45.6	37.4	29.4	23.6	20.1	17.4	18.4	19.0[*c] 13.4[*d]	17.4[*c] 11.4[*d]	11.1	11.0	---

[a] Percentage computed by compiler from data herein. See endnotes for source of data.
[b] Percentage computed by compiler from data herein is different from percentage given in source. The above percentage is the percentage computed by compiler.
[c] Previous urban definition (pre-1950).
[d] Current urban definition (1950 and after; see Glossary of Terms).
[e] Colored apprentices for life, by the act to abolish slavery passed April 18, 1846.
[f] Membership in the House of Representatives in 1789: 4.

GENERAL POPULATION STATISTICS, 1790-1990										
NEW MEXICO										
Item No.		1790 (or 1789)	1800	1810	1820	1830	1840	1850	1860	1870
1.	Population[1]	---	---	---	---	---	---	61,547[*e]	93,516[*e]	91,874
2.	Decennial rates of increase in population over preceding census[2]	---	---	---	---	---	---	---	51.9	-1.8
3.	Increase in population over previous census[1,3]	---	---	---	---	---	---	61,547	31,969	-,642
4.	Percent distribution of population[4]	---	---	---	---	---	---	0.3	0.3	0.2
5.	Population per square mile of land area[5,6]	---	---	---	---	---	---	.3	.4	.7
6.	Membership of House of Representatives at each apportionment[7]	---	---	---	---	---	---	---	---	---
7.	White population[8,9,10]	---	---	---	---	---	---	61,525	82,924	90,393
8.	Percentage increase in white population over preceding census[9,10,11]	---	---	---	---	---	---	---	34.8	9.0
9.	Black population[8,9,10]	---	---	---	---	---	---	22	85	172
10.	Percentage increase in Black population over preceding census[9,10,11,12,13,14]	---	---	---	---	---	---	---	286.4	102.4
11.	Percent Black in total population[1,8,9,10,14,15]	---	---	---	---	---	---	[*f]	0.1	0.2
12.	Number of slaves in the area enumerated in 1790 and in the added area[16]	---	---	---	---	---	---	---	---	---
13.	Urban population[17]	---	---	---	---	---	---	4,539	4,635	4,765
14.	Percent urban increase over preceding census[17]	---	---	---	---	---	---	---	2.1	2.8
15.	Rural population[17]	---	---	---	---	---	---	57,008	88,881	87,109
16.	Percent rural increase over preceding census[17]	---	---	---	---	---	---	---	55.9	-2.0
17.	Percent of urban to total population[17]	---	---	---	---	---	---	7.4	5.0	5.2
18.	Percent of rural to total population[17]	---	---	---	---	---	---	92.6	95.0	94.8

GENERAL POPULATION STATISTICS, 1790-1990 (Cont.)												
NEW MEXICO												
Item No.	1880	1890	1900	1910	1920	1930	1940	1950	1960	1970	1980	1990
1.	119,565	160,282	195,310	327,301	360,350	423,317	531,818	681,187	951,023	1,016,000	1,303,000	1,515,069
2.	30.1	34.1	21.9	67.6	10.1	17.5	25.6	28.1	39.6	6.8	28.1	16.3
3.	27,691	40,717[*b]	35,028[*b]	131,991[*a]	33,049[*a]	62,967[*a]	108,501[*a]	149,369[*a]	269,836	64,977	287,000[*a]	212,069[*b]
4.	0.2	0.3	0.3	0.4	0.3	0.3	0.4	0.5	0.5	0.5	---	0.6
5.	1.0	1.3	1.6	2.7	2.9	3.5	4.4	5.6	7.8	8.4	10.7	12.5
6.	---	---	---	1	1	1	2	2	2	2	3	---
7.	108,721	142,918	180,207	364,594	334,673	391,095	492,312	630,211	875,763	915,815	976,465	1,146,028
8.	20.3	31.5	26.1	102.3[*a]	-8.2	16.9[*a]	25.9[*a]	28.0[*a]	39.0[*a]	4.6[*a]	6.6[*a]	17.4[*b]
9.	1,015	1,956	1,610	1,628	5,733	2,850	4,672	8,408	17,063	19,555	24,042	30,210
10.	490.1	92.7	-17.7	1.1[*a]	252.1	-50.3	63.9[*a]	80.0[*a]	102.9[*a]	14.6[*a]	22.9	25.7[*b]
11.	0.9	1.3	0.8[*a]	0.5[*a]	1.6[*a]	0.7[*a]	0.9[*a]	1.2[*a]	1.8[*a]	1.9	1.8	2.0
12.	---	---	---	---	---	---	---	---	---	---	---	---
13.	6,635	9,970	27,381	46,571	64,960	106,816	176,401	314,636[*c] 341,889[*d]	588,177[*c] 626,479[*d]	708,775	939,963	---
14.	39.2	50.3	174.6	70.1	39.5	64.4	65.1	78.4[*c] ---[*d]	86.9[*c] 83.2[*d]	13.1	32.6	---
15.	112,930	150,312	167,929	280,730	295,390	316,501	355,417	366,551[*c] 339,298[*d]	362,846[*c] 324,544[*d]	307,225	362,931	---
16.	29.6	33.1	11.7	67.2	5.2	7.1	12.3	3.1[*c] ---[*d]	-1.0[*c] -4.3[*d]	-5.3	18.1	---
17.	5.5	6.2	14.0	14.2	18.0	25.2	33.2	46.2[*c] 50.2[*d]	61.8[*c] 65.9[*d]	69.8	72.1	---
18.	94.5	93.8	86.0	85.8	82.0	74.8	66.8	53.8[*c] 49.8[*d]	38.2[*c] 34.1[*d]	30.2	27.9	---

[a] Percentage computed by compiler from data herein. See endnotes for source of data.

[b] Percentage computed by compiler from data herein is different from percentage given in source. The above percentage is the percentage computed by compiler.

[c] Previous urban definition (pre-1950).

[d] Current urban definition (1950 and after; see Glossary of Terms).

[e] 1860 figure includes population of area taken to form part of Arizona Territory in 1863. 1850 figure is for Territory of New Mexico which included greater parts of present states of Arizona and New Mexico and smaller parts of Colorado and Nevada.

[f] Less than one-tenth of one percent.

GENERAL POPULATION STATISTICS, 1790-1990										
NEW YORK										
Item No.		1790 (or 1789)	1800	1810	1820	1830	1840	1850	1860	1870
1.	Population[1]	340,120	589,051	959,049	1,372,812	1,918,608	2,428,921	3,097,394	3,880,735	4,382,759
2.	Decennial rates of increase in population over preceding census[2]	---	73.2	62.8	43.1	39.8	26.6	27.5	25.3	12.9
3.	Increase in population over previous census[1,3]	---	248,931	369,998	413,763	545,796	510,313	668,473	783,341	502,024
4.	Percent distribution of population[4]	8.7	11.1	13.2	14.2	14.9	14.2	13.4	12.3	11.4
5.	Population per square mile of land area[5,6]	---	12.4	---	---	---	---	65.0	81.4	92.0
6.	Membership of House of Representatives at each apportionment[7]	10[*e]	17	27	34	40	34	33	31	33
7.	White population[8,9,10]	314,142	557,731	918,699	1,333,445	1,873,663	2,378,890	3,048,325	3,831,590	4,330,210
8.	Percentage increase in white population over preceding census[9,10,11]	---	77.5	64.7	45.1	40.5	27.0	28.1	25.7	13.0
9.	Black population[8,9,10]	25,978	31,320	40,350	39,367	44,945	50,031	49,069	49,005	52,081
10.	Percentage increase in Black population over preceding census[9,10,11,12,13,14]	---	20.6	28.8	2.4	14.2	11.3	1.9	0.1	6.3
11.	Percent Black in total population[1,8,9,10,14,15]	7.6[*a]	5.3[*a]	4.2[*a]	2.9[*a]	2.3[*a]	2.1[*a]	1.6	1.3	1.2
12.	Number of slaves in the area enumerated in 1790 and in the added area[16]	21,193	20,903	15,017	10,088	75	4	---	---	---
13.	Urban population[17]	39,213	74,757	121,488	160,996	286,618	471,266	873,414	1,524,344	2,189,455
14.	Percent urban increase over preceding census[17]	---	90.6	62.5	32.5	78.0	64.4	85.3	74.5	43.6
15.	Rural population[17]	300,907	514,294	837,561	1,211,816	1,631,990	1,957,655	2,223,980	2,356,391	2,193,304
16.	Percent rural increase over preceding census[17]	---	70.9	62.9	44.7	34.7	20.0	13.6	6.0	-6.9
17.	Percent of urban to total population[17]	11.5	12.7	12.7	11.7	14.9	19.4	28.2	39.3	50.0
18.	Percent of rural to total population[17]	88.5	87.3	87.3	88.3	85.1	80.6	71.8	60.7	50.0

GENERAL POPULATION STATISTICS, 1790-1990 (Cont.)

NEW YORK

Item No.	1880	1890	1900	1910	1920	1930	1940	1950	1960	1970	1980	1990
1.	5,082,871	6,003,174	7,268,894	9,113,614	10,385,227	12,588,066	13,479,142	14,830,192	16,782,304	18,237,000	17,558,000	17,990,455
2.	16.0	18.1	21.1	25.4	14.0	21.2	7.1	10.0	13.2	8.7	-3.7	2.5
3.	700,112	70,092[*b]	7,268,894[*b]	1,844,720[*a]	1,271,613[*a]	2,202,839[*a]	891,076[*a]	1,351,050[*a]	1,952,112	1,454,696[*b]	-679,000[*a]	432,455[*b]
4.	10.1	9.5	9.5	9.9	9.8	10.2	10.2	9.8	9.4	9.0	---	7.2
5.	106.7	126.0	152.5	191.2	217.9	264.2	281.2	309.3	350.6	381.3	370.6	381.0
6.	34	34	37	43	43	45	45	43	41	39	34	---
7.	5,016,022	5,923,955	7,456,881	---	10,172,027	12,153,491	12,879,546	13,872,095	15,287,071	15,834,090	13,961,106	13,385,255
8.	15.8	18.1	20.8	---	13.4	19.5[*a]	6.0[*a]	7.7[*a]	10.2[*a]	3.6[*a]	-11.8[*a]	-4.1
9.	65,104	70,092	99,232	---	498,483	412,814	571,221	918,191	1,417,511	2,168,949	2,401,842	2,859,055
10.	25.0	7.7	41.6	---	47.9	-17.2	38.4[*a]	60.7[*a]	54.4[*a]	53.0[*a]	10.7	19.0
11.	1.3	1.2	1.4[*a]	---	4.8[*a]	3.3[*a]	4.2[*a]	6.2[*a]	8.4[*a]	11.9	13.7	15.9
12.	---	---	---	---	---	---	---	---	---	---	---	---
13.	2,868,529	3,910,278	5,298,111	7,188,131	8,588,586	10,521,952	11,163,393	11,907,044[*c] 12,682,446[*d]	12,220,702[*c] 14,331,925[*d]	15,602,486	14,858,068	---
14.	31.0	36.3	35.5	35.7	19.5	22.5	6.1	6.6[*c] ---[*d]	2.6[*c] 13.0[*d]	8.9	-4.9	---
15.	2,214,342	2,092,896	1,970,783	1,925,483	1,796,641	2,066,114	2,313,249	2,923,148[*c] 2,147,746[*d]	4,561,602[*c] 2,450,379[*d]	2,634,481	2,700,004	---
16.	1.0	-5.5	-5.8	-2.3	-6.7	15.0	12.0	26.4[*c] ---[*d]	56.1[*c] 14.1[*d]	7.5	3.4	---
17.	56.4	65.1	72.9	78.9	82.7	83.6	82.8	80.3[*c] 85.5[*d]	72.8[*c] 85.4[*d]	85.6	84.6	---
18.	43.6	34.9	27.1	21.1	17.3	16.4	17.2	19.7[*c] 14.5[*d]	27.2[*c] 14.6[*d]	14.4	15.4	---

[a] Percentage computed by compiler from data herein. See endnotes for source of data.
[b] Percentage computed by compiler from data herein is different from percentage given in source. The above percentage is the percentage computed by compiler.
[c] Previous urban definition (pre-1950).
[d] Current urban definition (1950 and after; see Glossary of Terms).
[e] Membership in the House of Representatives in 1789: 6.

GENERAL POPULATION STATISTICS, 1790-1990										
NORTH CAROLINA										
Item No.		1790 (or 1789)	1800	1810	1820	1830	1840	1850	1860	1870
1.	Population[1]	353,751	478,103	555,500	638,829	737,987	753,419	869,039	992,622	1,071,361
2.	Decennial rates of increase in population over preceding census[2]	---	21.4	16.2	15.0	15.5	2.1	15.3	14.2	7.9
3.	Increase in population over previous census[1,3]	---	124,352[*b]	77,397	83,329	99,158	15,432	115,620	123,583	78,739
4.	Percent distribution of population[4]	10.0	9.0	7.7	6.6	5.7	4.4	3.7	3.2	2.8
5.	Population per square mile of land area[5,6]	---	9.8	---	---	---	---	17.8	20.4	22.0
6.	Membership of House of Representatives at each apportionment[7]	10[*e]	12	13	13	13	9	8	7	8
7.	White population[8,9,10]	288,204	337,764	376,410	419,200	472,843	484,870	553,028	629,942	678,470
8.	Percentage increase in white population over preceding census[9,10,11]	---	17.2	11.4	11.4	12.8	2.5	14.1	13.9	7.7
9.	Black population[8,9,10]	105,547	140,339	179,090	219,629	265,144	268,549	316,011	361,522	391,650
10.	Percentage increase in Black population over preceding census[9,10,11,12,13,14]	---	33.0	27.6	22.6	20.7	1.3	17.7	14.4	8.3
11.	Percent Black in total population[1,8,9,10,14,15]	29.8[*a]	29.4[*a]	32.2[*a]	34.4[*a]	35.9[*a]	35.6[*a]	36.4	36.4	36.6
12.	Number of slaves in the area enumerated in 1790 and in the added area[16]	100,783	133,296	168,824	204,917	245,601	245,817	288,548	331,059	---
13.	Urban population[17]	---	---	---	12,502	10,455	13,310	21,109	24,554	36,218
14.	Percent urban increase over preceding census[17]	---	---	---	---	-16.4	27.3	58.6	16.3	47.5
15.	Rural population[17]	393,751	478,103	555,500	626,327	727,532	740,109	847,930	968,068	1,035,143
16.	Percent rural increase over preceding census[17]	---	21.4	16.2	12.8	16.2	1.7	14.6	14.2	6.9
17.	Percent of urban to total population[17]	---	---	---	2.0	1.4	1.8	2.4	2.5	3.4
18.	Percent of rural to total population[17]	100.0	100.0	100.0	98.0	98.6	98.2	97.6	97.5	96.6

GENERAL POPULATION STATISTICS, 1790-1990 (Cont.)												
NORTH CAROLINA												
Item No.	1880	1890	1900	1910	1920	1930	1940	1950	1960	1970	1980	1990
1.	1,399,750	1,617,949	1,893,810	2,206,287	2,559,123	32,170,276	3,571,623	4,061,929	4,556,155	5,082,059	5,881,766	6,628,637
2.	30.7	15.6	17.1	16.5	16.0	23.9	12.7	13.7	12.2	11.5	15.7	12.7
3.	328,389	248,497[*b]	275,863[*b]	312,477[*a]	352,836[*a]	611,153[*a]	401,347[*a]	490,306[*a]	494,226	525,904	799,707[*a]	746,871
4.	2.8	2.6	2.5	2.4	2.4	2.6	2.7	2.7	2.5	2.5	---	2.7
5.	28.7	33.2	38.9	45.3	52.5	65.0	72.7	82.7	93.2	104.1	120.4	136.1
6.	9	9	10	10	10	11	12	12	11	11	11	---
7.	867,242	1,055,328	1,263,603	1,500,511	1,783,779	2,234,958	2,567,635	2,983,121	3,399,285	3,901,767	4,453,010	5,008,491
8.	27.8	21.7	19.7	18.7[*a]	18.9	25.3[*a]	14.9[*a]	16.2[*a]	14.0[*a]	14.8[*a]	14.1[*a]	12.5[*b]
9.	531,277	561,018	624,469	697,843	763,407	918,647	981,298	1,047,353	1,116,021	1,126,478	1,316,050	1,456,323
10.	35.7	5.6	11.3	11.7[*a]	9.4	20.3	6.8[*a]	6.7[*a]	6.6[*a]	0.9[*a]	16.8	10.7[*b]
11.	38.0	34.7	33.0[*a]	31.6[*a]	29.8[*a]	29.0[*a]	27.5[*a]	25.8[*a]	24.5[*a]	22.2	22.4	22.0
12.	---	---	---	---	---	---	---	---	---	---	---	---
13.	55,116	115,759	186,790	318,474	490,370	809,847	974,175	1,238,193[*c] 1,368,101[*d]	1,647,085[*c] 1,801,921[*d]	2,285,168	2,822,852	---
14.	52.2	110.0	61.4	70.5	54.0	65.2	20.3	27.1[*c] ---[*d]	33.0[*c] 31.7[*d]	26.8	22.2	---
15.	1,344,634	1,502,190	1,707,020	1,887,813	2,068,753	2,360,429	2,597,448	2,823,736[*c] 2,693,828[*d]	2,909,070[*c] 2,754,234[*d]	2,796,891	3,058,914	---
16.	29.9	11.7	13.6	10.6	9.6	14.1	10.0	8.7[*c] ---[*d]	3.0[*c] 2.2[*d]	1.5	10.4	---
17.	3.9	7.2	9.9	14.4	19.2	25.5	27.3	30.5[*c] 33.7[*d]	36.2[*c] 39.5[*d]	45.0	48.0	---
18.	96.1	92.8	90.1	85.6	80.8	74.5	72.7	69.5[*c] 66.3[*d]	63.8[*c] 60.5[*d]	55.0	52.0	---

[a] Percentage computed by compiler from data herein. See endnotes for source of data.

[b] Percentage computed by compiler from data herein is different from percentage given in source. The above percentage is the percentage computed by compiler.

[c] Previous urban definition (pre-1950).

[d] Current urban definition (1950 and after; see Glossary of Terms).

[*] Membership in the House of Representatives in 1789: 5.

GENERAL POPULATION STATISTICS, 1790-1990										
NORTH DAKOTA										
Item No.		1790 (or 1789)	1800	1810	1820	1830	1840	1850	1860	1870
1.	Population[1]	---	---	---	---	---	---	---	4,837[*e]	2,405[*h]
2.	Decennial rates of increase in population over preceding census[2]	---	---	---	---	---	---	---	---	193.2[*e]
3.	Increase in population over previous census[1,3]	---	---	---	---	---	---	---	4,837[*e]	-2,432[*b,e,h]
4.	Percent distribution of population[4]	---	---	---	---	---	---	---	---	---
5.	Population per square mile of land area[5,6]	---	---	---	---	---	---	---	[*f]	0.1[*f]
6.	Membership of House of Representatives at each apportionment[7]	---	---	---	---	---	---	---	---	---
7.	White population[8,9,10]	---	---	---	---	---	---	---	2,576[*e]	12,887[*e]
8.	Percentage increase in white population over preceding census[9,10,11]	---	---	---	---	---	---	---	---	400.3[*e]
9.	Black population[8,9,10]	---	---	---	---	---	---	---	---	94[*e]
10.	Percentage increase in Black population over preceding census[9,10,11,12,13,14]	---	---	---	---	---	---	---	---	---
11.	Percent Black in total population[1,8,9,10,14,15]	---	---	---	---	---	---	---	---	3.9[*b,e]
12.	Number of slaves in the area enumerated in 1790 and in the added area[16]	---	---	---	---	---	---	---	---	---
13.	Urban population[17]	---	---	---	---	---	---	---	---	---
14.	Percent urban increase over preceding census[17]	---	---	---	---	---	---	---	---	---
15.	Rural population[17]	---	---	---	---	---	---	---	[*g]	2,405
16.	Percent rural increase over preceding census[17]	---	---	---	---	---	---	---	---	---
17.	Percent of urban to total population[17]	---	---	---	---	---	---	---	---	---
18.	Percent of rural to total population[17]	---	---	---	---	---	---	---	[*g]	100.0

GENERAL POPULATION STATISTICS, 1790-1990 (Cont.)

NORTH DAKOTA

Item No.	1880	1890	1900	1910	1920	1930	1940	1950	1960	1970	1980	1990
1.	36,909[*h]	190,983	319,146	577,056	646,872	680,845	641,935	619,636	632,446	617,761	652,717	638,800
2.	1,434.7[*h]	417.4[*h]	67.1	80.8	12.1	5.3	-5.7	-3.5	2.1	-2.3	5.7	-2.1
3.	34,504[*b,h]	154,074[*b,h]	128,163[*b]	257,910[*a]	69,816[*a]	33,973[*a]	-38,910[*a]	-22,299[*a]	12,810	-14,685	34,956[*a]	-13,917
4.	0.1	0.3	0.4	0.6	0.6	0.6	0.5	0.4	0.4	0.3	---	0.3
5.	0.9[*f]	2.7	4.5	8.2	9.2	9.7	9.2	8.8	9.1	8.9	9.4	9.3
6.	1	1	2	3	3	2	2	2	2	1	1	---
7.	36,192[*h]	182,407	311,712	569,855	639,954	671,851	631,464	608,448	619,538	599,485	625,536	604,142
8.	108.8[*b,h]	404.0[*b,h,i]	70.9	82.8[*a]	12.3	5.0[*a]	-6.0[(*a)]	-3.6[*a]	1.8[*a]	-3.2[*a]	4.3[*a]	-3.4
9.	113[*h]	373	286	617	467	377	201	257	777	2,494	2,568	3,524
10.	20.2[*b,h]	230.1[*b,h,i]	-23.3	115.7[*a]	-24.3	-19.3	-46.7[*a]	27.9[*a]	202.3[*a]	221.0[*a]	3.0	37.2
11.	0.3[*h]	0.2	0.1[*a]	0.1[*a]	0.1[*a]	0.1[*a]	[*j]	[*j]	0.1[*a]	0.4	0.4	0.6
12.	---	---	---	---	---	---	---	---	---	---	---	---
13.	2,693	10,643	23,413	63,236	88,239	113,306	131,923	164,817[*c] 164,817[*d]	221,694[*c] 222,708[*d]	273,442	318,310	---
14.	---	295.2	120.0	170.1	39.5	28.4	16.4	24.9[*c] ---[*d]	34.5[*c] 35.1[*d]	22.8	16.4	---
15.	34,216	180,340	295,733	513,820	558,633	567,539	510,012	454,819[*c] 454,819[*d]	410,752[*c] 409,738[*d]	344,319	334,407	---
16.	1,000+	427.1	64.0	73.7	8.7	1.6	-10.1	-10.8[*c] ---[*d]	-9.7[*c] -9.9[*d]	-16.0	-2.9	---
17.	7.3	5.6	7.3	11.0	13.6	16.6	20.6	26.6[*c] 26.6[*d]	35.1[*c] 35.2[*d]	44.3	48.8	---
18.	92.7	94.4	92.7	89.0	86.4	83.4	79.4	73.4[*c] 73.4[*d]	64.9[*c] 64.8[*d]	55.7	51.2	---

[a] Percentage computed by compiler from data herein. See endnotes for source of data.
[b] Percentage computed by compiler from data herein is different from percentage given in source. The above percentage is the percentage computed by compiler.
[c] Previous urban definition (pre-1950).
[d] Current urban definition (1950 and after; see Glossary of Terms).
[e] Dakota Territory (same data listed for South Dakota).
[f] Dakota Territory: less than one-tenth of 1 in 1860, 0.1 in 1870, and 0.9 in 1880.
[g] In 1860 there were 4,837 persons enumerated in Dakota Territory, all of whom were living in rural territory.
[h] Based on the population of the area of Dakota Territory which became North Dakota on November 2, 1889.
[i] Dakota Territory; includes persons specially enumerated in 1890.
[j] Less than one-tenth of one percent.

GENERAL POPULATION STATISTICS, 1790-1990										
OHIO										
Item No.		1790 (or 1789)	1800	1810	1820	1830	1840	1850	1860	1870
1.	Population[1]	---	45,365[*e]	230,760	581,434	937,903	1,519,467	1,980,329	2,339,511	2,665,260
2.	Decennial rates of increase in population over preceding census[2]	---	---	408.7	152.0	61.3	62.0	30.3	18.1	13.9
3.	Increase in population over previous census[1,3]	---	45,365	185,395	350,674	356,469	581,564	460,862	359,182	325,749
4.	Percent distribution of population[4]	---	0.9	3.2	6.0	7.3	8.9	8.5	7.4	6.9
5.	Population per square mile of land area[5,6]	---	1.1	---	---	---	---	48.6	57.4	65.4
6.	Membership of House of Representatives at each apportionment[7]	---	1	6	14	19	21	21	19	20
7.	White population[8,9,10]	---	45,028	228,861	576,711	928,329	1,502,422	1,955,050	2,302,808	2,601,946
8.	Percentage increase in white population over preceding census[9,10,11]	---	---	408.3	152.0	61.0	61.8	30.2	17.8	13.0
9.	Black population[8,9,10]	---	337	1,899	4,723	9,574	17,345	25,279	36,673	63,213
10.	Percentage increase in Black population over preceding census[9,10,11,12,13,14]	---	---	463.5	148.7	102.7	81.2	45.7	45.1	72.4
11.	Percent Black in total population[1,8,9,10,14,15]	---	0.7[*a]	0.8[*a]	0.8[*a]	1.0[*a]	1.1[*a]	1.3	1.6	2.4
12.	Number of slaves in the area enumerated in 1790 and in the added area[16]	---	---	---	---	6	3	---	---	---
13.	Urban population[17]	---	---	2,540	9,642	36,658	83,491	242,418	400,435	682,922
14.	Percent urban increase over preceding census[17]	---	---	---	279.6	280.2	127.8	190.4	65.2	70.5
15.	Rural population[17]	---	45,365	228,220	571,792	901,245	1,435,976	1,737,911	1,939,076	1,982,338
16.	Percent rural increase over preceding census[17]	---	---	403.1	150.5	57.6	59.3	21.0	11.6	2.2
17.	Percent of urban to total population[17]	---	---	1.1	1.7	3.9	5.5	12.2	17.1	25.6
18.	Percent of rural to total population[17]	---	100.0	98.9	98.3	96.1	94.5	87.8	82.9	74.7

GENERAL POPULATION STATISTICS, 1790-1990 (Cont.)

OHIO

Item No.	1880	1890	1900	1910	1920	1930	1940	1950	1960	1970	1980	1990
1.	3,198,062	3,672,329	4,157,545	4,767,121	5,759,394	6,646,697	6,907,612	7,946,627	9,706,397	10,652,017	10,797,630	10,847,115
2.	20.0	14.8	13.2	14.7	20.8	15.4	3.9	15.0	22.1	9.7	1.3	0.5
3.	532,802	474,267[*b]	485,216[*b]	609,576[*a]	992,273[*a]	887,303[*a]	260,915[*a]	1,039,015[*a]	1,759,770	945,620	145,613[*a]	49,485
4.	6.4	5.8	5.5	5.2	5.4	5.4	5.2	5.3	5.4	5.2	---	4.4
5.	78.5	90.1	102.1	117.0	141.4	163.4	168.0	193.8	236.6	260.0	263.3	264.9
6.	21	21	21	22	22	24	23	23	24	23	21	---
7.	3,117,920	3,584,805	4,060,204	4,654,897	5,571,893	6,335,173	6,566,531	7,428,222	8,909,698	9,646,997	9,597,266	9,521,756
8.	19.8	15.0	13.3	14.6[*a]	19.7	13.7[*a]	3.7[*a]	13.1[*a]	19.9[*a]	8.3[*a]	-0.5[*a]	-0.8
9.	79,900	87,113	96,901	111,452	186,187	309,304	339,461	513,072	786,097	970,477	1,076,734	1,154,826
10.	26.4	9.0	11.2	15.0[*a]	67.1	66.1	9.7[*a]	51.1[*a]	53.2[*a]	23.5[*a]	10.9	7.3
11.	2.5	2.4	2.3[*a]	2.3[*a]	3.2[*a]	4.7[*a]	4.9[*a]	6.5[*a]	8.1[*a]	9.1	10.0	10.6
12.	---	---	---	---	---	---	---	---	---	---	---	---
13.	1,030,769	1,510,153	1,998,382	2,665,143	3,677,136	4,507,371	4,612,986	5,346,336[*c] 5,578,274[*d]	6,537,805[*c] 7,123,162[*d]	8,025,775	7,918,259	---
14.	50.9	46.5	32.3	33.4	38.0	22.6	2.3	15.9[*c] ---[*d]	22.3[*c] 27.7[*d]	12.7	-1.3	---
15.	2,167,293	2,162,176	2,159,163	2,101,978	2,082,258	2,139,326	2,294,626	2,600,291[*c] 2,368,353[*d]	3,168,592[*c] 2,583,235[*d]	2,626,242	2,879,371	---
16.	9.3	-0.2	-0.1	-2.6	-0.9	2.7	7.3	13.3[*c] ---[*d]	21.9[*c] 9.1[*d]	1.7	9.6	---
17.	32.2	41.1	48.1	55.9	63.8	67.8	66.8	67.3[*c] 70.2[*d]	67.4[*c] 73.4[*d]	75.3	73.3	---
18.	67.8	58.9	51.9	44.1	36.2	32.2	33.2	32.7[*c] 29.8[*d]	32.6[*c] 26.6[*d]	24.7	26.7	---

[a] Percentage computed by compiler from data herein. See endnotes for source of data.
[b] Percentage computed by compiler from data herein is different from percentage given in source. The above percentage is the percentage computed by compiler.
[c] Previous urban definition (pre-1950).
[d] Current urban definition (1950 and after; see Glossary of Terms).
[e] Population of territory northwest of the Ohio River.

GENERAL POPULATION STATISTICS, 1790-1990										
OKLAHOMA										
Item No.		1790 (or 1789)	1800	1810	1820	1830	1840	1850	1860	1870
1.	Population[1]	---	---	---	---	---	---	---	---	---
2.	Decennial rates of increase in population over preceding census[2]	---	---	---	---	---	---	---	---	---
3.	Increase in population over previous census[1,3]	---	---	---	---	---	---	---	---	---
4.	Percent distribution of population[4]	---	---	---	---	---	---	---	---	---
5.	Population per square mile of land area[5,6]	---	---	---	---	---	---	---	---	---
6.	Membership of House of Representatives at each apportionment[7]	---	---	---	---	---	---	---	---	---
7.	White population[8,9,10]	---	---	---	---	---	---	---	---	---
8.	Percentage increase in white population over preceding census[9,10,11]	---	---	---	---	---	---	---	---	---
9.	Black population[8,9,10]	---	---	---	---	---	---	---	---	---
10.	Percentage increase in Black population over preceding census[9,10,11,12,13,14]	---	---	---	---	---	---	---	---	---
11.	Percent Black in total population[1,8,9,10,14,15]	---	---	---	---	---	---	---	---	---
12.	Number of slaves in the area enumerated in 1790 and in the added area[16]	---	---	---	---	---	---	---	---	---
13.	Urban population[17]	---	---	---	---	---	---	---	---	---
14.	Percent urban increase over preceding census[17]	---	---	---	---	---	---	---	---	---
15.	Rural population[17]	---	---	---	---	---	---	---	---	---
16.	Percent rural increase over preceding census[17]	---	---	---	---	---	---	---	---	---
17.	Percent of urban to total population[17]	---	---	---	---	---	---	---	---	---
18.	Percent of rural to total population[17]	---	---	---	---	---	---	---	---	---

GENERAL POPULATION STATISTICS, 1790-1990 (Cont.)												
OKLAHOMA												
Item No.	1880	1890	1900	1910	1920	1930	1940	1950	1960	1970	1980	1990
1.	---	258,657	790,391	1,657,155	2,028,283	2,396,040	2,336,434	2,233,351	2,328,284	2,559,229	3,025,290	3,145,585
2.	---	---	205.6	109.7	22.4	18.1	-2.5	-4.4	4.3	9.9	18.2	4.0
3.	---	258,657[*b]	531,734[*a]	866,764[*a]	371,128[*a]	367,757[*a]	-59,606[*a]	-103,083[*a]	94,933	230,945	466,061[*a]	120,295
4.	---	0.4	1.0	1.8	1.9	1.9	1.8	1.5	1.3	1.3	---	1.3
5.	---	3.7[*e]	11.4[*e]	23.9	29.2	34.5	33.7	32.4	33.8	37.2	44.1	45.8
6.	---	---	5	8	8	9	8	6	6	6	6	---
7.	---	172,554[*f]	670,204[*f]	1,444,531	1,821,194	2,130,778	2,104,228	2,032,526	2,107,900	2,280,362	2,597,783	2,583,512
8.	---	---	288.4[*b]	115.5[*a]	26.1	17.0[*a]	-1.2[*a]	-3.4[*a]	3.7[*a]	8.2[*a]	13.9[*a]	-0.5
9.	---	21,609[*f]	55,684[*f]	137,612	149,408	172,198	168,849	145,503	153,084	171,892	204,658	233,801
10.	---	---	157.7[*b]	147.1[*a]	8.6	15.3	-1.9[*a]	-13.8[*a]	5.2[*a]	12.3[*a]	19.1	14.2
11.	---	8.4[*b]	7.0[*a]	8.3[*a]	7.4[*a]	7.2[*a]	7.2[*a]	6.5[*a]	6.6[*a]	6.7	6.8	7.4
12.	---	---	---	---	---	---	---	---	---	---	---	---
13.	---	9,484	58,417	318,975	538,017	821,681	879,663	1,107,252[*c] 1,139,481[*d]	1,419,793[*c] 1,464,786[*d]	1,740,137	2,035,082	---
14.	---	---	516.0	446.0	68.7	52.7	7.1	25.9[*c] ---[*d]	28.2[*c] 28.5[*d]	18.8	16.9	---
15.	---	249,173	731,974	1,338,180	1,490,266	1,574,359	1,456,771	1,126,099[*c] 1,093,870[*d]	908,491[*c] 863,498[*d]	819,092	990,208	---
16.	---	---	193.8	82.8	11.4	5.6	-7.5	-22.7[*c] ---[*d]	-19.3[*c] -21.1[*d]	-5.2	20.9	---
17.	---	3.7	7.4	19.2	26.5	34.3	37.6	49.6[*c] 51.0[*d]	61.0[*c] 62.9[*d]	68.0	67.3	---
18.	---	96.3	92.6	80.8	73.5	65.7	62.4	50.4[*c] 49.0[*d]	39.0[*c] 37.1[*d]	32.0	32.7	---

[a] Percentage computed by compiler from data herein. See endnotes for source of data.
[b] Percentage computed by compiler from data herein is different from percentage given in source. The above percentage is the percentage computed by compiler.
[c] Previous urban definition (pre-1950).
[d] Current urban definition (1950 and after; see Glossary of Terms).
[e] Oklahoma and Indian Territory combined. Separate data are as follows: Indian Territory, 5.9 in 1890 and 12.7 in 1900; Oklahoma, 2.0 in 1890 and 10.3 in 1900.
[f] Includes Indian Territory.

GENERAL POPULATION STATISTICS, 1790-1990										
OREGON										
Item No.		1790 (or 1789)	1800	1810	1820	1830	1840	1850	1860	1870
1.	Population[1]	---	---	---	---	---	---	12,093	52,465	90,923
2.	Decennial rates of increase in population over preceding census[2]	---	---	---	---	---	---	---	333.8	73.3
3.	Increase in population over previous census[1,3]	---	---	---	---	---	---	12,093[*b]	40,372[*b]	38,458
4.	Percent distribution of population[4]	---	---	---	---	---	---	0.1	0.2	0.2
5.	Population per square mile of land area[5,6]	---	---	---	---	---	---	[*e]	.5	1.0
6.	Membership of House of Representatives at each apportionment[7]	---	---	---	---	---	---	1	1	1
7.	White population[8,9,10]	---	---	---	---	---	---	13,087	52,160	86,929
8.	Percentage increase in white population over preceding census[9,10,11]	---	---	---	---	---	---	---	298.6	66.7
9.	Black population[8,9,10]	---	---	---	---	---	---	207	128	346
10.	Percentage increase in Black population over preceding census[9,10,11,12,13,14]	---	---	---	---	---	---	---	-38.2	170.3
11.	Percent Black in total population[1,8,9,10,14,15]	---	---	---	---	---	---	1.6	0.2	0.4
12.	Number of slaves in the area enumerated in 1790 and in the added area[16]	---	---	---	---	---	---	---	---	---
13.	Urban population[17]	---	---	---	---	---	---	---	2,874	8,293
14.	Percent urban increase over preceding census[17]	---	---	---	---	---	---	---	---	188.6
15.	Rural population[17]	---	---	---	---	---	---	12,093	49,591	82,630
16.	Percent rural increase over preceding census[17]	---	---	---	---	---	---	---	310.1	66.6
17.	Percent of urban to total population[17]	---	---	---	---	---	---	---	5.5	9.1
18.	Percent of rural to total population[17]	---	---	---	---	---	---	100.0	94.5	90.9

GENERAL POPULATION STATISTICS, 1790-1990 (Cont.)

OREGON

Item No.	1880	1890	1900	1910	1920	1930	1940	1950	1960	1970	1980	1990
1.	174,768	317,704	413,536	672,765	783,389	953,786	1,089,684	1,521,341	1,768,687	2,091,385	2,633,000	2,842,321
2.	92.2	81.8	30.2	62.7	16.4	21.8	14.2	39.6	16.3	18.2	25.9	7.9
3.	83,845	142,936[*b]	95,832[*b]	259,229[*a]	110,624[*a]	170,397[*a]	135,898[*a]	431,657[*a]	247,346	322,698	541,615[*a]	209,321[*b]
4.	0.3	0.5	0.5	0.7	0.7	0.8	0.8	1.0	1.0	1.0	---	1.1
5.	1.8	3.3	4.3	7.0	8.2	10.0	11.3	15.8	18.4	21.7	27.4	29.6
6.	1	2	2	3	3	3	4	4	4	4	5	---
7.	163,075	301,982	394,582	655,090	769,146	938,597	1,075,731	1,497,128	1,732,037	2,032,079	2,490,192	2,636,787
8.	87.6	85.2	30.7	66.0[*a]	17.4	22.0[*a]	14.6[*a]	39.2[*a]	15.7[*a]	17.3[*a]	22.5[*a]	5.9
9.	487	1,186	1,405	1,492	2,144	2,234	2,565	11,529	18,133	26,308	37,059	46,178
10.	40.8	143.5	-6.8	6.2[*a]	43.7	4.2	14.8[*a]	349.5[*a]	57.3[*a]	266.2[*a]	44.2	24.6
11.	0.3	0.4	0.3[*a]	0.2[*a]	0.3[*a]	0.2[*a]	0.2[*a]	0.8[*a]	1.0[*a]	1.3	1.4	1.6
12.	---	---	---	---	---	---	---	---	---	---	---	---
13.	25,852	88,491	133,180	307,060	390,346	489,746	531,675	732,247[*c] 819,318[*d]	943,861[*c] 1,100,122[*d]	1,402,704	1,788,354	---
14.	211.7	242.3	50.5	130.6	27.1	25.5	8.6	37.7[*c] ---[*d]	28.9[*c] 34.3[*d]	27.5	27.5	---
15.	148,916	229,213	280,356	365,705	393,043	464,040	558,009	789,094[*c] 702,023[*d]	824,826[*c] 668,565[*d]	688,681	844,751	---
16.	80.2	53.9	22.3	30.4	7.5	18.1	20.3	41.4[*c] ---[*d]	4.5[*c] -4.8[*d]	3.0	22.7	---
17.	14.8	27.9	32.2	45.6	49.8	51.3	48.8	48.1[*c] 53.9[*d]	53.4[*c] 62.2[*d]	67.1	67.9	---
18.	85.2	72.1	67.8	54.4	50.2	48.7	51.2	51.9[*c] 46.1[*d]	46.6[*c] 37.8[*d]	32.9	32.1	---

[a] Percentage computed by compiler from data herein. See endnotes for source of data.

[b] Percentage computed by compiler from data herein is different from percentage given in source. The above percentage is the percentage computed by compiler.

[c] Previous urban definition (pre-1950).

[d] Current urban definition (1950 and after; see Glossary of Terms).

[e] Less than one-tenth of one percent.

GENERAL POPULATION STATISTICS, 1790-1990										
PENNSYLVANIA										
Item No.		1790 (or 1789)	1800	1810	1820	1830	1840	1850	1860	1870
1.	Population[1]	434,373	602,365	810,091	1,049,458	1,348,233	1,724,033	2,311,786	2,906,215	3,521,951
2.	Decennial rates of increase in population over preceding census[2]	---	38.7	34.5	29.5	28.5	27.9	34.1	25.7	21.2
3.	Increase in population over previous census[1,3]	---	167,992	207,726	239,367	298,775	375,800	587,753	594,429	615,736
4.	Percent distribution of population[4]	11.1	11.3	11.2	10.9	10.5	10.1	10.0	9.2	9.1
5.	Population per square mile of land area[5,6]	---	13.4	---	---	---	---	51.6	64.8	78.6
6.	Membership of House of Representatives at each apportionment[7]	13[*e]	18	23	26	28	24	25	24	27
7.	White population[8,9,10]	424,099	586,095	786,804	1,019,045	1,309,900	1,676,115	2,258,160	2,849,259	3,456,609
8.	Percentage increase in white population over preceding census[9,10,11]	---	38.2	34.2	29.5	28.5	28.0	34.7	26.2	21.3
9.	Black population[8,9,10]	10,274	16,270	23,287	30,413	38,333	47,918	53,626	56,949	65,294
10.	Percentage increase in Black population over preceding census[9,10,11,12,13,14]	---	58.4	43.1	30.6	26.0	25.0	11.9	6.2	14.7
11.	Percent Black in total population[1,8,9,10,14,15]	2.4[*a]	2.7[*a]	2.9[*a]	2.9[*a]	2.8[*a]	2.8[*a]	2.3	2.0	1.9
12.	Number of slaves in the area enumerated in 1790 and in the added area[16]	3,707	1,706	795	211	403	64	---	---	---
13.	Urban population[17]	44,096	68,354	103,785	136,465	205,964	307,977	544,654	894,706	1,312,833
14.	Percent urban increase over preceding census[17]	---	55.0	51.8	31.5	50.9	49.5	76.8	64.3	46.7
15.	Rural population[17]	390,277	534,011	706,306	912,993	1,142,269	1,416,056	1,767,132	2,011,509	2,209,118
16.	Percent rural increase over preceding census[17]	---	36.8	32.3	29.3	25.1	24.0	24.8	13.8	9.8
17.	Percent of urban to total population[17]	10.2	11.3	12.8	13.0	15.3	17.9	23.6	30.8	37.3
18.	Percent of rural to total population[17]	89.8	88.7	87.2	87.0	84.7	82.1	76.4	69.2	62.7

GENERAL POPULATION STATISTICS, 1790-1990 (Cont.)

PENNSYLVANIA

Item No.	1880	1890	1900	1910	1920	1930	1940	1950	1960	1970	1980	1990
1.	4,282,891	5,258,113	6,302,115	7,665,111	8,720,017	96,331,350	9,900,180	10,498,012	11,319,366	11,793,909	11,863,895	11,881,643
2.	21.6	22.8	19.9	21.6	13.8	10.5	2.8	6.0	7.8	4.2	.5	0.1
3.	760,940	975,222[*b]	1,044,002[*b]	1,362,996[*a]	1,054,906[*a]	911,333[*a]	268,830[*a]	597,832[*a]	821,354	474,543	69,986[*a]	17,748
4.	8.5	8.3	8.3	8.3	8.2	7.8	7.5	6.9	6.3	5.8	---	4.8
5.	95.5	117.3	140.6	174.0	194.5	214.8	219.8	233.1	251.4	262.3	264.3	265.1
6.	28	30	32	36	36	34	33	30	27	25	23	---
7.	4,197,016	5,148,258	6,141,661	---	8,432,726	---	9,426,989	9,853,848	10,454,004	10,737,732	10,654,325	10,520,201
8.	21.4	22.7	19.3	---	12.9	---	---	4.5[*a]	6.1[*a]	2.7[*a]	-0.8[*a]	-1.3[*b]
9.	85,535	107,596	156,846	---	284,568	424,257	420,472	638,485	852,750	1,016,514	1,047,609	1,089,795
10.	31.0	25.8	45.8	---	46.7	49.1[*b]	-0.9[*a]	51.8[*a]	33.6[*a]	19.2[*a]	3.1	4.0[*b]
11.	2.0	2.1	2.5[*a]	---	3.3[*a]	4.4[*a]	4.2[*a]	6.1[*a]	7.5[*a]	8.6	8.8	9.2
12.	---	---	---	---	---	---	---	---	---	---	---	---
13.	1,783,378	2,557,397	3,448,610	4,630,669	5,672,453	6,533,511	6,586,877	6,985,409[*c] 7,403,036[*d]	7,419,910[*c] 8,102,051[*d]	8,430,410	8,220,851	---
14.	35.8	43.4	34.8	34.3	22.5	15.2	0.8	6.1[*c] ---[*d]	6.2[*c] 9.4[*d]	4.1	-2.6	---
15.	2,499,513	2,700,716	2,853,505	3,034,442	3,047,564	3,097,839	3,313,303	3,512,603[*c] 3,094,976[*d]	3,899,456[*c] 3,217,315[*d]	3,363,499	3,643,044	---
16.	13.1	8.0	5.7	6.3	0.4	1.6	7.0	6.0[*c] ---[*d]	11.0[*c] 4.0[*d]	4.5	8.5	---
17.	41.6	48.6	54.7	60.4	65.1	67.8	66.5	66.5[*c] 70.5[*c]	65.6[*c] 71.6[*d]	71.5	69.3	---
18.	58.4	51.4	45.3	39.6	34.9	32.2	33.5	33.5[*c] 29.5[*d]	34.4[*c] 28.4[*d]	28.5	30.7	---

[a] Percentage computed by compiler from data herein. See endnotes for source of data.
[b] Percentage computed by compiler from data herein is different from percentage given in source. The above percentage is the percentage computed by compiler.
[c] Previous urban definition (pre-1950).
[d] Current urban definition (1950 and after; see Glossary of Terms).
[e] Membership in the House of Representatives in 1789: 8.

GENERAL POPULATION STATISTICS, 1790-1990										
RHODE ISLAND										
Item No.		1790 (or 1789)	1800	1810	1820	1830	1840	1850	1860	1870
1.	Population[1]	68,825	69,122	76,931	83,059	97,199	108,830	147,545	174,620	217,353
2.	Decennial rates of increase in population over preceding census[2]	---	0.4	11.3	8.0	17.0	12.0	35.6	18.4	24.5
3.	Increase in population over previous census[1,3]	---	297	7,809	6,128	14,140	11,631	38,715	27,075	42,733
4.	Percent distribution of population[4]	1.8	1.3	1.1	0.9	0.8	0.6	0.6	0.6	0.6
5.	Population per square mile of land area[5,6]	---	64.8	---	---	---	--	138.3	163.7	203.7
6.	Membership of House of Representatives at each apportionment[7]	2[*e]	2	2	2	2	2	2	2	2
7.	White population[8,9,10]	64,470	65,438	73,214	79,457	93,621	105,587	143,875	170,649	212,219
8.	Percentage increase in white population over preceding census[9,10,11]	---	1.5	11.9	8.5	17.8	12.8	36.3	18.6	24.4
9.	Black population[8,9,10]	4,355	3,684	3,717	3,602	3,578	3,243	3,670	3,952	4,980
10.	Percentage increase in Black population over preceding census[9,10,11,12,13,14]	---	-15.4	0.9	-3.1	-0.7	-9.4	13.2	7.7	26.0
11.	Percent Black in total population[1,8,9,10,14,15]	6.3[*a]	5.3[*a]	4.8[*a]	4.3[*a]	3.7[*a]	3.0[*a]	2.5	2.3	2.3
12.	Number of slaves in the area enumerated in 1790 and in the added area[16]	958	380	108	48	17	5	---	---	---
13.	Urban population[17]	13,096	14,353	17,978	19,086	30,372	47,662	82,084	110,535	162,107
14.	Percent urban increase over preceding census[17]	---	9.6	25.3	6.2	59.1	56.9	72.2	34.7	46.7
15.	Rural population[17]	55,729	54,769	58,953	63,973	66,827	61,168	65,461	64,085	55,246
16.	Percent rural increase over preceding census[17]	---	-1.7	7.6	8.5	4.5	-8.5	7.0	-2.1	-13.8
17.	Percent of urban to total population[17]	19.0	20.8	23.4	23.0	31.2	43.8	55.6	63.3	74.6
18.	Percent of rural to total population[17]	81.0	79.2	76.6	77.0	68.8	56.2	44.4	36.7	25.4

GENERAL POPULATION STATISTICS, 1790-1990 (Cont.)												
RHODE ISLAND												
Item No.	1880	1890	1900	1910	1920	1930	1940	1950	1960	1970	1980	1990
1.	276,531	345,506	428,556	542,610	604,397	687,497	713,346	791,896	859,488	946,725	947,154	1,003,464
2.	27.2	24.9	24.0	26.6	11.4	13.7	3.8	11.0	8.5	10.1	-.3	5.9
3.	59,178	68,975	83,050	114,054[*a]	61,787[*a]	83,100[*a]	25,849[*a]	146,142[*a]	67,592	87,237	429[*a]	56,310
4.	0.6	0.5	0.6	0.6	0.6	0.6	0.5	0.5	0.5	0.5	---	0.4
5.	259.2	323.8	401.6	508.5	566.4	644.3	674.2	748.5	819.3	902.5	897.8	960.3
6.	2	2	2	3	3	2	2	2	2	2	2	---
7.	269,939	337,859	419,050	532,492	593,980	677,026	701,805	777,015	833,712	914,757	896,692	917,375
8.	27.2	25.2	24.0	27.1[*a]	11.5	14.0[*a]	3.7[*a]	10.7[*a]	7.3[*a]	9.7[*a]	-2.0[*a]	2.3
9.	6,488	7,393	9,092	9,529	10,036	9,913	11,024	13,903	18,332	25,338	27,584	38,861
10.	30.3	13.9	23.0	4.8[*a]	5.3	-1.2	11.2[*a]	26.1[*a]	31.9[*a]	38.2[*a]	8.9	40.9
11.	2.4	2.1	2.1[*a]	1.8[*a]	1.7[*a]	1.4[*a]	1.5[*a]	1.8[*a]	2.1[*a]	2.7	2.9	3.9
12.	---	---	---	---	---	---	---	---	---	---	---	---
13.	226,618	294,843	378,471	493,938	555,146	635,429	653,383	688,942[*c] 791,896[*d]	772,638[*c] 742,897[*d]	824,930	824,004	---
14.	39.8	30.1	28.4	30.5	12.4	14.5	2.8	5.4[*c] ---[*d]	12.1[*c] 11.3[*d]	11.0	-0.1	---
15.	49,913	50,663	50,085	48,672	49,251	52,068	59,963	102,954[*c] 124,684[*d]	86,850[*c] 116,591[*d]	121,795	123,150	---
16.	-9.7	1.5	-1.1	-2.8	1.2	5.7	15.2	71.7[*c] ---[*d]	-15.6[*c] -6.5[*d]	4.5	1.1	---
17.	82.0	85.3	88.3	91.0	91.9	92.4	91.6	87.0[*c] 84.3[*d]	89.9[*c] 86.4[*d]	87.1	87.0	---
18.	18.0	14.7	11.7	9.0	8.1	7.6	8.4	13.0[*c] 15.7[*d]	10.1[*c] 13.6[*d]	12.9	13.0	---

[a] Percentage computed by compiler from data herein. See endnotes for source of data.

[b] Percentage computed by compiler from data herein is different from percentage given in source. The above percentage is the percentage computed by compiler.

[c] Previous urban definition (pre-1950).

[d] Current urban definition (1950 and after; see Glossary of Terms).

[e] Membership in the House of Representatives in 1789: 1.

GENERAL POPULATION STATISTICS, 1790-1990										
SOUTH CAROLINA										
Item No.		1790 (or 1789)	1800	1810	1820	1830	1840	1850	1860	1870
1.	Population[1]	249,073	345,591	415,115	502,741	581,185	594,398	668,507	703,708	705,606
2.	Decennial rates of increase in population over preceding census[2]	---	38.8	20.1	21.1	15.6	2.3	12.5	5.3	0.3
3.	Increase in population over previous census[1,3]	---	96,518	69,524	87,626	78,444	13,213	74,109	35,201	1,898
4.	Percent distribution of population[4]	6.3	6.5	5.7	5.2	4.5	3.5	2.9	2.2	1.8
5.	Population per square mile of land area[5,6]	---	11.3	---	---	---	---	21.9	23.1	23.1
6.	Membership of House of Representatives at each apportionment[7]	6[*e]	8	9	9	9	7	6	4	5
7.	White population[8,9,10]	140,178	196,255	214,196	237,440	257,863	259,084	274,563	291,300	289,667
8.	Percentage increase in white population over preceding census[9,10,11]	---	40.0	9.1	10.9	8.6	0.5	6.0	6.1	-0.6
9.	Black population[8,9,10]	108,895	149,336	200,919	265,301	323,322	335,314	393,944	412,320	415,814
10.	Percentage increase in Black population over preceding census[9,10,11,12,13,14]	---	37.1	34.5	32.0	21.9	3.7	17.5	4.7	0.8
11.	Percent Black in total population[1,8,9,10,14,15]	43.7[*a]	43.2[*a]	48.4[*a]	52.8[*a]	55.6[*a]	56.4[*a]	58.9	58.6	58.9
12.	Number of slaves in the area enumerated in 1790 and in the added area[16]	107,094	146,151	196,365	258,475	315,401	327,038	384,984	402,406	---
13.	Urban population[17]	16,359	18,824	24,711	24,780	33,599	33,601	49,045	48,574	61,011
14.	Percent urban increase over preceding census[17]	---	15.1	31.3	0.3	35.6	---	46.0	-1.0	25.6
15.	Rural population[17]	232,714	326,767	390,404	477,961	547,586	560,797	619,462	655,134	644,595
16.	Percent rural increase over preceding census[17]	---	40.4	19.5	22.4	14.6	2.4	10.5	5.8	-1.6
17.	Percent of urban to total population[17]	6.6	5.4	6.0	4.9	5.8	5.7	7.3	6.9	8.6
18.	Percent of rural to total population[17]	93.4	94.6	94.0	95.1	94.2	94.3	92.7	93.1	91.4

GENERAL POPULATION STATISTICS, 1790-1990 (Cont.)												
SOUTH CAROLINA												
Item No.	1880	1890	1900	1910	1920	1930	1940	1950	1960	1970	1980	1990
1.	995,577	1,151,149	1,340,316	1,515,400	1,683,724	1,738,765	1,899,804	2,117,027	2,382,594	2,590,516	3,121,820	3,486,703
2.	41.1	15.6	16.4	13.1	11.1	3.3	9.3	11.4	12.5	8.7	20.5	11.7
3.	289,971	155,572	189,167	175,084[*a]	168,324[*a]	55,041[*a]	161,039[*a]	217,223[*a]	265,567	207,922	531,304[*a]	364,883
4.	20	1.8	1.8	1.6	1.6	1.4	1.4	1.4	1.3	1.3	---	1.4
5.	32.6	37.7	44.0	49.7	55.2	57.0	62.1	69.9	78.7	85.7	103.4	115.8
6.	7	7	7	7	7	6	6	6	6	6	6	---
7.	391,105	462,008	557,807	679,161	818,538	944,049	1,084,308	1,293,405	1,551,022	1,794,430	2,145,122	2,406,974
8.	35.0	18.1	20.7	21.8[*a]	20.5	15.3[*a]	14.9[*a]	19.3[*a]	19.9[*a]	15.7[*a]	19.5[*a]	12.2[*b]
9.	604,332	688,934	782,321	835,843	864,719	793,681	814,164	822,077	829,291	789,041	948,146	1,039,884
10.	45.3	14.0	13.6	6.8[*a]	3.5	-8.2	2.6[*a]	1.0[*a]	0.9[*a]	-4.9[*a]	20.2	9.7[*b]
11.	60.7	59.9	58.4[*a]	55.2[*a]	51.4[*a]	45.6[*a]	42.9[*a]	38.8[*a]	34.8[*a]	30.5	30.4	29.8
12.	---	---	---	---	---	---	---	---	---	---	---	---
13.	74,539	116,183	171,256	224,832	293,987	371,080	466,111	653,039[*c] 777,921[*d]	817,675[*c] 981,386[*d]	1,232,195	1,689,253	---
14.	22.2	55.9	47.4	31.3	30.8	26.2	25.6	40.1[*c] ---[*d]	25.2[*c] 26.2[*d]	25.6	35.1	---
15.	921,038	1,034,966	1,169,060	1,290,568	1,389,737	1,367,685	1,433,693	1,463,988[*c] 1,339,106[*d]	1,564,919[*c] 1,401,208[*d]	1,358,321	1,432,567	---
16.	42.9	12.4	13.0	10.4	7.7	-1.6	4.8	2.1[*c] ---[*d]	6.9[*c] 4.6[*d]	-3.1	6.9	---
17.	7.5	10.1	12.8	14.8	17.5	21.3	24.5	30.8[*c] 36.7[*d]	34.3[*c] 41.2[*d]	47.6	54.1	---
18.	92.5	89.9	87.2	85.2	82.5	78.7	75.5	69.2[*c] 63.3[*d]	65.7[*c] 58.8[*d]	52.4	45.9	---

[a] Percentage computed by compiler from data herein. See endnotes for source of data.
[b] Percentage computed by compiler from data herein is different from percentage given in source. The above percentage is the percentage computed by compiler.
[c] Previous urban definition (pre-1950).
[d] Current urban definition (1950 and after; see Glossary of Terms).
[*] Membership in the House of Representatives in 1789: 5.

GENERAL POPULATION STATISTICS, 1790-1990										
SOUTH DAKOTA										
Item No.		1790 (or 1789)	1800	1810	1820	1830	1840	1850	1860	1870
1.	Population[1]	---	---	---	---	---	---	---	4,837[*e]	11,776[*h]
2.	Decennial rates of increase in population over preceding census[2]	---	---	---	---	---	---	---	---	193.2[*e]
3.	Increase in population over previous census[1,3]	---	---	---	---	---	---	---	4,837[*e]	6,939[*b,e,h]
4.	Percent distribution of population[4]	---	---	---	---	---	---	---	---	---
5.	Population per square mile of land area[5,6]	---	---	---	---	---	---	---	[*f]	[*f]
6.	Membership of House of Representatives at each apportionment[7]	---	---	---	---	---	---	---	---	---
7.	White population[8,9,10]	---	---	---	---	---	---	---	2,576[*e]	12,887[*e]
8.	Percentage increase in white population over preceding census[9,10,11]	---	---	---	---	---	---	---	---	400.3[*e]
9.	Black population[8,9,10]	---	---	---	---	---	---	---	---	94[*e]
10.	Percentage increase in Black population over preceding census[9,10,11,12,13,14]	---	---	---	---	---	---	---	---	---
11.	Percent Black in total population[1,8,9,10,14,15]	---	---	---	---	---	---	---	---	0.8[*b,e]
12.	Number of slaves in the area enumerated in 1790 and in the added area[16]	---	---	---	---	---	---	---	---	---
13.	Urban population[17]	---	---	---	---	---	---	---	---	---
14.	Percent urban increase over preceding census[17]	---	---	---	---	---	---	---	---	---
15.	Rural population[17]	---	---	---	---	---	---	---	[*g]	11,776
16.	Percent rural increase over preceding census[17]	---	---	---	---	---	---	---	---	---
17.	Percent of urban to total population[17]	---	---	---	---	---	---	---	---	---
18.	Percent of rural to total population[17]	---	---	---	---	---	---	---	[*g]	100.0

GENERAL POPULATION STATISTICS, 1790-1990 (Cont.)

SOUTH DAKOTA

Item No.	1880	1890	1900	1910	1920	1930	1940	1950	1960	1970	1980	1990
1.	98,268*[h]	348,600	401,570	583,888	636,547	692,849	642,961	652,740	680,514	665,507	690,768	696,004
2.	734.5*[h]	254.7*[h]	15.2	45.4	9.0	8.8	-7.2	1.5	4.3	-2.2	3.7	0.8
3.	86,492*[b,h]	250,332*[b]	55,970*[b]	182,318*[a]	52,659*[a]	56,302*[a]	-49,888*[a]	9,779*[a]	27,774	-15,007	25,261*[a]	5,236
4.	0.2	0.6	0.5	0.6	0.6	0.6	0.5	0.4	0.4	0.3	---	0.3
5.	*[f]	4.5	5.2	7.6	8.3	9.0	8.4	8.5	9.0	8.8	9.1	9.2
6.	2	2	2	3	3	2	2	2	2	2	1	---
7.	96,955*[h]	328,010	380,714	563,771	619,147	670,269	619,075	628,504	653,098	630,333	638,955	637,515
8.	652.3 *[b,h]	2238.3*[b,h,i]	16.1	48.1*[a]	9.8	8.3*[a]	-7.6*[a]	1.5*[a]	3.9*[a]	-3.5*[a]	1.4*[a]	-0.2*[b]
9.	288*[h]	541	465	817	832	646	474	727	1,114	1,627	2,144	3,258
10.	206.4*[b,h]	87.8*[b,h,i]	-14.0	75.7*[a]	1.8	-22.4	-26.6*[a]	53.4*[a]	53.2*[a]	46.1*[a]	31.8	52.0
11.	0.3*[e]	0.2	0.1*[a]	0.1*[a]	0.1*[a]	0.1*[a]	0.1*[a]	0.1*[a]	0.2*[a]	0.2	0.3	0.5
12.	---	---	---	---	---	---	---	---	---	---	---	---
13.	7,208	28,555	40,936	76,469	101,872	130,907	158,087	216,157*[c] 216,710*[d]	265,328*[c] 267,180*[d]	296,628	320,777	---
14.	---	296.2	43.4	86.8	33.2	28.5	20.8	36.7*[c] ---*[d]	22.7*[c] 23.3*[d]	11.0	8.1	---
15.	91,060	320,045	360,634	507,419	534,675	561,942	484,874	436,583*[c] 436,030*[d]	415,186*[c] 413,334*[d]	368,879	369,991	---
16.	673.3	251.5	12.7	40.7	5.4	5.1	-13.7	-10.0*[c] ---*[d]	-4.9*[c] -5.2*[d]	-10.8	0.3	---
17.	7.3	8.2	10.2	13.1	16.0	18.9	24.6	33.1*[c] 33.2*[d]	39.0*[c] 39.3*[d]	44.6	46.4	---
18.	92.7	91.8	89.8	86.9	84.0	81.1	75.4	66.9*[c] 66.8*[d]	61.0*[c] 60.7*[d]	55.4	53.6	---

[a] Percentage computed by compiler from data herein. See endnotes for source of data.
[b] Percentage computed by compiler from data herein is different from <u>percentage</u> given in source. The above percentage is the percentage computed by compiler.
[c] Previous urban definition (pre-1950).
[d] Current urban definition (1950 and after; see Glossary of Terms).
[e] Dakota Territory (same data listed for North Dakota).
[f] Dakota Territory: less than one-tenth of 1 in 1860, 0.1 in 1870, and 0.9 in 1880.
[g] In 1860 there were 4,837 persons enumerated in Dakota Territory, all of whom were living in rural territory.
[h] Based on the population of the area of Dakota Territory which became South Dakota on November 2, 1889.
[i] Dakota Territory; includes persons specially enumerated in 1890.

GENERAL POPULATION STATISTICS, 1790-1990										
TENNESSEE										
Item No.		1790 (or 1789)	1800	1810	1820	1830	1840	1850	1860	1870
1.	Population[1]	35,961	105,602	261,727	422,823	681,904	829,210	1,002,717	1,109,801	1,258,520
2.	Decennial rates of increase in population over preceding census[2]	---	195.9	147.8	61.6	61.3	201.6	20.9	10.7	13.4
3.	Increase in population over previous census[1,3]	---	69,641[*b]	156,125	161,096	259,081	147,306	173,507	107,084	148,719
4.	Percent distribution of population[4]	0.9	2.0	3.6	4.4	5.3	4.9	4.3	3.5	3.3
5.	Population per square mile of land area[5,6]	---	2.5	---	---	---	---	24.1	26.6	30.2
6.	Membership of House of Representatives at each apportionment[7]	1	3	6	9	13	11	10	8	10
7.	White population[8,9,10]	31,913	91,709	215,875	339,979	535,746	640,627	756,836	826,722	936,119
8.	Percentage increase in white population over preceding census[9,10,11]	---	187.4	135.4	57.5	57.6	19.6	18.1	9.2	13.2
9.	Black population[8,9,10]	3,778	13,893	45,852	82,844	146,458	188,583	245,881	283,019	322,331
10.	Percentage increase in Black population over preceding census[9,10,11,12,13,14]	---	267.7	230.0	80.7	76.4	29.0	30.4	15.1	13.9
11.	Percent Black in total population[1,8,9,10,14,15]	10.5[*a]	13.2[*a]	17.5[*a]	19.6[*a]	21.5[*a]	22.7[*a]	24.5	25.5	25.6
12.	Number of slaves in the area enumerated in 1790 and in the added area[16]	3,417	13,584	44,535	80,107	141,603	183,059	239,459	275,719	---
13.	Urban population[17]	---	---	---	---	5,566	6,929	21,983	46,541	94,237
14.	Percent urban increase over preceding census[17]	---	---	---	---	---	24.5	217.3	111.7	102.5
15.	Rural population[17]	35,691	105,602	261,727	422,823	676,338	822,281	980,734	1,063,260	1,164,283
16.	Percent rural increase over preceding census[17]	---	195.9	147.8	61.6	60.0	21.6	19.3	8.4	9.5
17.	Percent of urban to total population[17]	---	---	---	---	0.8	0.8	2.2	4.2	7.5
18.	Percent of rural to total population[17]	100.0	100.0	100.0	100.0	99.2	99.2	97.8	95.8	92.5

GENERAL POPULATION STATISTICS, 1790-1990 (Cont.)												
TENNESSEE												
Item No.	1880	1890	1900	1910	1920	1930	1940	1950	1960	1970	1980	1990
1.	1,542,359	1,767,518	2,020,616	2,184,789	2,337,885	2,616,556	2,915,841	3,291,718	3,567,089	3,923,687	4,591,120	4,877,185
2.	22.6	14.6	143.	8.1	7.0	11.9	11.4	12.9	8.4	10.1	16.9	6.2
3.	283,839	225,159	253,098	164,173[*a]	153,096[*a]	278,671[*a]	299,285[*a]	375,877[*a]	275,371	356,598	668,433[*a]	286,065
4.	3.1	2.8	2.7	2.4	2.2	2.1	2.2	2.2	2.0	1.9	---	2.0
5.	37.0	42.4	48.5	52.4	56.1	62.4	69.5	78.8	86.2	94.2	111.6	118.3
6.	10	10	10	10	10	9	10	9	9	8	9	---
7.	1,138,831	1,336,637	1,540,186	1,711,432	1,885,993	2,138,644	2,406,906	2,760,257	2,977,753	3,293,930	2,835,078	4,048,068
8.	21.7	17.4	15.2	11.1[*a]	10.2	-13.4[*a]	12.5[*a]	14.7[*a]	7.9[*a]	10.6[*a]	16.4[*a]	5.6[*a]
9.	403,151	430,678	480,243	473,088	451,758	477,046	508,736	530,603	586,876	621,261	725,949	778,035
10.	25.1	6.8	11.5	-1.5[*a]	-4.5	5.6[*b]	6.6[*a]	4.3[*a]	10.6[*a]	5.9[*a]	16.9	7.2
11.	26.1	24.4	23.8[*a]	21.7[*a]	19.3[*a]	18.2[*a]	17.4[*a]	16.1[*a]	16.5[*a]	15.8	15.8	16.0
12.	---	---	---	---	---	---	---	---	---	---	---	---
13.	115,984	238,394	326,639	441,045	611,226	896,538	1,027,206	1,269,159[*c] 1,452,602[*d]	1,631,698[*c] 1,864,828[*d]	2,305,307	2,773,573	---
14.	23.1	105.5	37.0	35.0	38.6	46.7	14.6	23.1[*c] ---[*d]	29.1[*c] 28.4[*d]	23.6	19.6	---
15.	1,426,375	1,529,124	1,693,977	1,743,744	1,726,659	1,720,018	1,888,635	2,027,559[*c] 1,839,116[*d]	1,935,391[*c] 1,702,261[*d]	1,618,380	1,817,547	---
16.	22.5	7.2	10.8	2.9	-1.0	-0.4	9.8	7.4[*c] ---[*d]	-4.5[*c] -7.4[*d]	-4.9	13.2	---
17.	7.5	13.5	16.2	20.2	26.1	34.3	35.2	38.4[*c] 44.1[*d]	45.7[*c] 52.3[*d]	58.8	60.4	---
18.	92.5	86.5	83.8	79.8	73.9	65.7	64.8	61.6[*c] 55.9[*d]	54.3[*c] 47.7[*d]	41.2	39.6	---

[a] Percentage computed by compiler from data herein. See endnotes for source of data.

[b] Percentage computed by compiler from data herein is different from percentage given in source. The above percentage is the percentage computed by compiler.

[c] Previous urban definition (pre-1950).

[d] Current urban definition (1950 and after; see Glossary of Terms).

GENERAL POPULATION STATISTICS, 1790-1990										
TEXAS										
Item No.		1790 (or 1789)	1800	1810	1820	1830	1840	1850	1860	1870
1.	Population[1]	---	---	---	---	---	---	212,592	604,215	818,579
2.	Decennial rates of increase in population over preceding census[2]	---	---	---	---	---	---	---	184.2	35.5
3.	Increase in population over previous census[1,3]	---	---	---	---	---	---	212,592	391,623	214,364
4.	Percent distribution of population[4]	---	---	---	---	---	---	0.9	1.9	2.1
5.	Population per square mile of land area[5,6]	---	---	---	---	---	---	.8	2.3	3.1
6.	Membership of House of Representatives at each apportionment[7]	---	---	---	---	---	2	2	4	6
7.	White population[8,9,10]	---	---	---	---	---	---	154,034	420,891	564,700
8.	Percentage increase in white population over preceding census[9,10,11]	---	---	---	---	---	---	---	173.2	34.2
9.	Black population[8,9,10]	---	---	---	---	---	---	58,558	182,921	253,475
10.	Percentage increase in Black population over preceding census[9,10,11,12,13,14]	---	---	---	---	---	---	---	212.4	38.6
11.	Percent Black in total population[1,8,9,10,14,15]	---	---	---	---	---	---	27.5	30.3	31.0
12.	Number of slaves in the area enumerated in 1790 and in the added area[16]	---	---	---	---	---	---	58,161	182,566	---
13.	Urban population[17]	---	---	---	---	---	---	7,665	26,615	54,521
14.	Percent urban increase over preceding census[17]	---	---	---	---	---	---	---	247.2	104.9
15.	Rural population[17]	---	---	---	---	---	---	204,927	577,600	764,058
16.	Percent rural increase over preceding census[17]	---	---	---	---	---	---	---	181.9	32.3
17.	Percent of urban to total population[17]	---	---	---	---	---	---	3.6	4.4	6.7
18.	Percent of rural to total population[17]	---	---	---	---	---	---	96.4	95.6	93.3

GENERAL POPULATION STATISTICS, 1790-1990 (Cont.)

TEXAS

Item No.	1880	1890	1900	1910	1920	1930	1940	1950	1960	1970	1980	1990
1.	1,591,749	2,235,527	3,048,710	3,896,542	4,663,228	5,824,715	6,414,824	7,711,194	9,579,677	11,196,730	14,229,191	16,986,510
2.	94.5	40.4	36.4	27.8	19.7	24.9	10.1	20.2	24.2	16.9	27.1	19.4
3.	773,170	643,778[*b]	813,183[*b]	847,832[*a]	766,686[*a]	1,161,487[*a]	590,109[*a]	1,296,370[*a]	1,868,483	1,617,053	3,032,461[*a]	2,757,319
4.	3.2	3.5	4.0	4.2	4.4	4.7	4.9	5.1	5.3	5.5	---	6.8
5.	6.1	8.5	11.6	14.8	17.8	22.1	24.3	29.3	36.5	42.7	54.3	64.9
6.	11	13	16	18	18	21	21	22	23	24	27	---
7.	1,197,237	1,745,935	2,426,669	3,204,848	3,918,165	4,967,172	5,487,545	6,726,534	8,374,831	9,717,128	11,197,663	12,774,762
8.	112.0	45.8	39.0	32.1[*a]	22.3	26.8[*a]	10.5[*a]	22.6[*a]	24.5[*a]	16.0[*a]	15.2[*a]	14.1
9.	393,384	488,171	620,722	690,049	741,694	854,964	924,391	977,458	1,187,125	1,399,005	1,710,250	2,021,632
10.	55.2	24.1	27.2	11.2[*a]	7.5	15.3	8.1[*a]	5.7[*a]	21.5[*a]	17.8[*a]	22.2	18.2
11.	24.7	21.8	20.4[*a]	17.7[*a]	15.9[*a]	14.7[*a]	14.4[*a]	12.7[*a]	12.4[*a]	12.5	12.0	11.9
12.	---	---	---	---	---	---	---	---	---	---	---	---
13.	146,795	349,511	520,759	938,104	1,512,689	2,389,348	2,911,389	4,612,666[*c] 4,838,060[*d]	6,963,114[*c] 7,187,470[*d]	8,920,946	11,333,017	---
14.	169.2	138.1	49.0	80.1	61.2	58.0	21.8	58.4[*c] ---[*d]	51.0[*c] 48.6[*d]	24.1	27.0	---
15.	1,444,954	1,886,016	2,527,951	2,958,438	3,150,539	3,435,367	3,503,435	3,098,528[*c] 2,873,134[*d]	2,616,563[*c] 2,392,207[*d]	2,275,784	2,896,174	---
16.	89.1	30.5	34.0	17.0	6.5	9.0	2.0	-11.6[*c] ---[*d]	-15.6[*c] -16.7[*d]	-4.9	27.3	---
17.	9.2	15.6	17.1	24.1	32.4	41.0	45.4	59.8[*c] 62.7[*d]	72.7[*c] 75.0[*d]	79.7	79.6	---
18.	90.8	84.4	82.9	75.9	67.6	59.0	54.6	40.2[*c] 37.3[*d]	27.3[*c] 25.0[*d]	20.3	20.4	---

[a] Percentage computed by compiler from data herein. See endnotes for source of data.
[b] Percentage computed by compiler from data herein is different from percentage given in source. The above percentage is the percentage computed by compiler.
[c] Previous urban definition (pre-1950).
[d] Current urban definition (1950 and after; see Glossary of Terms).

GENERAL POPULATION STATISTICS, 1790-1990

UTAH

Item No.		1790 (or 1789)	1800	1810	1820	1830	1840	1850	1860	1870
1.	Population[1]	---	---	---	---	---	---	11,380	40,273[*f]	86,786
2.	Decennial rates of increase in population over preceding census[2]	---	---	---	---	---	---	---	253.9	115.5
3.	Increase in population over previous census[1,3]	---	---	---	---	---	---	11,380	28,893	46,513
4.	Percent distribution of population[4]	---	---	---	---	---	---	---	0.1	0.2
5.	Population per square mile of land area[5,6]	---	---	---	---	---	---	[*e]	.3	1.1
6.	Membership of House of Representatives at each apportionment[7]	---	---	---	---	---	---	---	---	---
7.	White population[8,9,10]	---	---	---	---	---	---	11,330	40,125	86,044
8.	Percentage increase in white population over preceding census[9,10,11]	---	---	---	---	---	---	---	254.1	114.4
9.	Black population[8,9,10]	---	---	---	---	---	---	50	59	118
10.	Percentage increase in Black population over preceding census[9,10,11,12,13,14]	---	---	---	---	---	---	---	18.0	100.0
11.	Percent Black in total population[1,8,9,10,14,15]	---	---	---	---	---	---	0.4	0.2	0.1
12.	Number of slaves in the area enumerated in 1790 and in the added area[16]	---	---	---	---	---	---	26	29	---
13.	Urban population[17]	---	---	---	---	---	---	---	8,236	15,981
14.	Percent urban increase over preceding census[17]	---	---	---	---	---	---	---	---	94.0
15.	Rural population[17]	---	---	---	---	---	---	11,380	32,037	70,805
16.	Percent rural increase over preceding census[17]	---	---	---	---	---	---	---	181.5	121.0
17.	Percent of urban to total population[17]	---	---	---	---	---	---	---	20.5	18.4
18.	Percent of rural to total population[17]	---	---	---	---	---	---	100.0	79.5	81.6

GENERAL POPULATION STATISTICS, 1790-1990 (Cont.)												
UTAH												
Item No.	1880	1890	1900	1910	1920	1930	1940	1950	1960	1970	1980	1990
1.	143,963	210,779	276,749	373,351	449,396	507,847	550,310	688,862	890,627	1,059,273	1,461,000	1,722,850
2.	65.9	46.4	31.3	34.9	20.4	13.0	8.4	25.2	29.3	18.9	37.9	17.9
3.	57,177	66,816[*b]	65,970[*b]	96,602[*a]	76,045[*a]	58,451[*a]	42,463[*a]	138,552[*a]	201,765	168,646	401,727[*a]	261,850[*b]
4.	0.3	0.3	0.4	0.4	0.4	0.4	0.4	0.5	0.5	0.5	---	0.7
5.	1.8	2.6	3.4	4.5	5.5	6.2	6.7	8.4	10.8	12.9	17.8	21.0
6.	1	1	2	2	2	2	2	2	2	2	3	---
7.	142,423	205,925	272,465	366,583	441,901	499,967	542,920	676,909	873,828	1,031,926	1,382,550	1,615,845
8.	65.5	44.6	32.3	34.5[*a]	20.5	13.1[*a]	8.6[*a]	24.7[*a]	29.1[*a]	18.1[*a]	34.0[*a]	16.9
9.	232	588	672	1,144	1,446	1,108	1,235	2,729	4,148	6,617	9,225	11,576
10.	96.6	153.4	14.3	70.2[*a]	26.4	-23.4	11.5[*a]	121.0[*a]	52.0[*a]	59.5[*a]	39.4	25.5
11.	0.2	0.3	0.2[*a]	0.3[*a]	0.3[*a]	0.2[*a]	0.2[*a]	0.4[*a]	0.5[*a]	0.6	0.6	0.7
12.	---	---	---	---	---	---	---	---	---	---	---	---
13.	33,665	75,155	105,427	172,934	215,584	266,264	305,493	432,993[*c] 449,855[*d]	592,027[*c] 667,158[*d]	851,472	1,233,060	---
14.	110.7	123.2	40.3	64.0	24.7	23.5	14.7	41.7[*c] ---[*d]	36.7[*c] 48.3[*d]	27.6	44.8	---
15.	110,298	135,624	171,322	200,417	233,812	241,583	244,817	255,869[*c] 239,007[*d]	298,600[*c] 223,469[*d]	207,801	227,977	---
16.	55.8	23.0	26.3	17.0	16.7	3.3	1.3	4.5[*c] ---[*d]	16.7[*c] -6.5[*d]	-7.0	9.7	---
17.	23.4	35.7	38.1	46.3	48.0	52.4	55.5	62.9[*c] 65.3[*d]	66.5[*c] 74.9[*d]	80.4	84.4	---
18.	76.6	64.3	61.9	53.7	52.0	47.6	44.5	37.1[*c] 34.7[*d]	33.5[*c] 25.1[*d]	19.6	15.6	---

[a] Percentage computed by compiler from data herein. See endnotes for source of data.
[b] Percentage computed by compiler from data herein is different from percentage given in source. The above percentage is the percentage computed by compiler.
[c] Previous urban definition (pre-1950).
[d] Current urban definition (1950 and after; see Glossary of Terms).
[e] Less than one-tenth of one percent.
[f] Population of Utah Territory exclusive of that part of present state of Colorado taken to form Colorado Territory in 1861.

GENERAL POPULATION STATISTICS, 1790-1990										
VERMONT										
Item No.		1790 (or 1789)	1800	1810	1820	1830	1840	1850	1860	1870
1.	Population[1]	85,425	154,465	217,895	235,981	280,652	291,948	314,120	315,098	330,551
2.	Decennial rates of increase in population over preceding census[2]	---	80.8	41.1	8.3	18.9	4.0	7.6	0.3	4.9
3.	Increase in population over previous census[1,3]	---	69,040	63,430	18,086	44,671	11,296	22,172	978	15,453
4.	Percent distribution of population[4]	2.2	2.9	3.0	2.4	2.2	1.7	1.4	1.0	0.9
5.	Population per square mile of land area[5,6]	---	16.9	---	---	---	---	34.4	34.5	36.2
6.	Membership of House of Representatives at each apportionment[7]	2	4	6	5	5	4	3	3	3
7.	White population[8,9,10]	85,154	153,908	217,145	235,078	279,771	294,218	313,402	314,369	329,613
8.	Percentage increase in white population over preceding census[9,10,11]	---	80.7	41.1	8.3	19.0	4.1	7.6	0.3	4.8
9.	Black population[8,9,10]	271	557	750	903	881	730	718	709	924
10.	Percentage increase in Black population over preceding census[9,10,11,12,13,14]	---	105.5	34.7	20.4	-2.4	-17.1	4.6	-1.3	30.3
11.	Percent Black in total population[1,8,9,10,14,15]	0.3[*a]	0.4[*a]	0.3[*a]	0.4[*a]	0.3[*a]	0.3[*a]	0.2	0.2	0.3
12.	Number of slaves in the area enumerated in 1790 and in the added area[16]	---	---	---	---	---	---	---	---	---
13.	Urban population[17]	---	---	---	---	---	---	6,110	6,213	22,960
14.	Percent urban increase over preceding census[17]	---	---	---	---	---	---	---	1.7	269.5
15.	Rural population[17]	85,425	154,465	217,895	235,981	280,652	291,948	308,010	308,885	307,591
16.	Percent rural increase over preceding census[17]	---	80.8	41.1	8.3	18.9	4.0	5.5	0.3	-0.4
17.	Percent of urban to total population[17]	---	---	---	---	---	---	1.9	2.0	6.9
18.	Percent of rural to total population[17]	100.0	100.0	100.0	100.0	100.0	100.0	98.1	98.0	93.1

GENERAL POPULATION STATISTICS, 1790-1990 (Cont.)												
VERMONT												
Item No.	1880	1890	1900	1910	1920	1930	1940	1950	1960	1970	1980	1990
1.	332,286	332,422	343,641	355,956	352,428	359,611	359,231	377,747	389,881	444,330	511,456	562,758
2.	0.5	---	3.4	3.6	-1.0	2.0	-0.1	5.2	3.2	14.0	15.0	10.0
3.	1,735	136	11,219	12,315[*a]	-3,528[*a]	7,183[*a]	-380[*a]	18,516[*a]	12,134	54,444	67,126[*a]	51,302
4.	0.7	0.5	0.5	0.4	0.3	0.3	0.3	0.2	0.2	0.2	---	0.2
5.	36.4	36.4	37.7	39.0	38.6	39.4	38.7	40.7	42.0	47.9	55.2	60.8
6.	2	2	2	2	2	1	1	1	1	1	1	---
7.	331,248	331,418	342,771	354,298	354,817	358,906	358,806	377,188	389,092	442,553	506,736	555,088
8.	0.5	0.4	3.4	3.4[*a]	0.1	1.2[*a]	[*e]	5.1[*a]	3.2[*a]	13.7[*a]	14.5[*a]	9.5
9.	1,057	937	828	1,621	572	568	384	443	519	761	1,135	1,951
10.	14.4	11.4	11.8	95.8[*a]	-64.7	-0.7	-32.4[*a]	15.4[*a]	17.2[*a]	46.6[*a]	49.1	71.9
11.	0.3	0.3	0.2[*a]	0.5[*a]	0.2[*a]	0.2[*a]	0.1[*a]	0.1[*a]	0.1[*a]	0.2	0.2	0.3
12.	---	---	---	---	---	---	---	---	---	---	---	---
13.	33,367	50,638	75,831	98,917	109,976	118,766	123,239	137,612	144,116[*c] 149,921[*d]	142,889	172,735	---
14.	45.3	51.8	49.8	30.4	11.2	8.0	3.8	11.7	4.7[*c] 8.9[*d]	-4.7	20.9	---
15.	298,919	281,784	267,810	257,039	242,452	240,845	235,992	240,135	245,765[*c] 239,960[*d]	301,441	338,721	---
16.	-2.8	-5.7	-5.0	-4.0	-5.7	-0.7	-2.0	1.8	2.3[*c] -0.1[*d]	25.6	12.4	---
17.	10.0	15.2	22.1	27.8	31.2	33.0	34.3	36.4	37.0[*c] 38.5[*d]	32.2	33.8	---
18.	90.0	84.8	77.9	72.2	68.8	67.0	65.7	63.6	63.0[*c] 61.5[*d]	67.8	66.2	---

[a] Percentage computed by compiler from data herein. See endnotes for source of data.
[b] Percentage computed by compiler from data herein is different from percentage given in source. The above percentage is the percentage computed by compiler.
[c] Previous urban definition (pre-1950).
[d] Current urban definition (1950 and after; see Glossary of Terms).
[e] Less than one-tenth of one percent.

GENERAL POPULATION STATISTICS, 1790-1990										
VIRGINIA										
Item No.		1790 (or 1789)	1800	1810	1820	1830	1840	1850	1860	1870
1.	Population[1]	691,737[*f]	807,557[*f]	877,683[*f]	938,261[*f]	1,044,054[*f]	1,025,227[*f]	1,119,348[*f]	1,219,630[*f]	1,225,163
2.	Decennial rates of increase in population over preceding census[2]	---	16.7[*f]	8.7[*f]	6.9[*f]	11.3[*f]	-1.8[*f]	9.2[*f]	9.0[*f]	0.5
3.	Increase in population over previous census[1,3]	---	115,820[*b,f]	70,126[*b,f]	60,578[*b,f]	105,793[*b,f]	-18,827[*b,f]	94,121[*b,f]	100,282[*b,f]	5,533[*b]
4.	Percent distribution of population[4]	17.6[*f]	15.2[*f]	12.1[*f]	9.7[*f]	8.1[*f]	6.0[*f]	4.8[*f]	3.9[*f]	3.2
5.	Population per square mile of land area[5,6]	---	13.7[*g]	---	---	---	---	22.1[*g]	24.8[*g]	30.4
6.	Membership of House of Representatives at each apportionment[7]	19[*e,g]	22[*g]	23[*g]	22[*g]	21[*g]	15[*g]	13[*g]	11[*g]	9
7.	White population[8,9,10]	442,117[*g]	514,280[*g]	554,514[*g]	603,335[*g]	694,300[*g]	740,968[*g]	894,800[*g]	1,047,299[*g]	712,089
8.	Percentage increase in white population over preceding census[9,10,11]	---	16.3[*g]	7.2[*g]	9.4[*g]	15.1[*g]	6.7[*g]	20.8[*g]	17.0[*g]	-32.0
9.	Black population[8,9,10]	305,493[*g]	365,920[*g]	423,086[*g]	462,031[*g]	517,105[*g]	498,829[*g]	526,861[*g]	548,907[*g]	512,841
10.	Percentage increase in Black population over preceding census[9,10,11,12,13,14]	---	19.8[*g]	15.6[*g]	9.2[*g]	11.9[*g]	-3.5[*g]	5.6[*g]	4.2[*g]	-6.6
11.	Percent Black in total population[1,8,9,10,14,15]	44.2[*a,g]	45.3[*a,g]	48.2[*a,g]	49.2[*a,g]	49.5[*a,g]	48.7[*a,g]	47.1[*g]	45.0[*g]	41.8
12.	Number of slaves in the area enumerated in 1790 and in the added area[16]	287,959[*f]	339,796[*f,h]	383,521[*f,h]	411,886[*f,h]	453,698[*f,h]	431,873[*f,h]	452,028[*f]	472,494[*f]	---
13.	Urban population[17]	12,296[*f]	21,155[*f]	31,823[*f]	35,453[*f]	50,375[*f]	70,968[*f]	89,255[*f]	115,879[*f]	145,618
14.	Percent urban increase over preceding census[17]	---	72.0[*f]	50.4[*f]	11.4[*f]	42.1[*f]	40.9[*f]	25.8[*f]	29.8[*f]	25.7
15.	Rural population[17]	679,441[*f]	786,402[*f]	845,860[*f]	902,808[*f]	993,679[*f]	954,259[*f]	1,030,093[*f]	1,103,751[*f]	1,079,545
16.	Percent rural increase over preceding census[17]	---	15.7[*f]	7.6[*f]	6.7[*f]	10.1[*f]	-4.0[*f]	7.9[*f]	7.2[*f]	-2.2
17.	Percent of urban to total population[17]	1.8[*f]	2.6[*f]	3.6[*f]	3.8[*f]	4.8[*f]	6.9[*f]	8.0[*f]	9.5[*f]	11.9
18.	Percent of rural to total population[17]	98.2[*f]	97.4[*f]	96.4[*f]	96.2[*f]	95.2[*f]	93.1[*f]	92.0[*f]	90.5[*f]	88.1

GENERAL POPULATION STATISTICS, 1790-1990 (Cont.)

VIRGINIA

Item No.	1880	1890	1900	1910	1920	1930	1940	1950	1960	1970	1980	1990
1.	1,512,565	1,655,980	1,854,184	2,061,612	2,309,187	2,421,851	2,677,773	3,318,680	3,966,949	4,648,494	5,346,818	6,187,358
2.	23.5	9.5	12.0	11.2	12.0	4.9	10.6	23.9	19.5	17.2	14.9	15.7
3.	287,402	143,415	198,204	207,428[*a]	247,575[*a]	112,664[*a]	255,922[*a]	640,907[*a]	648,269	681,545	698,324[*a]	840,540
4.	3.0	2.6	2.4	2.2	2.2	2.0	2.0	2.2	2.2	2.3	---	2.5
5.	37.6	41.1	46.1	51.2	57.4	60.2	67.1	83.2	99.6	116.9	134.7	156.3
6.	10	10	10	10	10	9	9	10	10	10	10	---
7.	880,858	1,020,122	1,192,855	1,389,809	1,617,909	1,770,441	2,015,583	2,581,555	3,142,443	3,761,514	4,229,734	4,791,739
8.	23.7	15.8	16.9	16.5[*a]	16.4	9.4[*a]	13.8[*a]	28.1[*a]	21.7[*a]	19.7[*a]	12.4[*a]	13.3
9.	631,616	635,438	660,722	671,096	620,017	650,165	661,449	734,211	816,258	861,368	1,008,311	1,162,994
10.	23.2	0.6	4.0	1.6[*a]	-7.6	4.9[*b]	1.7[*a]	11.0[*a]	11.2[*a]	5.5[*a]	17.1	15.3
11.	41.8	38.4	35.6[*a]	32.6[*a]	26.9[*a]	26.8[*a]	24.7[*a]	22.1[*a]	20.6[*a]	18.4[*b]	18.9	18.8
12.	---	---	---	---	---	---	---	---	---	---	---	---
13.	189,079	282,721	340,067	476,529	673,984	785,537	944,675	1,375,036[*c] 1,560,115[*d]	1,932,468[*c] 2,204,913[*d]	2,934,841	3,529,423	---
14.	29.8	49.5	20.3	40.1	41.4	16.6	20.3	45.6[*c] ---[*d]	40.5[*c] 41.3[*d]	33.1	20.1	---
15.	1,323,486	1,373,259	1,514,117	1,585,083	1,635,203	1,636,314	1,733,098	1,943,644[*c] 1,758,565[*d]	2,034,481[*c] 1,762,036[*d]	1,713,653	1,817,395	---
16.	22.6	3.8	10.3	4.7	3.2	0.1	5.9	12.1[*c] ---[*d]	4.7[*c] 0.2[*d]	-2.8	6.3	---
17.	12.5	17.1	18.3	23.1	29.2	32.4	35.3	41.4[*c] 47.0[*d]	48.7[*c] 55.6[*d]	63.1	66.0	---
18.	87.5	82.9	81.7	76.9	70.8	67.6	64.7	58.6[*c] 53.0[*d]	51.3[*c] 44.4[*d]	36.9	34.0	---

[a] Percentage computed by compiler from data herein. See endnotes for source of data.
[b] Percentage computed by compiler from data herein is different from percentage given in source. The above percentage is the percentage computed by compiler.
[c] Previous urban definition (pre-1950).
[d] Current urban definition (1950 and after; see Glossary of Terms).
[e] Membership in the House of Representatives in 1789: 10.
[f] Does not include the area later set off as West Virginia.
[g] Includes the area later set off as West Virginia.
[h] Alexandria County, which from 1800 to 1840, inclusive, formed a part of the District of Columbia, is here included with Virginia.

GENERAL POPULATION STATISTICS, 1790-1990										
WASHINGTON										
Item No.		1790 (or 1789)	1800	1810	1820	1830	1840	1850	1860	1870
1.	Population[1]	---	---	---	---	---	---	1,201[*e]	11,594[*e]	23,955
2.	Decennial rates of increase in population over preceding census[2]	---	---	---	---	---	---	---	865.4	106.6
3.	Increase in population over previous census[1,3]	---	---	---	---	---	---	---	10,393[*b]	12,361
4.	Percent distribution of population[4]	---	---	---	---	---	---	---	---	0.1
5.	Population per square mile of land area[5,6]	---	---	---	---	---	---	---	0.1	0.4
6.	Membership of House of Representatives at each apportionment[7]	---	---	---	---	---	---	---	---	---
7.	White population[8,9,10]	---	---	---	---	---	---	---	11,138	22,195
8.	Percentage increase in white population over preceding census[9,10,11]	---	---	---	---	---	---	---	---	99.3
9.	Black population[8,9,10]	---	---	---	---	---	---	---	30	207
10.	Percentage increase in Black population over preceding census[9,10,11,12,13,14]	---	---	---	---	---	---	---	---	590.0
11.	Percent Black in total population[1,8,9,10,14,15]	---	---	---	---	---	---	---	0.3	0.9
12.	Number of slaves in the area enumerated in 1790 and in the added area[16]	---	---	---	---	---	---	---	---	---
13.	Urban population[17]	---	---	---	---	---	---	---	---	---
14.	Percent urban increase over preceding census[17]	---	---	---	---	---	---	---	---	---
15.	Rural population[17]	---	---	---	---	---	---	1,201	11,594	23,955
16.	Percent rural increase over preceding census[17]	---	---	---	---	---	---	---	865.4	106.6
17.	Percent of urban to total population[17]	---	---	---	---	---	---	---	---	---
18.	Percent of rural to total population[17]	---	---	---	---	---	---	100.0	100.0	100.0

GENERAL POPULATION STATISTICS, 1790-1990 (Cont.)												
WASHINGTON												
Item No.	1880	1890	1900	1910	1920	1930	1940	1950	1960	1970	1980	1990
1.	75,116	357,232	518,103	1,141,990	1,356,621	1,563,396	1,736,191	2,378,963	2,853,214	3,409,169	4,130,163	4,866,692
2.	213.6	375.6	45.0	120.4	18.8	15.2	11.1	37.0	19.9	19.5	21.1	17.8
3.	51,161	282,116[*b]	160,871[*b]	623,887[*a]	214,631[*a]	206,775[*a]	172,795[*a]	642,772[*a]	474,251	555,955	720,994[*a]	736,529[*b]
4.	0.1	0.6	0.7	1.2	1.3	1.3	1.3	1.6	1.6	1.7	---	2.0
5.	1.1	5.3	7.8	17.1	20.3	23.4	25.9	35.6	42.8	51.2	62.1	73.1
6.	1	2	3	5	5	6	6	7	7	7	8	---
7.	67,199	340,829	496,304	1,109,111	1,319,777	1,521,661	1,698,147	2,316,496	2,751,675	3,251,055	3,777,296	4,308,937
8.	202.8	407.2	45.6	123.5[*a]	19.0	15.3[*a]	11.6[*a]	36.4[*a]	18.8[*a]	18.1[*a]	16.2[*a]	14.1[*b]
9.	325	1,602	2,514	6,058	6,883	6,840	7,424	30,691	48,738	71,308	105,544	149,801
10.	57.0	392.9	56.9	141.0[*a]	13.6	-0.6	8.5[*a]	313.4[*a]	58.8[*a]	46.3[*a]	48.0	41.9
11.	0.4	0.5	0.5[*a]	0.5[*a]	0.5[*a]	0.4[*a]	0.4[*a]	1.3[*a]	1.7[*a]	2.1	2.6	3.1
12.	---	---	---	---	---	---	---	---	---	---	---	---
13.	7,121	127,178	211,477	605,530	742,801	884,539	921,969	1,274,152[*c] 1,503,166[*d]	1,666,500[*c] 1,943,249[*d]	2,476,468	3,037,014	---
14.	---	1,686.0	66.3	186.3	22.7	19.1	4.2	38.2[*c] ---[*d]	30.8[*c] 29.3[*d]	27.4	21.4	---
15.	67,995	230,054	306,626	536,460	613,820	678,857	814,222	1,104,811[*c] 875,797[*d]	1,186,714[*c] 909,965[*d]	932,701	1,095,142	---
16.	183.8	238.3	33.3	75.0	14.4	10.6	19.9	35.7[*c] ---[*d]	7.4[*c] 3.9[*d]	2.5	20.6	---
17.	9.5	35.6	40.8	53.0	54.8	56.6	53.1	53.6[*c] 63.2[*d]	58.4[*c] 68.1[*d]	72.6	73.5	---
18.	90.5	64.4	59.2	47.0	45.2	43.4	46.9	46.4[*c] 36.8[*d]	41.6[*c] 31.9[*d]	27.4	26.5	---

[a] Percentage computed by compiler from data herein. See endnotes for source of data.
[b] Percentage computed by compiler from data herein is different from percentage given in source. The above percentage is the percentage computed by compiler.
[c] Previous urban definition (pre-1950).
[d] Current urban definition (1950 and after; see Glossary of Terms).
[e] 1860 figure includes population of Idaho and parts of Montana and Wyoming. 1850 figure is population of those parts of Oregon Territory taken to form part of Washington Territory in 1853 and 1859.

GENERAL POPULATION STATISTICS, 1790-1990										
WEST VIRGINIA										
Item No.		1790 (or 1789)	1800	1810	1820	1830	1840	1850	1860	1870
1.	Population[1]	55,873[*e]	78,592[*e]	105,469[*e]	136,808[*e]	176,924[*e]	224,537[*e]	302,313[*e]	376,688[*e]	442,014
2.	Decennial rates of increase in population over preceding census[2]	---	40.7[*e]	34.2[*e]	29.7[*e]	29.31[*e]	26.9[*e]	34.6[*e]	24.6[*e]	17.3
3.	Increase in population over previous census[1,3]	---	---	26,877[*e]	31,339[*e]	40,116[*e]	47,613[*e]	77,776[*e]	74,375[*e]	65,326[*b]
4.	Percent distribution of population[4]	1.4[*e]	1.5[*e]	1.5[*e]	1.4[*e]	1.4[*e]	1.3[*e]	1.3[*e]	1.2[*e]	1.1
5.	Population per square mile of land area[5,6]	*f	*f	*f	*f	*f	*f	*f	*f	18.4
6.	Membership of House of Representatives at each apportionment[7]	*f	*f	*f	*f	*f	*f	*f	*f	3
7.	White population[8,9,10]	*f	*f	*f	*f	*f	*f	*f	*f	424,033
8.	Percentage increase in white population over preceding census[9,10,11]	*f	*f	*f	*f	*f	*f	*f	*f	---
9.	Black population[8,9,10]	*f	*f	*f	*f	*f	*f	*f	*f	17,980
10.	Percentage increase in Black population over preceding census[9,10,11,12,13,14]	*f	*f	*f	*f	*f	*f	*f	*f	---
11.	Percent Black in total population[1,8,9,10,14,15]	*f	*f	*f	*f	*f	*f	*f	*f	4.1
12.	Number of slaves in the area enumerated in 1790 and in the added area[16]	4,668[*e]	7,172[*e]	10,836[*e]	15,119[*e]	17,673[*e]	18,488[*e]	20,500[*e]	18,371[*e]	---
13.	Urban population[17]	---	---	---	---	---	7,885[*e]	11,435[*e]	20,077[*e]	36,009
14.	Percent urban increase over preceding census[17]	---	---	---	---	---	---	45.0[*e]	75.6[*e]	79.4
15.	Rural population[17]	55,873[*e]	78,592[*e]	105,469[*e]	136,808[*e]	176,924[*e]	216,652[*e]	290,878[*e]	356,611[*e]	406,005
16.	Percent rural increase over preceding census[17]	---	40.7[*e]	34.2[*e]	29.7[*e]	29.3[*e]	22.5[*e]	34.3[*e]	22.6[*e]	13.9
17.	Percent of urban to total population[17]	---	---	---	---	---	3.5[*e]	3.8[*e]	5.3[*e]	8.1
18.	Percent of rural to total population[17]	100.0[*e]	100.0[*e]	100.0[*e]	100.0[*e]	100.0[*e]	96.5[*e]	96.2[*e]	94.7[*e]	91.9

GENERAL POPULATION STATISTICS, 1790-1990 (Cont.)												
WEST VIRGINIA												
Item No.	1880	1890	1900	1910	1920	1930	1940	1950	1960	1970	1980	1990
1.	618,457	762,794	958,800	1,221,119	1,463,701	1,729,205	1,901,974	2,005,552	1,860,421	1,744,237	1,949,644	1,793,477
2.	39.9	23.3	25.7	27.4	19.9	18.1	10.0	5.4	-7.2	-6.2	11.8	-8.0
3.	176,443	144,337	196,006	262,319[*a]	242,582[*a]	265,504[*a]	172,769[*a]	103,578[*a]	-145,131	-116,184	205,407[*a]	-156,167
4.	1.2	1.2	1.3	1.3	1.4	1.4	1.4	1.3	1.0	0.9	---	0.7
5.	25.7	31.8	39.9	50.8	60.9	72.0	79.0	83.3	77.2	72.5	80.8	74.5
6.	4	4	5	6	6	6	6	6	5	4	4	---
7.	592,537	730,077	915,233	1,156,817	1,377,235	1,614,191	1,784,102	1,890,282	1,770,133	1,673,480	1,874,751	1,725,523
8.	39.7	23.2	25.4	26.4[*a]	19.1	17.2[*a]	10.5[*a]	6.0[*a]	-6.4[*a]	-5.5[*a]	12.0[*a]	-8.0
9.	25,886	32,690	43,499	64,173	86,345	114,893	177,754	114,867	89,378	67,342	65,051	56,295
10.	44.0	26.3	33.1	47.5[*a]	34.6	33.1	54.7[*a]	-35.4[*a]	-22.2[*a]	-24.7[*a]	-3.4	-13.5
11.	4.2	4.3	4.5[*a]	5.3[*a]	5.9[*a]	6.6[*a]	9.3[*a]	5.7[*a]	4.8[*a]	3.9	3.3	3.1
12.	---	---	---	---	---	---	---	---	---	---	---	---
13.	54,050	81,365	125,465	228,242	369,007	491,504	534,292	640,606[*c] 694,487[*d]	665,504[*c] 711,101[*d]	679,491	705,319	---
14.	50.1	50.5	54.2	81.9	61.7	33.2	8.7	19.9[*c] ---[*d]	3.9[*c] 2.4[*d]	-4.4	3.5	---
15.	564,407	681,429	833,335	992,877	1,094,694	1,237,701	1,367,682	1,364,946[*c] 1,311,065[*d]	1,194,917[*c] 1,149,320[*d]	1,064,746	1,244,325	---
16.	39.0	20.7	22.3	19.1	10.3	13.1	10.5	-0.2[*c] ---[*d]	-12.5[*c] -12.3[*d]	-7.4	17.1	---
17.	8.7	10.7	13.1	18.7	25.2	28.4	28.1	31.9[*c] 34.6[*d]	35.8[*c] 38.2[*d]	39.0	36.2	---
18.	91.3	89.3	86.9	81.3	74.8	71.6	71.9	68.1[*c] 65.4[*d]	64.2[*c] 61.8[*d]	61.0	63.8	---

[a] Percentage computed by compiler from data herein. See endnotes for source of data.
[b] Percentage computed by compiler from data herein is different from percentage given in source. The above percentage is the percentage computed by compiler.
[c] Previous urban definition (pre-1950).
[d] Current urban definition (1950 and after; see Glossary of Terms).
[e] Based on population of the area of Virginia later separated to form West Virginia.
[f] The area which became West Virginia is included in the Virginia totals.

GENERAL POPULATION STATISTICS, 1790-1990										
WISCONSIN										
Item No.		1790 (or 1789)	1800	1810	1820	1830	1840	1850	1860	1870
1.	Population[1]	---	---	---	---	---	30,945[*f]	305,391	775,881	1,054,670
2.	Decennial rates of increase in population over preceding census[2]	---	---	---	---	---	---	886.9	154.1	35.9
3.	Increase in population over previous census[1,3]	---	---	---	---	---	30,945	274,446	470,490	278,789
4.	Percent distribution of population[4]	---	---	---	---	---	0.2	1.3	2.5	2.7
5.	Population per square mile of land area[5,6]	---	---	---	---	---	---	5.5	14.0	19.1
6.	Membership of House of Representatives at each apportionment[7]	---	---	---	---	---	2	3	6	8
7.	White population[8,9,10]	---	---	---	---	---	30,749	304,756	773,693	1,051,351
8.	Percentage increase in white population over preceding census[9,10,11]	---	---	---	---	---	---	891.1	153.9	35.9
9.	Black population[8,9,10]	---	---	---	---	---	196	635	1,171	2,113
10.	Percentage increase in Black population over preceding census[9,10,11,12,13,14]	---	---	---	---	---	---	224.0	84.4	80.4
11.	Percent Black in total population[1,8,9,10,14,15]	---	---	---	---	---	0.6[*a]	0.2	0.2	0.2
12.	Number of slaves in the area enumerated in 1790 and in the added area[16]	---	---	---	---	31[*e]	11	---	---	---
13.	Urban population[17]	---	---	---	---	---	---	28,623	111,874	207,099
14.	Percent urban increase over preceding census[17]	---	---	---	---	---	---	---	290.9	85.1
15.	Rural population[17]	---	---	---	---	---	30,945	276,768	664,007	847,571
16.	Percent rural increase over preceding census[17]	---	---	---	---	---	---	794.4	139.9	27.6
17.	Percent of urban to total population[17]	---	---	---	---	---	---	9.4	14.4	19.6
18.	Percent of rural to total population[17]	---	---	---	---	---	100.0	90.6	85.6	80.4

GENERAL POPULATION STATISTICS, 1790-1990 (Cont.)												
WISCONSIN												
Item No.	1880	1890	1900	1910	1920	1930	1940	1950	1960	1970	1980	1990
1.	1,315,497	1,693,330	2,069,042	2,333,860	2,632,067	2,939,006	3,137,587	3,434,575	3,951,777	4,417,731	4,705,767	4,891,769
2.	24.7	28.7	22.2	12.8	12.8	11.7	6.8	9.5	15.1	11.8	6.5	4.0
3.	260,827	377,833[*b]	375,712[*b]	264,818[*a]	298,207[*a]	306,939[*a]	198,581[*a]	296,988[*a]	517,202	465,954	288,036[*a]	186,002
4.	2.6	2.7	2.7	2.5	2.5	2.4	2.4	2.3	2.2	2.2	---	2.0
5.	23.8	30.6	37.4	42.2	47.6	53.7	57.3	62.8	72.6	81.1	86.5	90.1
6.	9	10	11	11	11	10	10	10	10	9	9	---
7.	1,309,618	1,680,828	2,057,911	2,320,555	2,616,938	2,916,255	3,112,752	3,392,690	3,858,903	4,258,959	4,442,598	4,512,523
8.	24.6	28.3	22.4	12.8[*a]	12.8	11.4[*a]	6.7[*a]	9.0[*a]	13.7[*a]	10.4[*a]	4.3[*a]	1.6
9.	2,702	2,444	2,542	2,900	5,201	10,739	12,158	28,182	74,546	128,224	182,593	244,539
10.	27.9	-9.5	4.0	14.1[*a]	79.3	106.5	13.2[*a]	131.8[*a]	164.5[*a]	72.0[*a]	42.4	33.9
11.	0.2	0.1	0.1[*a]	0.1[*a]	0.2[*a]	0.4[*a]	0.4[*a]	0.8[*a]	1.9[*a]	2.9	3.9	5.0
12.	---	---	---	---	---	---	---	---	---	---	---	---
13.	317,204	562,286	790,213	1,004,320	1,244,858	1,553,843	1,679,144	1,949,260[*c] 1,987,888[*d]	2,452,295[*c] 2,522,179[*d]	2,910,418	3,020,732	---
14.	53.2	77.3	40.5	27.1	24.0	24.8	8.1	16.1[*c] ---[*d]	25.8[*c] 26.9[*d]	15.4	3.8	---
15.	998,293	1,131,044	1,278,829	1,329,540	1,387,209	1,385,163	1,458,443	1,485,315[*c] 1,446,687[*d]	1,499,482[*c] 1,429,598[*d]	1,507,313	1,685,035	---
16.	17.8	13.3	13.1	4.0	4.3	-0.1	5.3	1.8[*c] ---[*d]	1.0[*c] -1.2[*d]	5.4	11.8	---
17.	24.1	33.2	38.2	43.0	47.3	52.9	53.5	56.8[*c] 57.9[*d]	62.1[*c] 63.8[*d]	65.9	64.2	---
18.	75.9	66.8	61.8	57.0	52.7	47.1	46.5	43.2[*c] 42.1[*d]	37.9[*c] 36.2[*d]	34.1	35.8	---

[a] Percentage computed by compiler from data herein. See endnotes for source of data.
[b] Percentage computed by compiler from data herein is different from percentage given in source. The above percentage is the percentage computed by compiler.
[c] Previous urban definition (pre-1950).
[d] Current urban definition (1950 and after; see Glossary of Terms).
[e] Reported as for Washington County, Mississippi Territory.
[f] Includes population of that part of Minnesota northeast of the Mississippi River.

GENERAL POPULATION STATISTICS, 1790-1990										
WYOMING										
Item No.		1790 (or 1789)	1800	1810	1820	1830	1840	1850	1860	1870
1.	Population[1]	---	---	---	---	---	---	---	---	9,118
2.	Decennial rates of increase in population over preceding census[2]	---	---	---	---	---	---	---	---	---
3.	Increase in population over previous census[1,3]	---	---	---	---	---	---	---	---	9,118
4.	Percent distribution of population[4]	---	---	---	---	---	---	---	---	---
5.	Population per square mile of land area[5,6]	---	---	---	---	---	---	---	---	.1
6.	Membership of House of Representatives at each apportionment[7]	---	---	---	---	---	---	---	---	---
7.	White population[8,9,10]	---	---	---	---	---	---	---	---	8,726
8.	Percentage increase in white population over preceding census[9,10,11]	---	---	---	---	---	---	---	---	---
9.	Black population[8,9,10]	---	---	---	---	---	---	---	---	183
10.	Percentage increase in Black population over preceding census[9,10,11,12,13,14]	---	---	---	---	---	---	---	---	---
11.	Percent Black in total population[1,8,9,10,14,15]	---	---	---	---	---	---	---	---	2.0
12.	Number of slaves in the area enumerated in 1790 and in the added area[16]	---	---	---	---	---	---	---	---	---
13.	Urban population[17]	---	---	---	---	---	---	---	---	---
14.	Percent urban increase over preceding census[17]	---	---	---	---	---	---	---	---	---
15.	Rural population[17]	---	---	---	---	---	---	---	---	9,118
16.	Percent rural increase over preceding census[17]	---	---	---	---	---	---	---	---	---
17.	Percent of urban to total population[17]	---	---	---	---	---	---	---	---	---
18.	Percent of rural to total population[17]	---	---	---	---	---	---	---	---	100.0

GENERAL POPULATION STATISTICS, 1790-1990 (Cont.)												
WYOMING												
Item No.	1880	1890	1900	1910	1920	1930	1940	1950	1960	1970	1980	1990
1.	20,789	62,555	92,531	145,965	194,402	225,565	250,742	290,529	330,066	332,416	469,557	453,588
2.	128.0	200.9	47.9	57.7	33.2	16.0	11.2	15.9	13.6	0.7	41.3	-3.4
3.	11,671	41,766[*b]	29,976[*b]	53,434[*a]	48,437[*a]	31,163[*a]	25,177[*a]	39,787[*a]	39,537	2,350	137,141[*a]	-15,969
4.	---	0.1	0.1	0.2	0.2	0.2	0.2	0.2	0.2	0.2	---	0.2
5.	.2	.6	.9	1.5	2.0	2.3	2.6	3.0	3.4	3.4	4.8	---
6.	1	1	1	1	1	1	1	1	1	1	---	---
7.	19,437	59,324	89,051	440,318	490,446	221,241	246,347	284,009	322,922	323,024	447,716	427,061
8.	122.7	205.2	50.1	394.5[*a]	11.4	-54.9[*a]	11.3[*a]	15.3[*a]	13.7[*a]	[*e]	38.6[*a]	-4.6[*b]
9.	298	922	940	2,235	1,375	1,250	956	2,557	2,483	2,568	3,364	3,606
10.	62.8	209.4	2.0	137.8[*a]	-38.5	-9.1	-23.5[*a]	167.5[*a]	-2.9[*a]	3.4[*a]	31.0	7.2
11.	1.4	1.5	1.0[*a]	1.5[*a]	0.7[*a]	0.6[*a]	0.4[*a]	0.9[*a]	0.8[*a]	0.8	0.7	0.8
12.	---	---	---	---	---	---	---	---	---	---	---	---
13.	6,152	21,484	26,657	43,221	57,095	70,097	93,577	144,618	187,551	201,111	294,639	---
14.	---	249.2	24.1	62.1	32.1	22.8	33.5	54.5	29.7	7.2	46.5	---
15.	14,637	41,071	65,874	102,744	137,307	155,468	157,165	145,911	142,515	131,305	174,918	---
16.	60.5	180.6	60.4	56.0	33.6	13.2	1.1	-7.2	-2.3	-7.9	33.2	---
17.	29.6	34.3	28.8	29.6	29.4	31.1	37.3	49.8	56.8	60.5	62.7	---
18.	70.4	65.7	71.2	70.4	70.6	68.9	62.7	50.2	43.2	39.5	37.3	---

[a] Percentage computed by compiler from data herein. See endnotes for source of data.
[b] Percentage computed by compiler from data herein is different from percentage given in source. The above percentage is the percentage computed by compiler.
[c] Previous urban definition (pre-1950).
[d] Current urban definition (1950 and after; see Glossary of Terms).
[e] Less than one-tenth of one percent.

GENERAL POPULATION STATISTICS, 1790-1990										
UNITED STATES[*e]										
Item No.		1790 (or 1789)	1800	1810	1820	1830	1840	1850	1860	1870
1.	Population[1]	3,929,214	5,308,483	7,239,881	9,638,453	12,866,020[*f]	17,068,953[*f]	23,191,876	31,443,321	38,558,371
2.	Decennial rates of increase in population over preceding census[2]	---	35.1	36.4	33.1	33.5	32.9	35.9	35.6	22.6
3.	Increase in population over previous census[1,3]	---	1,379,269	1,931,398	2,398,572	3,227,567[*f]	4,203,433[*f]	6,122,423[*f]	8,251,445	7,115,050
4.	Percent distribution of population[4]	100.0	100.0	100.0	100.0	100.0	100.0	100.0	100.0	100.0
5.	Population per square mile of land area[5,6]	---	6.1	---	---	---	---	7.9	10.6	13.0
6.	Membership of House of Representatives at each apportionment[7]	106	142	186	213	242	232	237	243	293
7.	White population[8,9,10]	3,172,006	4,306,446	5,862,073	7,866,797	10,532,060	14,189,705	19,553,068	26,922,537	33,589,377
8.	Percentage increase in white population over preceding census[9,10,11]	---	35.8	36.1	34.2	33.9	34.7	37.8	37.7	24.8
9.	Black population[8,9,10]	757,208	1,002,037	1,377,808	1,771,656	2,328,642	2,873,648	3,638,808	4,441,830	4,880,009
10.	Percentage increase in Black population over preceding census[9,10,11,12,13,14]	---	32.3	37.5	28.6	31.4	23.4	26.6	22.1	9.9
11.	Percent Black in total population[1,8,9,10,14,15]	19.3[*a]	18.9[*a]	19.0[*a]	18.4[*a]	18.1[*a]	16.8[*a]	15.7	14.1	12.7
12.	Number of slaves in the area enumerated in 1790 and in the added area[16]	697,624	893,602	1,191,362	1,538,022	2,009,043	2,487,355	3,204,313	2,953,760	---
13.	Urban population[17]	201,655	322,371	525,459	693,255	1,127,247[*f]	1,845,055[*f]	3,543,716	6,216,518	9,902,361
14.	Percent urban increase over preceding census[17]	---	59.9	63.0	31.9	62.6[*f]	63.7[*f]	92.1	75.4	59.3
15.	Rural population[17]	3,727,559	4,986,112	6,714,422	8,945,198	11,738,773[*f]	15,224,398[*f]	19,648,160	25,226,803	28,656,010
16.	Percent rural increase over preceding census[17]	---	33.8	34.7	33.2	31.2[*f]	29.7[*f]	29.1	28.4	13.6
17.	Percent of urban to total population[17]	5.1	6.1	7.3	7.2	8.8[*f]	10.8[*f]	15.3	19.8	25.7
18.	Percent of rural to total population[17]	94.9	93.9	92.7	92.8	91.2[*f]	89.2[*f]	84.7	80.2	74.3

GENERAL POPULATION STATISTICS, 1790-1990 (Cont.)

UNITED STATES[*e]

Item No.	1880	1890	1900	1910	1920	1930	1940	1950	1960	1970	1980	1990
1.	50,189,209	62,979,766[*g]	76,212,168	92,228,496	106,021,537	123,202,624	132,164,569	151,325,798	179,323,175	203,211,926	226,504,825	248,709,873
2.	30.1	25.5	20.7	21.0	15.0	16.2	7.3	14.5	18.5	13.3	11.4	9.8[*a]
3.	11,630,838[*b]	12,790,557[*b]	13,232,402[*b,h]	16,016,328[*a]	13,793,041[*a]	17,181,087[*a]	8,961,945[*a]	19,161,229[*a]	27,997,377	23,888,751	23,292,899[*a]	22,205,048
4.	100.0	100.0	100.0	100.0	100.0	100.0	100.0	100.0	100.0	100.0	100.0	100.0
5.	16.9	21.2	25.6	30.9	29.9	34.7	37.2	42.6	50.6	57.5	64.0	70.3
6.	332	357	391	435	435	435	435	437	435	435	435	---
7.	43,402,970	55,101,258[*i]	66,809,196	81,731,957	94,820,915	110,286,740	118,214,870	135,149,629	158,831,732	177,748,975	188,340,790	199,686,070
8.	29.2	27.0	21.2	22.3[*a]	16.0	16.3[*a]	7.2[*a]	14.3[*a]	17.5[*a]	11.9[*a]	6.0[*a]	6.0
9.	6,580,793	7,488,676[*i]	8,833,994	9,827,763	10,183,131	11,091,143	12,665,513	15,044,937	18,871,831	22,580,289	26,488,218	29,986,060
10.	34.9	13.8	18.0	11.2[*a]	6.5	13.6	14.2[*a]	18.8[*a]	25.4[*a]	19.7[*a]	17.3	13.2
11.	13.1[*b]	11.9[*b]	11.6[*a]	10.7[*a]	9.6[*a]	9.0[*a]	10.3[*a]	9.9[*a]	10.5[*a]	11.1	11.7	12.1
12.	---	---	---	---	---	---	---	---	---	---	---	---
13.	14,129,735	22,106,265	30,214,832	42,064,001	54,253,287	69,160,599	74,705,338	90,128,194[*c] 96,846,817[*d]	113,056,353[*c] 125,268,750[*d]	149,324,930	167,050,992	---
14.	42.7	56.5	36.7	39.2	29.0	27.5	8.0	20.6[*c] ---[*d]	25.4[*c] 29.3[*d]	19.2	11.6	---
15.	36,059,474	40,873,501	45,997,336	50,164,495	51,768,255	54,042,025	57,459,231	61,197,604[*c] 54,478,981[*d]	66,266,822[*c] 54,054,425[*d]	53,886,996	59,494,813	---
16.	25.8	13.4	12.5	9.1	3.2	4.4	6.3	6.5[*c] ---[*d]	8.3[*c] -0.8[*d]	-0.3	11.1	---
17.	28.2	35.1	39.6	45.6	51.2	56.1	56.5	59.6[*c] 64.0[*d]	63.0[*c] 69.9[*d]	73.5	73.7	---
18.	71.8	64.9	60.4	54.4	48.8	43.9	43.5	40.4[*c] 36.0[*d]	37.0[*c] 30.1[*d]	26.5	26.3	---

[a] Percentage computed by compiler from data herein. See endnotes for source of data.

[b] Percentage computed by compiler from data herein is different from percentage given in source. The above percentage is the percentage computed by compiler.

[c] Previous urban definition (pre-1950).

[d] Current urban definition (1950 and after; see Glossary of Terms).

[e] The United States' totals were taken from the source noted in the endnotes. It is not the sum of the state totals. The most common reasons they do not match are: 1) residents living in the territories—e.g. Indian Territory, Dakota Territory, Alaska and Hawaii before statehood—may be in the United States' totals, but they are not credited to any state; 2) military and civilian employees of the United States living abroad may be in the U.S. totals but they are not credited to any state; and 3) rounded percentages will rarely add up to 100%. See other endnotes and Glossary of Terms for specific explanations.

[f] Includes persons (6,100 in 1840 and 5,318 in 1830) on public ships in the service of the United States, not credited to any region, division, or state.

[g] Includes population (325,464) of Indian territory and Indian reservations specially enumerated in 1890 but not included in general report on population for 1890.

[h] Inclusive in 1900 of 91,219 persons in the military and Naval services of the United States (including civilian employees, etc.) stationed abroad, not credited to any state or territory, but exclusive of 63,592 persons in Alaska, 154,001 persons in Hawaii, 392,060 persons in Indian Territory, and 125,018 persons on Indian reservations credited to states and territories as follows: Arizona, 22,761; California, 2,874; Colorado, 1,145; Idaho, 2,625; Iowa, 385; Kansas, 2,026; Minnesota, 9,408; Montana, 11,770; Nevada, 1,673: New Mexico, 3,863; New York, 5,784; North Dakota, 6,907; Oklahoma, 16,090; Oregon, 3,772 Pennsylvania, 81; South Dakota, 17,683; Utah, 1,797; Washington, 6,317; Wisconsin, 6,126; Wyoming, 1,961.

[i] Includes persons living in Indian Territory and Indian reservations specially enumerated in 1890; Whites 117,368; Blacks 18,636.

General Agriculture Statistics, 1850–1990

GENERAL AGRICULTURE STATISTICS, 1850-1990										
ALABAMA										
Item No.		1850	1860	1870	1880	1890	1900	1910	1920	1930
1.	Number of farms[18,19,68,73,76,82,*a]	41,964	55,128	67,382	135,864	157,772	223,220	262,901	256,099	257,395
2.	Acres in farms[18,19,68,73,76,82]	12,137,681	19,104,545	14,961,178	18,855,334	19,853,000	20,685,427	20,732,312	19,576,856	17,554,635
3.	Acres improved land in farms[20,*a]	4,435,614	6,385,724	5,062,204	6,375,706	7,698,343	8,654,991	9,693,581	9,893,407	---
4.	Cropland harvested, acres[18,19,73,76,*a,b]	---	---	---	5,048,506	5,444,261	6,714,786	7,205,239	7,266,357	7,113,937
5.	Percentage increase in number of farms[18,19]	---	31.4	22.2	101.6	16.1	41.5	17.8	-2.6	0.5
6.	Percentage increase of land in farms[18,19]	---	57.4	-21.7	26.0	5.3	4.2	0.2	-5.6	-10.3
7.	Percentage increase of improved land in farms[20]	---	44.0	-20.7	25.9	20.7	12.4	12.0	2.1	---
8.	Average acreage per farm[18,19,66,73,76,78]	289.2	346.5	222.0	138.8	125.8	92.7	78.9	76.4	68.2
9.	Percentage increase in cropland harvested[18,19,*b]	---	---	---	---	7.8	23.3	7.3	0.8	-2.1
10.	Value of farms, dollars[18,19,64,73,76]	64,323,224	175,824,622	54,191,229	78,954,648	111,051,390	134,618,183	288,253,591	543,657,755	502,370,806
11.	Value of farms, percent increase[18,19]	---	173.3	-69.2	45.7	40.7	21.2	114.1	88.6	-7.6
12.	Average value per farm, dollars[18,19,64,73,76]	1,533	3,189	804	581	704	603	1,096	2,123	1,952
13.	Farms operated by owners[21,22,23,24,25,26,27,65,77*a]	---	---	---	72,215[*e]	81,141[*e]	93,472	103,929	107,089	90,372[*g]
14.	Value of livestock on farms, dollars[28,29,30,36,76,83*a]	21,690,112	43,411,711	21,352,076[*d]	23,787,681	30,776,730	36,105,799	65,594,834	112,824,748	75,098,775
15.	Average value of livestock per farm, dollars[19,28,29,30,36]	517	787	317[*d]	175	195	162	250[*c]	441[*c]	292[*c]
16.	Production of cotton in bales[28,29,30,67,74,83]	564,429	989,955	429,482	699,654	915,210	1,106,840[*f]	1,129,527[*f]	718,163[*f]	1,312,963[*f]
17.	Percent of total production of cotton[28,29,30]	22.9	18.4	14.3	12.2	12.2	11.6[*f]	10.6[*c,f]	6.3[*c,f]	9.0[*c,f]

GENERAL AGRICULTURE STATISTICS, 1850-1990

ALABAMA

Item No.		1850	1860	1870	1880	1890	1900	1910	1920	1930
18.	Production of wheat in bushels[31,32,35,36,69,74,84]	294,044	1,218,444	1,055,068	1,529,657	208,591	628,775	113,953	222,838	15,070
19.	Percent of total production of wheat[31,32,33,35,36]	.2926	.7039	.3667	.3329	.0445	.0955	.0167[*c]	.02361[*c]	.0019[*c]
20.	Production of corn in bushels[36,37,38,39,70,74,85]	28,754,048	33,226,282	16,977,948	25,451,278	30,072,161	35,053,047	30,695,737	43,699,100	35,683,874
21.	Percent of total production of corn[36,37,38,39]	4.9	4.0	2.2	1.4	1.4	1.3	1.2[*c]	1.9[*c]	1.7[*c]
22.	Production of oats in bushels[31,35,36,71,80,86]	2,965,696	682,179	770,866	3,039,639	3,230,455	1,882,060	3,251,146	1,120,384	245,616
23.	Percent of total production of oats[31,35,36]	2.0	0.4	0.3	0.7	0.4	0.2	0.3[*c]	0.1[*c]	[*c,j]
24.	Production of soybeans in bushels[36,40,41,72,74,76,87]	---	---	---	---	---	---	219	38,690	41,312[*h]
25.	Percent of total production of soybeans[36,40,41]	---	---	---	---	---	---	.8772[*c]	3.4084[*c]	.4770[*c]
26.	Production of hay crops in tons[31,34,42,43,44,74,76,88]	32,685	62,211	10,613	10,544	54,304	100,061	256,245	485,102	333,657
27.	Percent of total production of hay crops[31,34,42,43,44]	0.2[*c]	0.3	[*j]	[*j]	0.1	0.1[*c]	0.3[*c]	0.4[*c]	0.4[*c]

Item No.	GENERAL AGRICULTURE STATISTICS, 1850-1990 ALABAMA	1940	1950	1960	1970	1978	1982	1987	1990
1.	Number of farms[18,19,68,73,76,82,*a]	231,746	211,512	115,788	72,491	50,780	48,448	43,318	47,000
2.	Acres in farms[18,19,68,73,76,82]	19,143,391	20,888,784	16,542,730	13,654,215	11,147,825	10,200,547	9,145,753	10,300,000
3.	Acres improved land in farms[20,*a]	---	---	---	---	---	---	---	---
4.	Cropland harvested, acres[18,19,73,76,*a,b]	7,111,717	5,729,421	3,715,251	2,692,000	3,364,231	3,265,361	2,231,623	---
5.	Percentage increase in number of farms[18,19]	-10.0	-8.7	-45.3	-37.4[*c]	-29.9[*c]	-4.6[*c]	-10.6[*c]	8.5[*c]
6.	Percentage increase of land in farms[18,19]	9.1	9.1	-20.8	-17.5[*c]	-18.3[*c]	-8.5[*c]	-10.3[*c]	12.6[*c]
7.	Percentage increase of improved land in farms[20]	---	---	---	---	---	---	---	---
8.	Average acreage per farm[18,19,66,73,76,78]	82.6	98.8	142.9	188	220	211	211	226
9.	Percentage increase in cropland harvested[18,19,*b]	-0.03	-19.4	-35.2	-27.7[*c]	24.9[*c]	-2.9[*c]	-31.7[*c]	---
10.	Value of farms, dollars[18,19,64,79,81]	408,782,488	1,017,075,000[*i,k]	1,479,820,000[*i,k]	2,725,438,000	7,020,690,460	8,290,000,000	7,284,000,000	8,364,000,000
11.	Value of farms, percent increase[18,19]	-18.6	148.8[*i,k]	45.5[*i,k]	84.2[*c]	-158.0[*c]	18.1[*c]	-12.1[*c]	14.8[*c]
12.	Average value per farm, dollars[18,19,64,73,76]	1,764	4,809[*i,k]	12,780[*i,k]	37,596	138,257	171,210	168,161	177,957[*c]
13.	Farms operated by owners[21,22,23,24,25,26,27,65,77,*a]	95,107[*g]	123,463	83,539	65,239[*g]	46,697	45,171[*g]	40,466[*g]	---
14.	Value of livestock on farms, dollars[28,29,30,36,76,83,*a]	73,915,224	154,286,965	184,419,735	292,983,000	1,027,312,000	1,097,244,000	1,410,311,000	2,082,513,000
15.	Average value of livestock per farm, dollars[19,28,29,30,36]	319	729	1,593	4,041	20,231	22,648	32,557	44,309
16.	Production of cotton in bales[28,29,30,67,74,83]	772,711[*f]	824,290	683,491	507,000	287,622	421,367	380,936	383,000[*l,m]
17.	Percent of total production of cotton[28,29,30]	6.7[*c,f]	5.3[*c]	4.9[*c]	5.0[*c]	2.7[*c]	3.7[*c]	2.7[*c]	3.3[*c]

GENERAL AGRICULTURE STATISTICS, 1850-1990									
ALABAMA									
Item No.		1940	1950	1960	1970	1978	1982	1987	1990
18.	Production of wheat in bushels[31,32,35,36,69,74,84]	54,019	154,239	1,069,511	2,324,000	1,482,737	14,072,021	4,903,608	6,600,000
19.	Percent of total production of wheat[31,32,33,35,36]	.0076[a,c]	.0153[a,c]	.1013[a,c]	.1696[a,c]	.0922[a,c]	.5929[a,c]	.2598[a,c]	.3242[a,c]
20.	Production of corn in bushels[36,37,38,39,70,74,85]	31,028,109	40,972,309	62,580,000	12,535,000	22,723,611	20,144,774	15,623,257	14,580,000
21.	Percent of total production of corn[36,37,38,39]	1.3[a,c]	1.5[a,c]	1.5[a,c]	0.3[a,c]	0.3[a,c]	0.3[a,c]	0.2[a,c]	0.2[a,c]
22.	Production of oats in bushels[31,35,36,71,80,86]	934,428	1,306,543	3,084,158	1,064,000	---	---	1,250,000	1,375,000
23.	Percent of total production of oats[31,35,36]	0.1[a,c]	0.1[a,c]	0.3[a,c]	0.1[a,c]	---	---	0.4[a,c]	[a,c,j]
24.	Production of soybeans in bushels[36,40,41,72,74,76,87]	61,884[a,h]	921,320	2,678,541	14,312,000	31,251,395	36,402,694	11,633,904	11,970,000
25.	Percent of total production of soybeans[36,40,41]	.0707[a,c]	.4337[a,c]	.5195[a,c]	1.2736[a,c]	1.8147[a,c]	1.8293[a,c]	.6329[a,c]	.6212[a,c]
26.	Production of hay crops in tons[31,34,42,43,44,74,76,88]	605,683	416,581	490,612	791,000	1,029,089	1,113,671	1,186,655	1,540,000[a,n]
27.	Percent of total production of hay crops[31,34,42,43,44]	0.7[a,c]	0.5[a,c]	0.5[a,c]	0.6[a,c]	0.1[a,c]	0.9[a,c]	0.9[a,c]	1.0[a,c]

[a] See the Glossary of Terms for changing definitions, i.e. farm, improved land, cropland harvested, farm owners, and livestock.
[b] Prior to 1924, the data relate to the total acreage of crops for which figures are available, except for 1920 when 14,502,932 acres of corn cut for forage were excluded (as most of this was probably duplicated in the acreage of corn harvested for grain).
[c] Percentage computed by compiler from data herein. See endnotes for source of data.
[d] Values in gold, one-fifth less than currency values.
[e] Managers included with owners.
[f] Running square bales, counting round as half bales.
[g] Census listed the number of full and part time owners separately. Compiler added the two numbers for the above figure.
[h] Includes quantity of beans harvested from acreage grown with other crops as well as that from acreage grown alone.
[i] The total value for each state for 1950 was based on the average value per acre for farms in the sample, for which value of land and buildings was reported. The average value per farm and per acre was based on the total value of all farms.
[j] Less than one-tenth of one percent.
[k] Based on a sampling of farms.
[l] Production ginned and to be ginned.
[m] 480-pound net weight bales.
[n] Data avaliable for hay, all other only.

GENERAL AGRICULTURE STATISTICS, 1850-1990										
ALASKA										
Item No.		1850	1860	1870	1880	1890	1900	1910	1920	1930
1.	Number of farms[18,19,68,73,76,82,*a]	---	---	---	---	---	12	222	364	500
2.	Acres in farms[18,19,68,73,76,82]	---	---	---	---	---	159	42,544	90,652	525,942
3.	Acres improved land in farms[20,*a]	---	---	---	---	---	---	---	---	---
4.	Cropland harvested, acres[18,19,73,76,*a,b]	---	---	---	---	---	104	---	4,473	3,875
5.	Percentage increase in number of farms[18,19]	---	---	---	---	---	---	1,750[*c]	64.0	37.4
6.	Percentage increase of land in farms[18,19]	---	---	---	---	---	---	26,657[*c]	113.1	480.2
7.	Percentage increase of improved land in farms[20]	---	---	---	---	---	---	---	---	---
8.	Average acreage per farm[18,19,66,73,76,78]	---	---	---	---	---	13.3	191.6	249.0	1,051.9
9.	Percentage increase in cropland harvested[18,19,*b]	---	---	---	---	---	---	---	---	13.4
10.	Value of farms, dollars[18,19,64,79,81]	---	---	---	---	---	---	867,638	1,211,685	2,857,185
11.	Value of farms, percent increase[18,19]	---	---	---	---	---	---	---	39.7	135.8
12.	Average value per farm, dollars[18,19,64,73,76]	---	---	---	---	---	---	3,908	3,329	5,714
13.	Farms operated by owners[21,22,23,24,25,26,27,65,77*a]	---	---	---	---	---	---	---	---	---
14.	Value of livestock on farms, dollars[28,29,30,36,76,83*a]	---	---	---	---	[*j]	2,196	---	---	---
15.	Average value of livestock per farm, dollars[19,28,29,30,36]	---	---	---	---	[*j]	183	---	---	---
16.	Production of cotton in bales[28,29,30,67,74,83]	---	---	---	---	---	---	---	---	---
17.	Percent of total production of cotton[28,29,30]	---	---	---	---	---	---	---	---	---

GENERAL AGRICULTURE STATISTICS, 1850-1990										
ALASKA										
Item No.		1850	1860	1870	1880	1890	1900	1910	1920	1930
18.	Production of wheat in bushels[31,32,35,36,69,74,84]	---	---	---	---	---	---	---	---	---
19.	Percent of total production of wheat[31,32,33,35,36]	---	---	---	---	---	---	---	---	---
20.	Production of corn in bushels[36,37,38,39,70,74,85]	---	---	---	---	---	---	---	---	---
21.	Percent of total production of corn[36,37,38,39]	---	---	---	---	---	---	---	---	---
22.	Production of oats in bushels[31,35,36,71,80,86]	---	---	---	---	---	---	---	---	---
23.	Percent of total production of oats[31,35,36]	---	---	---	---	---	---	---	---	---
24.	Production of soybeans in bushels[36,40,41,72,74,76,87]	---	---	---	---	---	---	---	---	---
25.	Percent of total production of soybeans[36,40,41]	---	---	---	---	---	---	---	---	---
26.	Production of hay crops in tons[31,34,42,43,44,74,76,88]	---	---	---	---	---	113	---	---	---
27.	Percent of total production of hay crops[31,34,42,43,44]	---	---	---	---	---	*k	---	---	---

GENERAL AGRICULTURE STATISTICS, 1850-1990

ALASKA

Item No.		1940	1950	1960	1970	1978	1982	1987	1990
1.	Number of farms[18,19,68,73,76,82,*a]	623	525	367	332	383	570	574	580
2.	Acres in farms[18,19,68,73,76,82]	1,775,752	421,799	888,331	1,604,211	1,286,463	1,323,953	1,026,732	1,000,000
3.	Acres improved land in farms[20,*a]	---	---	---	---	---	---	---	---
4.	Cropland harvested, acres[18,19,73,76,*a,b]	7,305	6,450	14,482	---	20,538	25,694	28,949	---
5.	Percentage increase in number of farms[18,19]	24.6	-15.7	-30.1	-9.5[*c]	15.4[*c]	48.8[*c]	0.7[*c]	1.0[*c]
6.	Percentage increase of land in farms[18,19]	237.6	-76.3	110.6	80.6[*c]	-19.8[*c]	2.9[*c]	-22.4[*c]	-2.6[*c]
7.	Percentage increase of improved land in farms[20]	---	---	---	---	---	---	---	---
8.	Average acreage per farm[18,19,66,73,76,78]	2,850.3	803.4	2,420.5	4,831.9	3,359	2,323	1,789	1,683
9.	Percentage increase in cropland harvested[18,19,*b]	88.5	-11.7	124.5	---	---	25.1[*c]	12.7[*c]	---
10.	Value of farms, dollars[18,19,64,79,81]	3,841,045	6,544,000[*i]	17,755,000	20,432,000	459,156,869	264,000,000	317,000,000	---
11.	Value of farms, percent increase[18,19]	34.4	70.4[*i]	171.3	15.1[*c]	2,147.24[*c]	42.5[*c]	20.1[*c]	---
12.	Average value per farm, dollars[18,19,64,73,76]	6,165	12,465[*i]	48,379	61,541	364,527	463,849	553,000	---
13.	Farms operated by owners[21,22,23,24,25,26,27,65,77,*a]	---	---	3,389	290[*g]	326	515[*g]	520[*g]	---
14.	Value of livestock on farms, dollars[28,29,30,36,76,83,*a]	---	---	1,976,515	---	3,564,000	5,389,000	7,204,000	7,562,000
15.	Average value of livestock per farm, dollars[19,28,29,30,36]	---	---	5,386	---	9,306[*c]	9,454	12,551	13,038
16.	Production of cotton in bales[28,29,30,67,74,83]	---	---	---	---	---	---	---	---
17.	Percent of total production of cotton[28,29,30]	---	---	---	---	---	---	---	---

GENERAL AGRICULTURE STATISTICS, 1850-1990

ALASKA

Item No.		1940	1950	1960	1970	1978	1982	1987	1990
18.	Production of wheat in bushels[31,32,35,36,69,74,84]	---	---	---	---	2,855	2,802	*l	---
19.	Percent of total production of wheat[31,32,33,35,36]	---	---	---	---	.0002*c	.0001*c	---	---
20.	Production of corn in bushels[36,37,38,39,70,74,85]	---	---	---	---	---	---	---	---
21.	Percent of total production of corn[36,37,38,39]	---	---	---	---	---	---	---	---
22.	Production of oats in bushels[31,35,36,71,80,86]	---	11,616	50,559	---	---	---	---	---
23.	Percent of total production of oats[31,35,36]	---	*c,k	*c,k	---	---	---	---	---
24.	Production of soybeans in bushels[36,40,41,72,74,76,87]	---	---	---	---	---	---	---	---
25.	Percent of total production of soybeans[36,40,41]	---	---	---	---	---	---	---	---
26.	Production of hay crops in tons[31,34,42,43,44,74,76,88]	---	6,132	17,500	---	23,591	19,726	28,615	---
27.	Percent of total production of hay crops[31,34,42,43,44]	---	*c,k	*c,k	---	*c,k	*c,k	*c,k	---

[a] See the Glossary of Terms for changing definitions, i.e. farm, improved land, cropland harvested, farm owners, and livestock.

[b] Prior to 1924, the data relate to the total acreage of crops for which figures are available, except for 1920 when 14,502,932 acres of corn cut for forage were excluded (as most of this was probably duplicated in the acreage of corn harvested for grain).

[c] Percentage computed by compiler from data herein. See endnotes for source of data.

[d] Values in gold, one-fifth less than currency values.

[e] Managers included with owners.

[f] Running square bales, counting round as half bales.

[g] Census listed the number of full and part time owners separately. Compiler added the two numbers for the above figure.

[h] Includes quantity of beans harvested from acreage grown with other crops as well as that from acreage grown alone.

[i] The total value for each state for 1950 was based on the average value per acre for farms in the sample, for which value of land and buildings was reported. The average value per farm and per acre was based on the total value of all farms.

[j] Not reported prior to 1900.

[k] Less than one-tenth of one percent.

[l] Withheld to avoid disclosing data for individual farms.

GENERAL AGRICULTURE STATISTICS, 1850-1990										
ARIZONA										
Item No.		1850	1860	1870	1880	1890	1900	1910	1920	1930
1.	Number of farms[18,19,68,73,76,82,*a]	---	---	172	767	1,426	5,809	9,227	9,975	14,173
2.	Acres in farms[18,19,68,73,76,82]	---	---	21,807	135,573	1,297,033	1,935,327	1,246,613	5,802,126	10,526,627
3.	Acres improved land in farms[20,*a]	---	---	14,585	56,071	104,128	254,521	350,173	712,803	---
4.	Cropland harvested, acres[18,19,73,76,*a,b]	---	---	---	28,837	51,246	150,781	190,982	441,772	478,411
5.	Percentage increase in number of farms[18,19]	---	---	---	345.9	85.9	307.4	58.8	8.1	42.1
6.	Percentage increase of land in farms[18,19]	---	---	---	521.7	856.7	49.2	-35.6	365.4	81.4
7.	Percentage increase of improved land in farms[20]	---	---	---	284.4	85.7	144.4	37.6	103.6	---
8.	Average acreage per farm[18,19,66,73,76,78]	---	---	126.8	176.8	909.6	333.2	135.1	581.7	742.7
9.	Percentage increase in cropland harvested[18,19,*b]	---	---	---	---	77.7	194.2	26.7	131.3	8.3
10.	Value of farms, dollars18,19,64,79,81	---	---	129,072	1,127,946	7,222,230	13,682,960	47,285,310	172,325,321	184,230,656
11.	Value of farms, percent increase[18,19]	---	---	---	773.9	540.3	89.5	245.6	264.4	6.9
12.	Average value per farm, dollars[18,19,64,73,76]	---	---	750	1,471	5,065	2,355	5,125	17,276	12,999
13.	Farms operated by owners[21,22,23,24,25,26,27,65,77,*a]	---	---	---	666[*e]	1,313[*e]	4,985	8,203	7,869	11,294[*g]
14.	Value of livestock on farms, dollars[28,29,30,36,76,83,*a]	---	---	115,197[*d]	3,210,989[*k]	13,227,453[*k]	15,545,687	26,050,870	52,447,001	48,502,676
15.	Average value of livestock per farm, dollars[19,28,29,30,36]	---	---	670[*d]	4,186	9,276	2,676	2,823[*c]	5,258[*c]	3,422[*c]
16.	Production of cotton in bales[28,29,30,67,74,83]	---	---	---	---	---	15[*f]	11[*f]	59,351[*f]	149,488[*f]
17.	Percent of total production of cotton[28,29,30]	---	---	---	---	---	.0002[*c,f]	.0001[*c,f]	.5217[*c,f]	1.0257[*c,f]

GENERAL AGRICULTURE STATISTICS, 1850-1990										
ARIZONA										
Item No.		1850	1860	1870	1880	1890	1900	1910	1920	1930
18.	Production of wheat in bushels[31,32,35,36,69,74,84]	---	---	27,052	136,427	100,328	440,252	862,875	835,374	348,745
19.	Percent of total production of wheat[31,32,33,35,36]	---	---	.0094	.0297	.0214	.0669	.1263[*c]	.0884[*c]	.0436[*c]
20.	Production of corn in bushels[36,37,38,39],70,74,85	---	---	32,041	34,746	82,535	204,748	298,664	446,208	243,004
21.	Percent of total production of corn[36,37,38,39]	---	---	[*j]	[*j]	[*j]	[*j]	[*c,j]	[*c,j]	[*c,j]
22.	Production of oats in bushels[31,35,36,71,80,86]	---	---	25	564	33,996	43,246	189,312	377,785	79,755
23.	Percent of total production of oats[31,35,36]	---	---	[*j]	[*j]	[*j]	[*j]	[*c,j]	[*c,j]	[*c,j]
24.	Production of soybeans in bushels[36,40,41,72,74,76,87]	---	---	---	---	---	---	---	1,169	81[*h]
25.	Percent of total production of soybeans[36,40,41]	---	---	---	---	---	---	---	.1030[*c]	.0009[*c]
26.	Production of hay crops in tons[31,34,42,43,44,74,76,88]	---	---	109	5,606	63,947	117,504	260,878	480,342	302,214
27.	Percent of total production of hay crops[31,34,42,43,44]	---	---	[*j]	[*j]	0.1	0.2	0.3[*c]	0.4[*c]	0.4[*c]

GENERAL AGRICULTURE STATISTICS, 1850-1990

ARIZONA

Item No.		1940	1950	1960	1970	1978	1982	1987	1990
1.	Number of farms[18,19,68,73,76,82,*a]	18,468	10,412	7,233	5,890	6,298	7,334	7,669	7,800
2.	Acres in farms[18,19,68,73,76,82]	25,651,092	39,916,440	40,203,386	38,202,667	38,505,905	37,752,534	36,287,794	36,000,000
3.	Acres improved land in farms[20,*a]	---	---	---	---	---	---	---	---
4.	Cropland harvested, acres[18,19,73,76,*a,b]	525,974	883,717	1,018,757	1,042,000	1,106,631	1,047,213	865,817	---
5.	Percentage increase in number of farms[18,19]	30.3	-43.6	-30.5	-18.6[*c]	6.9[*c]	16.5[*c]	4.6[*c]	1.7[*c]
6.	Percentage increase of land in farms[18,19]	143.7	55.6	0.7	-5.0[*c]	0.8[*c]	-2.0[*c]	-3.9[*c]	-0.8[*c]
7.	Percentage increase of improved land in farms[20]	---	---	---	---	---	---	---	---
8.	Average acreage per farm[18,19,66,73,76,78]	1,338.9	3,833.7	5,558.3	6,486[*c]	6,114	5,148	4,732	4,444
9.	Percentage increase in cropland harvested[18,19,*b]	9.9	68.0	15.3	2.3	6.2	5.4[*c]	-17.3[*c]	---
10.	Value of farms, dollars[18,19,64,79,81]	153,676,675	603,851,000[*i]	1,950,911,000	2,664,000,000	7,550,313,214	10,972,000,000	10,111,000,000	7,730,000,000
11.	Value of farms, percent increase[18,19]	-16.6	292.9[*i]	223.1	36.6[*c]	183.0[*c]	45.3[*c]	-7.8[*c]	-23.5[*c]
12.	Average value per farm, dollars[18,19,64,73,76]	8,321	57,996[*i]	269,724	452,241	1,198,843	1,496,334	1,317,765	991,026
13.	Farms operated by owners[21,22,23,24,25,26,27,65,77,*a]	15,835[*g]	8,833	5,935[*g]	5,034[*g]	5,525	6,547[*g]	6,574[*g]	---
14.	Value of livestock on farms, dollars[28,29,30,36,76,83,*a]	30,288,632	90,105,299	144,798,414	---	654,031,000	720,068,000	731,863,000	819,246,000
15.	Average value of livestock per farm, dollars[19,28,29,30,36]	1,640[*c]	8,654	20,019	---	103,847	98,182	95,431	105,032
16.	Production of cotton in bales[28,29,30,67,74,83]	199,151[*f]	530,766	696,863	490,000	1,146,665	1,155,883	1,005,493	649,000[*l,m]
17.	Percent of total production of cotton[28,29,30]	1.7[*c]	3.4[*c]	5.0[*c]	4.8[*c]	0.1[*c]	0.1[*c]	7.6[*c]	5.6[*c]

GENERAL AGRICULTURE STATISTICS, 1850-1990									
ARIZONA									
Item No.		1940	1950	1960	1970	1978	1982	1987	1990
18.	Production of wheat in bushels[31,32,35,36,69,74,84]	610,206	707,505	3,066,639	10,350,000	7,535,554	11,891,456	7,991,708	10,772,000
19.	Percent of total production of wheat[31,32,33,35,36]	.0861[*c]	.0703[*c]	.2904[*c]	.7554[*c]	.4688[*c]	.5011[*c]	.4235[*c]	.5291[*c]
20.	Production of corn in bushels[36,37,38,39,70,74,85]	267,487	388,277	1,190,000	336,000	2,913,251	1,498,482	1,530,568	1,885,000
21.	Percent of total production of corn[36,37,38,39]	[*c,j]	[*c,j]	[*c,j]	[*c,j]	[*c,j]	[*c,j]	[*c,j]	[*c,j]
22.	Production of oats in bushels[31,35,36,71,80,86]	145,766	323,894	140,764	---	---	492,420	165,428	---
23.	Percent of total production of oats[31,35,36]	[*c,j]	[*c,j]	[*c,j]	---	---	0.1[*c]	0.1[*c]	---
24.	Production of soybeans in bushels[36,40,41,72,74,76,87]	33[*h]	---	3,685	---	94,359	---	---	---
25.	Percent of total production of soybeans[36,40,41]	.0000[*c]	---	.0007[*c]	---	.0055[*c]	---	---	---
26.	Production of hay crops in tons[31,34,42,43,44,74,76,88]	334,137	508,176	826,642	1,318,000	982,232	913,269	1,040,321	1,280,000[*n]
27.	Percent of total production of hay crops[31,34,42,43,44]	0.4[*c]	0.6[*c]	0.8[*c]	1.0[*c]	0.1[*c]	0.7[*c]	0.8[*c]	0.9[*c]

[a] See the Glossary of Terms for changing definitions, i.e. farm, improved land, cropland harvested, farm owners, and livestock.
[b] Prior to 1924, the data relate to the total acreage of crops for which figures are available, except for 1920 when 14,502,932 acres of corn cut for forage were excluded (as most of this was probably duplicated in the acreage of corn harvested for grain).
[c] Percentage computed by compiler from data herein. See endnotes for source of data.
[d] Values in gold, one-fifth less than currency values.
[e] Managers included with owners.
[f] Running square bales, counting round as half bales.
[g] Census listed the number of full and part time owners separately. Compiler added the two numbers for the above figure.
[h] Includes quantity of beans harvested from acreage grown with other crops as well as that from acreage grown alone.
[i] The total value for each state for 1950 was based on the average value per acre for farms in the sample, for which value of land and buildings was reported. The average value per farm and per acre was based on the total value of all farms.
[j] Less than one-tenth of one percent.
[k] Including estimated value of range animals.
[l] Production ginned and to be ginned.
[m] 480-pound net weight bales.
[n] Census had two separate listings: hay, alfalfa, and alfalfa mixtures; and hay, all other. Compiler added the two listings for the above figure.

GENERAL AGRICULTURE STATISTICS, 1850-1990

ARKANSAS

Item No.		1850	1860	1870	1880	1890	1900	1910	1920	1930
1.	Number of farms[18,19,68,73,76,82,*a]	17,758	39,004	49,424	94,433	124,760	178,694	214,678	232,604	242,334
2.	Acres in farms[18,19,68,73,76,82]	2,598,214	9,573,706	7,597,296	12,061,547	14,891,356	16,636,719	17,416,075	17,456,750	16,052,962
3.	Acres improved land in farms[20,*a]	781,530	1,983,313	1,859,821	3,595,603	5,475,043	6,953,735	8,076,254	9,210,556	---
4.	Cropland harvested, acres[18,19,73,76,*a,b]	---	---	---	2,755,901	3,982,999	5,017,894	5,376,484	6,465,305	6,581,834
5.	Percentage increase in number of farms[18,19]	---	119.6	26.7	91.1	32.1	43.2	20.1	8.4	4.2
6.	Percentage increase of land in farms[18,19]	---	268.5	-20.6	58.8	23.5	11.7	4.7	0.2	-8.0
7.	Percentage increase of improved land in farms[20]	---	153.8	-6.2	93.3	52.3	27.0	16.1	14.0	---
8.	Average acreage per farm[18,19,66,73,76,78]	146.3	245.4	153.7	127.7	119.4	93.1	81.1	75.0	66.2
9.	Percentage increase in cropland harvested[18,19,*b]	---	---	---	---	44.5	26.0	7.1	20.3	1.8
10.	Value of farms, dollars[18,19,64,79,81]	15,265,245	91,649,773	32,023,758	74,249,655	118,574,422	135,182,170	309,166,813	753,110,666	547,828,250
11.	Value of farms, percent increase[18,19]	---	500.4	-65.1	131.9	59.7	14.0	128.7	143.6	-27.3
12.	Average value per farm, dollars[18,19,64,73,76]	860	2,350	648	786	950	757	1.440	3,238	2,261
13.	Farms operated by owners[21,22,23,24,25,26,27,65,77,*a]	---	---	---	65,245[*e]	84,706[*e]	96,735	106,649	112,647	89,009[*g]
14.	Value of livestock on farms, dollars[28,29,30,36,76,83,*a]	6,647,969	22,096,977	13,778,005[*d]	20,472,425	30,772,880	37,483,771	74,058,292	127,852,580	68,573,100
15.	Average value of livestock per farm, dollars[19,28,29,30,36]	374	567	279[*d]	217	247	210	345[*c]	550[*c]	283[*c]
16.	Production of cotton in bales[28,29,30,67,74,83]	65,344	367,393	247,968	608,256	691,494	709,880[*f]	776,879[*f]	869,350[*f]	1,398,475[*f]
17.	Percent of total production of cotton[28,29,30]	2.6	6.8	8.2	10.6	9.3	7.4[*f]	7.3[*c,f]	7.6[*c,f]	9.6[*c,f]

GENERAL AGRICULTURE STATISTICS, 1850-1990										
ARKANSAS										
Item No.		1850	1860	1870	1880	1890	1900	1910	1920	1930
18.	Production of wheat in bushels[31,32,35,36,69,74,84]	199,639	957,601	741,736	1,269,715	955,668	2,449,970	526,414	2,051,405	153,281
19.	Percent of total production of wheat[31,32,33,35,36]	.1987	.5532	.2578	.2763	.2040	.3720	.0770[*c]	.2170[*c]	.0191[*c]
20.	Production of corn in bushels[36,37,38,39,70,74,85]	8,893,939	17,823,588	13,382,145	24,156,417	33,982,318	41,144,098	37,609,544	34,226,935	27,388,105
21.	Percent of total production of corn[36,37,38,39]	1.5	2.1	1.8	1.4	1.6	1.7	1.5[*c]	1.5[*c]	1.3[*c]
22.	Production of oats in bushels[31,35,36,71,80,86]	656,163	475,268	528,777	2,219,822	4,180,877	3,909,000	3,212,891	2,703,753	653,887
23.	Percent of total production of oats[31,35,36]	0.5	0.3	0.2	0.5	0.5	0.4	0.3[*c]	0.3[*c]	0.1[*c]
24.	Production of soybeans in bushels[36,40,41,72,74,76,87]	---	---	---	---	---	---	---	7,700	65,869[*h]
25.	Percent of total production of soybeans[36,40,41]	---	---	---	---	---	---	---	.6783[*c]	.7605[*c]
26.	Production of hay crops in tons[31,34,42,43,44,74,76,88]	3,976	9,356	6,839	20,630	164,399	271,616	472,367	906,928	675,342
27.	Percent of total production of hay crops[31,34,42,43,44]	[*c,k]	[*k]	[*k]	0.1	0.2	0.3	0.5[*c]	0.7[*c]	0.8[*c]

GENERAL AGRICULTURE STATISTICS, 1850-1990

ARKANSAS

Item No.		1940	1950	1960	1970	1978	1982	1987	1990
1.	Number of farms[18,19,68,73,76,82,*a]	216,674	182,429	95,007	60,433	51,751	50,525	48,242	47,000
2.	Acres in farms[18,19,68,73,76,82]	18,044,542	18,871,244	16,458,515	15,694,527	15,074,799	14,682,960	14,355,611	15,500,000
3.	Acres improved land in farms[20,*a]	---	---	---	---	---	---	---	---
4.	Cropland harvested, acres[18,19,73,76,*a,b]	6,609,833	5,930,093	5,324,541	7,322,000	7,572,049	7,484,316	6,477,365	---
5.	Percentage increase in number of farms[18,19]	-10.6	-15.8	-47.9	-36.4[*c]	-14.4[*c]	-2.4[*c]	-4.5[*c]	-2.6[*c]
6.	Percentage increase of land in farms[18,19]	12.4	4.6	-12.8	-4.6[*c]	-4.0[*c]	-6.4[*c]	-2.2[*c]	8.0[*c]
7.	Percentage increase of improved land in farms[20]	---	---	---	---	---	---	---	---
8.	Average acreage per farm[18,19,66,73,76,78]	83.3	103.4	173.2	260	291	291	298	320
9.	Percentage increase in cropland harvested[18,19,*b]	0.4	-10.3	-10.2	37.5[*c]	3.4[*c]	-1.2[*c]	-13.5[*c]	---
10.	Value of farms, dollars[18,19,64,79,81]	456,848,156	1,135,671,000[*i,j]	1,797,070,000[*i,j]	4,081,000,000	11,445,044,156	14,460,000,000	10,884,000,000	9,963,000,000
11.	Value of farms, percent increase[18,19]	-16.6	148.6[*i,j]	58.2[*i,j]	127.1[*c]	180.4[*c]	254.3[*c]	-24.7[*c]	-8.5[*c]
12.	Average value per farm, dollars[18,19,64,73,76]	2,108	6,225[*i,j]	18,915[*i,j]	68,000	221,156	286,402	225,604	211,979[*c]
13.	Farms operated by owners[21,22,23,24,25,26,27,65,77,*a]	100,636[*g]	113,283	72,044[*g]	52,763[*g]	45,959	45,371[*g]	42,838[*g]	---
14.	Value of livestock on farms, dollars[28,29,30,36,76,83,*a]	70,071,421	132,708,736	153,906,398	271,225,000	1,296,650,000	1,469,879,000	2,073,572,000	2,706,429,000
15.	Average value of livestock per farm, dollars[19,28,29,30,36]	323[*c]	727	1,620	4,488[*c]	25,056	29,092	42,983[*c]	57,584
16.	Production of cotton in bales[28,29,30,67,74,83]	1,351,209[*f]	1,584,307	1,484,003	1,048,000	648,790	525,887	816,723	851,000[*l,m]
17.	Percent of total production of cotton[28,29,30]	11.8[*c,f]	10.3[*c]	10.7[*c]	10.3[*c]	6.1[*c]	4.6[*c]	6.2[*c]	7.4[*c]

GENERAL AGRICULTURE STATISTICS, 1850-1990									
ARKANSAS									
Item No.		1940	1950	1960	1970	1978	1982	1987	1990
18.	Production of wheat in bushels[31,32,35,36,69,74,84]	353,443	289,454	2,945,711	10,725,000	8,792,162	61,332,564	33,241,332	52,800,000
19.	Percent of total production of wheat[31,32,33,35,36]	.0499[*c]	.0285[*c]	.2790[*c]	.7827[*c]	.5469[*c]	2.5843[*c]	1.7614[*c]	2.5936[*c]
20.	Production of corn in bushels[36,37,38,39,70,74,85]	33,762,323	21,626,026	14,945,000	1,575,000	1,351,741	2,389,882	5,802,912	7,076,000
21.	Percent of total production of corn[36,37,38,39]	1.5[*c]	0.8[*c]	0.3[*c]	[*c,k]	[*c,k]	[*c,k]	0.1[*c]	0.1[*c]
22.	Production of oats in bushels[31,35,36,71,80,86]	4,211,143	3,904,687	5,547,374	5,632,000	---	2,357,476	1,146,889	4,380,000
23.	Percent of total production of oats[31,35,36]	0.5[*c]	0.3[*c]	0.6[*c]	0.6[*c]	---	0.5[*c]	0.4[*c]	[*c,k]
24.	Production of soybeans in bushels[36,40,41,72,74,76,87]	551,788[*h]	6,134,516	52,349,152	97,043,000	103,394,661	98,603,852	73,279,691	76,800,000
25.	Percent of total production of soybeans[36,40,41]	.6300[*c]	2.8876[*c]	1.2770[*c]	8.6357[*c]	.6003[*c]	4.9550[*c]	3.9868[*c]	3.9859[*c]
26.	Production of hay crops in tons[31,34,42,43,44,74,76,88]	1,401,702	1,179,015	826,743	1,348,000	1,363,360	1,586,810	1,511,459	2,228,000[*n]
27.	Percent of total production of hay crops[31,34,42,43,44]	1.7[*c]	1.3[*c]	0.8[*c]	1.1[*c]	0.1[*c]	1.2[*c]	1.2[*c]	1.5[*c]

[a] See the Glossary of Terms for changing definitions, i.e. farm, improved land, cropland harvested, farm owners, and livestock.

[b] Prior to 1924, the data relate to the total acreage of crops for which figures are available, except for 1920 when 14,502,932 acres of corn cut for forage were excluded (as most of this was probably duplicated in the acreage of corn harvested for grain).

[c] Percentage computed by compiler from data herein. See endnotes for source of data.

[d] Values in gold, one-fifth less than currency values.

[e] Managers included with owners.

[f] Running square bales, counting round as half bales.

[g] Census listed the number of full and part time owners separately. Compiler added the two numbers for the above figure.

[h] Includes quantity of beans harvested from acreage grown with other crops as well as that from acreage grown alone.

[i] The total value for each state for 1950 was based on the average value per acre for farms in the sample, for which value of land and buildings was reported. The average value per farm and per acre was based on the total value of all farms.

[j] Based on a sampling of farms.

[k] Less than one-tenth of one percent.

[l] Production ginned and to be ginned.

[m] 480-pound net weight bales.

[n] Census had two separate listings: hay, alfalfa, and alfalfa mixtures; and hay, all other. Compiler added the two listings for the above figure.

GENERAL AGRICULTURE STATISTICS, 1850-1990

CALIFORNIA

Item No.		1850	1860	1870	1880	1890	1900	1910	1920	1930
1.	Number of farms[18,19,68,73,76,82,*a]	872	18,716	23,724	35,934	52,894	72,542	88,197	117,670	135,676
2.	Acres in farms[18,19,68,73,76,82]	3,893,985	8,730,034	11,427,105	16,593,742	21,427,293	28,828,951	27,931,444	29,365,667	30,422,581
3.	Acres improved land in farms[20,*a]	32,454	2,468,034	6,218,133	10,669,698	12,222,839	11,958,837	11,389,894	11,878,339	---
4.	Cropland harvested, acres[18,19,73,76,*a,b]	---	---	---	3,321,027	5,289,070	6,434,434	4,924,733	5,761,190	6,549,967
5.	Percentage increase in number of farms[18,19]	---	[*k]	26.8	51.5	47.2	37.1	21.6	33.4	15.3
6.	Percentage increase of land in farms[18,19]	---	124.2	30.9	45.2	29.1	34.5	-3.1	5.1	3.6
7.	Percentage increase of improved land in farms[20]	---	7,504.7[*c]	151.9	71.6	14.6	-2.2	-4.8	4.3	---
8.	Average acreage per farm[18,19,66,73,76,78]	4,465.6	466.4	481.7	461.8	405.0	397.4	316.7	249.6	224.4
9.	Percentage increase in cropland harvested[18,19,*b]	---	---	---	---	59.3	21.7	-23.5	17.0	13.7
10.	Value of farms, dollars[18,19,64,79,81]	3,874,041	48,726,804	141,240,028	262,051,282	697,116,630	707,912,960	1,450,601,488	3,073,811,109	3,419,470,764
11.	Value of farms, percent increase[18,19]	---	[*k]	189.9	85.5	166.0	1.5	104.9	111.9	11.2
12.	Average value per farm, dollars[18,19,64,73,76]	4,443	2,603	5,953	7,293	13,180	9,759	16,447	26,122	25,203
13.	Farms operated by owners[21,22,23,24,25,26,27,65,77,*a]	---	---	---	28,810[*e]	43,489[*e]	52,529	66,632	87,580	103,506[*g]
14.	Value of livestock on farms, dollars[28,29,30,36,76,83,*a]	3,351,058	35,585,017	37,964,752[*d]	41,498,417[*l]	65,575,427[*l]	67,303,325	127,599,938	221,141,462	199,107,567
15.	Average value of livestock per farm, dollars[19,28,29,30,36]	3,843	1,901	1,600[*d]	1,155	1,240	928	1,447[*c]	1,879[*c]	1,468[*c]
16.	Production of cotton in bales[28,29,30,67,74,83]	---	---	34	---	---	---	183	46,418	253,881
17.	Percent of total production of cotton[28,29,30]	---	---	[*j]	---	---	---	[*j]	0.4	1.7

GENERAL AGRICULTURE STATISTICS, 1850-1990										
CALIFORNIA										
Item No.		1850	1860	1870	1880	1890	1900	1910	1920	1930
18.	Production of wheat in bushels[31,32,35,36,69,74,84]	17,328	5,928,470	16,676,702	29,017,707	40,869,337	36,534,407	6,203,206	16,866,882	10,957,967
19.	Percent of total production of wheat[31,32,33,35,36]	.0172	3.4248	5.7956	6.3153	8.7258	5.5478	.9077[*c]	1.7841[*c]	1.3686[*c]
20.	Production of corn in bushels[36,37,38,39,70,74,85]	12,236	510,708	1,221,222	1,993,325	2,381,270	1,477,093	1,273,901	3,448,459	1,323,930
21.	Percent of total production of corn[36,37,38,39]	[*j]	0.1	0.2	0.1	0.1	[*j]	0.5[*c]	0.1[*c]	0.1[*c]
22.	Production of oats in bushels[31,35,36,71,80,86]	---	1,043,006	1,757,507	1,341,271	1,463,068	4,972,356	4,143,688	2,966,776	2,162,657
23.	Percent of total production of oats[31,35,36]	---	0.6	0.6	0.3	0.2	0.5	0.4[*c]	0.3[*c]	0.2[*c]
24.	Production of soybeans in bushels[36,40,41,72,74,76,87]	---	---	---	---	---	---	5,534	49,694	---
25.	Percent of total production of soybeans[36,40,41]	---	---	---	---	---	---	22.1661[*c]	4.3778[*c]	---
26.	Production of hay crops in tons[31,34,42,43,44,74,76,88]	2,038	305,655	551,773	1,045,119	2,218,285	3,035,266	4,331,885	4,469,973	4,098,993
27.	Percent of total production of hay crops[31,34,42,43,44]	[*c,j]	1.6	2.0	3.0	3.3	3.8	4.4[*c]	3.6[*c]	4.8[*c]

GENERAL AGRICULTURE STATISTICS, 1850-1990									
CALIFORNIA									
Item No.		1940	1950	1960	1970	1978	1982	1987	1990
1.	Number of farms[18,19,68,73,76,82,*a]	132,658	137,168	99,274	77,875	73,194	82,463	83,217	85,000
2.	Acres in farms[18,19,68,73,76,82]	30,524,324	36,613,291	36,887,948	35,328,360	32,727,202	32,156,894	30,598,178	30,800,000
3.	Acres improved land in farms[20,*a]	---	---	---	---	---	---	---	---
4.	Cropland harvested, acres[18,19,73,76,*a,b]	6,534,562	7,956,671	8,021,836	5,751,000	8,804,374	8,764,808	7,676,287	---
5.	Percentage increase in number of farms[18,19]	-2.2	3.4	-27.6	-21.6[*c]	-6.0[*c]	5.9[*c]	0.9[*c]	2.1[*c]
6.	Percentage increase of land in farms[18,19]	0.3	19.9	0.8	-3.2[*c]	-8.4[*c]	-10.0[*c]	-4.8[*c]	0.7[*c]
7.	Percentage increase of improved land in farms[20]	---	---	---	---	---	---	---	---
8.	Average acreage per farm[18,19,66,73,76,78]	230.1	266.9	371.6	454	447	390	368	373
9.	Percentage increase in cropland harvested[18,19,*b]	-0.2	21.8	0.8	-28.3[*c]	53.1[*c]	-0.4[*c]	-12.4[*c]	---
10.	Value of farms, dollars[18,19,64,79,81]	2,166,452,648	5,650,279,000[*i]	13,025,988,000	16,956,000,000	38,151,640,560	61,532,000,000	48,567,000,000	46,181,000,000
11.	Value of farms, percent increase[18,19]	-36.6	160.8[*i]	130.5	30.2[*c]	125.0[*c]	262.9[*c]	-21.1[*c]	-4.9[*c]
12.	Average value per farm, dollars[18,19,64,73,76]	16,331	41,192[*i]	131,212	218,000	521,240	746,577	538,668	543,306
13.	Farms operated by owners[21,22,23,24,25,26,27,65,77,*a]	103,834[*g]	118,312	86,245[*g]	68,088[*g]	64,431	73,248,000[*g]	72,857,000[*g]	---
14.	Value of livestock on farms, dollars[28,29,30,36,76,83,*a]	144,593,133	448,227,100	664,537,733	---	3,422,592,000	4,332,948,000	4,652,844,000	5,515,159,000
15.	Average value of livestock per farm, dollars[19,28,29,30,36]	1,090[*c]	3,268	6,694	---	46,761	52,544	55,912	64,884[*c]
16.	Production of cotton in bales[28,29,30,67,74,83]	435,397[*f]	1,230,532	1,791,260	1,160,000	1,911,050	2,872,637	2,619,934	2,661,000[*n,o]
17.	Percent of total production of cotton[28,29,30]	3.8[*c,f]	7.1[*c]	12.9[*c]	11.4[*c]	0.2[*c]	0.3[*c]	0.3[*c]	0.2[*c]

GENERAL AGRICULTURE STATISTICS, 1850-1990

CALIFORNIA

Item No.		1940	1950	1960	1970	1978	1982	1987	1990
18.	Production of wheat in bushels[31,32,35,36,69,74,84]	10,371,800	11,210,357	8,170,040	22,175,000	32,687,096	63,130,854	40,004,786	52,605,000
19.	Percent of total production of wheat[31,32,33,35,36]	1.4632[*c]	1.1137[*c]	.7737[*c]	1.6183[*c]	2.0333[*c]	2.6601[*c]	2.1199[*c]	2.5840[*c]
20.	Production of corn in bushels[36,37,38,39,70,74,85]	1,507,778	1,150,811	18,250,000	21,168,000	33,081,209	37,721,398	23,454,799	27,200,000
21.	Percent of total production of corn[36,37,38,39]	0.1[*c]	[*c,j]	0.4[*c]	[*c,j]	0.5[*c]	0.5[*c]	0.3[*c]	0.4[*c]
22.	Production of oats in bushels[31,35,36,71,80,86]	4,227,089	3,454,203	4,245,656	5,050,000	---	3,322,597	2,800,000	3,000,000
23.	Percent of total production of oats[31,35,36]	0.5[*c]	0.3[*c]	0.4[*c]	0.6[*c]	---	0.7[*c]	0.9[*c]	[*c,j]
24.	Production of soybeans in bushels[36,40,41,72,74,76,87]	661[*h]	---	436	---	4,980,999	17,063	[*m]	---
25.	Percent of total production of soybeans[36,40,41]	.0008[*c]	---	.0001[*c]	---	.0289[*c]	.0009[*c]	---	---
26.	Production of hay crops in tons[31,34,42,43,44,74,76,88]	4,115,627	4,988,046	6,328,534	7,774,000	6,195,765	6,485,070	7,304,837	8,524,000[*p]
27.	Percent of total production of hay crops[31,34,42,43,44]	5.0[*c]	5.6[*c]	6.0[*c]	6.1[*c]	0.5[*c]	5.0[*c]	5.7[*c]	5.8[*c]

[a] See the Glossary of Terms for changing definitions, i.e. farm, improved land, cropland harvested, farm owners, and livestock.
[b] Prior to 1924, the data relate to the total acreage of crops for which figures are available, except for 1920 when 14,502,932 acres of corn cut for forage were excluded (as most of this was probably duplicated in the acreage of corn harvested for grain).
[c] Percentage computed by compiler from data herein. See endnotes for source of data.
[d] Values in gold, one-fifth less than currency values.
[e] Managers included with owners.
[f] Running square bales, counting round as half bales.
[g] Census listed the number of full and part time owners separately. Compiler added the two numbers for the above figure.
[h] Includes quantity of beans harvested from acreage grown with other crops as well as that from acreage grown alone.
[i] The total value for each state for 1950 was based on the average value per acre for farms in the sample, for which value of land and buildings was reported. The average value per farm and per acre was based on the total value of all farms.
[j] Less than one-tenth of one percent.
[k] 1,000 percent or more.
[l] Including estimated value of range animals.
[m] Withheld to avoid disclosing data for individual farms.
[n] Production ginned and to be ginned.
[o] 480-pound net weight bales.
[p] Census had two separate listings: hay, alfalfa, and alfalfa mixtures; and hay, all other. Compiler added the two listings for the above figure.

GENERAL AGRICULTURE STATISTICS, 1850-1990										
COLORADO										
Item No.		1850	1860	1870	1880	1890	1900	1910	1920	1930
1.	Number of farms[18,19,68,73,76,82,*a]	---	---	1,738	4,506	16,389	24,700	46,170	59,934	59,956
2.	Acres in farms[18,19,68,73,76,82]	---	---	320,346	1,165,373	4,598,941	9,474,588	13,532,113	24,462,014	28,876,171
3.	Acres improved land in farms[20,*a]	---	---	95,594	616,169	1,823,520	2,273,968	4,302,101	7,744,757	---
4.	Cropland harvested, acres[18,19,73,76,*a,b]	---	---	---	213,238	865,788	1,549,503	2,614,312	5,052,863	6,750,398
5.	Percentage increase in number of farms[18,19]	---	---	---	159.3	263.7	50.7	86.9	29.8	.04
6.	Percentage increase of land in farms[18,19]	---	---	---	263.8	294.6	106.0	42.8	80.8	18.0
7.	Percentage increase of improved land in farms[20]	---	---	---	544.6	195.9	24.7	89.2	80.0	---
8.	Average acreage per farm[18,19,66,73,76,78]	---	---	184.3	258.6	280.6	383.6	293.1	408.1	481.6
9.	Percentage increase in cropland harvested[18,19,*b]	---	---	---	---	306.0	79.0	68.7	93.3	33.6
10.	Value of farms, dollars[18,19,64,79,81]	---	---	2,708,598	25,109,223	85,035,180	106,344,035	408,518,861	866,013,660	629,346,675
11.	Value of farms, percent increase[18,19]	---	---	---	827.0	238.7	25.1	284.2	112.0	-27.3
12.	Average value per farm, dollars[18,19,64,73,76]	---	---	1,558	5,572	5,189	4,305	8,848	14,449	10,497
13.	Farms operated by owners[21,22,23,24,25,26,27,65,77,*a]	---	---	---	3,922[*e]	14,546[*e]	18,239	36,993	45,291	38,426[*g]
14.	Value of livestock on farms, dollars[28,29,30,36,76,83,*a]	---	---	2,296,882[*d]	15,972,342[*k]	29,675,528[*k]	49,954,311	70,161,344	160,976,580	115,414,435
15.	Average value of livestock per farm, dollars[19,28,29,30,36]	---	---	1,322[*d]	3,545	1,811	2,022	1,520	2,686	1,925[*c]
16.	Production of cotton in bales[28,29,30,67,74,83]	---	---	---	---	---	---	---	---	---
17.	Percent of total production of cotton[28,29,30]	---	---	---	---	---	---	---	---	---

GENERAL AGRICULTURE STATISTICS, 1850-1990										
COLORADO										
Item No.		1850	1860	1870	1880	1890	1900	1910	1920	1930
18.	Production of wheat in bushels[31,32,35,36,69,74,84]	---	---	258,474	1,425,014	2,845,439	5,587,770	7,224,057	18,260,663	17,332,160
19.	Percent of total production of wheat[31,32,33,35,36]	---	---	.0898	.3101	.6075	.8485	1.0571	1.9315	2.1648
20.	Production of corn in bushels[36,37,38,39,70,74,85]	---	---	231,903	455,968	1,511,907	1,275,680	4,903,304	10,105,627	18,594,210
21.	Percent of total production of corn[36,37,38,39]	---	---	*j	*j	0.1	*j	0.2	0.4	0.9
22.	Production of oats in bushels[31,35,36,71,80,86]	---	---	332,940	640,900	2,514,480	3,080,130	7,642,855	4,535,527	4,704,838
23.	Percent of total production of oats[31,35,36]	---	---	0.1	0.2	0.3	0.3	0.8	0.4	0.5
24.	Production of soybeans in bushels[36,40,41,72,74,76,87]	---	---	---	---	---	---	---	4,882	2,498[*h]
25.	Percent of total production of soybeans[36,40,41]	---	---	---	---	---	---	---	.4301	.0288
26.	Production of hay crops in tons[31,34,42,43,44,74,76,88]	---	---	19,787	86,562	714,555	1,643,347	2,249,547	3,388,523	2,562,530
27.	Percent of total production of hay crops[31,34,42,43,44]	---	---	0.1	0.2	1.1	2.1	2.3	2.7	3.0

Item No.	GENERAL AGRICULTURE STATISTICS, 1850-1990 COLORADO	1940	1950	1960	1970	1978	1982	1987	1990
1.	Number of farms[18,19,68,73,76,82,*a]	51,436	45,578	33,390	27,950	26,907	27,111	27,284	26,500
2.	Acres in farms[18,19,68,73,76,82]	31,527,240	37,953,099	38,787,312	36,697,000	35,253,411	33,537,998	34,048,433	33,100,000
3.	Acres improved land in farms[20,*a]	---	---	---	---	---	---	---	---
4.	Cropland harvested, acres[18,19,73,76,*a,b]	4,769,671	6,892,904	5,879,446	5,686,000	5,844,805	6,036,679	5,522,216	---
5.	Percentage increase in number of farms[18,19]	-14.2	-11.4	-26.7	-16.3	-3.7	0.8[*c]	0.6	-2.9
6.	Percentage increase of land in farms[18,19]	9.2	20.4	2.2	-5.4	-12.1[*c]	-4.9[*c]	1.5	-2.8
7.	Percentage increase of improved land in farms[20]	---	---	---	---	---	---	---	---
8.	Average acreage per farm[18,19,66,73,76,78]	612.9	832.7	1,161.2	1,313	1,310	1,237	1,248	1,241
9.	Percentage increase in cropland harvested[18,19,*b]	-29.3	44.5	-14.7	-3.3	2.8	3.3[*c]	-8.5	---
10.	Value of farms, dollars[18,19,64,79,81]	388,343,847	1,211,818,000[*i]	2,053,281,000	3,471,000,000	11,219,896,116	15,228,000,000	12,519,000,000	12,277,000,000
11.	Value of farms, percent increase[18,19]	-38.3	212.1[*i]	69.4	69.0	223.2	35.7[*c]	-17.8[*c]	-1.9[*c]
12.	Average value per farm, dollars[18,19,64,73,76]	7,550	26,588[*i]	61,494	124,000	416,988	562,479	458,906	463,283
13.	Farms operated by owners[21,22,23,24,25,26,27,65,77,*a]	31,827	34,837	26,065[*g]	23,499[*g]	22,893	23,461[*g]	23,326[*g]	---
14.	Value of livestock on farms, dollars[28,29,30,36,76,83,*a]	71,597,078	261,143,142	339,975,962	---	2,016,422,000	2,093,574,000	2,361,197,000	3,029,345,000
15.	Average value of livestock per farm, dollars[19,28,29,30,36]	1,392	5,730	10,182	---	74,940	77,222	86,541	114,315
16.	Production of cotton in bales[28,29,30,67,74,83]	---	---	---	---	---	---	---	---
17.	Percent of total production of cotton[28,29,30]	---	---	---	---	---	---	---	---

GENERAL AGRICULTURE STATISTICS, 1850-1990

COLORADO

Item No.		1940	1950	1960	1970	1978	1982	1987	1990
18.	Production of wheat in bushels[31,32,35,36,69,74,84]	11,372,620	38,581,463	49,490,059	66,684,000	55,066,616	78,307,590	81,581,401	62,100,000
19.	Percent of total production of wheat[31,32,33,35,36]	1.6044	3.8330[*c]	4.6869	4.8666	3.4255	3.2996	4.3231	3.0504
20.	Production of corn in bushels[36,37,38,39,70,74,85]	4,682,852	11,616,645	26,182,000	33,600,000	78,311,274	94,879,902	98,919,585	134,850,000
21.	Percent of total production of corn[36,37,38,39]	0.2	0.4	0.6	0.8	1.2[*c]	1.3	1.5	1.8
22.	Production of oats in bushels[31,35,36,71,80,86]	2,840,414	6,584,168	3,781,050	5,120,000	---	1,851,419[*c]	2,271,543	3,025,000
23.	Percent of total production of oats[31,35,36]	0.3	0.6	0.4	0.6	---	0.4[*c]	0.7[*c]	0.8[*c]
24.	Production of soybeans in bushels[36,40,41,72,74,76,87]	1,532[*h]	223	50	---	75718	28,772	216,167	---
25.	Percent of total production of soybeans[36,40,41]	.0017	.0001	.0000	---	.0044	.0014	.1181	---
26.	Production of hay crops in tons[31,34,42,43,44,74,76,88]	1,669,054	2,252,850	2,272,678	3,187,000	3,005,902	2,923,775	3,088,681	3,450,000[*l]
27.	Percent of total production of hay crops[31,34,42,43,44]	2.0	2.5	2.1	2.5[*c]	2.3[*c]	2.3	2.4[*c]	2.3[*c]

[a] See the Glossary of Terms for changing definitions, i.e. farm, improved land, cropland harvested, farm owners, and livestock.
[b] Prior to 1924, the data relate to the total acreage of crops for which figures are available, except for 1920 when 14,502,932 acres of corn cut for forage were excluded (as most of this was probably duplicated in the acreage of corn harvested for grain).
[c] Percentage computed by compiler from data herein. See endnotes for source of data.
[d] Values in gold, one-fifth less than currency values.
[e] Managers included with owners.
[f] Running square bales, counting round as half bales.
[g] Census listed the number of full and part time owners separately. Compiler added the two numbers for the above figure.
[h] Includes quantity of beans harvested from acreage grown with other crops as well as that from acreage grown alone.
[i] The total value for each state for 1950 was based on the average value per acre for farms in the sample, for which value of land and buildings was reported. The average value per farm and per acre was based on the total value of all farms.
[j] Less than one-tenth of one percent.
[k] Including estimated value of range animals.
[l] Census had two separate listings: hay, alfalfa, and alfalfa mixtures; and hay all other. Compiler added the two listings for the above figure.

GENERAL AGRICULTURE STATISTICS, 1850-1990										
CONNECTICUT										
Item No.		1850	1860	1870	1880	1890	1900	1910	1920	1930
1.	Number of farms[18,19,68,73,76,82,*a]	22,445	25,180	25,508	30,598	26,350	26,948	26,815	22,655	17,195
2.	Acres in farms[18,19,68,73,76,82]	2,383,879	2,504,264	2,364,416	2,453,541	2,253,432	2,312,083	2,185,788	1,898,980	1,502,279
3.	Acres improved land in farms[20,*a]	1,768,178	1,830,807	1,646,752	1,642,188	1,379,419	1,064,525	988,252	701,086	---
4.	Cropland harvested, acres[18,19,73,76,*a,b]	---	---	---	715,235	626,859	603,357	534,846	458,934	372,147
5.	Percentage increase in number of farms[18,19]	---	12.2	1.3	10.0	-13.9	2.3	-0.5	-15.5	-24.1
6.	Percentage increase of land in farms[18,19]	---	5.0	-5.6	3.8	-8.2	2.6	-5.5	-13.1	-20.9
7.	Percentage increase of improved land in farms[20]	---	3.5	-10.1	-0.3	-16.0	-22.8	-7.2	-29.1	---
8.	Average acreage per farm[18,19,66,73,76,78]	106.2	99.5	92.7	80.2	85.5	85.8	81.5	83.8	87.4
9.	Percentage increase in cropland harvested[18,19,*b]	---	---	---	---	-12.4	-3.7	-11.4	-14.2	-18.9
10.	Value of farms, dollars[18,19,64,79,81]	72,726,422	90,830,005	99,393,106	121,063,910	95,000,595	97,425,068	138,319,221	190,270,827	227,412,905
11.	Value of farms, percent increase[18,19]	---	24.9	9.4	21.8	-21.5	2.6	42.0	37.6	19.5
12.	Average value per farm, dollars[18,19,64,73,76]	3,240	3,607	3,897	3,957	3,605	3,615	5,158	8,399	13,226
13.	Farms operated by owners[21,22,23,24,25,26,27,65,77,*a]	---	---	---	27,472[*e]	23,310[*e]	22,705	23,234	19,666	15,586
14.	Value of livestock on farms, dollars[28,29,30,36,*a]	7,467,490	11,311,079	14,036,030[*d]	10,959,296	9,974,618	10,932,212	14,163,902	23,472,693	20,433,530
15.	Average value of livestock per farm, dollars[19,28,29,30,36]	333	449	550[*d]	358	379	406	528	1,036	1,188[*c]
16.	Production of cotton in bales[28,29,30,67,74,83]	---	---	---	---	---	---	---	---	---
17.	Percent of total production of cotton[28,29,30]	---	---	---	---	---	---	---	---	---

GENERAL AGRICULTURE STATISTICS, 1850-1990										
CONNECTICUT										
Item No.		1850	1860	1870	1880	1890	1900	1910	1920	1930
18.	Production of wheat in bushels[31,32,35,36,69,74,84]	41,762	52,401	38,144	38,742	7,482	8,660	11,869	50,102	3,575
19.	Percent of total production of wheat[31,32,33,35,36]	.0416	.0303	.0133	.0084	.0016	.0013	.0017	.0053	.0004
20.	Production of corn in bushels[36,37,38,39],70,74,85	1,935,043	2,059,835	1,570,364	1,880,421	1,471,979	1,931,510	2,530,542	2,062,495	576,428
21.	Percent of total production of corn[36,37,38,39]	0.3	0.2	0.2	0.1	0.1	*j	0.1	0.1	*j
22.	Production of oats in bushels[31,35,36,71,80,86]	1,258,738	1,522,218	1,114,595	1,009,706	593,691	316,380	273,804	295,050	38,357
23.	Percent of total production of oats[31,35,36]	0.9	0.9	0.4	0.3	0.1	*j	*j	*j	*j
24.	Production of soybeans in bushels[36,40,41,72,74,76,87]	---	---	---	---	---	---	---	260	159*h
25.	Percent of total production of soybeans[36,40,41]	---	---	---	---	---	---	---	.0229	.0018
26.	Production of hay crops in tons[31,34,42,43,44,74,76,88]	516,131	562,425	563,328	564,079	612,906	535,336	549,487	627,787	326,189
27.	Percent of total production of hay crops[31,34,42,43,44]	3.7*c	2.9	2.1	1.6	0.9	0.7	0.6	0.5	0.4

GENERAL AGRICULTURE STATISTICS, 1850-1990									
CONNECTICUT									
Item No.		1940	1950	1960	1970	1978	1982	1987	1990
1.	Number of farms[18,19,68,73,76,82,*a]	21,163	15,615	8,292	4,490	3,519	3,754	3,580	3,900
2.	Acres in farms[18,19,68,73,76,82]	1,512,151	1,272,352	884,443	541,000	455,731	444,242	398,400	420,000
3.	Acres improved land in farms[20,*a]	---	---	---	---	---	---	---	---
4.	Cropland harvested, acres[18,19,73,76,*a,b]	362,577	308,500	237,512	144,000	169,681	171,229	153,715	---
5.	Percentage increase in number of farms[18,19]	23.1	-26.2	-46.9	-45.9	-21.6[*c]	-6.7[*c]	-4.6	8.9
6.	Percentage increase of land in farms[18,19]	0.7	-15.9	-30.5	-38.8	-15.8	-2.5[*c]	-10.3	5.4
7.	Percentage increase of improved land in farms[20]	---	---	---	---	---	---	---	---
8.	Average acreage per farm[18,19,66,73,76,78]	71.5	81.5	106.7	121	130	118	111	110
9.	Percentage increase in cropland harvested[18,19,*b]	-2.6	-14.9	-23.0	-39.4	17.8	0.9[*c]	10.2	---
10.	Value of farms, dollars[18,19,64,79,81]	204,761,302	315,251,000[*i]	392,810,000	499,000,000	982,751,130	1,188,000,000	1,674,000,000	2,313,000,000
11.	Value of farms, percent increase[18,19]	-10.0	54.0[*i]	24.6	27.0	96.9[*c]	20.9[*c]	40.9	38.2
12.	Average value per farm, dollars[18,19,64,73,76]	9,675	20,189[*i]	47,372	111,000	279,270	316,317	467,677	593,077
13.	Farms operated by owners[21,22,23,24,25,26,27,65,77,*a]	19,270	14,689	7,779[*g]	4,149[*g]	3,198	3,421[*g]	3,304[*g]	---
14.	Value of livestock on farms, dollars[28,29,30,36,76,83,*a]	15,673,608	32,153,005	37,860,241	---	142,995,000	183,266,000	193,039,000	195,833,000
15.	Average value of livestock per farm, dollars[19,28,29,30,36]	741	2,059	4,566	---	40,635	48,819	53,922	50,214
16.	Production of cotton in bales[28,29,30,67,74,83]	---	---	---	---	---	---	---	---
17.	Percent of total production of cotton[28,29,30]	---	---	---	---	---	---	---	---

GENERAL AGRICULTURE STATISTICS, 1850-1990									
CONNECTICUT									
Item No.		1940	1950	1960	1970	1978	1982	1987	1990
18.	Production of wheat in bushels[31,32,35,36,69,74,84]	3,048	---	4,974	---	8,713	8,141	2,652	---
19.	Percent of total production of wheat[31,32,33,35,36]	.0004	---	.0005	---	.0005	.0003	.0001	---
20.	Production of corn in bushels[36,37,38,39,70,74,85]	363,312	231,019	2,132,000	---	339,904	628,384	335,317	---
21.	Percent of total production of corn[36,37,38,39]	*j	*j	*j	---	*c,j	*j	*j	---
22.	Production of oats in bushels[31,35,36,71,80,86]	54,262	50,652	41,051	---	---	---	30,000	30,025
23.	Percent of total production of oats[31,35,36]	*j	*j	*j	---	---	---	*c,j	*c,j
24.	Production of soybeans in bushels[36,40,41,72,74,76,87]	740*h	573	---	---	---	1,282	*k	---
25.	Percent of total production of soybeans[36,40,41]	.0008	.0003	---	---	---	.0001	---	---
26.	Production of hay crops in tons[31,34,42,43,44,74,76,88]	341,646	349,082	326,505	203,000	190,992	190,034	184,080	171,000*l
27.	Percent of total production of hay crops[31,34,42,43,44]	0.4	0.4	0.3	0.2	0.1*c	0.1	0.1	0.1

[a] See the Glossary of Terms for changing definitions, i.e. farm, improved land, cropland harvested, farm owners, and livestock.
[b] Prior to 1924, the data relate to the total acreage of crops for which figures are available, except for 1920 when 14,502,932 acres of corn cut for forage were excluded (as most of this was probably duplicated in the acreage of corn harvested for grain).
[c] Percentage computed by compiler from data herein. See endnotes for source of data.
[d] Values in gold, one-fifth less than currency values.
[e] Managers included with owners.
[f] Running square bales, counting round as half bales.
[g] Census listed the number of full and part time owners separately. Compiler added the two numbers for the above figure.
[h] Includes quantity of beans harvested from acreage grown with other crops as well as that from acreage grown alone.
[i] The total value for each state for 1950 was based on the average value per acre for farms in the sample, for which value of land and buildings was reported. The average value per farm and per acre was based on the total value of all farms.
[j] Less than one-tenth of one percent.
[k] Withheld to avoid disclosing data for individual farms.
[l] Census had two separate listings: hay, alfalfa, and alfalfa mixtures; and hay, all other. Compiler added the two listings for the above figure.

GENERAL AGRICULTURE STATISTICS, 1850-1990										
DELAWARE										
Item No.		1850	1860	1870	1880	1890	1900	1910	1920	1930
1.	Number of farms[18,19,68,73,76,82,*a]	6,063	6,658	7,615	8,749	9,381	9,687	10,836	10,140	9,707
2.	Acres in farms[18,19,68,73,76,82]	956,144	1,004,295	1,052,322	1,090,245	1,055,692	1,066,228	1,038,866	944,511	900,815
3.	Acres improved land in farms[20,*a]	580,862	637,065	698,115	746,958	762,655	754,010	713,538	653,052	---
4.	Cropland harvested, acres[18,19,73,76,*a,b]	---	---	---	353,170	373,011	437,168	438,522	448,422	407,609
5.	Percentage increase in number of farms[18,19]	---	9.8	14.4	14.9	7.2	3.3	11.9	-6.4	-4.3
6.	Percentage increase of land in farms[18,19]	---	5.0	4.8	3.6	-3.2	1.0	-2.6	-9.1	-4.6
7.	Percentage increase of improved land in farms[20]	---	9.7	9.6	7.0	2.1	-1.1	-5.4	-8.5	---
8.	Average acreage per farm[18,19,66,73,76,78]	157.7	150.8	138.2	124.6	112.5	110.1	95.9	93.1	92.8
9.	Percentage increase in cropland harvested[18,19,*b]	---	---	---	---	5.6	17.2	0.3	2.3	-9.1
10.	Value of farms, dollars[18,19,64,79,81]	18,880,031	31,426,357	37,370,296	36,789,672	39,586,080	34,436,040	53,155,983	64,755,631	66,941,747
11.	Value of farms, percent increase[18,19]	---	66.5	18.9	-1.6	7.6	-13.0	54.4	21.8	3.4
12.	Average value per farm, dollars[18,19,64,73,76]	3,114	4,720	4,907	4,205	4,220	3,555	4,905	6,386	6,896
13.	Farms operated by owners[21,22,23,24,25,26,27,65,77,*a]	---	---	---	5,041[*e]	4,978[*e]	4,680	6,178	6,010	6,260
14.	Value of livestock on farms, dollars[28,29,30,36,76,83,*a]	1,849,281	3,144,706	3,405,859[*d]	3,420,080	4,198,810	4,111,054	6,817,123	8,600,665	9,031,037
15.	Average value of livestock per farm, dollars[19,28,29,30,36]	305	472	447[*d]	391	448	424	629	848	930
16.	Production of cotton in bales[28,29,30,67,74,83]	---	---	---	---	---	---	---	---	---
17.	Percent of total production of cotton[28,29,30]	---	---	---	---	---	---	---	---	---

GENERAL AGRICULTURE STATISTICS, 1850-1990

DELAWARE

Item No.		1850	1860	1870	1880	1890	1900	1910	1920	1930
18.	Production of wheat in bushels[31,32,35,36,69,74,84]	482,511	912,941	895,477	1,175,272	1,501,050	1,870,570	1,643,572	1,571,567	1,975,161
19.	Percent of total production of wheat[31,32,33,35,36]	.4802	.5274	.3112	.2558	.3205	.2841	.2405	.1662	.2467[*c]
20.	Production of corn in bushels[36,37,38,39,70,74,85]	3,145,542	3,892,337	3,010,390	3,894,264	3,097,164	4,736,580	4,839,548	3,686,109	3,466,565
21.	Percent of total production of corn[36,37,38,39]	0.5	0.5	0.4	0.2	0.1	0.2	0.2	0.2	0.2
22.	Production of oats in bushels[31,35,36,71,80,86]	604,518	1,046,910	554,388	378,508	382,900	131,960	98,239	70,791	52,947
23.	Percent of total production of oats[31,35,36]	0.4	0.6	0.2	0.1	[*j]	[*j]	[*j]	[*j]	[*j]
24.	Production of soybeans in bushels[36,40,41,72,74,76,87]	---	---	---	---	---	---	---	3,561	211,191[*h]
25.	Percent of total production of soybeans[36,40,41]	---	---	---	---	---	---	---	.3137	2.4384
26.	Production of hay crops in tons[31,34,42,43,44,74,76,88]	30,159	36,973	41,890	49,632	105,231	79,303	103,686	104,356	82,485
27.	Percent of total production of hay crops[31,34,42,43,44]	0.2[*c]	0.2	0.2	0.1	0.2	0.1	0.1	0.1	0.1

GENERAL AGRICULTURE STATISTICS, 1850-1990

DELAWARE

Item No.		1940	1950	1960	1970	1978	1982	1987	1990
1.	Number of farms[18,19,68,73,76,82,*a]	8,994	7,448	5,208	3,710	3,398	3,338	2,966	2,900
2.	Acres in farms[18,19,68,73,76,82]	895,507	851,291	762,526	674,000	669,646	655,465	608,245	570,000
3.	Acres improved land in farms[20,*a]	---	---	---	---	---	---	---	---
4.	Cropland harvested, acres[18,19,73,76,*a,b]	378,448	389,283	416,197	443,000	496,756	499,986	441,502	---
5.	Percentage increase in number of farms[18,19]	-7.3	-17.2	-30.1	-28.8	-8.4	-1.8	-11.1	-2.2
6.	Percentage increase of land in farms[18,19]	-0.6	-4.9	-10.4	-11.6	-0.6	-2.1	-7.2	-6.3
7.	Percentage increase of improved land in farms[20]	---	---	---	---	---	---	---	---
8.	Average acreage per farm[18,19,66,73,76,78]	99.6	114.3	146.4	182	197	196	205	197
9.	Percentage increase in cropland harvested[18,19,*b]	-7.2	2.9	6.9	6.4	12.1	0.7	11.7	---
10.	Value of farms, dollars[18,19,64,79,81]	54,898,828	97,141,000[*i,k]	179,943,000[*i,k]	336,000,000	963,649,014	1,218,000,000	1,096,000,000	1,308,000,000
11.	Value of farms, percent increase[18,19]	-18.0	76.9[*i,k]	85.2[*i,k]	86.7	187.0	26.4	-10.0	19.3
12.	Average value per farm, dollars[18,19,64,73,76]	6,104	13,043[*i,k]	34,551[*i,k]	91,000	283,593	364,843	369,751	451,034
13.	Farms operated by owners[21,22,23,24,25,26,27,65,77,*a]	5,956	6,111	4,453[*g]	3,246[*g]	3,001	2,947[*g]	2,682[*g]	---
14.	Value of livestock on farms, dollars[28,29,30,36,76,83,*a]	5,861,253	9,865,410	9,904,430	8,818,000	218,310,000	260,286,000	347,456,000	459,832,000
15.	Average value of livestock per farm, dollars[19,28,29,30,36]	652	1,325	1,902	2,377	64,247	77,977	117,146	158,563
16.	Production of cotton in bales[28,29,30,67,74,83]	---	---	---	---	---	---	---	---
17.	Percent of total production of cotton[28,29,30]	---	---	---	---	---	---	---	---

GENERAL AGRICULTURE STATISTICS, 1850-1990									
DELAWARE									
Item No.		1940	1950	1960	1970	1978	1982	1987	1990
18.	Production of wheat in bushels[31,32,35,36,69,74,84]	1,131,176	1,030,309	617,917	798,000	572,030	2,234,788	1,827,869	3,108,000
19.	Percent of total production of wheat[31,32,33,35,36]	.1596	.1024	.0585	.0582	.0356	.0942	.0969	.1527
20.	Production of corn in bushels[36,37,38,39,70,74,85]	3,597,583	4,159,065	8,586,000	13,690,000	14,980,373	14,880,293	9,875,539	13,300,000
21.	Percent of total production of corn[36,37,38,39]	0.2	0.1	0.2	0.3	.220	0.2	0.1	0.2
22.	Production of oats in bushels[31,35,36,71,80,86]	37,488	155,708	204,217	150,000	---	67,034	34,955	---
23.	Percent of total production of oats[31,35,36]	*j	*j	*j	*j	---	*j	*j	---
24.	Production of soybeans in bushels[36,40,41,72,74,76,87]	330,531*h	871,406	3,246,234	3,402,000	7,501,262	6,373,519	4,143,975	7,250,000
25.	Percent of total production of soybeans[36,40,41]	.3774	.4102	.6296	.3027	.0436	.3203	.2255	.3763
26.	Production of hay crops in tons[31,34,42,43,44,74,76,88]	78,992	82,146	69,463	76,000	46,439	38,149	43,254	73,000*l
27.	Percent of total production of hay crops[31,34,42,43,44]	0.1	0.1	0.1	0.1	*j	*j	*j	*c,j

[a] See the Glossary of Terms for changing definitions, i.e. farm, improved land, cropland harvested, farm owners, and livestock.
[b] Prior to 1924, the data relate to the total acreage of crops for which figures are available, except for 1920 when 14,502,932 acres of corn cut for forage were excluded (as most of this was probably duplicated in the acreage of corn harvested for grain).
[c] Percentage computed by compiler from data herein. See endnotes for source of data.
[d] Values in gold, one-fifth less than currency values.
[e] Managers included with owners.
[f] Running square bales, counting round as half bales.
[g] Census listed the number of full and part time owners separately. Compiler added the two numbers for the above figure.
[h] Includes quantity of beans harvested from acreage grown with other crops as well as that from acreage grown alone.
[i] The total value for each state for 1950 was based on the average value per acre for farms in the sample, for which value of land and buildings was reported. The average value per farm and per acre was based on the total value of all farms.
[j] Less than one-tenth of one percent.
[k] Based on a sampling of farms.
[l] Census had two separate listings: hay, alfalfa, and alfalfa mixtures; and hay, all other. Compiler added the two listings for the above figure.

GENERAL AGRICULTURE STATISTICS, 1850-1990

DISTRICT OF COLUMBIA

Item No.		1850	1860	1870	1880	1890	1900	1910	1920	1930
1.	Number of farms[18,19,68,73,76,82,*a]	267	238	209	435	382	269	217	204	104
2.	Acres in farms[18,19,68,73,76,82]	27,454	34,263	11,677	18,146	11,745	8,489	6,063	5,668	3,071
3.	Acres improved land in farms[20,*a]	16,267	17,474	8,266	12,632	9,898	5,934	5,133	4,258	---
4.	Cropland harvested, acres[18,19,73,76,*a,b]	---	---	---	4,568	2,522	3,396	2,982	2,230	1,737
5.	Percentage increase in number of farms[18,19]	---	-10.9	-12.2	108.1	-12.2	-29.6	-19.3	-6.0	-49.0
6.	Percentage increase of land in farms[18,19]	---	24.8	-65.9	55.4	-35.3	-27.7	-28.6	-6.5	-45.8
7.	Percentage increase of improved land in farms[20]	---	7.4	-52.7	52.8	-21.6	-40.0	-13.5	-17.0	---
8.	Average acreage per farm[18,19,66,73,76,78]	102.8	144.0	55.9	41.7	30.7	31.6	27.9	27.8	29.5
9.	Percentage increase in cropland harvested[18,19,*b]	---	---	---	---	-44.8	34.7	-12.2	-25.2	-22.1
10.	Value of farms, dollars[18,19,64,79,81]	1,730,460	2,989,267	3,040,184	3,632,403	6,471,120	11,273,990	8,231,343	5,577,369	7,143,712
11.	Value of farms, percent increase[18,19]	---	72.8	1.7	19.5	78.1	74.2	-27.0	-32.2	28.1
12.	Average value per farm, dollars[18,19,64,73,76]	6,481	12,560	14,546	8,350	16,940	41,911	37,932	27,340	68,690
13.	Farms operated by owners[21,22,23,24,25,26,27,65,77,*a]	---	---	---	269[*e]	242[*e]	133	118	100	59
14.	Value of livestock on farms, dollars[28,29,30,36,76,83,*a]	71,643	109,640	91,933[*d]	123,300	129,120	125,326	152,840	246,366	109,163
15.	Average value of livestock per farm, dollars[19,28,29,30,36]	268	461	440[*d]	283	338	466	704	1,208	1,050[*c]
16.	Production of cotton in bales[28,29,30,67,74,83]	---	---	---	---	---	---	---	---	---
17.	Percent of total production of cotton[28,29,30]	---	---	---	---	---	---	---	---	---

GENERAL AGRICULTURE STATISTICS, 1850-1990

DISTRICT OF COLUMBIA

Item No.		1850	1860	1870	1880	1890	1900	1910	1920	1930
18.	Production of wheat in bushels[31,32,35,36,69,74,84]	17,370	12,760	3,782	6,402	600	410	---	200	---
19.	Percent of total production of wheat[31,32,33,35,36]	.0173	.0074	.0013	.0014	.0001	.0001	---	.0000	---
20.	Production of corn in bushels[36,37,38,39,70,74,85]	65,230	80,840	28,020	29,750	10,755	14,980	12,667	15,663	2,595
21.	Percent of total production of corn[36,37,38,39]	[*j]	[*j]	[*j]	[*j]	[*j]	[*j]	[*j]	[*j]	[*j]
22.	Production of oats in bushels[31,35,36,71,80,86]	8,134	29,548	8,500	7,440	1,371	620	375	315	---
23.	Percent of total production of oats[31,35,36]	[*j]	[*j]	[*j]	[*j]	[*j]	[*j]	[*j]	[*j]	---
24.	Production of soybeans in bushels[36,40,41,72,74,76,87]	---	---	---	---	---	---	---	---	---
25.	Percent of total production of soybeans[36,40,41]	---	---	---	---	---	---	---	---	---
26.	Production of hay crops in tons[31,34,42,43,44,74,76,88]	2,279	3,180	2,019	3,759	1,868	2,241	2,148	2,265	881
27.	Percent of total production of hay crops[31,34,42,43,44]	[*c,j]	[*j]	[*j]	[*j]	[*j]	[*j]	[*j]	[*j]	[*j]

Item No.	GENERAL AGRICULTURE STATISTICS, 1850-1990 DISTRICT OF COLUMBIA	1940	1950	1960	1970	1978	1982	1987	1990
1.	Number of farms[18,19,68,73,76,82,*a]	65	28	---	---	---	---	---	---
2.	Acres in farms[18,19,68,73,76,82]	2,341	1,265	---	---	---	---	---	---
3.	Acres improved land in farms[20,*a]	---	---	---	---	---	---	---	---
4.	Cropland harvested, acres[18,19,73,76,*a,b]	1,017	266	---	---	---	---	---	---
5.	Percentage increase in number of farms[18,19]	-37.5	-56.9	---	---	---	---	---	---
6.	Percentage increase of land in farms[18,19]	-23.8	-46.0	---	---	---	---	---	---
7.	Percentage increase of improved land in farms[20]	---	---	---	---	---	---	---	---
8.	Average acreage per farm[18,19,66,73,76,78]	36.0	45.2	---	---	---	---	---	---
9.	Percentage increase in cropland harvested[18,19,*b]	-41.5	-73.8	---	---	---	---	---	---
10.	Value of farms, dollars[18,19,64,79,81]	5,942,900	4,666,000[*i]	---	---	---	---	---	---
11.	Value of farms, percent increase[18,19]	-16.8	-21.5[*i]	---	---	---	---	---	---
12.	Average value per farm, dollars[18,19,64,73,76]	91,429	166,643[*i]	---	---	---	---	---	---
13.	Farms operated by owners[21,22,23,24,25,26,27,65,77,*a]	30	18	---	---	---	---	---	---
14.	Value of livestock on farms, dollars[28,29,30,36,76,83,*a]	76,510	51,428	---	---	---	---	---	---
15.	Average value of livestock per farm, dollars[19,28,29,30,36]	1,177[*c]	1,837	---	---	---	---	---	---
16.	Production of cotton in bales[28,29,30,67,74,83]	---	---	---	---	---	---	---	---
17.	Percent of total production of cotton[28,29,30]	---	---	---	---	---	---	---	---

GENERAL AGRICULTURE STATISTICS, 1850-1990

DISTRICT OF COLUMBIA

Item No.		1940	1950	1960	1970	1978	1982	1987	1990
18.	Production of wheat in bushels[31,32,35,36,69,74,84]	---	---	---	---	---	---	---	---
19.	Percent of total production of wheat[31,32,33,35,36]	---	---	---	---	---	---	---	---
20.	Production of corn in bushels[36,37,38,39,70,74,85]	1,762	496	---	---	---	---	---	---
21.	Percent of total production of corn[36,37,38,39]	*j	*j	---	---	---	---	---	---
22.	Production of oats in bushels[31,35,36,71,80,86]	---	---	---	---	---	---	---	---
23.	Percent of total production of oats[31,35,36]	---	---	---	---	---	---	---	---
24.	Production of soybeans in bushels[36,40,41,72,74,76,87]	---	---	---	---	---	---	---	---
25.	Percent of total production of soybeans[36,40,41]	---	---	---	---	---	---	---	---
26.	Production of hay crops in tons[31,34,42,43,44,74,76,88]	781	404	---	---	---	---	---	---
27.	Percent of total production of hay crops[31,34,42,43,44]	*j	*j	---	---	---	---	---	---

[a] See the Glossary of Terms for changing definitions, i.e. farm, improved land, cropland harvested, farm owners, and livestock.
[b] Prior to 1924, the data relate to the total acreage of crops for which figures are available, except for 1920 when 14,502,932 acres of corn cut for forage were excluded (as most of this was probably duplicated in the acreage of corn harvested for grain).
[c] Percentage computed by compiler from data herein. See endnotes for source of data.
[d] Values in gold, one-fifth less than currency values.
[e] Managers included with owners.
[f] Running square bales, counting round as half bales.
[g] Census listed the number of full and part time owners separately. Compiler added the two numbers for the above figure.
[h] Includes quantity of beans harvested from acreage grown with other crops as well as that from acreage grown alone.
[i] The total value for each state for 1950 was based on the average value per acre for farms in the sample, for which value of land and buildings was reported. The average value per farm and per acre was based on the total value of all farms.
[j] Less than one-tenth of one percent.

GENERAL AGRICULTURE STATISTICS, 1850-1990										
FLORIDA										
Item No.		1850	1860	1870	1880	1890	1900	1910	1920	1930
1.	Number of farms[18,19,68,73,76,82,*a]	4,304	6,568	10,241	23,438	34,228	40,814	50,016	54,005	58,966
2.	Acres in farms[18,19,68,73,76,82]	1,595,289	2,920,228	2,373,541	3,297,324	3,674,486	4,363,891	5,253,538	6,046,691	5,026,617
3.	Acres improved land in farms[20,*a]	349,049	654,213	736,172	947,640	1,145,693	1,511,653	1,805,408	2,297,271	---
4.	Cropland harvested, acres[18,19,73,76,*a,b]	---	---	---	684,630	715,633	1,019,968	1,223,078	1,237,009	1,454,254
5.	Percentage increase in number of farms[18,19]	---	52.6	55.9	128.9	46.0	19.2	22.5	8.0	9.2
6.	Percentage increase of land in farms[18,19]	---	83.1	-18.7	38.9	11.4	18.8	20.4	15.1	-16.9
7.	Percentage increase of improved land in farms[20]	---	87.4	12.5	28.7	20.9	31.9	19.4	27.2	---
8.	Average acreage per farm[18,19,66,73,76,78]	370.7	444.6	231.8	140.7	107.4	106.9	105.0	112.0	85.2
9.	Percentage increase in cropland harvested[18,19,*b]	---	---	---	---	4.5	42.5	19.9	1.1	17.6
10.	Value of farms, dollars[18,19,69,79,81]	6,323,109	16,435,727	7,958,336	20,291,835	72,745,180	40,799,838	118,145,989	281,449,404	423,346,262
11.	Value of farms, percent increase[18,19]	---	159.9	-51.6	155.0	258.5	-43.9	189.6	138.2	50.4
12.	Average value per farm, dollars[18,19,64,73,76]	1,469	2,502	777	866	2,125	1,000	2,362	5,212	7,179
13.	Farms operated by owners[21,22,23,24,25,26,27,65,77,*a]	---	---	---	16,198[*e]	26,140[*e]	28,984	35,399	38,487	39,394
14.	Value of livestock on farms, dollars[28,29,30,36,76,83,*a]	2,880,058	5,553,356	4,169,726[*d]	6,920,980[*k]	7,142,980	11,166,016	20,591,187	35,300,540	23,474,662
15.	Average value of livestock per farm, dollars[19,28,29,30,36]	669	846	407[*d]	295	209	274	412	654	398
16.	Production of cotton in bales[28,29,30,67,74,83]	45,131	65,153	39,789	54,997	57,928	61,856[*f]	65,056[*f]	19,538[*f]	34,426[*f]
17.	Percent of total production of cotton[28,29,30]	1.8	1.2	1.3	1.0	0.8	0.7[*f]	0.6[*f]	0.2[*f]	0.2[*f]

GENERAL AGRICULTURE STATISTICS, 1850-1990										
FLORIDA										
Item No.		1850	1860	1870	1880	1890	1900	1910	1920	1930
18.	Production of wheat in bushels[31,32,35,36,69,74,84]	1,027	2,808	---	422	290	800	137	249	---
19.	Percent of total production of wheat[31,32,33,35,36]	.0010	.0016	---	.0001	.0001	.0001	.0000	.0000	.0000
20.	Production of corn in bushels[36,37,38,39,70,74,85]	1,996,809	2,834,391	2,225,056	3,174,234	3,701,264	5,311,050	7,023,767	8,831,112	6,617,724
21.	Percent of total production of corn[36,37,38,39]	0.3	0.3	0.3	0.2	0.2	0.2	0.3	0.4	0.3
22.	Production of oats in bushels[31,35,36,71,80,86]	66,586	46,899	114,204	468,112	391,321	297,430	606,380	222,226	15,534
23.	Percent of total production of oats[31,35,36]	*j	*j	*j	0.1	*j	*j	0.1	*j	*j
24.	Production of soybeans in bushels[36,40,41,72,74,76,87]	---	---	---	---	---	---	---	993	2,591
25.	Percent of total production of soybeans[36,40,41]	---	---	---	---	---	---	---	.0875	.0299
26.	Production of hay crops in tons[31,34,42,43,44,74,76,88]	2,510	11,478	17	179	8,373	22,381	55,462	90,118	36,725
27.	Percent of total production of hay crops[31,34,42,43,44]	*c,j	0.1	*j	*j	*j	*j	0.1	0.1	*j

GENERAL AGRICULTURE STATISTICS, 1850-1990									
FLORIDA									
Item No.		1940	1950	1960	1970	1978	1982	1987	1990
1.	Number of farms[18,19,68,73,76,82,*a]	62,248	56,921	45,100	35,586	36,109	36,352	36,556	41,000
2.	Acres in farms[18,19,68,73,76,82]	8,337,708	16,527,536	15,236,521	14,032,000	13,016,288	12,814,216	11,194,090	10,900,000
3.	Acres improved land in farms[20,*a]	---	---	---	---	---	---	---	---
4.	Cropland harvested, acres[18,19,73,76,*a,b]	1,679,622	1,728,232	1,881,879	1,038,000	2,705,674	2,643,147	2,240,831	---
5.	Percentage increase in number of farms[18,19]	5.6	-8.6	-20.8	-21.1	1.5	0.7[*c]	0.6	12.2
6.	Percentage increase of land in farms[18,19]	65.9	98.2	-7.8	-7.9	-7.2	-1.6[*c]	-12.6	-2.6
7.	Percentage increase of improved land in farms[20]	---	---	---	---	---	---	---	---
8.	Average acreage per farm[18,19,66,73,76,78]	133.9	290.4	337.8	394	360	353	306	273
9.	Percentage increase in cropland harvested[18,19,*b]	15.5	2.9	8.9	-44.8	160.7[*c]	-2.3[*c]	-15.22	---
10.	Value of farms, dollars[18,19,64,79,81]	324,377,874	945,871,000[*i,l]	3,317,285,000[*i,l]	4,976,000,000	14,700,623,862	20,085,000,000	19,884,000,000	21,995,000,000
11.	Value of farms, percent increase[18,19]	-23.4	191.6[*i,l]	250.7[*i,l]	50.0	195.4[*c]	36.6[*c]	-1.0	10.6[*c]
12.	Average value per farm, dollars[18,19,64,73,76]	5,211	16,617[*i,l]	73,554[*i,l]	140,000	47,118	552,586	543,830	536,463
13.	Farms operated by owners[21,22,23,24,25,26,27,65,77,*a]	44,935	48,966	41,282[*g]	33,229[*g]	33,317	33,865[*g]	33,951[*g]	---
14.	Value of livestock on farms, dollars[28,29,30,36,76,83,*a]	26,929,375	101,673,014	172,470,807	303,317,000	858,522,000	1,003,144,000	1,033,560,000	1,260,281,000
15.	Average value of livestock per farm, dollars[19,28,29,30,36]	433	1,786	3,824	8,524[*c]	23,776	27,595	28,273	30,739
16.	Production of cotton in bales[28,29,30,67,74,83]	11,424[*f]	17,502	13,665	7,400	2,317	10,882	32,805	29,000[*m,n]
17.	Percent of total production of cotton[28,29,30]	0.1[*f]	0.1	0.1	0.1	[*c,j]	0.1[*c]	0.2[*c]	0.3[*c]

GENERAL AGRICULTURE STATISTICS, 1850-1990									
FLORIDA									
Item No.		1940	1950	1960	1970	1978	1982	1987	1990
18.	Production of wheat in bushels[31,32,35,36,69,74,84]	---	---	170,113	1,102,000	340,049	2,771,217	1,246,973	1,885,000
19.	Percent of total production of wheat[31,32,33,35,36]	---	---	.0162	.0804	.0212[*c]	.1168	.0661	.0926
20.	Production of corn in bushels[36,37,38,39,70,74,85]	5,190,717	3,845,324	16,281,000	8,050,000	1,5207,531	12,559,553	6,628,740	5,920,000
21.	Percent of total production of corn[36,37,38,39]	0.2	0.1	0.4	0.2	0.2	0.2	0.1	0.1
22.	Production of oats in bushels[31,35,36,71,80,86]	22,765	49,144	316,343	564,000	---	1,595,873[*c]	494,959[*c]	---
23.	Percent of total production of oats[31,35,36]	[*j]	[*j]	[*j]	0.1	---	0.3[*c]	0.2[*c]	---
24.	Production of soybeans in bushels[36,40,41,72,74,76,87]	671[*h]	70,849	707,117	5,152,000	7,928,276	8,529,087	2,257,392	2,640,000
25.	Percent of total production of soybeans[36,40,41]	.0008	.0334[*c]	.1371	.4585	.4604[*c]	.4286	.1228	.1370
26.	Production of hay crops in tons[31,34,42,43,44,74,76,88]	49,336	17,355	127,963	286,000	626,432	721,190	687,019	598,000[*o]
27.	Percent of total production of hay crops[31,34,42,43,44]	0.1	[*j]	0.1	0.2	[*j]	0.6	0.5	0.4[*c]

[a] See the Glossary of Terms for changing definitions, i.e. farm, improved land, cropland harvested, farm owners, and livestock.
[b] Prior to 1924, the data relate to the total acreage of crops for which figures are available, except for 1920 when 14,502,932 acres of corn cut for forage were excluded (as most of this was probably duplicated in the acreage of corn harvested for grain).
[c] Percentage computed by compiler from data herein. See endnotes for source of data.
[d] Values in gold, one-fifth less than currency values.
[e] Managers included with owners.
[f] Running square bales, counting round as half bales.
[g] Census listed the number of full and part time owners separately. Compiler added the two numbers for the above figure.
[h] Includes quantity of beans harvested from acreage grown with other crops as well as that from acreage grown alone.
[i] The total value for each state for 1950 was based on the average value per acre for farms in the sample, for which value of land and buildings was reported. The average value per farm and per acre was based on the total value of all farms.
[j] Less than one-tenth of one percent.
[k] Including estimated value of range animals.
[l] Based on a sampling of farms.
[m] Production ginned and to be ginned.
[n] 480-pound net weight bales.
[o] Data available for hay, all other only.

GENERAL AGRICULTURE STATISTICS, 1850-1990										
GEORGIA										
Item No.		**1850**	**1860**	**1870**	**1880**	**1890**	**1900**	**1910**	**1920**	**1930**
1.	Number of farms[18,19,68,73,76,82,*a]	51,759	62,003	69,956	138,626	171,071	224,691	291,027	310,732	255,598
2.	Acres in farms[18,19,68,73,76,82]	22,821,379	26,650,490	23,647,941	26,043,282	25,200,435	26,392,057	26,953,413	25,441,061	22,078,630
3.	Acres improved land in farms[20,*a]	6,378,479	8,062,758	6,831,856	8,204,720	9,582,866	10,615,644	12,298,017	13,055,209	---
4.	Cropland harvested, acres[18,19,73,76,*a,b]	---	---	---	6,400,009	6,917,305	8,267,290	9,662,383	10,470,079	8,337,145
5.	Percentage increase in number of farms[18,19]	---	19.8	12.8	98.2	23.4	31.3	29.5	6.8	-17.7
6.	Percentage increase of land in farms[18,19]	---	16.8	-11.3	10.1	-3.2	4.7	2.1	-5.6	-13.2
7.	Percentage increase of improved land in farms[20]	---	26.4	-15.3	20.1	16.8	10.8	15.8	6.2	---
8.	Average acreage per farm[18,19,66,73,76,78]	440.9	429.8	338.0	187.9	147.3	117.5	92.6	81.9	86.4
9.	Percentage increase in cropland harvested[18,19,*b]	---	---	---	---	8.1	19.5	16.9	8.4	-20.4
10.	Value of farms, dollars[18,19,64,79,81]	95,753,445	157,072,803	75,647,574	111,910,540	152,006,230	183,370,120	479,204,332	1,138,298,627	577,338,409
11.	Value of farms, percent increase[18,19]	---	64.0	-51.8	47.9	35.8	20.6	161.3	137.5	-49.3
12.	Average value per farm, dollars[18,19,64,73,76]	1,850	2,533	1,081	807	889	816	1,647	3,663	2,259
13.	Farms operated by owners[21,22,23,24,25,26,27,65,77,*a]	---	---	---	76,451[*e]	79,477[*e]	88,529	98,628	102,123	79,802
14.	Value of livestock on farms, dollars[28,29,30,36,76,83,*a]	25,728,416	38,372,734	24,125,055[*d]	25,930,352	31,477,990	35,200,507	80,393,993	155,043,349	74,573,493
15.	Average value of livestock per farm, dollars[19,28,29,30,36]	497	619	345[*d]	187	184	157	276	499	292
16.	Production of cotton in bales[28,29,30,67,74,83]	499,091	701,840	473,934	814,441	1,191,846	1,287,992[*f]	1,992,408[*f]	1,681,907[*f]	1,344,488[*f]
17.	Percent of total production of cotton[28,29,30]	20.2	13.0	15.7	14.1	15.9	13.5[*f]	18.7[*f]	14.8[*f]	9.2[*f]

GENERAL AGRICULTURE STATISTICS, 1850-1990										
GEORGIA										
Item No.		1850	1860	1870	1880	1890	1900	1910	1920	1930
18.	Production of wheat in bushels[31,32,35,36,69,74,84]	1,088,534	2,544,913	2,127,017	3,159,771	1,096,312	1,765,947	752,858	1,085,972	409,472
19.	Percent of total production of wheat[31,32,33,35,36]	1.0833	1.4702	.7392	.6877	.2341	.2682	.1102	.1149	.0511
20.	Production of corn in bushels[36,37,38,39,70,74,85]	30,080,099	30,776,293	17,646,459	23,202,018	29,261,422	34,032,230	39,374,569	51,492,033	39,492,897
21.	Percent of total production of corn[36,37,38,39]	5.1	3.7	2.3	1.3	1.4	1.3	1.5	2.2	1.9
22.	Production of oats in bushels[31,35,36,71,80,86]	3,820,044	1,231,817	1,904,601	5,548,743	4,767,821	3,115,610	6,199,243	2,758,851	1,165,731
23.	Percent of total production of oats[31,35,36]	2.6	0.7	0.7	1.4	0.6	0.3	0.6	0.3	0.1
24.	Production of soybeans in bushels[36,40,41,72,74,76,87]	---	---	---	---	---	---	40	12,602	68,089[*h]
25.	Percent of total production of soybeans[36,40,41]	---	---	---	---	---	---	.1602	1.1102	.7861
26.	Production of hay crops in tons[31,34,42,43,44,74,76,88]	23,449	46,448	10,518	14,409	69,769	150,224	265,631	436,096	216,682
27.	Percent of total production of hay crops[31,34,42,43,44]	0.2[*c]	0.2	[*m]	[*m]	0.1	0.2	0.3	0.4	0.3

GENERAL AGRICULTURE STATISTICS, 1850-1990									
GEORGIA									
Item No.		1940	1950	1960	1970	1978	1982	1987	1990
1.	Number of farms[18,19,68,73,76,82,*a]	216,033	198,191	106,350	67,431	51,405	49,630	43,552	49,000
2.	Acres in farms[18,19,68,73,76,82]	23,683,631	25,751,055	19,657,615	15,806,000	13,416,833	12,291,885	10,744,718	12,500,000
3.	Acres improved land in farms[20,*a]	---	---	---	---	---	---	---	---
4.	Cropland harvested, acres[18,19,73,76,*a,b]	8,802,593	7,098,147	4,917,975	3,848,000	4,687,895	4,761,260	3,298,268	---
5.	Percentage increase in number of farms[18,19]	-15.5	-8.3	-46.3	-36.6	-23.8	-3.5[*c]	-12.2	12.5[*c]
6.	Percentage increase of land in farms[18,19]	7.3	8.7	-23.7	-19.6	-15.1	-8.4[*c]	-12.6	16.3
7.	Percentage increase of improved land in farms[20]	---	---	---	---	---	---	---	---
8.	Average acreage per farm[18,19,66,73,76,78]	109.6	129.9	184.8	234	261	248	247	263
9.	Percentage increase in cropland harvested[18,19,*b]	5.6	-19.4	-30.7	-21.8	21.8[*c]	1.6[*c]	-30.7	---
10.	Value of farms, dollars[18,19,64,79,81]	480,344,531	1,114,506,000[*i,j]	1,908,362,000[*j]	3,701,000,000	10,291,332,405	11,166,000,000	9,852,000,000	12,253,000,000
11.	Value of farms, percent increase[18,19]	-16.8	132.0[*i,j]	71.2[*j]	93.9	178.0	8.5	-11.8	24.4
12.	Average value per farm, dollars[18,19,64,73,76]	2,223	5,623[*i,j]	17,944[*j]	55,000	200,201	225,092	226,217	250,061
13.	Farms operated by owners[21,22,23,24,25,26,27,65,77,*a]	85,181	112,527	79,883	61,258[*g]	46,766	45,900[*g]	40,437[*g]	---
14.	Value of livestock on farms, dollars[28,29,30,36,76,83,*a]	81,791,694	143,680,254	181,936,798	321,503,000	1,427,458,000	1,586,691,000	1,808,928,000	2,268,105,000
15.	Average value of livestock per farm, dollars[19,28,29,30,36]	379	725	1,711	4,768	27,769	31,970	41,535	47,252
16.	Production of cotton in bales[28,29,30,67,74,83]	905,088[*f]	609,967	521,374	292,000	103,409	192,496	286,188	342,000[*k,l]
17.	Percent of total production of cotton[28,29,30]	7.9[*f]	4.0	3.7	2.1[*c]	1.0[*c]	1.7[*c]	2.2[*c]	3.0[*c]

GENERAL AGRICULTURE STATISTICS, 1850-1990									
GEORGIA									
Item No.		1940	1950	1960	1970	1978	1982	1987	1990
18.	Production of wheat in bushels[31,32,35,36,69,74,84]	1,630,159	1,414,825	2,027,201	3,600,000	3,286,853	31,864,435	13,269,742	22,400,000
19.	Percent of total production of wheat[31,32,33,35,36]	.2300	.1406	.1920	.2627	.2045[a,c]	1.3427	.7032	1.1003
20.	Production of corn in bushels[36,37,38,39,70,74,85]	37,603,790	37,837,343	81,909,000	44,206,000	76,812,159	60,031,978	43,332,343	52,250,000
21.	Percent of total production of corn[36,37,38,39]	1.7	1.4	1.9	1.1[a,c]	1.1[a,c]	0.8	0.6	0.7
22.	Production of oats in bushels[31,35,36,71,80,86]	3,664,951	6,762,532	7,967,379	4,048,000	---	3,996,376	1,467,182	4,130,000
23.	Percent of total production of oats[31,35,36]	0.4	0.6	0.8	0.4	---	0.8[a,c]	0.5	1.1[a,c]
24.	Production of soybeans in bushels[36,40,41,72,74,76,87]	67,637[a,h]	135,737	1,028,050	11,880,000	2,7148,555	51,993,159	16,725,741	28,600,000
25.	Percent of total production of soybeans[36,40,41]	.0772	.0639	.1994	1.0572	1.57643	2.6127	.9100	1.4843
26.	Production of hay crops in tons[31,34,42,43,44,74,76,88]	524,985	315,410	472,725	863,000	940,893	1,090,697	1,076,223	1,620,000[a,n]
27.	Percent of total production of hay crops[31,34,42,43,44]	0.6	0.4	0.4	0.7[a,c]	0.7[a,c]	0.8	0.8	1.1[a,c]

[a] See the Glossary of Terms for changing definitions, i.e. farm, improved land, cropland harvested, farm owners, and livestock.
[b] Prior to 1924, the data relate to the total acreage of crops for which figures are available, except for 1920 when 14,502,932 acres of corn cut for forage were excluded (as most of this was probably duplicated in the acreage of corn harvested for grain).
[c] Percentage computed by compiler from data herein. See endnotes for source of data.
[d] Values in gold, one-fifth less than currency values.
[e] Managers included with owners.
[f] Running square bales, counting round as half bales.
[g] Census listed the number of full and part time owners separately. Compiler added the two numbers for the above figure.
[h] Includes quantity of beans harvested from acreage grown with other crops as well as that from acreage grown alone.
[i] The total value for each state for 1950 was based on the average value per acre for farms in the sample, for which value of land and buildings was reported. The average value per farm and per acre was based on the total value of all farms.
[j] Based on a sampling of farms.
[k] Production ginned and to be ginned.
[l] 480-pound net weight bales.
[m] Less than one-tenth of one percent.
[n] Data available for hay, all other only.

GENERAL AGRICULTURE STATISTICS, 1850-1990										
HAWAII[*j]										
Item No.		1850	1860	1870	1880	1890	1900	1910	1920	1930
1.	Number of farms[18,19,68,73,76,82,*a]	---	---	---	---	---	2,273	4,320	5,284	5,955
2.	Acres in farms[18,19,68,73,76,82]	---	---	---	---	---	2,609,613	2,590,600	2,702,245	2,815,026
3.	Acres improved land in farms[20,*a]	---	---	---	---	---	---	---	---	---
4.	Cropland harvested, acres[18,19,73,76,*a,b]	---	---	---	---	---	---	---	---	---
5.	Percentage increase in number of farms[18,19]	---	---	---	---	---	---	90.1	22.3	12.7
6.	Percentage increase of land in farms[18,19]	---	---	---	---	---	---	-0.7	4.3	4.2
7.	Percentage increase of improved land in farms[20]	---	---	---	---	---	---	---	---	---
8.	Average acreage per farm[18,19,66,73,76,78]	---	---	---	---	---	1,148.1	599.7	511.4	472.7
9.	Percentage increase in cropland harvested[18,19,*b]	---	---	---	---	---	---	---	---	---
10.	Value of farms, dollars[18,19,64,79,81]	---	---	---	---	---	60,029,956	82,931,701	129,131,324	111,780,432
11.	Value of farms, percent increase[18,19]	---	---	---	---	---	---	38.2	55.7	-13.4
12.	Average value per farm, dollars[18,19,64,73,76]	---	---	---	---	---	26,410	19,197	24,438	18,771
13.	Farms operated by owners[21,22,23,24,25,26,27,65,77,*a]	---	---	---	---	---	---	---	---	---
14.	Value of livestock on farms, dollars[28,29,30,36,76,83,*a]	---	---	---	---	---	2,570,142	---	---	---
15.	Average value of livestock per farm, dollars[19,28,29,30,36]	---	---	---	---	---	1,130	---	---	---
16.	Production of cotton in bales[28,29,30,67,74,83]	---	---	---	---	---	---	4	8	97
17.	Percent of total production of cotton[28,29,30]	---	---	---	---	---	---	*k	*k	*k

GENERAL AGRICULTURE STATISTICS, 1850-1990										
HAWAII*j										
Item No.		1850	1860	1870	1880	1890	1900	1910	1920	1930
18.	Production of wheat in bushels[31,32,35,36,69,74,84]	---	---	---	---	---	---	---	---	---
19.	Percent of total production of wheat[31,32,33,35,36]	---	---	---	---	---	---	---	---	---
20.	Production of corn in bushels[36,37,38,39,70,74,85]	---	---	---	---	---	115,909	83,780	115,130	35,857
21.	Percent of total production of corn[36,37,38,39]	---	---	---	---	---	*k	*k	*k	*k
22.	Production of oats in bushels[31,35,36,71,80,86]	---	---	---	---	---	---	---	---	---
23.	Percent of total production of oats[31,35,36]	---	---	---	---	---	---	---	---	---
24.	Production of soybeans in bushels[36,40,41,72,74,76,87]	---	---	---	---	---	---	---	---	---
25.	Percent of total production of soybeans[36,40,41]	---	---	---	---	---	---	---	---	---
26.	Production of hay crops in tons[31,34,42,43,44,74,76,88]	---	---	---	---	---	271	---	---	---
27.	Percent of total production of hay crops[31,34,42,43,44]	---	---	---	---	---	*k	---	---	---

GENERAL AGRICULTURE STATISTICS, 1850-1990									
HAWAII[*j]									
Item No.		1940	1950	1960	1970	1978	1982	1987	1990
1.	Number of farms[18,19,68,73,76,82,*a]	4,995	5,750	6,242	3,896	4,310	4,595	4,870	4,600
2.	Acres in farms[18,19,68,73,76,82]	2,485,648	2,432,069	2,461,454	2,058,000	1,988,282	1,957,501	1,721,521	1,710,000
3.	Acres improved land in farms[20,*a]	---	---	---	---	---	---	---	---
4.	Cropland harvested, acres[18,19,73,76,*a,b]	184,553	159,497	176,410	120,000	158,639	155,960	152,719	---
5.	Percentage increase in number of farms[18,19]	-16.1	15.0	8.6	-37.6	10.6	6.6[*c]	6.0	-5.5
6.	Percentage increase of land in farms[18,19]	-11.7	-2.2	1.2	-16.4	-3.4	-1.5[*c]	-12.1	-0.7
7.	Percentage increase of improved land in farms[20]	---	---	---	---	---	---	---	---
8.	Average acreage per farm[18,19,66,73,76,78]	497.6	423.0	394.3	528	461	426	353	370
9.	Percentage increase in cropland harvested[18,19,*b]	---	-13.6	10.6	32.0	32.2	-1.7[*c]	-2.1[*c]	---
10.	Value of farms, dollars[18,19,64,79,81]	112,788,201	195,277,000[*i]	---	611,000,000	1,797,045,880	3,575,000,000	2,938,000,000	---
11.	Value of farms, percent increase[18,19]	0.9	73.1[*i]	---	---	194.1	98.9[*c]	-17.8[*c]	-17.8
12.	Average value per farm, dollars[18,19,64,73,76]	22,580	33,961[*i]	---	157,000	413,948	778,471	603,435	---
13.	Farms operated by owners[21,22,23,24,25,26,27,65,77,*a]	---	---	3,713[*g]	2,411[*g]	2,824	3,126[*g]	3,317[*g]	---
14.	Value of livestock on farms, dollars[28,29,30,36,76,83,*a]	---	---	45,988,385	---	88,230,000	102,539,000	111,424,000	88,444,000
15.	Average value of livestock per farm, dollars[19,28,29,30,36]	---	---	7,368	---	20,471	22,315	22,880	19,227
16.	Production of cotton in bales[28,29,30,67,74,83]	57[*f]	---	---	---	---	---	---	---
17.	Percent of total production of cotton[28,29,30]	[*f,k]	---	---	---	---	---	---	---

GENERAL AGRICULTURE STATISTICS, 1850-1990

HAWAII*[j]

Item No.		1940	1950	1960	1970	1978	1982	1987	1990
18.	Production of wheat in bushels[31,32,35,36,69,74,84]	---	---	---	---	---	---	---	---
19.	Percent of total production of wheat[31,32,33,35,36]	---	---	---	---	---	--	---	---
20.	Production of corn in bushels[36,37,38,39,70,74,85]	29,143	17,213	---	---	849	*l	---	---
21.	Percent of total production of corn[36,37,38,39]	*k	*k	---	---	---	---	---	---
22.	Production of oats in bushels[31,35,36,71,80,86]	---	---	---	---	---	---	---	---
23.	Percent of total production of oats[31,35,36]	---	---	---	---	---	---	---	---
24.	Production of soybeans in bushels[36,40,41,72,74,76,87]	---	---	---	---	---	---	---	---
25.	Percent of total production of soybeans[36,40,41]	---	---	---	---	---	---	---	---
26.	Production of hay crops in tons[31,34,42,43,44,74,76,88]	---	3,915	3,884	---	5,711	1,660	5,818	---
27.	Percent of total production of hay crops[31,34,4,43,44]	---	*k	*k	---	*k	*k	*k	---

[a] See the Glossary of Terms for changing definitions, i.e. farm, improved land, cropland harvested, farm owners, and livestock.
[b] Prior to 1924, the data relate to the total acreage of crops for which figures are available, except for 1920 when 14,502,932 acres of corn cut for forage were excluded (as most of this was probably duplicated in the acreage of corn harvested for grain).
[c] Percentage computed by compiler from data herein. See endnotes for source of data.
[d] Values in gold, one-fifth less than currency values.
[e] Managers included with owners.
[f] Running square bales, counting round as half bales.
[g] Census listed the number of full and part time owners separately. Compiler added the two numbers for the above figure.
[h] Includes quantity of beans harvested from acreage grown with other crops as well as that from acreage grown alone.
[i] The total value for each state for 1950 was based on the average value per acre for farms in the sample, for which value of land and buildings was reported. The average value per farm and per acre was based on the total value of all farms.
[j] Acquired in 1898.
[k] Less than one-tenth of one percent.
[l] Withheld to avoid disclosing data for individual farms.

GENERAL AGRICULTURE STATISTICS, 1850-1990										
IDAHO										
Item No.		1850	1860	1870	1880	1890	1900	1910	1920	1930
1.	Number of farms[18,19,68,73,76,82,*a]	---	---	414	1,885	6,603	17,471	30,807	42,106	41,674
2.	Acres in farms[18,19,68,73,76,82]	---	---	77,139	327,798	1,302,256	3,204,903	5,283,604	8,375,873	9,346,908
3.	Acres improved land in farms[20,*a]	---	---	26,603	197,407	606,362	1,413,118	2,778,740	4,511,680	---
4.	Cropland harvested, acres[18,19,73,76,*a,b]	---	---	---	78,878	300,469	918,124	1,638,479	2,706,312	3,150,097
5.	Percentage increase in number of farms[18,19]	---	---	---	355.3	250.3	164.6	76.3	36.7	-1.0
6.	Percentage increase of land in farms[18,19]	---	---	---	324.9	297.3	146.1	64.9	58.5	11.6
7.	Percentage increase of improved land in farms[20]	---	---	---	642.0	207.2	133.0	96.6	62.4	---
8.	Average acreage per farm[18,19,66,73,76,78]	---	---	186.3	173.9	197.2	183.4	171.5	198.9	224.3
9.	Percentage increase in cropland harvested[18,19,*b]	---	---	---	---	280.9	205.6	78.5	65.2	16.4
10.	Value of farms, dollars[18,19,64,79,81]	---	---	394,288	2,832,890	17,431,580	42,318,183	245,065,825	581,511,964	417,249,572
11.	Value of farms, percent increase[18,19]	---	---	---	618.5	515.3	142.8	479.1	137.3	-28.3
12.	Average value per farm, dollars[18,19,64,73,76]	---	---	952	1,503	2,640	2,422	7.955	13,811	10,012
13.	Farms operated by owners[21,22,23,24,25,26,27,65,77,*a]	---	---	---	1,796[*e]	6,298[*e]	15,585	27,169	34,647	30,512
14.	Value of livestock on farms, dollars[28,29,30,36,76,83,*a]	---	---	416,464[*d]	4,023,800[*k]	7,253,490	21,657,974	49,775,309	96,208,693	71,641,683
15.	Average value of livestock per farm, dollars[19,28,29,30,36]	---	---	1,006[*d]	2,135	1,099	1,240	1,616	2,285	1,719[*c]
16.	Production of cotton in bales[28,29,30,67,74,83]	---	---	---	---	---	---	---	---	---
17.	Percent of total production of cotton[28,29,30]	---	---	---	---	---	---	---	---	---

GENERAL AGRICULTURE STATISTICS, 1850-1990										
IDAHO										
Item No.		1850	1860	1870	1880	1890	1900	1910	1920	1930
18.	Production of wheat in bushels[31,32,35,36]	---	---	75,650	540,589	1,176,878	5,340,180	10,237,609	17,877,113	28,591,357
19.	Percent of total production of wheat[31,32,33,35,36]	---	---	.0263	.1177	.2513	.8109	1.4981	1.8910	3.5710
20.	Production of corn in bushels[36,37,38,39,70,74,85]	---	---	5,750	16,408	24,695	11,528	318,181	640,569	700,187
21.	Percent of total production of corn[36,37,38,39]	---	---	*j	*j	*j	*j	*j	*j	*j
22.	Production of oats in bushels[31,35,36,71,80,86]	---	---	100,119	462,236	587,407	1,956,498	11,328,106	3,069,132	4,244,701
23.	Percent of total production of oats[31,35,36]	---	---	*j	0.1	0.1	0.2	1.1	0.3	0.4
24.	Production of soybeans in bushels[36,40,41,72,74,76,87]	---	---	---	---	---	---	---	3,951	2,204*h
25.	Percent of total production of soybeans[36,40,41]	---	---	---	---	---	---	---	.3481	.0254
26.	Production of hay crops in tons[31,34,42,43,44,74,76,88]	---	---	6,985	40,053	269,104	899,125	1,584,617	2,313,921	2,332,919
27.	Percent of total production of hay crops[31,34,42,43,44]	---	---	*j	0.1	0.4	1.1	1.6	1.9	2.7

GENERAL AGRICULTURE STATISTICS, 1850-1990									
IDAHO									
Item No.		1940	1950	1960	1970	1978	1982	1987	1990
1.	Number of farms[18,19,68,73,76,82,*a]	43,663	40,284	33,670	25,475	24,249	24,714	24,142	21,800
2.	Acres in farms[18,19,68,73,76,82]	10,297,745	13,224,192	15,232,401	14,417,000	14,699,100	13,921,639	13,931,875	13,700,000
3.	Acres improved land in farms[20,*a]	---	---	---	---	---	---	---	---
4.	Cropland harvested, acres[18,19,73,76,*a,b]	2,935,350	3,647,885	3,832,164	3,904,000	4,820,928	4,887,805	4,349,122	---
5.	Percentage increase in number of farms[18,19]	4.8	-7.7	-16.4	-24.3	-4.8	1.9[*c]	-2.3	-9.7
6.	Percentage increase of land in farms[18,19]	10.2	28.4	15.2	-5.4	2.0	-5.3[*c]	0.1	-1.7
7.	Percentage increase of improved land in farms[20]	---	---	---	---	---	---	---	----
8.	Average acreage per farm[18,19,66,73,76,78]	235.8	328.3	452.4	566	606	563	577	614
9.	Percentage increase in cropland harvested[18,19,*b]	-6.8	24.3	5.1	1.9	23.5	1.4[*c]	-11.0	---
10.	Value of farms, dollars[18,19,64,79,81]	339,194,391	923,292,000[*i]	1,701,283,000	2,545,000,000	8,448,545,592	11,353,000,000	8,126,000,000	8,512,000,000
11.	Value of farms, percent increase[18,19]	-18.7	172.2[*i]	-84.3	49.6	232	34.4[*c]	-28.4	4.8
12.	Average value per farm, dollars[18,19,64,73,76]	7,768	22,920[*i]	50,528	100,000	348,408	459,965	336,615	390,459
13.	Farms operated by owners[21,22,23,24,25,26,27,65,77,*a]	32,225	32,837	28,438[*g]	22,660[*g]	21,496	22,058[*g]	21,223[*g]	---
14.	Value of livestock on farms, dollars[28,29,30,36,76,83,*a]	50,990,044	150,085,606	211,190,774	---	836,360,000	1,070,863,000	1,172,149	1,153,678,000
15.	Average value of livestock per farm, dollars[19,28,29,30,36]	1,168	3,726	6,272	---	34,491	43,330	48,552	52,921
16.	Production of cotton in bales[28,29,30,67,74,83]	---	---	---	---	---	---	---	---
17.	Percent of total production of cotton[28,29,30]	---	---	---	---	---	---	---	---

GENERAL AGRICULTURE STATISTICS, 1850-1990									
IDAHO									
Item No.		1940	1950	1960	1970	1978	1982	1987	1990
18.	Production of wheat in bushels[31,32,35,36,69,74,84]	22,323,077	34,872,882	38,412,559	42,734,000	69,166,361	87,980,724	83,250,152	91,420,000
19.	Percent of total production of wheat[31,32,33,35,36]	3.1492	3.4646	3.6378	3.1188	4.3026	3.7072	4.4115	4.4906
20.	Production of corn in bushels[36,37,38,39,70,74,85]	1,392,614	713,747	5,600,000	2,430,000	4,959,574	8,082,179	5,687,256	6,250,000
21.	Percent of total production of corn[36,37,38,39]	0.1	*j	0.1	0.1*c	0.1*c	0.1	0.1	0.1
22.	Production of oats in bushels[31,35,36,71,80,86]	6,611,917	6,248,875	5,768,999	5,775,000	---	2,794,994	2,700,000	4,080,000
23.	Percent of total production of oats[31,35,36]	0.8	0.5	0.6	0.6	---	0.6*c	0.6	1.1
24.	Production of soybeans in bushels[36,40,41,72,74,76,87]	144*h	35	---	---	45,632	*l	18,707	---
25.	Percent of total production of soybeans[36,40,41]	.0002	.0000	---	---	.0027	---	.0010	---
26.	Production of hay crops in tons[31,34,42,43,44,74,76,88]	2,222,833	2,316,160	2,869,466	3,957,000	3,956,186	3,846,435	3,563,558	4,043,000*m
27.	Percent of total production of hay crops[31,34,42,43,44]	2.7	2.6	2.7	3.1	3.0	3.0	2.8	2.8*c

[a] See the Glossary of Terms for changing definitions, i.e. farm, improved land, cropland harvested, farm owners, and livestock.
[b] Prior to 1924, the data relate to the total acreage of crops for which figures are available, except for 1920 when 14,502,932 acres of corn cut for forage were excluded (as most of this was probably duplicated in the acreage of corn harvested for grain).
[c] Percentage computed by compiler from data herein. See endnotes for source of data.
[d] Values in gold, one-fifth less than currency values.
[e] Managers included with owners.
[f] Running square bales, counting round as half bales.
[g] Census listed the number of full and part time owners separately. Compiler added the two numbers for the above figure.
[h] Includes quantity of beans harvested from acreage grown with other crops as well as that from acreage grown alone.
[i] The total value for each state for 1950 was based on the average value per acre for farms in the sample, for which value of land and buildings was reported. The average value per farm and per acre was based on the total value of all farms.
[j] Less than one-tenth of one percent.
[k] Including estimated value of range animals.
[l] Withheld to avoid disclosing data for individual farms.
[m] Census had two separate listings: hay, alfalfa, and alfalfa mixtures; and hay, all other. Compiler added the two listings for the above figure.

GENERAL AGRICULTURE STATISTICS, 1850-1990										
ILLINOIS										
Item No.		1850	1860	1870	1880	1890	1900	1910	1920	1930
1.	Number of farms[18,19,68,73,76,82,*a]	76,208	143,310	202,803	255,741	240,681	264,151	251,872	237,181	214,497
2.	Acres in farms[18,19,68,73,76,82]	12,037,412	20,911,989	25,882,861	31,673,645	30,498,227	32,794,728	32,522,937	31,974,775	30,695,339
3.	Acres improved land in farms[20,*a]	5,039,545	13,096,374	19,329,952	26,115,154	25,669,060	27,699,219	28,048,323	27,294,533	---
4.	Cropland harvested, acres[18,19,73,76,*a,b]	---	---	---	16,939,089	17,950,065	20,519,034	20,273,916	20,372,347	18,958,337
5.	Percentage increase in number of farms[18,19]	---	88.1	41.5	26.1	-5.9	9.8	-4.6	-5.8	-9.6
6.	Percentage increase of land in farms[18,19]	---	73.7	23.8	22.4	-3.7	7.5	-0.8	-1.7	-4.0
7.	Percentage increase of improved land in farms[20]	---	159.9	47.6	35.1	-1.7	7.9	1.3	-2.7	---
8.	Average acreage per farm[18,19,66,73,76,78]	158.0	145.9	127.6	123.8	126.7	124.2	129.1	134.8	143.1
9.	Percentage increase in cropland harvested[18,19,*b]	---	---	---	---	6.0	14.3	-1.2	0.5	-6.9
10.	Value of farms, dollars[18,19,64,79,81]	96,133,290	408,944,033	736,405,077	1,009,594,580	1,262,870,587	1,765,581,550	3,552,792,570	5,997,993,566	3,336,049,028
11.	Value of farms, percent increase[18,19]	---	325.4	80.1	37.1	25.1	39.8	99.5	70.3	-44.4
12.	Average value per farm, dollars[18,19,64,73,76]	1,261	2,854	3,631	3,948	5,247	6,684	13,986	25,289	15,553
13.	Farms operated by owners[21,22,23,24,25,26,27,65,77,*a]	---	---	---	175,497[*e]	158,848[*e]	158,503	145,107	132,574	119,892[*g]
14.	Value of livestock on farms, dollars[28,29,30,36,76,83,*a]	24,209,258	72,501,225	119,805,358[*d]	132,437,762	180,431,662	193,758,037	308,804,431	446,154,064	289,505,765
15.	Average value of livestock per farm, dollars[19,28,29,30,36]	318	506	591[*d]	518	750	734	1,226	1,881	1,350
16.	Production of cotton in bales[28,29,30,67,74,83]	---	1,482	465	---	---	---	---	---	826[*f]
17.	Percent of total production of cotton[28,29,30]	---	[*j]	[*j]	---	---	---	---	---	[*f,j]

GENERAL AGRICULTURE STATISTICS, 1850-1990										
ILLINOIS										
Item No.		1850	1860	1870	1880	1890	1900	1910	1920	1930
18.	Production of wheat in bushels[31,32,35,36,69,74,84]	9,414,575	23,837,023	30,128,405	51,110,502	37,389,444	19,795,500	37,830,732	70,890,917	30,150,949
19.	Percent of total production of wheat[31,32,33,35,36]	9.3690	13.7703	10.4705	11.1235	7.9828	3.0060	5.5358	7.4985	3.7658
20.	Production of corn in bushels[36,37,38,39,70,74,85]	57,616,981	115,171,777	129,921,395	325,792,481	289,697,256	398,149,140	390,218,676	285,346,031	275,850,367
21.	Percent of total production of corn[36,37,38,39]	9.7	13.7	17.1	18.6	13.7	14.9	15.3	12.2	12.9
22.	Production of oats in bushels[31,35,36,71,80,86]	10,087,241	15,220,029	42,780,851	63,189,200	137,624,828	180,305,630	150,386,074	129,104,668	128,257,740
23.	Percent of total production of oats[31,35,36]	6.9	8.8	15.2	15.5	17.0	19.1	14.9	12.2	12.9
24.	Production of soybeans in bushels[36,40,41,72,74,76,87]	---	---	---	---	---	---	---	23,812	3,249,996[*h]
25.	Percent of total production of soybeans[36,40,41]	---	---	---	---	---	---	---	2.0977	37.5237
26.	Production of hay crops in tons[31,34,42,43,44,74,76,88]	601,952	1,774,554	2,747,339	3,276,319	4,911,104	3,948,563	4,355,397	5,973,076	3,610,648
27.	Percent of total production of hay crops[31,34,42,43,44]	4.4	9.3	10.1	9.3	7.3	5.0	4.5	4.8	4.2

GENERAL AGRICULTURE STATISTICS, 1850-1990									
ILLINOIS									
Item No.		1940	1950	1960	1970	1978	1982	1987	1990
1.	Number of farms[18,19,68,73,76,82*a]	213,439	195,268	154,644	123,565	104,690	98,483	88,786	83,000
2.	Acres in farms[18,19,68,73,76,82]	31,032,572	30,978,495	30,327,261	29,913,000	29,472,473	28,726,114	28,526,664	28,500,000
3.	Acres improved land in farms[20*a]	---	---	---	---	---	---	---	---
4.	Cropland harvested, acres[18,19,73,76,*a,b]	18,270,025	20,364,489	20,967,738	20,004,000	22,676,226	23,008,244	20,102,388	---
5.	Percentage increase in number of farms[18,19]	-0.5	-8.5	-20.8	-20.1	-15.3	-5.9[*c]	-9.8[*c]	-6.5[*c]
6.	Percentage increase of land in farms[18,19]	1.1	-0.2	-2.1	-1.4	-1.5[*c]	-2.5[*c]	-0.7	-0.1
7.	Percentage increase of improved land in farms[20]	---	---	---	----	---	---	---	---
8.	Average acreage per farm[18,19,66,73,76,78]	145.4	158.6	196.1	242	282	292	321	331
9.	Percentage increase in cropland harvested[18,19,*b]	-3.6	11.5	3.0	-4.6	13.4	15.0	-12.6	---
10.	Value of farms, dollars[18,19,64,79,81]	2,537,117,306	5,394,905,000[*i]	9,579,602,000	14,643,000,000	54,932,727,420	53,061,000,000	35,779,000,000	35,035,000,000
11.	Value of farms, percent increase[18,19]	-23.9	112.6[*i]	77.6	52.9	275.1[*c]	-3.4[*c]	-32.6	-2.1
12.	Average value per farm, dollars[18,19,64,73,76]	11,887	27,628[*i]	61,946	119,000	524,718	538,886	402,970	422,108
13.	Farms operated by owners[21,22,23,24,25,26,27,65,77,*a]	119,830	127,005	102,461[*g]	92,580[*g]	81,738	78,765[*g]	71,563[*g]	---
14.	Value of livestock on farms, dollars[28,29,30,36,76,83,*a]	209,239,272	564,483,012	707,495,509	590,040,000	2,013,039,000	2,221,076,000	2,217,865,000	2,476,972,000
15.	Average value of livestock per farm, dollars[19,28,29,30,36]	980	2,891	4,575	4,775	19,229	22,553	24,980	29,843
16.	Production of cotton in bales[28,29,30,67,74,83]	4,169[*f]	2,031	1,106	200	---	---	---	---
17.	Percent of total production of cotton[28,29,30]	[*f,j]	[*j]	[*j]	[*j]	---	---	---	---

GENERAL AGRICULTURE STATISTICS, 1850-1990									
ILLINOIS									
Item No.		1940	1950	1960	1970	1978	1982	1987	1990
18.	Production of wheat in bushels[31,32,35,36,69,74,84]	38,107,733	42,427,820	42,484,623	35,748,000	31,325,922	62,046,957	48,850,664	105,020
19.	Percent of total production of wheat[31,32,33,35,36]	5.3760	4.2151	4.0235	2.6089	1.9487[*c]	2.6114	2.5887	.0052[*c]
20.	Production of corn in bushels[36,37,38,39,70,74,85]	382,457,687	457,731,394	673,350,000	735,560,000	1,181,849,723	1,425,129,317	1,168,644,485	1,322,250,000
21.	Percent of total production of corn[36,37,38,39]	16.5	16.5	15.7	17.9	17.4[*c]	19.0	17.4	17.6
22.	Production of oats in bushels[31,35,36,71,80,86]	92,108,749	148,343,869	85,906,342	34,272,000	---	10,268,768	13,110,000	16,000,000
23.	Percent of total production of oats[31,35,36]	10.6	13.1	8.6	3.8	---	2.0[*c]	4.2	4.3[*c]
24.	Production of soybeans in bushels[36,40,41,72,74,76,87]	44,771,860[*h]	73,390,475	120,910,225	210,800,000	30,1061,189	335,976,354	329,323,117	354,000,000
25.	Percent of total production of soybeans[36,40,41]	51.1149	34.5465	23.4491	18.7508	1.74816	16.8833	17.9169	18.3724
26.	Production of hay crops in tons[31,34,42,43,44,74,76,88]	3,794,655	3,444,072	4,391,318	3,378,000	3,134,558	2,729,197	2,720,838	3,526,000[*k]
27.	Percent of total production of hay crops[31,34,42,43,44]	4.6	3.9	4.1	2.7	2.4[*c]	2.1	2.1	2.4[*c]

[a] See the Glossary of Terms for changing definitions, i.e. farm, improved land, cropland harvested, farm owners, and livestock.
[b] Prior to 1924, the data relate to the total acreage of crops for which figures are available, except for 1920 when 14,502,932 acres of corn cut for forage were excluded (as most of this was probably duplicated in the acreage of corn harvested for grain).
[c] Percentage computed by compiler from data herein. See endnotes for source of data.
[d] Values in gold, one-fifth less than currency values.
[e] Managers included with owners.
[f] Running square bales, counting round as half bales.
[g] Census listed the number of full and part time owners separately. Compiler added the two numbers for the above figure.
[h] Includes quantity of beans harvested from acreage grown with other crops as well as that from acreage grown alone.
[i] The total value for each state for 1950 was based on the average value per acre for farms in the sample, for which value of land and buildings was reported. The average value per farm and per acre was based on the total value of all farms.
[j] Less than one-tenth of one percent.
[k] Census had two separate listings: hay, alfalfa, and alfalfa mixtures; and hay, all other. Compiler added the two listings for the above figure.

GENERAL AGRICULTURE STATISTICS, 1850-1990										
INDIANA										
Item No.		1850	1860	1870	1880	1890	1900	1910	1920	1930
1.	Number of farms[18,19,68,73,76,82,*a]	93,896	131,826	161,289	194,013	198,167	221,897	215,485	205,126	181,570
2.	Acres in farms[18,19,68,73,76,82]	12,793,422	16,388,292	18,119,648	20,420,983	20,362,516	21,619,623	21,299,823	21,063,332	19,688,675
3.	Acres improved land in farms[20,*a]	5,046,543	8,242,183	10,104,279	13,933,738	15,107,482	16,680,358	16,931,252	16,680,212	---
4.	Cropland harvested, acres[18,19,73,76,*a,b]	---	---	---	8,261,961	9,812,393	11,134,726	11,331,395	11,850,661	10,213,813
5.	Percentage increase in number of farms[18,19]	---	40.4	22.3	20.3	2.1	12.0	-2.9	-4.8	-11.5
6.	Percentage increase of land in farms[18,19]	---	28.1	10.6	12.7	-0.3	6.2	-1.5	-1.1	-6.5
7.	Percentage increase of improved land in farms[20]	---	63.3	22.6	37.9	8.4	10.4	1.5	-1.5	---
8.	Average acreage per farm[18,19,66,73,76,78]	136.2	124.3	112.3	105.3	102.8	97.4	98.8	102.7	108.4
9.	Percentage increase in cropland harvested[18,19,*b]	---	---	---	---	18.8	13.5	1.8	4.6	-13.8
10.	Value of farms, dollars[18,19,64,79,81]	136,385,173	356,712,175	507,843,351	635,236,111	754,789,110	841,735,340	1,594,275,596	2,653,643,973	1,415,542,192
11.	Value of farms, percent increase[18,19]	---	161.5	42.4	25.1	18.8	11.5	89.4	66.4	-46.7
12.	Average value per farm, dollars[18,19,64,73,76]	1,453	2,706	3,149	3,274	3,809	3,793	7,899	12,937	7,796
13.	Farms operated by owners[21,22,23,24,25,26,27,65,77,*a]	---	---	---	147,963[*e]	147,885[*e]	156,227	148,501	137,210	125,517
14.	Value of livestock on farms, dollars[28,29,30,36,76,83,*a]	22,478,555	41,855,539	67,021,426[*d]	71,068,758	93,361,422	109,550,761	173,860,101	261,264,188	175,235,615
15.	Average value of livestock per farm, dollars[19,28,29,30,36]	239	318	416[*d]	366	471	494	807	1,274	965[*c]
16.	Production of cotton in bales[28,29,30,67,74,83]	14	---	3	---	---	---	---	---	---
17.	Percent of total production of cotton[28,29,30]	[*j]	---	[*j]	---	---	---	---	---	---

GENERAL AGRICULTURE STATISTICS, 1850-1990										
INDIANA										
Item No.		1850	1860	1870	1880	1890	1900	1910	1920	1930
18.	Production of wheat in bushels[31,32,35,36,69,74,84]	6,214,458	16,848,267	27,747,222	47,284,853	37,318,798	34,986,280	33,935,972	45,207,862	25,190,384
19.	Percent of total production of wheat[31,32,33,35,36]	6.1844	9.7330	9.6430	10.2909	7.9677	5.3128	4.9659	4.7819	3.1462
20.	Production of corn in bushels[36,37,38,39,70,74,85]	52,964,363	71,588,919	51,094,538	115,482,300	108,843,094	178,967,070	195,496,433	158,603,938	114,871,320
21.	Percent of total production of corn[36,37,38,39]	8.9	8.5	6.7	6.6	5.1	6.7	7.7	6.8	5.4
22.	Production of oats in bushels[31,35,36,71,80,86]	5,655,014	5,317,831	8,590,409	15,599,518	31,491,661	34,565,070	50,607,913	52,529,723	47,465,387
23.	Percent of total production of oats[31,35,36]	3.9	3.1	3.0	3.8	3.9	3.7	5.0	5.0	4.8
24.	Production of soybeans in bushels[36,40,41,72,74,76,87]	---	--	---	---	---	---	---	23,010	1,379,279[*h]
25.	Percent of total production of soybeans[36,40,41]	---	---	---	---	---	---	---	2.0271	15.9248
26.	Production of hay crops in tons[31,34,42,43,44,74,76,88]	403,230	622,426	1,076,768	1,361,083	2,741,045	2,905,608	2,882,822	3,911,063	2,450,101
27.	Percent of total production of hay crops[31,34,42,43,44]	2.9	3.3	3.9	3.9	4.1	3.7	2.9	3.2	2.9

GENERAL AGRICULTURE STATISTICS, 1850-1990									
INDIANA									
Item No.		1940	1950	1960	1970	1978	1982	1987	1990
1.	Number of farms[18,19,68,73,76,82,*a]	184,549	166,627	128,160	101,479	82,483	77,180	70,506	68,000
2.	Acres in farms[18,19,68,73,76,82]	19,800,778	19,658,677	18,613,046	17,573,000	16,824,438	16,294,268	16,170,895	16,300,000
3.	Acres improved land in farms[20,*a]	---	---	---	---	---	---	---	---
4.	Cropland harvested, acres[18,19,73,76,*a,b]	9,711,028	11,000,662	11,147,102	10,392,000	11,809,491	12,136,310	10,706,298	---
5.	Percentage increase in number of farms[18,19]	1.6	-9.7	-23.1	-20.8	-18.7	-6.4	-8.6	-3.6
6.	Percentage increase of land in farms[18,19]	0.6	-0.7	-5.3	-5.6	-4.3	-3.2	-0.8	0.8
7.	Percentage increase of improved land in farms[20]	---	---	---	---	---	---	---	---
8.	Average acreage per farm[18,19,66,73,76,78]	107.3	118.0	145.2	173	204	211	229	231
9.	Percentage increase in cropland harvested[18,19,*b]	-4.9	13.3	1.3	-6.8	13.6	2.8	-11.8	---
10.	Value of farms, dollars[18,19,64,79,81]	1,251,491,614	2,691,273,000[*i]	4,932,749,000	7,136,000,000	26,659,577,879	26,128,000,000	18,716,000,000	17,404,000,000
11.	Value of farms, percent increase[18,19]	-11.6	115.0[*i]	83.3	44.6	274.0	-2.0	-28.4	-7.0
12.	Average value per farm, dollars[18,19,64,73,76]	6,781	16,151[*i]	38,489	70,000	323,213	338,549	265,446	255,941
13.	Farms operated by owners[21,22,23,24,25,26,27,65,77,*a]	131,263	133,980	106,047[*g]	89,105[*g]	72,818	68,567[*g]	62,841[*g]	---
14.	Value of livestock on farms, dollars[28,29,30,36,76,83,*a]	134,156,789	331,212,725	408,035,166	---	1,432,237,000	1,787,521,000	1,940,549,000	2,059,601,000
15.	Average value of livestock per farm, dollars[19,28,29,30,36]	727	1,988	3,184	---	17,364	23,160	27,523	30,288
16.	Production of cotton in bales[28,29,30,67,74,83]	---	---	---	---	---	---	---	---
17.	Percent of total production of cotton[28,29,30]	---	---	---	---	---	---	---	---

Item No.	GENERAL AGRICULTURE STATISTICS, 1850-1990 INDIANA	1940	1950	1960	1970	1978	1982	1987	1990
18.	Production of wheat in bushels[31,32,35,36,69,74,84]	25,653,913	36,621,026	30,941,720	29,799,000	22,175,789	37,007,361	30,789,151	51,920,000
19.	Percent of total production of wheat[31,32,33,35,36]	3.6165	3.6382	2.9303	2.1748	1.3795	1.5594	1.6316	2.5503
20.	Production of corn in bushels[36,37,38,39,70,74,85]	187,635,164	219,032,305	325,314,000	371,998,000	626,525,204	712,234,375	619,045,978	691,600,000
21.	Percent of total production of corn[36,37,38,39]	8.1	7.9	7.6	9.1	9.2	9.5	9.2	9.2
22.	Production of oats in bushels[31,35,36,71,80,86]	22,607,221	48,759,882	33,428,856	15,423,000	---	---	6,365,000	6,840,000
23.	Percent of total production of oats[31,35,36]	2.6	4.3	3.3	1.7	---	---	2.0	1.8[*c]
24.	Production of soybeans in bushels[36,40,41,72,74,76,87]	13,763,282[*h]	30,818,984	58,440,247	101,618,000	134,853,388	161,462,876	169,749,051	168,350,000
25.	Percent of total production of soybeans[36,40,41]	15.7132	14.5072	11.3338	9.0428	.78305	8.1137	9.2353	8.7373
26.	Production of hay crops in tons[31,34,42,43,44,74,76,88]	2,637,420	2,160,180	2,510,632	2,204,000	2,038,362	1,841,243	1,892,446	2,365,000[*k]
27.	Percent of total production of hay crops[31,34,42,43,44]	3.2	2.4	2.4	1.7	1.6	1.4	1.5	1.6[*c]

[a] See the Glossary of Terms for changing definitions, i.e. farm, improved land, cropland harvested, farm owners, and livestock.
[b] Prior to 1924, the data relate to the total acreage of crops for which figures are available, except for 1920 when 14,502,932 acres of corn cut for forage were excluded (as most of this was probably duplicated in the acreage of corn harvested for grain).
[c] Percentage computed by compiler from data herein. See endnotes for source of data.
[d] Values in gold, one-fifth less than currency values.
[e] Managers included with owners.
[f] Running square bales, counting round as half bales.
[g] Census listed the number of full and part time owners separately. Compiler added the two numbers for the above figure.
[h] Includes quantity of beans harvested from acreage grown with other crops as well as that from acreage grown alone.
[i] The total value for each state for 1950 was based on the average value per acre for farms in the sample, for which value of land and buildings was reported. The average value per farm and per acre was based on the total value of all farms.
[j] Less than one-tenth of one percent.
[k] Census had two separate listings: hay, alfalfa, and alfalfa mixtures; and hay, all other. Compiler added the two listings for the above figure.

GENERAL AGRICULTURE STATISTICS, 1850-1990

IOWA

Item No.		1850	1860	1870	1880	1890	1900	1910	1920	1930
1.	Number of farms[18,19,68,73,76,82,*a]	14,805	61,163	116,292	185,351	201,903	228,622	217,044	213,439	214,928
2.	Acres in farms[18,19,68,73,76,82]	2,736,064	10,069,907	15,541,793	24,752,700	30,491,541	34,574,337	33,930,688	33,474,896	34,019,332
3.	Acres improved land in farms[20,*a]	824,682	3,792,792	9,396,467	19,866,541	25,428,899	29,897,552	29,491,199	28,606,951	---
4.	Cropland harvested, acres[18,19,73,76,*a,b]	---	---	---	13,982,995	18,219,553	21,985,377	20,374,925	20,422,591	22,275,868
5.	Percentage increase in number of farms[18,19]	---	313.1	90.1	59.4	8.9	13.2	-5.1	-1.7	0.7
6.	Percentage increase of land in farms[18,19]	---	268.0	54.3	59.3	23.2	13.4	-1.9	-1.3	1.6
7.	Percentage increase of improved land in farms[20]	---	359.9	147.7	111.4	28.0	17.6	-1.4	-3.0	---
8.	Average acreage per farm[18,19,66,73,76,78]	184.8	164.6	133.6	133.5	151.0	151.2	156.3	156.8	158.3
9.	Percentage increase in cropland harvested[18,19,*b]	---	---	---	---	30.3	20.7	-7.3	0.2	9.1
10.	Value of farms, dollars[18,19,64,79,81]	16,657,567	119,899,547	314,129,953	567,430,227	857,581,022	1,497,554,790	3,257,379,400	7,601,772,290	4,224,506,083
11.	Value of farms, percent increase[18,19]	---	619.8	162.0	80.6	51.1	74.6	117.5	133.4	-44.4
12.	Average value per farm, dollars[18,19,64,73,76]	1,125	1,960	2,701	3,061	4,247	6,550	15,008	35,616	19,655
13.	Farms operated by owners[21,22,23,24,25,26,27,65,77,*a]	---	---	---	141,177[*e]	145,183[*e]	147,305	133,003	121,888	111,333
14.	Value of livestock on farms, dollars[28,29,30,36,76,83,*a]	3,689,275	22,476,293	66,389,706[*d]	124,715,103	206,436,242	278,830,096	393,003,196	613,926,268	496,965,755
15.	Average value of livestock per farm, dollars[19,28,29,30,36]	249	367	571[*d]	673	1,023	1,220	1,811	2,876[*c]	2,312[*c]
16.	Production of cotton in bales[28,29,30,67,74,83]	---	---	---	---	---	---	---	---	---
17.	Percent of total production of cotton[28,29,30]	---	---	---	---	---	---	---	---	---

GENERAL AGRICULTURE STATISTICS, 1850-1990										
IOWA										
Item No.		1850	1860	1870	1880	1890	1900	1910	1920	1930
18.	Production of wheat in bushels[31,32,35,36,69,74,84]	1,530,581	8,449,403	29,435,692	31,154,205	8,249,786	22,769,440	8,055,944	21,591,928	7,990,286
19.	Percent of total production of wheat[31,32,33,35,36]	1.5232	4.8811	10.2298	6.7803	1.7614	3.4576	1.1788	2.2839	.9980
20.	Production of corn in bushels[36,37,38,39,70,74,85]	8,656,799	42,410,686	68,935,065	275,014,247	313,130,782	383,453,190	341,750,460	371,362,393	389,000,414
21.	Percent of total production of corn[36,37,38,39]	1.5	5.0	9.1	15.7	14.8	14.4	13.4	15.8	18.3
22.	Production of oats in bushels[31,35,36,71,80,86]	1,524,345	5,887,645	21,005,142	50,610,591	146,679,289	168,364,170	128,198,055	187,045,705	208,070,091
23.	Percent of total production of oats[31,35,36]	1.0	3.4	7.4	12.4	18.1	17.8	12.7	17.7[*c]	21.0
24.	Production of soybeans in bushels[36,40,41,72,74,76,87]	---	---	---	---	---	---	---	3,098	573,711[*h]
25.	Percent of total production of soybeans[36,40,41]	---	---	---	---	---	---	---	.2729	6.6239
26.	Production of hay crops in tons[31,34,42,43,44,74,76,88]	89,055	813,173	1,777,339	3,613,941	7,264,700	6,600,169	7,827,696	7,744,315	5,384,422
27.	Percent of total production of hay crops[31,34,42,43,44]	0.6[*c]	4.3	6.5	10.3	10.9	8.3	8.0	6.3	6.3

GENERAL AGRICULTURE STATISTICS, 1850-1990									
IOWA									
Item No.		1940	1950	1960	1970	1978	1982	1987	1990
1.	Number of farms[18,19,68,73,76,82,*a]	213,318	203,159	174,707	140,354	121,339	115,413	105,180	104,000
2.	Acres in farms[18,19,68,73,76,82]	34,148,673	34,264,639	33,830,950	33,570,000	33,258,233	32,611,964	31,638,130	33,500,000
3.	Acres improved land in farms[20,*a]	---	---	---	---	---	---	---	---
4.	Cropland harvested, acres[18,19,73,76,*a,b]	20,076,641	22,547,337	22,873,407	20,687,000	23,622,212	24,137,670	20,484,178	20,656,000
5.	Percentage increase in number of farms[18,19]	-0.7	-4.8	-14.0	-19.7	-13.6	-4.9	-8.9	-1.1
6.	Percentage increase of land in farms[18,19]	0.4	0.3	-1.3	-0.8	-0.9	-1.9	-3.0	5.9
7.	Percentage increase of improved land in farms[20]	---	---	---	---	---	---	---	---
8.	Average acreage per farm[18,19,66,73,76,78]	160.1	168.7	193.6	239	274	283	301	319
9.	Percentage increase in cropland harvested[18,19,*b]	-9.9	12.3	1.5	-9.6	14.2	2.2	-15.1	0.8
10.	Value of farms, dollars[18,19,64,79,81]	2,690,744,215	5,506,670,000[*i]	8,586,924,100	13,150,000,000	51,831,288,579	54,349,000,000	29,830,000,000	34,869,000,000
11.	Value of farms, percent increase[18,19]	-36.3	104.7[*i]	55.9	53.1	294.2	5.0	-45.1	16.9[*c]
12.	Average value per farm, dollars[18,19,64,73,76]	12,614	27,105[*i]	49,150	94,000	427,161	471,011	283,597	335,279
13.	Farms operated by owners[21,22,23,24,25,26,27,65,77,*a]	110,616	125,062	113,223[*g]	106,605[*g]	94,776	91,361	83,433[*g]	---
14.	Value of livestock on farms, dollars[28,29,30,36,76,83,*a]	335,772,837	889,797,868	1,236,974,635	---	5,039,742,000	5,685,846	5,266,682,000	5,882,149,000
15.	Average value of livestock per farm, dollars[19,28,29,30,36]	1,574	4,380	7,080	---	41,534	49,000	50,073	56,559
16.	Production of cotton in bales[28,29,30,67,74,83]	---	---	---	---	---	---	---	---
17.	Percent of total production of cotton[28,29,30]	---	---	---	---	---	---	---	---

GENERAL AGRICULTURE STATISTICS, 1850-1990									
IOWA									
Item No.		1940	1950	1960	1970	1978	1982	1987	1990
18.	Production of wheat in bushels[31,32,35,36,69,74,84]	6,567,597	7,077,705	3,257,682	1,400,000	986,591	2,845,239	1,180,360	3,290,000
19.	Percent of total production of wheat[31,32,33,35,36]	.9265	.7032	.3085	.1022	.0614	.1199	.0625	.1576
20.	Production of corn in bushels[36,37,38,39,70,74,85]	469,786,611	503,589,858	811,265,000	859,140,000	1,389,912,254	1,466,953,043	1,274,388,346	1,445,500,000
21.	Percent of total production of corn[36,37,38,39]	20.3	18.1	18.9	21.0	20.5	19.5	19.0	19.2
22.	Production of oats in bushels[31,35,36,71,74,85]	155,348,088	233,533,684	184,086,771	94,105,000	---	45,769,302	37,050,000	54,000,000
23.	Percent of total production of oats[31,35,36]	17.9	20.5	18.4	10.4	---	9.0	9.9	14.5
24.	Production of soybeans in bushels[36,40,41,72,74,76,87]	11,359,475[*h]	29,596,245	62,106,812	184,600,000	265,870,687	291,189,890	326,081,351	322,920,000
25.	Percent of total production of soybeans[36,40,41]	12.9688	13.9316	12.0449	16.4273	1.5438	14.6327	17.7406	16.7563
26.	Production of hay crops in tons[31,34,42,43,44,74,76,88]	5,051,371	4,830,842	8,140,050	6,910,000	6,728,686	6,201,756	5,612,944	6,650,000[*j]
27.	Percent of total production of hay crops[31,34,42,43,44]	6.1	5.4	7.6	5.4	5.2	4.8	4.4	4.5[*c]

[a] See the Glossary of Terms for changing definitions, i.e. farm, improved land, cropland harvested, farm owners, and livestock.
[b] Prior to 1924, the data relate to the total acreage of crops for which figures are available, except for 1920 when 14,502,932 acres of corn cut for forage were excluded (as most of this was probably duplicated in the acreage of corn harvested for grain).
[c] Percentage computed by compiler from data herein. See endnotes for source of data.
[d] Values in gold, one-fifth less than currency values.
[e] Managers included with owners.
[f] Running square bales, counting round as half bales.
[g] Census listed the number of full and part time owners separately. Compiler added the two numbers for the above figure.
[h] Includes quantity of beans harvested from acreage grown with other crops as well as that from acreage grown alone.
[i] The total value for each state for 1950 was based on the average value per acre for farms in the sample, for which value of land and buildings was reported. The average value per farm and per acre was based on the total value of all farms.
[j] Census had two separate listings: hay, alfalfa, and alfalfa mixtures; and hay, all other. Compiler added the two listings for the above figure.

GENERAL AGRICULTURE STATISTICS, 1850-1990										
KANSAS										
Item No.		1850	1860	1870	1880	1890	1900	1910	1920	1930
1.	Number of farms[18,19,68,73,76,82,*a]	---	10,400	38,202	138,561	166,617	173,098	177,841	165,286	166,042
2.	Acres in farms[18,19,68,73,76,82]	---	1,778,400	5,656,879	21,417,468	30,214,456	41,662,970	43,384,799	45,425,179	46,975,647
3.	Acres improved land in farms[20,*a]	---	405,468	1,971,003	10,739,566	22,303,301	25,040,550	29,904,067	30,600,760	---
4.	Cropland harvested, acres[18,19,73,76,*a,b]	---	---	---	7,063,676	14,618,304	18,077,048	19,900,750	21,908,887	24,308,361
5.	Percentage increase in number of farms[18,19]	---	---	267.3	262.7	20.2	3.9	2.7	-7.1	0.5
6.	Percentage increase of land in farms[18,19]	---	---	218.1	278.6	41.1	37.9	4.1	4.7	3.4
7.	Percentage increase of improved land in farms[20]	---	---	386.1	444.9	107.7	12.3	19.4	2.3	---
8.	Average acreage per farm[18,19,66,73,76,78]	---	171.0	148.0	154.6	181.3	240.7	244.0	274.8	282.9
9.	Percentage increase in cropland harvested[18,19,*b]	---	---	---	---	107.0	23.7	10.1	10.1	11.0
10.	Value of farms, dollars[18,19,64,79,81]	---	12,258,239	72,261,632	235,178,936	559,726,046	643,652,770	1,737,556,172	2,830,063,918	2,281,101,631
11.	Value of farms, percent increase[18,19]	---	---	489.5	225.4	138.0	15.0	170.0	62.9	-19.4
12.	Average value per farm, dollars[18,19,64,73,76]	---	1,179	1,892	1,697	3,359	3,718	9,770	17,122	13,738
13.	Farms operated by owners[21,22,23,24,25,26,27,65,77,*a]	---	---	---	115,910[*e]	119,576[*e]	110,443	111,108	97,090	94,762
14.	Value of livestock on farms, dollars[28,29,30,36,76,83,*a]	---	3,332,450	18,538,548[*d]	62,704,149[*j]	128,068,305	190,956,936	253,523,577	318,025,292	246,394,684[*c]
15.	Average value of livestock per farm, dollars[19,28,29,30,36]	---	320	485[*d]	453	769	1,103	1,426	1,924	1,484
16.	Production of cotton in bales[28,29,30,67,74,83]	---	61	7	---	212	70[*f]	10[*f]	---	455[*f]
17.	Percent of total production of cotton[28,29,30]	---	[*j]	[*j]	---	[*j]	[*f,j]	[*f,j]	---	[*f,j]

GENERAL AGRICULTURE STATISTICS, 1850-1990										
KANSAS										
Item No.		1850	1860	1870	1880	1890	1900	1910	1920	1930
18.	Production of wheat in bushels[31,32,35,36,69,74,84]	---	194,173	2,391,198	17,324,141	30,399,871	38,778,450	77,577,115	148,475,729	148,482,595
19.	Percent of total production of wheat[31,32,33,35,36]	---	.1122	.8310	3.7704	6.6058	5.8886	11.3520	15.7050	18.5453
20.	Production of corn in bushels[36,37,38,39,70,74,85]	---	6,150,727	17,025,525	105,729,325	259,574,568	229,937,430	154,651,703	59,719,831	101,355,511
21.	Percent of total production of corn[36,37,38,39]	---	0.7	2.2	6.0	12.2	8.6	6.1	2.5[*c]	4.9
22.	Production of oats in bushels[31,35,36,71,80,86]	---	88,325	4,097,925	8,180,385	44,629,034	24,469,980	22,923,641	36,257,356	21,526,565
23.	Percent of total production of oats[31,35,36]	---	0.1	1.5	2.0	5.5	2.6	2.3	3.4[*c]	2.2[*c]
24.	Production of soybeans in bushels[36,40,41,72,74,76,87]	---	---	---	---	---	---	---	1,160	29,906[*h]
25.	Percent of total production of soybeans[36,40,41]	---	---	---	---	---	---	---	.1022	.3453
26.	Production of hay crops in tons[31,34,42,43,44,74,76,88]	---	56,232	490,289	1,601,932	4,854,960	7,066,671	5,963,525	7,378,683	2,628,183
27.	Percent of total production of hay crops[31,34,42,43,44]	---	0.3	1.8	4.6	7.3	8.9	6.1	6.0	3.1

GENERAL AGRICULTURE STATISTICS, 1850-1990

KANSAS

Item No.		1940	1950	1960	1970	1978	1982	1987	1990
1.	Number of farms[18,19,68,73,76,82,*a]	156,327	131,394	104,347	86,057	74,171	73,315	68,579	69,000
2.	Acres in farms[18,19,68,73,76,82]	48,173,635	48,611,366	50,152,870	49,390,000	47,499,831	47,052,213	46,628,519	47,900,000
3.	Acres improved land in farms[20,*a]	---	---	---	---	---	---	---	---
4.	Cropland harvested, acres[18,19,73,76,*a,b]	17,816,498	21,493,734	20,528,357	18,853,000	18,987,644	20,186,974	17,729,394	26,780,000
5.	Percentage increase in number of farms[18,19]	-5.9	-15.9	-20.6	-17.5	-13.8	-1.2	-6.5	-0.6
6.	Percentage increase of land in farms[18,19]	2.6	0.9	3.2	-1.5	-3.8	-0.9	-0.9	-2.7
7.	Percentage increase of improved land in farms[20]	---	---	---	---	---	---	---	---
8.	Average acreage per farm[18,19,66,73,76,78]	308.2	370.0	480.6	574	640	642	680	694
9.	Percentage increase in cropland harvested[18,19,*b]	-26.7	20.6	-4.5	-8.2	0.7	6.3	-12.2	51.1
10.	Value of farms, dollars[18,19,64,79,81]	1,421,387,464	3,198,628,000[*i]	5,017,473,000	7,842,501,000	23,895,30,215	28,076,000,000	19,068,000	18,695,000,000
11.	Value of farms, percent increase[18,19]	-37.7	125.0[*i]	56.9	56.3	205.0	258.0	-32.1	-2.0
12.	Average value per farm, dollars[18,1964,73,76]	9,092	24,344[*i]	48,084	91,131	322,165	384,197	278,047	270,942
13.	Farms operated by owners[21,22,23,24,25,26,27,65,77,*a]	85,475	91,815	77,949[*g]	70,152[*g]	61,708	61,696[*g]	57,923[*g]	---
14.	Value of livestock on farms, dollars[28,29,30,36,76,83,*a]	138,722,051	459,386,405	589,746,446	---	3,554,701,000	4,047,815,000	4,783,060,000	4,896,215,000
15.	Average value of livestock per farm, dollars[19,28,29,30,36]	887	3,496	5,652	---	47,925	55,211	69,745	70,960
16.	Production of cotton in bales[28,29,30,67,74,83]	156[*f]	15	13	---	---	---	595	200
17.	Percent of total production of cotton[28,29,30]	[*f,j]	[*j]	[*j]	---	---	---	[*j]	[*j]

Item No.	GENERAL AGRICULTURE STATISTICS, 1850-1990 KANSAS	1940	1950	1960	1970	1978	1982	1987	1990
18.	Production of wheat in bushels[31,32,35,36,69,74,84]	112,413,657	145,657,700	199,604,763	299,013,000	26,8457,130	372,590,045	292,999,442	213,600,000
19.	Percent of total production of wheat[31,32,33,35,36]	15.8586	14.4709	18.9033	21.8222	16.7000	15.6996	15.5264	10.4921
20.	Production of corn in bushels[36,37,38,39,70,74,85]	31,880,109	61,785,287	81,630,000	79,670,000	154,173,376	130,662,235	144,133,581	155,000,000
21.	Percent of total production of corn[36,37,38,39]	1.4	2.2	1.9	1.9	2.3	1.7	2.1	2.1
22.	Production of oats in bushels[31,35,36,71,80,86]	20,929,707	15,145,436	16,080,168	10,250,000	---	7,799,056	6,510,000	9,000,000
23.	Percent of total production of oats[31,35,36]	---	---	---	1.1	---	1.5	2.1	2.4
24.	Production of soybeans in bushels[36,40,41,72,74,76,87]	88,322[*h]	3,577,605	8,715,280	15,075,000	26436742	43,042,471	55,789,994	49,950,000
25.	Percent of total production of soybeans[36,40,41]	.1008	1.6841	1.6902	1.3415	1.535	2.1629	3.0353	2.5924
26.	Production of hay crops in tons[31,34,42,43,44,74,76,88]	1,389,193	3,167,662	3,388,855	4,102,000	4,462,796	5,092,039	5,080,847	5,620,000[*k]
27.	Percent of total production of hay crops[31,34,42,43,44]	1.7	3.6	3.2	3.2	.3414	4.0	3.9	3.8[*c]

[a] See the Glossary of Terms for changing definitions, i.e. farm, improved land, cropland harvested, farm owners, and livestock.
[b] Prior to 1924, the data relate to the total acreage of crops for which figures are available, except for 1920 when 14,502,932 acres of corn cut for forage were excluded (as most of this was probably duplicated in the acreage of corn harvested for grain).
[c] Percentage computed by compiler from data herein. See endnotes for source of data.
[d] Values in gold, one-fifth less than currency values.
[e] Managers included with owners.
[f] Running square bales, counting round as half bales.
[g] Census listed the number of full and part time owners separately. Compiler added the two numbers for the above figure.
[h] Includes quantity of beans harvested from acreage grown with other crops as well as that from acreage grown alone.
[i] The total value for each state for 1950 was based on the average value per acre for farms in the sample, for which value of land and buildings was reported. The average value per farm and per acre was based on the total value of all farms.
[j] Less than one-tenth of one percent.
[k] Census had two separate listings: hay, alfalfa, and alfalfa mixtures; and hay, all other. Compiler added the two listings for the above figure.

GENERAL AGRICULTURE STATISTICS, 1850-1990										
KENTUCKY										
Item No.		1850	1860	1870	1880	1890	1900	1910	1920	1930
1.	Number of farms[18,19,68,73,76,82,*a]	74,777	90,814	118,422	166,453	179,264	234,667	259,185	270,626	246,499
2.	Acres in farms[18,19,68,73,76,82]	16,949,748	19,163,261	18,660,106	21,495,240	21,412,229	21,979,422	22,189,127	21,612,772	19,927,286
3.	Acres improved land in farms[20,*a]	5,968,270	7,644,208	8,103,850	10,731,683	11,818,882	13,741,968	14,354,471	13,975,746	---
4.	Cropland harvested, acres[18,19,73,76,*a,b]	---	---	---	5,245,337	5,616,453	6,349,926	6,046,819	6,300,850	5,330,821
5.	Percentage increase in number of farms[18,19]	---	21.4	30.4	40.6	7.7	30.9	10.4	4.4	-8.9
6.	Percentage increase of land in farms[18,19]	---	13.1	-2.6	15.2	-0.4	2.6	1.0	-2.6	-7.8
7.	Percentage increase of improved land in farms[20]	---	28.1	6.0	32.4	10.1	16.3	4.5	-2.6	---
8.	Average acreage per farm[18,19,66,73,76,78]	226.7	211.0	157.6	129.1	119.4	93.7	85.6	79.9	80.8
9.	Percentage increase in cropland harvested[18,19,*b]	---	---	---	---	7.1	13.1	-4.8	4.2	-15.4
10.	Value of farms, dollars[18,19,64,79,81]	155,021,262	291,496,955	248,991,133	299,298,631	346,339,360	382,004,890	635,459,372	1,305,158,936	871,448,632
11.	Value of farms, percent increase[18,19]	---	88.0	-14.6	20.2	15.7	10.3	66.3	105.4	-33.2
12.	Average value per farm, dollars[18,19,64,73,76]	2,073	3,210	2,103	1,798	1,932	1,628	2,452	4,823	3,535
13.	Farms operated by owners[21,22,23,24,25,26,27,65,77,*a]	---	---	---	122,426[*c]	134,529[*c]	155,996	170,332	179,327	157,403
14.	Value of livestock on farms, dollars[28,29,30,36,76,83,*a]	29,661,436	61,868,237	53,029,874[*d]	49,670,567	70,924,400	73,739,106	117,486,662	158,387,284	120,931,359
15.	Average value of livestock per farm, dollars[19,28,29,30,36]	397	681	448[*d]	298	396	314	453	585	491[*c]
16.	Production of cotton in bales[*28,29,30,67,74,83]	758	---	1,080	1,367	873	1,369[*f]	3,469[*f]	2,967[*f]	8,955[*f]
17.	Percent of total production of cotton[28,29,30]	[*k]	---	[*k]	[*k]	[*k]	[*f,k]	[*f,k]	[*f,k]	0.1[*f]

GENERAL AGRICULTURE STATISTICS, 1850-1990										
KENTUCKY										
Item No.		1850	1860	1870	1880	1890	1900	1910	1920	1930
18.	Production of wheat in bushels[31,32,35,36,69,74,84]	2,142,822	7,394,809	5,728,704	11,356,113	10,707,462	14,264,500	8,739,260	10,375,129	2,483,443
19.	Percent of total production of wheat[31,32,33,35,36]	2.1325	4.2719	1.9909	2.4715	2.2861	2.1661	1.2788	1.0974	.3102
20.	Production of corn in bushels[36,37,38,39,70,74,85]	58,672,591	64,043,633	50,091,006	72,852,263	78,434,817	73,974,220	83,348,024	71,518,484	61,008,387
21.	Percent of total production of corn[36,37,38,39]	9.9	7.6	6.6	4.2	3.7	2.8	3.3	3.0	2.9
22.	Production of oats in bushels[31,35,36,71,80,86]	8,201,311	4,617,029	6,620,103	4,580,738	8,775,814	4,009,830	2,406,064	2,791,447	731,543
23.	Percent of total production of oats[31,35,36]	5.6	2.7	2.4	1.1	1.1	0.4	0.2	0.3	0.1
24.	Production of soybeans in bushels[36,40,41,72,74,76,87]	---	---	---	---	---	---	27	11,178	70,189[*h]
25.	Percent of total production of soybeans[36,40,41]	---	---	---	---	---	---	.1081	.9847	.8104
26.	Production of hay crops in tons[31,34,42,43,44,74,76,88]	113,747	158,476	204,399	218,739	652,995	655,066	985,815	1,368,436	1,306,228
27.	Percent of total production of hay crops[31,34,42,43,44]	0.8[*c]	0.8	0.8	0.6	1.0	0.8	1.0	1.1	1.5

GENERAL AGRICULTURE STATISTICS, 1850-1990									
KENTUCKY									
Item No.		**1940**	**1950**	**1960**	**1970**	**1978**	**1982**	**1987**	**1990**
1.	Number of farms[18,19,68,73,76,82,*a]	252,894	218,476	150,986	125,069	102,263	101,642	92,453	93,000
2.	Acres in farms[18,19,68,73,76,82]	20,294,016	19,441,774	17,030,675	15,968,000	14,606,168	14,179,284	14,012,700	14,100,000
3.	Acres improved land in farms[20,*a]	---	---	---	---	---	---	---	---
4.	Cropland harvested, acres[18,19,73,76,*a,b]	5,271,623	5,053,682	4,012,962	3,511,000	4,511,837	4,835,631	4,250,284	---
5.	Percentage increase in number of farms[18,19]	2.6	-13.6	-30.9	-17.2	-18.2	-0.6	-9.0	0.6
6.	Percentage increase of land in farms[18,19]	1.8	-4.2	-12.4	-6.2	-8.5	-2.9	-1.2	0.6
7.	Percentage increase of improved land in farms[20]	---	---	---	---	---	---	---	---
8.	Average acreage per farm[18,19,66,73,76,78]	80.2	89.0	112.8	128	143	140	152	148
9.	Percentage increase in cropland harvested[18,19,*b]	-1.1	-4.1	-20.6	-12.5	28.5	7.2	-12.1	---
10.	Value of farms, dollars[18,19,64,79,81]	776,494,098	1,572,256,000[*i,j]	2,305,473,000[*j]	4,041,000,000	12,704,439,279	14,661,000,000	12,545,000,000	11,745,000,000
11.	Value of farms, percent increase[18,19]	-10.9	102.5[*i,j]	46.6[*j]	75.3	212.4	15.4	-14.4	-6.4
12.	Average value per farm, dollars[18,19,64,73,76]	3,070	7,196[*i,j]	15,269[*j]	32,000	124,233	144,427	135,696	126,290
13.	Farms operated by owners[21,22,23,24,25,26,27,65,77,*a]	168,604	168,948	126,253[*g]	113,441[*g]	91,335	90,527[*g]	84,149[*g]	---
14.	Value of livestock on farms, dollars[28,29,30,36,76,83,*a]	103,422,377	257,415,282	306,353,207	---	864,066,000	1,018,573,000	1,185,689,000	1,698,323,000
15.	Average value of livestock per farm, dollars[19,28,29,30,36]	409	1,178	2,029	---	8,449	10,021	12,825	18,262
16.	Production of cotton in bales[28,29,30,67,74,83]	15,704[*f]	12,887	10,653	2,400	44	---	---	---
17.	Percent of total production of cotton[28,29,30]	0.1[*f]	0.1	0.1	[*k]	[*k]	---	---	---

Item No.	GENERAL AGRICULTURE STATISTICS, 1850-1990 KENTUCKY	1940	1950	1960	1970	1978	1982	1987	1990
18.	Production of wheat in bushels[31,32,35,36,69,74,84]	3,658,612	4,490,750	3,877,314	6,120,000	5,994,647	19,653,581	12,752,191	22,500,000
19.	Percent of total production of wheat[31,32,33,35,36]	.5161	.4461	.3672	.4466	.3729	.8281	.6758	1.1052
20.	Production of corn in bushels[36,37,38,39,70,74,85]	61,052,096	71,009,754	85,775,000	49,400,000	110,068,935	131,668,799	104,364,883	136,880,000
21.	Percent of total production of corn[36,37,38,39]	2.6	2.6	2.0	1.2	1.6	1.8	1.6	1.8
22.	Production of oats in bushels[31,35,36,71,80,86]	479,844	1,273,321	1,621,283	846,000	---	227,364	364,000	480,000
23.	Percent of total production of oats[31,35,36]	0.1	0.1	0.2	0.1	---	*k	0.1	0.1
24.	Production of soybeans in bushels[36,40,41,72,74,76,87]	277,410*h	2,266,108	4,015,319	15,066,000	35,761,994	44,292,449	27,138,451	36,855,000
25.	Percent of total production of soybeans[36,40,41]	.3167	1.0667	.7787	1.3407	2.0766	2.2258	1.4765	1.9128
26.	Production of hay crops in tons[31,34,42,43,44,74,76,88]	1,857,481	2,117,541	2,139,978	3,059,000	2,731,736	2,787,331	3,291,951	5,501,000*l
27.	Percent of total production of hay crops[31,34,42,43,44]	2.3	2.4	2.0	2.4	2.1	2.2	2.6	3.7*c

[a] See the Glossary of Terms for changing definitions, i.e. farm, improved land, cropland harvested, farm owners, and livestock.
[b] Prior to 1924, the data relate to the total acreage of crops for which figures are available, except for 1920 when 14,502,932 acres of corn cut for forage were excluded (as most of this was probably duplicated in the acreage of corn harvested for grain).
[c] Percentage computed by compiler from data herein. See endnotes for source of data.
[d] Values in gold, one-fifth less than currency values.
[e] Managers included with owners.
[f] Running square bales, counting round as half bales.
[g] Census listed the number of full and part time owners separately. Compiler added the two numbers for the above figure.
[h] Includes quantity of beans harvested from acreage grown with other crops as well as that from acreage grown alone.
[i] The total value for each state for 1950 was based on the average value per acre for farms in the sample, for which value of land and buildings was reported. The average value per farm and per acre was based on the total value of all farms.
[j] Based on a sampling of farms.
[k] Less than one-tenth of one percent.
[l] Census had two separate listings: hay, alfalfa, and alfalfa mixtures; and hay all other. Compiler added the two listings for the above figure.

GENERAL AGRICULTURE STATISTICS, 1850-1990										
LOUISIANA										
Item No.		1850	1860	1870	1880	1890	1900	1910	1920	1930
1.	Number of farms[18,19,68,73,76,82,*a]	13,422	17,328	28,481	48,292	69,294	115,969	120,546	135,463	161,445
2.	Acres in farms[18,19,68,73,76,82]	4,989,043	9,298,576	7,025,817	8,273,506	9,544,219	11,059,127	10,439,481	10,019,822	9,355,437
3.	Acres improved land in farms[20,*a]	1,590,025	2,707,108	2,045,640	2,739,972	3,774,668	4,666,532	5,276,016	5,626,226	---
4.	Cropland harvested, acres[18,19,73,76,*a,b]	---	---	---	1,913,360	2,477,134	3,408,944	3,586,348	3,924,267	4,068,151
5.	Percentage increase in number of farms[18,19]	---	29.1	64.4	69.6	43.5	67.4	3.9	12.4	19.2
6.	Percentage increase of land in farms[18,19]	---	86.4	-24.4	17.8	15.4	15.9	-5.6	-4.0	-6.6
7.	Percentage increase of improved land in farms[20]	---	70.3	-24.4	33.9	37.8	23.6	13.1	6.6	---
8.	Average acreage per farm[18,19,66,73,76,78]	371.7	536.6	246.7	171.3	137.7	95.4	86.6	74.0	57.9
9.	Percentage increase in cropland harvested[18,19,*b]	---	---	---	---	29.5	37.6	5.2	9.4	3.7
10.	Value of farms, dollars[18,19,64,79,81]	75,814,398	204,789,662	54,572,337	58,989,117	85,381,270	141,130,610	237,544,450	474,038,793	418,191,773
11.	Value of farms, percent increase[18,19]	---	170.1	-73.4	8.1	44.7	65.3	68.3	99.6	-11.8
12.	Average value per farm, dollars[18,19,64,73,76]	5,649	11,818	1,916	1,222	1,232	1,217	1,971	3,499	2,590
13.	Farms operated by owners[21,22,23,24,25,26,27,65,77,*a]	---	---	---	31,286[*e]	38,539[*e]	47,701	52,989	57,254	53,159[*g]
14.	Value of livestock on farms, dollars[28,29,30,36,76,83,*a]	11,152,275	24,546,940	12,743,351[*d]	12,345,905	17,898,380	28,869,506	44,699,485	83,072,876	55,320,377
15.	Average value of livestock per farm, dollars[19,28,29,30,36]	831	1,417	447[*d]	256	258	249	371	613	343
16.	Production of cotton in bales[28,29,30,67,74,83]	178,737	777,738	350,832	508,569	659,180	709,041[*f]	268,909[*f]	306,791[*f]	798,828[*f]
17.	Percent of total production of cotton[28,29,30]	7.2	14.5	11.7	8.8	8.8	7.4[*f]	2.5[*f]	2.7[*f]	5.5[*f]

GENERAL AGRICULTURE STATISTICS, 1850-1990										
LOUISIANA										
Item No.		1850	1860	1870	1880	1890	1900	1910	1920	1930
18.	Production of wheat in bushels[31,32,35,36,69,74,84]	417	32,208	9,906	5,034	257	2,345	488	5,788	144
19.	Percent of total production of wheat[31,32,33,35,36]	.0004	.0186	.0034	.0011	.0001	.0004	.0001	.0006	.0000
20.	Production of corn in bushels[36,37,38,39,70,74,85]	10,266,373	16,853,745	7,596,628	9,889,689	13,081,954	22,062,580	26,010,361	21,675,602	18,279,702
21.	Percent of total production of corn[36,37,38,39]	1.7	2.0	1.0	0.6	0.6	0.8	1.0	0.9	0.9
22.	Production of oats in bushels[31,35,36,71,80,86]	89,637	89,377	17,782	229,840	297,271	316,070	420,033	489,380	201,315
23.	Percent of total production of oats[31,35,36]	0.1	0.1	*j	0.1	*j	*j	*j	*j	*j
24.	Production of soybeans in bushels[36,40,41,72,74,76,87]	---	---	---	---	---	---	133	4,443	191,161*h
25.	Percent of total production of soybeans[36,40,41]	---	---	---	---	---	---	.5327	.3914	2.2071
26.	Production of hay crops in tons[31,34,42,43,44,74,76,88]	25,752	52,721	8,776	29,579	40,601	163,443	247,218	274,993	216,217
27.	Percent of total production of hay crops[31,34,42,43,44]	0.2*c	0.3	*j	0.1	0.1	0.2	0.3	0.2	0.3

GENERAL AGRICULTURE STATISTICS, 1850-1990									
LOUISIANA									
Item No.		1940	1950	1960	1970	1978	1982	1987	1990
1.	Number of farms[18,19,68,73,76,82,*a]	150,007	124,181	74,438	42,269	31,370	31,628	27,350	34,000
2.	Acres in farms[18,19,68,73,76,82]	9,996,108	11,202,278	10,347,328	9,789,000	9,295,029	8,928,827	8,007,173	9,000,000
3.	Acres improved land in farms[20,*a]	---	---	---	---	---	---	---	---
4.	Cropland harvested, acres[18,19,73,76,*a,b]	4,051,670	3,148,881	2,425,936	3,914,000	4,838,520	4,699,323	3,599,678	---
5.	Percentage increase in number of farms[18,19]	-7.1	-17.2	-40.1	-43.2	25.8	8.2	-13.5	24.3
6.	Percentage increase of land in farms[18,19]	6.8	12.1	-7.6	-5.4	-5.0	-3.9	-10.3	12.4
7.	Percentage increase of improved land in farms[20]	---	---	---	---	---	---	---	---
8.	Average acreage per farm[18,19,66,73,76,78]	66.6	90.2	139	232	296	282	293	266
9.	Percentage increase in cropland harvested[18,19,*b]	-0.4	-22.3	-23.0	61.3	23.6	-2.9	-23.4	---
10.	Value of farms, dollars[18,19,64,79,81]	353,873,506	920,939,000[*i]	1,765,573,000[*k]	3,145,000,000	9,111,541,980	12,070,000,000	7,348,000,000	6,858,000,000
11.	Value of farms, percent increase[18,19]	-15.4	160.3[*i]	91.7[*k]	78.1	189.7	32.5	-39.1	-6.7
12.	Average value per farm, dollars[18,19,64,73,76]	2,359	7,416[*i]	23,719[*k]	74,000	290,454	381,817	268,630	214,312
13.	Farms operated by owners[21,22,23,24,25,26,27,65,77,*a]	60,312	74,394	56,019[*g]	35,504[*g]	27,118	27,750[*g]	23,664[*g]	---
14.	Value of livestock on farms, dollars[28,29,30,36,76,83,*a]	60,646,142	147,861,044	197,452,676	246,352,000	372,655,000	411,482,000	410,304,000	637,067,000
15.	Average value of livestock per farm, dollars[19,28,29,30,36]	404	1,191	2,653	5,828	11,879	13,010	15,002	18,737
16.	Production of cotton in bales[28,29,30,67,74,83]	717,713[*f]	607,186	479,298	521,000	470,675	788,360	921,867	868,000[*l,m]
17.	Percent of total production of cotton[28,29,30]	6.3[*f]	3.9	3.4	5.1	4.4	6.9	6.9	7.5

GENERAL AGRICULTURE STATISTICS, 1850-1990									
LOUISIANA									
Item No.		1940	1950	1960	1970	1978	1982	1987	1990
18.	Production of wheat in bushels[31,32,35,36,69,74,84]	601	---	709,068	957,000	400,487	13,515,660	4,654,627	10,850,000
19.	Percent of total production of wheat[31,32,33,35,36]	.0001	---	.0672	.0698	.0249	.5695	.2467	.5330
20.	Production of corn in bushels[36,37,38,39,70,74,85]	22,444,412	13,030,057	17,490,000	4,998,000	1,991,356	2,769,934	19,097,307	12,540,000
21.	Percent of total production of corn[36,37,38,39]	1.0	0.5	0.4	0.1	j	*j	0.3	0.2
22.	Production of oats in bushels[31,35,36,71,80,86]	1,455,521	1,225,671	1,843,835	1,872,000	---	---	37,050,000	40,800,000
23.	Percent of total production of oats[31,35,36]	0.2	0.1	0.2	0.2	---	---	11.8	10.9
24.	Production of soybeans in bushels[36,40,41,72,74,76,87]	198,317[*h]	303,225	4,326,633	37,980,000	74,258,151	67,702,197	40,524,474	33,600,000
25.	Percent of total production of soybeans[36,40,41]	.2264	.1427	.8391	3.3798	4.3119	3.4021	2.2047	1.7438
26.	Production of hay crops in tons[31,34,42,43,44,74,76,88]	388,978	333,684	529,700	606,000	683,284	742,992	717,887	781,000[*n]
27.	Percent of total production of hay crops[31,34,42,43,44]	0.5	0.4	0.5	0.5	0.5	0.6	0.6	0.5[*c]

[a] See the Glossary of Terms for changing definitions, i.e. farm, improved land, cropland harvested, farm owners, and livestock.
[b] Prior to 1924, the data relate to the total acreage of crops for which figures are available, except for 1920 when 14,502,932 acres of corn cut for forage were excluded (as most of this was probably duplicated in the acreage of corn harvested for grain).
[c] Percentage computed by compiler from data herein. See endnotes for source of data.
[d] Values in gold, one-fifth less than currency values.
[e] Managers included with owners.
[f] Running square bales, counting round as half bales.
[g] Census listed the number of full and part time owners separately. Compiler added the two numbers for the above figure.
[h] Includes quantity of beans harvested from acreage grown with other crops as well as that from acreage grown alone.
[i] The total value for each state for 1950 was based on the average value per acre for farms in the sample, for which value of land and buildings was reported. The average value per farm and per acre was based on the total value of all farms.
[j] Less than one-tenth of one percent.
[k] Based on a sampling of farms.
[l] Production ginned and to be ginned.
[m] 480-pound net weight bales.
[n] Census had two separate listings: hay, alfalfa, and alfalfa mixtures; and hay, all other. Compiler added the two listings for the above figure.

GENERAL AGRICULTURE STATISTICS, 1850-1990										
MAINE										
Item No.		1850	1860	1870	1880	1890	1900	1910	1920	1930
1.	Number of farms[18,19,68,73,76,82,*a]	46,760	55,698	59,804	64,309	62,013	59,299	60,016	48,227	39,006
2.	Acres in farms[18,19,68,73,76,82]	4,555,393	5,727,671	5,838,058	6,552,578	6,179,925	6,299,946	6,296,859	5,425,968	4,639,938
3.	Acres improved land in farms[20,*a]	2,039,596	2,704,133	2,917,793	3,484,908	3,044,666	2,386,889	2,360,657	1,977,329	---
4.	Cropland harvested, acres[18,19,73,76,*a,b]	---	---	---	1,536,711	1,521,766	1,543,277	1,588,065	1,530,027	1,304,014
5.	Percentage increase in number of farms[18,19]	---	19.1	7.4	7.5	-3.6	-4.4	1.2	-19.6	-19.1
6.	Percentage increase of land in farms[18,19]	---	25.7	1.9	12.2	-5.7	1.9	[*j]	-13.8	-14.5
7.	Percentage increase of improved land in farms[20]	---	32.6	7.9	19.4	-12.6	-21.6	-1.1	-16.2	---
8.	Average acreage per farm[18,19,66,73,76,78]	97.4	102.8	97.6	101.9	99.7	106.2	104.9	112.5	119.0
9.	Percentage increase in cropland harvested[18,19,*b]	---	---	---	---	-1.0	1.4	2.9	-3.7	-14.8
10.	Value of farms, dollars[18,19,64,79,81]	54,861,748	78,688,525	82,369,561	102,357,615	98,567,730	96,502,150	159,619,626	204,108,971	194,279,884
11.	Value of farms, percent increase[18,19]	---	43.4	4.7	24.3	-3.7	-2.1	65.4	27.9	-4.8
12.	Average value per farm, dollars[18,19,64,73,76]	1,173	1,413	1,377	1,592	1,589	1,627	2,660	4,232	4,981
13.	Farms operated by owners[21,22,23,24,25,26,27,65,77,*a]	---	---	---	61,528[*e]	58,643[*e]	55,607	56,454	45,437	36,748
14.	Value of livestock on farms, dollars[28,29,30,36,76,83,*a]	9,705,726	15,437,533	18,685,703[*d]	16,499,376	18,280,140	17,106,034	25,161,839	39,780,102	25,988,049
15.	Average value of livestock per farm, dollars[19,28,29,30,36]	208	277	312[*d]	257	295	289	419	825	666[*c]
16.	Production of cotton in bales[28,29,30,67,74,83]	---	---	---	---	---	---	---	---	---
17.	Percent of total production of cotton[28,29,30]	---	---	---	---	---	---	---	---	---

GENERAL AGRICULTURE STATISTICS, 1850-1990										
MAINE										
Item No.		1850	1860	1870	1880	1890	1900	1910	1920	1930
18.	Production of wheat in bushels[31,32,35,36,69,74,84]	296,259	233,876	278,793	665,714	79,826	116,720	85,119	261,185	39,474
19.	Percent of total production of wheat[31,32,33,35,36]	.2948	.1351	.0969	.1449	.0170	.0177	.0125	.0276	.0049
20.	Production of corn in bushels[36,37,38,39,70,74,85]	1,750,056	1,546,071	1,089,888	960,633	380,662	645,040	648,882	288,281	63,393
21.	Percent of total production of corn[36,37,38,39]	0.3	0.2	0.1	0.1	*j	*j	*j	*j	*j
22.	Production of oats in bushels[31,35,36,71,80,86]	2,181,037	2,988,939	2,351,354	2,265,575	3,668,909	3,799,435	4,232,309	8,600,617	3,942,774
23.	Percent of total production of oats[31,35,36]	1.5	1.7	0.8	0.6	0.5	0.4	0.4	0.8	0.4
24.	Production of soybeans in bushels[36,40,41,72,74,76,87]	---	---	---	---	---	---	---	2,096	322*h
25.	Percent of total production of soybeans[36,40,41]	---	---	---	---	---	---	---	.1846	.0037
26.	Production of hay crops in tons[31,34,42,43,44,74,76,88]	755,889	975,803	1,053,415	1,107,788	1,192,228	1,133,932	1,113,390	1,303,472	884,740
27.	Percent of total production of hay crops[31,34,42,43,44]	5.5*c	5.1	3.9	3.1	1.8	1.4	1.1	1.1	1.0

GENERAL AGRICULTURE STATISTICS, 1850-1990

MAINE

Item No.		1940	1950	1960	1970	1978	1982	1987	1990
1.	Number of farms[18,19,68,73,76,82,*a]	38,980	30,358	17,360	7,971	6,775	7,003	6,269	7,300
2.	Acres in farms[18,19,68,73,76,82]	4,223,297	4,181,613	3,081,987	1,760,000	1,500,390	1,468,674	1,342,588	1,450,000
3.	Acres improved land in farms[20,*a]	---	---	---	---	---	---	---	---
4.	Cropland harvested, acres[18,19,73,76,*a,b]	1,146,613	932,028	698,188	435,000	463,029	457,076	410,891	---
5.	Percentage increase in number of farms[18,19]	-0.1	-22.1	-42.8	-54.1	-15.0	3.4	-10.5	16.4
6.	Percentage increase of land in farms[18,19]	-9.0	-1.0	-26.3	-42.9	-14.8	-2.1	-8.6	8.0
7.	Percentage increase of improved land in farms[20]	---	---	---	---	---	---	---	---
8.	Average acreage per farm[18,19,66,73,76,78]	108.3	137.7	177.5	221	221	210	214	199
9.	Percentage increase in cropland harvested[18,19,*b]	-12.1	-18.7	-25.1	-37.7	6.4	-1.3	-10.1	---
10.	Value of farms, dollars[18,19,64,79,81]	124,082,841	226,518,000[*i]	256,157,000	283,000,000	799,632,925	1,053,000,000	1,321,000,000	1,984,000,000
11.	Value of farms, percent increase[18,19]	-36.1	82.6[*i]	13.1	10.5	183.0	31.7	25.5	50.2
12.	Average value per farm, dollars[18,19,64,73,76]	3,183	7,462[*i]	14,756	35,000	118,027	150,487	210,777	271,781
13.	Farms operated by owners[21,22,23,24,25,26,27,65,77,*a]	36,250	29,473	16,830[*g]	7,686[*g]	6,496	6,709[*g]	5,997[*g]	---
14.	Value of livestock on farms, dollars[28,29,30,36,76,83,*a]	16,870,129	30,392,754	37,638,175	---	287,117,000	256,578,000	247,656,000	219,895,000
15.	Average value of livestock per farm, dollars[19,28,29,30,36]	433	1,001	2,168	---	42,379	36,638	39,505	30,123
16.	Production of cotton in bales[28,29,30,67,74,83]	---	---	---	---	---	---	---	---
17.	Percent of total production of cotton[28,29,30]	---	---	---	---	---	---	---	---

GENERAL AGRICULTURE STATISTICS, 1850-1990

MAINE

Item No.		1940	1950	1960	1970	1978	1982	1987	1990
18.	Production of wheat in bushels[31,32,35,36,69,74,84]	28,756	---	8,453	---	41,475	35,394	25,012	---
19.	Percent of total production of wheat[31,32,33,35,36]	.0041	---	.0008	---	.0026	.0015	.0013	---
20.	Production of corn in bushels[36,37,38,39,70,74,85]	206,886	53,716	451,000	---	374,766	647,910	485,087	---
21.	Percent of total production of corn[36,37,38,39]	[*j]	[*j]	[*j]	---	[*j]	[*j]	[*j]	---
22.	Production of oats in bushels[31,35,36,71,80,86]	3,358,212	2,807,378	2,350,822	1,485,000	---	---	2,850,000	2,015,000
23.	Percent of total production of oats[31,35,36]	0.4	0.2	0.2	0.2	---	---	0.9	0.5
24.	Production of soybeans in bushels[36,40,41,72,74,76,87]	491[*h]	---	---	---	---	2,986	---	---
25.	Percent of total production of soybeans[36,40,41]	.0006	---	---	---	---	.0002	---	---
26.	Production of hay crops in tons[31,34,42,43,44,74,76,88]	746,225	619,969	563,121	408,000	367,396	414,555	393,393	420,000[*k]
27.	Percent of total production of hay crops[31,34,42,43,44]	0.9	0.7	0.5	0.3	0.3	0.3	0.3	0.3

[a] See the Glossary of Terms for changing definitions, i.e. farm, improved land, cropland harvested, farm owners, and livestock.
[b] Prior to 1924, the data relate to the total acreage of crops for which figures are available, except for 1920 when 14,502,932 acres of corn cut for forage were excluded (as most of this was probably duplicated in the acreage of corn harvested for grain).
[c] Percentage computed by compiler from data herein. See endnotes for source of data.
[d] Values in gold, one-fifth less than currency values.
[e] Managers included with owners.
[f] Running square bales, counting round as half bales.
[g] Census listed the number of full and part time owners separately. Compiler added the two numbers for the above figure.
[h] Includes quantity of beans harvested from acreage grown with other crops as well as that from acreage grown alone.
[i] The total value for each state for 1950 was based on the average value per acre for farms in the sample, for which value of land and buildings was reported. The average value per farm and per acre was based on the total value of all farms.
[j] Less than one-tenth of one percent.
[k] Census had two separate listings: hay, alfalfa, and alfalfa mixtures; and hay, all other. Compiler added the two listings for the above figure.

GENERAL AGRICULTURE STATISTICS, 1850-1990

MARYLAND

Item No.		1850	1860	1870	1880	1890	1900	1910	1920	1930
1.	Number of farms[18,19,68,73,76,82,*a]	21,860	25,494	27,000	40,517	40,798	46,012	48,923	47,908	43,203
2.	Acres in farms[18,19,68,73,76,82]	4,634,350	4,835,571	4,512,579	5,119,831	4,952,390	5,170,075	5,057,140	4,757,999	4,374,398
3.	Acres improved land in farms[20,*a]	2,797,905	3,002,267	2,914,007	3,342,700	3,412,908	3,516,352	3,354,767	3,136,728	---
4.	Cropland harvested, acres[18,19,73,76,*a,b]	---	---	---	1,680,192	1,662,333	1,940,093	1,931,972	1,991,030	1,741,615
5.	Percentage increase in number of farms[18,19]	---	16.6	5.9	50.1	0.7	12.8	6.3	-2.1	-9.8
6.	Percentage increase of land in farms[18,19]	---	4.3	-6.7	13.5	-3.3	4.4	-2.2	-5.9	-8.1
7.	Percentage increase of improved land in farms[20]	---	7.3	-2.9	14.7	2.1	3.0	-4.6	-6.5	---
8.	Average acreage per farm[18,19,66,73,76,78]	212.0	189.7	167.1	126.4	121.4	112.4	103.4	99.3	101.3
9.	Percentage increase in cropland harvested[18,19,*b]	---	---	---	---	-1.1	16.7	-0.4	3.1	-12.5
10.	Value of farms, dollars[18,19,64,79,81]	87,178,545	145,973,677	136,295,747	165,503,341	175,058,550	175,178,310	241,737,123	386,596,850	356,170,168
11.	Value of farms, percent increase[18,19]	---	67.4	-6.6	21.4	5.8	0.1	38.0	59.9	-7.9
12.	Average value per farm, dollars[18,19,64,73,76]	3,988	5,726	5,048	4,085	4,291	3,807	4,941	8,070	8,244
13.	Farms operated by owners[21,22,23,24,25,26,27,65,77,*a]	---	---	---	27,978[*e]	28,154[*e]	29,513	33,519	32,805	30,823
14.	Value of livestock on farms, dollars[28,29,30,36,76,83,*a]	7,997,634	14,667,853	14,746,958[*d]	15,865,728	19,194,320	20,855,877	32,570,134	48,071,250	43,303,575
15.	Average value of livestock per farm, dollars[19,28,29,30,36]	366	575	546[*d]	392	470	454	666	1,003	1,002
16.	Production of cotton in bales[28,29,30,67,74,83]	---	---	---	---	---	---	---	---	---
17.	Percent of total production of cotton[28,29,30]	---	---	---	---	---	---	---	---	---

GENERAL AGRICULTURE STATISTICS, 1850-1990										
MARYLAND										
Item No.		1850	1860	1870	1880	1890	1900	1910	1920	1930
18.	Production of wheat in bushels[31,32,35,36,69,74,84]	4,494,680	6,103,480	5,774,503	8,004,864	8,348,177	9,671,800	9,463,457	9,620,526	9,095,169
19.	Percent of total production of wheat[31,32,33,35,36]	4.4729	3.5259	2.0068	1.7421	1.7824	1.4687	1.3848	1.0176	1.1360
20.	Production of corn in bushels[36,37,38,39,70,74,85]	10,749,858	13,449,422	11,701,817	15,968,533	14,928,147	19,766,510	17,911,436	21,083,076	14,543,218
21.	Percent of total production of corn[36,37,38,39]	1.8	1.6	1.5	0.9	0.7	0.7	0.7	0.9	0.7
22.	Production of oats in bushels[31,35,36,71,80,86]	2,242,151	3,959,298	3,221,643	1,794,872	2,019,658	1,109,560	1,160,663	1,082,994	1,164,583
23.	Percent of total production of oats[31,35,36]	1.5	2.3	1.1	0.4	0.2	0.1	0.1	0.1	0.1
24.	Production of soybeans in bushels[36,40,41,72,74,76,87]	---	---	---	---	---	---	---	11,572	54,363[*h]
25.	Percent of total production of soybeans[36,40,41]	---	---	---	---	---	---	---	46.3510	.6277
26.	Production of hay crops in tons[31,34,42,43,44,74,76,88]	157,956	191,744	223,119	264,567	494,157	415,197	477,711	573,131	474,940
27.	Percent of total production of hay crops[31,34,42,43,44]	1.1[*c]	1.0	0.8	0.8	0.7	0.5	0.5	0.5	0.6

Item No.	GENERAL AGRICULTURE STATISTICS, 1850-1990 MARYLAND	1940	1950	1960	1970	1978	1982	1987	1990
1.	Number of farms[18,19,68,73,76,82,*a]	42,110	36,107	25,122	17,181	15,540	16,183	14,776	15,200
2.	Acres in farms[18,19,63,73,76,82]	4,197,827	4,055,529	3,456,769	2,803,000	2,614,439	2,557,728	2,396,629	2,250,000
3.	Acres improved land in farms[20,*a]	---	---	---	---	---	---	---	---
4.	Cropland harvested, acres[18,19,73,76,*a,b]	1,608,856	1,531,421	1,455,921	1,323,000	1,477,316	1,528,994	1,346,913	---
5.	Percentage increase in number of farms[18,19]	-2.5	-14.3	-30.4	-31.6	-9.6	4.1	-8.7	2.9
6.	Percentage increase of land in farms[18,19]	-4.0	-3.4	-14.8	-18.9	-6.7	-2.2	-6.3	-6.1
7.	Percentage increase of improved land in farms[20]	---	---	---	---	---	---	---	---
8.	Average acreage per farm[18,19,66,73,76,78]	99.7	112.3	137.6	163	168	158	162	147
9.	Percentage increase in cropland harvested[18,19,*b]	-7.6	-4.8	-4.9	-9.1	11.7	3.5	-11.9	---
10.	Value of farms, dollars[18,19,64,79,81]	273,980,352	507,225,000[*i,j]	982,152,000[*j]	1,793,000,000	4,645,216,800	5,378,000,000	5,419,000,000	5,206,000,000
11.	Value of farms, percent increase[18,19]	-23.1	85.1[*i,j]	93.6[*j]	82.6	159.1	15.8	0.8	-3.9
12.	Average value per farm, dollars[18,19,64,73,76]	6,506	14,048[*i,j]	39,095[*j]	104,000	298,920	332,301	366,788	342,500
13.	Farms operated by owners[21,22,23,24,25,26,27,65,77,*a]	30,458	29,058	20,916[*g]	14,796[*g]	13,370	14,191[*g]	13,068[*g]	---
14.	Value of livestock on farms, dollars[28,29,30,36,76,83,*a]	31,456,509	71,892,868	88,980,601	105,168,000	517,434,000	689,815,000	736,006,000	828,464,000
15.	Average value of livestock per farm, dollars[19,28,29,30,36]	747	1,991	3,542	6,121	33,297	42,626	49,811	54,504
16.	Production of cotton in bales[28,29,30,67,74,83]	---	---	---	----	---	---	---	---
17.	Percent of total production of cotton[28,29,30]	---	---	---	---	---	---	---	---

GENERAL AGRICULTURE STATISTICS, 1850-1990

MARYLAND

Item No.		1940	1950	1960	1970	1978	1982	1987	1990
18.	Production of wheat in bushels[31,32,35,36,69,74,84]	6,581,115	5,719,200	3,708,867	4,181,000	2,589,498	5,635,641	6,766,273	8,600,000
19.	Percent of total production of wheat[31,32,33,35,36]	.9284	.5682	.3512	.3051	.16108	.2375	.3586	.4224
20.	Production of corn in bushels[36,37,38,39,70,74,85]	15,449,757	16,761,266	26,838,000	40,172,000	55,103,713	62,845,256	31,941,714	44,000,000
21.	Percent of total production of corn[36,37,38,39]	0.7	0.6	0.6	1.0	0.8	0.8	0.5	0.6
22.	Production of oats in bushels[31,35,36,71,80,86]	827,623	1,224,576	2,147,604	1,456,000	---	873,176	896,000	1,230,000
23.	Percent of total production of oats[31,35,36]	0.1	0.1	0.2	0.2	---	0.2	0.3	0.3
24.	Production of soybeans in bushels[36,40,41,72,74,76,87]	179,789[a,h]	928,440	4,439,382	5,112,000	11,434,269	11,290,198	9,352,369	16,500,000
25.	Percent of total production of soybeans[36,40,41]	.2053	.4370	.8610	.4549	.6634	.5673	.5088	.8563
26.	Production of hay crops in tons[31,34,42,43,44,74,76,88]	519,699	628,583	768,810	735,000	587,186	533,939	593,854	629,000[a,l]
27.	Percent of total production of hay crops[31,34,42,43,44]	0.6	0.7	0.7	0.6	0.4	0.4	0.5	0.4[a,c]

a See the Glossary of Terms for changing definitions, i.e. farm, improved land, cropland harvested, farm owners, and livestock.
b Prior to 1924, the data relate to the total acreage of crops for which figures are available, except for 1920 when 14,502,932 acres of corn cut for forage were excluded (as most of this was probably duplicated in the acreage of corn harvested for grain).
c Percentage computed by compiler from data herein. See endnotes for source of data.
d Values in gold, one-fifth less than currency values.
e Managers included with owners.
f Running square bales, counting round as half bales.
g Census listed the number of full and part time owners separately. Compiler added the two numbers for the above figure.
h Includes quantity of beans harvested from acreage grown with other crops as well as that from acreage grown alone.
i The total value for each state for 1950 was based on the average value per acre for farms in the sample, for which value of land and buildings was reported. The average value per farm and per acre was based on the total value of all farms.
j Based on a sampling of farms.
k Less than one-tenth of one percent.
l Census had two separate listings: hay, alfalfa, and alfalfa mixtures; and hay, all other. Compiler added the two listings for the above figure.

GENERAL AGRICULTURE STATISTICS, 1850-1990										
MASSACHUSETTS										
Item No.		1850	1860	1870	1880	1890	1900	1910	1920	1930
1.	Number of farms[18,19,68,73,76,82,*a]	34,069	35,601	26,500	38,406	34,374	37,715	36,917	32,001	25,598
2.	Acres in farms[18,19,68,73,76,82]	3,356,012	3,338,724	2,730,283	3,359,079	2,988,282	3,147,064	2,875,941	2,494,477	2,005,461
3.	Acres improved land in farms[20,*a]	2,133,436	2,155,512	1,736,221	2,128,311	1,657,024	1,292,132	1,164,501	908,834	---
4.	Cropland harvested, acres[18,19,73,76,*a,b]	---	---	---	778,564	719,652	735,134	654,844	562,462	474,167
5.	Percentage increase in number of farms[18,19]	---	4.5	-25.6	44.9	-10.5	9.7	-2.1	-13.3	-20.0
6.	Percentage increase of land in farms[18,19]	---	-0.5	-18.2	23.0	-10.7	5.0	-8.6	-13.3	-19.6
7.	Percentage increase of improved land in farms[20]	---	1.0	-19.5	22.6	-22.1	-22.0	-9.9	-22.0	---
8.	Average acreage per farm[18,19,66,73,76,78]	98.5	93.8	103.0	87.5	87.2	83.4	77.9	77.9	78.3
9.	Percentage increase in cropland harvested[18,19,*b]	---	---	---	---	-7.6	2.2	-10.9	-14.1	-15.7
10.	Value of farms, dollars[18,19,64,79,81]	109,076,347	123,255,948	93,146,227	146,197,415	127,538,284	158,019,290	194,168,765	247,587,831	261,222,390
11.	Value of farms, percent increase[18,19]	---	13.0	-24.4	57.0	-12.8	23.9	22.9	27.5	5.5
12.	Average value per farm, dollars[18,19,64,73,76]	3,202	3,462	3,515	3,807	3,710	4,190	5,260	7,737	10,205
13.	Farms operated by owners[21,22,23,24,25,26,27,65,77,*a]	---	---	---	35,266[*e]	31,177[*e]	32,581	32,075	28,087	23,198
14.	Value of livestock on farms, dollars[28,29,30,36,76,83,*a]	9,647,710	12,737,744	13,639,383[*d]	12,957,004	14,200,178	15,798,464	20,741,366	33,524,157	23,842,014
15.	Average value of livestock per farm, dollars[19,28,29,30,36]	283	358	515[*d]	337	413	419	562	1,048	931[*c]
16.	Production of cotton in bales[28,29,30,67,74,83]	---	---	---	---	---	---	---	---	---
17.	Percent of total production of cotton[28,29,30]	---	---	---	---	---	---	---	---	---

GENERAL AGRICULTURE STATISTICS, 1850-1990										
MASSACHUSETTS										
Item No.		1850	1860	1870	1880	1890	1900	1910	1920	1930
18.	Production of wheat in bushels[31,32,35,36,69,74,84]	31,211	119,783	34,648	15,768	1,813	1,750	2,404	33,253	3,625
19.	Percent of total production of wheat[31,32,33,35,36]	.0311	.0692	.0120	.0034	.0004	.0003	.0004	.0035	.0005
20.	Production of corn in bushels[36,37,38,39,70,74,85]	2,345,490	2,157,063	1,397,807	1,797,768	1,330,101	1,539,980	2,029,381	1,515,933	349,387
21.	Percent of total production of corn[36,37,38,39]	0.4	0.2	0.2	0.1	0.1	*j	0.1	0.1	*j
22.	Production of oats in bushels[31,35,36,71,80,86]	1,165,146	1,180,075	797,664	645,159	388,819	240,990	268,500	287,881	39,704
23.	Percent of total production of oats[31,35,36]	0.8	0.7	0.3	0.2	*j	*j	*j	*j	*j
24.	Production of soybeans in bushels[36,40,41,72,74,76,87]	---	---	---	---	---	---	53	573	87*h
25.	Percent of total production of soybeans[36,40,41]	---	---	---	---	---	---	.2123	.0505	.0010
26.	Production of hay crops in tons[31,34,42,43,44,74,76,88]	651,807	665,331	597,455	684,679	793,167	848,950	832,727	820,905	421,070
27.	Percent of total production of hay crops[31,34,42,43,44]	4.7*c	3.5	2.2	1.9	1.2	1.1	0.9	0.7	0.5

GENERAL AGRICULTURE STATISTICS, 1850-1990									
MASSACHUSETTS									
Item No.		1940	1950	1960	1970	1978	1982	1987	1990
1.	Number of farms[18,19,68,73,76,82,*a]	31,897	22,220	11,179	5,703	4,946	5,401	6,216	6,900
2.	Acres in farms[18,19,68,73,76,82]	1,937,963	1,660,389	1,142,341	701,000	617,359	612,819	615,185	680,000
3.	Acres improved land in farms[20,*a]	---	---	---	---	---	---	---	---
4.	Cropland harvested, acres[18,19,73,76,*a,b]	456,267	376,036	290,682	153,000	197,405	197,769	194,874	---
5.	Percentage increase in number of farms[18,19]	24.6	-30.3	-49.7	-49.0	-13.3	9.1	15.1	11.0
6.	Percentage increase of land in farms[18,19]	-3.4	-14.3	-31.2	-38.6	-11.9	-0.7	0.4	10.5
7.	Percentage increase of improved land in farms[20]	---	---	---	---	---	---	---	---
8.	Average acreage per farm[18,19,66,73,76,78]	60.8	74.7	102.2	123	125	113	99	99
9.	Percentage increase in cropland harvested[18,19,*b]	-3.8	-17.6	-22.7	-47.4	29.0	0.2	-1.5	---
10.	Value of farms, dollars[18,19,64,79,81]	212,014,287	314,710,000[*i]	354,285,000	396,000,000	906,794,694	1,111,000,000	2,154,000,000	2,571,000,000
11.	Value of farms, percent increase[18,19]	-18.8	48.4[*i]	12.6	11.8	129.0	22.5	93.9	19.4
12.	Average value per farm, dollars[18,19,64,73,76]	6,647	14,163[*i]	31,692	69,000	183,339	205,677	346,530	372,609
13.	Farms operated by owners[21,22,23,24,25,26,27,65,77,*a]	29,072	21,206	10,667[*g]	5,413[*g]	4,625	5,002[*g]	5,762[*g]	---
14.	Value of livestock on farms, dollars[28,29,30,36,76,83,*a]	19,721,839	40,028,165	41,342,112	---	111,915,000	142,008,000	124,609,000	115,937,000
15.	Average value of livestock per farm, dollars[19,28,29,30,36]	618	1,801	3,698	---	22,627	26,293	20,047	16,803
16.	Production of cotton in bales[28,29,30,67,74,83]	---	---	---	---	---	---	---	---
17.	Percent of total production of cotton[28,29,30]	---	---	---	---	---	---	---	---

Item No.	GENERAL AGRICULTURE STATISTICS, 1850-1990 MASSACHUSETTS	1940	1950	1960	1970	1978	1982	1987	1990
18.	Production of wheat in bushels[31,32,35,36,69,74,84]	5,503	---	8,459	---	---	1,276	6,056	8,600
19.	Percent of total production of wheat[31,32,33,35,36]	.0008	.0008	.0008	---	---	.0001	.0003	.0004
20.	Production of corn in bushels[36,37,38,39,70,74,85]	311,229	214,271	1,728,000	---	401,871	591,680	626,829	---
21.	Percent of total production of corn[36,37,38,39]	*j	*j	*j	---	*j	*j	*j	---
22.	Production of oats in bushels[31,35,36,71,80,86]	66,924	45,990	42,983	---	---	26,675	8,175	---
23.	Percent of total production of oats[31,35,36]	*j	*j	*j	---	---	*j	*j	---
24.	Production of soybeans in bushels[36,40,41,72,74,76,87]	668*h	6	---	---	---	*k	---	---
25.	Percent of total production of soybeans[36,40,41]	.0008	.0000	---	---	---	---	---	---
26.	Production of hay crops in tons[31,34,42,43,44,74,76,88]	410,845	398,522	365,857	239,000	244,457	241,584	250,559	237,000*l
27.	Percent of total production of hay crops[31,34,42,43,44]	0.5	0.4	0.3	0.2	0.2	0.2	0.2	0.2*c

[a] See the Glossary of Terms for changing definitions, i.e. farm, improved land, cropland harvested, farm owners, and livestock.
[b] Prior to 1924, the data relate to the total acreage of crops for which figures are available, except for 1920 when 14,502,932 acres of corn cut for forage were excluded (as most of this was probably duplicated in the acreage of corn harvested for grain).
[c] Percentage computed by compiler from data herein. See endnotes for source of data.
[d] Values in gold, one-fifth less than currency values.
[e] Managers included with owners.
[f] Running square bales, counting round as half bales.
[g] Census listed the number of full and part time owners separately. Compiler added the two numbers for the above figure.
[h] Includes quantity of beans harvested from acreage grown with other crops as well as that from acreage grown alone.
[i] The total value for each state for 1950 was based on the average value per acre for farms in the sample, for which value of land and buildings was reported. The average value per farm and per acre was based on the total value of all farms.
[j] Less than one-tenth of one percent.
[k] Withheld to avoid disclosing data for individual farms.
[l] Census had two separate listings: hay, alfalfa, and alfalfa mixtures; and hay, all other. Compiler added the two listings for the above figure.

GENERAL AGRICULTURE STATISTICS, 1850-1990

MICHIGAN

Item No.		1850	1860	1870	1880	1890	1900	1910	1920	1930
1.	Number of farms[18,19,68,73,76,82,*a]	34,089	62,422	98,786	154,008	172,344	203,261	206,960	196,447	169,372
2.	Acres in farms[18,19,68,73,76,82]	4,383,890	7,030,834	10,019,142	13,807,240	14,785,636	17,561,698	18,940,614	19,032,961	17,118,951
3.	Acres improved land in farms[20,*a]	1,929,110	3,476,296	5,096,939	8,296,862	9,865,350	11,799,250	12,832,078	12,925,521	---
4.	Cropland harvested, acres[18,19,73,76,*a,b]	---	---	---	4,764,811	6,116,504	7,741,175	8,198,578	9,169,921	7,738,221
5.	Percentage increase in number of farms[18,19]	---	83.1	58.3	55.9	11.9	17.9	1.8	-5.1	-13.8
6.	Percentage increase of land in farms[18,19]	---	60.4	42.5	37.8	7.1	18.8	7.9	0.5	-10.1
7.	Percentage increase of improved land in farms[20]	---	80.2	46.6	62.8	18.9	19.6	8.8	0.7	---
8.	Average acreage per farm[18,19,66,73,76,78]	128.6	112.6	101.4	89.7	85.8	86.4	91.5	96.9	101.1
9.	Percentage increase in cropland harvested[18,19,*b]	---	---	---	---	28.4	26.6	5.9	11.8	-15.6
10.	Value of farms, dollars[18,19,64,79,81]	51,872,446	160,836,495	318,592,463	499,103,181	556,190,670	582,517,710	901,138,299	1,436,686,210	1,160,651,607
11.	Value of farms, percent increase[18,19]	---	210.1	98.1	56.7	11.4	4.7	54.7	59.4	-19.2
12.	Average value per farm, dollars[18,19,64,73,76]	1,522	2,577	3,225	3,241	3,227	2,866	4,354	7,313	6,853
13.	Farms operated by owners[21,22,23,24,25,26,27,65,77,*a]	---	---	---	138,597[*e]	148,208[*e]	168,814	172,310	159,406	141,647
14.	Value of livestock on farms, dollars[28,29,30,36,76,83,*a]	8,008,734	23,714,771	39,847,895[*d]	55,720,113	69,564,985	79,042,644	137,803,795	204,258,632	162,105,215
15.	Average value of livestock per farm, dollars[19,28,29,30,36]	235	380	403[*d]	362	404	389	666	1,040	957[*c]
16.	Production of cotton in bales[28,29,30,67,74,83]	---	---	---	---	---	---	---	---	---
17.	Percent of total production of cotton[28,29,30]	---	---	---	---	---	---	---	---	---

GENERAL AGRICULTURE STATISTICS, 1850-1990										
MICHIGAN										
Item No.		1850	1860	1870	1880	1890	1900	1910	1920	1930
18.	Production of wheat in bushels[31,32,35,36,69,74,84]	4,925,889	8,336,368	16,265,773	35,532,543	24,771,171	20,535,140	16,025,791	20,411,825	13,711,136
19.	Percent of total production of wheat[31,32,33,35,36]	4.9021	4.8158	5.3053	7.7332	5.2888	3.1183	2.3451	2.1591	1.7125
20.	Production of corn in bushels[36,37,38,39,70,74,85]	5,641,420	12,444,676	14,086,238	32,461,452	28,785,579	44,584,130	52,906,842	45,088,912	15,635,217
21.	Percent of total production of corn[36,37,38,39]	1.0	1.5	1.9	1.8	1.4	1.7	2.1	1.9	0.7
22.	Production of oats in bushels[31,35,36,71,80,86]	2,866,056	4,036,980	8,954,466	18,190,793	36,961,193	36,338,145	43,869,502	36,956,425	33,523,336
23.	Percent of total production of oats[31,35,36]	2.0	2.3	3.2	4.5	4.6	3.9	4.4	3.5	3.4
24.	Production of soybeans in bushels[36,40,41,72,74,76,87]	---	---	---	---	---	---	---	78,515	13,251[*g]
25.	Percent of total production of soybeans[36,40,41]	---	---	---	---	---	---	---	6.9168	.1530
26.	Production of hay crops in tons[31,34,42,43,44,74,76,88]	404,934	768,256	1,290,923	1,393,845	2,385,155	2,703,214	3,634,196	5,778,578	3,495,495
27.	Percent of total production of hay crops[31,34,42,43,44]	2.9[*c]	4.0	4.7	4.0	3.6	3.4	3.7	4.7	4.1

GENERAL AGRICULTURE STATISTICS, 1850-1990									
MICHIGAN									
Item No.		1940	1950	1960	1970	1978	1982	1987	1990
1.	Number of farms[18,19,68,73,76,82,*a]	187,589	155,589	111,817	77,946	60,426	58,661	51,172	54,000
2.	Acres in farms[18,19,68,73,76,82]	18,037,995	17,269,992	14,782,507	11,901,000	11,038,419	10,942,172	10,316,861	10,800,000
3.	Acres improved land in farms[20,*a]	---	---	---	---	---	---	---	---
4.	Cropland harvested, acres[18,19,73,76,*a,b]	7,862,858	7,797,346	7,154,811	5,297,000	6,774,229	7,255,909	6,172,468	---
5.	Percentage increase in number of farms[18,19]	10.8	-17.1	-28.1	-30.3	-22.5	-2.9	-12.8	5.5
6.	Percentage increase of land in farms[18,19]	5.4	-4.3	-14.4	-19.5	-7.2	-0.9	-5.7	4.7
7.	Percentage increase of improved land in farms[20]	---	---	---	---	---	---	---	---
8.	Average acreage per farm[18,19,66,73,76,78]	96.2	111.0	132.2	153	183	187	202	196
9.	Percentage increase in cropland harvested[18,19,*b]	1.6	-0.8	-8.2	-26.0	27.9	7.1	-14.9	---
10.	Value of farms, dollars[18,19,64,79,81]	912,545,223	1,701,440,000[*i]	2,855,261,000	3,883,000,000	10,584,882,846	13,389,000,000	10,034,000,000	9,841,000,000
11.	Value of farms, percent increase[18,19]	-21.4	86.4[*i]	67.8	36.0	173.0	26.5	-25.1	-1.9
12.	Average value per farm, dollars[18,19,64,73,76]	4,865	10,935[*i]	25,535	50,000	175,171	228,238	196,065	182,241
13.	Farms operated by owners[21,22,23,24,25,26,27,65,77,*a]	154,928	141,145	103,594	73,698[*g]	56,595	55,012[*g]	48,089[*g]	---
14.	Value of livestock on farms, dollars[28,29,30,36,76,83,*a]	136,685,230	262,833,558	297,330,001	---	916,517,000	1,223,652,000	1,272,276,000	1,398,322,000
15.	Average value of livestock per farm, dollars[19,28,29,30,36]	729	1,689	2,659	---	15,168	20,860	24,863	25,895
16.	Production of cotton in bales[28,29,30,67,74,83]	---	---	---	---	---	---	---	---
17.	Percent of total production of cotton[28,29,30]	---	---	---	---	---	---	---	---

GENERAL AGRICULTURE STATISTICS, 1850-1990									
MICHIGAN									
Item No.		1940	1950	1960	1970	1978	1982	1987	1990
18.	Production of wheat in bushels[31,32,35,36,69,74,84]	15,804,411	31,710,009	34,597,340	22,035,000	14,669,977	20,764,229	16,465,394	33,920,000
19.	Percent of total production of wheat[31,32,33,35,36]	2.2296	3.1503	3.2765	1.6081	.9126	.8749	.8725	1.6662
20.	Production of corn in bushels[36,37,38,39,70,74,85]	47,287,199	64,393,111	121,240,000	114,076,000	184,697,964	256,473,754	189,779,819	222,610,000
21.	Percent of total production of corn[36,37,38,39]	2.0	2.3	2.8	2.8	2.7	3.4	2.8	3.0
22.	Production of oats in bushels[31,35,36,71,80,86]	41,102,609	44,870,017	36,282,364	27,086,000	---	24,770,648	17,100,000	20,100,000
23.	Percent of total production of oats[31,35,36]	4.7	3.9	3.6	3.0	---	4.9	5.5	5.4
24.	Production of soybeans in bushels[36,40,41,72,74,76,87]	824,505[a,h]	1,279,178	5,417,149	13,624,000	21,174,856	34,307,197	36,267,622	38,880,000
25.	Percent of total production of soybeans[36,40,41]	.9413	.6021	1.0506	1.2124	1.2296	1.7240	1.9732	2.1078
26.	Production of hay crops in tons[31,34,42,43,44,74,76,88]	3,378,166	2,868,700	3,477,938	3,260,000	3,599,083	3,476,731	3,323,175	5,205,000[a,j]
27.	Percent of total production of hay crops[31,34,42,43,44]	4.1	3.2	3.3	2.6	2.8	2.7	2.6	3.5

[a] See the Glossary of Terms for changing definitions, i.e. farm, improved land, cropland harvested, farm owners, and livestock.
[b] Prior to 1924, the data relate to the total acreage of crops for which figures are available, except for 1920 when 14,502,932 acres of corn cut for forage were excluded (as most of this was probably duplicated in the acreage of corn harvested for grain).
[c] Percentage computed by compiler from data herein. See endnotes for source of data.
[d] Values in gold, one-fifth less than currency values.
[e] Managers included with owners.
[f] Running square bales, counting round as half bales.
[g] Census listed the number of full and part time owners separately. Compiler added the two numbers for the above figure.
[h] Includes quantity of beans harvested from acreage grown with other crops as well as that from acreage grown alone.
[i] The total value for each state for 1950 was based on the average value per acre for farms in the sample, for which value of land and buildings was reported. The average value per farm and per acre was based on the total value of all farms.
[j] Census had two separate listings: hay, alfalfa, and alfalfa mixtures; and hay, all other. Compiler added the two listings for the above figure.

GENERAL AGRICULTURE STATISTICS, 1850-1990										
MINNESOTA										
Item No.		1850	1860	1870	1880	1890	1900	1910	1920	1930
1.	Number of farms[18,19,68,73,76,82,*a]	157	18,181	46,500	92,386	116,851	154,659	156,137	178,478	185,255
2.	Acres in farms[18,19,68,73,76,82]	28,881	2,711,968	6,483,828	13,403,019	18,663,645	26,248,498	27,675,823	30,221,758	30,913,367
3.	Acres improved land in farms[20,*a]	5,035	556,250	2,322,102	7,246,693	11,127,953	18,442,585	19,643,533	21,481,710	---
4.	Cropland harvested, acres[18,19,73,76,*a,b]	---	---	---	5,287,758	9,419,785	15,119,570	14,731,464	16,364,914	18,445,306
5.	Percentage increase in number of farms[18,19]	---	[*k]	155.8	98.7	26.5	32.4	1.0	14.3	3.8
6.	Percentage increase of land in farms[18,19]	---	[*k]	139.1	106.7	39.2	40.6	5.4	9.2	2.3
7.	Percentage increase of improved land in farms[20]	---	10,948[*c]	317.5	212.1	53.6	65.7	6.5	9.4	---
8.	Average acreage per farm[18,19,66,73,76,78]	183.9	149.2	139.4	145.1	159.7	169.7	177.3	169.3	166.9
9.	Percentage increase in cropland harvested[18,19,*b]	---	---	---	---	78.1	60.5	-2.6	11.1	12.7
10.	Value of farms, dollars[18,19,64,79,81]	161,948	27,505,922	78,277,954	193,724,260	340,059,470	669,522,315	1,262,441,426	3,301,168,325	2,125,093,278
11.	Value of farms, percent increase[18,19]	---	[*k]	184.6	147.5	75.5	96.9	88.6	161.5	-35.6
12.	Average value per farm, dollars[18,19,64,73,76]	1,032	1,513	1,683	2,097	2,910	4,329	8,085	18,496	11,471
13.	Farms operated by owners[21,22,23,24,25,26,27,65,77,*a]	---	---	---	83,933[*e]	101,717[*e]	126,809	122,104	132,744	126,570
14.	Value of livestock on farms, dollars[28,29,30,36,76,83,*a]	92,859	3,642,841	16,095,073[*d]	31,904,821	57,725,683	89,063,097	161,641,146	305,163,825	300,970,571
15.	Average value of livestock per farm, dollars[19,28,29,30,36]	591	200	346[*d]	345	494	576	1,035	1,710	1,625[*c]
16.	Production of cotton in bales[28,29,30,67,74,83]	---	---	---	---	---	---	---	---	---
17.	Percent of total production of cotton[28,29,30]	---	---	---	---	---	---	---	---	---

GENERAL AGRICULTURE STATISTICS, 1850-1990										
MINNESOTA										
Item No.		1850	1860	1870	1880	1890	1900	1910	1920	1930
18.	Production of wheat in bushels[31,32,35,36,69,74,84]	1,401	2,186,993	18,866,073	34,601,030	52,300,247	95,278,660	57,094,412	37,616,384	19,760,092
19.	Percent of total production of wheat[31,32,33,35,36]	.0014	1.2634	6.5565	7.5304	11.1663	14.4683	8.3547	3.9789	2.4680
20.	Production of corn in bushels[36,37,38,39,70,74,85]	16,725	2,941,952	4,743,117	14,831,741	24,696,446	47,256,920	67,897,051	84,786,096	104,419,048
21.	Percent of total production of corn[36,37,38,39]	*j	0.3	0.6	0.8	1.2	1.8	2.7	3.6	4.9
22.	Production of oats in bushels[31,35,36,71,80,86]	30,582	2,176,002	10,678,261	23,382,158	49,958,791	74,054,150	93,897,717	89,108,151	126,221,063
23.	Percent of total production of oats[31,35,36]	*j	1.3	3.8	5.7	6.2	7.8	9.3	8.4	12.7
24.	Production of soybeans in bushels[36,40,41,72,74,76,87]	---	---	---	---	---	---	---	2,909	3,380
25.	Percent of total production of soybeans[36,40,41]	---	---	---	---	---	---	---	.2563	.0390
26.	Production of hay crops in tons[31,34,42,43,44,74,76,88]	2,019	179,482	695,053	1,637,109	3,135,241	4,339,328	6,037,527	7,915,689	5,549,722
27.	Percent of total production of hay crops[31,34,42,43,44]	*c,j	0.9	2.6	4.7	4.7	5.5	6.2	6.4	6.5

GENERAL AGRICULTURE STATISTICS, 1850-1990									
MINNESOTA									
Item No.		1940	1950	1960	1970	1978	1982	1987	1990
1.	Number of farms[18,19,68,73,76,82,*a]	197,351	179,101	145,662	110,747	98,671	94,382	85,079	89,000
2.	Acres in farms[18,19,68,73,76,82]	32,606,962	32,883,163	30,796,097	28,845,000	28,459,790	27,708,456	26,573,819	30,000,000
3.	Acres improved land in farms[20,*a]	---	---	---	---	---	---	---	---
4.	Cropland harvested, acres[18,19,73,76,*a,b]	18,807,114	19,709,121	18,917,911	16,958,000	19,122,640	19,722,645	16,635,264	---
5.	Percentage increase in number of farms[18,19]	6.5	-9.2	-18.7	-24.0	-10.9	-4.3	-9.9	4.6
6.	Percentage increase of land in farms[18,19]	5.48	0.8	-6.3	-6.3	-1.3	-2.6	-4.1	12.9
7.	Percentage increase of improved land in farms[20]	---	---	---	---	---	---	---	---
8.	Average acreage per farm[18,19,66,73,76,78]	165.2	183.6	211.4	260	288	294	312	333
9.	Percentage increase in cropland harvested[18,19,*b]	2.0	4.8	-4.0	-10.4	12.8	3.1	-15.7	---
10.	Value of farms, dollars[18,19,64,79,81]	1,443,021,290	2,777,312,000[*i]	4,749,296,000	6,512,000,000	25,762,603,416	32,326,000,000	18,616,000,000	18,071,000,000
11.	Value of farms, percent increase[18,19]	-32.1	92.5[*i]	71.0	37.1	296.0	25.5	-42.4	-2.9
12.	Average value per farm, dollars[18,19,64,73,76]	7,312	15,507[*i]	32,605	59,000	261,096	342,593	218,808	203,045
13.	Farms operated by owners[21,22,23,24,25,26,27,65,77]	132,903	141,330	131,481	97,827[*g]	86,781	82,752[*g]	74,568[*g]	---
14.	Value of livestock on farms, dollars[28,29,30,36,76,83,*a]	227,946,324	535,226,163	652,645,858	---	2,448,134,000	3,268,146,000	3,175,549,000	3,757,696,000
15.	Average value of livestock per farm, dollars[19,28,29,30,36]	1,155	2,988	4,481	---	24,811	34,627	37,325	42,221
16.	Production of cotton in bales[28,29,30,67,74,83]	---	---	---	---	---	---	---	---
17.	Percent of total production of cotton[28,29,30]	---	---	---	---	---	---	---	---

GENERAL AGRICULTURE STATISTICS, 1850-1990									
MINNESOTA									
Item No.		1940	1950	1960	1970	1978	1982	1987	1990
18.	Production of wheat in bushels[31,32,35,36,69,74,84]	20,341,862	18,163,607	21,535,651	22,882,000	80,968,259	111,500,972	97,967,169	102,504,000
19.	Percent of total production of wheat[31,32,33,35,36]	2.8697	1.8045	2.0395	1.6699	5.0368	4.6982	5.1914	5.0350
20.	Production of corn in bushels[36,37,38,39,70,74,85]	162,766,107	207,669,742	339,913,000	390,490,000	569,665,483	610,113,278	567,384,166	700,000,000
21.	Percent of total production of corn[36,37,38,39]	7.0	7.5	7.9	9.5	8.4	8.1	8.4	9.3
22.	Production of oats in bushels[31,35,36,71,80,86]	143,070,552	165,008,851	157,080,385	167,700,000	---	76,684,380	45,600,000	46,750,000
23.	Percent of total production of oats[31,35,36]	16.4	14.5	15.7	18.5	---	15.2	14.6	12.5
24.	Production of soybeans in bushels[36,40,41,72,74,76,87]	466,585[*h]	12,912,013	41,379,627	82,124,000	122,566,278	151,240,357	166,025,760	185,000,000
25.	Percent of total production of soybeans[36,40,41]	.5327	5.0780	8.0251	7.3081	.7117	7.5982	9.0327	9.6014
26.	Production of hay crops in tons[31,34,42,43,44,74,76,88]	6,131,243	5,094,940	6,404,474	8,155,000	7,292,173	6,623,748	5,920,884	6,400,000[*l]
27.	Percent of total production of hay crops[31,34,42,43,44]	7.4	5.7	6.0	6.4	5.6	5.2	4.6	4.4

[a] See the Glossary of Terms for changing definitions, i.e. farm, improved land, cropland harvested, farm owners, and livestock.
[b] Prior to 1924, the data relate to the total acreage of crops for which figures are available, except for 1920 when 14,502,932 acres of corn cut for forage were excluded (as most of this was probably duplicated in the acreage of corn harvested for grain).
[c] Percentage computed by compiler from data herein. See endnotes for source of data.
[d] Values in gold, one-fifth less than currency values.
[e] Managers included with owners.
[f] Running square bales, counting round as half bales.
[g] Census listed the number of full and part time owners separately. Compiler added the two numbers for the above figure.
[h] Includes quantity of beans harvested from acreage grown with other crops as well as that from acreage grown alone.
[i] The total value for each state for 1950 was based on the average value per acre for farms in the sample, for which value of land and buildings was reported. The average value per farm and per acre was based on the total value of all farms.
[j] Less than one-tenth of one percent.
[k] 1,000 percent or more.
[l] Census had two separate listings: hay, alfalfa, and alfalfa mixtures; and hay, all other. Compiler added the two listings for the above figure.

Item No.	GENERAL AGRICULTURE STATISTICS, 1850-1990 MISSISSIPPI	1850	1860	1870	1880	1890	1900	1910	1920	1930
1.	Number of farms[18,19,68,73,76,82,*a]	33,960	42,840	68,023	101,772	144,318	220,803	274,382	272,101	312,663
2.	Acres in farms[18,19,68,73,76,82]	10,490,419	15,839,684	13,121,113	15,855,462	17,572,547	18,240,736	18,557,533	18,196,979	17,332,195
3.	Acres improved land in farms[20,*a]	3,444,358	5,065,755	4,209,146	5,216,937	6,849,390	7,594,428	9,008,310	9,325,677	---
4.	Cropland harvested, acres[18,19,73,76,*a,b]	---	---	---	3,980,356	4,873,809	5,570,380	6,158,719	6,359,538	6,597,112
5.	Percentage increase in number of farms[18,19]	---	26.1	58.8	49.6	41.8	53.0	24.3	-0.8	14.9
6.	Percentage increase of land in farms[18,19]	---	51.0	-17.2	20.8	10.8	3.8	1.7	-1.9	-4.8
7.	Percentage increase of improved land in farms[20]	---	47.1	-16.9	23.9	31.3	10.9	18.6	3.5	---
8.	Average acreage per farm[18,19,66,73,76,78]	308.9	369.7	192.9	155.8	121.8	82.6	67.6	66.9	55.4
9.	Percentage increase in cropland harvested[18,19,*b]	---	---	---	---	22.4	14.3	10.6	3.3	3.7
10.	Value of farms, dollars[18,19,64,79,81]	54,738,634	190,760,367	65,373,261	92,844,915	127,423,157	152,007,000	334,162,289	789,896,778	568,322,065
11.	Value of farms, percent increase[18,19]	---	248.5	-65.7	42.0	37.2	19.3	119.8	136.4	-28.1
12.	Average value per farm, dollars[18,19,64,73,76]	1,612	4,453	961	912	883	688	1,218	2,903	1,818
13.	Farms operated by owners[21,22,23,24,25,26,27,65,77,*a]	---	---	---	57,214[*e]	68,058[*e]	82,021	92,066	91,310	86,047[*g]
14.	Value of livestock on farms, dollars[28,29,30,36,76,83,*a]	19,403,662	41,891,692	23,952,190[*d]	24,285,717	33,936,435	42,657,222	75,247,033	134,973,821	82,711,344
15.	Average value of livestock per farm, dollars[19,28,29,30,36]	571	978	352[*d]	239	235	193	274	496	265
16.	Production of cotton in bales[28,29,30,67,74,83]	484,292	1,202,507	564,938	963,111	1,154,725	1,313,798[*f]	1,127,156[*f]	957,527[*f]	1,875,108[*f]
17.	Percent of total production of cotton[28,29,30]	19.6	22.3	18.8	16.7	15.5	13.8[*f]	10.6[*f]	8.4[*f]	12.9[*f]

GENERAL AGRICULTURE STATISTICS, 1850-1990										
MISSISSIPPI										
Item No.		1850	1860	1870	1880	1890	1900	1910	1920	1930
18.	Production of wheat in bushels[31,32,35,36,69,74,84]	137,990	587,925	274,479	218,890	16,570	37,257	4,670	54,685	6,435
19.	Percent of total production of wheat[31,32,33,35,36]	.1373	.3396	.0955	.0476	.0035	.0057	.0007	.0058	.0008
20.	Production of corn in bushels[36,37,38,39,70,74,85]	22,446,552	29,057,682	15,637,316	21,340,800	26,148,144	38,789,920	28,428,667	38,095,228	34,935,657
21.	Percent of total production of corn[36,37,38,39]	3.8	3.5	2.1	1.2	1.2	1.5	1.1	1.6	1.6
22.	Production of oats in bushels[31,35,36,71,80,86]	1,503,288	221,235	414,586	1,959,620	1,362,290	862,805	1,268,785	760,417	265,034
23.	Percent of total production of oats[31,35,36]	1.0	0.1	0.2	0.5	0.2	0.1	0.1	0.1	*m
24.	Production of soybeans in bushels[36,40,41,72,74,76,87]	---	---	---	---	---	---	152	24,839	76,719*h
25.	Percent of total production of soybeans[36,40,41]	---	---	---	---	---	---	.6088	2.1882	.8858
26.	Production of hay crops in tons[31,34,42,43,44,74,76,88]	12,504	32,901	8,324	7,694	85,054	129,332	284,337	574,316	409,285
27.	Percent of total production of hay crops[31,34,42,43,44]	0.1*c	0.2	*m	*m	0.1	0.2	0.3	0.5	0.5

GENERAL AGRICULTURE STATISTICS, 1850-1990									
MISSISSIPPI									
Item No.		1940	1950	1960	1970	1978	1982	1987	1990
1.	Number of farms[18,19,68,73,76,82,*a]	291,092	251,383	138,142	72,577	44,104	42,415	34,074	40,000
2.	Acres in farms[18,19,68,73,76,82]	19,156,058	20,710,770	18,630,263	16,040,000	13,210,879	12,421,651	10,746,190	13,000,000
3.	Acres improved land in farms[20,*a]	---	---	---	---	---	---	---	---
4.	Cropland harvested, acres[18,19,73,76,*a,b]	6,952,931	6,136,206	4,564,307	5,064,000	5,848,897	5,799,772	4,272,651	---
5.	Percentage increase in number of farms[18,19]	-6.9	-13.6	-45.0	-47.5	-39.2	-3.8	-19.7	17.4
6.	Percentage increase of land in farms[18,19]	10.5	8.1	-10.0	-13.9	-17.6	-6.0	-13.5	21.0
7.	Percentage increase of improved land in farms[20]	---	---	---	---	---	---	---	---
8.	Average acreage per farm[18,19,66,73,76,78]	65.8	82.4	134.9	221	300	293	315	324
9.	Percentage increase in cropland harvested[18,19,*b]	5.4	-11.7	-25.6	11.0	15.5	-0.8	-26.3	---
10.	Value of farms, dollars[18,19,64,79,81]	474,986,062	1,147,791,000[*i,j]	1,974,266,000[*j]	3,746,000,000	8,849,291,184	10,923,000,000	7,333,000,000	9,149,000,000
11.	Value of farms, percent increase[18,19]	-16.4	141.6[*i,j]	72.0[*j]	89.7	136.2	-88.4	-32.9	24.8
12.	Average value per farm, dollars[18,19,64,73,76]	1,632	4,566[*i,j]	14,2921[*j]	52,000	200,646	257,819	215,209	228,725
13.	Farms operated by owners[21,22,23,24,25,26,27,65,77,*a]	97,266	120,729	93,810[*g]	65,997[*g]	40,404	39,203[*g]	30,961[*g]	---
14.	Value of livestock on farms, dollars[28,29,30,36,76,83,*a]	83,197,684	173,935,645	227,838,994	389,653,000	716,433,000	796,015,000	948,989,000	1,321,676,000
15.	Average value of livestock per farm, dollars[19,28,29,30,36]	286	692	1,649	4,102	16,244	18,767	27,851	33,042
16.	Production of cotton in bales[28,29,30,67,74,83]	1,533,092[*f]	1,496,902	1,560,581	1,631,000	1,338,394	1,641,939	1,654,648	1,555,000[k,l]
17.	Percent of total production of cotton[28,29,30]	13.4[*f]	9.7	11.2	16.0[*c]	12.5	14.4[*c]	12.5[*c]	13.5[*c]

GENERAL AGRICULTURE STATISTICS, 1850-1990									
MISSISSIPPI									
Item No.		1940	1950	1960	1970	1978	1982	1987	1990
18.	Production of wheat in bushels[31,32,35,36,69,74,84]	38,974	109,066	784,273	4,930,000	1,853,571	29,185,697	9,674,702	15,300,000
19.	Percent of total production of wheat[31,32,33,35,36]	.0055	.0108	.0743	.3598	.1153	1.2298	.5127	.7515
20.	Production of corn in bushels[36,37,38,39,70,74,85]	36,034,812	37,933,711	42,501,000	6,944,000	4,935,672	4,757,736	9,369,093	9,800,000
21.	Percent of total production of corn[36,37,38,39]	1.6	1.4	1.0	0.2	0.1	0.1	0.1	0.1
22.	Production of oats in bushels[31,35,36,71,80,86]	4,185,456	2,606,871	7,428,642	3,360,000	--	613,125	257,147	20,100,000
23.	Percent of total production of oats[31,35,36]	0.4	0.2	0.7	0.4	---	0.1	0.1	5.4[*c]
24.	Production of soybeans in bushels[36,40,41,72,74,76,87]	264,945[*h]	2,825,484	21,037,945	55,512,000	73,505,537	81,944,364	41,329,519	40,000,000
25.	Percent of total production of soybeans[36,40,41]	.3025	1.3300	4.0801	4.9399	4.2682	4.1178	2.2485	2.0760
26.	Production of hay crops in tons[31,34,42,43,44,74,76,88]	1,003,449	709,699	700,697	1,061,000	960,499	1,148,110	1,092,059	1,560,000[*n]
27.	Percent of total production of hay crops[31,34,42,43,44]	1.2	0.8	0.7	0.8	.07348	0.9	0.8	1.1

[a] See the Glossary of Terms for changing definitions, i.e. farm, improved land, cropland harvested, farm owners, and livestock.
[b] Prior to 1924, the data relate to the total acreage of crops for which figures are available, except for 1920 when 14,502,932 acres of corn cut for forage were excluded (as most of this was probably duplicated in the acreage of corn harvested for grain).
[c] Percentage computed by compiler from data herein. See endnotes for source of data.
[d] Values in gold, one-fifth less than currency values.
[e] Managers included with owners.
[f] Running square bales, counting round as half bales.
[g] Census listed the number of full and part time owners separately. Compiler added the two numbers for the above figure.
[h] Includes quantity of beans harvested from acreage grown with other crops as well as that from acreage grown alone.
[i] The total value for each state for 1950 was based on the average value per acre for farms in the sample, for which value of land and buildings was reported. The average value per farm and per acre was based on the total value of all farms.
[j] Based on a sampling of farms.
[k] Production ginned and to be ginned.
[l] 480-pound net weight bales.
[m] Less than one-tenth of one percent.
[n] Data available for hay, all other only.

GENERAL AGRICULTURE STATISTICS, 1850-1990

MISSOURI

Item No.		1850	1860	1870	1880	1890	1900	1910	1920	1930
1.	Number of farms[18,19,68,73,76,82,*a]	54,458	92,792	148,328	215,575	238,043	284,886	277,244	263,004	255,940
2.	Acres in farms[18,19,68,73,76,82]	9,732,670	19,984,810	21,707,220	27,879,276	30,780,290	33,997,873	34,591,248	34,774,679	33,743,019
3.	Acres improved land in farms[20,*a]	2,938,425	6,246,871	9,130,615	16,745,031	19,792,313	22,900,043	24,581,186	24,832,966	---
4.	Cropland harvested, acres[18,19,73,76,*a,b]	---	---	---	10,041,817	12,861,453	14,351,177	14,335,588	15,419,907	13,175,947
5.	Percentage increase in number of farms[18,19]	---	70.4	59.8	45.3	10.4	19.7	-2.7	-5.1	-2.7
6.	Percentage increase of land in farms[18,19]	---	105.3	8.6	28.4	10.4	10.5	1.7	0.5	-3.0
7.	Percentage increase of improved land in farms[20]	---	112.6	46.2	83.4	18.2	15.7	7.3	1.0	---
8.	Average acreage per farm[18,19,66,73,76,78]	178.7	215.4	146.3	129.3	129.3	119.3	124.8	132.2	131.8
9.	Percentage increase in cropland harvested[18,19,*a,b]	---	---	---	---	28.1	11.6	-0.1	7.6	-14.6
10.	Value of farms, dollars[18,19,64,79,81]	63,225,543	230,632,126	314,326,438	375,633,307	625,858,361	843,979,213	1,716,204,386	3,062,967,700	1,796,246,519
11.	Value of farms, percent increase[18,19]	---	264.8	36.3	19.5	66.6	34.9	103.3	78.5	-41.4
12.	Average value per farm, dollars18,19,64,73,76	1,161	2,485	2,119	1,742	2,629	2,963	6,190	11,646	7,018
13.	Farms operated by owners[21,22,23,24,25,26,27,65,77,*a]	---	---	---	156,703[*e]	174,285[*e]	196,158	192,285	185,030	165,318
14.	Value of livestock on farms, dollars[28,29,30,36,76,83,*a]	19,887,580	53,693,673	67,428,218[*d]	95,785,282	138,701,173	160,540,004	285,839,108	389,839,045	257,955,342
15.	Average value of livestock per farm, dollars[19,28,29,30,36]	365	579	455[*d]	444	583	564	1,031	1,482	1,008
16.	Production of cotton in bales[28,29,30,67,74,83]	---	41,188	1,246	20,318	15,856	25,576[*f]	54,498[*f]	63,808[*f]	225,351[*f]
17.	Percent of total production of cotton[28,29,30]	---	0.8	0.1	0.4	0.2	0.3[*f]	0.5[*f]	0.6[*f]	1.5[*f]

GENERAL AGRICULTURE STATISTICS, 1850-1990										
MISSOURI										
Item No.		1850	1860	1870	1880	1890	1900	1910	1920	1930
18.	Production of wheat in bushels[31,32,35,36,69,74,84]	2,981,652	4,227,586	14,315,926	24,966,627	30,113,821	23,072,768	29,837,429	65,210,462	15,116,509
19.	Percent of total production of wheat[31,32,33,35,36]	2.9672	2.4422	4.9752	5.4336	6.4294	3.5037	4.3662	6.8976	1.8880
20.	Production of corn in bushels[36,37,38,39,70,74,85]	36,214,537	72,892,157	66,034,075	202,414,413	196,999,016	208,844,870	191,427,087	146,342,036	112,348,071
21.	Percent of total production of corn[36,37,38,39]	6.1	8.7	8.7	11.5	9.3	7.8	7.5	6.2	5.3
22.	Production of oats in bushels[31,35,36,71,80,86]	5,278,079	3,680,870	16,578,313	20,670,958	39,820,149	20,545,350	24,828,501	40,493,700	19,050,770
23.	Percent of total production of oats[31,35,36]	3.6	2.1	5.9	5.1	4.9	2.2	2.5	3.8	1.9
24.	Production of soybeans in bushels[36,40,41]	---	---	---	---	---	---	---	18,315	725,114[*h]
25.	Percent of total production of soybeans[36,40,41]	---	---	---	---	---	---	---	1.6134[*c]	8.3720
26.	Production of hay crops in tons[31,34,42,43,44,74,76,88]	116,925	401,070	615,611	1,083,929	3,567,635	4,062,199	4,116,289	4,357,970	3,564,805
27.	Percent of total production of hay crops[31,34,42,43,44]	0.9	2.1	2.3	3.1	5.3	5.1	4.2	3.5	4.2

GENERAL AGRICULTURE STATISTICS, 1850-1990									
MISSOURI									
Item No.		1940	1950	1960	1970	1978	1982	1987	1990
1.	Number of farms[18,19,68,73,76,82,*a]	256,100	230,045	168,672	137,067	114,963	112,447	106,105	108,000
2.	Acres in farms[18,19,68,73,76,82]	34,739,598	35,123,143	33,155,226	32,420,000	30,098,727	29,266,609	29,209,187	30,400,000
3.	Acres improved land in farms[20,*a]	---	---	---	---	---	---	---	---
4.	Cropland harvested, acres[18,19,73,76,*a,b]	12,399,860	12,263,847	12,177,822	11,273,000	12,433,661	12,725,378	11,655,304	---
5.	Percentage increase in number of farms[18,19]	0.1	-10.2	-26.7	-18.7	-16.1	-2.2	-5.6	1.8
6.	Percentage increase of land in farms[18,19]	3.0	1.1	-5.6	-2.2	-7.2	-2.8	-0.2	4.1
7.	Percentage increase of improved land in farms[20]	---	---	---	---	---	---	---	---
8.	Average acreage per farm[18,19,66,73,76,78]	135.6	152.7	196.6	237	262	260	275	281
9.	Percentage increase in cropland harvested[18,19,*b]	-5.9	-1.1	-0.7	-7.4	10.3	2.3	-8.4	4.1
10.	Value of farms, dollars[18,19,64,79,81]	1,107,302,598	2,235,939,000[*i]	3,726,715,000	7,269,000,000	21,972,878,190	25,094,000,000	18,634,000,000	18,432,000,000
11.	Value of farms, percent increase[18,19]	-38.4	101.9[*i]	66.7	95.1	202.0	14.2	-25.7	-1.1
12.	Average value per farm, dollars[18,19,64,73,76]	4,324	9,720[*i]	22,094	53,000	191,130	223,247	175,612	170,667
13.	Farms operated by owners[21,22,23,24,25,26,27,65,77,*a]	163,763	183,101	143,855[*g]	124,270[*g]	103,865	102,021[*g]	96,667[*g]	---
14.	Value of livestock on farms, dollars[28,29,30,36,76,83,*a]	188,775,965	493,729,253	606,400,133	839,800,000	1,919,122,000	2,060,191,000	2,184,138,000	2,270,615,000
15.	Average value of livestock per farm, dollars[19,28,29,30,36]	737	2,146	3,595	6,127	16,693	18,321	20,585	21,024
16.	Production of cotton in bales[28,29,30,67,74,83]	433,196[*f]	472,043	482,119	224,000	181,018	179,134	305,767	269,000[*j,k]
17.	Percent of total production of cotton[28,29,30]	3.8[*f]	3.1	3.5	2.2	1.8	1.6	2.3	2.3

GENERAL AGRICULTURE STATISTICS, 1850-1990									
MISSOURI									
Item No.		1940	1950	1960	1970	1978	1982	1987	1990
18.	Production of wheat in bushels[31,32,35,36,69,74,84]	30,890,536	25,999,611	35,731,219	31,222,000	27,277,966	68,338,008	31,939,663	86,950,000
19.	Percent of total production of wheat[31,32,33,35,36]	4.3578	2.5830	3.3839	2.2786	1.69687	2.8795	1.6925	4.2710
20.	Production of corn in bushels[36,37,38,39,70,74,85]	124,058,341	129,968,135	232,485,000	173,057,000	184789444	178,722,297	218,093,408	219,840,000
21.	Percent of total production of corn[36,37,38,39]	5.4	4.7	5.4	4.2	2.7	2.4	3.2	2.9
22.	Production of oats in bushels[31,35,36,71,80,86]	34,771,104	30,223,572	15,645,290	9,184,000	---	2,840,632	2,712,492	3,600,000
23.	Percent of total production of oats[31,35,36]	4.0	2.7	1.6	1.0	---	0.6	0.9	1.0
24.	Production of soybeans in bushels[36,40,41,72,74,76,87]	1,090,829[*h]	16,738,422	47,441,259	88,358,000	140836086	153,691,360	148,272,506	123,975,000
25.	Percent of total production of soybeans[36,40,41]	1.2454	7.8791	9.2007	7.8629	.8178	7.7232	8.0668	6.3213
26.	Production of hay crops in tons[31,34,42,43,44,74,76,88]	3,259,443	4,392,710	3,882,963	5,535,000	5,749,474	5,575,960	5,409,063	6,764,000[*l]
27.	Percent of total production of hay crops[31,34,42,43,44]	4.0	4.9	3.6	4.3	4.4	4.3	4.2	4.6

[a] See the Glossary of Terms for changing definitions, i.e. farm, improved land, cropland harvested, farm owners, and livestock.
[b] Prior to 1924, the data relate to the total acreage of crops for which figures are available, except for 1920 when 14,502,932 acres of corn cut for forage were excluded (as most of this was probably duplicated in the acreage of corn harvested for grain).
[c] Percentage computed by compiler from data herein. See endnotes for source of data.
[d] Values in gold, one-fifth less than currency values.
[e] Managers included with owners.
[f] Running square bales, counting round as half bales.
[g] Census listed the number of full and part time owners separately. Compiler added the two numbers for the above figure.
[h] Includes quantity of beans harvested from acreage grown with other crops as well as that from acreage grown alone.
[i] The total value for each state for 1950 was based on the average value per acre for farms in the sample, for which value of land and buildings was reported. The average value per farm and per acre was based on the total value of all farms.
[j] Production ginned and to be ginned.
[k] 480-pound net weight bales.
[l] Census had two separate listings: hay, alfalfa, and alfalfa mixtures; and hay, all other. Compiler added the two listings for the above figure.

GENERAL AGRICULTURE STATISTICS, 1850-1990										
MONTANA										
Item No.		1850	1860	1870	1880	1890	1900	1910	1920	1930
1.	Number of farms[18,19,68,73,76,82,*a]	---	---	851	1,519	5,603	13,370	26,214	57,677	47,495
2.	Acres in farms[18,19,68,73,76,82]	---	---	139,537	405,683	1,964,197	11,844,454	13,545,603	35,070,656	44,659,152
3.	Acres improved land in farms[20,*a]	---	---	84,674	262,611	915,517	1,736,701	3,640,309	11,007,278	---
4.	Cropland harvested, acres[18,19,73,76,*a,b]	---	---	---	100,726	381,399	1,146,093	1,848,113	3,812,033	7,840,979
5.	Percentage increase in number of farms[18,19]	---	---	---	78.5	268.9	138.6	96.1	120.0	-17.7
6.	Percentage increase of land in farms[18,19]	---	---	---	190.7	384.2	503.0	14.4	158.9	27.3
7.	Percentage increase of improved land in farms[20]	---	---	---	210.1	248.6	89.7	109.6	202.4	---
8.	Average acreage per farm[18,19,66,73,76,78]	---	---	164.0	267.1	350.6	885.9	516.7	608.1	940.3
9.	Percentage increase in cropland harvested[18,19,*b]	---	---	---	---	278.7	200.5	61.3	106.3	105.7
10.	Value of farms, dollars[18,19,64,79,81]	---	---	583,355	3,234,504	25,512,340	62,026,090	251,625,930	776,767,529	527,610,002
11.	Value of farms, percent increase[18,19]	---	---	---	454.5	688.7	143.1	305.7	208.7	-32.1
12.	Average value per farm, dollars[18,19,64,73,76]	---	---	685	2,129	4,553	4,639	9,599	13,468	11,109
13.	Farms operated by owners[21,22,23,24,25,26,27,65,77,*a]	---	---	---	1,439[*e]	5,333[*e]	11,661	23,365	50,271	35,353
14.	Value of livestock on farms, dollars[28,29,30,36,76,83,*a]	---	---	1,454,954[*d]	9,170,554[*k]	33,266,752[*k]	52,161,833	85,663,187	154,189,567	118,531,951
15.	Average value of livestock per farm, dollars[19,28,29,30,36]	---	---	1,710[*d]	6,037	5,937	3,901	3,268	2,673	2,496[*c]
16.	Production of cotton in bales[28,29,30,67,74,83]	---	---	---	---	---	---	---	---	---
17.	Percent of total production of cotton[28,29,30]	---	---	---	---	---	---	---	---	---

GENERAL AGRICULTURE STATISTICS, 1850-1990

MONTANA

Item No.		1850	1860	1870	1880	1890	1900	1910	1920	1930
18.	Production of wheat in bushels[31,32,35,36,69,74,84]	---	---	181,184	469,688	457,607	1,899,683	6,251,945	7,799,647	40,558,049
19.	Percent of total production of wheat[31,32,33,35,36]	---	---	.0630	.1022	.0977	.2885	.9149	.8250	5.0656
20.	Production of corn in bushels[36,37,38,39,70,74,85]	---	---	320	5,649	14,225	75,838	274,103	159,410	258,667
21.	Percent of total production of corn[36,37,38,39]	---	---	*j	*j	*j	*j	*j	*j	*j
22.	Production of oats in bushels[31,35,36,71,80,86]	---	---	149,367	900,915	1,535,615	3,746,231	13,805,735	2,583,908	4,809,018
23.	Percent of total production of oats[31,35,36]	---	---	0.1	0.2	0.2	0.5	1.4	0.2	0.5
24.	Production of soybeans in bushels[36,40,41,72,74,76,87]	---	---	---	---	---	---	---	831	1,973[*h]
25.	Percent of total production of soybeans[36,40,41]	---	---	---	---	---	---	---	.0732	.0228
26.	Production of hay crops in tons[31,34,42,43,44,74,76,88]	---	---	18,727	62,709	268,689	1,059,268	1,693,333	1,349,464	2,235,052
27.	Percent of total production of hay crops[31,34,42,43,44]	---	---	0.1	0.2	0.4	1.3	1.7	1.1	2.6

GENERAL AGRICULTURE STATISTICS, 1850-1990									
MONTANA									
Item No.		1940	1950	1960	1970	1978	1982	1987	1990
1.	Number of farms[18,19,68,73,76,82,*a]	41,823	35,085	28,959	24,951	23,565	23,570	24,568	24,700
2.	Acres in farms[18,19,68,73,76,82]	46,451,594	59,247,434	64,081,391	62,918,000	61,690,919	60,539,209	60,203,993	60,500,000
3.	Acres improved land in farms[20,*a]	---	---	---	---	---	---	---	---
4.	Cropland harvested, acres[18,19,73,76,*a,b]	5,748,069	7,576,173	8,158,899	8,269,000	8,741,043	9,365,775	9,128,013	---
5.	Percentage increase in number of farms[18,19]	-11.9	-16.1	-17.5	-13.8	-5.6	0.2	4.2	0.5
6.	Percentage increase of land in farms[18,19]	4.0	27.5	8.2	-1.8	-2.0	-1.9	-2.5	0.5
7.	Percentage increase of improved land in farms[20]	---	---	---	---	---	---	---	---
8.	Average acreage per farm[18,19,66,73,76,78]	1,110.7	1,688.7	2,212.8	2,522	2,618	2,568	2,451	2,453
9.	Percentage increase in cropland harvested[18,19,*b]	-26.7	31.8	7.7	1.3	5.7	7.1	-2.5	---
10.	Value of farms, dollars[18,19,64,79,81]	350,178,461	999,061,000[*i]	2,222,921,000	3,748,000,000	12,083,919,915	15,866,000,000	12,418,000,000	10,131,000,000
11.	Value of farms, percent increase[18,19]	-33.6	185.3[*i]	122.5	68.6	222.4	31.3	-21.7	-18.4
12.	Average value per farm, dollars[18,19,64,73,76]	8,373	28,475[*i]	76,761	150,000	512,791	677,995	505,526	410,162
13.	Farms operated by owners[21,22,23,24,25,26,27,65,77,*a]	29,884	29,663	24,559[*g]	21,986[*g]	20,800	20,901[*g]	21,391[*g]	---
14.	Value of livestock on farms, dollars[28,29,30,36,76,83,*a]	82,255,039	253,353,908	391,958,404	---	688,968,000	787,989,000	908,084,000	863,679,000
15.	Average value of livestock per farm, dollars[19,28,29,30,36]	1,967	7,221	13,535	---	29,237	33,432	36,962	34,967
16.	Production of cotton in bales[28,29,30,67,74,83]	---	---	---	---	---	---	---	---
17.	Percent of total production of cotton[28,29,30]	---	---	---	---	---	---	---	---

GENERAL AGRICULTURE STATISTICS, 1850-1990									
MONTANA									
Item No.		1940	1950	1960	1970	1978	1982	1987	1990
18.	Production of wheat in bushels[31,32,35,36,69,74,84]	40,349,690	52,516,438	70,909,534	85,167,000	134,207,558	159,093,238	143,802,744	145,030.000
19.	Percent of total production of wheat[31,32,33,35,36]	5.6923	5.2174	6.7154	6.2155	8.3486	6.7036	7.6203	7.1239
20.	Production of corn in bushels[36,37,38,39,70,74,85]	861,232	157,643	3,404,000	288,000	1,251,164	1,933,434	1,471,198	320,000
21.	Percent of total production of corn[36,37,38,39]	*j	*j	*j	*j	*j	*j	*j	*j
22.	Production of oats in bushels[31,35,36,71,80,86]	7,897,726	5,215,651	7,084,953	17,976,000	---	8,068,970	6,356,871	6,670,000
23.	Percent of total production of oats[31,35,36]	0.9	0.5	0.7	2.0	---	1.6	2.0	1.8
24.	Production of soybeans in bushels[36,40,41,72,74,76,87]	146*h	---	---	---	000	14,918	*l	---
25.	Percent of total production of soybeans[36,40,41]	.0002	---	---	---	---	.0007	---	---
26.	Production of hay crops in tons[31,34,42,43,44,74,76,88]	2,026,040	1,895,946	2,751,315	4,112,000	4,319,247	4,335,853	3,858,349	4,470,000*m
27.	Percent of total production of hay crops[31,34,42,43,44]	2.5	2.1	2.6	3.2	3.3	3.4	3.0	3.0

[a] See the Glossary of Terms for changing definitions, i.e. farm, improved land, cropland harvested, farm owners, and livestock.
[b] Prior to 1924, the data relate to the total acreage of crops for which figures are available, except for 1920 when 14,502,932 acres of corn cut for forage were excluded (as most of this was probably duplicated in the acreage of corn harvested for grain).
[c] Percentage computed by compiler from data herein. See endnotes for source of data.
[d] Values in gold, one-fifth less than currency values.
[e] Managers included with owners.
[f] Running square bales, counting round as half bales.
[g] Census listed the number of full and part time owners separately. Compiler added the two numbers for the above figure.
[h] Includes quantity of beans harvested from acreage grown with other crops as well as that from acreage grown alone.
[i] The total value for each state for 1950 was based on the average value per acre for farms in the sample, for which value of land and buildings was reported. The average value per farm and per acre was based on the total value of all farms.
[j] Less than one-tenth of one percent.
[k] Including estimated value of range animals.
[l] Withheld to avoid disclosing data for individual farms.
[m] Census had two separate listings: hay, alfalfa, and alfalfa mixtures; and hay, all other. Compiler added the two listings for the above figure.

GENERAL AGRICULTURE STATISTICS, 1850-1990										
NEBRASKA										
Item No.		1850	1860	1870	1880	1890	1900	1910	1920	1930
1.	Number of farms[18,19,68,73,76,82,*a]	---	2,789	12,301	63,387	113,608	121,525	129,678	124,417	129,458
2.	Acres in farms[18,19,68,73,76,82]	---	631,214	2,073,781	9,944,826	21,593,444	29,911,779	38,622,021	42,225,475	44,708,565
3.	Acres improved land in farms[20,*a]	---	118,789	647,031	5,504,702	15,247,705	18,432,595	24,382,577	23,109,624	---
4.	Cropland harvested, acres[18,19,73,76,*a,b]	---	---	---	4,019,116	10,724,838	15,044,428	17,231,205	18,936,108	21,399,340
5.	Percentage increase in number of farms[18,19]	---	---	341.1	415.3	79.2	7.0	6.7	-4.1	4.1
6.	Percentage increase of land in farms[18,19]	---	---	228.5	379.6	117.1	38.5	29.0	9.3	5.9
7.	Percentage increase of improved land in farms[20]	---	---	444.7	750.8	177.0	20.9	32.3	-5.2	---
8.	Average acreage per farm[18,19,66,73,76,78]	---	226.3	168.6	156.9	190.1	246.1	297.8	339.4	345.4
9.	Percentage increase in cropland harvested[18,19,*b]	---	---	---	---	166.8	40.3	14.5	9.9	13.0
10.	Value of farms, dollars[18,19,64,79,81]	---	3,878,326	24,193,749	105,932,541	402,358,913	577,660,020	1,813,346,935	3,712,107,760	2,495,203,071
11.	Value of farms, percent increase[18,19]	---	---	523.8	337.9	279.8	43.6	213.9	104.7	-32.8
12.	Average value per farm, dollars[18,19,64,73,76]	---	1,391	1,967	1,671	3,542	4,753	13,983	29,836	19,274
13.	Farms operated by owners[21,22,23,24,25,26,27,65,77,*a]	---	---	---	51,963[*e]	85,525[*e]	75,583	79,250	69,672	67,418
14.	Value of livestock on farms, dollars[28,29,30,36,76,83,*a]	---	1,128,771	5,240,948[*d]	40,350,265[*j]	92,971,920	145,349,587	222,222,004	336,443,784	288,546,065
15.	Average value of livestock per farm, dollars[19,28,29,30,36]	---	405	426[*d]	637	818	1,196	1,714	2,704	2,229
16.	Production of cotton in bales[28,29,30,67,74,83]	---	---	---	---	---	---	---	---	---
17.	Percent of total production of cotton[28,29,30]	---	---	---	---	---	---	---	---	---

GENERAL AGRICULTURE STATISTICS, 1850-1990										
NEBRASKA										
Item No.		1850	1860	1870	1880	1890	1900	1910	1920	1930
18.	Production of wheat in bushels[31,32,35,36,69,74,84]	---	147,867	2,125,086	13,847,007	10,571,059	24,924,520	47,685,745	57,843,598	53, 867,855
19.	Percent of total production of wheat[31,32,33,35,36]	---	.0854	.7385	3.0136	2.2570	3.7848	6.9779	6.1184	6.7280
20.	Production of corn in bushels[36,37,38,39,70,74,85]	---	1,482,080	4,736,710	65,450,135	215,895,996	210,974,740	180,132,807	160,391,314	216,020,274
21.	Percent of total production of corn[36,37,38,39]	---	0.2	0.6	3.7	10.2	7.9	7.1	6.8	10.1
22.	Production of oats in bushels[31,35,36,71,80,86]	---	74,502	1,477,562	6,555,875	43,843,640	58,007,140	53,360,185	59,819,545	70,733,080
23.	Percent of total production of oats[31,35,36]	---	0.1	0.5	1.6	5.4	6.1	5.3	5.7	7.1
24.	Production of soybeans in bushels[36,40,41,72,74,76,87]	---	---	---	---	---	---	---	1,184	1,785[*h]
25.	Percent of total production of soybeans[36,40,41]	---	---	---	---	---	---	---	.1043	.0206
26.	Production of hay crops in tons[31,34,42,43,44,74,76,88]	---	24,458	169,354	786,722	3,115,398	3,502,380	5,785,847	6,172,052	4,574,577
27.	Percent of total production of hay crops[31,34,42,43,44]	---	0.1	0.6	2.2	4.7	4.4	5.9	5.0	5.4

GENERAL AGRICULTURE STATISTICS, 1850-1990

NEBRASKA

Item No.		1940	1950	1960	1970	1978	1982	1987	1990
1.	Number of farms[18,19,68,73,76,82,*a]	121,062	107,183	90,475	72,257	63,768	60,243	60,502	57,000
2.	Acres in farms[18,19,68,73,76,82]	47,343,981	47,466,828	47,755,708	45,834,000	46,113,973	44,961,371	45,305,441	47,100,000
3.	Acres improved land in farms[20,*a]	---	---	---	---	---	---	---	---
4.	Cropland harvested, acres[18,19,73,76,*a,b]	17,304,802	19,406,990	18,057,090	15,408,000	16,371,595	17,075,625	15,276,151	---
5.	Percentage increase in number of farms[18,19]	-6.5	-11.5	-15.6	-20.1	-11.7	-5.5	0.4	-5.8
6.	Percentage increase of land in farms[18,19]	5.9	0.3	0.6	-4.0	0.6	-2.5	0.8	4.0
7.	Percentage increase of improved land in farms[20]	---	---	---	---	---	---	---	---
8.	Average acreage per farm[18,19,66,73,76,78]	391.1	442.9	527.8	634	723	746	749	826
9.	Percentage increase in cropland harvested[18,19,*b]	-19.1	12.1	-7.0	-14.7	6.3	4.3	-10.5	---
10.	Value of farms, dollars[18,19,64,79,81]	1,137,808,019	2,735,039,000[*i]	4,233,856,000	7,076,000,000	24,416,894,736	31,910,000,000	20,828,000,000	19,830,000,000
11.	Value of farms, percent increase[18,19]	-54.4	140.4[*i]	54.8	67.1	245.0	30.7	-34.7	-4.8
12.	Average value per farm, dollars[18,19,64,73,76]	9,399	25,517[*i]	46,796	98,000	382,902	532,741	344,253	347,895
13.	Farms operated by owners[21,22,23,24,25,26,27,65,77,*a]	56,561	65,103	58,617[*g]	54,503[*g]	50,081	47,923[*g]	47,662[*g]	---
14.	Value of livestock on farms, dollars[28,29,30,36,76,83,*a]	160,581,094	495,179,724	748,150,364	1,171,050,000	3,430,583,000	4,245,931,000	4,528,016,000	6,037,490,000
15.	Average value of livestock per farm, dollars[19,28,29,30,36]	1,326	4,620	8,269	16,207	53,798	70,480	74,841	105,921
16.	Production of cotton in bales[28,29,30,67,74,83]	---	---	---	---	---	---	---	---
17.	Percent of total production of cotton[28,29,30]	---	---	---	---	---	---	---	---

GENERAL AGRICULTURE STATISTICS, 1850-1990									
NEBRASKA									
Item No.		1940	1950	1960	1970	1978	1982	1987	1990
18.	Production of wheat in bushels[31,32,35,36,69,74,84]	34,676,159	52,599,446	64,921,062	97,204,000	72,979,509	87,959,769	76,826,252	55,350,000
19.	Percent of total production of wheat[31,32,33,35,36]	4.8919	5.2257	6.1483	7.0940	4.5398	3.7063	4.0711	2.7188
20.	Production of corn in bushels[36,37,38,39,70,74,85]	71,886,032	224,259,108	330,285,000	360,375,000	707,687,558	676,484,963	749,231,198	852,000,000
21.	Percent of total production of corn[36,37,38,39]	3.1	8.0	7.7	8.8	10.4	9.0	11.1	11.3
22.	Production of oats in bushels[31,35,36,71,80,86]	18,225,518	42,290,850	30,996,174	24,276,000	---	22,158,999	13,643,509	8,640,000
23.	Percent of total production of oats[31,35,36]	2.1	3.7	3.1	2.7	---	4.4	4.4	2.3
24.	Production of soybeans in bushels[36,40,41,72,74,76,87]	20,566[*h]	421,961	3,431,626	17,864,000	37,689,210	70,218,107	78,147,991	81,920,000
25.	Percent of total production of soybeans[36,40,41]	.0235	.1986	.6655	1.5897	2.18849	3.5286	4.2517	4.2516
26.	Production of hay crops in tons[31,34,42,43,44,74,76,88]	2,449,278	5,076,863	6,077,179	5,999,000	6,751,689	6,711,376	5,951,228	5,705,000[*k]
27.	Percent of total production of hay crops[31,34,42,43,44]	3.0	5.7	5.7	4.7	5.2	5.2	4.6	3.9

[a] See the Glossary of Terms for changing definitions, i.e. farm, improved land, cropland harvested, farm owners, and livestock.
[b] Prior to 1924, the data relate to the total acreage of crops for which figures are available, except for 1920 when 14,502,932 acres of corn cut for forage were excluded (as most of this was probably duplicated in the acreage of corn harvested for grain).
[c] Percentage computed by compiler from data herein. See endnotes for source of data.
[d] Values in gold, one-fifth less than currency values.
[e] Managers included with owners.
[f] Running square bales, counting round as half bales.
[g] Census listed the number of full and part time owners separately. Compiler added the two numbers for the above figure.
[h] Includes quantity of beans harvested from acreage grown with other crops as well as that from acreage grown alone.
[i] The total value for each state for 1950 was based on the average value per acre for farms in the sample, for which value of land and buildings was reported. The average value per farm and per acre was based on the total value of all farms.
[j] Including estimated value of range animals.
[k] Census had two separate listings: hay, alfalfa, and alfalfa mixtures; and hay, all other. Compiler added the two listings for the above figure.

GENERAL AGRICULTURE STATISTICS, 1850-1990										
NEVADA										
Item No.		1850	1860	1870	1880	1890	1900	1910	1920	1930
1.	Number of farms[18,19,68,76,82,*a]	---	91	1,036	1,404	1,277	2,184	2,689	3,163	3,442
2.	Acres in farms[18,19,68,73,76,82]	---	56,118	208,510	530,862	1,661,416	2,565,647	2,714,757	2,357,163	4,080,906
3.	Acres improved land in farms[20,*a]	---	14,132	92,644	344,423	723,052	572,946	752,117	594,741	---
4.	Cropland harvested, acres[18,19,73,76,*a,b]	---	---	---	104,422	157,048	326,526	392,387	389,281	397,504
5.	Percentage increase in number of farms[18,19]	---	---	---	35.5	-9.0	71.0	23.1	17.6	8.8
6.	Percentage increase of land in farms[18,19]	---	---	271.6	154.6	213.0	54.4	5.8	-13.2	73.1
7.	Percentage increase of improved land in farms[20]	---	---	555.6	271.8	109.9	-20.8	31.3	-20.9	---
8.	Average acreage per farm[18,19,66,73,76,78]	---	616.7	201.3	378.1	1,301.0	1,174.7	1,009.6	745.2	1,185.6
9.	Percentage increase in cropland harvested[18,19,*b]	---	---	---	---	50.4	107.9	20.2	-0.8	2.1
10.	Value of farms, dollars[18,19,64,79,81]	---	302,340	1,485,505	5,408,325	12,339,410	15,615,710	39,609,339	66,255,214	64,111,000
11.	Value of farms, percent increase[18,19]	---	---	391.3	264.1	128.2	26.6	153.7	67.3	-3.2
12.	Average value per farm, dollars[18,19,64,73,76]	---	3,322	1,434	3,852	9,663	7,150	14,730	20,947	18,626
13.	Farms operated by owners[21,22,23,24,25,26,27,65,77,*a]	---	---	---	1,268[*e]	1,181[*e]	1,809	2,175	2,699	2,770
14.	Value of livestock on farms, dollars[28,29,30,36,76,83,*a]	---	177,638	1,445,449[*d]	4,233,749[*k]	5,801,820	12,169,565	19,213,930	29,893,525	28,770,741
15.	Average value of livestock per farm, dollars[19,28,29,30,36]	---	1,952	1,395[*d]	3,015	4,543	5,572	7,145	9,451	8,359[*c]
16.	Production of cotton in bales[28,29,30,67,74,83]	---	---	106	---	---	18[*f]	---	---	---
17.	Percent of total production of cotton[28,29,30]	---	---	[*j]	---	---	[*f,j]	---	---	---

GENERAL AGRICULTURE STATISTICS, 1850-1990										
NEVADA										
Item No.		1850	1860	1870	1880	1890	1900	1910	1920	1930
18.	Production of wheat in bushels[31,32,35,36,69,74,84]	---	3,631	228,866	69,298	81,486	450,812	396,075	464,151	355,890
19.	Percent of total production of wheat[31,32,33,35,36]	---	.0021	.0795	.0151	.0174	.0685	.0580	.0491	.0445
20.	Production of corn in bushels[36,37,38,39,70,74,85]	---	460	9,660	12,891	6,540	14,614	20,779	14,714	34,798
21.	Percent of total production of corn[36,37,38,39]	---	*j	*j	*j	*j	*j	*j	*j	*j
22.	Production of oats in bushels[31,35,36,71,80,86]	---	1,082	55,916	186,860	99,126	151,176	334,973	75,000	102,024
23.	Percent of total production of oats[31,35,36]	---	*j	*j	*j	*j	*j	*j	*j	*j
24.	Production of soybeans in bushels[36,40,41,72,74,76,87]	---	---	---	---	---	---	---	---	---
25.	Percent of total production of soybeans[36,40,41]	---	---	---	---	---	---	---	---	---
26.	Production of hay crops in tons[31,34,42,43,44,74,76,88]	---	2,213	33,855	95,853	225,827	419,812	521,954	547,559	544,737
27.	Percent of total production of hay crops[31,34,42,43,44]	---	*j	0.1	0.3	0.3	0.5	0.5	0.4	0.6

Item No.	GENERAL AGRICULTURE STATISTICS, 1850-1990 NEVADA	1940	1950	1960	1970	1978	1982	1987	1990
1.	Number of farms[18,19,68,73,76,82,*a]	3,573	3,110	2,354	2,112	2,399	2,719	3,027	2,500
2.	Acres in farms[18,19,68,73,76,82]	3,785,106	7,063,525	10,942,936	10,708,000	10,427,111	9,980,201	9,988,520	8,900,000
3.	Acres improved land in farms[20,*a]	---	---	---	---	---	---	---	---
4.	Cropland harvested, acres[18,19,73,76,*a,b]	435,855	421,202	337,529	547,000	585,486	605,082	526,067	---
5.	Percentage increase in number of farms[18,19]	3.8	-13.0	-24.3	-10.3	13.6	13.3	11.3	-17.4
6.	Percentage increase of land in farms[18,19]	-7.2	86.6	54.9	-2.1	-2.6	-4.3	8.3	-10.9
7.	Percentage increase of improved land in farms[20]	---	---	---	---	---	---	---	---
8.	Average acreage per farm[18,19,66,73,76,78]	1,059.4	2,271.2	4,648.7	5,070	4,346	3,671	3,300	3,560
9.	Percentage increase in cropland harvested[18,19,*b]	9.6	-3.4	-19.9	62.1	7.0	3.3	-13.1	---
10.	Value of farms, dollars[18,19,64,73,76]	47,594,384	135,907,000[*i]	334,206,000	571,000,000	1,922,014,027	2,509,000,000	2,272,000,000	1,749,000,000
11.	Value of farms, percent increase[18,19]	-25.8	185.6[*i]	145.9	70.9	237.0	30.5	-9.4	-23.0
12.	Average value per farm, dollars[18,19,64,73,76]	13,321	43,700[*i]	141,974	271,000	801,173	925,540	749,936	699,600
13.	Farms operated by owners[21,22,23,24,25,26,27,65,77,*a]	2,940	2,782	2,091[*g]	1,934[*g]	2,199	2,484[*g]	2,756[*g]	---
14.	Value of livestock on farms, dollars[28,29,30,36,76,83,*a]	21,211,895	64,763,909	82,277,749	---	140,206,000	129,999,000	174,773,000	218,350,000
15.	Average value of livestock per farm, dollars[19,28,29,30,36]	5,937	20,824	34,952	---	58,444	47,811	57,738	87,340
16.	Production of cotton in bales[28,29,30,67,74,83]	---	499	5,972	2,500	1,372	803	---	---
17.	Percent of total production of cotton[28,29,30]	---	*j	*j	*j	*j	*j	---	---

Item No.	GENERAL AGRICULTURE STATISTICS, 1850-1990 NEVADA	1940	1950	1960	1970	1978	1982	1987	1990
18.	Production of wheat in bushels[31,32,35,36,69,74,84]	351,129	486,644	577,506	810,000	1,053,253	1,386,182	1,096,511	1,200,000
19.	Percent of total production of wheat[31,32,33,35,36]	.0495	.0483	.0547	.0591	.065519	.0584	.0581	.0589
20.	Production of corn in bushels[36,37,38,39,70,74,85]	62,304	13,094	220,000	---	---	*l	151,128	---
21.	Percent of total production of corn[36,37,38,39]	*j	*j	*j	---	---	---	*j	---
22.	Production of oats in bushels[31,35,36,71,80,86]	117,255	186,400	119,857	156,000	---	129,299	48,862	---
23.	Percent of total production of oats[31,35,36]	*j	*j	*j	*j	---	*j	*j	---
24.	Production of soybeans in bushels[36,40,41,72,74,76,87]	---	---	---	---	---	---	---	---
25.	Percent of total production of soybeans[36,40,41]	---	---	---	---	---	---	---	---
26.	Production of hay crops in tons[31,34,42,43,44,74,76,88]	565,675	565,301	513,054	834,000	1,079,592	1,254,889	1,223,895	1,463,000*m
27.	Percent of total production of hay crops[31,34,42,43,44]	0.7	0.6	0.5	0.7	0.8	1.0	1.0	1.0

[a] See the Glossary of Terms for changing definitions, i.e. farm, improved land, cropland harvested, farm owners, and livestock.
[b] Prior to 1924, the data relate to the total acreage of crops for which figures are available, except for 1920 when 14,502,932 acres of corn cut for forage were excluded (as most of this was probably duplicated in the acreage of corn harvested for grain).
[c] Percentage computed by compiler from data herein. See endnotes for source of data.
[d] Values in gold, one-fifth less than currency values.
[e] Managers included with owners.
[f] Running square bales, counting round as half bales.
[g] Census listed the number of full and part time owners separately. Compiler added the two numbers for the above figure.
[h] Includes quantity of beans harvested from acreage grown with other crops as well as that from acreage grown alone.
[i] The total value for each state for 1950 was based on the average value per acre for farms in the sample, for which value of land and buildings was reported. The average value per farm and per acre was based on the total value of all farms.
[j] Less than one-tenth of one percent.
[k] Including estimated value of range animals.
[l] Withheld to avoid disclosing data for individual farms.
[m] Census had two separate listings: hay, alfalfa, and alfalfa mixtures; and hay, all other. Compiler added the two listings for the above figure.

GENERAL AGRICULTURE STATISTICS, 1850-1990										
NEW HAMPSHIRE										
Item No.		1850	1860	1870	1880	1890	1900	1910	1920	1930
1.	Number of farms[18,19,68,73,76,82,*a]	29,229	30,501	29,642	32,181	29,151	29,324	27,053	20,523	14,906
2.	Acres in farms[18,19,68,73,76,82]	3,392,414	3,744,625	3,605,994	3,721,173	3,459,018	3,609,864	3,249,458	2,603,806	1,960,061
3.	Acres improved land in farms[20,*a]	2,251,488	2,367,034	2,334,487	2,308,112	1,727,387	1,076,879	929,185	702,902	---
4.	Cropland harvested, acres[18,19,73,76,*a,b]	---	---	---	791,924	736,380	688,107	593,093	508,276	380,105
5.	Percentage increase in number of farms[18,19]	---	4.4	-2.8	8.6	-9.4	0.6	-7.7	-24.1	-27.4
6.	Percentage increase of land in farms[18,19]	---	10.4	-3.7	3.2	-7.0	4.4	-10.0	-19.9	-24.7
7.	Percentage increase of improved land in farms[20]	---	5.1	-1.4	-1.1	-25.2	-37.7	-13.7	-24.4	---
8.	Average acreage per farm[18,19,66,73,76,78]	116.1	122.8	121.7	115.6	118.7	123.1	120.1	126.9	131.5
9.	Percentage increase in cropland harvested[18,19,*b]	---	---	---	---	-7.0	-6.6	-13.8	-14.3	-25.2
10.	Value of farms, dollars[18,19,64,79,81]	55,245,997	69,689,761	64,471,451	75,834,389	66,162,600	70,124,360	85,916,061	89,995,870	77,355,327
11.	Value of farms, percent increase[18,19]	---	26.1	-7.5	17.6	-12.8	6.0	22.5	4.7	-14.0
12.	Average value per farm, dollars[18,19,64,73,76]	1,890	2,285	2,175	2,356	2,270	2,391	3,176	4,385	5,190
13.	Farms operated by owners[21,22,23,24,25,26,27,65,77,*a]	---	---	---	29,566[*e]	26,827[*e]	26,450	24,493	18,604	13,755
14.	Value of livestock on farms, dollars[28,29,30,36,76,83,*a]	8,871,901	10,924,627	12,197,236[*d]	9,812,064	10,450,125	10,554,646	11,910,478	19,160,923	13,314,025
15.	Average value of livestock per farm, dollars[19,28,29,30,36]	304	358	411[*d]	305	358	360	440	934	893[*c]
16.	Production of cotton in bales[28,29,30,67,74,83]	---	---	---	---	---	---	---	---	---
17.	Percent of total production of cotton[28,29,30]	---	---	---	---	---	---	---	---	---

GENERAL AGRICULTURE STATISTICS, 1850-1990										
NEW HAMPSHIRE										
Item No.		1850	1860	1870	1880	1890	1900	1910	1920	1930
18.	Production of wheat in bushels[31,32,35,36,69,74,84]	185,658	238,965	193,621	169,316	35,192	4,035	1,311	21,968	376
19.	Percent of total production of wheat[31,32,33,35,36]	.1848	.1380	.0673	.0368	.0075	.0006	.0002	.0023	.0000
20.	Production of corn in bushels[36,37,38,39,70,74,85]	1,573,670	1,414,628	1,277,768	1,350,248	988,806	1,080,720	916,263	482,738	111,977
21.	Percent of total production of corn[36,37,38,39]	0.3	0.2	0.2	0.1	[*j]	0.4	[*j]	[*j]	[*j]
22.	Production of oats in bushels[31,35,36,71,80,86]	973,381	1,329,233	1,146,451	1,017,620	892,243	497,110	386,419	485,367	126,083
23.	Percent of total production of oats[31,35,36]	0.7[*c]	0.8	0.4	0.3	0.1	0.1	[*j]	[*j]	[*j]
24.	Production of soybeans in bushels[36,40,41,72,74,76,87]	---	---	---	---	---	---	---	801	55[*h]
25.	Percent of total production of soybeans[36,40,41]	---	---	---	---	---	---	---	.0706	.0006
26.	Production of hay crops in tons[31,34,42,43,44,74,76,88]	598,854	642,741	612,648	588,170	659,368	653,265	582,579	587,958	362,899
27.	Percent of total production of hay crops[31,34,42,43,44]	4.3[*c]	3.4	2.3	1.7	1.0	0.8	0.6	0.5	0.4

GENERAL AGRICULTURE STATISTICS, 1850-1990									
NEW HAMPSHIRE									
Item No.		1940	1950	1960	1970	1978	1982	1987	1990
1.	Number of farms[18,19,68,73,76,82,*a]	16,554	13,391	6,542	2,902	2,508	2,757	2,515	3,000
2.	Acres in farms[18,19,68,73,76,82]	1,809,314	1,713,731	1,124,312	613,000	484,631	469,582	426,237	490,000
3.	Acres improved land in farms[20,*a]	---	---	---	---	---	---	---	---
4.	Cropland harvested, acres[18,19,73,76,*a,b]	371,611	290,199	205,767	112,000	124,510	116,613	106,629	---
5.	Percentage increase in number of farms[18,19]	11.1	-19.1	-51.1	-55.6	-13.6	9.9	-8.8	19.3
6.	Percentage increase of land in farms[18,19]	-7.7	-5.3	-34.4	-46.9	-21.0	-3.1	-9.2	15.0
7.	Percentage increase of improved land in farms[20]	---	---	---	---	---	---	---	---
8.	Average acreage per farm[18,19,66,73,76,78]	109.3	128.0	171.9	211	193	170	169	159
9.	Percentage increase in cropland harvested[18,19,*b]	-2.2	-21.9	-29.1	-45.6	11.2	-6.3	-9.2	---
10.	Value of farms, dollars[18,19,64,79,81]	62,206,391	124,845,000[*i]	118,058,000	146,000,000	425,697,888	555,000,000	900,000,000	1,133,000,000
11.	Value of farms, percent increase[18,19]	-19.6	100.7[*i]	-5.4	23.7	192.0	30.4	62.2	25.9
12.	Average value per farm, dollars[18,19,64,73,76]	3,758	9,323[*i]	18,046	50,000	169,736	201,171	358,279	390,690
13.	Farms operated by owners[21,22,23,24,25,26,27,65,77,*a]	15,342	12,856	6,344[*g]	2,820[*g]	2,389	2,628[*g]	2,393[*g]	---
14.	Value of livestock on farms, dollars[28,29,30,36,76,83,*a]	9,534,049	18,004,115	20,201,800	---	65,498,000	76,312,000	71,775,000	63,172,000
15.	Average value of livestock per farm, dollars[19,28,29,30,36]	576	1,344	3,088	---	26,116	27,679	28,539	21,057
16.	Production of cotton in bales[28,29,30,67,74,83]	---	---	---	---	---	---	---	---
17.	Percent of total production of cotton[28,29,30]	---	---	---	---	---	---	---	---

GENERAL AGRICULTURE STATISTICS, 1850-1990

NEW HAMPSHIRE

Item No.		1940	1950	1960	1970	1978	1982	1987	1990
18.	Production of wheat in bushels[31,32,35,36,69,74,84]	779	---	127	---	---	•k	•k	---
19.	Percent of total production of wheat[31,32,33,35,36]	.0001	---	.0000	---	---	---	---	---
20.	Production of corn in bushels[36,37,38,39,70,74,85]	143,642	66,186	564,000	---	154,182	145,792	102,358	---
21.	Percent of total production of corn[36,37,38,39]	•j	•j	•j	---	.0022657	•j	•j	---
22.	Production of oats in bushels[31,35,36,71,80,86]	90,490	50,635	24,874	---	---	7,610	5,940	---
23.	Percent of total production of oats[31,35,36]	•j	•j	•j	---	---	•j	•j	---
24.	Production of soybeans in bushels[36,40,41,72,74,76,87]	283•h	---	---	---	265	•k	•k	---
25.	Percent of total production of soybeans[36,40,41]	.0003	---	---	---	.000154	---	---	---
26.	Production of hay crops in tons[31,34,42,43,44,74,76,88]	354,257	301,556	253,249	204,000	171,222	165,999	164,829	167,000•l
27.	Percent of total production of hay crops[31,34,42,43,44]	0.4	0.3	0.2	0.2	0.1	0.1	0.1	0.1

[a] See the Glossary of Terms for changing definitions, i.e. farm, improved land, cropland harvested, farm owners, and livestock.
[b] Prior to 1924, the data relate to the total acreage of crops for which figures are available, except for 1920 when 14,502,932 acres of corn cut for forage were excluded (as most of this was probably duplicated in the acreage of corn harvested for grain).
[c] Percentage computed by compiler from data herein. See endnotes for source of data.
[d] Values in gold, one-fifth less than currency values.
[e] Managers included with owners.
[f] Running square bales, counting round as half bales.
[g] Census listed the number of full and part time owners separately. Compiler added the two numbers for the above figure.
[h] Includes quantity of beans harvested from acreage grown with other crops as well as that from acreage grown alone.
[i] The total value for each state for 1950 was based on the average value per acre for farms in the sample, for which value of land and buildings was reported. The average value per farm and per acre was based on the total value of all farms.
[j] Less than one-tenth of one percent.
[k] Withheld to avoid disclosing data for individual farms.
[l] Census had two separate listings: hay, alfalfa, and alfalfa mixtures; and hay, all other. Compiler added the two listings for the above figure.

GENERAL AGRICULTURE STATISTICS, 1850-1990

NEW JERSEY

Item No.		1850	1860	1870	1880	1890	1900	1910	1920	1930
1.	Number of farms[18,19,68,73,76,82,*a]	23,905	27,646	30,652	34,307	30,828	34,650	33,487	29,702	25,378
2.	Acres in farms[18,19,68,73,76,82]	2,752,946	2,983,525	2,989,511	2,929,773	2,662,009	2,840,966	2,573,857	2,282,585	1,758,027
3.	Acres improved land in farms[20,*a]	1,767,991	1,944,441	1,976,474	2,096,297	1,999,117	1,977,042	1,803,336	1,555,607	---
4.	Cropland harvested, acres[18,19,73,76,*a,b]	---	---	---	1,249,117	1,126,552	1,212,772	1,114,903	997,541	776,954
5.	Percentage increase in number of farms[18,19]	---	15.6	10.9	11.9	-10.1	12.4	-3.4	-11.3	-14.6
6.	Percentage increase of land in farms[18,19]	---	8.4	0.2	-2.0	-9.1	6.7	-9.4	-11.3	-23.0
7.	Percentage increase of improved land in farms[20]	---	10.0	1.6	6.1	-4.6	-1.1	-8.8	-13.7	---
8.	Average acreage per farm[18,19,66,73,76,78]	115.2	107.9	97.5	85.4	86.4	82.0	76.9	76.8	69.3
9.	Percentage increase in cropland harvested[18,19,*b]	---	---	---	---	-9.8	7.7	-8.1	-10.5	-22.1
10.	Value of farms, dollars[18,19,64,79,81]	120,237,511	180,250,338	206,018,701	190,895,833	159,262,840	162,591,010	217,134,519	250,323,986	298,845,113
11.	Value of farms, percent increase[18,19]	---	49.9	14.3	-7.3	-16.6	2.1	33.5	15.3	19.4
12.	Average value per farm, dollars[18,19,64,73,76]	5,030	6,520	6,721	5,564	5,166	4,692	6,484	8,428	11,776
13.	Farms operated by owners[21,22,23,24,25,26,27,65,77,*a]	---	---	---	25,869[*c]	22,442[*c]	23,434	24,133	21,889	20,771
14.	Value of livestock on farms, dollars[28,29,30,36,76,83,*a]	10,679,291	16,134,693	17,154,770[*d]	14,861,412	15,811,430	17,612,620	24,588,639	36,064,757	29,403,397
15.	Average value of livestock per farm, dollars[19,28,29,30,36]	447	584	560[*d]	433	513	508	734	1,214	1,159[*c]
16.	Production of cotton in bales[28,29,30,67,74,83]	---	---	---	---	---	---	---	---	---
17.	Percent of total production of cotton[28,29,30]	---	---	---	---	---	---	---	---	---

GENERAL AGRICULTURE STATISTICS, 1850-1990										
NEW JERSEY										
Item No.		1850	1860	1870	1880	1890	1900	1910	1920	1930
18.	Production of wheat in bushels[31,32,35,36,69,74,84]	1,601,190	1,763,218	2,301,433	1,901,739	1,823,382	1,902,590	1,489,233	1,378,269	1,100,937
19.	Percent of total production of wheat[31,32,33,35,36]	1.5934	1.0186	.7998	.4139	.3893	.2889	.2179	.1458	.1375
20.	Production of corn in bushels[36,37,38,39,70,74,85]	8,759,704	9,723,336	8,745,384	11,150,705	8,637,011	10,978,800	10,000,731	8,776,107	4,978,926
21.	Percent of total production of corn[36,37,38,39]	1.5	1.2	1.1	0.6	0.4	0.4	0.4	0.4	0.2
22.	Production of oats in bushels[31,35,36,71,80,86]	3,578,063	4,539,132	4,009,830	3,710,573	2,837,293	1,601,610	1,376,752	1,477,319	815,609
23.	Percent of total production of oats[31,35,36]	2.3	2.6	1.4	0.9	0.4	0.2	0.1	0.1	0.1
24.	Production of soybeans in bushels[36,40,41,72,74,76,87]	---	---	---	---	---	---	---	1,886	3,164[*h]
25.	Percent of total production of soybeans[36,40,41]	---	---	---	---	---	---	---	.1617	.0365
26.	Production of hay crops in tons[31,34,42,43,44,74,76,88]	435,950	508,726	521,975	518,990	661,791	465,137	569,973	558,503	327,062
27.	Percent of total production of hay crops[31,34,42,43,44]	3.2[*c]	2.7	1.9	1.5	1.0	0.6	0.6	0.5	0.4

GENERAL AGRICULTURE STATISTICS, 1850-1990									
NEW JERSEY									
Item No.		**1940**	**1950**	**1960**	**1970**	**1978**	**1982**	**1987**	**1990**
1.	Number of farms[18,19,68,73,76,82,*a]	25,835	24,838	15,459	8,493	7,984	8,277	9,032	8,100
2.	Acres in farms[18,19,68,73,76,82]	1,874,402	1,725,441	1,379,002	1,036,000	987,309	916,331	894,426	870,000
3.	Acres improved land in farms[20,*a]	---	---	---	---	---	---	---	---
4.	Cropland harvested, acres[18,19,73,76,*a,b]	778,809	781,820	657,877	374,000	584,406	570,031	484,805	---
5.	Percentage increase in number of farms[18,19]	1.8	-3.9	-37.8	-45.1	-6.0	3.7	9.1	-10.3
6.	Percentage increase of land in farms[18,19]	6.6	-7.9	-20.1	-24.9	-4.7	-7.2	-15.0	-2.7
7.	Percentage increase of improved land in farms[20]	---	---	---	---	---	---	---	---
8.	Average acreage per farm[18,19,66,73,76,78]	72.6	69.5	89.2	122	124	111	99	106
9.	Percentage increase in cropland harvested[18,19,*b]	0.2	0.4	-15.9	-43.2	56.3	-2.5	-15.0	---
10.	Value of farms, dollars[18,19,64,79,81]	227,805,686	505,278,000[*i]	717,251,000	1,131,000,000	2,548,357,072	2,840,000,000	3,579,000,000	6,010,000,000
11.	Value of farms, percent increase[18,19]	-23.8	121.8[*i]	42.0	57.7	125.3	11.4	26.0	67.9
12.	Average value per farm, dollars[18,19,64,73,76]	8,818	20,343[*i]	46,397	133,000	319,183	343,137	396,198	741,975
13.	Farms operated by owners[21,22,23,24,25,26,27,65,77,*a]	21,370	22,611	13,952[*g]	7,504[*g]	7,032	7,428[*g]	8,192[*g]	---
14.	Value of livestock on farms, dollars[28,29,30,36,76,83,*a]	27,671,943	65,466,857	71,424,719	---	102,885,000	113,928,000	125,423,000	195,873,000
15.	Average value of livestock per farm, dollars[19,28,29,30,36]	1,071	2,636	4,620	---	12,886	13,764	13,887	24,182
16.	Production of cotton in bales[28,29,30,67,74,83]	---	---	---	---	---	---	---	---
17.	Percent of total production of cotton[28,29,30]	---	---	---	---	---	---	---	---

GENERAL AGRICULTURE STATISTICS, 1850-1990

NEW JERSEY

Item No.		1940	1950	1960	1970	1978	1982	1987	1990
18.	Production of wheat in bushels[31,32,35,36,69,74,84]	1,103,347	1,860,994	1,331,834	1,216,000	706,983	1,461,995	869,823	1,365,000
19.	Percent of total production of wheat[31,32,33,35,36]	.1557	.1849	.1261	.0887	.043979	.0616	.0461	.0670
20.	Production of corn in bushels[36,37,38,39,70,74,85]	4,475,692	4,592,239	12,160,000	5,070,000	7,807,146	10,186,110	7,570,456	7,242,000
21.	Percent of total production of corn[36,37,38,39]	0.2	0.2	0.3	0.1	0.1	0.1	0.1	0.1
22.	Production of oats in bushels[31,35,36,71,80,86]	914,204	1,049,597	934,814	400,000	---	325,025	260,000	264,000
23.	Percent of total production of oats[31,35,36]	0.1	0.1	0.1	*j	---	0.1	0.1	0.1
24.	Production of soybeans in bushels[36,40,41,72,74,76,87]	48,984*h	310,048	696,946	1,225,000	5,259,919	4,109,956	3,153,039	3,616,000
25.	Percent of total production of soybeans[36,40,41]	.0559	.1459	.1352	.1090	.3054267	.2065	.1715	.1877
26.	Production of hay crops in tons[31,34,42,43,44,74,76,88]	323,542	390,415	430,569	331,000	295,413	265,054	262,323	241,000*k
27.	Percent of total production of hay crops[31,34,42,43,44]	0.4	0.4	0.4	0.3	0.2	0.2	0.2	0.2

[a] See the Glossary of Terms for changing definitions, i.e. farm, improved land, cropland harvested, farm owners, and livestock.

[b] Prior to 1924, the data relate to the total acreage of crops for which figures are available, except for 1920 when 14,502,932 acres of corn cut for forage were excluded (as most of this was probably duplicated in the acreage of corn harvested for grain).

[c] Percentage computed by compiler from data herein. See endnotes for source of data.

[d] Values in gold, one-fifth less than currency values.

[e] Managers included with owners.

[f] Running square bales, counting round as half bales.

[g] Census listed the number of full and part time owners separately. Compiler added the two numbers for the above figure.

[h] Includes quantity of beans harvested from acreage grown with other crops as well as that from acreage grown alone.

[i] The total value for each state for 1950 was based on the average value per acre for farms in the sample, for which value of land and buildings was reported. The average value per farm and per acre was based on the total value of all farms.

[j] Less than one-tenth of one percent.

[k] Census had two separate listings: hay, alfalfa, and alfalfa mixtures; and hay, all other. Compiler added the two listings for the above figure.

Item No.		1850	1860	1870	1880	1890	1900	1910	1920	1930
GENERAL AGRICULTURE STATISTICS, 1850-1990										
NEW MEXICO										
1.	Number of farms[18,19,68,73,76,82,*a]	3,750	5,086	4,480	5,053	4,458	12,311	35,676	29,844	31,404
2.	Acres in farms[18,19,68,73,76,82]	290,571	1,414,909	833,549	631,131	787,882	5,130,878	11,270,021	24,409,633	30,822,034
3.	Acres improved land in farms[20,*a]	166,201	149,274	143,007	237,392	263,106	326,873	1,467,191	1,717,224	---
4.	Cropland harvested, acres[18,19,73,76,*a,b]	---	---	---	116,839	88,649	196,023	632,769	1,131,832	1,493,998
5.	Percentage increase in number of farms[18,19]	---	35.6	-11.9	12.8	11.8	176.2	189.8	-16.3	5.2
6.	Percentage increase of land in farms[18,19]	---	386.9	-41.1	-24.3	24.8	551.2	119.7	116.6	26.3
7.	Percentage increase of improved land in farms[20]	---	-10.2	-4.2	66.0	10.8	24.2	348.9	17.0	---
8.	Average acreage per farm[18,19,66,73,76,78]	77.5	278.2	186.1	124.9	176.7	416.8	315.9	817.9	981.5
9.	Percentage increase in cropland harvested[18,19,*b]	---	---	---	---	-24.1	121.1	222.8	78.9	32.0
10.	Value of farms, dollars[18,19,64,79,81]	1,653,922	2,707,386	1,808,111	5,514,399	8,140,800	20,888,814	111,830,999	221,814,212	207,859,492
11.	Value of farms, percent increase[18,19]	---	63.7	-33.2	205.0	47.6	156.6	435.4	98.3	-6.3
12.	Average value per farm, dollars[18,19,64,73,76]	441	532	404	1,091	1,826	1,697	3,135	7,432	6,619
13.	Farms operated by owners[21,22,23,24,25,26,27,65,77,*a]	---	---	---	4,645[*e]	4,257[*e]	10,674	33,398	25,756	24,740
14.	Value of livestock on farms, dollars[28,29,30,36,76,83,*a]	1,494,629	4,499,746	1,911,326[*d]	10,914,800[*k]	25,111,201[*k]	31,727,400	43,494,679	93,626,418	72,147,017
15.	Average value of livestock per farm, dollars[19,28,29,30,36]	399	885	427[*d]	2,160	5,633	2,577	1,219	3,137	2,297[*c]
16.	Production of cotton in bales[28,29,30,67,74,83]	---	19	---	---	---	---	206[*f]	5,399[*f]	90,805[*f]
17.	Percent of total production of cotton[28,29,30]	---	[*j]	---	---	---	---	[*f,j]	[*f,j]	0.6[*f]

GENERAL AGRICULTURE STATISTICS, 1850-1990										
NEW MEXICO										
Item No.		1850	1860	1870	1880	1890	1900	1910	1920	1930
18.	Production of wheat in bushels[31,32,35,36,69,74,84]	196,516	434,309	352,822	706,641	343,484	603,303	499,799	2,437,213	4,431,748
19.	Percent of total production of wheat[31,32,33,35,36]	.1956	.2509	.1226	.1538	.0733	.0916	.0731	.2578	.5535
20.	Production of corn in bushels[36,37,38,39,70,74,85]	365,411	709,304	640,823	633,786	583,489	677,305	1,164,970	4,737,182	3,822,545
21.	Percent of total production of corn[36,37,38,39]	0.1	0.1	0.1	*j	*j	*j	*j	0.2	0.2
22.	Production of oats in bushels[31,35,36,71,80,86]	5	7,246	67,660	156,527	193,832	342,777	720,560	1,085,311	453,362
23.	Percent of total production of oats[31,35,36]	*j	*j	*j	*j	*j	*j	*j	0.1	*j
24.	Production of soybeans in bushels[36,40,41,72,74,76,87]	---	---	---	---	---	---	---	52,190	2,340*h
25.	Percent of total production of soybeans[36,40,41]	---	---	---	---	---	---	---	4.5977	.0270
26.	Production of hay crops in tons[31,34,42,43,44,74,76,88]	---	1,113	4,209	11,025	47,253	195,324	433,504	660,811	321,921
27.	Percent of total production of hay crops[31,34,42,43,44]	---	*j	*j	*j	0.1	0.3	0.4	0.5	0.4

Item No.	GENERAL AGRICULTURE STATISTICS, 1850-1990 NEW MEXICO	1940	1950	1960	1970	1978	1982	1987	1990
1.	Number of farms[18,19,68,73,76,82,*a]	34,105	23,599	15,919	11,641	12,311	13,484	14,249	13,500
2.	Acres in farms[18,19,68,73,76,82]	38,860,427	47,521,809	46,293,207	46,792,000	47,934,714	47,096,085	46,018,005	44,500,000
3.	Acres improved land in farms[20,*a]	---	---	---	---	---	---	---	---
4.	Cropland harvested, acres[18,19,73,76,*a,b]	1,572,507	1,897,813	1,076,947	1,029,000	1,208,928	1,297,305	989,214	---
5.	Percentage increase in number of farms[18,19]	8.6	-30.8	-32.5	-26.9	5.8	9.5	5.7	-5.3
6.	Percentage increase of land in farms[18,19]	26.0	22.3	-2.6	1.1	2.4	-1.7	-2.3	-3.3
7.	Percentage increase of improved land in farms[20]	---	---	---	---	---	---	---	---
8.	Average acreage per farm[18,19,66,73,76,78]	1,139.4	2,013.7	2,908.0	4,020	3,894	3,493	3,230	3,179
9.	Percentage increase in cropland harvested[18,19,*b]	5.3	20.7	-43.3	-4.5	17.5	7.3	-2.3	---
10.	Value of farms, dollars[18,19,64,79,81]	187,525,814	713,360,000[*i]	1,086,207,000	1,960,000,000	6,634,250,168	8,322,000,000	8,291,000,000	6,337,000,000
11.	Value of farms, percent increase[18,19]	-9.8	280.4[*i]	52.3	80.4	238.5	25.4	-0.4	-23.6
12.	Average value per farm, dollars[18,19,64,73,76]	5,498	30,228[*i]	58,233	168,000	538,888	618,708	582,012	469,407
13.	Farms operated by owners[21,22,23,24,25,26,27,65,77,*a]	28,030	20,264	13,922[*g]	10,233[*g]	11,018	12,237[*g]	12,846[*g]	---
14.	Value of livestock on farms, dollars[28,29,30,36,76,83,*a]	45,319,272	162,111,348	166,560,690	---	604,348,000	618,332,000	798,624,000	1,045,979,000
15.	Average value of livestock per farm, dollars[19,28,29,30,36]	1,329	6,869	10,463	---	49,090	45,857	56,048	77,480
16.	Production of cotton in bales[28,29,30,67,74,83]	100,138[*f]	261,283	299,669	143,000	118,536	88,282	113,013	80,000[*m,n]
17.	Percent of total production of cotton[28,29,30]	0.9[*f]	1.7	2.2	1.4	1.1	0.8	0.9	0.7

GENERAL AGRICULTURE STATISTICS, 1850-1990									
NEW MEXICO									
Item No.		1940	1950	1960	1970	1978	1982	1987	1990
18.	Production of wheat in bushels[31,32,35,36,69,74,84]	3,092,256	4,960,810	3,613,411	5,152,000	5,482,576	10,026,475	8,820,030	3,200,000
19.	Percent of total production of wheat[31,32,33,35,36]	.4362	.4928	.3422	.3760	.34105	.4225	.4674	.1965
20.	Production of corn in bushels[36,37,38,39,70,74,85]	1,967,780	1,212,860	1,584,000	1,071,000	6,423,473	6,901,030	5,300,378	9,765,000
21.	Percent of total production of corn[36,37,38,39]	0.1	*j	*j	*j	0.1	0.1	0.1	0.1
22.	Production of oats in bushels[31,35,36,71,80,86]	42,428	430,616	305,807	---	---	260,277	243,044	---
23.	Percent of total production of oats[31,35,36]	*j	*j	*j	---	---	0.1	0.1	---
24.	Production of soybeans in bushels[36,40,41,72,74,76,87]	509*h	---	11,347	---	59,550	42,818	*l	---
25.	Percent of total production of soybeans[36,40,41]	.0006	---	.0022	---	.0035	.0022	---	---
26.	Production of hay crops in tons[31,34,42,43,44,74,76,88]	377,671	396,990	559,248	1,044,000	1,042,578	1,042,289	960,735	1,332,000*o
27.	Percent of total production of hay crops[31,34,42,43,44]	0.5	0.4	0.5	0.8	0.8	0.8	0.7	0.9

[a] See the Glossary of Terms for changing definitions, i.e. farm, improved land, cropland harvested, farm owners, and livestock.
[b] Prior to 1924, the data relate to the total acreage of crops for which figures are available, except for 1920 when 14,502,932 acres of corn cut for forage were excluded (as most of this was probably duplicated in the acreage of corn harvested for grain).
[c] Percentage computed by compiler from data herein. See endnotes for source of data.
[d] Values in gold, one-fifth less than currency values.
[e] Managers included with owners.
[f] Running square bales, counting round as half bales.
[g] Census listed the number of full and part time owners separately. Compiler added the two numbers for the above figure.
[h] Includes quantity of beans harvested from acreage grown with other crops as well as that from acreage grown alone.
[i] The total value for each state for 1950 was based on the average value per acre for farms in the sample, for which value of land and buildings was reported. The average value per farm and per acre was based on the total value of all farms.
[j] Less than one-tenth of one percent.
[k] Including estimated value of range animals.
[l] Withheld to avoid disclosing data for individual farms.
[m] Production ginned and to be ginned.
[n] 480-pound net weight bales.
[o] Census had two separate listings: hay, alfalfa, and alfalfa mixtures; and hay, all other. Compiler added the two listings for the above figure.

GENERAL AGRICULTURE STATISTICS, 1850-1990

NEW YORK

Item No.		1850	1860	1870	1880	1890	1900	1910	1920	1930
1.	Number of farms[18,19,68,73,76,82,*a]	170,621	196,990	216,253	241,058	226,223	226,720	215,597	193,195	159,806
2.	Acres in farms[18,19,68,73,76,82]	19,119,084	20,974,958	22,190,810	23,780,754	21,961,562	22,648,109	22,030,367	20,632,803	17,979,633
3.	Acres improved land in farms[20,*a]	12,408,964	14,358,403	15,627,206	17,717,862	16,389,380	15,599,986	14,844,039	13,158,781	---
4.	Cropland harvested, acres[18,19,73,76,*a,b]	---	---	---	8,698,831	8,889,349	9,041,199	8,387,731	8,147,816	6,958,936
5.	Percentage increase in number of farms[18,19]	---	15.5	9.8	11.5	-6.2	0.2	-4.9	-10.4	-17.3
6.	Percentage increase of land in farms[18,19]	---	9.7	5.8	7.2	-7.6	3.1	-2.7	-6.3	-12.9
7.	Percentage increase of improved land in farms[20]	---	15.7	8.8	13.4	-7.5	-4.8	-4.8	-11.4	---
8.	Average acreage per farm[18,19,66,73,76,78]	112.1	106.5	102.6	98.7	97.1	99.9	102.2	106.8	112.5
9.	Percentage increase in cropland harvested[18,19,*b]	---	---	---	---	2.2	1.7	-7.2	-2.9	-14.6
10.	Value of farms, dollars[18,19,64,79,81]	554,546,642	803,343,593	1,018,286,213	1,056,176,741	968,127,286	888,134,180	1,184,745,829	1,425,061,740	1,315,904,741
11.	Value of farms, percent increase[18,19]	---	44.9	26.8	3.7	-8.3	-8.3	33.4	20.3	-7.7
12.	Average value per farm, dollars[18,19,64,73,76]	3,250	4,078	4,709	4,381	4,280	3,917	5,495	7,376	8,234
13.	Farms operated by owners[21,22,23,24,25,26,27,65,77,*a]	---	---	---	201,186[*e]	180,472[*e]	168,698	166,674	151,717	136,041
14.	Value of livestock on farms, dollars[28,29,30,36,76,83,*a]	73,570,499	103,856,296	140,706,169[*d]	117,868,283	124,523,965	125,583,715	183,090,844	313,554,695	221,634,355
15.	Average value of livestock per farm, dollars[19,28,29,30,36]	431	527	651[*d]	489	550	554	849	1,623	1,387[*c]
16.	Production of cotton in bales[28,29,30,67,74,83]	---	---	---	---	---	---	---	---	---
17.	Percent of total production of cotton[28,29,30]	---	---	---	---	---	---	---	---	---

GENERAL AGRICULTURE STATISTICS, 1850-1990										
NEW YORK										
Item No.		1850	1860	1870	1880	1890	1900	1910	1920	1930
18.	Production of wheat in bushels[31,32,35,36,69,74,84]	13,121,498	8,681,105	12,178,462	11,587,766	8,304,539	10,412,675	6,664,121	9,135,268	3,817,648
19.	Percent of total production of wheat[31,32,33,35,36]	13.0580	5.0149	4.2324	2.5219	1.7731	1.5812	.9752	.9963	.4768
20.	Production of corn in bushels[36,37,38,39,70,74,85]	17,858,400	20,061,049	16,462,825	25,690,156	15,109,969	20,024,850	18,115,634	14,109,202	4,283,820
21.	Percent of total production of corn[36,37,38,39]	3.0	2.4	2.2	1.5	0.7	0.8	0.7	0.6	0.2
22.	Production of oats in bushels[31,35,36,71,80,86]	26,552,814	35,175,134	35,293,625	37,575,506	38,896,479	40,785,900	34,795,277	21,595,461	12,775,284
23.	Percent of total production of oats[31,35,36]	18.1	20.4	12.5	9.2	4.8	4.3	3.5	2.0	1.3
24.	Production of soybeans in bushels[36,40,41,72,74,76,87]	---	---	---	---	---	---	5	16,556	3,781
25.	Percent of total production of soybeans[36,40,41]	---	---	---	---	---	---	.0200	1.4585	.0437
26.	Production of hay crops in tons[31,34,42,43,44,74,76,88]	3,728,797	3,564,793	5,614,205	5,255,642	6,675,658	6,319,475	7,056,980	9,472,345	5,154,974
27.	Percent of total production of hay crops[31,34,42,43,44]	27.0[*c]	18.7	20.6	14.9	10.0	8.0	7.2	7.7	6.0

GENERAL AGRICULTURE STATISTICS, 1850-1990

NEW YORK

Item No.		1940	1950	1960	1970	1978	1982	1987	1990
1.	Number of farms[18,19,68,73,76,82,*a]	153,238	124,977	82,356	51,909	43,075	42,207	37,743	38,500
2.	Acres in farms[18,19,68,73,76,82]	17,170,337	16,016,721	13,489,516	10,148,000	9,461,060	9,189,559	8,416,228	8,400,000
3.	Acres improved land in farms[20,*a]	---	---	---	---	---	---	---	---
4.	Cropland harvested, acres[18,19,73,76,*a,b]	6,581,296	5,791,673	5,032,671	3,925,000	4,348,591	4,430,198	3,899,819	---
5.	Percentage increase in number of farms[18,19]	-4.1	-18.4	-34.1	-37.0	-17.0	-2.0	-10.6	2.0
6.	Percentage increase of land in farms[18,19]	-4.5	-6.7	-15.8	-24.8	-6.8	-2.9	-8.4	-0.2
7.	Percentage increase of improved land in farms[20]	---	---	---	---	---	---	---	---
8.	Average acreage per farm[18,19,66,73,76,78]	112.1	128.2	163.8	196	220	218	223	215
9.	Percentage increase in cropland harvested[18,19,*b]	-5.4	-12.0	-13.1	-22.0	10.8	1.9	-12.0	---
10.	Value of farms, dollars[18,19,64,79,81]	947,073,893	1,467,452,000[*i]	1,971,252,000	2,772,000,000	6,314,665,775	7,509,000,000	8,263,000,000	8,615,000,000
11.	Value of farms, percent increase[18,19]	-28.0	54.9[*i]	34.3	40.6	128	18.9	10.0	4.3
12.	Average value per farm, dollars[18,19,64,73,76]	6,180	11,742[*i]	23,936	53,000	146,597	177,988	218,934	223,766
13.	Farms operated by owners[21,22,23,24,25,26,27,65,77,*a]	132,100	116,510	77,910[*g]	49,434[*g]	40,525	39,822[*g]	35,571[*g]	---
14.	Value of livestock on farms, dollars[28,29,30,36,76,83,*a]	173,442,063	349,390,932	450,166,186	---	1,325,936,000	1,769,216,000	1,740,508,000	1,983,159,000
15.	Average value of livestock per farm, dollars[19,28,29,30,36]	1,132	2,796	5,466	---	30,782	41,918	35,517	51,511
16.	Production of cotton in bales[28,29,30,67,74,83]	---	---	---	---	---	---	---	---
17.	Percent of total production of cotton[28,29,30]	---	---	---	---	---	---	---	---

GENERAL AGRICULTURE STATISTICS, 1850-1990									
NEW YORK									
Item No.		1940	1950	1960	1970	1978	1982	1987	1990
18.	Production of wheat in bushels[31,32,35,36,69,74,84]	6,543,906	10,337,917	7,259,656	6,579,000	2,191,852	4,951,504	3,622,242	5,850,000
19.	Percent of total production of wheat[31,32,33,35,36]	.9232	1.1128	.6875	.4801	.136348	---	---	---
20.	Production of corn in bushels[36,37,38,39,70,74,85]	6,859,795	7,703,216	33,405,000	22,041,000	50,651,462	70,349,704	65,911,889	53,010,000
21.	Percent of total production of corn[36,37,38,39]	0.3	0.3	0.8	0.5	0.7	0.9	0.9	0.7
22.	Production of oats in bushels[31,35,36,71,80,86]	19,490,828	16,220,320	32,386,104	22,554,000	---	16,151,602	9,562,189	9,145,000
23.	Percent of total production of oats[31,35,36]	2.2	1.4	3.2	2.5	---	3.2	3.1	2.4
24.	Production of soybeans in bushels[36,40,41,72,74,76,87]	97,375[*h]	75,577	39,283	120,000	539,809	583,577	942,410	---
25.	Percent of total production of soybeans[36,40,41]	.1112	.0356	.0076	.0107	.031345	.0293	.0513	---
26.	Production of hay crops in tons[31,34,42,43,44,74,76,88]	4,385,674	4,402,336	5,390,738	5,798,000	4,810,961	5,056,408	4,861,661	4,538,000[*j]
27.	Percent of total production of hay crops[31,34,42,43,44]	5.3	4.9	5.1	4.5	3.7	3.9	3.8	3.1

[a] See the Glossary of Terms for changing definitions, i.e. farm, improved land, cropland harvested, farm owners, and livestock.
[b] Prior to 1924, the data relate to the total acreage of crops for which figures are available, except for 1920 when 14,502,932 acres of corn cut for forage were excluded (as most of this was probably duplicated in the acreage of corn harvested for grain).
[c] Percentage computed by compiler from data herein. See endnotes for source of data.
[d] Values in gold, one-fifth less than currency values.
[e] Managers included with owners.
[f] Running square bales, counting round as half bales.
[g] Census listed the number of full and part time owners separately. Compiler added the two numbers for the above figure.
[h] Includes quantity of beans harvested from acreage grown with other crops as well as that from acreage grown alone.
[i] The total value for each state for 1950 was based on the average value per acre for farms in the sample, for which value of land and buildings was reported. The average value per farm and per acre was based on the total value of all farms.
[j] Census had two separate listings: hay, alfalfa, and alfalfa mixtures; and hay, all other. Compiler added the two listings for the above figure.

GENERAL AGRICULTURE STATISTICS, 1850-1990										
NORTH CAROLINA										
Item No.		1850	1860	1870	1880	1890	1900	1910	1920	1930
1.	Number of farms[18,19,68,73,76,82,*a]	56,963	75,203	93,565	157,609	178,359	224,637	253,725	269,763	279,708
2.	Acres in farms[18,19,68,73,76,82]	20,996,983	23,762,969	19,835,410	22,363,558	22,651,896	22,749,356	22,439,129	20,021,736	18,055,103
3.	Acres improved land in farms[20,*a]	5,453,975	6,517,284	5,258,742	6,481,191	7,828,569	8,327,106	8,813,056	8,198,409	---
4.	Cropland harvested, acres[18,19,73,76,*a,b]	---	---	---	4,634,339	5,205,938	5,609,144	5,737,037	5,850,997	5,809,741
5.	Percentage increase in number of farms[18,19]	---	32.0	24.4	68.4	13.2	25.9	12.9	6.3	3.7
6.	Percentage increase of land in farms[18,19]	---	13.2	-16.5	12.7	1.3	0.4	-1.4	-10.8	-9.8
7.	Percentage increase of improved land in farms[20]	---	19.5	-19.3	23.2	20.8	6.4	5.8	-7.0	---
8.	Average acreage per farm[18,19,66,73,76,78]	368.6	316.0	212.0	141.9	127.0	101.3	88.4	74.2	64.5
9.	Percentage increase in cropland harvested[18,19,*b]	---	---	---	---	12.3	7.7	2.3	2.0	-0.7
10.	Value of farms, dollars[18,19,64,79,81]	67,891,766	143,301,065	62,568,866	135,793,602	183,977,010	194,655,920	456,624,607	1,076,392,960	844,121,809
11.	Value of farms, percent increase[18,19]	---	111.1	-56.3	117.0	35.5	5.8	134.6	135.7	-21.6
12.	Average value per farm, dollars[18,19,64,73,76]	1,192	1,906	669	862	1,031	867	1,800	3,990	3,018
13.	Farms operated by owners[21,22,23,24,25,26,27,65,77,*a]	---	---	---	104,887[*e]	117,469[*e]	130,572	145,320	151,376	141,445
14.	Value of livestock on farms, dollars[28,29,30,36,76,83,*a]	17,717,647	31,130,805	17,595,174[*d]	22,414,659	25,547,280	30,106,173	62,649,984	119,152,672	78,537,148
15.	Average value of livestock per farm, dollars[19,28,29,30,36]	311	414	188[*d]	142	143	134	247	442	281
16.	Production of cotton in bales[28,29,30,67,74,83]	73,845	145,514	144,935	389,598	336,261	459,707[*f]	665,132[*f]	858,406[*f]	764,328[*f]
17.	Percent of total production of cotton[28,29,30]	3.0	2.7	4.8	6.8	4.5	4.8[*f]	6.2[*f]	7.5[*f]	5.2[*f]

GENERAL AGRICULTURE STATISTICS, 1850-1990										
NORTH CAROLINA										
Item No.		1850	1860	1870	1880	1890	1900	1910	1920	1930
18.	Production of wheat in bushels[31,32,35,36,69,74,84]	2,130,102	4,743,706	2,859,879	3,397,393	4,292,035	4,342,351	3,827,145	4,744,528	3,623,003
19.	Percent of total production of wheat[31,32,33,35,36]	2.1198	2.7404	.9939	.7394	.9164	.6594	.560	.5019	.4525
20.	Production of corn in bushels[36,37,38,39,70,74,85]	27,941,051	30,078,564	18,454,215	28,019,839	25,783,623	34,818,860	34,063,531	40,998,317	35,608,833
21.	Percent of total production of corn[36,37,38,39]	4.7	3.6	2.4	1.6	1.2	1.3	1.3	1.8	1.7
22.	Production of oats in bushels[31,35,36,71,80,86]	4,032,078	2,781,860	3,220,105	3,838,068	4,512,762	2,454,768	2,782,508	1,671,308	949,082
23.	Percent of total production of oats[31,35,36]	2.8	1.6	1.1	0.9	0.6	0.3	0.3	0.2	0.1
24.	Production of soybeans in bushels[36,40,41,72,74,76,87]	---	---	---	---	---	---	13,313	498,048	1,047,201[*h]
25.	Percent of total production of soybeans[36,40,41]	---	---	---	---	---	---	53.3245[*c]	43.8754	12.0907
26.	Production of hay crops in tons[31,34,42,43,44,74,76,88]	145,653	181,365	83,540	89,528	191,262	246,820	371,126	491,995	500,741
27.	Percent of total production of hay crops[31,34,42,43,44]	1.1[*c]	1.0	0.3	0.3	0.3	0.3	0.4	0.4	0.6

GENERAL AGRICULTURE STATISTICS, 1850-1990									
NORTH CAROLINA									
Item No.		1940	1950	1960	1970	1978	1982	1987	1990
1.	Number of farms[18,19,68,73,76,82,*a]	278,276	288,508	190,567	119,386	81,706	72,792	59,284	62,000
2.	Acres in farms[18,19,68,73,76,82]	18,845,338	19,317,937	15,887,724	12,734,000	10,998,652	10,320,832	9,447,705	9,700,000
3.	Acres improved land in farms[20,*a]	---	---	---	---	---	---	---	---
4.	Cropland harvested, acres[18,19,73,76,*a,b]	6,125,386	5,782,407	4,746,364	4,022,000	4,467,045	4,659,283	3,779,164	---
5.	Percentage increase in number of farms[18,19]	-0.5	3.7	-33.9	-37.4	-31.6	-10.9	-18.6	4.6
6.	Percentage increase of land in farms[18,19]	4.4	2.5	-17.8	-19.9	-13.6	-6.2	-8.5	2.7
7.	Percentage increase of improved land in farms[20]	---	---	---	---	---	---	---	---
8.	Average acreage per farm[18,19,66,73,76,78]	67.7	67.0	83.4	107	135	142	159	154
9.	Percentage increase in cropland harvested[18,19,*b]	5.4	-5.6	-17.9	-15.3	11.1	4.3	-19.0	---
10.	Value of farms, dollars[18,19,64,79,81]	736,708,125	1,905,714,000[*i,j]	2,948,972,000[*j]	4,244,000,000	11,558,457,584	13,669,000,000	11,845,000,000	11,821,000,000
11.	Value of farms, percent increase[18,19]	-12.7	158.7[*i,j]	54.7[*j]	43.9	172.3	18.3	-13.3	-0.2
12.	Average value per farm, dollars[18,19,64,73,76]	2,647	6,605[*i,j]	15,475[*j]	36,000	141,464	187,840	199,781	190,661
13.	Farms operated by owners[21,22,23,24,25,26,27,65,77,*a]	154,235	177,507	132,166[*g]	101,514[*g]	70,008	64,097[*g]	53,538[*g]	---
14.	Value of livestock on farms, dollars[28,29,30,36,76,83,*a]	89,925,652	146,286,671	155,842,492	221,178,000	1,310,309,000	1,602,642,000	2,104,430,000	2,652,798,000
15.	Average value of livestock per farm, dollars[19,28,29,30,36]	323	507	818	1,853	16,037	22,017	35,497	42,787
16.	Production of cotton in bales[28,29,30,67,74,83]	458,146	472,389	318,638	155,000	47,261	92,248	93,720	141,000[*l,m]
17.	Percent of total production of cotton[28,29,30]	4.0	3.1	2.3	1.5	0.4	0.8	0.7	1.2

GENERAL AGRICULTURE STATISTICS, 1850-1990

NORTH CAROLINA

Item No.		1940	1950	1960	1970	1978	1982	1987	1990
18.	Production of wheat in bushels[31,32,35,36,69,74,84]	4,968,759	4,581,881	8,609,247	8,514,000	4,312,796	20,682,804	15,091,015	21,420,000
19.	Percent of total production of wheat[31,32,33,35,36]	.7010	.4552	.8153	.6214	.26828	.8715	.7997	1.0522
20.	Production of corn in bushels[36,37,38,39,70,74,85]	50,797,461	58,054,020	85,914,000	70,000,000	113,677,738	133,576,411	71,595,021	88,350,000
21.	Percent of total production of corn[36,37,38,39]	2.2	2.1	2.0	1.7	1.7	1.8	*k	1.2
22.	Production of oats in bushels[31,35,36,71,80,86]	3,038,823	6,821,344	10,055,957	6,448,000	---	3,050,914	2,293,375	9,145,000
23.	Percent of total production of oats[31,35,36]	0.4	0.6	1.0	0.7	---	0.6	0.7	2.5
24.	Production of soybeans in bushels[36,40,41,72,74,76,87]	1,650,314*h	2,990,624	8,472,872	20,808,000	35,093,482	42,285,536	31,368,069	41,850,000
25.	Percent of total production of soybeans[36,40,41]	1.8841	1.4078	1.6432	1.8517	2.03776	2.1249	1.7610	2.1720
26.	Production of hay crops in tons[31,34,42,43,44,74,76,88]	970,831	980,532	779,754	583,000	673,400	647,953	795,954	1,161,000*n
27.	Percent of total production of hay crops[31,34,42,43,44]	1.2	1.1	0.7	0.5	0.5	0.5	0.6	0.8

[a] See the Glossary of Terms for changing definitions, i.e. farm, improved land, cropland harvested, farm owners, and livestock.
[b] Prior to 1924, the data relate to the total acreage of crops for which figures are available, except for 1920 when 14,502,932 acres of corn cut for forage were excluded (as most of this was probably duplicated in the acreage of corn harvested for grain).
[c] Percentage computed by compiler from data herein. See endnotes for source of data.
[d] Values in gold, one-fifth less than currency values.
[e] Managers included with owners.
[f] Running square bales, counting round as half bales.
[g] Census listed the number of full and part time owners separately. Compiler added the two numbers for the above figure.
[h] Includes quantity of beans harvested from acreage grown with other crops as well as that from acreage grown alone.
[i] The total value for each state for 1950 was based on the average value per acre for farms in the sample, for which value of land and buildings was reported. The average value per farm and per acre was based on the total value of all farms.
[j] Based on a sampling of farms.
[k] Less than one-tenth of one percent.
[l] Production ginned and to be ginned.
[m] 480-pound net weight bales.
[n] Census had two separate listings: hay, alfalfa, and alfalfa mixtures; and hay, all other. Compiler added the two listings for the above figure.

GENERAL AGRICULTURE STATISTICS, 1850-1990										
NORTH DAKOTA										
Item No.		1850	1860	1870	1880	1890	1900	1910	1920	1930
1.	Number of farms[18,19,68,73,76,82,*a]	---	123[*j]	1,720[*j]	3,790[*k]	27,611	45,332	74,360	77,690	77,975
2.	Acres in farms[18,19,68,73,76,82]	---	26,448[*j]	302,376[*j]	1,027,845[*k]	7,660,333	15,542,640	28,426,650	36,214,751	38,657,894
3.	Acres improved land in farms[20,*a]	---	2,115[*j]	42,645[*j]	259,543[*k]	4,658,015	9,644,520	20,455,092	24,563,178	---
4.	Cropland harvested, acres[18,19,73,76,*a,b]	---	---	---	642,035	3,856,054	7,821,704	15,888,756	19,422,855	21,254,660
5.	Percentage increase in number of farms[18,19]	---	---	[*j,m]	120.3[*k]	628.5	64.2	64.0	4.5	0.4
6.	Percentage increase of land in farms[18,19]	---	---	[*j,m]	239.9[*k]	645.3	102.9	82.9	27.4	6.7
7.	Percentage increase of improved land in farms[20]	---	---	1,916.3[*c]	508.6[*k]	1,694.7[*c]	107.1	112.1	20.1	---
8.	Average acreage per farm[18,19,66,73,76,78]	---	215.0[*j]	175.8[*j]	271.2[*k]	277.4	342.9	382.3	466.1	495.8
9.	Percentage increase in cropland harvested[18,19,*b]	---	---	---	---	500.6	102.8	103.1	22.2	9.4
10.	Value of farms, dollars[18,19,64,79,81]	---	96,445[*j]	1,668,211[*j]	8,575,114[*k]	75,310,305	198,780,700	822,656,744	1,488,521,495	951,225,446
11.	Value of farms, percent increase[18,19]	---	---	[*j,m]	414.0	778.2	163.9	313.9	80.9	-36.1
12.	Average value per farm, dollars[18,19,64,73,76]	---	784[*j]	970[*j]	2,263[*k]	2,728	4,385	11,063	19,160	12,199
13.	Farms operated by owners[21,22,23,24,25,26,27,65,77,*a]	---	---	---	16,757[*e,k]	25,698[*e]	40,972	63,212	56,917	50,105
14.	Value of livestock on farms, dollars[28,29,30,36,76,83,*a]	---	39,116[*j]	623,962[*d,j]	1,448,053[*k,n]	18,787,294	42,430,491	108,249,866	157,034,635	116,588,924
15.	Average value of livestock per farm, dollars[19,28,29,30,36]	---	318[*j]	363[*d,j]	433[*k]	680	936	1,456	2,021	1,495
16.	Production of cotton in bales[28,29,30,67,74,83]	---	---	---	---	---	---	---	---	---
17.	Percent of total production of cotton[28,29,30]	---	---	---	---	---	---	---	---	---

GENERAL AGRICULTURE STATISTICS, 1850-1990										
NORTH DAKOTA										
Item No.		1850	1860	1870	1880	1890	1900	1910	1920	1930
18.	Production of wheat in bushels[31,32,35,36,69,74,84]	---	945[*j]	170,662[*j]	1,737,343[*k]	26,403,365	59,888,810	116,781,886	61,540,404	95,574,408
19.	Percent of total production of wheat[31,32,33,35,36]	---	.0005[*j]	.0593[*j]	0.3781[*k]	5.6372	9.0943	17.0889	6.5094	11.9371
20.	Production of corn in bushels[36,37,38,39,70,74,85]	---	20,269[*j]	133,140[*j]	2,000,864	178,729	1,284,870	4,941,152	3,876,883	2,172,643
21.	Percent of total production of corn[36,37,38,39]	---	[*j,l]	[*j,l]	0.1	[*l]	[*l]	0.2	0.2	0.1
22.	Production of oats in bushels[31,35,36,71,80,86]	---	2,540[*j]	114,327[*j]	728,811[*k]	5,773,129	22,125,331	65,886,702	30,294,074	31,174,936
23.	Percent of total production of oats[31,35,36]	---	[*j,l]	[*j,l]	0.5[*k]	0.7	2.3	6.5	2.9	3.1
24.	Production of soybeans in bushels[36,40,41,72,74,76,87]	---	---	---	---	---	---	---	110	195[*h]
25.	Percent of total production of soybeans[36,40,41]	---	---	---	---	---	---	---	.0097[*c]	.0023[*c]
26.	Production of hay crops in tons[31,34,42,43,44,74,76,88]	---	855[*j]	13,347[*j]	308,036[*k]	531,472	1,747,390	3,010,582	3,145,407	2,362,585
27.	Percent of total production of hay crops[31,34,42,43,44]	---	[*j,l]	0.1[*j]	0.9[*k]	0.8	2.2	3.1	2.5	2.8

GENERAL AGRICULTURE STATISTICS, 1850-1990									
NORTH DAKOTA									
Item No.		1940	1950	1960	1970	1978	1982	1987	1990
1.	Number of farms[18,19,68,73,76,82,*a]	73,962	65,401	54,928	46,381	40,357	36,431	35,289	34,000
2.	Acres in farms[18,19,68,73,76,82]	37,936,136	41,194,044	41,465,717	43,118,000	41,702,370	40,206,005	40,336,869	40,500,000
3.	Acres improved land in farms[20,*a]	---	---	---	---	---	---	---	---
4.	Cropland harvested, acres[18,19,73,76,*a,b]	15,536,632	20,352,760	19,357,711	17,643,000	18,978,609	20,308,135	18,363,910	---
5.	Percentage increase in number of farms[18,19]	-5.1	-11.6	-16.0	-15.6	-13.0	-9.7	-3.1	-3.7
6.	Percentage increase of land in farms[18,19]	-1.9	8.6	0.7	4.0	-3.3	-3.6	0.3	0.4
7.	Percentage increase of improved land in farms[20]	---	---	---	---	---	---	---	---
8.	Average acreage per farm[18,19,66,73,76,78]	512.9	629.9	754.9	930	1,033	1,104	1,143	1,209
9.	Percentage increase in cropland harvested[18,19,*b]	-26.9	31.0	-4.9	-8.9	7.6	7.0	-9.6	---
10.	Value of farms, dollars[18,19,64,79,81]	490,197,358	1,188,860,000[*i]	2,140,991,000	4,045,000,000	14,564,922,014	17,609,000,000	12,934,000,000	12,171,000,000
11.	Value of farms, percent increase[18,19]	-48.5	142.5[*i]	80.1	88.9	260.1	20.9	-26.5	-5.9
12.	Average value per farm, dollars[18,19,64,73,76]	6,628	18,178[*i]	38,978	87,000	360,902	486,939	366,475	357,971
13.	Farms operated by owners[21,22,23,24,25,26,27,65,77,*a]	40,391	50,976	44,253	39,696[*g]	33,492	30,197[*g]	28,979[*g]	---
14.	Value of livestock on farms, dollars[28,29,30,36,76,83,*a]	79,478,711	201,506,486	292,523,424	402,870,000	495,583,000	534,455,000	690,946,000	813,451,000
15.	Average value of livestock per farm, dollars[19,28,29,30,36]	1,075	3,081	5,326	8,686	12,280	14,670	19,580	23,925
16.	Production of cotton in bales[28,29,30,67,74,83]	---	---	---	---	---	---	---	---
17.	Percent of total production of cotton[28,29,30]	---	---	---	---	---	---	---	---

GENERAL AGRICULTURE STATISTICS, 1850-1990

NORTH DAKOTA

Item No.		1940	1950	1960	1970	1978	1982	1987	1990
18.	Production of wheat in bushels[31,32,35,36,69,74,84]	69,261,286	105,579,644	94,798,822	152,826,000	268,471,784	295,849,566	248,678,425	242,320,000
19.	Percent of total production of wheat[31,32,33,35,36]	9.7709	10.4892	8.9778	11.1534	1.6700	12.4660	13.1778	11.9028
20.	Production of corn in bushels[36,37,38,39,70,74,85]	6,630,344	11,465,677	22,126,000	6,500,000	20,262,366	34,122,728	46,983,098	34,875,000
21.	Percent of total production of corn[36,37,38,39]	0.3	0.4	0.5	0.2	0.3	0.5	0.7	0.5
22.	Production of oats in bushels[31,35,36,71,80,86]	33,104,454	32,220,244	39,116,923	115,541,000	---	47,655,524	31,162,857	20,150,000
23.	Percent of total production of oats[31,35,36]	3.8	2.8	3.9	12.7	---	9.4	10.0	5.4
24.	Production of soybeans in bushels[36,40,41,72,74,76,87]	9,966[*h]	226,044	2,430,630	2,715,000	4,108,667	8,800,232	15,034,325	13,860,000
25.	Percent of total production of soybeans[36,40,41]	.0114	.1064	.4714	.2416	.23857	.4422	.8179	.7193
26.	Production of hay crops in tons[31,34,42,43,44,74,76,88]	2,392,734	2,901,939	2,968,110	4,414,000	4,914,517	4,190,010	4,030,165	3,020,000[*o]
27.	Percent of total production of hay crops[31,34,42,43,44]	2.9	3.3	2.8	3.5	3.8	3.3	3.1	2.1

[a] See the Glossary of Terms for changing definitions, i.e. farm, improved land, cropland harvested, farm owners, and livestock.

[b] Prior to 1924, the data relate to the total acreage of crops for which figures are available, except for 1920 when 14,502,932 acres of corn cut for forage were excluded (as most of this was probably duplicated in the acreage of corn harvested for grain).

[c] Percentage computed by compiler from data herein. See endnotes for source of data.

[d] Values in gold, one-fifth less than currency values.

[e] Managers included with owners.

[f] Running square bales, counting round as half bales.

[g] Census listed the number of full and part time owners separately. Compiler added the two numbers for the above figure.

[h] Includes quantity of beans harvested from acreage grown with other crops as well as that from acreage grown alone.

[i] The total value for each state for 1950 was based on the average value per acre for farms in the sample, for which value of land and buildings was reported. The average value per farm and per acre was based on the total value of all farms.

[j] Dakota Territory.

[k] North Dakota and South Dakota admitted as states in 1889. Figures for 1880 obtained by consolidating data for the counties which then occupied the area now known as North Dakota.

[l] Less then one-tenth of one percent.

[m] 1,000 percent or more.

[n] Including estimated value of range animals.

[o] Census had two separate listings: hay, alfalfa, and alfalfa mixtures; and hay, all other. Compiler added the two listings for the above figure.

GENERAL AGRICULTURE STATISTICS, 1850-1990

OHIO

Item No.		1850	1860	1870	1880	1890	1900	1910	1920	1930
1.	Number of farms[18,19,68,73,76,82,*a]	143,807	179,889	195,953	247,189	251,430	276,719	272,045	256,695	219,296
2.	Acres in farms[18,19,68,73,76,82]	17,997,493	20,472,141	21,712,420	24,529,226	23,352,408	24,501,985	24,105,708	23,515,888	21,514,059
3.	Acres improved land in farms[20,*a]	9,851,493	12,625,394	14,469,133	18,081,091	18,338,824	19,244,472	19,227,969	18,542,353	---
4.	Cropland harvested, acres[18,19,73,76,*a,b]	---	---	---	9,086,811	10,038,131	11,614,165	11,431,610	11,783,788	10,115,652
5.	Percentage increase in number of farms[18,19]	---	25.1	8.9	26.1	1.7	10.1	-1.7	-5.6	-14.6
6.	Percentage increase of land in farms[18,19]	---	13.7	6.1	13.0	-4.8	4.9	-1.6	-2.4	-8.5
7.	Percentage increase of improved land in farms[20]	---	28.2	14.6	25.0	1.4	4.9	-0.1	-3.6	---
8.	Average acreage per farm[18,19,66,73,76,78]	125.2	113.8	110.8	99.2	92.9	88.5	88.6	91.6	98.1
9.	Percentage increase in cropland harvested[18,19,*b]	---	---	---	---	10.5	15.7	-1.6	3.1	-14.2
10.	Value of farms, dollars[18,19,64,79,81]	358,758,603	678,132,991	843,572,181	1,127,497,353	1,050,031,828	1,036,615,180	1,654,152,406	2,661,435,949	1,693,030,716
11.	Value of farms, percent increase[18,19]	---	89.0	24.4	33.7	-6.9	-1.3	59.6	60.9	-36.4
12.	Average value per farm, dollars[18,19,64,73,76]	2,495	3,770	4,305	4,561	4,176	3,746	6,080	10,368	7,720
13.	Farms operated by owners[21,22,23,24,25,26,27,65,77,*a]	---	---	---	199,562[*c]	193,895[*c]	197,361	192,104	177,986	159,849
14.	Value of livestock on farms, dollars[28,29,30,36,76,83,*a]	44,121,741	80,384,819	96,240,422[*d]	103,707,730	116,181,690	125,954,616	197,332,112	287,655,118	216,139,273
15.	Average value of livestock per farm, dollars[19,28,29,30,36]	307	447	491[*d]	420	462	455	725	1,121	986
16.	Production of cotton in bales[28,29,30,67,74,83]	---	---	---	---	---	---	---	---	---
17.	Percent of total production of cotton[28,29,30]	---	---	---	---	---	---	---	---	---

GENERAL AGRICULTURE STATISTICS, 1850-1990										
OHIO										
Item No.		1850	1860	1870	1880	1890	1900	1910	1920	1930
18.	Production of wheat in bushels[31,32,35,36,69,74,84]	14,487,351	15,119,047	27,882,159	46,014,869	35,559,208	50,376,800	30,663,704	58,124,351	30,289,579
19.	Percent of total production of wheat[31,32,33,35,36]	14.4173	8.7340	9.6899	10.0145	7.5921	7.6498	4.4871	6.1481	3.7831
20.	Production of corn in bushels[36,37,38,39,70,74,85]	59,078,695	73,543,190	67,501,144	111,877,124	113,892,318	152,055,390	157,513,300	149,844,626	102,177,194
21.	Percent of total production of corn[36,37,38,39]	10.0	8.8	8.9	6.4	5.4	5.7	6.2[*c]	6.4[*c]	4.8[*c]
22.	Production of oats in bushels[31,35,36,71,80,86]	13,472,742	15,409,234	25,347,549	28,664,505	40,136,732	42,050,910	57,591,046	46,818,330	44,730,590
23.	Percent of total production of oats[31,35,36]	9.2	8.9	9.0	7.0	5.0	4.5	5.7	4.4	4.5
24.	Production of soybeans in bushels[36,40,41,72,74,76,87]	---	---	---	---	---	---	424	17,441	316,462[*h]
25.	Percent of total production of soybeans[36,40,41]	---	---	---	---	---	---	1.6983[*c]	1.5365[*c]	3.6538
26.	Production of hay crops in tons[31,34,42,43,44,74,76,88]	1,443,142	1,564,502	2,289,565	2,212,133	3,981,070	3,629,722	4,522,066	5,637,908	3,456,552
27.	Percent of total production of hay crops[31,34,42,43,44]	10.4	8.2	8.4	6.3	6.0	4.6	4.6	4.6	4.1

GENERAL AGRICULTURE STATISTICS, 1850-1990									
OHIO									
Item No.		1940	1950	1960	1970	1978	1982	1987	1990
1.	Number of farms[18,19,68,73,76,82,*a]	233,783	199,359	140,353	111,332	89,131	86,934	79,277	84,000
2.	Acres in farms[18,19,68,73,76,82]	21,907,523	20,969,411	18,506,796	17,111,000	15,788,833	15,404,054	14,997,381	15,700,000
3.	Acres improved land in farms[20,*a]	---	---	---	---	---	---	---	---
4.	Cropland harvested, acres[18,19,73,76,*a,b]	9,771,609	10,295,590	9,743,467	8,792,000	10,213,858	10,396,323	9,297,596	---
5.	Percentage increase in number of farms[18,19]	6.6	-14.7	-29.6	-20.7	-20.0	-2.5	-8.8	6.0
6.	Percentage increase of land in farms[18,19]	1.8	-4.3	-11.7	-7.5	-7.7	-2.4	-2.6	4.7
7.	Percentage increase of improved land in farms[20]	---	---	---	---	---	---	---	---
8.	Average acreage per farm[18,19,66,73,76,78]	93.7	105.2	131.9	154	177	177	189	182
9.	Percentage increase in cropland harvested[18,19,*b]	-3.4	5.4	-5.4	-9.8	16.2	1.8	-10.6	---
10.	Value of farms, dollars[18,19,64,79,81]	1,443,917,176	2,858,969,000[*i]	4,573,139,000	6,819,000,000	23,493,594,635	23,287,000,000	18,023,000,000	16,389,000,000
11.	Value of farms, percent increase[18,19]	-14.7	98.0[*i]	60.0	49.1	245	-1.0	-22.6	-9.1
12.	Average value per farm, dollars[18,19,64,73,76]	6,176	14,341[*i]	32,583	65,000	263,585	267,899	227,341	195,107
13.	Farms operated by owners[21,22,23,24,25,26,27,65,77,*a]	171,156	162,995	117,039[*g]	98,032[*g]	78,231	77,145[*g]	70,529[*g]	---
14.	Value of livestock on farms, dollars[28,29,30,36,76,83,*a]	156,908,404	352,494,542	426,117,231	405,840,000	1,258,660,000	1,523,522,000	1,683,281,000	1,836,394,000
15.	Average value of livestock per farm, dollars[19,28,29,30,36]	671	1,768	3,036	3,645	14,122	17,525	21,233	21,862
16.	Production of cotton in bales[28,29,30,67,74,83]	---	---	---	---	---	---	---	---
17.	Percent of total production of cotton[28,29,30]	---	---	---	---	---	---	---	---

GENERAL AGRICULTURE STATISTICS, 1850-1990

OHIO

Item No.		1940	1950	1960	1970	1978	1982	1987	1990
18.	Production of wheat in bushels[31,32,35,36,69,74,84]	37,074,406	53,039,880	29,499,714	35,927,000	36,576,855	47,417,971	42,452,489	62,730,000
19.	Percent of total production of wheat[31,32,33,35,36]	5.2302	5.2694	2.7937	2.6220	2.2753	1.9980	2.2496	3.0813
20.	Production of corn in bushels[36,37,38,39,70,74,85]	156,303,520	168,046,185	246,708,000	232,078,000	350,988,744	417,724,837	355,339,490	342,200,000
21.	Percent of total production of corn[36,37,38,39]	6.8	6.0	5.8	5.7	5.2	5.6	5.3	4.5
22.	Production of oats in bushels[31,35,36,71,80,86]	30,764,247	42,281,470	47,930,525	29,870,000	---	20,554,883	13,781,000	15,750,000
23.	Percent of total production of oats[31,35,36]	3.5	3.7	4.8	3.3	---	4.1	4.4	4.2
24.	Production of soybeans in bushels[36,40,41,72,74,76,87]	10,293,393[a,h]	18,794,324	35,430,327	68,799,000	121,071,160	124,408,037	132,974,160	125,370,000
25.	Percent of total production of soybeans[36,40,41]	11.7517	8.8469	6.8713	6.1223	.70302	6.2517	7.2345	6.5066
26.	Production of hay crops in tons[31,34,42,43,44,74,76,88]	3,280,279	3,003,753	3,564,094	2,913,000	3,412,559	2,931,179	3,236,378	4,553,000[a,j]
27.	Percent of total production of hay crops[31,34,42,43,44]	4.0	3.4	3.3	2.3	.26107	2.3	2.5	3.1

[a] See the Glossary of Terms for changing definitions, i.e. farm, improved land, cropland harvested, farm owners, and livestock.
[b] Prior to 1924, the data relate to the total acreage of crops for which figures are available, except for 1920 when 14,502,932 acres of corn cut for forage were excluded (as most of this was probably duplicated in the acreage of corn harvested for grain).
[c] Percentage computed by compiler from data herein. See endnotes for source of data.
[d] Values in gold, one-fifth less than currency values.
[e] Managers included with owners.
[f] Running square bales, counting round as half bales.
[g] Census listed the number of full and part time owners separately. Compiler added the two numbers for the above figure.
[h] Includes quantity of beans harvested from acreage grown with other crops as well as that from acreage grown alone.
[i] The total value for each state for 1950 was based on the average value per acre for farms in the sample, for which value of land and buildings was reported. The average value per farm and per acre was based on the total value of all farms.
[j] Census had two separate listings: hay, alfalfa, and alfalfa mixtures; and hay, all other. Compiler added the two listings for the above figure.

GENERAL AGRICULTURE STATISTICS, 1850-1990

OKLAHOMA

Item No.		1850	1860	1870	1880[*j]	1890	1900	1910	1920	1930
1.	Number of farms[18,19,68,73,76,82,*a]	---	---	---	---	8,826[*m]	108,000[*q]	190,192	191,988	203,866
2.	Acres in farms[18,19,68,73,76,82]	---	---	---	---	1,606,423[*m]	22,988,339[*q]	28,859,353	31,951,934	33,790,817
3.	Acres improved land in farms[20,*a]	---	---	---	---	563,728	8,574,187[*q]	17,551,337	18,125,321	---
4.	Cropland harvested, acres[18,19,73,76,*a,b]	---	---	---	35,000[*j]	122,932[*m]	6,317,711[*q]	11,921,670	15,132,769	15,553,185
5.	Percentage increase in number of farms[18,19]	---	---	---	---	---	[*s,q]	76.1	0.9	6.2
6.	Percentage increase of land in farms[18,19]	---	---	---	---	---	[*s,q]	25.5	10.7	5.8
7.	Percentage increase of improved land in farms[20]	---	---	---	---	---	1,421.0[*q]	104.7	3.3	---
8.	Average acreage per farm[18,19,66,73,76,78]	---	---	---	---	182.0[*m]	212.9[*q]	151.7	166.4	165.8
9.	Percentage increase in cropland harvested[18,19,*b]	---	---	---	---	251.2[*m]	[*s,q]	88.7	26.9	2.8
10.	Value of farms, dollars[18,19,64,79,81]	---	---	---	---	8,581,170[*m]	170,804,675[*q]	738,677,224	1,363,865,294	1,242,723,526
11.	Value of farms, percent increase[18,19]	---	---	---	---	---	[*s,q]	332.5	84.6	-8.9
12.	Average value per farm, dollars[18,19,64,73,76]	---	---	---	---	972[*m]	1,582[*q]	3,884	7,104	6,096
13.	Farms operated by owners[21,22,23,24,25,26,27,65,77,*a]	---	---	---	---	8,761[*e,p]	60,209[*p]	85,404	93,217	77,714
14.	Value of livestock on farms, dollars[28,29,30,36,76,83,*a]	---	---	---	11,375,000[*k,l]	9,182,999[*n]	96,208,263[*q]	152,432,792	215,927,703	141,827,981
15.	Average value of livestock per farm, dollars[19,28,29,30,36]	---	---	---	---	1,040	877	802	1,125	696
16.	Production of cotton in bales[28,29,30,67,74,83]	---	---	---	---	425[*o]	70,675[*f]	555,742[*f]	1,006,242[*f]	1,130,415[*f]
17.	Percent of total production of cotton[28,29,30]	---	---	---	---	[*o,r]	0.7[*f]	5.2[*f]	8.8[*f]	7.8[*f]

GENERAL AGRICULTURE STATISTICS, 1850-1990										
OKLAHOMA										
Item No.		1850	1860	1870	1880	1890	1900	1910	1920	1930
18.	Production of wheat in bushels[31,32,35,36,69,74,84]	---	---	---	---	30,175[*p]	20,328,300[*p]	14,008,334	65,761,843	51,184,128
19.	Percent of total production of wheat[31,32,33,35,36]	---	---	---	---	.0064[*p]	3.0869[*p]	2.0499	6.9560	6.3928
20.	Production of corn in bushels[36,37,38,39,70,74,85]	---	---	---	---	234,315[*o]	38,239,880	94,283,407	53,851,093	44,830,439
21.	Percent of total production of corn[36,37,38,39]	---	---	---	---	[*r]	1.4	3.7	2.3	2.1
22.	Production of oats in bushels[31,35,36,71,80,86]	---	---	---	---	76,194[*p]	9,511,740[*p]	16,606,154	45,470,191	16,196,880
23.	Percent of total production of oats[31,35,36]	---	---	---	---	[*p,r]	1.0[*p]	1.7	4.3	1.6
24.	Production of soybeans in bushels[36,40,41,72,74,76,87]	---	---	---	---	---	---	---	2,968	52,893[*h]
25.	Percent of total production of soybeans[36,40,41]	---	---	---	---	---	---	---	.2615	.6107
26.	Production of hay crops in tons[31,34,42,43,44,74,76,88]	---	---	---	---	40,473[*o,p]	1,617,905[*p]	1,447,296	2,946,614	1,139,961
27.	Percent of total production of hay crops[31,34,42,43,44]	---	---	---	---	0.1[*o,p]	2.0[*p]	1.5	2.4	1.3

Item No.	GENERAL AGRICULTURE STATISTICS, 1850-1990 OKLAHOMA	1940	1950	1960	1970	1978	1982	1987	1990
1.	Number of farms[18,19,68,73,76,82,*a]	179,687	142,246	94,676	83,037	72,237	72,523	70,228	70,000
2.	Acres in farms[18,19,68,73,76,82]	34,803,317	36,006,603	35,800,688	36,008,000	33,737,292	32,369,206	31,541,977	33,000,000
3.	Acres improved land in farms[20,*a]	---	---	---	---	---	---	---	---
4.	Cropland harvested, acres[18,19,73,76,*a,b]	12,766,219	11,896,040	8,975,117	8,116,000	8,585,011	8,961,353	7,319,193	---
5.	Percentage increase in number of farms[18,19]	-11.9	-20.8	-33.4	-12.3	-13.0	0.4	-3.2	-0.3
6.	Percentage increase of land in farms[18,19]	3.0	3.5	-0.6	0.6	-6.3	-4.1	-2.6	4.6
7.	Percentage increase of improved land in farms[20]	---	---	---	---	---	---	---	---
8.	Average acreage per farm[18,19,66,73,76,78]	193.7	253.1	378.1	434	467	446	449	478
9.	Percentage increase in cropland harvested[18,19,*b]	-17.9	-6.8	-24.6	-9.6	5.8	4.4	-18.3	4.6
10.	Value of farms, dollars[18,19,64,79,81]	831,140,748	1,851,460,000[*i]	3,002,221,000[*t]	6,214,000,000	17,037,674,346	22,556,000,000	15,102,000,000	15,143,000,000
11.	Value of farms, percent increase[18,19]	-33.1	122.8[*i]	62.2[*t]	107.0	174.2	32.4	-33.0	0.3
12.	Average value per farm, dollars[18,19,64,73,76]	4,625	13,016[*i]	31,710[*t]	75,000	235,858	311,642	215,024	216,329
13.	Farms operated by owners[21,22,23,24,25,26,27,65,77,*a]	81,086	97,038	76,385[*g]	71,325[*g]	63,674	64,770[*g]	62,960[*g]	---
14.	Value of livestock on farms, dollars[28,29,30,36,76,83,*a]	108,484,682	300,241,879	408,083,219	812,887,000	1,712,670,000	1,702,366,000	2,104,842,000	2,363,125,000
15.	Average value of livestock per farm, dollars[19,28,29,30,36]	604	2,111	4,310	9,790	23,709	23,441	29,972	33,759
16.	Production of cotton in bales[28,29,30,67,74,83]	520,591[*f]	567,792	364,833	193,000	336,710	235,262	306,388	173,000[*u,v]
17.	Percent of total production of cotton[28,29,30]	4.5[*f]	3.7	2.6	1.9	3.2	2.1	2.3	1.5

GENERAL AGRICULTURE STATISTICS, 1850-1990									
OKLAHOMA									
Item No.		1940	1950	1960	1970	1978	1982	1987	1990
18.	Production of wheat in bushels[31,32,35,36,69,74,84]	58,492,919	78,682,555	83,737,347	98,202,000	124,604,327	171,665,099	113,464,955	153,900,000
19.	Percent of total production of wheat[31,32,33,35,36]	8.2518	7.8170	7.9302	7.1669	.77512	7.2333	6.0126	7.5596
20.	Production of corn in bushels[36,37,38,39,70,74,85]	25,341,206	19,204,157	8,316,000	4,758,000	3,764,346	3,652,498	8,019,226	9,204,000
21.	Percent of total production of corn[36,37,38,39]	1.1	0.7	0.2	0.1	0.1	*r	0.1	0.1
22.	Production of oats in bushels[31,35,36,71,80,86]	21,078,534	8,162,279	12,213,451	7,400,000	---	3,111,780	1,277,283	2,040,000
23.	Percent of total production of oats[31,35,36]	2.4	0.7	1.2	0.8	---	0.1	0.4	0.5
24.	Production of soybeans in bushels[36,40,41,72,74,76,87]	7,580*h	163,381	1,511,094	3,009,000	5,023,617	4,632,732	5,622,675	6,840,000
25.	Percent of total production of soybeans[36,40,41]	.0087	.0769	.2931	.2678	.2917054	.2328	.3059	.3550
26.	Production of hay crops in tons[31,34,42,43,44,74,76,88]	1,124,768	1,655,980	1,751,573	2,806,000	2,907,928	3,044,714	3,430,874	5,115,000*w
27.	Percent of total production of hay crops[31,34,42,43,44]	1.4	1.9	1.6	2.2	2.2	2.4	2.7	3.5

[a] See the Glossary of Terms for changing definitions, i.e. farm, improved land, cropland harvested, farm owners, and livestock.
[b] Prior to 1924, the data relate to the total acreage of crops for which figures are available, except for 1920 when 14,502,932 acres of corn cut for forage were excluded (as most of this was probably duplicated in the acreage of corn harvested for grain).
[c] Percentage computed by compiler from data herein. See endnotes for source of data.
[d] Values in gold, one-fifth less than currency values.
[e] Managers included with owners.
[f] Running square bales, counting round as half bales.
[g] Census listed the number of full and part time owners separately. Compiler added the two numbers for the above figure.
[h] Includes quantity of beans harvested from acreage grown with other crops as well as that from acreage grown alone.
[i] The total value for each state for 1950 was based on the average value per acre for farms in the sample, for which value of land and buildings was reported. The average value per farm and per acre was based on the total value of all farms.
[j] There was not enumeration of farms in 1880 in what is now known as Oklahoma; the figure shown under cropland harvested consists of cotton acreage reported for Indian Territory by special agent.
[k] Figures for 1880 are for Indian Territory.
[l] Including estimated value of range animals.
[m] The 1890 figures for number of farms, farm acreage, and value are for Oklahoma Territory alone, no data for these items being available for Indian Territory; the percent of total land area in farms is based on the total land area of Oklahoma Territory plus Indian Territory; acreage shown under cropland harvested includes 35,078 acres of cotton in Indian Territory estimated from a special survey.
[n] The 1890 figures for value of livestock include Indian Territory.
[o] Included in Indian Territory prior to 1890.
[p] Figures for 1900 include Indian Territory; those for 1890 are for Oklahoma Territory alone, no data being available for Indian Territory.
[q] Figures for 1900 are for Oklahoma Territory and Indian Territory.
[r] Less than one-tenth of one percent.
[s] 1,000 percent or more.
[t] Based on a sampling of farms.
[u] Production ginned and to be ginned.
[v] 480-pound net weight bales.
[w] Census had two separate listings: hay, alfalfa, and alfalfa mixtures; and hsy, all other. Compiler added the two listings for the above figure.

GENERAL AGRICULTURE STATISTICS, 1850-1990										
OREGON										
Item No.		1850	1860	1870	1880	1890	1900	1910	1920	1930
1.	Number of farms[18,19,68,73,76,82,*a]	1,164	5,806	7,587	16,217	25,530	35,837	45,502	50,206	55,153
2.	Acres in farms[18,19,68,73,76,82]	432,808	2,060,539	2,389,252	4,214,712	6,909,888	10,071,328	11,685,110	13,542,318	16,548,678
3.	Acres improved land in farms[20,*a]	132,857	896,414	1,116,290	2,198,645	3,516,000	3,328,308	4,274,803	4,913,851	---
4.	Cropland harvested, acres[18,19,73,76,*a,b]	---	---	---	799,724	1,317,490	2,027,856	2,281,288	2,804,265	2,906,324
5.	Percentage increase in number of farms[18,19]	---	398.8	30.7	113.7	57.4	40.4	27.0	10.3	9.9
6.	Percentage increase of land in farms[18,19]	---	376.1	16.0	76.4	63.9	45.8	16.0	15.9	22.2
7.	Percentage increase of improved land in farms[20]	---	574.7	24.5	97.0	59.9	-5.3	28.4	14.9	---
8.	Average acreage per farm[18,19,66,73,76,78]	371.8	354.9	314.9	259.9	270.7	281.0	256.8	269.7	300.1
9.	Percentage increase in cropland harvested[18,19,*b]	---	---	---	---	64.7	53.9	12.5	22.9	3.6
10.	Value of farms, dollars[18,19,64,79,81]	2,849,170	15,200,593	22,352,989	56,908,575	115,819,200	132,337,514	455,576,309	675,213,284	630,827,927
11.	Value of farms, percent increase[18,19]	---	433.5	47.1	154.6	103.5	14.3	244.3	48.2	-6.6
12.	Average value per farm, dollars[18,19,64,73,76]	2,448	2,618	2,946	3,509	4,537	3,693	10,012	13,449	11,438
13.	Farms operated by owners[21,22,23,24,25,26,27,65,77,*a]	---	---	---	13,938[*e]	22,324[*e]	28,963	37,796	39,863	44,521
14.	Value of livestock on farms, dollars[28,29,30,36,76,83,*a]	1,876,189	5,946,255	6,828,675[*d]	17,110,392[*k]	22,648,830	33,917,048	59,461,828	101,779,342	82,291,512
15.	Average value of livestock per farm, dollars[19,28,29,30,36]	1,612	1,024	900[*d]	1,055	887	946	1,307	2,027	1,492[*c]
16.	Production of cotton in bales[28,29,30,67,74,83]	---	---	---	---	---	---	---	---	---
17.	Percent of total production of cotton[28,29,30]	---	---	---	---	---	---	---	---	---

GENERAL AGRICULTURE STATISTICS, 1850-1990										
OREGON										
Item No.		1850	1860	1870	1880	1890	1900	1910	1920	1930
18.	Production of wheat in bushels[31,32,35,36,69,74,84]	211,943	826,776	2,340,746	7,480,010	9,296,734	14,508,636	12,456,751	19,526,765	21,526,667
19.	Percent of total production of wheat[31,32,33,35,36]	.2109	.4476	.8135	1.6279	1.9849	2.2032	1.8228	2.0654	2.6887
20.	Production of corn in bushels[36,37,38,39,70,74,85]	2,918	76,122	72,138	126,862	238,203	359,523	451,757	846,642	788,450
21.	Percent of total production of corn[36,37,38,39]	*j	*j	*j	*j	*j	*j	*j	*j	*j
22.	Production of oats in bushels[31,35,36,71,80,86]	61,214	885,673	2,029,909	4,385,650	5,948,594	6,725,828	10,881,286	8,357,406	7,613,345
23.	Percent of total production of oats[31,35,36]	*j	0.5	0.7	1.1	0.7	0.7	1.1	0.8	0.8
24.	Production of soybeans in bushels[36,40,41,72,74,76,87]	---	---	---	---	---	---	---	313	88*h
25.	Percent of total production of soybeans[36,40,41]	---	---	---	---	---	---	---	.0276	.0010
26.	Production of hay crops in tons[31,34,42,43,44,74,76,88]	373	27,986	75,357	266,187	632,115	1,117,400	1,598,543	2,163,207	1,827,537
27.	Percent of total production of hay crops[31,34,42,43,44]	*c,j	0.1	0.3	0.8	0.9	1.4	1.6	1.8	2.1

Item No.	GENERAL AGRICULTURE STATISTICS, 1850-1990 OREGON	1940	1950	1960	1970	1978	1982	1987	1990
1.	Number of farms[18,19,68,73,76,82,*a]	61,829	59,827	42,573	29,063	28,503	34,087	32,014	36,500
2.	Acres in farms[18,19,68,73,76,82]	17,988,307	20,327,683	21,236,298	18,018,000	18,053,960	17,739,782	17,809,165	17,800,000
3.	Acres improved land in farms[20,*a]	---	---	---	---	---	---	---	---
4.	Cropland harvested, acres[18,19,73,76,*a,b]	2,824,316	3,218,767	3,118,451	2,322,000	3,209,647	3,305,714	2,832,663	---
5.	Percentage increase in number of farms[18,19]	12.1	-3.2	-28.8	-31.7	-1.9	19.6	-6.1	14.0
6.	Percentage increase of land in farms[18,19]	8.7	13.0	4.5	-15.2	0.2	-1.7	0.4	-5.1
7.	Percentage increase of improved land in farms[20]	---	---	---	---	---	---	---	---
8.	Average acreage per farm[18,19,66,73,76,78]	290.9	339.8	498.8	620	633	520	556	481
9.	Percentage increase in cropland harvested[18,19,*b]	-2.8	14.0	-3.1	-25.5	38.2	3.0	-14.3	---
10.	Value of farms, dollars[18,19,64,79,81]	476,817,354	1,216,088,000[*i]	1,856,543,000	2,707,000,000	8,588,181,924	12,665,000,000	9,597,000,000	8,288,000,000
11.	Value of farms, percent increase[18,19]	-24.4	155.0[*i]	52.7	45.8	217.3	47.5	-24.2	-13.6
12.	Average value per farm, dollars[18,19,64,73,76]	7,712	20,327[*i]	43,608	93,000	301,308	371,644	299,755	227,068
13.	Farms operated by owners[21,22,23,24,25,26,27,65,77,*a]	50,137	54,351	39,303[*g]	26,877[*g]	26,416	31,652[*g]	29,317[*g]	---
14.	Value of livestock on farms, dollars[28,29,30,36,76,83,*a]	55,976,484	141,039,827	200,545,543	---	573,058,000	705,134,000	797,451,000	754,695,000
15.	Average value of livestock per farm, dollars[19,28,29,30,36]	905	2,357	4,711	---	20,105	20,686	24,909	20,677
16.	Production of cotton in bales[28,29,30,67,74,83]	---	---	---	---	---	---	---	---
17.	Percent of total production of cotton[28,29,30]	---	---	---	---	---	---	---	---

GENERAL AGRICULTURE STATISTICS, 1850-1990									
OREGON									
Item No.		1940	1950	1960	1970	1978	1982	1987	1990
18.	Production of wheat in bushels[31,32,35,36,69,74,84]	15,358,147	21,860,159	27,897,641	27,658,000	45,726,181	58,924,228	51,875,186	53,835,000
19.	Percent of total production of wheat[31,32,33,35,36]	2.1666	2.1718	2.6240	2.0119	2.84448	2.4892	2.7489	2.6444
20.	Production of corn in bushels[36,37,38,39,70,74,85]	1,061,576	484,349	3,840,000	864,000	1,306,917	7,187,740	2,490,000	3,520,000
21.	Percent of total production of corn[36,37,38,39]	[*j]	[*j]	0.1	[*j]	[*j]	0.1	[*j]	[*j]
22.	Production of oats in bushels[31,35,36,71,80,86]	8,167,826	8,688,687	6,475,778	5,406,000	---	5,267,490	5,200,000	6,860,000
23.	Percent of total production of oats[31,35,36]	0.9	0.8	0.6	0.6	---	1.0	1.7	1.8
24.	Production of soybeans in bushels[36,40,41,72,74,76,87]	6[*h]	141	2,240	---	2,651	---	289	---
25.	Percent of total production of soybeans[36,40,41]	.0000	.0001	.0004	---	.0002	---	.0000	---
26.	Production of hay crops in tons[31,34,42,43,44,74,76,88]	1,809,973	1,511,298	1,771,122	2,369,000	2,509,847	2,482,717	2,340,999	2,890,000[*l]
27.	Percent of total production of hay crops[31,34,42,43,44]	2.2	1.7	1.7	1.9	1.9	1.9	1.8	2.0

[a] See the Glossary of Terms for changing definitions, i.e. farm, improved land, cropland harvested, farm owners, and livestock.
[b] Prior to 1924, the data relate to the total acreage of crops for which figures are available, except for 1920 when 14,502,932 acres of corn cut for forage were excluded (as most of this was probably duplicated in the acreage of corn harvested for grain).
[c] Percentage computed by compiler from data herein. See endnotes for source of data.
[d] Values in gold, one-fifth less than currency values.
[e] Managers included with owners.
[f] Running square bales, counting round as half bales.
[g] Census listed the number of full and part time owners separately. Compiler added the two numbers for the above figure.
[h] Includes quantity of beans harvested from acreage grown with other crops as well as that from acreage grown alone.
[i] The total value for each state for 1950 was based on the average value per acre for farms in the sample, for which value of land and buildings was reported. The average value per farm and per acre was based on the total value of all farms.
[j] Less than one-tenth of one percent.
[k] Including estimated value of range animals.
[l] Census had two separate listings: hay, alfalfa, and alfalfa mixtures; and hay, all other. Compiler added the two listings for the above figure.

Item No.		1850	1860	1870	1880	1890	1900	1910	1920	1930
GENERAL AGRICULTURE STATISTICS, 1850-1990										
PENNSYLVANIA										
1.	Number of farms[18,19,68,73,76,82,*a]	127,577	156,357	174,041	213,542	211,557	224,248	219,295	202,250	172,419
2.	Acres in farms[18,19,68,73,76,82]	14,923,347	17,012,140	17,994,200	19,791,341	18,364,370	19,371,015	18,586,832	17,657,513	15,309,485
3.	Acres improved land in farms[20,*a]	8,628,619	10,463,296	11,515,965	13,423,007	13,210,597	13,209,183	12,673,519	11,847,719	---
4.	Cropland harvested, acres[18,19,73,76,*a,b]	---	---	---	7,653,439	7,993,154	8,365,475	7,826,562	7,874,646	6,587,707
5.	Percentage increase in number of farms[18,19]	---	22.6	11.3	22.7	-0.9	6.0	-2.2	-7.8	-14.7
6.	Percentage increase of land in farms[18,19]	---	14.0	5.8	10.0	-7.2	5.5	-4.0	-5.0	-13.3
7.	Percentage increase of improved land in farms[20]	---	21.3	10.1	16.6	-1.6	[*j]	-4.1	-6.5	---
8.	Average acreage per farm[18,19,66,73,76,78]	116.9	108.8	103.4	92.7	86.8	86.4	84.8	87.3	88.8
9.	Percentage increase in cropland harvested[18,19,*b]	---	---	---	---	4.4	4.7	-6.4	0.6	-16.3
10.	Value of farms, dollars[18,19,64,79,81]	407,876,099	662,050,707	834,785,265	975,689,410	922,240,233	898,272,750	1,041,068,755	1,326,752,028	1,203,017,645
11.	Value of farms, percent increase[18,19]	---	62.3	26.1	16.9	-5.5	-2.6	15.9	27.4	-9.3
12.	Average value per farm, dollars[18,19,64,78,76]	3,197	4,234	4,796	4,569	4,359	4,006	4,747	6,560	6,977
13.	Farms operated by owners[21,22,23,24,25,26,27,65,77,*a]	---	---	---	168,220[*e]	162,219[*e]	162,279	164,229	153,498	142,283[*g]
14.	Value of livestock on farms, dollars[28,29,30,36,76,83,*a]	41,500,053	69,672,726	92,517,660	84,242,877	101,652,758	102,439,183	141,480,052	238,774,641	177,131,940
15.	Average value of livestock per farm, dollars[19,28,29,30,36]	325	446	532	395	480	457	645	1,181	1,027[*c]
16.	Production of cotton in bales[28,29,30,67,74,83]	---	---	---	---	---	---	---	---	---
17.	Percent of total production of cotton[28,29,30]	---	---	---	---	---	---	---	---	---

GENERAL AGRICULTURE STATISTICS, 1850-1990										
PENNSYLVANIA										
Item No.		1850	1860	1870	1880	1890	1900	1910	1920	1930
18.	Production of wheat in bushels[31,32,35,36,69,74,84]	15,367,691	13,042,165	19,672,967	19,462,405	21,595,499	20,632,680	21,564,479	23,453,978	17,410,853
19.	Percent of total production of wheat[31,32,33,35,36]	15.2934	7.5343	6.8369	4.2357	4.6107	3.1331	3.1556	2.4808	2.1746
20.	Production of corn in bushels[36,37,38,39,70,74,85]	19,835,214	28,196,821	34,702,006	45,821,531	42,318,279	51,869,780	41,494,237	61,450,012	35,294,020
21.	Percent of total production of corn[36,37,38,39]	3.4	3.4	4.6	2.6	2.0	1.9	1.6	2.6	1.7
22.	Production of oats in bushels[31,35,36,71,80,86]	21,538,156	27,387,147	36,478,585	33,841,439	36,197,409	37,242,810	28,172,686	29,188,172	22,921,194
23.	Percent of total production of oats[31,35,36]	14.7	15.9	12.9	8.3	4.5	3.9	2.8	2.8	2.3
24.	Production of soybeans in bushels[36,40,41,72,74,76,87]	---	---	---	---	---	---	---	11,374	7,860[*h]
25.	Percent of total production of soybeans[36,40,41]	---	---	---	---	---	---	---	1.0020	.0907
26.	Production of hay crops in tons[31,34,42,43,44,74,76,88]	1,842,970	2,245,413	2,848,219	2,811,517	4,331,582	3,766,834	3,678,207	5,111,084	3,166,308
27.	Percent of total production of hay crops[31,34,42,43,44]	13.3[*c]	11.8	10.4	8.0	6.5	4.8	3.8	4.1	3.7

GENERAL AGRICULTURE STATISTICS, 1850-1990

PENNSYLVANIA

Item No.		1940	1950	1960	1970	1978	1982	1987	1990
1.	Number of farms[18,19,68,73,76,82,*a]	169,027	146,887	100,052	62,824	56,202	55,535	51,549	53,000
2.	Acres in farms[18,19,68,73,76,82]	14,594,134	14,112,841	11,861,727	8,901,000	8,543,661	8,297,713	7,866,289	8,100,000
3.	Acres improved land in farms[20,*a]	---	---	---	---	---	---	---	---
4.	Cropland harvested, acres[18,19,73,76,*a,b]	6,097,116	5,637,292	4,853,664	4,242,000	4,263,952	4,363,789	4,080,153	4,240,000
5.	Percentage increase in number of farms[18,19]	-2.0	-13.1	-31.9	-37.2	-10.5	-1.2	-7.2	-2.8
6.	Percentage increase of land in farms[18,19]	-4.7	-3.3	-16.0	-25.0	-4.0	-2.9	-5.2	3.0
7.	Percentage increase of improved land in farms[20]	---	---	---	---	---	---	---	---
8.	Average acreage per farm[18,19,66,73,76,78]	86.3	96.1	118.6	142	152	149	153	152
9.	Percentage increase in cropland harvested[18,19,*b]	-7.4	-7.5	-13.9	-12.7	0.5	2.3	-6.5	3.9
10.	Value of farms, dollars[18,19,64,79,81]	864,199,795	1,512,755,000[*i]	2,190,314,000	3,319,000,000	10,878,346,716	12,538,000,000	12,337,000,000	18,488,000,000
11.	Value of farms, percent increase[18,19]	-28.2	75.0[*i]	44.8	51.5	227.8	15.3	-1.6	49.9
12.	Average value per farm, dollars[18,19,64,73,76]	5,113	10,299[*i]	21,892	53,000	193,558	225,794	239,333	348,830
13.	Farms operated by owners[21,22,23,24,25,26,27,65,77,*a]	140,169[*g]	132,338	90,548[*g]	57,947[*g]	51,223	50,440[*g]	46,487[*g]	---
14.	Value of livestock on farms, dollars[28,29,30,36,76,83,*a]	135,439,416	283,005,759	407,201,145	---	1,527,183,000	2,096,220,000	2,250,857,000	2,713,767,000
15.	Average value of livestock per farm, dollars[19,28,29,30,36]	801	1,927	4,070	---	27,173	37,746	43,664	51,203
16.	Production of cotton in bales[28,29,30,67,74,83]	---	---	---	---	---	---	---	---
17.	Percent of total production of cotton[28,29,30]	---	---	---	---	---	---	---	---

GENERAL AGRICULTURE STATISTICS, 1850-1990									
PENNSYLVANIA									
Item No.		1940	1950	1960	1970	1978	1982	1987	1990
18.	Production of wheat in bushels[31,32,35,36,69,74,84]	18,082,994	19,777,724	13,213,071	9,834,000	6,310,367	7,790,790	7,663,537	7,955,000
19.	Percent of total production of wheat[31,32,33,35,36]	2.5510	1.9649	1.2513	.7177	.392548	.3283	.4061	.3098
20.	Production of corn in bushels[36,37,38,39,70,74,85]	43,136,868	49,509,946	76,800,000	80,155,000	113,599,487	119,837,016	99,282,796	98,880,000
21.	Percent of total production of corn[36,37,38,39]	1.9	1.8	1.8	2.0	1.7	1.6	1.5	1.3
22.	Production of oats in bushels[31,35,36,71,80,86]	23,197,536	21,870,117	28,481,774	24,795,000	---	18,088,854	13,881,340	13,770,000
23.	Percent of total production of oats[31,35,36]	2.7	1.9	2.8	2.7	---	3.6	4.4	3.7
24.	Production of soybeans in bushels[36,40,41,72,74,76,87]	159,533*[h]	403,782	228,581	896,000	2,345,762	3,827,271	6,020,707	10,370,000
25.	Percent of total production of soybeans[36,40,41]	.1821	.1901	.0443	.0796	.1362	.1923	.3276	.5382
26.	Production of hay crops in tons[31,34,42,43,44,74,76,88]	2,667,892	3,047,200	4,082,560	4,396,000	4,379,817	4,230,141	4,477,463	4,709,000*[k]
27.	Percent of total production of hay crops[31,34,42,43,44]	3.2	3.4	3.8	3.4	3.4	3.3	3.5	3.2

[a] See the Glossary of Terms for changing definitions, i.e. farm, improved land, cropland harvested, farm owners, and livestock.
[b] Prior to 1924, the data relate to the total acreage of crops for which figures are available, except for 1920 when 14,502,932 acres of corn cut for forage were excluded (as most of this was probably duplicated in the acreage of corn harvested for grain).
[c] Percentage computed by compiler from data herein. See endnotes for source of data.
[d] Values in gold, one-fifth less than currency values.
[e] Managers included with owners.
[f] Running square bales, counting round as half bales.
[g] Census listed the number of full and part time owners separately. Compiler added the two numbers for the above figure.
[h] Includes quantity of beans harvested from acreage grown with other crops as well as that from acreage grown alone.
[i] The total value for each state for 1950 was based on the average value per acre for farms in the sample, for which value of land and buildings was reported. The average value per farm and per acre was based on the total value of all farms.
[j] Less than one-tenth of one percent decrease.
[k] Census had two separate listings: hay, alfalfa, and alfalfa mixtures; and hay, all other. Compiler added the two listings for the above figure.

GENERAL AGRICULTURE STATISTICS, 1850-1990										
RHODE ISLAND										
Item No.		1850	1860	1870	1880	1890	1900	1910	1920	1930
1.	Number of farms[18,19,68,73,76,82,*a]	5,385	5,406	5,368	6,216	5,500	5,498	5,292	4,083	3,322
2.	Acres in farms[18,19,68,73,76,82]	553,938	521,224	502,308	514,813	469,281	455,602	443,308	331,600	279,361
3.	Acres improved land in farms[20,*a]	356,487	335,128	289,030	298,486	274,491	187,354	178,344	132,855	---
4.	Cropland harvested, acres[18,19,73,76,*a,b]	---	---	---	128,267	112,367	92,415	84,207	62,045	55,214
5.	Percentage increase in number of farms[18,19]	---	0.4	-0.7	15.8	-11.5	*j	-3.7	-22.8	-18.6
6.	Percentage increase of land in farms[18,19]	---	-5.9	-3.6	2.5	-8.8	-2.9	-2.7	-25.2	-15.8
7.	Percentage increase of improved land in farms[20]	---	-6.0	-13.8	3.3	-8.0	-31.7	-4.8	-25.5	---
8.	Average acreage per farm[18,19,66,73,76,78]	102.9	96.4	93.6	82.8	85.3	82.9	83.8	81.2	84.1
9.	Percentage increase in cropland harvested[18,19,*b]	---	---	---	---	-12.4	-17.8	-8.9	-26.3	-11.0
10.	Value of farms, dollars[18,19,64,79,81]	17,070,802	19,550,553	17,259,974	25,882,079	21,873,479	23,125,260	27,932,860	26,387,926	34,507,749
11.	Value of farms, percent increase[18,19]	---	14.5	-11.7	50.0	-15.5	5.7	20.8	-5.5	30.8
12.	Average value per farm, dollars[18,19,64,73,76]	3,170	3,616	3,215	4,164	3,977	4,206	5,278	6,463	10,388
13.	Farms operated by owners[21,22,23,24,25,26,27,65,77,*a]	---	---	---	4,980[*e]	4,470[*e]	4,182	4,087	3,245	2,808
14.	Value of livestock on farms, dollars[28,29,30,36,76,83,*a]	1,532,637	2,042,044	2,508,106[*d]	2,254,142	2,364,970	2,593,659	3,276,472	4,840,279	3,878,364
15.	Average value of livestock per farm, dollars[19,28,29,30,36]	285	378	467[*d]	363	430	472	619	1,186	1,168[*c]
16.	Production of cotton in bales[28,29,30,67,74,83]	---	---	---	---	---	---	---	---	---
17.	Percent of total production of cotton[28,29,30]	---	---	---	---	---	---	---	---	---

GENERAL AGRICULTURE STATISTICS, 1850-1990

RHODE ISLAND

Item No.		1850	1860	1870	1880	1890	1900	1910	1920	1930
18.	Production of wheat in bushels[31,32,35,36,69,74,84]	49	1,131	784	240	91	310	208	2,275	496
19.	Percent of total production of wheat[31,32,33,35,36]	.0000	.0007	.0003	.0001	.0000	.0000	.0000	.0002	.0001
20.	Production of corn in bushels[36,37,38,39,70,74,85]	539,201	461,497	311,957	372,967	253,810	288,220	398,193	310,901	76,463
21.	Percent of total production of corn[36,37,38,39]	0.1	*j	*j	*j	*j	*j	*j	*j	*j
22.	Production of oats in bushels[31,35,36,71,80,86]	213,232	244,453	157,010	159,339	100,520	47,120	48,212	34,507	10,576
23.	Percent of total production of oats[31,35,36]	0.1	0.1	0.1	*j	*j	*j	*j	*j	*j
24.	Production of soybeans in bushels[36,40,41,72,74,76,87]	---	---	---	---	---	---	---	156	34*h
25.	Percent of total production of soybeans[36,40,41]	---	---	---	---	---	---	---	.0137	.0004
26.	Production of hay crops in tons[31,34,42,43,44,74,76,88]	74,818	82,722	89,045	82,646	101,392	75,410	80,309	82,725	43,311
27.	Percent of total production of hay crops[31,34,42,43,44]	0.5*c	0.4	0.3	0.2	0.1	*j	0.1	0.1	0.1

GENERAL AGRICULTURE STATISTICS, 1850-1990									
RHODE ISLAND									
Item No.		1940	1950	1960	1970	1978	1982	1987	1990
1.	Number of farms[18,19,68,73,76,82,*a]	3,014	2,598	1,395	700	674	728	701	770
2.	Acres in farms[18,19,68,73,76,82]	221,913	191,052	137,930	69,000	66,233	62,466	58,685	71,000
3.	Acres improved land in farms[20,*a]	---	---	---	---	---	---	---	---
4.	Cropland harvested, acres[18,19,73,76,*a,b]	48,753	39,782	33,512	18,000	23,704	21,252	18,498	---
5.	Percentage increase in number of farms[18,19]	-9.3	-13.8	-46.3	-49.8	-3.7	8.0	-3.7	9.8
6.	Percentage increase of land in farms[18,19]	-20.6	-13.9	-27.8	-50.0	-4.0	-5.7	-6.1	21.0
7.	Percentage increase of improved land in farms[20]	---	---	---	---	---	---	---	---
8.	Average acreage per farm[18,19,66,73,76,78]	73.6	73.5	98.9	98	98	86	84	95
9.	Percentage increase in cropland harvested[18,19,*b]	-11.7	-18.4	-15.8	-46.3	31.7	-5.7	-6.1	21.0
10.	Value of farms, dollars[18,19,64,79,81]	26,334,374	44,328,000[*i]	52,411,000	50,000,000	159,357,864	173,000,000	295,000,000	481,000,000
11.	Value of farms, percent increase[18,19]	-23.7	68.3[*i]	18.2	-4.6	219.0	8.6	70.5	63.1
12.	Average value per farm, dollars[18,19,64,73,76]	8,737	17,062[*i]	37,571	72,000	236,436	237,141	420,279	650,000
13.	Farms operated by owners[21,22,23,24,25,26,27,65,77,*a]	2,634[*g]	2,391	1,275[*g]	609[*g]	628	661[*g]	627[*g]	---
14.	Value of livestock on farms, dollars[28,29,30,36,76,83,*a]	2,603,499	5,323,344	6,058,484	---	10,546,000	12,237,000	11,100,000	12,524,000
15.	Average value of livestock per farm, dollars[19,28,29,30,36]	864	2,049	4,343	---	15,647	16,809	15,835	16,265
16.	Production of cotton in bales[28,29,30,67,74,83]	---	---	---	---	---	---	---	---
17.	Percent of total production of cotton[28,29,30]	---	---	---	---	---	---	---	---

GENERAL AGRICULTURE STATISTICS, 1850-1990									
RHODE ISLAND									
Item No.		1940	1950	1960	1970	1978	1982	1987	1990
18.	Production of wheat in bushels[31,32,35,36,69,74,84]	1,051	---	641	---	*k	*k	*k	---
19.	Percent of total production of wheat[31,32,33,35,36]	.0001	---	.0001	---	---	---	---	---
20.	Production of corn in bushels[36,37,38,39,70,74,85]	46,684	35,803	264,000	---	23,162	10,902	7,585	---
21.	Percent of total production of corn[36,37,38,39]	*j	*j	*j	---	*j	*j	*j	---
22.	Production of oats in bushels[31,35,36,71,80,86]	5,889	4,880	2,955	---	---	---	---	---
23.	Percent of total production of oats[31,35,36]	*j	*j	*j	---	---	---	---	---
24.	Production of soybeans in bushels[36,40,41,72,74,76,87]	322*h	---	---	---	---	---	---	---
25.	Percent of total production of soybeans[36,40,41]	.0004	---	---	---	---	---	---	---
26.	Production of hay crops in tons[31,34,42,43,44,74,76,88]	41,609	34,664	37,236	25,000	20,914	17,708	14,125	17,000*l
27.	Percent of total production of hay crops[31,34,42,43,44]	0.1	*j	*j	*j	*j	*j	*j	*j

[a] See the Glossary of Terms for changing definitions, i.e. farm, improved land, cropland harvested, farm owners, and livestock.
[b] Prior to 1924, the data relate to the total acreage of crops for which figures are available, except for 1920 when 14,502,932 acres of corn cut for forage were excluded (as most of this was probably duplicated in the acreage of corn harvested for grain).
[c] Percentage computed by compiler from data herein. See endnotes for source of data.
[d] Values in gold, one-fifth less than currency values.
[e] Managers included with owners.
[f] Running square bales, counting round as half bales.
[g] Census listed the number of full and part time owners separately. Compiler added the two numbers for the above figure.
[h] Includes quantity of beans harvested from acreage grown with other crops as well as that from acreage grown alone.
[i] The total value for each state for 1950 was based on the average value per acre for farms in the sample, for which value of land and buildings was reported. The average value per farm and per acre was based on the total value of all farms.
[j] Less than one-tenth of one percent.
[k] Withheld to avoid disclosing data for individual farms.
[l] Census had two separate listings: hay, alfalfa, and alfalfa mixtures; and hay, all other. Compiler added the two listings for the above figure.

GENERAL AGRICULTURE STATISTICS, 1850-1990										
SOUTH CAROLINA										
Item No.		1850	1860	1870	1880	1890	1900	1910	1920	1930
1.	Number of farms[18,19,68,73,76,82,*a]	29,967	33,171	51,889	93,864	115,008	155,355	176,434	192,693	157,931
2.	Acres in farms[18,19,68,73,76,82]	16,217,700	16,195,919	12,105,280	13,457,613	13,184,652	13,985,014	13,512,028	12,426,675	10,393,113
3.	Acres improved land in farms[20,*a]	4,072,651	4,572,060	3,010,539	4,132,050	5,255,237	5,775,741	6,097,999	6,184,159	---
4.	Cropland harvested, acres[18,19,73,76,*a,b]	---	---	---	3,230,554	3,900,873	4,722,151	5,152,845	5,396,980	4,136,809
5.	Percentage increase in number of farms[18,19]	---	10.7	56.4	80.9	22.5	35.1	13.6	9.2	-18.0
6.	Percentage increase of land in farms[18,19]	---	-0.1	-25.3	11.2	-2.0	6.1	-3.4	-8.0	-16.4
7.	Percentage increase of improved land in farms[20]	---	12.3	-34.2	37.3	27.2	9.9	5.6	1.4	---
8.	Average acreage per farm[18,19,66,73,76,78]	541.2	488.2	233.3	143.4	114.6	90.0	76.6	64.5	65.8
9.	Percentage increase in cropland harvested[18,19,*b]	---	---	---	---	20.7	21.1	9.1	4.7	-23.3
10.	Value of farms, dollars[18,19,64,79,81]	82,431,684	139,652,508	35,847,010	68,677,482	99,104,600	126,761,530	332,888,081	813,484,200	379,190,630
11.	Value of farms, percent increase[18,19]	---	69.4	-74.3	91.6	44.3	27.9	162.6	144.4	-53.4
12.	Average value per farm, dollars[18,19,64,73,76]	2,751	4,210	691	732	862	816	1,887	4,222	2,401
13.	Farms operated by owners[21,22,23,24,25,26,27,65,77,*a]	---	---	---	46,645[*e]	51,428[*e]	59,417	64,350	67,724	54,470[*g]
14.	Value of livestock on farms, dollars[28,29,30,36,76,83,*a]	15,060,015	23,934,465	9,954,808[*d]	12,199,510	16,572,410	20,199,859	45,131,380	91,518,155	38,888,439
15.	Average value of livestock per farm, dollars[19,28,29,30,36]	503	722	192[*d]	130	144	130	256	475	246
16.	Production of cotton in bales[28,29,30,67,74,83]	300,901	353,412	224,500	522,548	747,190	881,422[*f]	1,279,866[*f]	1,476,645[*f]	835,963[*f]
17.	Percent of total production of cotton[28,29,30]	12.2	6.6	7.5	9.1	10.0	9.2[*f]	12.0[*f]	13.0[*f]	5.7[*f]

GENERAL AGRICULTURE STATISTICS, 1850-1990										
SOUTH CAROLINA										
Item No.		1850	1860	1870	1880	1890	1900	1910	1920	1930
18.	Production of wheat in bushels[31,32,35,36,69,74,84]	1,068,277	1,285,631	783,610	962,358	658,351	1,017,319	310,614	630,911	505,206
19.	Percent of total production of wheat[31,32,33,35,36]	1.0631	.7427	.2723	.2094	.1406	.1545	.0455	.0667	.0631
20.	Production of corn in bushels[36,37,38,39,70,74,85]	16,271,454	15,065,606	7,614,207	11,767,099	13,770,417	17,429,610	20,871,946	27,472,013	19,325,825
21.	Percent of total production of corn[36,37,38,39]	2.8	1.8	1.0	0.7	0.6	0.7	0.8	1.2	0.9
22.	Production of oats in bushels[31,35,36,71,80,86]	2,322,155	936,974	613,593	2,715,505	3,019,119	2,661,670	5,745,291	3,597,835	2,229,914
23.	Percent of total production of oats[31,35,36]	1.6	0.5	0.2	0.7	0.4	0.3	0.6	0.3	0.2
24.	Production of soybeans in bushels[36,40,41,72,74,76,87]	---	---	---	---	---	---	12	7,087	47,326[*h]
25.	Percent of total production of soybeans[36,40,41]	---	---	---	---	---	---	.0481[*c]	.6243	.5464
26.	Production of hay crops in tons[31,34,42,43,44,74,76,88]	20,925	87,587	10,665	2,706	27,000	108,886	191,467	297,871	149,765
27.	Percent of total production of hay crops[31,34,42,43,44]	0.2[*c]	0.5	[*m]	[*m]	[*m]	0.1	0.2	0.2	0.2

GENERAL AGRICULTURE STATISTICS, 1850-1990									
SOUTH CAROLINA									
Item No.		1940	1950	1960	1970	1978	1982	1987	1990
1.	Number of farms[18,19,68,73,76,82,*a]	137,558	139,364	78,172	39,559	26,706	24,929	20,517	24,500
2.	Acres in farms[18,19,68,73,76,82]	11,238,697	11,878,793	9,149,492	6,992,000	6,045,719	5,589,799	4,758,631	5,200,000
3.	Acres improved land in farms[20,*a]	---	---	---	---	---	---	---	---
4.	Cropland harvested, acres[18,19,73,76,*a,b]	4,321,962	3,959,822	2,694,196	2,353,000	2,524,147	2,474,025	1,589,636	---
5.	Percentage increase in number of farms[18,19]	-12.9	1.3	-43.9	-49.4	-32.5	-6.7	-17.7	19.4
6.	Percentage increase of land in farms[18,19]	8.1	5.7	-23.0	-23.6	-13.5	-7.5	-14.9	9.3
7.	Percentage increase of improved land in farms[20]	---	---	---	---	---	---	---	---
8.	Average acreage per farm[18,19,66,73,76,78]	81.7	85.2	117	177	226	224	232	208
9.	Percentage increase in cropland harvested[18,19,*b]	4.5	-8.4	-32.0	-12.7	7.3	-2.0	-35.8	---
10.	Value of farms, dollars[18,19,64,79,81]	338,494,517	820,349,000[*i,j]	1,226,146,000[*j]	1,826,000,000	4,581,627,948	5,193,000,000	4,127,000,000	5,051,000,000
11.	Value of farms, percent increase[18,19]	-10.7	142.4[*i,j]	49.5[*j]	48.9	151.0	13.3	-20.5	22.4
12.	Average value per farm, dollars[18,19,64,73,76]	2,461	5,886[*i,j]	15,685[*j]	46,000	171,558	208,524	201,169	202,040
13.	Farms operated by owners[21,22,23,24,25,26,27,65,77,*a]	59,867	75,777	53,717[*g]	34,662[*g]	24,043	22,769[*g]	19,057[*g]	---
14.	Value of livestock on farms, dollars[28,29,30,36,76,83,*a]	43,092,480	72,268,009	77,363,569	107,971,000	311,804,000	367,536,000	427,398,000	576,522,000
15.	Average value of livestock per farm, dollars[19,28,29,30,36]	313	519	990	2,729	11,675	14,743	20,831	23,532
16.	Production of cotton in bales[28,29,30,67,74,83]	849,982[*f]	543,936	411,120	211,000	114,401	147,897	102,078	154,000[*k,l]
17.	Percent of total production of cotton[28,29,30]	7.4[*f]	3.5	3.0	2.1	1.1	1.3	0.8	1.3

GENERAL AGRICULTURE STATISTICS, 1850-1990

SOUTH CAROLINA

Item No.		1940	1950	1960	1970	1978	1982	1987	1990
18.	Production of wheat in bushels[31,32,35,36,69,74,84]	2,121,624	1,603,107	3,116,662	2,835,000	1,745,494	14,810,264	7,558,179	17,835,000
19.	Percent of total production of wheat[31,32,33,35,36]	.2993	.1593	.2952	.2069	.1085817	.6241	.4005	.8761
20.	Production of corn in bushels[36,37,38,39,70,74,85]	23,527,406	23,624,155	24,975,000	10,854,000	29,268,243	31,085,287	22,143,190	30,940,000
21.	Percent of total production of corn[36,37,38,39]	1.0	0.9	0.6	0.3	0.4	0.4	0.3	0.4
22.	Production of oats in bushels[31,35,36,71,80,86]	5,302,558	6,964,541	10,375,067	3,154,000	---	2,150,861	1,396,040	2,360,000
23.	Percent of total production of oats[31,35,36]	0.6	0.6	1.0	0.3	---	0.4	0.4	0.6
24.	Production of soybeans in bushels[36,40,41,72,74,76,87]	76,677[a,h]	460,938	6,598,313	20,254,000	29,082,744	29,039,562	12,872,219	20,160,000
25.	Percent of total production of soybeans[36,40,41]	.0875	.2170	1.2797	1.8024	1.68874	1.4593	.7003	1.0463
26.	Production of hay crops in tons[31,34,42,43,44,74,76,88]	404,812	360,109	311,558	378,000	405,556	414,498	432,109	564,000[a,n]
27.	Percent of total production of hay crops[31,34,42,43,44]	0.5	0.4	0.3	0.3	0.3	0.3	0.3	0.4

[a] See the Glossary of Terms for changing definitions, i.e. farm, improved land, cropland harvested, farm owners, and livestock.
[b] Prior to 1924, the data relate to the total acreage of crops for which figures are available, except for 1920 when 14,502,932 acres of corn cut for forage were excluded (as most of this was probably duplicated in the acreage of corn harvested for grain).
[c] Percentage computed by compiler from data herein. See endnotes for source of data.
[d] Values in gold, one-fifth less than currency values.
[e] Managers included with owners.
[f] Running square bales, counting round as half bales.
[g] Census listed the number of full and part time owners separately. Compiler added the two numbers for the above figure.
[h] Includes quantity of beans harvested from acreage grown with other crops as well as that from acreage grown alone.
[i] The total value for each state for 1950 was based on the average value per acre for farms in the sample, for which value of land and buildings was reported. The average value per farm and per acre was based on the total value of all farms.
[j] Based on a sampling of farms.
[k] Production ginned and to be ginned.
[l] 480-pound net weight bales.
[m] Less then one-tenth of one percent.
[n] Data available for hay, all other only.

GENERAL AGRICULTURE STATISTICS, 1850-1990										
SOUTH DAKOTA										
Item No.		1850	1860	1870	1880	1890	1900	1910	1920	1930
1.	Number of farms[18,19,68,73,76,82,*a]	---	123[*j]	1,720[*j]	13,645[*k]	50,158	52,622	77,644	74,637	83,157
2.	Acres in farms[18,19,68,73,76,82]	---	26,448[*j]	302,376[*j]	2,772,811[*k]	11,396,460	19,070,616	26,016,892	34,636,491	36,470,083
3.	Acres improved land in farms[20,*a]	---	2,115[*j]	42,645[*j]	890,870[*k]	6,959,293	11,285,983	15,827,208	18,199,250	---
4.	Cropland harvested, acres[18,19,73,76,*a,b]	---	---	---	---	5,647,880	8,843,905	12,226,772	14,655,116	17,856,178
5.	Percentage increase in number of farms[18,19]	---	---	[*j,n]	---	267.6	4.9	47.6	-3.9	11.4
6.	Percentage increase of land in farms[18,19]	---	---	[*j,n]	---	311.0	67.3	36.4	33.1	5.3
7.	Percentage increase of improved land in farms[20]	---	---	---	---	681.2	62.2	40.2	15.0	---
8.	Average acreage per farm[18,19,66,73,76,78]	---	215.0[*j]	175.8[*j]	227.2[*k]	362.4	335.1	464.1	402.6	438.6
9.	Percentage increase in cropland harvested[18,19,*a]	---	---	---	---	---	56.6	38.3	19.9	21.8
10.	Value of farms, dollars[18,19,64,79,81]	---	96,445[*j]	1,668,211[*j]	13,825,970[*k]	107,466,335	220,133,190	1,005,080,807	2,472,893,681	1,285,153,538
11.	Value of farms, percent increase[18,19]	---	---	[*j,n]	---	677.3	104.8	356.6	146.0	-48.0
12.	Average value per farm, dollars[18,19,64,73,76]	---	784[*j]	970[*j]	1,013[*k]	2,143	4,183	12,945	33,132	15,455
13.	Farms operated by owners[21,22,23,24,25,26,27,65,77,*a]	---	---	---	13,045[*e,k]	43,555[*e]	40,640	57,984	47,815	45,609
14.	Value of livestock on farms, dollars[28,29,30,36,76,83,*a]	---	39,116[*j]	623,962[*d,j]	6,107,221[*k]	29,689,509[*l]	65,173,432	127,229,200	238,568,263	186,622,264
15.	Average value of livestock per farm, dollars[19,28,29,30,36]	---	318[*j]	363[*d,j]	433[*k]	592	1,238	1,639	3,196	2,244
16.	Production of cotton in bales[28,29,30,67,74,83]	---	---	---	---	---	---	---	---	---
17.	Percent of total production of cotton[28,29,30]	---	---	---	---	---	---	---	---	---

GENERAL AGRICULTURE STATISTICS, 1850-1990										
SOUTH DAKOTA										
Item No.		1850	1860	1870	1880	1890	1900	1910	1920	1930
18.	Production of wheat in bushels[31,32,35,36,69,74,84]	---	945[*j]	170,662[*j]	1,092,946[*k]	16,541,138	41,889,380	47,059,590	31,086,995	34,044,975
19.	Percent of total production of wheat[31,32,33,35,36]	---	.0005[*j]	.0593[*j]	.2379[*k]	3.5316	6.3610	6.8863	3.2882	4.2522
20.	Production of corn in bushels[36,37,38,39,70,74,85]	---	20,269[*j]	133,140[*j]	[*j]	13,152,008	32,402,540	55,558,737	69,060,782	84,569,812
21.	Percent of total production of corn[36,37,38,39]	---	[*j,m]	[*j,m]	[*j]	0.6	1.2	2.2	2.9	4.0
22.	Production of oats in bushels[31,35,36,71,80,86]	---	2,540[*j]	114,327[*j]	1,488,321[*k]	7,469,846	19,421,490	43,565,676	51,091,904	62,480,531
23.	Percent of total production of oats[31,35,36]	---	[*j,m]	[*j,m]	0.4[*c,k]	0.9	2.1	4.3	4.8	6.3
24.	Production of soybeans in bushels[36,40,41,72,74,76,87]	---	---	---	---	----	----	----	---	419[*h]
25.	Percent of total production of soybeans[36,40,41]	---	---	---	---	---	---	---	---	.0048
26.	Production of hay crops in tons[31,34,42,43,44,74,76,88]	---	855[*j]	13,374[*j]	276,484[*k]	1,541,524	2,378,392	3,651,706	4,262,132	2,645,277
27.	Percent of total production of hay crops[31,34,42,43,44]	---	[*j,m]	[*c,j,m]	0.8[*k]	2.3	3.3	3.7	3.4	3.1

GENERAL AGRICULTURE STATISTICS, 1850-1990

SOUTH DAKOTA

Item No.		1940	1950	1960	1970	1978	1982	1987	1990
1.	Number of farms[18,19,68,73,76,82,*a]	72,454	66,452	55,727	45,726	38,741	37,148	36,376	35,000
2.	Acres in farms[18,19,68,73,76,82]	39,473,584	44,785,529	44,850,666	45,584,000	44,422,328	43,810,988	44,157,503	44,300,000
3.	Acres improved land in farms[20,*a]	---	---	---	---	---	---	---	---
4.	Cropland harvested, acres[18,19,73,76,*a,b]	12,297,291	17,527,893	14,236,384	14,185,000	13,855,939	14,433,490	12,982,611	---
5.	Percentage increase in number of farms[18,19]	-12.9	-8.3	-16.1	-17.9	-15.3	-4.1	-2.1	-3.8
6.	Percentage increase of land in farms[18,19]	8.2	13.5	0.1	1.6	-2.6	-1.4	0.8	0.3
7.	Percentage increase of improved land in farms[20]	---	---	---	---	---	---	---	---
8.	Average acreage per farm[18,19,66,73,76,78]	544.8	674.0	804.8	997	1,147	1,179	1,214	1,266
9.	Percentage increase in cropland harvested[18,19,*a]	-31.1	42.5	-18.8	-36.1	-2.3	4.2	-10.1	---
10.	Value of farms, dollars[18,19,64,79,81]	505,452,178	1,401,787,000[*i]	2,276,544,000	3,815,000,000	11,465,515,173	15,429,000,000	11,871,000,000	9,001,000,000
11.	Value of farms, percent increase[18,19]	-60.7	177.3[*i]	62.4	67.6	201.0	34.6	-23.1	-24.2
12.	Average value per farm, dollars[18,19,64,73,76]	6,976	21,095[*i]	40,852	83,000	295,953	418,940	326,333	257,171
13.	Farms operated by owners[21,22,23,24,25,26,27,65,77,*a]	33,803	46,031	40,783[*g]	37,849[*g]	32,555	31,211[*g]	30,401[*g]	---
14.	Value of livestock on farms, dollars[28,29,30,36,76,83*a]	104,156,465	364,750,026	549,434,105	837,900,000	1,333,982,000	1,635,131,00	1,862,125,000	2,312,649,000
15.	Average value of livestock per farm, dollars[19,28,29,30,36]	1,438	5,489	9,859	18,324	3,458	44,017	51,191	66,076
16.	Production of cotton in bales[28,29,30,67,74,83]	---	---	---	---	---	---	---	---
17.	Percent of total production of cotton[28,29,30]	---	---	---	---	---	---	---	---

GENERAL AGRICULTURE STATISTICS, 1850-1990									
SOUTH DAKOTA									
Item No.		1940	1950	1960	1970	1978	1982	1987	1990
18.	Production of wheat in bushels[31,32,35,36,69,74,84]	17,592,727	30,462,570	17,240,094	39,282,000	64,231,362	85,895,594	91,141,128	83,080,000
19.	Percent of total production of wheat[31,32,33,35,36]	2.4819	3.0264	1.6327	2.8668	3.9956	3.6193	4.8297	4.0809
20.	Production of corn in bushels[36,37,38,39,70,74,85]	40,755,611	76,149,324	79,774,000	102,336,000	168,736,099	174,109,203	199,208,883	190,800,000
21.	Percent of total production of corn[36,37,38,39]	1.8	2.7	1.9	2.5	2.5	2.3	3.0	2.5
22.	Production of oats in bushels[31,35,36,71,80,86]	43,101,900	62,578,547	39,751,143	102,336,000	---	97,763,987	41,997,525	44,000,000
23.	Percent of total production of oats[31,35,36]	5.0	5.5	4.0	11.3	---	19.3	13.4	11.8
24.	Production of soybeans in bushels[36,40,41,72,74,76,87]	5,369[*h]	386,845	1,510,924	4,323,000	11,435,996	22,315,924	40,074,670	48,880,000
25.	Percent of total production of soybeans[36,40,41]	.0178	.1821	.2930	.3847	.66405	1.1214	2.0138	2.5368
26.	Production of hay crops in tons[31,34,42,43,44,74,76,88]	1,727,320	2,966,293	3,263,593	5,519,000	6,838,623	6,594,617	5,682,824	4,290,000[*o]
27.	Percent of total production of hay crops[31,34,42,43,44]	2.1	3.3	3.2	4.3	5.2	5.1	4.4	2.9

[a] See the Glossary of Terms for changing definitions, i.e. farm, improved land, cropland harvested, farm owners, and livestock.
[b] Prior to 1924, the data relate to the total acreage of crops for which figures are available, except for 1920 when 14,502,932 acres of corn cut for forage were excluded (as most of this was probably duplicated in the acreage of corn harvested for grain).
[c] Percentage computed by compiler from data herein. See endnotes for source of data.
[d] Values in gold, one-fifth less than currency values.
[e] Managers included with owners.
[f] Running square bales, counting round as half bales.
[g] Census listed the number of full and part time owners separately. Compiler added the two numbers for the above figure.
[h] Includes quantity of beans harvested from acreage grown with other crops as well as that from acreage grown alone.
[i] The total value for each state for 1950 was based on the average value per acre for farms in the sample, for which value of land and buildings was reported. The average value per farm and per acre was based on the total value of all farms.
[j] Dakota Territory (combining area that became North and South Dakota in 1889).
[k] North Dakota and South Dakota admitted as states in 1889. Figures for 1880 obtained by consolidating data for the counties which then occupied the area now known as South Dakota.
[l] Including estimated value of range animals.
[m] Less than one-tenth of one percent.
[n] 1,000 percent or more.
[o] Census had two separate listings: hay, alfalfa, and alfalfa mixtures; and hay, all other. Compiler added the two listings for the above figure.

GENERAL AGRICULTURE STATISTICS, 1850-1990										
TENNESSEE										
Item No.		1850	1860	1870	1880	1890	1900	1910	1920	1930
1.	Number of farms[18,19,68,73,76,82,*a]	72,735	82,368	118,141	165,650	174,412	224,623	246,012	252,774	245,657
2.	Acres in farms[18,19,68,73,76,82]	18,984,022	20,669,165	19,581,214	20,666,915	20,161,583	20,342,058	20,041,657	19,510,856	18,003,241
3.	Acres improved land in farms[20,*a]	5,175,173	6,795,337	6,843,278	8,496,556	9,362,555	10,245,950	10,890,484	11,185,302	---
4.	Cropland harvested, acres[18,19,73,76,*a,b]	---	---	---	5,601,179	5,777,345	6,680,504	6,365,143	6,787,384	6,106,300
5.	Percentage increase in number of farms[18,19]	---	13.2	43.4	40.2	5.3	28.8	9.5	2.7	-2.8
6.	Percentage increase of land in farms[18,19]	---	8.9	-5.3	5.5	-2.4	0.9	-1.5	-2.6	-7.7
7.	Percentage increase of improved land in farms[20]	---	31.3	0.7	24.2	10.2	9.4	6.3	2.7	---
8.	Average acreage per farm[18,19,66,73,76,78]	261.0	250.9	165.7	124.8	115.6	90.6	81.5	77.2	73.3
9.	Percentage increase in cropland harvested[18,19,*b]	---	---	---	---	3.1	15.6	-4.7	6.6	-10.0
10.	Value of farms, dollars[18,19,64,79,81]	97,851,212	271,358,985	174,994,997	206,749,837	242,700,540	265,150,750	480,522,587	1,024,979,894	743,222,363
11.	Value of farms, percent increase[18,19]	---	177.3	-35.5	18.1	17.4	9.3	81.2	113.3	-27.5
12.	Average value per farm, dollars[18,19,64,73,76]	1,345	3,294	1,481	1,248	1,392	1,180	1,953	4,055	3,025
13.	Farms operated by owners[21,22,23,24,25,26,27,65,77,*a]	---	---	---	108,454[*e]	120,622[*e]	132,197	144,125	148,082	131,526[*g]
14.	Value of livestock on farms, dollars[28,29,30,36,76,83,*a]	29,978,016	60,211,425	44,067,260[*d]	43,651,470	60,254,230	60,818,605	110,706,078	173,522,135	104,252,201
15.	Average value of livestock per farm, dollars[19,28,29,30,36]	412	731	373[*d]	264	345	271	450	687	424
16.	Production of cotton in bales[28,29,30,67,74,83]	194,532	296,464	181,842	330,621	190,579	234,592[*f]	264,562[*f]	306,974[*f]	503,816[*f]
17.	Percent of total production of cotton[28,29,30]	7.9	5.5	6.0	5.7	2.5	2.5[*f]	2.5[*f]	2.7[*f]	3.5[*f]

GENERAL AGRICULTURE STATISTICS, 1850-1990										
TENNESSEE										
Item No.		1850	1860	1870	1880	1890	1900	1910	1920	1930
18.	Production of wheat in bushels[31,32,35,36,69,74,84]	1,619,386	5,459,268	6,188,916	7,331,353	8,300,789	11,924,010	6,516,539	6,362,357	2,480,846
19.	Percent of total production of wheat[31,32,33,35,36]	1.6116	3.1537	2.1508	1.5956	1.7723	1.8107	.9536	.6730	.3099
20.	Production of corn in bushels[36,37,38,39,70,74,85]	52,276,223	52,089,926	41,343,614	62,764,429	63,635,350	67,307,390	67,682,489	70,639,252	61,045,986
21.	Percent of total production of corn[36,37,38,39]	8.8	6.2	5.4	3.6	3.0	2.5	2.7	3.0	2.9
22.	Production of oats in bushels[31,35,36,71,80,86]	7,703,086	2,267,814	4,513,315	4,722,190	7,355,100	2,725,330	4,720,692	2,413,409	478,230
23.	Percent of total production of oats[31,35,36]	5.3[*c]	1.3	1.6	1.2	0.9	0.3	0.5	0.2	[*j]
24.	Production of soybeans in bushels[36,40,41,72,74,76,87]	---	---	---	---	---	---	2,037	49,731	126,154[*h]
25.	Percent of total production of soybeans[36,40,41]	---	---	---	---	---	---	8.2	4.4	1.5
26.	Production of hay crops in tons[31,34,42,43,44,74,76,88]	74,091	143,499	116,582	186,698	630,417	679,450	1,100,838	1,679,312	1,298,808
27.	Percent of total production of hay crops[31,34,42,43,44]	0.5[*c]	0.8	0.4	0.5	0.9	0.9	1.1	1.4	1.5

GENERAL AGRICULTURE STATISTICS, 1850-1990

TENNESSEE

Item No.		1940	1950	1960	1970	1978	1982	1987	1990
1.	Number of farms[18,19,68,73,76,82,*a]	247,617	231,631	157,688	121,406	86,910	90,565	79,711	89,000
2.	Acres in farms[18,19,68,73,76,82]	18,492,898	18,534,380	16,081,285	15,057,000	12,680,809	12,474,931	11,731,386	12,400,000
3.	Acres improved land in farms[20,*a]	---	---	---	---	---	---	---	---
4.	Cropland harvested, acres[18,19,73,76,*a,b]	6,158,662	5,575,106	4,116,418	3,697,000	4,409,331	4,548,895	3,854,302	---
5.	Percentage increase in number of farms[18,19]	0.8	-6.5	-31.9	-23.0	-28.4	4.2	-12.0	11.7
6.	Percentage increase of land in farms[18,19]	2.7	0.2	-13.2	-6.4	-15.8	1.6	-6.0	5.7
7.	Percentage increase of improved land in farms[20]	---	---	---	---	---	---	---	---
8.	Average acreage per farm[18,19,66,73,76,78]	74.7	80.0	102	124	146	138	147	138
9.	Percentage increase in cropland harvested[18,19,*b]	0.9	-9.5	-26.2	-10.2	19.3	3.2	-15.3	---
10.	Value of farms, dollars[18,19,64,79,81]	664,474,267	1,431,966,000[*i,k]	2,095,354,000[*k]	4,028,000,000	10,884,434,580	12,592,000,000	11,648,000,000	14,418,000,000
11.	Value of farms, percent increase[18,19]	-10.6	115.5[*i,k]	46.3[*k]	92.2	170.2	15.7	-7.5	23.8
12.	Average value per farm, dollars[18,19,64,73,76]	2,683	6,182[*i,k]	13,288[*k]	33,000	125,238	139,141	146,126	162,000
13.	Farms operated by owners[21,22,23,24,25,26,27,65,77,*a]	147,443	163,521	127,134[*g]	112,261[*g]	80,778	84,046[*g]	74,859[*g]	---
14.	Value of livestock on farms, dollars[28,29,30,36,76,83,*a]	97,706,469	215,817,363	256,564,677	403,401,000	737,132,000	835,033,000	915,807,000	1,110,601,000
15.	Average value of livestock per farm, dollars[19,28,29,30,36]	395	932	1,627	3,323	8,482	9,220	11,489	12,479
16.	Production of cotton in bales[28,29,30,67,74,83]	436,126	616,742	620,385	392,000	232,005	306,159	566,890	476,000[*l,m]
17.	Percent of total production of cotton[28,29,30]	3.8	4.0	4.5	3.9	2.2	2.7	4.3	4.1

Item No.	GENERAL AGRICULTURE STATISTICS, 1850-1990 TENNESSEE	1940	1950	1960	1970	1978	1982	1987	1990
18.	Production of wheat in bushels[31,32,35,36,69,74,84]	3,886,315	3,487,713	3,468,671	7,378,000	5,092,917	25,038,992	12,749,682	18,900,000
19.	Percent of total production of wheat[31,32,33,35,36]	.5483	.3465	.3285	.5385	.3168142	1.0551	.6756	.9284
20.	Production of corn in bushels[36,37,38,39,70,74,85]	54,904,608	56,099,664	65,560,000	22,760,000	42,165,218	48,544,140	47,899,079	56,710,000
21.	Percent of total production of corn[36,37,38,39]	2.4	2.0	1.5	0.6	0.6	0.6	0.7	0.8
22.	Production of oats in bushels[31,35,36,71,80,86]	1,046,786	4,281,486	4,163,506	1,800,000	---	306,298	282,028	---
23.	Percent of total production of oats[31,35,36]	0.1	0.4	0.4	0.2	---	0.1	0.1	---
24.	Production of soybeans in bushels[36,40,41,72,74,76,87]	104,163[a,h]	2,849,621	8,159,730	27,991,000	49,101,186	55,353,433	27,367,017	29,760,000
25.	Percent of total production of soybeans[36,40,41]	.1189	1.3414	1.5825	2.4909	2.85114	2.7816	1.4889	1.5445
26.	Production of hay crops in tons[31,34,42,43,44,74,76,88]	2,087,502	2,029,708	1,615,273	2,036,000	1,833,474	1,923,652	2,161,679	3,499,000[a,n]
27.	Percent of total production of hay crops[31,34,42,43,44]	2.5	2.3	1.5	1.6	1.4	1.5	1.7	2.4

[a] See the Glossary of Terms for changing definitions, i.e. farm, improved land, cropland harvested, farm owners, and livestock.
[b] Prior to 1924, the data relate to the total acreage of crops for which figures are available, except for 1920 when 14,502,932 acres of corn cut for forage were excluded (as most of this was probably duplicated in the acreage of corn harvested for grain).
[c] Percentage computed by compiler from data herein. See endnotes for source of data.
[d] Values in gold, one-fifth less than currency values.
[e] Managers included with owners.
[f] Running square bales, counting round as half bales.
[g] Census listed the number of full and part time owners separately. Compiler added the two numbers for the above figure.
[h] Includes quantity of beans harvested from acreage grown with other crops as well as that from acreage grown alone.
[i] The total value for each state for 1950 was based on the average value per acre for farms in the sample, for which value of land and buildings was reported. The average value per farm and per acre was based on the total value of all farms.
[j] Less than one-tenth of one percent.
[k] Based on a sampling of farms.
[l] Production ginned and to be ginned.
[m] 480-pound net weight bales.
[n] Census had two separate listings: hay, alfalfa, and alfalfa mixtures; and hay, all other. Compiler added the two listings for the above figure.

GENERAL AGRICULTURE STATISTICS, 1850-1990										
TEXAS										
Item No.		1850	1860	1870	1880	1890	1900	1910	1920	1930
1.	Number of farms[18,19,68,73,76,82,*a]	12,198	42,891	61,125	174,184	228,126	352,190	417,770	436,033	495,489
2.	Acres in farms[18,19,68,73,76,82]	11,496,339	25,344,028	18,396,523	36,292,219	51,406,937	125,807,017	112,435,067	114,020,621	124,707,130
3.	Acres improved land in farms[20,*a]	643,976	2,650,781	2,964,836	12,650,314	20,746,215	19,576,076	27,360,666	31,227,503	---
4.	Cropland harvested, acres[18,19,73,76,*a,b]	---	---	---	5,356,360	8,393,489	15,112,549	18,389,092	25,030,834	30,634,370
5.	Percentage increase in number of farms[18,19]	---	251.6	42.5	185.0	31.0	54.4	18.6	4.4	13.6
6.	Percentage increase of land in farms[18,19]	---	120.5	-27.4	97.3	41.6	144.7	-10.6	1.4	9.4
7.	Percentage increase of improved land in farms[20]	---	311.6	11.8	326.7	64.0	-5.6	39.8	14.1	---
8.	Average acreage per farm[18,19,66,73,76,78]	942.5	590.9	301.0	208.4	225.3	357.2	269.1	261.5	251.7
9.	Percentage increase in cropland harvested[18,19,*b]	---	---	---	---	56.7	80.1	21.7	36.1	22.4
10.	Value of farms, dollars[18,19,64,79,81]	16,550,008	88,101,320	48,119,960	170,468,886	399,971,289	691,773,613	1,843,208,395	3,700,173,319	3,597,406,986
11.	Value of farms, percent increase[18,19]	---	432.3	-45.4	254.3	134.6	73.0	166.4	100.7	-2.8
12.	Average value per farm, dollars[18,19,64,73,76]	1,357	2,054	787	979	1,753	1,964	4,412	8,486	7,260
13.	Farms operated by owners[21,22,23,24,25,26,27,65,77,*a]	---	---	---	108,716[*e]	132,616[*e]	174,639	195,863	201,210	190,515
14.	Value of livestock on farms, dollars[28,29,30,36,76,83,*a]	10,412,927	42,825,447	29,940,155[*d]	76,563,987[*j]	138,409,274[*j]	240,576,955	318,646,509	592,926,006	453,716,794
15.	Average value of livestock per farm, dollars[19,28,29,30,36]	854	998	490[*d]	440	607	683	763	1,360	916
16.	Production of cotton in bales[28,29,30,67,74,83]	58,072	431,463	350,628	805,284	1,471,242	2,506,212[*f]	2,455,174[*f]	2,971,757[*f]	3,793,392[*f]
17.	Percent of total production of cotton[28,29,30]	2.4	8.0	11.6	14.0	19.7	26.3[*f]	23.1[*f]	26.1[*f]	26.0[*f]

GENERAL AGRICULTURE STATISTICS, 1850-1990										
TEXAS										
Item No.		1850	1860	1870	1880	1890	1900	1910	1920	1930
18.	Production of wheat in bushels[31,32,35,36,69,74,84]	41,729	1,478,345	415,112	2,567,737	4,283,344	12,266,320	2,560,891	36,427,255	44,077,764
19.	Percent of total production of wheat[31,32,33,35,36]	.0415	.8540	.1443	.5588	.9145	1.8627	.3747	3.8531	5.5053
20.	Production of corn in bushels[36,37,38,39,70,74,85]	6,028,876	16,500,702	20,554,538	29,065,172	69,112,150	109,970,350	75,498,695	108,377,282	66,251,026
21.	Percent of total production of corn[36,37,38,39]	1.0	2.0	2.7	1.7	3.3	4.1	3.0	4.6	3.1
22.	Production of oats in bushels[31,35,36,71,80,86]	199,017	985,889	762,663	4,893,359	12,581,360	24,190,668	7,034,617	63,989,423	27,260,261
23.	Percent of total production of oats[31,35,36]	0.1	0.6	0.3	1.2	1.6	2.6	0.7	6.1	2.8
24.	Production of soybeans in bushels[36,40,41,72,74,76,87]	---	---	---	---	---	---	5	7,084	13,404[*h]
25.	Percent of total production of soybeans[36,40,41]	---	---	---	---	---	---	.0200	.6241	.1548
26.	Production of hay crops in tons[31,34,42,43,44,74,76,88]	8,354	11,865	18,982	48,530	528,500	1,466,452	1,329,245	3,657,356	650,992
27.	Percent of total production of hay crops[31,34,42,43,44]	0.1[*c]	0.1	0.1	0.1	0.8	1.9	1.4	3.0	0.8

GENERAL AGRICULTURE STATISTICS, 1850-1990

TEXAS

Item No.		1940	1950	1960	1970	1978	1982	1987	1990
1.	Number of farms[18,19,68,73,76,82,*a]	418,002	331,567	227,071	213,550	175,395	185,020	188,788	186,000
2.	Acres in farms[18,19,68,73,76,82]	137,683,372	145,389,014	143,217,559	142,567,000	135,619,617	131,310,306	130,502,792	132,000,000
3.	Acres improved land in farms[20,*a]	---	---	---	---	---	---	---	---
4.	Cropland harvested, acres[18,19,73,76,*a,b]	26,044,008	28,107,865	22,236,473	19,042,000	20,598,823	20,761,160	16,521,315	---
5.	Percentage increase in number of farms[18,19]	-15.6	-20.7	-31.5	-6.0	-17.9	5.5	2.0	-1.5
6.	Percentage increase of land in farms[18,19]	10.4	5.6	-1.5	-0.5	-4.9	-3.2	-0.6	1.1
7.	Percentage increase of improved land in farms[20]	---	---	---	---	---	---	---	---
8.	Average acreage per farm[18,19,66,73,76,78]	329.4	438.5	630.7	668	773	710	691	710
9.	Percentage increase in cropland harvested[18,19,*b]	-15.0	7.9	-20.8	-14.4	8.2	0.8	-20.4	---
10.	Value of farms, dollars[18,19,64,79,81]	2,589,978,936	6,718,426,000[*i,k]	11,759,366,000[*k]	21,170,000,000	51,649,091,835	71,334,000,000	70,746,000,000	58,476,000,000
11.	Value of farms, percent increase[18,19]	-28.0	159.4[*i,k]	75.0[*k]	80.0	144.0	38.1	-0.8	-17.3
12.	Average value per farm, dollars[18,19,64,73,76]	6,196	20,263[*i,k]	51,787[*k]	99,000	294,473	386,138	374,742	314,387
13.	Farms operated by owners[21,22,23,24,25,26,27,65,77,*a]	210,182	228,372	178,049[*g]	178,265[*g]	150,379	161,802[*g]	166,387[*g]	---
14.	Value of livestock on farms, dollars[28,29,30,36,76,83,*a]	344,946,306	1,019,560,574	1,244,715,031	1,996,142,000	5,534,746,000	5,910,665,000	7,586,244,000	7,712,149,000
15.	Average value of livestock per farm, dollars[19,28,29,30,36]	825	3,075	5,482	9,347	31,556	31,946	40,184	41,463
16.	Production of cotton in bales[28,29,30,67,74,83]	2,724,442	5,549,667	4,155,986	3,209,100	3,746,038	2,715,950	4,071,552	2,870,000[*l,m]
17.	Percent of total production of cotton[28,29,30]	23.7	36.0	29.9	31.6	35.1	24.0	30.7	25.0

GENERAL AGRICULTURE STATISTICS, 1850-1990									
TEXAS									
Item No.		1940	1950	1960	1970	1978	1982	1987	1990
18.	Production of wheat in bushels[31,32,35,36,69,74,84]	28,096,367	75,277,232	50,116,390	54,408,000	55,182,535	123,039,757	98,226,965	60,000,000
19.	Percent of total production of wheat[31,32,33,35,36]	3.9636	7.4787	4.7462	3.9707	3.4327	5.1844	5.2052	2.9472
20.	Production of corn in bushels[36,37,38,39,70,74,85]	69,649,829	44,077,397	42,728,000	33,232,000	115,710,749	110,164,572	123,806,676	148,400,000
21.	Percent of total production of corn[36,37,38,39]	3.0	1.6	1.0	0.8	1.7	1.5	1.8	2.0
22.	Production of oats in bushels[31,35,36,71,80,86]	32,306,788	25,647,630	18,667,883	29,032,000	---	9,040,211	8,690,781	6,600,000
23.	Percent of total production of oats[31,35,36]	3.7	2.3	1.9	3.2	---	1.8	2.8	1.8
24.	Production of soybeans in bushels[36,40,41,72,74,76,87]	16,000[*h]	4,694	1,266,775	4,424,000	15,872,788	17,783,050	4,235,367	12,450,000
25.	Percent of total production of soybeans[36,40,41]	.0183	.0022	.2457	.3931	.92168	.8936	.2304	.6461
26.	Production of hay crops in tons[31,34,42,43,44,74,76,88]	1,152,387	1,542,820	1,908,767	4,037,000	5,189,390	5,689,779	6,684,785	9,582,000[*n]
27.	Percent of total production of hay crops[31,34,42,43,44]	1.4	1.7	1.8	3.2	4.0	4.4	5.2	6.5

[a] See the Glossary of Terms for changing definitions, i.e. farm, improved land, cropland harvested, farm owners, and livestock.
[b] Prior to 1924, the data relate to the total acreage of crops for which figures are available, except for 1920 when 14,502,932 acres of corn cut for forage were excluded (as most of this was probably duplicated in the acreage of corn harvested for grain).
[c] Percentage computed by compiler from data herein. See endnotes for source of data.
[d] Values in gold, one-fifth less than currency values.
[e] Managers included with owners.
[f] Running square bales, counting round as half bales.
[g] Census listed the number of full and part time owners separately. Compiler added the two numbers for the above figure.
[h] Includes quantity of beans harvested from acreage grown with other crops as well as that from acreage grown alone.
[i] The total value for each state for 1950 was based on the average value per acre for farms in the sample, for which value of land and buildings was reported. The average value per farm and per acre was based on the total value of all farms.
[j] Including estimated value of range animals.
[k] Based on a sampling of farms.
[l] Production ginned and to be ginned.
[m] 480-pound net weight bales.
[n] Census had two separate listings: hay, alfalfa, and alfalfa mixtures; and hay, all other. Compiler added the two listings for the above figure.

GENERAL AGRICULTURE STATISTICS, 1850-1990										
UTAH										
Item No.		1850	1860	1870	1880	1890	1900	1910	1920	1930
1.	Number of farms[18,19,68,73,76,82,*a]	926	3,635	4,908	9,452	10,517	19,387	21,676	25,662	27,159
2.	Acres in farms[18,19,68,73,76,82]	46,849	89,911	148,361	655,524	1,323,705	4,116,951	3,397,699	5,050,410	5,613,101
3.	Acres improved land in farms[20,*a]	16,333	77,219	118,755	416,105	548,223	1,032,117	1,368,211	1,715,380	---
4.	Cropland harvested, acres[18,19,73,76,*a,b]	---	---	---	189,509	289,138	669,824	755,370	1,030,464	1,159,890
5.	Percentage increase in number of farms[18,19]	---	292.5	35.0	92.6	11.3	84.3	11.8	18.4	5.8
6.	Percentage increase of land in farms[18,19]	---	91.9	65.0	341.8	101.9	211.0	-17.5	48.6	11.1
7.	Percentage increase of improved land in farms[20]	---	372.8	53.8	250.4	31.7	88.3	32.6	25.4	---
8.	Average acreage per farm[18,19,66,73,76,78]	50.6	24.7	30.2	69.4	125.9	212.4	156.7	196.8	206.7
9.	Percentage increase in cropland harvested[18,19,*b]	---	---	---	---	52.6	131.7	12.8	36.4	12.6
10.	Value of farms, dollars[18,19,64,79,81]	311,799	1,333,355	1,838,338	14,015,178	28,402,780	50,778,350	117,545,332	243,751,758	221,223,172
11.	Value of farms, percent increase[18,19]	---	327.6	37.9	662.4	102.7	78.8	131.5	107.4	-9.2
12.	Average value per farm, dollars[18,19,64,73,76]	337	367	375	1,483	2,701	2,619	5,423	9,499	8,135
13.	Farms operated by owners[21,22,23,24,25,26,27,65,77,*a]	---	---	---	9,019[*e]	9,974[*e]	17,363	19,762	22,579	23,608
14.	Value of livestock on farms, dollars[28,29,30,36,76,83,*a]	546,968	1,516,707	1,719,851[*d]	4,371,638[*k]	9,914,766[*k]	21,474,241	28,781,691	54,008,183	53,942,783
15.	Average value of livestock per farm, dollars[19,28,29,30,36]	591	417	350[*d]	463	943	1,108	1,328	2,105	1,986[*c]
16.	Production of cotton in bales[28,29,30,67,74,83]	---	136	22	---	---	5[*f]	---	---	---
17.	Percent of total production of cotton[28,29,30]	---	[*j]	[*j]	---	---	[*f,j]	---	---	---

GENERAL AGRICULTURE STATISTICS, 1850-1990										
UTAH										
Item No.		1850	1860	1870	1880	1890	1900	1910	1920	1930
18.	Production of wheat in bushels[31,32,35,36,69,74,84]	107,702	384,892	558,473	1,169,199	1,515,465	3,413,470	3,943,910	4,100,979	5,309,953
19.	Percent of total production of wheat[31,32,33,35,36]	.1072	.2223	.1941	.2545	.3236	.5183	.5771	.4338	.6632
20.	Production of corn in bushels[36,37,38,39,70,74,85]	9,899	90,482	95,557	163,342	84,760	250,020	169,688	265,361	232,123
21.	Percent of total production of corn[36,37,38,39]	*j	*j	*j	*j	*j	0.5	*j	*j	*j
22.	Production of oats in bushels[31,35,36,71,80,86]	10,900	63,211	65,650	418,082	597,947	1,436,225	3,221,289	1,724,392	1,741,902
23.	Percent of total production of oats[31,35,36]	*c,j	*j	*j	0.1	0.1	0.2	0.3	0.2	0.2
24.	Production of soybeans in bushels[36,40,41,72,74,76,87]	---	---	---	---	---	---	---	562	5,006*h
25.	Percent of total production of soybeans[36,40,41]	---	---	---	---	---	---	---	.0495	.0578
26.	Production of hay crops in tons[31,34,42,43,44,74,76,88]	4,805	19,235	27,305	92,735	301,901	850,962	1,016,075	1,018,986	1,372,709
27.	Percent of total production of hay crops[31,34,42,43,44]	*c,j	0.1	0.1	0.3	0.4	1.1	1.0	0.8	1.6

GENERAL AGRICULTURE STATISTICS, 1850-1990									
UTAH									
Item No.		1940	1950	1960	1970	1978	1982	1987	1990
1.	Number of farms[18,19,68,73,76,82,*a]	25,411	24,176	17,811	13,045	12,764	13,984	14,066	13,200
2.	Acres in farms[18,19,68,73,76,82]	7,302,007	10,865,165	12,688,518	11,313,000	10,470,564	9,772,942	9,989,073	11,300,000
3.	Acres improved land in farms[20,*a]	---	---	---	---	---	---	---	---
4.	Cropland harvested, acres[18,19,73,76,*a,b]	966,088	1,279,469	1,062,246	1,050,000	1,163,141	1,118,486	1,076,886	---
5.	Percentage increase in number of farms[18,19]	-6.4	-4.9	-26.3	-26.8	-2.2	9.6	0.6	-6.2
6.	Percentage increase of land in farms[18,19]	30.1	48.8	16.8	-10.8	-7.4	-6.7	2.2	13.1
7.	Percentage increase of improved land in farms[20]	---	---	---	---	---	---	---	---
8.	Average acreage per farm[18,19,66,73,76,78]	287.4	449.4	712.4	867	820	699	710	869
9.	Percentage increase in cropland harvested[18,19,*b]	-16.7	32.4	-17.0	-1.2	10.8	-3.8	-3.7	---
10.	Value of farms, dollars[18,19,64,79,81]	154,358,365	471,242,000[*i]	755,028,000	1,040,000,000	4,087,466,776	5,445,000,000	4,259,000,000	4,840,000,000
11.	Value of farms, percent increase[18,19]	-30.2	205.3[*i]	60.2	37.7	293	33.2	-21.8	13.6
12.	Average value per farm, dollars[18,19,64,73,76]	6,074	19,492[*i]	42,391	80,000	320,234	389,678	302,838	366,667
13.	Farms operated by owners[21,22,23,24,25,26,27,65,77,*a]	21,906	22,225	16,715[*g]	12,292[*g]	12,045	12,995[*g]	13,071[*g]	---
14.	Value of livestock on farms, dollars[28,29,30,36,76,83,*a]	32,255,135	103,817,181	124,092,880	---	363,831,000	425,195,000	487,442,000	576,140,000
15.	Average value of livestock per farm, dollars[19,28,29,30,36]	1,269	4,294	6,967	---	28,505	30,406	34,654	43,647
16.	Production of cotton in bales[28,29,30,67,74,83]	---	---	---	---	---	---	---	---
17.	Percent of total production of cotton[28,29,30]	---	---	---	---	---	---	---	---

GENERAL AGRICULTURE STATISTICS, 1850-1990

UTAH

Item No.		1940	1950	1960	1970	1978	1982	1987	1990
18.	Production of wheat in bushels[31,32,35,36,69,74,84]	4,059,709	8,540,829	5,305,000	5,976,000	6,672,767	6,662,449	7,149,004	5,950,000
19.	Percent of total production of wheat[31,32,33,35,36]	.5727	.8485	.5024	.4361	.41509	.2087	.3788	.2923
20.	Production of corn in bushels[36,37,38,39,70,74,85]	231,695	136,228	3,050,000	---	1,183,487	1,617,750	2,559,872	2,640,000
21.	Percent of total production of corn[36,37,38,39]	*j	*j	0.1	---	*j	*j	*j	*j
22.	Production of oats in bushels[31,35,36,71,80,86]	1,924,428	1,822,982	921,562	1,160,000	---	784,230	699,305	1,258,000
23.	Percent of total production of oats[31,35,36]	0.2	0.2	0.1	0.1	---	0.2	0.2	0.3
24.	Production of soybeans in bushels[36,40,41,72,74,76,87]	238*h	---	---	---	*l	---	*l	---
25.	Percent of total production of soybeans[36,40,41]	.0003	---	---	---	---	---	---	---
26.	Production of hay crops in tons[31,34,42,43,44,74,76,88]	901,465	1,121,928	1,240,486	1,592,000	1,759,548	1,877,759	1,962,334	1,986,000*m
27.	Percent of total production of hay crops[31,34,42,43,44]	1.1	1.3	1.2	1.2	1.3	1.5	1.5	1.4

[a] See the Glossary of Terms for changing definitions, i.e. farm, improved land, cropland harvested, farm owners, and livestock.
[b] Prior to 1924, the data relate to the total acreage of crops for which figures are available, except for 1920 when 14,502,932 acres of corn cut for forage were excluded (as most of this was probably duplicated in the acreage of corn harvested for grain).
[c] Percentage computed by compiler from data herein. See endnotes for source of data.
[d] Values in gold, one-fifth less than currency values.
[e] Managers included with owners.
[f] Running square bales, counting round as half bales.
[g] Census listed the number of full and part time owners separately. Compiler added the two numbers for the above figure.
[h] Includes quantity of beans harvested from acreage grown with other crops as well as that from acreage grown alone.
[i] The total value for each state for 1950 was based on the average value per acre for farms in the sample, for which value of land and buildings was reported. The average value per farm and per acre was based on the total value of all farms.
[j] Less than one-tenth of one percent.
[k] Including estimated value of range animals.
[l] Withheld to avoid disclosing data for individual farms.
[m] Census had two separate listings: hay, alfalfa, and alfalfa mixtures; and hay, all other. Compiler added the two listings for the above figure.

GENERAL AGRICULTURE STATISTICS, 1850-1990										
VERMONT										
Item No.		1850	1860	1870	1880	1890	1900	1910	1920	1930
1.	Number of farms[18,19,68,73,76,82,*a]	29,763	31,556	33,827	35,522	32,573	33,104	32,709	29,075	24,898
2.	Acres in farms[18,19,68,73,76,82]	4,125,822	4,274,414	4,528,804	4,882,588	4,395,646	4,724,440	4,663,577	4,235,811	3,896,097
3.	Acres improved land in farms[20,*a]	2,601,409	2,823,157	3,073,257	3,286,461	2,655,943	2,126,624	1,633,965	1,691,595	---
4.	Cropland harvested, acres[18,19,73,76,*a,b]	---	---	---	1,264,536	1,211,187	1,203,513	1,203,795	1,143,361	1,073,693
5.	Percentage increase in number of farms[18,19]	---	6.0	7.2	5.0	-8.3	1.6	-1.2	-11.1	-14.4
6.	Percentage increase of land in farms[18,19]	---	3.6	6.0	7.8	-10.0	7.5	-1.3	-9.2	-8.0
7.	Percentage increase of improved land in farms[20]	---	8.5	8.9	6.9	-19.2	-19.9	-23.2	3.5	---
8.	Average acreage per farm[18,19,66,73,76,78]	138.6	135.5	133.9	137.5	134.9	142.7	142.6	145.7	156.5
9.	Percentage increase in cropland harvested[18,19,*b]	---	---	---	---	-4.2	-0.6	[*j]	-5.0	-6.1
10.	Value of farms, dollars[18,19,64,79,81]	63,367,227	94,289,045	111,493,660	109,346,010	80,427,490	83,071,620	112,588,275	159,117,159	145,935,241
11.	Value of farms, percent increase[18,19]	---	48.8	18.2	-1.9	-26.4	3.3	35.5	41.3	-8.3
12.	Average value per farm, dollars[18,19,64,73,76]	2,129	2,988	3,296	3,078	2,469	2,509	3,442	5,473	5,861
13.	Farms operated by owners[21,22,23,24,25,26,27,65,77,*a]	---	---	---	30,760[*e]	27,816[*e]	27,669	28,065	25,121	22,009[*g]
14.	Value of livestock on farms, dollars[28,29,30,36,76,83,*a]	12,643,228	16,241,989	19,111,068[*d]	16,586,195	16,644,320	17,841,317	22,642,766	42,385,331	36,071,729
15.	Average value of livestock per farm, dollars[19,28,29,30,36]	425	515	565[*d]	467	511	539	692	1,458	1,449[*c]
16.	Production of cotton in bales[28,29,30,67,74,83]	---	---	---	---	---	---	---	---	---
17.	Percent of total production of cotton[28,29,30]	---	---	---	---	---	---	---	---	---

GENERAL AGRICULTURE STATISTICS, 1850-1990										
VERMONT										
Item No.		1850	1860	1870	1880	1890	1900	1910	1920	1930
18.	Production of wheat in bushels[31,32,35,36,69,74,84]	535,955	437,037	454,703	337,257	164,720	34,650	14,087	176,003	13,248
19.	Percent of total production of wheat[31,32,33,35,36]	.5334	.2525	.1580	.0734	.0352	.0053	.0021	.0186	.0017
20.	Production of corn in bushels[36,37,38,39,70,74,85]	2,032,396	1,525,411	1,699,882	2,014,271	1,700,688	2,322,450	1,715,133	937,375	259,170
21.	Percent of total production of corn[36,37,38,39]	0.3	0.2	0.2	0.1	0.1	0.5	0.1	*j	*j
22.	Production of oats in bushels[31,35,36,71,80,86]	2,307,734	3,630,267	3,602,430	3,742,282	3,316,141	2,742,140	2,141,357	2,369,349	1,010,660
23.	Percent of total production of oats[31,35,36]	1.6	2.1	1.3	0.9	0.4	0.3	0.2	0.2	0.1
24.	Production of soybeans in bushels[36,40,41,72,74,76,87]	---	---	---	---	---	---	---	639	47*h
25.	Percent of total production of soybeans[36,40,41]	---	---	---	---	---	---	---	.0563	.0005
26.	Production of hay crops in tons[31,34,42,43,44,74,76,88]	866,153	940,178	1,020,669	1,052,183	1,205,953	1,329,972	1,502,780	1,696,508	1,141,206
27.	Percent of total production of hay crops[31,34,42,43,44]	6.3*c	4.9	3.7	3.0	1.8	1.7	1.5	1.4	1.3

GENERAL AGRICULTURE STATISTICS, 1850-1990									
VERMONT									
Item No.		1940	1950	1960	1970	1978	1982	1987	1990
1.	Number of farms[18,19,68,73,76,82,*a]	23,582	19,043	12,099	6,874	5,852	6,315	5,877	7,000
2.	Acres in farms[18,19,68,73,76,82]	3,666,835	3,527,381	2,945,343	1,916,000	1,633,049	1,574,441	1,407,868	1,510,000
3.	Acres improved land in farms[20,*a]	---	---	---	---	---	---	---	---
4.	Cropland harvested, acres[18,19,73,76,*a,b]	1,022,581	858,512	743,448	577,000	554,957	547,848	488,253	---
5.	Percentage increase in number of farms[18,19]	-5.3	-19.2	-36.5	-43.2	-14.9	7.9	-6.9	19.1
6.	Percentage increase of land in farms[18,19]	-5.9	-3.8	-16.5	-34.9	-14.8	-3.6	-10.6	7.3
7.	Percentage increase of improved land in farms[20]	---	---	---	---	---	---	---	---
8.	Average acreage per farm[18,19,66,73,76,78]	155.5	185.2	243.4	279	279	249	240	214
9.	Percentage increase in cropland harvested[18,19,*b]	-4.8	-16.0	-13.4	-22.4	-3.8	-1.3	-10.9	---
10.	Value of farms, dollars[18,19,64,79,81]	111,108,534	196,405,000[*i]	240,003,000	429,000,000	1,064,707,028	1,305,000,000	1,521,000,000	2,273,000,000
11.	Value of farms, percent increase[18,19]	-23.9	76.8[*i]	22.2	78.7	148.2	22.6	16.6	49.4
12.	Average value per farm, dollars[18,19,64,73,76]	4,712	10,314[*i]	19,837	62,000	181,939	206,616	258,713	---
13.	Farms operated by owners[21,22,23,24,25,26,27,65,77,*a]	20,952	18,014	11,608[*g]	6,638[*g]	5,520	5,926[*g]	5,472[*g]	324,714
14.	Value of livestock on farms, dollars[28,29,30,36,76,83,*a]	28,065,322	58,492,869	75,171,592	---	254,162,000	349,348,000	350,351,000	---
15.	Average value of livestock per farm, dollars[19,28,29,30,36]	1,190	3,072	6,213	---	43,432	55,320	59,614	397,771,000
16.	Production of cotton in bales[28,29,30,67,74,83]	---	---	---	---	---	---	---	56,824
17.	Percent of total production of cotton[28,29,30]	---	---	---	---	---	---	---	0.5

GENERAL AGRICULTURE STATISTICS, 1850-1990									
VERMONT									
Item No.		1940	1950	1960	1970	1978	1982	1987	1990
18.	Production of wheat in bushels[31,32,35,36,69,74,84]	4,282	---	19,859	---	10,622	10,366	15,114	---
19.	Percent of total production of wheat[31,32,33,35,36]	.0006	---	.0019	---	.00066	.0004	.0008	---
20.	Production of corn in bushels[36,37,38,39,70,74,85]	277,530	102,038	3,172,000	---	514,903	1,173,189	1,031,941	---
21.	Percent of total production of corn[36,37,38,39]	*j	*j	0.1	---	*j	*j	*j	---
22.	Production of oats in bushels[31,35,36,71,80,86]	997,954	390,603	761,728	246,000	---	70,621	28,475	---
23.	Percent of total production of oats[31,35,36]	0.1	*j	0.1	*j	---	*j	*j	---
24.	Production of soybeans in bushels[36,40,41,72,74,76,87]	1,397*h	64	---	---	*k	*k	*k	---
25.	Percent of total production of soybeans[36,40,41]	.0016	.0000	---	---	---	---	---	---
26.	Production of hay crops in tons[31,34,42,43,44,74,76,88]	1,137,876	977,639	1,042,246	904,000	847,192	886,084	869,548	754,000*l
27.	Percent of total production of hay crops[31,34,42,43,44]	1.4	1.1	1.0	0.7	0.6	0.7	0.7	0.5

a See the Glossary of Terms for changing definitions, i.e. farm, improved land, cropland harvested, farm owners, and livestock.

b Prior to 1924, the data relate to the total acreage of crops for which figures are available, except for 1920 when 14,502,932 acres of corn cut for forage were excluded (as most of this was probably duplicated in the acreage of corn harvested for grain).

c Percentage computed by compiler from data herein. See endnotes for source of data.

d Values in gold, one-fifth less than currency values.

e Managers included with owners.

f Running square bales, counting round as half bales.

g Census listed the number of full and part time owners separately. Compiler added the two numbers for the above figure.

h Includes quantity of beans harvested from acreage grown with other crops as well as that from acreage grown alone.

i The total value for each state for 1950 was based on the average value per acre for farms in the sample, for which value of land and buildings was reported. The average value per farm and per acre was based on the total value of all farms.

j Less than one-tenth of one percent.

k Withheld to avoid disclosing data for individual farms.

l Census had two separate listings: hay, alfalfa, and alfalfa mixtures; and hay, all other. Compiler added the two listings for the above figure.

GENERAL AGRICULTURE STATISTICS, 1850-1990										
VIRGINIA										
Item No.		1850	1860	1870	1880	1890	1900	1910	1920	1930
1.	Number of farms[18,19,68,73,76,82,*a]	77,013[*j]	92,605[*j]	73,849	118,517	127,600	167,886	184,018	186,242	170,610
2.	Acres in farms[18,19,68,73,76,82]	26,152,311[*j]	31,117,036[*j]	18,145,911	19,835,785	19,104,951	19,907,883	19,495,636	18,561,112	16,728,620
3.	Acres improved land in farms[20,*a]	10,360,135[*j]	11,437,821[*j]	8,165,040	8,510,113	9,125,545	10,094,805	9,870,058	9,460,492	---
4.	Cropland harvested, acres[18,19,73,76,*a,b]	---	---	---	3,844,702	3,781,053	4,345,537	4,256,226	4,579,830	3,975,307
5.	Percentage increase in number of farms[18,19]	---	20.2[*j]	-20.3	60.5	7.7	31.6	9.6	1.2	-8.4
6.	Percentage increase of land in farms[18,19]	---	19.0[*j]	-41.7	9.3	-3.7	4.2	-2.1	-4.8	-9.9
7.	Percentage increase of improved land in farms[20]	---	10.4[*j]	-28.6	4.2	7.2	10.6	-2.2	-4.1	---
8.	Average acreage per farm[18,19,66,73,76,78]	339.6[*j]	336.0[*j]	245.7	167.4	149.7	118.6	105.9	99.7	98.1
9.	Percentage increase in cropland harvested[18,19,*a,b]	---	---	---	---	-1.7	14.9	-2.1	7.6	-13.2
10.	Value of farms, dollars[18,19,64,79,81]	216,401,543[*j]	371,761,661[*j]	170,416,676	216,028,107	254,490,600	271,578,200	532,058,062	1,024,435,025	855,849,672
11.	Value of farms, percent increase[18,19]	---	71.8[*j]	-54.2	26.8	17.8	6.7	95.9	92.5	-16.5
12.	Average value per farm, dollars[18,19,64,73,76]	2,810[*j]	4,014[*j]	2,308	1,823	1,994	1,618	2,891	5,501	5,016
13.	Farms operated by owners[21,22,23,24,25,26,27,65,77,*a]	---	---	---	83,531[*e]	93,311[*e]	114,155	133,664	136,363	121,104
14.	Value of livestock on farms, dollars[28,29,30,36,76,83,*a]	33,656,659[*j]	47,803,049[*j]	22,550,135[*d]	25,953,315	33,404,281	42,026,737	74,891,438	121,969,281	92,128,480
15.	Average value of livestock per farm, dollars[19,28,29,30,36]	437[*j]	516[*j]	305[*d]	219	262	250	407	655	540
16.	Production of cotton in bales[28,29,30,67,74,83]	3,947[*j]	12,727[*j]	183	19,595	5,375	10,789[*f]	10,480[*f]	24,887[*f]	52,442[*f]
17.	Percent of total production of cotton[28,29,30]	0.2[*j]	0.2[*j]	[*c,n]	0.3	0.1	0.1[*f]	0.1[*f]	0.2[*f]	0.4[*f]

GENERAL AGRICULTURE STATISTICS, 1850-1990										
VIRGINIA										
Item No.		1850	1860	1870	1880	1890	1900	1910	1920	1930
18.	Production of wheat in bushels[31,32,35,36,69,74,84]	11,212,616[*j]	13,130,977[*j]	7,398,787	7,826,174	7,904,092	8,907,510	8,076,989	11,446,027	8,575,461
19.	Percent of total production of wheat[31,32,33,35,36]	11.1584[*j]	7.5856[*j]	2.5713	1.7033	1.6876	1.3526	1.1819	1.2107	1.0711
20.	Production of corn in bushels[36,37,38,39,70,74,85]	35,254,319[*j]	38,319,999[*j]	17,649,304	29,119,761	27,172,493	36,748,410	38,295,141	42,302,978	32,772,810
21.	Percent of total production of corn[36,37,38,39]	6.0[*j]	4.6[*j]	2.3	1.7	1.3	1.4	1.5	1.8	1.5
22.	Production of oats in bushels[31,35,36,71,80,86]	10,179,144[*j]	10,186,720[*j]	6,857,555	5,333,181	5,695,100	3,269,430	2,884,495	1,958,609	1,127,824
23.	Percent of total production of oats[31,35,36]	6.9[*j]	5.9[*j]	2.4	1.3	0.7	0.3	0.3	0.2	0.1
24.	Production of soybeans in bushels[36,40,41,72,74,76,87]	---	---	---	---	---	---	415	111,353	261,234
25.	Percent of total production of soybeans[36,40,41]	---	---	---	---	---	---	1.6623	9.8096	3.0161
26.	Production of hay crops in tons[31,34,42,43,44,74,76,88]	369,098[*j]	445,133[*j]	199,883	286,823	656,153	627,979	824,051	1,334,838	980,737
27.	Percent of total production of hay crops[31,34,42,43,44]	2.7[*c,j]	2.3[*j]	0.7	0.8	1.0	0.8	0.8	1.1	1.2

GENERAL AGRICULTURE STATISTICS, 1850-1990

VIRGINIA

Item No.		1940	1950	1960	1970	1978	1982	1987	1990
1.	Number of farms[18,19,68,73,76,82,*a]	174,885	150,997	97,623	64,572	49,936	51,859	44,799	46,000
2.	Acres in farms[18,19,68,73,76,82]	16,444,907	15,572,295	13,125,802	10,650,000	9,459,429	9,436,854	8,676,336	8,900,000
3.	Acres improved land in farms[20,*a]	---	---	---	---	---	---	---	---
4.	Cropland harvested, acres[18,19,73,76,*a,b]	3,840,189	3,313,849	2,857,848	2,612,000	2,599,660	2,779,282	2,406,976	---
5.	Percentage increase in number of farms[18,19]	2.5	-13.7	-35.3	-33.9	-22.7	-3.9	-13.6	2.7
6.	Percentage increase of land in farms[18,19]	-1.7	-5.3	-15.7	-18.9	-11.2	-0.2	-8.1	2.6
7.	Percentage increase of improved land in farms[20]	---	---	---	---	---	---	---	---
8.	Average acreage per farm[18,19,66,73,76,78]	94.0	103.1	134.5	165	189	182	194	191
9.	Percentage increase in cropland harvested[18,19,*b]	-3.4	-13.7	-13.8	-8.6	-0.5	6.9	-13.4	---
10.	Value of farms, dollars[18,19,64,79,81]	674,975,424	1,277,084,000[*i,k]	1,819,248,000[*k]	3,047,000,000	8,571,913,888	10,622,000,000	10,409,000,000	12,339,000,000
11.	Value of farms, percent increase[18,19]	-21.1	89.2[*i,k]	42.5[*k]	67.5	181.3	23.9	-2.0	18.5
12.	Average value per farm, dollars[18,19,64,73,76]	3,860	8,458[*i,k]	18,635[*k]	47,000	171,658	205,034	232,374	28,239
13.	Farms operated by owners[21,22,23,24,25,26,27,65,77,*a]	126,674[*g]	124,547	82,959	59,163[*g]	45,601	47,794[*g]	41,500[*g]	---
14.	Value of livestock on farms, dollars[28,29,30,36,76,83,*a]	73,061,191	186,707,909	214,725,607	269,201,000	757,676,000	977,612,000	1,123,391,000	1,378,752,000
15.	Average value of livestock per farm, dollars[19,28,29,30,36]	418	1,237	2,200	4,169	15,173	18,851	25,076	29,973
16.	Production of cotton in bales[28,29,30,67,74,83,83]	12,865[*f]	18,722	12,476	3,400	140	338	1,546	2,700[*l,m]
17.	Percent of total production of cotton[28,29,30]	0.1[*f]	0.1	0.1	[*n]	[*n]	[*n]	[*n]	[*n]

GENERAL AGRICULTURE STATISTICS, 1850-1990

VIRGINIA

Item No.		1940	1950	1960	1970	1978	1982	1987	1990
18.	Production of wheat in bushels[31,32,35,36,69,74,84]	7,211,524	6,864,798	5,996,456	7,260,000	4,427,658	10,873,751	8,065,684	12,650,000
19.	Percent of total production of wheat[31,32,33,35,36]	1.0174	.6820	.5679	.5298	.27543	.4582	.4274	.6214
20.	Production of corn in bushels[36,37,38,39,70,74,85]	33,600,920	33,150,002	37,352,000	31,144,000	50,865,163	58,283,179	20,941,850	40,150,000
21.	Percent of total production of corn[36,37,38,39]	1.5	1.2	0.9	2.8	0.7	0.8	0.3	0.5
22.	Production of oats in bushels[31,35,36,71,80,86]	1,159,760	2,568,203	3,858,101	2,448,000	---	546,609	511,222	495,000
23.	Percent of total production of oats[31,35,36]	0.1	0.2	0.4	0.3	---	---	0.2	0.1
24.	Production of soybeans in bushels[36,40,41,72,75,76,87]	594,890[a,h]	2,284,808	5,733,425	6,441,000	13,015,028	17,698,179	10,421,715	17,280,000
25.	Percent of total production of soybeans[36,40,41]	.6792	1.0755	1.1119	.5732	.7557	.8894	.5670	.8968
26.	Production of hay crops in tons[31,34,42,43,44,75,76,88]	1,201,339	1,504,043	1,620,013	1,778,000	1,535,228	1,714,484	1,832,905	2,565,000[a,o]
27.	Percent of total production of hay crops[31,34,42,43,44]	1.5	1.7	1.5	1.4	1.2	1.3	1.4	1.7[a,c]

[a] See the Glossary of Terms for changing definitions, i.e. farm, improved land, cropland harvested, farm owners, and livestock.
[b] Prior to 1924, the data relate to the total acreage of crops for which figures are available, except for 1920 when 14,502,932 acres of corn cut for forage were excluded (as most of this was probably duplicated in the acreage of corn harvested for grain).
[c] Percentage computed by compiler from data herein. See endnotes for source of data.
[d] Values in gold, one-fifth less than currency values.
[e] Managers included with owners.
[f] Running square bales, counting round as half bales.
[g] Census listed the number of full and part time owners separately. Compiler added the two numbers for the above figure.
[h] Includes quantity of beans harvested from acreage grown with other crops as well as that from acreage grown alone.
[i] The total value for each state for 1950 was based on the average value per acre for farms in the sample, for which value of land and buildings was reported. The average value per farm and per acre was based on the total value of all farms.
[j] Virginia totals includes the area now known as West Virginia.
[k] Based on a sampling of farms.
[l] Production ginned and to be ginned.
[m] 480-pound net weight bales.
[n] Less than one-tenth of one percent.
[o] Census had two separate listings: hay, alfalfa, and alfalfa mixtures; and hay, all other. Compiler added the two listings for the above figure.

GENERAL AGRICULTURE STATISTICS, 1850-1990										
WASHINGTON										
Item No.		1850	1860	1870	1880	1890	1900	1910	1920	1930
1.	Number of farms[18,19,68,73,76,82,*a]	---	1,330	3,127	6,529	18,056	33,202	56,192	66,288	70,904
2.	Acres in farms[18,19,68,73,76,82]	---	366,156	649,139	1,409,421	4,179,190	8,499,297	11,712,235	13,244,720	13,533,778
3.	Acres improved land in farms[20,*a]	---	81,869	192,016	484,346	1,820,832	3,465,960	6,373,311	7,129,343	---
4.	Cropland harvested, acres[18,19,73,76,*a,b]	---	---	---	201,261	809,266	1,901,381	3,431,273	4,001,852	3,658,514
5.	Percentage increase in number of farms[18,19]	---	---	135.1	108.8	176.6	83.9	69.2	18.0	7.0
6.	Percentage increase of land in farms[18,19]	---	---	77.3	117.1	196.5	103.4	37.8	13.1	2.2
7.	Percentage increase of improved land in farms[20]	---	---	134.5	152.2	275.9	90.4	83.9	11.9	---
8.	Average acreage per farm[18,19,66,73,76,78]	---	275.3	207.6	215.9	231.4	256.0	208.4	199.8	190.9
9.	Percentage increase in cropland harvested[18,19,*b]	---	---	---	---	302.1	135.0	80.5	16.6	-8.6
10.	Value of farms, dollars[18,19,68,73,76,82]	---	2,217,842	3,978,341	13,844,224	83,461,660	115,609,710	571,968,457	920,392,341	773,662,602
11.	Value of farms, percent increase[18,19]	---	---	79.4	248.0	502.9	38.5	394.8	60.9	-15.9
12.	Average value per farm, dollars[18,19,64,73,76]	---	1,668	1,272	2,120	4,622	3,482	10,179	13,885	10,911
13.	Farms operated by owners[21,22,23,24,25,26,27,65,77*a]	---	---	---	6,058[*e]	16,529[*e]	28,020	47,505	52,701	57,588
14.	Value of livestock on farms, dollars[28,29,30,36,76,83*a]	---	1,099,911	2,103,343[*d]	5,974,307[*k]	14,113,110	22,159,207	48,865,110	82,316,130	63,449,390
15.	Average value of livestock per farm, dollars[19,28,29,30,36]	---	827	673[*d]	915	782	667	870	1,242	895[*c]
16.	Production of cotton in bales[28,29,30,67,74,83]	---	---	---	---	---	---	---	---	---
17.	Percent of total production of cotton[28,29,30]	---	---	---	---	---	---	---	---	---

GENERAL AGRICULTURE STATISTICS, 1850-1990										
WASHINGTON										
Item No.		1850	1860	1870	1880	1890	1900	1910	1920	1930
18.	Production of wheat in bushels[31,32,35,36,69,74,84]	---	86,219	217,043	1,921,322	6,345,426	21,187,527	40,920,390	41,837,909	42,588,762
19.	Percent of total production of wheat[31,32,33,35,36]	---	.0498	.0754	.4181	1.3548	3.2174	5.9879	4.4254	5.3193
20.	Production of corn in bushels[36,37,38,39,70,74,85]	---	4,712	21,781	39,183	156,413	218,706	563,025	901,905	349,100
21.	Percent of total production of corn[36,37,38,39]	---	*j	*j	*j	*j	*j	*j	*j	*j
22.	Production of oats in bushels[31,35,36,71,80,86]	---	134,334	255,169	1,571,706	2,273,182	5,336,486	13,228,003	8,073,481	5,776,632
23.	Percent of total production of oats[31,35,36]	---	0.1	0.1	0.4	0.3	0.6	1.3	0.8	0.6
24.	Production of soybeans in bushels[36,40,41,72,74,76,87]	---	---	---	---	---	---	---	295	---
25.	Percent of total production of soybeans[36,40,41]	---	---	---	---	---	---	---	.0260	---
26.	Production of hay crops in tons[31,34,42,43,44,74,76,88]	---	4,580	30,233	106,819	395,770	826,897	1,399,597	1,973,173	1,474,663
27.	Percent of total production of hay crops[31,34,42,43,44]	---	*j	0.1	0.3	0.6	1.1	1.4	1.6	1.7

Item No.	GENERAL AGRICULTURE STATISTICS, 1850-1990 WASHINGTON	1940	1950	1960	1970	1978	1982	1987	1990
1.	Number of farms[18,19,68,73,76,82,*a]	81,686	69,820	51,577	34,033	30,987	36,080	33,559	37,000
2.	Acres in farms[18,19,68,73,76,82]	15,181,815	17,369,245	18,716,972	17,559,000	16,721,836	16,469,678	16,115,568	16,000,000
3.	Acres improved land in farms[20.*a]	---	---	---	---	---	---	---	---
4.	Cropland harvested, acres[18,19,73,76,*a,b]	3,569,803	4,236,705	4,412,466	4,110,000	5,014,228	5,278,772	4,597,476	---
5.	Percentage increase in number of farms[18,19]	15.2	-14.5	-26.1	-34.0	-9.0	16.4	-7.0	10.3
6.	Percentage increase of land in farms[18,19]	12.2	14.4	7.8	-6.2	-4.8	-1.5	-2.2	-0.7
7.	Percentage increase of improved land in farms[20]	---	---	---	---	---	---	---	---
8.	Average acreage per farm[18,19,66,73,76,78]	185.9	248.8	362.9	516	540	456	480	421
9.	Percentage increase in cropland harvested[18,19,*b]	-2.4	18.7	4.1	-6.9	22.0	5.3	-12.9	---
10.	Value of farms, dollars[18,19,64,79,81]	593,366,445	1,470,208,000[*i]	2,454,524,000	3,930,000,000	11,114,386,173	15,271,000,000	11,948,000,000	11,625,000,000
11.	Value of farms, percent increase[18,19]	-23.3	147.8[*i]	67.0	60.1	183.0	37.4	-21.8	-2.7
12.	Average value per farm, dollars[18,19,64,73,76]	7,264	21,057[*i]	47,590	115,000	358,679	423,352	355,976	---
13.	Farms operated by owners[21,22,23,24,25,26,27,65,77,*a]	66,561[*g]	62,740	46,664[*g]	31,005[*g]	28,224	33,068[*g]	30,203[*g]	314,189
14.	Value of livestock on farms, dollars[28,29,30,36,76,83,*a]	48,460,103	118,064,962	182,509,821	---	781,28,000	1,116,418,000	1,230,978,000	---
15.	Average value of livestock per farm, dollars[19,28,29,30,36]	---	1,691	3,539	---	25,214	30,943	36,681	1,395,640,000
16.	Production of cotton in bales[28,29,30,67,74,83]	593	---	---	---	---	---	---	---
17.	Percent of total production of cotton[28,29,30]	[*j]	---	---	---	---	---	---	---

GENERAL AGRICULTURE STATISTICS, 1850-1990

WASHINGTON

Item No.		1940	1950	1960	1970	1978	1982	1987	1990
18.	Production of wheat in bushels[31,32,35,36,69,74,84]	44,029,287	57,678,231	73,470,299	97,075,000	123,527,226	128,069,408	114,781,997	110,610,000
19.	Percent of total production of wheat[31,32,33,35,36]	6.2114	5.7302	6.9579	7.0846	.7684	5.3964	6.0824	5.4332
20.	Production of corn in bushels[36,37,38,39,70,74,85]	484,013	449,829	7,040,000	4,558,000	7,770,743	20,807,328	15,956,710	15,750,000
21.	Percent of total production of corn[36,37,38,39]	*j	*j	0.2	0.1	0.1	0.3	0.2	0.2
22.	Production of oats in bushels[31,35,36.71,80,86]	7,798,436	5,947,558	5,931,702	9,635,000	---	1,787,357	1,659,582	2,835,000
23.	Percent of total production of oats[31,35,36]	0.9	0.5	0.6	1.1	---	0.4	0.5	0.8
24.	Production of soybeans in bushels[36,40,41,72,74,76,87]	654*h	---	1,116	---	67,890	---	*l	---
25.	Percent of total production of soybeans[36,40,41]	.0007	---	.0002	---	.0039	---	---	---
26.	Production of hay crops in tons[31,34,42,43,44,74,76,88]	1,631,776	1,367,257	1,798,215	2,335,000	2,541,298	2,206,096	2,574,944	2,814,000*m
27.	Percent of total production of hay crops[31,34,42,43,44]	2.0	1.5	1.7	1.8	1.9	1.7	2.0	1.9*c

[a] See the Glossary of Terms for changing definitions, i.e. farm, improved land, cropland harvested, farm owners, and livestock.
[b] Prior to 1924, the data relate to the total acreage of crops for which figures are available, except for 1920 when 14,502,932 acres of corn cut for forage were excluded (as most of this was probably duplicated in the acreage of corn harvested for grain).
[c] Percentage computed by compiler from data herein. See endnotes for source of data.
[d] Values in gold, one-fifth less than currency values.
[e] Managers included with owners.
[f] Running square bales, counting round as half bales.
[g] Census listed the number of full and part time owners separately. Compiler added the two numbers for the above figure.
[h] Includes quantity of beans harvested from acreage grown with other crops as well as that from acreage grown alone.
[i] The total value for each state for 1950 was based on the average value per acre for farms in the sample, for which value of land and buildings was reported. The average value per farm and per acre was based on the total value of all farms.
[j] Less than one-tenth of one percent.
[k] Including estimated value of range animals.
[l] Withheld to avoid disclosing data for individual farms.
[m] Census had two separate listings: hay, alfalfa, and alfalfa mixtures; and hay, all other. Compiler added the two listings for the above figure.

GENERAL AGRICULTURE STATISTICS, 1850-1990										
WEST VIRGINIA										
Item No.		1850	1860	1870	1880	1890	1900	1910	1920	1930
1.	Number of farms[18,19,68,73,76,82,*a]	*j	*j	39,778	62,674	72,773	92,874	96,685	87,289	82,641
2.	Acres in farms[18,19,68,73,76,82]	*j	*j	8,528,394	101,193,779	10,321,326	10,654,513	10,026,442	9,569,790	8,802,348
3.	Acres improved land in farms[20,*a]	*j	*j	2,580,254	3,792,327	4,554,000	5,498,981	5,521,757	5,520,308	---
4.	Cropland harvested, acres[18,19,73,76,*a,b]	---	---	---	1,506,407	1,771,976	1,992,403	1,874,382	1,891,515	1,655,380
5.	Percentage increase in number of farms[18,19]	---	*j	---	57.6	16.1	27.6	4.1	-9.7	-5.3
6.	Percentage increase of land in farms[18,19]	---	*j	---	19.5	1.3	3.2	-5.9	-4.6	-8.0
7.	Percentage increase of improved land in farms[20]	---	*j	---	47.0	20.1	20.8	0.4	0.9[*c]	---
8.	Average acreage per farm[18,19,66,73,76,78]	*j	*j	214.4	162.6	141.8	114.7	103.7	109.6	106.5
9.	Percentage increase in cropland harvested[18,19,*b]	---	---	---	---	17.6	12.4	-5.9	0.9	-12.5
10.	Value of farms, dollars[18,19,64,79,81]	*j	*j	81,283,505	133,147,175	151,880,300	168,295,670	264,390,954	410,783,406	341,976,394
11.	Value of farms, percent increase[18,19]	---	*j	---	63.8	14.1	10.8	57.1	55.4	-16.8
12.	Average value per farm, dollars[18,19,64,73,76]	*j	*j	2,043	2,124	2,687	1,812	2,735	4,706	4,138
13.	Farms operated by owners[21,22,23,24,25,26,27,65,77*a]	---	---	---	50,673[*e]	59,858[*e]	71,529	75,978	72,101	66,573
14.	Value of livestock on farms, dollars[28,29,30,36,76,83*a]	*j	*j	13,740,336[*d]	17,742,387	23,964,610	30,571,259	43,336,073	67,261,153	54,070,701
15.	Average value of livestock per farm, dollars[19,28,29,30,36]	*j	*j	345[*d]	283	329	329	448	771	654
16.	Production of cotton in bales[28,29,30,67,74,83]	*j	*j	2	---	---	---	---	---	---
17.	Percent of total production of cotton[28,29,30]	*j	*j	*k	---	---	---	---	---	---

GENERAL AGRICULTURE STATISTICS, 1850-1990

WEST VIRGINIA

Item No.		1850	1860	1870	1880	1890	1900	1910	1920	1930
18.	Production of wheat in bushels[31,32,35,36,69,74,84]	*j	*j	2,483,543	4,001,711	3,634,197	4,326,150	2,575,996	3,747,812	1,360,285
19.	Percent of total production of wheat[31,32,33,35,36]	*j	*j	.8531	.8709	.7759	.6569	.3769	.3964	.1699
20.	Production of corn in bushels[36,37,38,39,70,74,85]	*j	*j	8,197,865	14,090,609	13,730,506	16,610,730	17,119,097	17,010,357	11,656,200
21.	Percent of total production of corn[36,37,38,39]	*j	*j	1.1	0.8	0.6	0.6	0.7	0.7	0.5
22.	Production of oats in bushels[31,35,36,71,80,86]	*j	*j	2,413,749	1,908,505	2,946,653	1,833,840	1,728,806	3,054,668	1,514,150
23.	Percent of total production of oats[31,35,36]	*j	*j	0.9	0.5	0.4	0.2	0.2	0.3	0.2
24.	Production of soybeans in bushels[36,40,41,72,74,76,87]	---	---	---	---	---	---	---	7,871	10,714*h
25.	Percent of total production of soybeans[36,40,41,74,76,88]	---	---	---	---	---	---	---	.6934	.1237
26.	Production of hay crops in tons[31,34,42,43,44]	*j	*j	224,164	232,338	550,645	541,084	639,152	896,279	744,480
27.	Percent of total production of hay crops[31,34,42,43,44]	*j	*j	0.8	0.7	0.8	0.7	0.7	0.7	0.9

GENERAL AGRICULTURE STATISTICS, 1850-1990

WEST VIRGINIA

Item No.		1940	1950	1960	1970	1978	1982	1987	1990
1.	Number of farms[18,19,68,73,76,82,*a]	99,282	81,434	44,011	23,142	17,475	18,742	17,237	20,500
2.	Acres in farms[18,19,68,73,76,82]	8,908,803	8,214,626	6,062,594	4,341,000	3,529,266	3,559,051	3,372,955	3,700,000
3.	Acres improved land in farms[20,*a]	---	---	---	---	---	---	---	---
4.	Cropland harvested, acres[18,19,73,76,*a,b]	1,564,754	1,218,239	831,884	723,000	560,652	576,889	553,517	---
5.	Percentage increase in number of farms[18,19]	20.1	-17.9	-46.0	-47.4	-24.5	7.3	-8.0	18.9
6.	Percentage increase of land in farms[18,19]	1.2	-7.8	-26.2	-28.4	-18.7	0.8	-5.2	9.7
7.	Percentage increase of improved land in farms[20]	---	---	---	---	---	---	---	---
8.	Average acreage per farm[18,19,66,73,76,78]	89.7	100.9	137.8	188	202	190	196	176
9.	Percentage increase in cropland harvested[18,19,*b]	-5.5	-22.1	-31.7	-13.1	-22.5	2.9	-4.1	---
10.	Value of farms, dollars[18,19,64,79,81]	269,827,285	487,209,000[*i,l]	450,246,000[*l]	589,000,000	2,082,198,675	2,421,000,000	2,255,000,000	2,048,000,000
11.	Value of farms, percent increase[18,19]	-21.1	80.6[*i,l]	-7.6[*l]	30.8	254.0	16.3	-6.9	-9.2
12.	Average value per farm, dollars[18,19,64,73,76]	2,718	5,983[*i,l]	10,230[*l]	25,000	119,153	129,390	130,802	99,902
13.	Farms operated by owners[21,22,23,24,25,26,27,65,77,*a]	76,325[*g]	72,863	40,956[*g]	22,348[*g]	16,739	17,960[*g]	16,445[*g]	---
14.	Value of livestock on farms, dollars[28,29,30,36,76,83,*a]	36,515,689	80,663,228	78,018,091	---	148,877,000	184,923,000	221,390,000	268,615,000
15.	Average value of livestock per farm, dollars[19,28,29,30,36]	368	991	1,773	2,901	8,519	9,867	12,844	13,103
16.	Production of cotton in bales[28,29,30,67,74,83]	---	---	---	---	---	---	---	---
17.	Percent of total production of cotton[28,29,30]	---	---	---	---	---	---	---	---

GENERAL AGRICULTURE STATISTICS, 1850-1990									
WEST VIRGINIA									
Item No.		1940	1950	1960	1970	1978	1982	1987	1990
18.	Production of wheat in bushels[31,32,35,36,69,74,84]	1,782,392	1,208,423	512,221	462,000	178,288	244,165	316,337	516,000
19.	Percent of total production of wheat[31,32,33,35,36]	.2514	.1201	.0485	.0337	.0110	.0103	.0168	.0253
20.	Production of corn in bushels[36,37,38,39,70,74,85]	12,391,025	9,659,976	7,650,000	3,120,000	5,544,781	7,416,016	3,257,345	4,370,000
21.	Percent of total production of corn[36,37,38,39]	0.5	0.3	0.2	0.1	0.1	0.1	[*k]	0.1
22.	Production of oats in bushels[31,35,36,71,80,86]	996,908	825,058	1,016,809	473,000	---	383,792	227,284	300,000
23.	Percent of total production of oats[31,35,36]	0.1	0.1	0.1	0.1	---	0.1	0.1	0.1
24.	Production of soybeans in bushels[36,40,41,72,74,76,87]	11,805[*h]	22,414	8,265	---	72,655	162,710	174,205	---
25.	Percent of total production of soybeans[36,40,41]	.0135	.0106	.0016	---	.0042	.0082	.0093	---
26.	Production of hay crops in tons[31,34,42,43,44,74,76,88]	759,769	919,585	819,609	873,000	715,828	669,643	673,598	1,036,000[*m]
27.	Percent of total production of hay crops[31,34,42,43,44]	0.9	1.0	0.8	0.7	0.5	0.5	0.5	0.7

[a] See the Glossary of Terms for changing definitions, i.e. farm, improved land, cropland harvested, farm owners, and livestock.
[b] Prior to 1924, the data relate to the total acreage of crops for which figures are available, except for 1920 when 14,502,932 acres of corn cut for forage were excluded (as most of this was probably duplicated in the acreage of corn harvested for grain).
[c] Percentage computed by compiler from data herein. See endnotes for source of data.
[d] Values in gold, one-fifth less than currency values.
[e] Managers included with owners.
[f] Running square bales, counting round as half bales.
[g] Census listed the number of full and part time owners separately. Compiler added the two numbers for the above figure.
[h] Includes quantity of beans harvested from acreage grown with other crops as well as that from acreage grown alone.
[i] The total value for each state for 1950 was based on the average value per acre for farms in the sample, for which value of land and buildings was reported. The average value per farm and per acre was based on the total value of all farms.
[j] Included in Virginia totals.
[k] Less than one-tenth of one percent.
[l] Based on a sampling of farms.
[m] Census had two separate listings: hay, alfalfa, and alfalfa mixtures; and hay, all other. Compiler added the two listings for the above figure.

GENERAL AGRICULTURE STATISTICS, 1850-1990										
WISCONSIN										
Item No.		1850	1860	1870	1880	1890	1900	1910	1920	1930
1.	Number of farms[18,19,68,73,76,82,*a]	20,177	69,270	102,904	134,322	146,409	169,795	177,127	189,295	181,767
2.	Acres in farms[18,19,68,73,76,82]	2,976,658	7,893,587	11,715,321	15,353,118	16,787,988	19,862,727	21,060,066	22,148,223	21,874,155
3.	Acres improved land in farms[20,*a]	1,045,499	3,746,167	5,899,343	9,162,528	9,793,931	11,246,972	11,907,606	12,452,216	---
4.	Cropland harvested, acres[18,19,73,76,*a,b]	---	---	---	5,825,463	6,738,193	8,214,711	8,555,080	9,590,633	9,618,331
5.	Percentage increase in number of farms[18,19]	---	243.3	48.6	30.5	9.0	16.0	4.3	6.9	-4.0
6.	Percentage increase of land in farms[18,19]	---	165.2	48.4	31.1	9.3	18.3	6.0	5.2	-1.2
7.	Percentage increase of improved land in farms[20]	---	258.3	57.5	55.3	6.9	14.8	5.9	4.6	---
8.	Average acreage per farm[18,19,66,73,76,78]	147.5	114.0	113.8	114.3	114.7	117.0	118.9	117.0	120.3
9.	Percentage increase in cropland harvested[18,19,*b]	---	---	---	---	15.7	21.9	4.1	12.1	0.3
10.	Value of farms, dollars[18,19,68,73,76,82]	28,528,563	131,117,164	240,331,251	357,709,507	477,524,507	686,147,660	1,201,632,723	2,187,881,973	1,731,517,017
11.	Value of farms, percent increase[18,19]	---	359.6	83.3	48.8	33.5	43.7	75.1	82.1	-20.9
12.	Average value per farm, dollars[18,19,64,73,76]	1,414	1,893	2,335	2,663	3,262	4,041	6,784	11,558	9,526
13.	Farms operated by owners[21,22,23,24,25,26,27,65,77*a]	---	---	---	122,163[*e]	129,681[*e]	145,408	151,022	159,610	146,987
14.	Value of livestock on farms, dollars[28,29,30,36,76,83*a]	4,897,385	17,807,375	36,248,705[*d]	46,508,643	63,784,377	96,327,649	158,529,483	322,312,115	307,384,493
15.	Average value of livestock per farm, dollars[19,28,29,30,36]	243	257	352[*d]	346	436	567	895	1,703	1,691
16.	Production of cotton in bales[28,29,30,67,74,83]	---	---	---	---	---	---	---	---	---
17.	Percent of total production of cotton[28,29,30]	---	---	---	---	---	---	---	---	---

GENERAL AGRICULTURE STATISTICS, 1850-1990

WISCONSIN

Item No.		1850	1860	1870	1880	1890	1900	1910	1920	1930
18.	Production of wheat in bushels[31,32,35,36,69,74,84]	4,286,131	15,657,458	25,606,344	24,884,689	11,698,922	9,005,170	2,641,476	7,328,444	1,835,704
19.	Percent of total production of wheat[31,32,33,35,36]	4.2654	9.0451	8.8990	5.4158	2.4978	1.3675	.3865	.7752	.2293
20.	Production of corn in bushels[36,37,38,39,70,74,85]	1,988,979	7,517,300	15,033,998	34,230,579	34,024,216	53,309,810	49,163,034	44,547,398	26,019,264
21.	Percent of total production of corn[36,37,38,39]	0.3	0.9	2.0	2.0	1.6	2.0	1.9	1.9	1.2
22.	Production of oats in bushels[31,35,36,71,80,86]	3,414,672	11,059,260	20,180,016	32,905,320	60,739,052	84,040,800	71,349,038	68,296,223	68,694,665
23.	Percent of total production of oats[31,35,36]	2.3	6.4	7.2	8.1	7.5	8.9	7.1	6.5	6.9
24.	Production of soybeans in bushels[36,40,41,72,74,76,87]	---	---	---	---	---	---	---	16,838	18,451[*h]
25.	Percent of total production of soybeans[36,40,41]	---	---	---	---	---	---	---	1.4833	.2130
26.	Production of hay crops in tons[31,34,42,43,44,74,76,88]	275,662	855,037	1,287,651	1,907,429	2,981,521	3,275,169	5,003,761	10,642,835	6,226,633
27.	Percent of total production of hay crops[31,34,42,43,44]	2.0	4.5	4.7	5.4	4.5	4.1	5.1	8.6	7.3

GENERAL AGRICULTURE STATISTICS, 1850-1990									
WISCONSIN									
Item No.		1940	1950	1960	1970	1978	1982	1987	1990
1.	Number of farms[18,19,68,73,76,82,*a]	186,735	168,561	131,215	98,973	86,505	82,199	75,131	80,000
2.	Acres in farms[18,19,68,73,76,82]	22,876,494	23,221,095	21,156,223	18,109,000	17,838,982	17,234,127	16,606,567	17,600,000
3.	Acres improved land in farms[20,*a]	---	---	---	---	---	---	---	---
4.	Cropland harvested, acres[18,19,73,76,*a,b]	9,815,964	10,112,027	9,599,094	8,662,000	9,863,051	10,062,154	9,335,007	---
5.	Percentage increase in number of farms[18,19]	2.7	-9.7	-22.2	-24.6	-12.6	-5.0	-8.6	6.5
6.	Percentage increase of land in farms[18,19]	4.6	1.5	-8.9	-14.4	-1.5	-3.4	-3.6	6.0
7.	Percentage increase of improved land in farms[20]	---	---	---	---	---	---	---	---
8.	Average acreage per farm[18,19,66,73,76,78]	122.5	137.8	161.2	183	206	210	221	217
9.	Percentage increase in cropland harvested[18,19,*b]	2.1	3.0	-5.1	-9.8	13.9	2.0	-7.2	---
10.	Value of farms, dollars[18,19,64,79,81]	1,188,559,407	2,056,925,000[*i]	2,796,049,000	4,201,000,000	15,146,592,975	19,102,000,000	13,740,000,000	11,641,000,000
11.	Value of farms, percent increase[18,19]	-31.4	73.1[*i]	35.9	50.2	261.0	26.1	-28.1	-15.3
12.	Average value per farm, dollars[18,19,64,73,76]	6,365	12,203[*i]	21,309	42,000	175,095	232,606	182,950	145,512
13.	Farms operated by owners[21,22,23,24,25,26,27,65,77,*a]	142,728	141,652	115,524[*g]	91,978[*g]	80,334	75,146[*g]	68,769[*g]	---
14.	Value of livestock on farms, dollars[28,29,30,36,76,83,*a]	256,503,605	647,940,946	781,784,850	998,620,000	2,773,506,000	3,911,160,000	3,973,245,000	4,581,226,000
15.	Average value of livestock per farm, dollars[19,28,29,30,36]	1,374	3,844	5,958	10,090	32,062	47,582	52,884	57,265
16.	Production of cotton in bales[28,29,30,67,74,83]	---	---	---	---	---	---	---	---
17.	Percent of total production of cotton[28,29,30]	---	---	---	---	---	---	---	---

GENERAL AGRICULTURE STATISTICS, 1850-1990

WISCONSIN

Item No.		1940	1950	1960	1970	1978	1982	1987	1990
18.	Production of wheat in bushels[31,32,35,36,69,74,84]	969,713	2,257,414	1,816,643	1,422,000	1,522,724	5,505,837	4,236,394	9,320,000
19.	Percent of total production of wheat[31,32,33,35,36]	.1368	.2243	.1720	.1038	.0947	.2320	.2245	0.4578
20.	Production of corn in bushels[36,37,38,39,70,74,85]	44,552,990	83,974,114	184,990,000	143,520,000	288,060,992	332,327,822	311,689,830	310,800
21.	Percent of total production of corn[36,37,38,39]	1.9	3.0	4.3	3.5	3.8	4.4	4.6	4.1
22.	Production of oats in bushels[31,35,36,71,80,86]	64,514,885	112,840,761	121,399,193	104,594,000	---	46,411,629	37,458,060	46,860,000
23.	Percent of total production of oats[31,35,36]	7.4	9.9	12.1	11.5	---	9.2	12.0	12.5
24.	Production of soybeans in bushels[36,40,41,72,74,76,87]	166,355[*h]	273,702	1,851,320	3,213,000	6,602,755	10,619,901	11,491,031	15,170,000
25.	Percent of total production of soybeans[36,40,41]	.1899	.1288	.3590	.2859	.3834	.5337	.6252	.7873
26.	Production of hay crops in tons[31,34,42,43,44,74,76,88]	5,764,323	5,705,604	8,866,854	10,601,000	12,908,132	11,846,550	12,407,639	8,080,000[*j]
27.	Percent of total production of hay crops[31,34,42,43,44]	7.0	6.4	8.3	8.3	9.9	9.2	9.6	5.5[*c]

[a] See the Glossary of Terms for changing definitions, i.e. farm, improved land, cropland harvested, farm owners, and livestock.
[b] Prior to 1924, the data relate to the total acreage of crops for which figures are available, except for 1920 when 14,502,932 acres of corn cut for forage were excluded (as most of this was probably duplicated in the acreage of corn harvested for grain).
[c] Percentage computed by compiler from data herein. See endnotes for source of data.
[d] Values in gold, one-fifth less than currency values.
[e] Managers included with owners.
[f] Running square bales, counting round as half bales.
[g] Census listed the number of full and part time owners separately. Compiler added the two numbers for the above figure.
[h] Includes quantity of beans harvested from acreage grown with other crops as well as that from acreage grown alone.
[i] The total value for each state for 1950 was based on the average value per acre for farms in the sample, for which value of land and buildings was reported. The average value per farm and per acre was based on the total value of all farms.
[j] Census had two separate listings: hay, alfalfa, and alfalfa mixtures; and hay, all other. Compiler added the two listings for the above figure.

GENERAL AGRICULTURE STATISTICS, 1850-1990										
WYOMING										
Item No.		1850	1860	1870	1880	1890	1900	1910	1920	1930
1.	Number of farms[18,19,68,73,76,82,*a]	---	---	175	457	3,125	6,095	10,987	15,748	16,011
2.	Acres in farms[18,19,68,73,76,82]	---	---	4,341	124,433	1,830,432	8,124,536	8,543,010	11,809,351	23,525,234
3.	Acres improved land in farms[20,*a]	---	---	338	83,122	476,831	792,332	1,256,160	2,102,005	---
4.	Cropland harvested, acres[18,19,73,76,*a,b]	---	---	---	25,397	196,516	435,621	786,650	1,153,633	2,007,751
5.	Percentage increase in number of farms[18,19]	---	---	---	161.1	583.8	95.0	80.3	43.3	1.7
6.	Percentage increase of land in farms[18,19]	---	---	---	[*k]	[*k]	343.9	5.2	38.2	99.2
7.	Percentage increase of improved land in farms[20]	---	---	---	262.4	473.6	66.2	58.5	67.3	---
8.	Average acreage per farm[18,19,66,73,76,78]	---	---	24.8	272.3	585.7	1,333.0	777.6	749.9	1,469.3
9.	Percentage increase in cropland harvested[18,19,*b]	---	---	---	---	673.8	121.7	80.6	46.7	74.0
10.	Value of farms, dollars[18,19,64,79,81]	---	---	14,550	835,895	14,460,880	26,965,530	97,915,277	234,748,125	206,852,171
11.	Value of farms, percent increase[18,19]	---	---	---	[*k]	[*k]	86.5	263.1	139.7	-11.9
12.	Average value per farm, dollars[18,19,64,73,76]	---	---	83	1,829	4,627	4,424	8,912	14,907	12,919
13.	Farms operated by owners[21,22,23,24,25,26,27,65,77,*a]	---	---	---	444[*c]	2,993[*c]	5,185	9,779	13,403	12,195
14.	Value of livestock on farms, dollars[28,29,30,36,76,83,*a]	---	---	353,435[*d]	9,182,107	18,785,301	39,145,877	65,605,510	87,884,516	81,997,660
15.	Average value of livestock per farm, dollars[19,28,29,30,36]	---	---	2,020[*d]	20,092	6,011	6,423	5,971	5,581	5,121[*c]
16.	Production of cotton in bales[28,29,30,67,74,83]	---	---	---	---	---	---	---	---	---
17.	Percent of total production of cotton[28,29,30]	---	---	---	---	---	---	---	---	---

GENERAL AGRICULTURE STATISTICS, 1850-1990										
WYOMING										
Item No.		1850	1860	1870	1880	1890	1900	1910	1920	1930
18.	Production of wheat in bushels[31,32,35,36,69,74,84]	---	---	---	4,674	74,450	348,890	738,698	1,445,227	4,298,085
19.	Percent of total production of wheat[31,32,33,35,36]	---	---	---	.0010	.0159	.0530	.1081	.1529	.5368
20.	Production of corn in bushels[36,37,38,39,70,74,85]	---	---	---	---	25,172	38,000	176,354	388,512	1,062,206
21.	Percent of total production of corn[36,37,38,39]	---	---	---	---	*j	*j	*j	*j	*j
22.	Production of oats in bushels[31,35,36,71,80,86]	---	---	100	22,512	388,505	763,370	3,361,425	1,006,552	3,197,152
23.	Percent of total production of oats[31,35,36]	---	---	*j	*j	*j	0.1	0.3	0.1	0.3
24.	Production of soybeans in bushels[36,40,41,72,74,76,87]	---	---	---	---	---	---	---	97	1,121
25.	Percent of total production of soybeans[36,40,41]	---	---	---	---	---	---	---	.0085	.0129
26.	Production of hay crops in tons[31,34,42,43,4474,76,88]	---	---	3,180	23,516	147,963	462,101	853,802	882,539	1,212,804
27.	Percent of total production of hay crops[31,34,42,43,44]	---	---	*j	0.1	0.2	0.6	0.9	0.7	1.4

GENERAL AGRICULTURE STATISTICS, 1850-1990

WYOMING

Item No.		1940	1950	1960	1970	1978	1982	1987	1990
1.	Number of farms[18,19,68,73,76,82,*a]	15,018	12,614	9,744	8,838	8,040	8,861	9,205	8,900
2.	Acres in farms[18,19,68,73,76,82]	28,025,979	34,420,892	36,199,666	35,476,374	33,627,257	33,500,453	33,595,135	34,800
3.	Acres improved land in farms[20,*a]	---	---	---	---	---	---	---	---
4.	Cropland harvested, acres[18,19,73,76,*a,b]	1,534,800	1,900,646	1,679,024	1,739,000	1,780,333	1,813,830	1,717,027	2,150,000
5.	Percentage increase in number of farms[18,19]	-6.2	-16.0	-22.8	-9.3	-9.0	10.2	3.9	-3.3
6.	Percentage increase of land in farms[18,19]	19.1	22.8	5.2	-2.0	-5.2	-0.4	0.3	3.6
7.	Percentage increase of improved land in farms[20]	---	---	---	---	---	---	---	---
8.	Average acreage per farm[18,19,66,73,76,78]	1,866.2	2,728.8	3,715.1	4,014	4,182	3,781	3,650	3,910
9.	Percentage increase in cropland harvested[18,19,*b]	-23.6	23.8	-11.7	3.6	2.4	1.9	-5.3	25.2
10.	Value of farms, dollars[18,19,64,79,81]	158,971,294	454,862,000[*i]	774,130,000	1,445,270,000	4,812,928,920	6,484,000,000	4,909,000,000	4,730,000,000
11.	Value of farms, percent increase[18,19]	-23.1	186.1[*i]	70.2	86.7	233.0	34.7	-24.3	-3.6
12.	Average value per farm, dollars[18,19,64,73,76]	10,585	36,060[*i]	79,447	163,529	598,623	732,875	533,284	531,461
13.	Farms operated by owners[21,22,23,24,25,26,27,65,77,*a]	11,125	10,257	7,959[*g]	7,512[*g]	7,018	7,734[*g]	7,967[*g]	---
14.	Value of livestock on farms, dollars[28,29,30,36,76,83,*a]	61,389,424	178,884,767	228,594,276	---	441,198,000	478,221,000	552,028,000	609,574,000
15.	Average value of livestock per farm, dollars[19,28,29,30,36]	4,088	14,181	23,460	---	54,875	53,969	59,971	68,492
16.	Production of cotton in bales[28,29,30,67,74,83]	---	---	---	---	---	---	---	---
17.	Percent of total production of cotton[28,29,30]	---	---	---	---	---	---	---	---

GENERAL AGRICULTURE STATISTICS, 1850-1990

WYOMING

Item No.		1940	1950	1960	1970	1978	1982	1987	1990
18.	Production of wheat in bushels[31,32,35,36,69,74,84]	1,798,012	6,657,448	5,268,442	6,259,000	6,641,767	9,169,664	7,207,742	4,708,000
19.	Percent of total production of wheat[31,32,33,35,36]	.2537	.6614	.4989	.4,568	.4132	.3864	.3819	.2313
20.	Production of corn in bushels[36,37,38,39,70,74,85]	711,398	249,252	1,800,000	1,674,000	2,564,619	4,681,878	4,304,628	3,845,000
21.	Percent of total production of corn[36,37,38,39]	*j	*j	*j	*j	*j	0.6	0.1	0.1
22.	Production of oats in bushels[31,35,36,71,80,86]	2,256,994	3,372,029	3,022,956	4,560,000	---	2,286,662	2,205,000	1,410,000
23.	Percent of total production of oats[31,35,36]	0.3	0.3	0.3	0.5	---	0.5	0.7	0.4
24.	Production of soybeans in bushels[36,40,41,72,74,76,87]	28*h	22	---	---	4,280	---	---	---
25.	Percent of total production of soybeans[36,40,41]	.0000	.0000	---	---	.0002	---	---	---
26.	Production of hay crops in tons[31,34,42,43,44,74,76,88]	961,533	1,147,358	1,276,017	1,853,000	1,903,450	1,935,538	1,904,291	1,776,000*m
27.	Percent of total production of hay crops[31,34,42,43,44]	1.2	1.3	1.2	1.5	1.5	1.5	1.5	1.2

[a] See the Glossary of Terms for changing definitions, i.e. farm, improved land, cropland harvested, farm owners, and livestock.
[b] Prior to 1924, the data relate to the total acreage of crops for which figures are available, except for 1920 when 14,502,932 acres of corn cut for forage were excluded (as most of this was probably duplicated in the acreage of corn harvested for grain).
[c] Percentage computed by compiler from data herein. See endnotes for source of data.
[d] Values in gold, one-fifth less than currency values.
[e] Managers included with owners.
[f] Running square bales, counting round as half bales.
[g] Census listed the number of full and part time owners separately. Compiler added the two numbers for the above figure.
[h] Includes quantity of beans harvested from acreage grown with other crops as well as that from acreage grown alone.
[i] The total value for each state for 1950 was based on the average value per acre for farms in the sample, for which value of land and buildings was reported. The average value per farm and per acre was based on the total value of all farms.
[j] Less than one-tenth of one percent.
[k] 1,000 percent or more.
[l] Including estimated value of range animals.
[m] Census had two separate listings: hay, alfalfa, and alfalfa mixtures; and hay, all other. Compiler added the two listings for the above figure.

GENERAL AGRICULTURE STATISTICS, 1850-1990										
UNITED STATES										
Item No.		1850	1860	1870	1880	1890	1900	1910	1920	1930
1.	Number of farms[18,19,68,73,76,82,*a]	1,449,073	2,044,077	2,659,985	4,008,907	4,564,641	5,737,372[*m] 5,739,657[*n]	6,361,502[*m] 6,366,044[*n]	6,448,343[*m] 6,453,991[*n]	6,288,648[*m] 6,295,103[*n]
2.	Acres in farms[18,19,68,73,76,82]	293,560,614	407,212,538	407,735,041	536,081,835	623,218,619	838,591,774[*m] 841,201,546[*n]	878,798,325[*m] 881,431,469[*n]	955,883,715[*m] 958,676,612[*n]	986,771,016[*m] 990,111,984[*n]
3.	Acres improved land in farms[20,*a]	113,032,614	163,110,720	188,921,099	284,771,042	357,616,755	414,498,487	478,451,750	503,073,007	---
4.	Cropland harvested, acres[18,19,73,76,*a,b]	---	---	---	166,186,584	219,705,564	283,218,280	311,293,382	348,603,729	359,242,091
5.	Percentage increase in number of farms[18,19]	---	41.1	30.1	50.7	13.9	25.7[*m] 25.7[*n]	10.9[*m] 10.9[*n]	1.4[*m] 1.4[*n]	-2.5[*m] -1.3[*n]
6.	Percentage increase of land in farms[18,19]	---	38.7	0.1	31.5	16.3	34.6[*m] 35.0[*n]	4.8[*m] 4.8[*n]	8.8[*m] 8.8[*n]	3.2[*m] 6.8[*n]
7.	Percentage increase of improved land in farms[20]	---	44.3	15.8	50.7	25.6	15.9	15.4	5.1	---
8.	Average acreage per farm[18,19,66,73,76,78]	202.6	199.2	153.3	133.7	136.5	146.2[*c,m] 146.6[*n]	138.1[*c,m] 138.5[*n]	148.2[*c,m] 98.5[*n]	156.9[*c,m] 157.3[*n]
9.	Percentage increase in cropland harvested[18,19,*b]	---	---	---	---	32.2	28.9	9.9	12.0	4.3
10.	Value of farms, dollars[18,19,64,79,81]	3,271,575,426	6,645,045,007	7,444,054,462	10,197,096,776	13,279,252,649	16,614,647,491	34,801,125,697[*m] 34,968,724,375[*n]	66,316,002,602[*m] 66,446,345,611[*n]	47,879,838,358[*m] 47,994,475,975[*n]
11.	Value of farms, percent increase[18,19]	---	103.1	12.0	37.0	30.2	25.1	109.5[*m] 110.5[*n]	90.6[*m] 90.5[*n]	-27.8[*m] -27.8[*n]
12.	Average value per farm, dollars[18,19,64,73,76]	2,258	3,251	2,799	2,544	2,909	2,896	5,471[*m] 5,480[*n]	10,284[*m] 10,295[*n]	7,614[*m] 7,624[*n]
13.	Farms operated by owners[21,22,23,24,25,26,27,65,77,*a]	---	---	---	2,984,306[*e]	3,269,728[*e]	3,653,323	3,948,722[*k]	3,925,090	3,568,394[*g]
14.	Value of livestock on farms, dollars[28,29,30,36,76,83,*a]	544,180,516	1,089,329,915	1,229,889,609[*d]	1,576,884,707[*j]	2,308,767,573[*j]	3,075,477,703	4,925,173,610	8,013,324,808	---
15.	Average value of livestock per farm, dollars[19,28,29,30,36]	376	533	462[*d]	393	506	536	774[*c]	1,243[*c]	---
16.	Production of cotton in bales[28,29,30,67,74,83]	2,469,093	5,387,052	3,011,996	5,755,359	7,472,511	9,534,707[*f]	10,649,272[*f]	11,376,138[*f]	14,574,502[*f]
17.	Percent of total production of cotton[28,29,30]	100	100	100	100	100	100[*f]	100[*f]	100[*f]	100[*f]

GENERAL AGRICULTURE STATISTICS, 1850-1990

UNITED STATES

Item No.		1850	1860	1870	1880	1890	1900	1910	1920	1930
18.	Production of wheat in bushels[31,32,35,36,69,74,84]	100,485,944	173,104,934	287,745,626	459,483,137	468,373,968	658,534,252	683,379,259	945,403,215	800,648,955
19.	Percent of total production of wheat[31,32,33,35,36]	100	100	100	100	100	100	100	100	100
20.	Production of corn in bushels[36,37,38,39,70,74,85]	592,071,104	838,792,742	760,944,549	1,754,591,676	2,122,327,547	2,666,440,279	2,552,273,410	2,345,947,637	2,130,787,639
21.	Percent of total production of corn[36,37,38,39]	100	100	100	100	100	100	100	100	100
22.	Production of oats in bushels[31,35,36,71,80,86]	146,584,179	172,643,185	282,107,157	407,858,999	809,250,666	943,389,375	1,007,142,980	1,055,182,798	992,746,912
23.	Percent of total production of oats[31,35,36]	100	100	100	100	100	100	100	100	100
24.	Production of soybeans in bushels[36,40,41,72,74,76,87]	---	---	---	---	---	143,388	24,966	1,135,141	8,661,188[*h]
25.	Percent of total production of soybeans[36,40,41]	---	---	---	---	---	100	100	100	100
26.	Production of hay crops in tons[31,34,42,43,44,74,76,88]	13,838,642	19,083,896	27,316,048	35,150,711	66,831,480	79,251,562	97,755,296	123,549,499	85,280,764
27.	Percent of total production of hay crops[31,34,42,43,44]	100	100	100	100	100	100	100	100	100

GENERAL AGRICULTURE STATISTICS, 1850-1990									
UNITED STATES									
Item No.		1940	1950	1960	1970	1978	1982	1987	1990
1.	Number of farms[18,19,68,73,76,82,*a]	6,096,799[*m] 6,102,417[*n]	5,382,162[*m] 5,388,437[*n]	3,703,894[*m] 3,710,503[*n]	2,730,250	2,257,775	2,240,976	2,087,759	2,143,150
2.	Acres in farms[18,19,68,73,76,82]	1,060,852,374[*m] 1,065,113,774[*n]	1,158,565,852[*m] 1,161,419,720[*n]	1,120,157,789[*m] 1,123,507,574[*n]	1,063,346,489[*m] 1,123,507,574[*n]	1,014,777,234	986,796,579	964,470,625	987,420,000
3.	Acres improved land in farms[20,*a]	---	---	---	---	---	---	---	---
4.	Cropland harvested, acres[18,19,73,76,*a,b]	321,242,435[*m] 321,434,288[*n]	344,398,550[*m] 344,564,497[*n]	311,285,249[*m] 311,476,141[*n]	273,016,000	317,145,955	326,306,462	282,223,880	330,877,000
5.	Percentage increase in number of farms[18,19]	-3.1[*m] -3.1[*n]	-11.7[*m] -11.7[*n]	-31.2[*m] -31.1[*n]	-26.3[*c,m] -26.4[*c,n]	-4.6[*c,m] -9.7[*c,n]	-0.7[*c]	-6.8[*c]	2.7[*c]
6.	Percentage increase of land in farms[18,19]	0.6	1.5	-3.3	---	-4.6[*c]	-4.7[*c]	-0.2[*c]	2.4[*c]
7.	Percentage increase of improved land in farms[20]	---	---	---	---	---	---	---	---
8.	Average acreage per farm[18,19,66,73,76,78]	174.0[*m] 174.5[*n]	215.3[*m] 215.5[*n]	302.4[*m] 302.8[*n]	390	450	440	462	456
9.	Percentage increase in cropland harvested[18,19,*b]	-10.6[*m] -10.5[*n]	7.2[*m] 7.2[*n]	-9.6[*m] -9.6[*n]	-12.3[*c,m] -12.3[*c,n]	16.2[*c]	2.9[*c]	-13.5[*c]	17.2[*c]
10.	Value of farms, dollars[18,19,64,79,81]	33,641,738,726[*m] 33,758,367,972[*n]	75,260,608,000[*i,m] 75,462,427,000[*n]	128,987,659,000	206,751,634,000	631,436,449,800	774,158,000,000	604,167,607,000	593,845,000,000
11.	Value of farms, percent increase[18,19]	-29.7[*c,m] -29.7[*c,n]	123.7[*i,l,m] 123.5[*c,n]	71.4[*m] 70.9[*n]	60.3[*c]	205.4[*c]	22.6[*c]	22.0[*c]	1.7[*c]
12.	Average value per farm, dollars[18,19,64,73,76]	5,518[*m] 5,532[*n]	13,983[*i,m] 14,005[*n]	34,825	75,714	279,672	345,869	289,387	277,443
13.	Farms operated by owners[21,22,23,24,25,26,27,65,77,*a]	3,699,177[*g]	3,914,506	2,951,064	2,377,327[*g]	1,979,014	1,982,022[*g]	1,847,559[*g]	---
14.	Value of livestock on farms, dollars[28,29,30,36,76,83,*a]	---	---	15,187,285,654	---	58,870,258,000	69,644,136,000	77,117,431,000	89,623,454,000
15.	Average value of livestock per farm, dollars[19,28,29,30,36]	---	---	4,093	---	26,074	31,078	36,938	41,872
16.	Production of cotton in bales[28,29,30,67,74,83]	11,481,357[*f]	15,419,458	13,913,505	10,192,100	10,686,447	11,375,524	13,280,143	11,503,900[*p,q]
17.	Percent of total production of cotton[28,29,30]	100[*f]	100	100	100	100	100	100	100

GENERAL AGRICULTURE STATISTICS, 1850-1990									
UNITED STATES									
Item No.		1940	1950	1960	1970	1978	1982	1987	1990
18.	Production of wheat in bushels[31,32,35,36,69,74,84]	708,851,598	1,006,559,285	1,055,924,506	1,370,225,000	1,607,540,430	2,373,246,659	1,887,103,964	2,035,818,000
19.	Percent of total production of wheat[31,32,33,35,36]	100	100	100	100	100	100	100	100
20.	Production of corn in bushels[36,37,38,39,70,74,85]	2,311,429,068	2,778,207,344	4,281,316,000*[n]	4,099,493,000	6,805,185,861	7,508,721,493	6,725,001,837	7,527,152,000
21.	Percent of total production of corn[36,37,38,39]	100	100	100	100	100	100	100	100
22.	Production of oats in bushels[31,35,36,71,80,86]	870,258,195	1,136,653,628	1,001,092,491	908,702,000	581,657,000	505,854,912	312,727,716	373,587,000
23.	Percent of total production of oats[31,35,36]	100	100	100	100	100	100	100	100
24.	Production of soybeans in bushels[36,40,41,72,74,76,87]	87,590,641*[h]	212,439,834	515,627,957	1,123,740,000	1,722,154,229	1,989,993,158	1,838,053,979	1,926,806,000
25.	Percent of total production of soybeans[36,40,41]	100	100	100	100	100	100	100	100
26.	Production of hay crops in tons[31,34,42,43,44,74,76,88]	82,413,269	89,009,493	106,589,630	127,465,000	130,713,685	128,474,661	128,816,054	146,985,000*[q]
27.	Percent of total production of hay crops[31,34,42,43,44]	100	100	100	100	100	100	100	100

[a] See the Glossary of Terms for changing definitions, i.e. farm, improved land, cropland harvested, farm owners, and livestock.
[b] Prior to 1924, the data relate to the total acreage of crops for which figures are available, except for 1920 when 14,502,932 acres of corn cut for forage were excluded (as most of this was probably duplicated in the acreage of corn harvested for grain).
[c] Percentage computed by compiler from data herein. See endnotes for source of data.
[d] Values in gold, one-fifth less than currency values.
[e] Managers included with owners.
[f] Running square bales, counting round as half bales.
[g] Census listed the number of full and part time owners separately. Compiler added the two numbers for the above figure.
[h] Includes quantity of beans harvested from acreage grown with other crops as well as that from acreage grown alone.
[i] The total value for each state for 1950 was based on the average value per acre for farms in the sample, for which value of land and buildings was reported. The average value per farm and per acre was based on the total value of all farms.
[j] Including estimated value of range animals.
[k] Data for conterminous area.
[l] Percentage computed by compiler from data herein is different from percentage given in source. The above percentage is the percentage computed by compiler.
[m] Excludes Alaska and Hawaii.
[n] Includes Alaska and Hawaii.
[o] Production ginned and to be ginned.
[p] 480-pound net weight bales.
[q] Census had two separate listings: hay, alfalfa, and alfalfa mixtures; and hay, all other. Compiler added the two listings for the above figure.

General Manufacturing Statistics, 1850–1890

GENERAL MANUFACTURING STATISTICS, 1850-1890[45]						
ALABAMA						
Item No.		1850	1860	1870	1880	1890
1.	Number of manufacturing establishments[45,46,47,48]	1,026	1,459	2,188	2,070	2,977
2.	Capital of manufacturing establishments[45,46,47,48]	3,450,606	9,098,181	5,714,032	9,668,008	46,122,571
3.	Average number of wage earners[45,46,47,48]	4,936	7,889	8,248	10,019	31,137
4.	Total wages[45,46,47,48]	1,105,824	2,132,940	2,227,968	2,500,504	10,799,747
5.	Cost of materials used in manufacturing[45,46,47,48]	2,224,960	5,489,963	7,592,837	8,545,520	28,432,281
6.	Value of manufactured product[45,46,47,48]	4,528,876	10,588,566	13,040,644	13,565,504	51,226,605

GENERAL MANUFACTURING STATISTICS, 1850-1890[45]						
ALASKA						
Item No.		1850	1860	1870	1880	1890
1.	Number of manufacturing establishments[45,46,47,48]	---	---	---	---	10
2.	Capital of manufacturing establishments[45,46,47,48]	---	---	---	---	105,727
3.	Average number of wage earners[45,46,47,48]	---	---	---	---	78
4.	Total wages[45,46,47,48]	---	---	---	---	18,625
5.	Cost of materials used in manufacturing[45,46,47,48]	---	---	---	---	30,198
6.	Value of manufactured product[45,46,47,48]	---	---	---	---	58,440

GENERAL MANUFACTURING STATISTICS, 1850-1890[45]						
ARIZONA						
Item No.		1850	1860	1870	1880	1890
1.	Number of manufacturing establishments[45,46,47,48]	---	---	18	66	76
2.	Capital of manufacturing establishments[45,46,47,48]	---	---	150,700	272,600	616,629
3.	Average number of wage earners[45,46,47,48]	---	---	84	220	458
4.	Total wages[45,46,47,48]	---	---	45,580	111,180	302,146
5.	Cost of materials used in manufacturing[45,46,47,48]	---	---	110,090	380,023	353,814
6.	Value of manufactured product[45,46,47,48]	---	---	185,410	618,365	947,547

GENERAL MANUFACTURING STATISTICS, 1850-1890[45]						
ARKANSAS						
Item No.		1850	1860	1870	1880	1890
1.	Number of manufacturing establishments[45,46,47,48]	261	518	1,079	1,202	2,073
2.	Capital of manufacturing establishments[45,46,47,48]	305,015	1,316,610	1,782,913	2,953,130	14,971,614
3.	Average number of wage earners[45,46,47,48]	842	1,877	3,206	4,557	14,143
4.	Total wages[45,46,47,48]	159,876	554,240	673,963	925,358	4,649,186
5.	Cost of materials used in manufacturing[45,46,47,48]	215,789	1,280,503	2,536,998	4,392,080	12,397,261
6.	Value of manufactured product[45,46,47,48]	537,908	2,880,578	4,629,234	6,756,159	22,659,179

GENERAL MANUFACTURING STATISTICS, 1850-1890[45]						
CALIFORNIA						
Item No.		1850	1860	1870	1880	1890
1.	Number of manufacturing establishments[45,46,47,48]	1,003	8,468	3,984	5,885	7,923
2.	Capital of manufacturing establishments[45,46,47,48]	1,006,197	22,043,096	39,728,202	61,243,784	146,797,102
3.	Average number of wage earners[45,46,47,48]	3,964	49,226	25,392	43,693	72,696
4.	Total wages[45,46,47,48]	3,717,180	28,402,287	13,136,722	21,065,905	41,172,918
5.	Cost of materials used in manufacturing[45,46,47,48]	1,201,154	27,051,674	35,351,193	72,607,709	120,243,683
6.	Value of manufactured product[45,46,47,48]	12,862,522	68,253,228	66,594,556	116,218,973	213,403,996

GENERAL MANUFACTURING STATISTICS, 1850-1890[45]						
COLORADO						
Item No.		1850	1860	1870	1880	1890
1.	Number of manufacturing establishments[45,46,47,48]	---	---	256	599	1,518
2.	Capital of manufacturing establishments[45,46,47,48]	---	---	2,835,605	4,311,714	26,651,840
3.	Average number of wage earners[45,46,47,48]	---	---	876	5,074	15,016
4.	Total wages[45,46,47,48]	---	---	528,221	2,314,427	9,872,405
5.	Cost of materials used in manufacturing[45,46,47,48]	---	---	1,593,280	8,806,762	20,848,516
6.	Value of manufactured product[45,46,47,48]	---	---	2,852,820	14,260,159	42,480,205

GENERAL MANUFACTURING STATISTICS, 1850-1890[45]

CONNECTICUT

Item No.		1850	1860	1870	1880	1890
1.	Number of manufacturing establishments[45,46,47,48]	3,737	3,019	5,128	4,488	6,822
2.	Capital of manufacturing establishments[45,46,47,48]	25,876,648	45,590,430	95,281,278	120,480,275	227,004,496
3.	Average number of wage earners[45,46,47,48]	50,731	64,469	89,523	112,915	140,514
4.	Total wages[45,46,47,48]	12,435,984	19,026,196	38,987,187	43,501,518	66,465,317
5.	Cost of materials used in manufacturing[45,46,47,48]	23,608,971	40,909,090	86,419,579	102,183,341	123,183,080
6.	Value of manufactured product[45,46,47,48]	47,114,585	81,924,555	161,065,474	185,697,211	248,336,364

GENERAL MANUFACTURING STATISTICS, 1850-1890[45]

DELAWARE

Item No.		1850	1860	1870	1880	1890
1.	Number of manufacturing establishments[45,46,47,48]	531	615	800	746	1,003
2.	Capital of manufacturing establishments[45,46,47,48]	2,978,945	5,452,887	10,839,093	15,655,822	33,695,400
3.	Average number of wage earners[45,46,47,48]	3,888	6,421	9,710	12,638	20,479
4.	Total wages[45,46,47,48]	936,924	1,905,754	3,692,195	4,267,349	8,630,475
5.	Cost of materials used in manufacturing[45,46,47,48]	2,864,607	6,028,918	10,206,397	12,828,461	21,161,752
6.	Value of manufactured product[45,46,47,48]	4,649,296	9,892,902	16,791,382	20,514,438	37,571,848

GENERAL MANUFACTURING STATISTICS, 1850-1890[45]						
DISTRICT OF COLUMBIA						
Item No.		1850	1860	1870	1880	1890
1.	Number of manufacturing establishments[45,46,47,48]	---	---	---	---	---
2.	Capital of manufacturing establishments[45,46,47,48]	---	---	---	---	---
3.	Average number of wage earners[45,46,47,48]	---	---	---	---	---
4.	Total wages[45,46,47,48]	---	---	---	---	---
5.	Cost of materials used in manufacturing[45,46,47,48]	---	---	---	---	---
6.	Value of manufactured product[45,46,47,48]	---	---	---	---	---

GENERAL MANUFACTURING STATISTICS, 1850-1890[45]						
FLORIDA						
Item No.		1850	1860	1870	1880	1890
1.	Number of manufacturing establishments[45,46,47,48]	103	185	659	426	805
2.	Capital of manufacturing establishments[45,46,47,48]	547,060	1,874,125	1,679,930	3,210,680	11,110,304
3.	Average number of wage earners[45,46,47,48]	991	2,454	2,749	5,504	13,119
4.	Total wages[45,46,47,48]	199,452	619,840	989,592	1,270,875	5,918,614
5.	Cost of materials used in manufacturing[45,46,47,48]	220,611	874,506	2,330,873	3,040,119	8,021,854
6.	Value of manufactured product[45,46,47,48]	668,335	2,447,969	4,685,403	5,546,448	18,222,890

GENERAL MANUFACTURING STATISTICS, 1850-1890[45]						
GEORGIA						
Item No.		1850	1860	1870	1880	1890
1.	Number of manufacturing establishments[45,46,47,48]	1,522	1,890	3,836	3,593	4,285
2.	Capital of manufacturing establishments[45,46,47,48]	5,456,483	10,890,875	13,930,125	20,672,410	56,921,580
3.	Average number of wage earners[45,46,47,48]	8,368	11,575	17,871	24,875	52,298
4.	Total wages[45,46,47,48]	1,709,664	2,925,148	4,844,508	5,266,152	14,623,996
5.	Cost of materials used in manufacturing[45,46,47,48]	3,404,917	9,986,532	18,583,731	24,143,939	35,774,480
6.	Value of manufactured product[45,46,47,48]	7,082,075	16,925,564	31,196,115	36,440,948	68,917,020

GENERAL MANUFACTURING STATISTICS, 1850-1890[45]						
HAWAII						
Item No.		1850	1860	1870	1880	1890
1.	Number of manufacturing establishments[45,46,47,48]	---	---	---	---	---
2.	Capital of manufacturing establishments[45,46,47,48]	---	---	---	---	---
3.	Average number of wage earners[45,46,47,48]	---	---	---	---	---
4.	Total wages[45,46,47,48]	---	---	---	---	---
5.	Cost of materials used in manufacturing[45,46,47,48]	---	---	---	---	---
6.	Value of manufactured product[45,46,47,48]	---	---	---	---	---

GENERAL MANUFACTURING STATISTICS, 1850-1890[45]						
IDAHO						
Item No.		1850	1860	1870	1880	1890
1.	Number of manufacturing establishments[45,46,47,48]	---	---	101	162	140
2.	Capital of manufacturing establishments[45,46,47,48]	---	---	742,300	677,215	1,048,916
3.	Average number of wage earners[45,46,47,48]	---	---	265	388	667
4.	Total wages[45,46,47,48]	---	---	112,372	136,326	255,907
5.	Cost of materials used in manufacturing[45,46,47,48]	---	---	691,785	844,874	638,678
6.	Value of manufactured product[45,46,47,48]	---	---	1,047,624	1,271,317	1,396,096

GENERAL MANUFACTURING STATISTICS, 1850-1890[45]						
ILLINOIS						
Item No.		1850	1860	1870	1880	1890
1.	Number of manufacturing establishments[45,46,47,48]	3,162	4,268	12,597	14,549	20,482
2.	Capital of manufacturing establishments[45,46,47,48]	6,217,765	27,548,563	94,368,057	140,652,066	502,004,512
3.	Average number of wage earners[45,46,47,48]	11,559	22,968	82,979	144,727	280,218
4.	Total wages[45,46,47,48]	3,204,336	7,637,921	31,100,244	57,429,085	142,873,265
5.	Cost of materials used in manufacturing[45,46,47,48]	8,959,327	35,558,782	127,600,077	289,843,907	529,019,089
6.	Value of manufactured product[45,46,47,48]	16,534,272	57,580,886	205,620,672	414,864,673	908,640,280

GENERAL MANUFACTURING STATISTICS, 1850-1890[45]

INDIANA

Item No.		1850	1860	1870	1880	1890
1.	Number of manufacturing establishments[45,46,47,48]	4,392	5,323	11,847	11,198	12,354
2.	Capital of manufacturing establishments[45,46,47,48]	7,750,402	18,451,121	52,052,425	65,742,962	131,605,366
3.	Average number of wage earners[45,46,47,48]	14,400	21,295	58,852	69,508	110,590
4.	Total wages[45,46,47,48]	3,728,844	6,318,335	18,366,780	21,960,888	42,577,258
5.	Cost of materials used in manufacturing[45,46,47,48]	10,369,700	27,142,597	63,135,492	100,262,917	130,119,106
6.	Value of manufactured product[45,46,47,48]	18,725,423	42,803,469	108,617,278	148,006,411	226,825,082

GENERAL MANUFACTURING STATISTICS, 1850-1890[45]

IOWA

Item No.		1850	1860	1870	1880	1890
1.	Number of manufacturing establishments[45,46,47,48]	522	1,939	6,566	6,921	7,440
2.	Capital of manufacturing establishments[45,46,47,48]	1,292,875	7,247,130	22,420,183	33,987,886	77,513,097
3.	Average number of wage earners[45,46,47,48]	1,707	6,307	25,032	28,372	51,037
4.	Total wages[45,46,47,48]	473,016	1,922,417	6,893,292	9,725,962	20,429,620
5.	Cost of materials used in manufacturing[45,46,47,48]	2,356,881	8,612,259	27,682,096	48,704,311	79,292,407
6.	Value of manufactured product[45,46,47,48]	3,551,783	13,971,325	46,534,322	71,045,926	125,049,183

GENERAL MANUFACTURING STATISTICS, 1850-1890[45]						
KANSAS						
Item No.		1850	1860	1870	1880	1890
1.	Number of manufacturing establishments[45,46,47,48]	---	344	1,477	2,803	4,471
2.	Capital of manufacturing establishments[45,46,47,48]	---	1,084,935	4,319,060	11,192,315	43,926,002
3.	Average number of wage earners[45,46,47,48]	---	1,735	6,844	12,062	28,237
4.	Total wages[45,46,47,48]	---	880,346	2,377,511	3,995,010	13,288,175
5.	Cost of materials used in manufacturing[45,46,47,48]	---	1,449,975	6,112,163	21,453,141	78,845,167
6.	Value of manufactured product[45,46,47,48]	---	4,357,408	11,775,833	30,843,777	110,219,805

GENERAL MANUFACTURING STATISTICS, 1850-1890[45]						
KENTUCKY						
Item No.		1850	1860	1870	1880	1890
1.	Number of manufacturing establishments[45,46,47,48]	3,609	3,450	5,390	5,328	7,745
2.	Capital of manufacturing establishments[45,46,47,48]	11,810,462	20,256,579	29,277,809	45,813,039	79,811,980
3.	Average number of wage earners[45,46,47,48]	21,476	21,258	30,636	37,391	56,558
4.	Total wages[45,46,47,48]	5,106,048	6,020,082	9,444,524	11,657,844	21,326,831
5.	Cost of materials used in manufacturing[45,46,47,48]	12,165,075	22,295,759	29,497,535	47,461,890	63,677,583
6.	Value of manufactured product[45,46,47,48]	21,710,212	37,931,240	54,625,809	75483,377	126,719,857

GENERAL MANUFACTURING STATISTICS, 1850-1890[45]						
LOUISIANA						
Item No.		1850	1860	1870	1880	1890
1.	Number of manufacturing establishments[45,46,47,48]	1,008	1,744	2,557	1,553	2,613
2.	Capital of manufacturing establishments[45,46,47,48]	5,032,424	7,151,172	18,313,974	11,462,468	34,754,121
3.	Average number of wage earners[45,46,47,48]	6,217	8,789	30,071	12,167	28,377
4.	Total wages[45,46,47,48]	2,033,928	3,683,679	4,593,470	4,360,371	10,122,569
5.	Cost of materials used in manufacturing[45,46,47,48]	2,459,508	6,738,486	12,412,023	14,442,506	33,282,724
6.	Value of manufactured product[45,46,47,48]	6,779,417	15,587,473	24,161,905	24,205,183	57,806,713

GENERAL MANUFACTURING STATISTICS, 1850-1890[45]						
MAINE						
Item No.		1850	1860	1870	1880	1890
1.	Number of manufacturing establishments[45,46,47,48]	3,974	3,810	5,550	4,481	5,010
2.	Capital of manufacturing establishments[45,46,47,48]	14,699,152	22,044,020	39,796,190	49,988,171	80,419,809
3.	Average number of wage earners[45,46,47,48]	28,020	34,619	49,180	52,954	70,374
4.	Total wages[45,46,47,48]	7,485,588	8,368,691	14,282,205	13,623,318	22,962,582
5.	Cost of materials used in manufacturing[45,46,47,48]	13,553,144	21,553,066	49,379,757	51,120,708	51,520,589
6.	Value of manufactured product[45,46,47,48]	24,661,057	38,193,254	79,497,521	79,829,793	95,689,500

GENERAL MANUFACTURING STATISTICS, 1850-1890[45]						
MARYLAND						
Item No.		1850	1860	1870	1880	1890
1.	Number of manufacturing establishments[45,46,47,48]	3,725	3,083	5,812	6,787	7,485
2.	Capital of manufacturing establishments[45,46,47,48]	14,934,450	23,230,608	36,438,729	56,742,384	119,667,316
3.	Average number of wage earners[45,46,47,48]	30,212	28,403	44,860	74,945	97,808
4.	Total wages[45,46,47,48]	7,403,832	7,190,672	12,682,817	18,904,965	34,441,414
5.	Cost of materials used in manufacturing[45,46,47,48]	17,690,836	25,494,007	46,897,032	66,937,846	92,059,390
6.	Value of manufactured product[45,46,47,48]	33,043,892	41,735,157	76,593,613	106,780,563	171,842,593

GENERAL MANUFACTURING STATISTICS, 1850-1890[45]						
MASSACHUSETTS						
Item No.		1850	1860	1870	1880	1890
1.	Number of manufacturing establishments[45,46,47,48]	8,852	8,176	13,212	14,352	26,923
2.	Capital of manufacturing establishments[45,46,47,48]	88,940,292	132,792,327	231,677,862	303,806,185	630,032,341
3.	Average number of wage earners[45,46,47,48]	177,461	217,421	279,380	352,255	447,270
4.	Total wages[45,46,47,48]	41,954,736	56,960,913	118,051,886	128,315,362	205,844,337
5.	Cost of materials used in manufacturing[45,46,47,48]	85,856,771	135,053,721	334,413,982	386,972,655	473,199,434
6.	Value of manufactured product[45,46,47,48]	157,743,994	255,545,922	553,912,568	631,135,284	888,160,403

GENERAL MANUFACTURING STATISTICS, 1850-1890[45]

MICHIGAN

Item No.		1850	1860	1870	1880	1890
1.	Number of manufacturing establishments[45,46,47,48]	2,033	3,448	9,455	8,873	12,127
2.	Capital of manufacturing establishments[45,46,47,48]	6,563,660	23,808,226	71,712,283	92,930,959	262,412,240
3.	Average number of wage earners[45,46,47,48]	9,344	23,190	63,694	77,591	148,674
4.	Total wages[45,46,47,48]	2,717,124	6,735,047	21,205,355	25,313,682	54,982,906
5.	Cost of materials used in manufacturing[45,46,47,48]	6,136,328	17,635,611	68,142,515	92,900,269	154,521,918
6.	Value of manufactured product[45,46,47,48]	11,169,002	32,658,356	118,394,676	150,715,025	277,896,706

GENERAL MANUFACTURING STATISTICS, 1850-1890[45]

MINNESOTA

Item No.		1850	1860	1870	1880	1890
1.	Number of manufacturing establishments[45,46,47,48]	5	562	2,270	3,493	7,505
2.	Capital of manufacturing establishments[45,46,47,48]	94,000	2,388,310	11,993,729	31,004,811	127,686,618
3.	Average number of wage earners[45,46,47,48]	63	2,123	11,290	21,247	69,790
4.	Total wages[45,46,47,48]	18,540	712,214	4,052,837	8,613,094	30,371,123
5.	Cost of materials used in manufacturing[45,46,47,48]	24,300	1,904,070	13,842,902	55,660,681	118,481,941
6.	Value of manufactured product[45,46,47,48]	58,300	3,373,172	23,110,700	76,065,198	192,033,478

GENERAL MANUFACTURING STATISTICS, 1850-1890[45]						
MISSISSIPPI						
Item No.		1850	1860	1870	1880	1890
1.	Number of manufacturing establishments[45,46,47,48]	947	976	1,731	1,479	1,698
2.	Capital of manufacturing establishments[45,46,47,48]	1,815,820	4,384,492	4,501,714	4,727,600	14,896,884
3.	Average number of wage earners[45,46,47,48]	3,154	4,775	5,941	5,827	14,465
4.	Total wages[45,46,47,48]	771,528	1,618,320	1,547,428	1,192,645	4,191,754
5.	Cost of materials used in manufacturing[45,46,47,48]	1,275,771	3,146,636	4,364,206	4,667,183	10,064,897
6.	Value of manufactured product[45,46,47,48]	2,912,068	6,590,687	8,154,758	7,518,302	18,705,834

GENERAL MANUFACTURING STATISTICS, 1850-1890[45]						
MISSOURI						
Item No.		1850	1860	1870	1880	1890
1.	Number of manufacturing establishments[45,46,47,48]	2,923	3,157	11,871	8,592	14,052
2.	Capital of manufacturing establishments[45,46,47,48]	8,576,607	20,034,220	80,257,244	72,507,844	189,558,546
3.	Average number of wage earners[45,46,47,48]	15,808	19,681	65,354	63,995	124,203
4.	Total wages[45,46,47,48]	4,692,648	6,669,916	31,055,445	24,309,716	59,643,429
5.	Cost of materials used in manufacturing[45,46,47,48]	12,798,351	23,849,941	115,533,269	110,798,392	177,582,382
6.	Value of manufactured product[45,46,47,48]	24,324,418	41,782,731	206,213,429	165,386,205	324,561,993

GENERAL MANUFACTURING STATISTICS, 1850-1890[45]						
MONTANA						
Item No.		1850	1860	1870	1880	1890
1.	Number of manufacturing establishments[45,46,47,48]	---	---	201	196	289
2.	Capital of manufacturing establishments[45,46,47,48]	---	---	1,794,300	899,390	4,293,794
3.	Average number of wage earners[45,46,47,48]	---	---	701	578	2,386
4.	Total wages[45,46,47,48]	---	---	370,843	318,759	1,652,413
5.	Cost of materials used in manufacturing[45,46,47,48]	---	---	1,316,331	1,006,442	2,375,093
6.	Value of manufactured product[45,46,47,48]	---	---	2,494,511	1,835,867	5,507,573

GENERAL MANUFACTURING STATISTICS, 1850-1890[45]						
NEBRASKA						
Item No.		1850	1860	1870	1880	1890
1.	Number of manufacturing establishments[45,46,47,48]	---	107	670	1,403	3,014
2.	Capital of manufacturing establishments[45,46,47,48]	---	266,575	2,169,963	4,881,150	37,569,508
3.	Average number of wage earners[45,46,47,48]	---	336	2,665	4,793	20,450
4.	Total wages[45,46,47,48]	---	105,332	1,429,913	1,742,311	10,271,478
5.	Cost of materials used in manufacturing[45,46,47,48]	---	237,215	2,902,074	8,208,478	67,334,532
6.	Value of manufactured product[45,46,47,48]	---	607,328	5,738,512	12,627,336	93,037,794

GENERAL MANUFACTURING STATISTICS, 1850-1890[45]						
NEVADA						
Item No.		1850	1860	1870	1880	1890
1.	Number of manufacturing establishments[45,46,47,48]	---	---	330	184	95
2.	Capital of manufacturing establishments[45,46,47,48]	---	---	5,127,790	1,323,300	1,211,269
3.	Average number of wage earners[45,46,47,48]	---	---	2,859	577	558
4.	Total wages[45,46,47,48]	---	---	2,498,473	461,807	376,535
5.	Cost of materials used in manufacturing[45,46,47,48]	---	---	10,315,984	1,049,794	439,058
6.	Value of manufactured product[45,46,47,48]	---	---	15,870,539	2,179,626	1,105,063

GENERAL MANUFACTURING STATISTICS, 1850-1890[45]						
NEW HAMPSHIRE						
Item No.		1850	1860	1870	1880	1890
1.	Number of manufacturing establishments[45,46,47,48]	3,211	2,592	3,342	3,181	3,229
2.	Capital of manufacturing establishments[45,46,47,48]	18,242,114	23,274,094	36,023,743	51,112,263	79,375,160
3.	Average number of wage earners[45,46,47,48]	27,092	32,340	40,783	48,831	60,111
4.	Total wages[45,46,47,48]	6,123,876	8,110,561	13,823,091	14,814,793	21,927,290
5.	Cost of materials used in manufacturing[45,46,47,48]	12,745,466	20,539,857	41,577,967	43,552,462	47,754,152
6.	Value of manufactured product[45,46,47,48]	23,164,503	37,586,453	71,038,249	73,978,028	85,779,549

GENERAL MANUFACTURING STATISTICS, 1850-1890[45]						
NEW JERSEY						
Item No.		1850	1860	1870	1880	1890
1.	Number of manufacturing establishments[45,46,47,48]	4,207	4,173	6,636	7,128	9,225
2.	Capital of manufacturing establishments[45,46,47,48]	22,993,258	40,521,048	79,606,719	106,226,593	250,805,745
3.	Average number of wage earners[45,46,47,48]	37,830	56,027	75,552	126,038	173,778
4.	Total wages[45,46,47,48]	9,364,740	16,277,337	32,648,409	46,083,015	82,944,118
5.	Cost of materials used in manufacturing[45,46,47,48]	22,011,871	41,429,100	103,415,245	165,285,779	189,365,740
6.	Value of manufactured product[45,46,47,48]	39,851,256	76,306,104	169,237,732	254,380,236	554,573,571

GENERAL MANUFACTURING STATISTICS, 1850-1890[45]						
NEW MEXICO						
Item No.		1850	1860	1870	1880	1890
1.	Number of manufacturing establishments[45,46,47,48]	23	82	182	144	127
2.	Capital of manufacturing establishments[45,46,47,48]	68,300	2,008,350	1,450,695	463,275	965,938
3.	Average number of wage earners[45,46,47,48]	81	1,074	427	557	849
4.	Total wages[45,46,47,48]	20,772	341,306	167,281	218,731	470,361
5.	Cost of materials used in manufacturing[45,46,47,48]	110,220	367,892	880,957	871,352	691,420
6.	Value of manufactured product[45,46,47,48]	249,010	1,249,123	1,489,863	1,284,846	1,516,195

GENERAL MANUFACTURING STATISTICS, 1850-1890[45]						
NEW YORK						
Item No.		1850	1860	1870	1880	1890
1.	Number of manufacturing establishments[45,46,47,48]	23,553	22,624	36,206	42,739	65,840
2.	Capital of manufacturing establishments[45,46,47,48]	99,904,405	172,895,652	366,994,320	514,246,575	1,130,161,195
3.	Average number of wage earners[45,46,47,48]	119,349	230,112	351,800	531,533	752,066
4.	Total wages[45,46,47,48]	49,131,000	65,446,759	142,466,758	198,634,029	370,380,559
5.	Cost of materials used in manufacturing[45,46,47,48]	134,655,674	214,813,061	452,065,452	679,612,545	871,264,085
6.	Value of manufactured product[45,46,47,48]	237,597,249	378,870,939	785,194,651	1,080,696,596	1,711,577,671

GENERAL MANUFACTURING STATISTICS, 1850-1890[45]						
NORTH CAROLINA						
Item No.		1850	1860	1870	1880	1890
1.	Number of manufacturing establishments[45,46,47,48]	2,663	3,689	3,642	3,802	3,667
2.	Capital of manufacturing establishments[45,46,47,48]	7,456,860	9,693,703	8,140,473	13,045,639	32,745,995
3.	Average number of wage earners[45,46,47,48]	14,601	14,217	13,622	18,109	33,625
4.	Total wages[45,46,47,48]	2,383,456	2,689,441	2,195,711	2,740,768	6,552,121
5.	Cost of materials used in manufacturing[45,46,47,48]	4,602,501	10,203,228	12,824,693	13,090,937	22,789,187
6.	Value of manufactured product[45,46,47,48]	9,111,050	16,678,698	19,021,327	20,095,037	40,375,450

GENERAL MANUFACTURING STATISTICS, 1850-1890[45]

NORTH DAKOTA

Item No.		1850	1860	1870	1880	1890
1.	Number of manufacturing establishments[45,46,47,48]	---	---	17	251	382
2.	Capital of manufacturing establishments[45,46,47,48]	---	---	19,200	771,428	2,894,553
3.	Average number of wage earners[45,46,47,48]	---	---	91	868	1,499
4.	Total wages[45,46,47,48]	---	---	21,106	339,375	759,132
5.	Cost of materials used in manufacturing[45,46,47,48]	---	---	105,997	1,523,761	3,087,161
6.	Value of manufactured product[45,46,47,48]	---	---	178,570	2,373,970	5,028,107

GENERAL MANUFACTURING STATISTICS, 1850-1890[45]

OHIO

Item No.		1850	1860	1870	1880	1890
1.	Number of manufacturing establishments[45,46,47,48]	10,622	11,123	22,773	20,699	28,673
2.	Capital of manufacturing establishments[45,46,47,48]	29,019,538	57,295,303	141,923,964	188,939,614	402,793,019
3.	Average number of wage earners[45,46,47,48]	51,491	75,602	137,202	183,609	292,982
4.	Total wages[45,46,47,48]	13,467,156	22,302,989	49,066,488	62,103,800	128,447,799
5.	Cost of materials used in manufacturing[45,46,47,48]	34,678,019	69,800,270	157,131,697	215,334,258	341,016,464
6.	Value of manufactured product[45,46,47,48]	62,692,279	121,691,148	269,713,610	348,298,390	641,688,064

GENERAL MANUFACTURING STATISTICS, 1850-1890[45]						
OKLAHOMA						
Item No.		1850	1860	1870	1880	1890
1.	Number of manufacturing establishments[45,46,47,48]	---	---	---	---	72
2.	Capital of manufacturing establishments[45,46,47,48]	---	---	---	---	95,519
3.	Average number of wage earners[45,46,47,48]	---	---	---	---	147
4.	Total wages[45,46,47,48]	---	---	---	---	52,326
5.	Cost of materials used in manufacturing[45,46,47,48]	---	---	---	---	56,518
6.	Value of manufactured product[45,46,47,48]	---	---	---	---	180,445

GENERAL MANUFACTURING STATISTICS, 1850-1890[45]						
OREGON						
Item No.		1850	1860	1870	1880	1890
1.	Number of manufacturing establishments[45,46,47,48]	52	309	969	1,080	1,523
2.	Capital of manufacturing establishments[45,46,47,48]	843,600	1,337,238	4,376,849	6,312,056	32,122,051
3.	Average number of wage earners[45,46,47,48]	285	978	2,884	3,473	16,760
4.	Total wages[45,46,47,48]	388,620	635,256	1,120,173	1,667,046	9,559,734
5.	Cost of materials used in manufacturing[45,46,47,48]	809,560	1,431,952	3,419,756	6,954,436	21,793,578
6.	Value of manufactured product[45,46,47,48]	2,236,640	2,976,761	6,877,387	10,931,232	41,432,174

GENERAL MANUFACTURING STATISTICS, 1850-1890[45]						
PENNSYLVANIA						
Item No.		1850	1860	1870	1880	1890
1.	Number of manufacturing establishments[45,46,47,48]	21,605	22,363	37,200	31,232	39,339
2.	Capital of manufacturing establishments[45,46,47,48]	94,473,810	190,055,904	406,821,845	474,510,993	991,243,115
3.	Average number of wage earners[45,46,47,48]	146,766	222,132	319,487	387,072	570,393
4.	Total wages[45,46,47,48]	37,163,232	60,369,165	127,976,594	134,055,904	263,375,215
5.	Cost of materials used in manufacturing[45,46,47,48]	87,206,377	153,477,698	421,197,673	465,020,563	773,734,637
6.	Value of manufactured product[45,46,47,48]	155,044,910	290,121,188	711,894,344	744,818,445	1,331,794,901

GENERAL MANUFACTURING STATISTICS, 1850-1890[45]						
RHODE ISLAND						
Item No.		1850	1860	1870	1880	1890
1.	Number of manufacturing establishments[45,46,47,48]	864	1,191	1,850	2,205	3,377
2.	Capital of manufacturing establishments[45,46,47,48]	12,935,676	24,278,295	66,557,322	75,575,943	126,483,401
3.	Average number of wage earners[45,46,47,48]	20,967	32,490	49,417	62,878	81,111
4.	Total wages[45,46,47,48]	5,047,080	8,760,125	19,354,256	21,355,619	33,239,313
5.	Cost of materials used in manufacturing[45,46,47,48]	13,186,703	19,858,515	73,154,109	58,103,443	76,253,023
6.	Value of manufactured product[45,46,47,48]	22,117,688	40,711,296	111,418,354	104,163,621	142,500,625

GENERAL MANUFACTURING STATISTICS, 1850-1890[45]						
SOUTH CAROLINA						
Item No.		1850	1860	1870	1880	1890
1.	Number of manufacturing establishments[45,46,47,48]	1,430	1,230	1,584	2,078	2,382
2.	Capital of manufacturing establishments[45,46,47,48]	6,053,265	6,931,756	5,400,418	11,205,894	29,276,261
3.	Average number of wage earners[45,46,47,48]	7,066	6,994	8,141	15,828	22,748
4.	Total wages[45,46,47,48]	1,127,712	1,380,027	1,543,715	2,836,289	5,474,739
5.	Cost of materials used in manufacturing[45,46,47,48]	2,787,534	5,198,881	5,855,736	9,885,538	18,873,666
6.	Value of manufactured product[45,46,47,48]	7,045,477	8,615,915	9,858,981	16,738,008	31,926,681

GENERAL MANUFACTURING STATISTICS, 1850-1890[45]						
SOUTH DAKOTA						
Item No.		1850	1860	1870	1880	1890
1.	Number of manufacturing establishments[45,46,47,48]	---	---	17	251	499
2.	Capital of manufacturing establishments[45,46,47,48]	---	---	79,200	771,428	3,207,796
3.	Average number of wage earners[45,46,47,48]	---	---	91	868	2,011
4.	Total wages[45,46,47,48]	---	---	21,106	339,375	832,693
5.	Cost of materials used in manufacturing[45,46,47,48]	---	---	105,997	1,523,761	3,523,840
6.	Value of manufactured product[45,46,47,48]	---	---	178,570	2,373,970	5,682,748

GENERAL MANUFACTURING STATISTICS, 1850-1890[45]						
TENNESSEE						
Item No.		1850	1860	1870	1880	1890
1.	Number of manufacturing establishments[45,46,47,48]	2,887	2,572	5,317	4,326	4,559
2.	Capital of manufacturing establishments[45,46,47,48]	6,527,729	14,426,261	15,595,295	20,092,845	51,475,092
3.	Average number of wage earners[45,46,47,48]	12,039	12,528	19,412	22,445	37,487
4.	Total wages[45,46,47,48]	2,247,492	3,370,687	5,390,630	5,254,775	13,557,180
5.	Cost of materials used in manufacturing[45,46,47,48]	5,166,886	9,416,514	19,657,027	23,834,262	40,463,782
6.	Value of manufactured product[45,46,47,48]	9,725,608	17,987,225	34,362,636	37,074,886	72,355,286

GENERAL MANUFACTURING STATISTICS, 1850-1890[45]						
TEXAS						
Item No.		1850	1860	1870	1880	1890
1.	Number of manufacturing establishments[45,46,47,48]	309	983	2,399	2,996	5,268
2.	Capital of manufacturing establishments[45,46,47,48]	539,290	3,272,450	5,284,110	9,245,561	46,815,181
3.	Average number of wage earners[45,46,47,48]	1,066	3,449	7,927	12,159	34,794
4.	Total wages[45,46,47,48]	322,368	1,162,756	1,787,835	3,343,087	15,148,495
5.	Cost of materials used in manufacturing[45,46,47,48]	394,642	3,367,372	6,273,193	12,956,269	36,152,308
6.	Value of manufactured product[45,46,47,48]	1,168,538	6,577,202	11,517,302	20,719,928	70,433,551

GENERAL MANUFACTURING STATISTICS, 1850-1890[45]						
UTAH						
Item No.		1850	1860	1870	1880	1890
1.	Number of manufacturing establishments[45,46,47,48]	14	148	533	640	531
2.	Capital of manufacturing establishments[45,46,47,48]	44,400	443,356	1,391,898	2,656,657	6,583,022
3.	Average number of wage earners[45,46,47,48]	51	389	1,534	2,495	4,349
4.	Total wages[45,46,47,48]	9,984	231,701	395,365	858,863	2,191,265
5.	Cost of materials used in manufacturing[45,46,47,48]	337,381	439,512	1,238,252	2,561,737	4,252,030
6.	Value of manufactured product[45,46,47,48]	291,220	900,153	2,343,019	4,324,992	8,911,047

GENERAL MANUFACTURING STATISTICS, 1850-1890[45]						
VERMONT						
Item No.		1850	1860	1870	1880	1890
1.	Number of manufacturing establishments[45,46,47,48]	1,849	1,883	3,270	2,874	3,031
2.	Capital of manufacturing establishments[45,46,47,48]	5,001,377	9,498,617	20,329,637	23,265,224	32,763,291
3.	Average number of wage earners[45,46,47,48]	8,445	10,497	18,686	17,540	22,119
4.	Total wages[45,46,47,48]	2,202,348	3,004,986	6,264,581	5,164,479	8,427,553
5.	Cost of materials used in manufacturing[45,46,47,48]	4,172,552	7,608,858	17,007,769	18,330,677	20,433,174
6.	Value of manufactured product[45,46,47,48]	8,570,920	14,637,807	32,184,606	31,354,366	38,340,066

GENERAL MANUFACTURING STATISTICS, 1850-1890[45]						
VIRGINIA						
Item No.		1850	1860	1870	1880	1890
1.	Number of manufacturing establishments[45,46,47,48]	4,740	5,385	5,933	5,710	5,915
2.	Capital of manufacturing establishments[45,46,47,48]	18,109,143	26,935,560	18,455,400	26,988,990	63,456,799
3.	Average number of wage earners[45,46,47,48]	29,110	36,174	26,974	40,184	53,566
4.	Total wages[45,46,47,48]	5,434,476	8,544,117	5,343,099	7,425,261	15,816,930
5.	Cost of materials used in manufacturing[45,46,47,48]	18,101,131	30,840,531	23,832,384	32,883,933	50,148,285
6.	Value of manufactured product[45,46,47,48]	29,602,507	50,652,124	38,364,322	51,780,992	88,363,824

GENERAL MANUFACTURING STATISTICS, 1850-1890[45]						
WASHINGTON						
Item No.		1850	1860	1870	1880	1890
1.	Number of manufacturing establishments[45,46,47,48]	---	52	269	261	1,543
2.	Capital of manufacturing establishments[45,46,47,48]	---	1,296,200	1,893,674	3,202,497	34,369,735
3.	Average number of wage earners[45,46,47,48]	---	870	1,026	1,147	18,677
4.	Total wages[45,46,47,48]	---	453,601	574,936	532,226	11,011,894
5.	Cost of materials used in manufacturing[45,46,47,48]	---	502,021	1,435,128	1,967,469	19,917,057
6.	Value of manufactured product[45,46,47,48]	---	1,406,921	2,851,052	3,250,134	41,768,022

GENERAL MANUFACTURING STATISTICS, 1850-1890[45]						
WEST VIRGINIA						
Item No.		1850	1860	1870	1880	1890
1.	Number of manufacturing establishments[45,46,47,48]	---	---	2,444	2,375	2,376
2.	Capital of manufacturing establishments[45,46,47,48]	---	---	11,084,520	13,883,390	28,118,030
3.	Average number of wage earners[45,46,47,48]	---	---	11,672	14,311	19,340
4.	Total wages[45,46,47,48]	---	---	4,322,164	4,313,965	6,911,779
5.	Cost of materials used in manufacturing[45,46,47,48]	---	---	14,503,701	14,027,388	23,729,089
6.	Value of manufactured product[45,46,47,48]	---	---	24,102,201	22,867,126	38,702,125

GENERAL MANUFACTURING STATISTICS, 1850-1890[45]						
WISCONSIN						
Item No.		1850	1860	1870	1880	1890
1.	Number of manufacturing establishments[45,46,47,48]	1,262	3,064	7,013	7,674	10,417
2.	Capital of manufacturing establishments[45,46,47,48]	3,382,148	15,831,581	41,981,872	73,821,802	246,515,404
3.	Average number of wage earners[45,46,47,48]	6,089	15,414	43,910	57,109	120,006
4.	Total wages[45,46,47,48]	1,712,496	4,268,708	13,575,642	18,814,917	42,958,267
5.	Cost of materials used in manufacturing[45,46,47,48]	5,414,931	17,137,334	45,851,266	85,796,178	145,437,016
6.	Value of manufactured product[45,46,47,48]	9,293,068	27,849,467	77,214,326	128,255,480	248,546,164

GENERAL MANUFACTURING STATISTICS, 1850-1890[45]						
WYOMING						
Item No.		1850	1860	1870	1880	1890
1.	Number of manufacturing establishments[45,46,47,48]	---	---	32	57	190
2.	Capital of manufacturing establishments[45,46,47,48]	---	---	889,400	364,675	1,411,184
3.	Average number of wage earners[45,46,47,48]	---	---	502	391	1,022
4.	Total wages[45,46,47,48]	---	---	347,578	187,798	787,169
5.	Cost of materials used in manufacturing[45,46,47,48]	---	---	280,156	601,214	1,084,432
6.	Value of manufactured product[45,46,47,48]	---	---	765,424	898,494	2,367,601

GENERAL MANUFACTURING STATISTICS, 1850-1890[45]						
UNITED STATES						
Item No.		1850	1860	1870	1880	1890
1.	Number of manufacturing establishments[45,46,47,48]	123,025	140,433	252,148	253,852	355,415
2.	Capital of manufacturing establishments[45,46,47,48]	533,245,351	1,009,855,715	2,118,208,769	2,790,272,606	6,525,156,486
3.	Average number of wage earners[45,46,47,48]	957,059	1,311,246	2,053,996	2,732,595	4,251,613
4.	Total wages[45,46,47,48]	236,755,461	378,878,966	775,584,343	947,953,795	1,891,228,321
5.	Cost of materials used in manufacturing[45,46,47,48]	555,123,822	1,031,605,092	2,488,427,242	3,396,823,549	5,162,044,076
6.	Value of manufactured product[45,46,47,48]	1,019,106,616	1,885,861,676	4,232,325,442	5,369,579,191	9,372,437,283

General Manufacturing Statistics, 1899–1989

GENERAL MANUFACTURING STATISTICS, 1899-1989[89,91]						
ALABAMA[*a]						
Item No.		1899	1909	1919	1929	1939
1.	Total establishments[90,*a]	2,000	3,398	3,522	2,848	1,982
2.	With 20 employees or more[90]	---	---	---	---	---
3.	All employees, number (1,000)	55.0	78.2	116.4	130.0	129.3
4.	Payroll ($1,000,000)	17.0	33.8	117.0	126.4	114.7
5.	Production workers, total (number) (1,000)	52.7	72.1	106.7	119.6	115.7
6.	Man hours (1,000,000)	---	---	---	---	---
7.	Wages ($1,000,000)	14.9	27.3	98.5	102.0	91.1
8.	Value added by manufacture ($1,000,000)	34.1	62.5	191.0	258.1	245.6
9.	Capital expenditures, new ($1,000,000)	---	---	---	---	---
10.	Percent of U.S. Employment	1.13	1.12	1.18	1.35	1.36
11.	Index of employment change (1958 = 100)	25	36	54	60	60
12.	U.S. index of employment change (1958 = 100)	30	45	63	62	61

GENERAL MANUFACTURING STATISTICS, 1899-1989[89,91] (Cont.)

ALABAMA[*a]

Item No.	1947	1954	1958	1963	1967	1972	1977	1982	1987	1989[*d]
1.	3,336	3,893	3,956[*b]	4,079	4,951	4,974	5,863	5,528	5,845	---
2.	---	1,152	1,195	1,257[*b]	1,446	1,630	1,855	1,968	2,072	---
3.	206.2	220.1[*b]	229.8	243.8	288.8	322.6	341.0	329.6	347.3	364.4
4.	444.9	690.0[*b]	920.0	1,162.4	1,602.8	2,396.8	3,773.2	5,234.4	6,962.5	7,787.3
5.	185.7	188.4	188.7	197.6	235.3	262.2	273.0	253.6	268.8	281.0
6.	---	357.8	363.2	391.0	466.6	519.3	525.2	479.8	530.7	550.9
7.	372.5	528.6	677.6	842.3	1,162.6	1,730.8	2,697.6	3,598.3	4,745.6	5,238.0
8.	877.4	1,319.2	1,770.5	2,325.2	3,525.5	5,064.8	8,405.9	12,045.7	18,652.1	20,583.4
9.	---	82.2	165.1[*c]	147.4	378.9	355.1	1,318.9	1,540.2	1,360.1	2,137.6
10.	1.44	1.37	1.43	1.44	1.49	1.70	1.74	1.73	1.83	1.91
11.	95	96	100	106	126	140 95	148 100	143 97	151 102	159 107
12.	91	100	100	106	121	119 97	122 100	119 97	118 97	119 97

[a] There were a number of changes in the definition of manufacturing industries through the years that affect historical comparability. See the Glossary of Terms for these changes. The changes have not appreciably affected the comparability of the historical data except for the figures on the number of establishments.

[b] Data for central administrative offices and auxiliaries included for the first time for other states but this information was not collected in Alaska and Hawaii in 1954. See the Glossary of Terms.

[c] Item 9 (1958) includes expenditures for plants under construction but not in operation prior to 1958, the data represents expenditures at operating manufacturing establishments only. See Glossary of Terms.

[d] The Census Data for 1972, 1977, 1983 and 1987 are from manufacturing. Data for 1989 are estimates based on a representative sample of establishments canvassed annually and may differ from results of a complete canvass of all establishments.

GENERAL MANUFACTURING STATISTICS, 1899-1989[89,91]						
ALASKA[*a,e]						
Item No.		1899	1909	1919	1929	1939
1.	Total establishments[90,*a]	48	152	147	---	230
2.	With 20 employees or more[90]	---	---	---	---	---
3.	All employees, number (1,000)	---	3.5	7.3	---	5.5
4.	Payroll ($1,000,000)	1.5	2.3	10.9	---	8.0
5.	Production workers, total (number) (1,000)	2.3	3.1	6.6	---	4.8
6.	Man hours (1,000,000)	---	---	---	---	---
7.	Wages ($1,000,000)	1.4	1.9	8.8	---	6.9
8.	Value added by manufacture ($1,000,000)	2.4	6.2	22.0	---	17.9
9.	Capital expenditures, new ($1,000,000)	---	---	---	---	---
10.	Percent of U.S. Employment	---	.04	.11	---	.06
11.	Index of employment change (1958 = 100)	---	72	152	---	114
12.	U.S. index of employment change (1958 = 100)	30	61	60	---	59

GENERAL MANUFACTURING STATISTICS, 1899-1989[89,91] (Cont.)										
ALASKA*[a]										
Item No.	1947	1954	1958	1963	1967	1972	1977	1982	1987	1989*[d]
1.	---	219	246*[e]	303	323	342	429	445	427	---
2.	---	68	69	73*[e]	95	91	128	144	104	---
3.	---	4.1*[b]	4.8	5.8	7.6	7.5	11.4	12.8	11.1	11.4
4.	---	20.4*[b]	25.7	39.7	55.6	75.1	166.0	269.5	271.7	304.3
5.	---	3.5	3.9	4.7	6.3	6.1	9.3	10.0	8.4	8.9
6.	---	7.0	7.3	9.2	11.7	11.6	16.9	18.3	16.7	17.8
7.	---	16.5	19.9	30.5	42.7	56.5	122.7	196.6	191.4	223.4
8.	---	40.2	64.6	85.0	130.4	170.4	504.2	769.2	834.0	1,176.7
9.	---	---	3.3*[c]	14.5	14.7	21.8	178.1	58.5	68.6	102.1
10.	---	.02	.03	.03	.04	.04	.06	.07	.06	.06
11.	---	85	100	121	158	156 66	238 100	267 112	231 97	238 100
12.	---	100	100	106	121	119 97	122 100	119 97	118 97	119 97

[a] There were a number of changes in the definition of manufacturing industries through the years that affect historical comparability. See the Glossary of Terms for these changes. The changes have not appreciably affected the comparability of the historical data except for the figures on the number of establishments.

[b] Data for central administrative offices and auxiliaries included for the first time for other states but this information was not collected in Alaska and Hawaii in 1954. See the Glossary of Terms.

[c] Item 9 (1958) includes expenditures for plants under construction but not in operation prior to 1958, the data represents expenditures at operating manufacturing establishments only. See Glossary of Terms.

[d] The Census Data for 1972, 1977, 1983 and 1987 are from manufacturing. Data for 1989 are estimates based on a representative sample of establishments canvassed annually and may differ from results of a complete canvass of all establishments.

[e] Data for central administrative offices and auxiliaries included for the first time. See the Glossary of Terms.

GENERAL MANUFACTURING STATISTICS, 1899-1989[89,91]						
ARIZONA[*a]						
Item No.		1899	1909	1919	1929	1939
1.	Total establishments[90,*a]	154	311	399	348	313
2.	With 20 employees or more[90]	---	---	---	---	---
3.	All employees, number (1,000)	3.3	6.9	9.7	12.2	8.0
4.	Payroll ($1,000,000)	2.6	6.3	14.7	19.3	11.0
5.	Production workers, total (number) (1,000)	3.1	6.4	8.3	10.6	5.9
6.	Man hours (1,000,000)	---	---	---	---	---
7.	Wages ($1,000,000)	2.3	5.5	11.7	15.1	7.0
8.	Value added by manufacture ($1,000,000)	12.6	16.7	27.5	32.3	31.6
9.	Capital expenditures, new ($1,000,000)	---	---	---	---	---
10.	Percent of U.S. Employment	.07	.10	.10	.13	.08
11.	Index of employment change (1958 = 100)	8	27	24	30	20
12.	U.S. index of employment change (1958 = 100)	30	44	61	60	59

GENERAL MANUFACTURING STATISTICS, 1899-1989[89,91] (Cont.)

ARIZONA*[a]

Item No.	1947	1954	1958	1963	1967	1972	1977	1982	1987	1989*[d]
1.	544	817	1,158*[b]	1,518	1,630	2,037	2,892	3,407	4,152	---
2.	125	175	257	339*[b]	424	597	677	854	1,129	---
3.	14.2	26.2*[b]	40.6	56.9	76.8	93.9	110.9	149.8	184.1	180.2
4.	39.3	110.7*[b]	213.3	347.5	543.2	855.1	1,462.9	3,036.9	4,669.0	5,039.6
5.	11.2	20.3	30.0	38.6	50.8	62.3	69.8	86.7	105.9	103.4
6.	24.3	42.3	61.4	77.5	101.8	121.1	135.0	165.2	214.2	209.0
7.	29.7	80.6	148.3	210.5	308.6	481.5	780.7	1,423.4	2,148.8	2,291.4
8.	83.8	192.5	360.2	627.1	995.3	1,879.6	3,332.9	6,162.4	11,299.0	11,670.7
9.	8.3	13.8	27.7*[c]	49.5	109.9	198.4	213.7	765.2	836.9	924.7
10.	.10	.16	.25	.34	.40	.49	.57	.78	.97	.95
11.	35	65	100	140	189	231 85	273 100	369 135	453 166	444 162
12.	89	100	100	106	121	119 97	122 100	119 97	118 97	119 97

[a] There were a number of changes in the definition of manufacturing industries through the years that affect historical comparability. See the Glossary of Terms for these changes. The changes have not appreciably affected the comparability of the historical data except for the figures on the number of establishments.

[b] Data for central administrative offices and auxiliaries included for the first time for other states but this information was not collected in Alaska and Hawaii in 1954. See the Glossary of Terms.

[c] Item 9 (1958) includes expenditures for plants under construction but not in operation prior to 1958, the data represents expenditures at operating manufacturing establishments only. See Glossary of Terms.

[d] The Census Data for 1972, 1977, 1983 and 1987 are from manufacturing. Data for 1989 are estimates based on a representative sample of establishments canvassed annually and may differ from results of a complete canvass of all establishments.

GENERAL MANUFACTURING STATISTICS, 1899-1989[89,91]						
ARKANSAS[*a]						
Item No.		1899	1909	1919	1929	1939
1.	Total establishments[90,*a]	1,746	2,925	3,044	1,731	1,115
2.	With 20 employees or more[90]	---	---	---	---	---
3.	All employees, number (1,000)	33.1	48.3	54.2	48.7	41.2
4.	Payroll ($1,000,000)	11.4	22.6	56.2	49.4	33.4
5.	Production workers, total (number) (1,000)	31.5	45.0	49.7	44.2	35.7
6.	Man hours (1,000,000)	---	---	---	---	---
7.	Wages ($1,000,000)	10.2	19.1	46.9	39.5	24.2
8.	Value added by manufacture ($1,000,000)	21.6	40.0	97.0	94.2	66.4
9.	Capital expenditures, new ($1,000,000)	---	---	---	---	---
10.	Percent of U.S. Employment	.68	.69	.55	.50	.43
11.	Index of employment change (1958 = 100)	37	54	61	55	46
12.	U.S. index of employment change (1958 = 100)	30	44	61	60	59

GENERAL MANUFACTURING STATISTICS, 1899-1989[89,91] (Cont.)										
ARKANSAS[*a]										
Item No.	1947	1954	1958	1963	1967	1972	1977	1982	1987	1989[*d]
1.	1,926	2,428	2,589[*b]	2,859	2,911	2,897	3,595	3,313	---	---
2.	---	568	666	840[*b]	927	1,053	1,101	1,161	---	---
3.	65.8	79.1[*b]	88.7	113.6	143.6	180.9	197.1	189.8	205.5	214.4
4.	125.2	211.8[*b]	292.7	439.6	665.6	1,151.7	1,932.4	2,823.7	3,814.6	4,154.7
5.	58.7	67.5	74.4	95.6	120.7	150.1	160.6	148.8	161.7	169.2
6.	---	134.5	144.7	191.8	239.6	298.4	310.4	279.1	326.3	333.2
7.	102.8	171.1	220.7	331.7	497.3	853.4	1,400.7	1,931.7	2,651.6	2,876.1
8.	267.5	457.0	591.7	960.9	1,557.7	2,799.8	4,881.6	7,755.3	10,826.9	12,280.3
9.	---	42.7	48.2[*c]	73.4	172.6	190.0	470.1	701.2	891.5	988.8
10.	.46	.49	.55	.67	.74	.95	1.01	.99	1.08	1.13
11.	74	89	100	128	162	204 92	222 100	214 96	232 104	242 109
12.	89	100	100	106	121	119 97	122 100	119 97	118 97	119 97

[a] There were a number of changes in the definition of manufacturing industries through the years that affect historical comparability. See the Glossary of Terms for these changes. The changes have not appreciably affected the comparability of the historical data except for the figures on the number of establishments.

[b] Data for central administrative offices and auxiliaries included for the first time for other states but this information was not collected in Alaska and Hawaii in 1954. See the Glossary of Terms.

[c] Item 9 (1958) includes expenditures for plants under construction but not in operation prior to 1958, the data represents expenditures at operating manufacturing establishments only. See Glossary of Terms.

[d] The Census Data for 1972, 1977, 1983 and 1987 are from manufacturing. Data for 1989 are estimates based on a representative sample of establishments canvassed annually and may differ from results of a complete canvass of all establishments.

GENERAL MANUFACTURING STATISTICS, 1899-1989[89,91]						
CALIFORNIA[*a]						
Item No.		1899	1909	1919	1929	1939
1.	Total establishments[90,*a]	4,997	7,659	10,282	12,019	11,558
2.	With 20 employees or more[90]	---	---	---	---	---
3.	All employees, number (1,000)	84.1	133.5	276.4	352.9	357.1
4.	Payroll ($1,000,000)	47.4	107.1	368.7	607.1	533.7
5.	Production workers, total (number) (1,000)	77.2	115.3	236.9	290.9	271.3
6.	Man hours (1,000,000)	---	---	---	---	---
7.	Wages ($1,000,000)	39.9	84.1	295.7	423.1	358.7
8.	Value added by manufacture ($1,000,000)	92.5	204.5	742.5	1,349.2	1,122.5
9.	Capital expenditures, new ($1,000,000)	---	---	---	---	---
10.	Percent of U.S. Employment	1.73	1.90	2.81	3.65	3.75
11.	Index of employment change (1958 = 100)	7	11	23	29	29
12.	U.S. index of employment change (1958 = 100)	30	44	61	60	59

GENERAL MANUFACTURING STATISTICS, 1899-1989[89,91] (Cont.)										
CALIFORNIA[*a]										
Item No.	1947	1954	1958	1963	1967	1972	1977	1982	1987	1989[*d]
1.	17,648	24,509	28,735[*b]	32,201	31,962	35,699	45,289	47,625	49,941	---
2.	4,991	6,642	7,858	9,079[*b]	10,012	11,149	12,883	14,467	15,695	---
3.	663.9	1,053.3[*b]	1,217.3	1,397.6	1,583.5	1,545.1	1,751.5	2,004.8	2,104.3	2,126.2
4.	2,064.5	4,807.4[*b]	6,876.3	9,612.2	12,514.5	15,483.1	24,671.5	42,630.0	57,147.8	63,492.6
5.	530.3	773.7	838.7	897.5	1,044.9	1,020.0	1,142.6	1,209.3	1,240.2	1,247.0
6.	1,070.3	1,534.9	1,656.7	1,791.4	2,089.7	1,974.9	2,224.2	2,317.6	2,432.9	2,484.6
7.	1,519.3	3,151.4	4,107.2	5,195.2	6,877.8	8,430.4	13,150.5	20,560.6	25,697.0	27,700.6
8.	3,994.0	8,597.5	12,048.0	17,185.0	23,393.6	31,175.2	54,862.4	94,388.4	132,637.5	147,502.3
9.	410.5	549.8	753.2[*c]	985.1	1,529.2	1,649.0	3,385.4	8,439.4	8,571.7	9,373.7
10.	4.64	6.54	7.60	8.24	8.19	8.12	8.94	10.49	11.10	11.17
11.	54	86	100	115	130	127 88	144 100	165 114	173 120	175 121
12.	89	100	100	106	121	119 97	122 100	119 97	118 97	119 97

[a] There were a number of changes in the definition of manufacturing industries through the years that affect historical comparability. See the Glossary of Terms for these changes. The changes have not appreciably affected the comparability of the historical data except for the figures on the number of establishments.

[b] Data for central administrative offices and auxiliaries included for the first time for other states but this information was not collected in Alaska and Hawaii in 1954. See the Glossary of Terms.

[c] Item 9 (1958) includes expenditures for plants under construction but not in operation prior to 1958, the data represents expenditures at operating manufacturing establishments only. See Glossary of Terms.

[d] The Census Data for 1972, 1977, 1983 and 1987 are from manufacturing. Data for 1989 are estimates based on a representative sample of establishments canvassed annually and may differ from results of a complete canvass of all establishments.

GENERAL MANUFACTURING STATISTICS, 1899-1989[89,91]						
COLORADO[*a]						
Item No.		1899	1909	1919	1929	1939
1.	Total establishments[90,*a]	1,323	2,034	2,230	1,548	1,219
2.	With 20 employees or more[90]	---	---	---	---	---
3.	All employees, number (1,000)	21.4	32.4	40.8	39.1	32.2
4.	Payroll ($1,000,000)	13.8	25.6	53.8	57.2	44.0
5.	Production workers, total (number) (1,000)	19.5	28.1	33.8	32.9	23.4
6.	Man hours (1,000,000)	---	---	---	---	---
7.	Wages ($1,000,000)	11.7	19.9	41.0	43.6	28.0
8.	Value added by manufacture ($1,000,000)	28.3	49.6	97.2	122.3	90.3
9.	Capital expenditures, new ($1,000,000)	---	---	---	---	---
10.	Percent of U.S. Employment	.44	.46	.41	.40	.34
11.	Index of employment change (1958 = 100)	28	42	53	50	42
12.	U.S. index of employment change (1958 = 100)	30	44	61	60	59

GENERAL MANUFACTURING STATISTICS, 1899-1989[89,91] (Cont.)										
COLORADO*[a]										
Item No.	1947	1954	1958	1963	1967	1972	1977	1982	1987	1989*[d]
1.	1,602	2,069	2,274*[b]	2,453	2,461	2,841	3,948	4,406	4,701	---
2.	425	490	535	593*[b]	664	834	961	1,167	1,098	---
3.	54.1	64.4*[b]	77.5	93.7	104.0	132.6	152.5	191.4	183.8	183.9
4.	144.2	254.8*[b]	405.0	596.0	730.5	1,297.8	2,124.8	3,983.2	4,958.4	5,476.6
5.	44.2	47.9	55.1	64.0	71.2	89.0	97.7	109.8	103.3	103.5
6.	92.6	95.8	112.0	128.5	143.4	176.7	190.1	207.5	204.0	210.7
7.	109.7	173.0	265.2	369.1	444.8	769.7	1,141.3	1,876.7	2,285.6	2,416.4
8.	286.8	472.4	781.9	1,193.8	1,509.2	2,504.3	4,471.8	8,056.8	12,045.8	13,519.4
9.	32.2	30.1	50.7*[c]	68.0	99.6	228.8	443.1	892.2	791.5	870.4
10.	.38	.04	.49	.55	.54	.70	.78	1.00	.97	.97
11.	70	81	100	121	134	171 87	197 100	247 126	237 121	237 121
12.	89	100	100	106	121	119 97	122 100	119 97	118 97	119 97

[a] There were a number of changes in the definition of manufacturing industries through the years that affect historical comparability. See the Glossary of Terms for these changes. The changes have not appreciably affected the comparability of the historical data except for the figures on the number of establishments.

[b] Data for central administrative offices and auxiliaries included for the first time for other states but this information was not collected in Alaska and Hawaii in 1954. See the Glossary of Terms.

[c] Item 9 (1958) includes expenditures for plants under construction but not in operation prior to 1958, the data represents expenditures at operating manufacturing establishments only. See Glossary of Terms.

[d] The Census Data for 1972, 1977, 1983 and 1987 are from manufacturing. Data for 1989 are estimates based on a representative sample of establishments canvassed annually and may differ from results of a complete canvass of all establishments.

GENERAL MANUFACTURING STATISTICS, 1899-1989[89,91]						
CONNECTICUT[*a]						
Item No.		1899	1909	1919	1929	1939
1.	Total establishments[90,*a]	3,382	4,251	4,571	3,129	2,809
2.	With 20 employees or more[90]	---	---	---	---	---
3.	All employees, number (1,000)	169.0	230.4	332.8	288.0	281.4
4.	Payroll ($1,000,000)	85.1	135.8	404.8	422.3	382.3
5.	Production workers, total (number) (1,000)	159.7	210.8	291.6	251.9	233.0
6.	Man hours (1,000,000)	---	---	---	---	---
7.	Wages ($1,000,000)	73.4	110.1	323.3	328.9	275.6
8.	Value added by manufacture ($1,000,000)	145.4	233.0	703.6	806.2	690.3
9.	Capital expenditures, new ($1,000,000)	---	---	---	---	---
10.	Percent of U.S. Employment	3.48	3.28	3.38	2.98	2.95
11.	Index of employment change (1958 = 100)	43	58	84	73	71
12.	U.S. index of employment change (1958 = 100)	30	44	61	60	59

GENERAL MANUFACTURING STATISTICS, 1899-1989[89,91] (Cont.)										
CONNECTICUT*[a]										
Item No.	1947	1954	1958	1963	1967	1972	1977	1982	1987	1989*[d]
1.	3,946	5,090	5,326*[b]	5,607	5,829	5,836	6,485	6,693	6,730	---
2.	---	1,864	1,874	2,050*[b]	2,309	2,231	2,366	2,537	2,446	---
3.	400.0	420.0*[b]	394.2	419.4	477.7	399.3	412.1	424.4	388.9	348.8
4.	1,149.3	1,751.0*[b]	1,967.1	2,583.8	3,494.3	3,860.0	5,852.3	9,059.6	11,110.6	11,187.9
5.	331.9	326.8	284.6	294.0	329.9	258.2	255.3	245.0	216.5	192.1
6.	---	652.0	563.8	601.7	684.6	520.9	509.0	478.8	440.6	398.4
7.	882.0	1,231.4	1,254.4	1,569.1	2,066.0	2,068.7	2,901.8	4,095.0	4,825.6	4,674.2
8.	1,896.7	2,877.5	3,200.3	4,495.9	6,389.8	6,828.3	10,933.9	16,373.4	22,348.9	22,457.3
9.	---	129.6	195.4*[c]	214.8	445.7	331.6	566.0	1,054.2	1,293.3	1,374.7
10.	2.80	2.60	2.46	2.47	2.47	2.10	2.10	2.22	2.05	1.83
11.	102	107	100	106	121	101 97	105 100	108 103	99 94	88 85
12.	89	100	100	106	121	119 97	122 100	119 97	118 97	119 97

[a] There were a number of changes in the definition of manufacturing industries through the years that affect historical comparability. See the Glossary of Terms for these changes. The changes have not appreciably affected the comparability of the historical data except for the figures on the number of establishments.

[b] Data for central administrative offices and auxiliaries included for the first time for other states but this information was not collected in Alaska and Hawaii in 1954. See the Glossary of Terms.

[c] Item 9 (1958) includes expenditures for plants under construction but not in operation prior to 1958, the data represents expenditures at operating manufacturing establishments only. See Glossary of Terms.

[d] The Census Data for 1972, 1977, 1983 and 1987 are from manufacturing. Data for 1989 are estimates based on a representative sample of establishments canvassed annually and may differ from results of a complete canvass of all establishments.

GENERAL MANUFACTURING STATISTICS, 1899-1989[89,91]						
DELAWARE[*a]						
Item No.		1899	1909	1919	1929	1939
1.	Total establishments[90,*a]	633	726	653	460	416
2.	With 20 employees or more[90]	---	---	---	---	---
3.	All employees, number (1,000)	21.8	23.3	33.2	26.6	23.4
4.	Payroll ($1,000,000)	9.8	12.6	44.9	37.4	29.1
5.	Production workers, total (number) (1,000)	20.6	21.2	29.0	23.6	19.8
6.	Man hours (1,000,000)	---	---	---	---	---
7.	Wages ($1,000,000)	8.5	10.3	37.2	29.1	21.2
8.	Value added by manufacture ($1,000,000)	16.6	21.9	79.5	69.2	54.1
9.	Capital expenditures, new ($1,000,000)	---	---	---	---	---
10.	Percent of U.S. Employment	.45	.33	.34	.27	.25
11.	Index of employment change (1958 = 100)	37	40	57	46	40
12.	U.S. index of employment change (1958 = 100)	30	44	61	60	59

GENERAL MANUFACTURING STATISTICS, 1899-1989[89,91] (Cont.)										
DELAWARE*[a]										
Item No.	1947	1954	1958	1963	1967	1972	1977	1982	1987	1989*[d]
1.	483	556	569*[b]	569	528	567	619	632	676	---
2.	---	209	222	243*[b]	253	243	231	248	264	---
3.	34.7	54.5*[b]	57.8	58.4	70.7	69.1	66.5	67.9	66.6	67.9
4.	92.9	267.4*[b]	347.6	429.6	588.4	754.5	1,140.6	1,742.9	2,090.8	2,409.4
5.	29.3	31.0	30.0	30.4	38.8	37.7	32.3	31.7	32.8	31.4
6.	---	60.5	57.3	61.5	75.8	73.9	63.0	60.5	65.2	64.7
7.	70.6	104.9	125.2	159.0	228.1	304.4	409.9	557.0	760.0	792.6
8.	183.1	353.1	419.8	658.2	958.4	1,291.9	1,595.7	2,466.7	3,866.0	4,654.4
9.	---	23.4	27.9*[c]	88.8	115.9	91.5	148.2	322.1	276.9	335.2
10.	.24	.34	.36	.34	.37	.36	.34	.35	.35	.36
11.	60	94	100	101	122	120 104	115 100	117 102	115 100	117 102
12.	89	100	100	106	121	119 97	122 100	119 97	118 97	119 97

[a] There were a number of changes in the definition of manufacturing industries through the years that affect historical comparability. See the Glossary of Terms for these changes. The changes have not appreciably affected the comparability of the historical data except for the figures on the number of establishments.

[b] Data for central administrative offices and auxiliaries included for the first time for other states but this information was not collected in Alaska and Hawaii in 1954. See the Glossary of Terms.

[c] Item 9 (1958) includes expenditures for plants under construction but not in operation prior to 1958, the data represents expenditures at operating manufacturing establishments only. See Glossary of Terms.

[d] The Census Data for 1972, 1977, 1983 and 1987 are from manufacturing. Data for 1989 are estimates based on a representative sample of establishments canvassed annually and may differ from results of a complete canvass of all establishments.

GENERAL MANUFACTURING STATISTICS, 1899-1989[89,91]						
DISTRICT OF COLUMBIA[*a]						
Item No.		1899	1909	1919	1929	1939
1.	Total establishments[90,*a]	491	518	568	547	452
2.	With 20 employees or more[90]	---	---	---	---	---
3.	All employees, number (1,000)	7.1	9.3	13.3	14.0	14.4
4.	Payroll ($1,000,000)	3.9	6.8	18.5	25.4	24.9
5.	Production workers, total (number) (1,000)	6.2	7.7	10.3	9.8	7.7
6.	Man hours (1,000,000)	---	---	---	---	---
7.	Wages ($1,000,000)	3.0	5.0	13.0	11.5	11.5
8.	Value added by manufacture ($1,000,000)	9.0	15.0	37.4	52.8	43.4
9.	Capital expenditures, new ($1,000,000)	---	---	---	---	---
10.	Percent of U.S. Employment	.13	.14	.14	.15	.12
11.	Index of employment change (1958 = 100)	44	63	68	68	84
12.	U.S. index of employment change (1958 = 100)	30	44	61	60	59

GENERAL MANUFACTURING STATISTICS, 1899-1989[89,91] (Cont.)										
DISTRICT OF COLUMBIA*[a]										
Item No.	1947	1954	1958	1963	1967	1972	1977	1982	1987	1989*[d]
1.	428	484	561*[b]	617	593	564	555	514	488	---
2.	156	148	142	167*[b]	155	135	130	127	124	---
3.	17.8	20.7*[b]	21.3	22.1	23.1	19.4	18.6	16.7	17.0	14.4
4.	55.9	92.3*[b]	114.0	147.6	178.7	220.0	297.6	393.7	494.1	531.8
5.	10.0	11.8	11.2	11.3	11.7	9.4	7.5	6.4	5.2	4.3
6.	21.3	22.4	21.3	21.3	21.7	16.5	13.3	12.0	10.7	9.4
7.	27.7	44.7	52.8	64.7	77.4	96.7	102.3	125.3	118.8	113.3
8.	99.1	157.2	198.1	256.8	332.8	389.0	610.2	928.6	1,525.4	1,631.5
9.	4.5	6.5	14.7*[c]	13.0	17.0	18.9	18.1	55.1	43.6	44.1
10.	.13	.13	.13	.13	.12	.10	.10	.09	.09	.08
11.	97	100	100	104	108	91 104	87 100	78 90	80 91	68 77
12.	89	100	100	106	121	119 97	122 100	119 97	118 97	119 97

[a] There were a number of changes in the definition of manufacturing industries through the years that affect historical comparability. See the Glossary of Terms for these changes. The changes have not appreciably affected the comparability of the historical data except for the figures on the number of establishments.

[b] Data for central administrative offices and auxiliaries included for the first time for other states but this information was not collected in Alaska and Hawaii in 1954. See the Glossary of Terms.

[c] Item 9 (1958) includes expenditures for plants under construction but not in operation prior to 1958, the data represents expenditures at operating manufacturing establishments only. See Glossary of Terms.

[d] The Census Data for 1972, 1977, 1983 and 1987 are from manufacturing. Data for 1989 are estimates based on a representative sample of establishments canvassed annually and may differ from results of a complete canvass of all establishments.

GENERAL MANUFACTURING STATISTICS, 1899-1989[89,91]						
FLORIDA[*a,e]						
Item No.		1899	1909	1919	1929	1939
1.	Total establishments[90,*a]	---	1,275	2,503	2,212	1,976
2.	With 20 employees or more[90]	---	---	---	---	---
3.	All employees, number (1,000)	---	37.3	80.1	71.3	62.6
4.	Payroll ($1,000,000)	---	12.2	78.0	66.7	55.4
5.	Production workers, total (number) (1,000)	---	35.5	74.2	64.9	51.1
6.	Man hours (1,000,000)	---	---	---	---	---
7.	Wages ($1,000,000)	---	10.9	67.1	54.6	36.8
8.	Value added by manufacture ($1,000,000)	---	21.3	120.2	135.5	115.9
9.	Capital expenditures, new ($1,000,000)	---	---	---	---	---
10.	Percent of U.S. Employment	---	.77	.81	.74	.66
11.	Index of employment change (1958 = 100)	---	22	47	42	37
12.	U.S. index of employment change (1958 = 100)	---	30	61	60	59

GENERAL MANUFACTURING STATISTICS, 1899-1989[89,91] (Cont.)										
FLORIDA[*a]										
Item No.	1947	1954	1958	1963	1967	1972	1977	1982	1987	1989[*d]
1.	2,807	4,792	6,349[*b]	7,377	7,950	10,275	12,399	13,723	---	---
2.	755	1,065	1,526	1,826[*b]	2,186	2,893	2,915	3,599	---	---
3.	78.7	123.9[*b]	171.3	215.4	285.1	342.9	358.0	454.4	499.3	496.6
4.	168.8	389.3[*b]	680.5	1,102.3	1,754.7	2,750.3	4,133.1	7,773.2	10,954.0	11,880.9
5.	66.0	97.3	125.1	148.4	197.3	242.0	249.6	292.2	308.7	309.4
6.	139.9	198.5	247.8	301.3	399.8	481.5	485.2	566.6	614.7	611.9
7.	128.2	270.7	434.5	626.2	990.0	1,580.8	2,335.5	3,955.8	5,222.7	5,582.1
8.	350.0	797.7	1,410.8	2,352.0	3,682.7	5,786.8	9,255.1	18,111.8	27,574.2	28,844.4
9.	50.1	104.6	152.3	152.3	300.7	463.0	737.3	1,960.6	1,910.7	1,887.3
10.	.55	.77	1.07	1.07	1.48	1.80	1.83	2.37	2.63	2.61
11.	46	72	100	126[*e]	166	200 96	209 100	265 127	291 139	290 139
12.	89	100	100	100	121	119 97	122 100	119 97	118 97	119 97

[a] There were a number of changes in the definition of manufacturing industries through the years that affect historical comparability. See the Glossary of Terms for these changes. The changes have not appreciably affected the comparability of the historical data except for the figures on the number of establishments.

[b] Data for central administrative offices and auxiliaries included for the first time for other states but this information was not collected in Alaska and Hawaii in 1954. See the Glossary of Terms.

[c] Item 9 (1958) includes expenditures for plants under construction but not in operation prior to 1958, the data represents expenditures at operating manufacturing establishments only. See Glossary of Terms.

[d] The Census Data for 1972, 1977, 1983 and 1987 are from manufacturing. Data for 1989 are estimates based on a representative sample of establishments canvassed annually and may differ from results of a complete canvass of all establishments.

[e] Percentage computed by compiler from data herein is different from percentages given in source. The above percentage is the percentage computed by compiler.

GENERAL MANUFACTURING STATISTICS, 1899-1989[89,91]						
GEORGIA[*a]						
Item No.		1899	1909	1919	1929	1939
1.	Total establishments[90,*a]	3,015	4,792	4,608	4,179	3,055
2.	With 20 employees or more[90]	---	---	---	---	---
3.	All employees, number (1,000)	87.2	112.9	135.3	171.7	177.0
4.	Payroll ($1,000,000)	23.2	43.9	125.5	140.7	142.0
5.	Production workers, total (number) (1,000)	83.3	104.6	122.6	158.8	155.9
6.	Man hours (1,000,000)	---	---	---	---	---
7.	Wages ($1,000,000)	20.0	34.8	100.1	110.4	106.2
8.	Value added by manufacture ($1,000,000)	45.2	85.9	251.1	294.6	280.0
9.	Capital expenditures, new ($1,000,000)	---	---	---	---	---
10.	Percent of U.S. Employment	1.80	1.61	1.38	1.78	1.86
11.	Index of employment change (1958 = 100)	28	36	43	55	56
12.	U.S. index of employment change (1958 = 100)	30	44	61	60	39

GENERAL MANUFACTURING STATISTICS, 1899-1989[89,91] (Cont.)

GEORGIA[*a]

Item No.	1947	1954	1958	1963	1967	1972	1977	1982	1987	1989[*d]
1.	4,755	5,655	5,860[*b]	6,249	6,976	7,627	8,623	8,534	9,165	---
2.	---	1,713	1,844	2,056[*b]	2,268	2,663	2,906	3,148	3,509	---
3.	250.0	303.0[*b]	314.1	354.0	423.1	467.5	484.7	503.0	569.9	568.1
4.	484.3	853.5[*b]	1,075.0	1,505.6	2,231.2	3,336.0	5,124.5	7,905.7	11,933.1	12,794.5
5.	225.8	260.1	261.1	290.0	339.3	368.6	376.2	369.4	409.4	410.5
6.	---	503.5	500.3	582.4	684.6	737.5	740.6	705.0	820.1	830.5
7.	399.9	642.6	775.9	1073.0	1,522.2	2,242.8	3,404.4	4,863.9	7,239.9	7,638.2
8.	1,016.1	1,592.4	2,102.3	3,254.0	4,683.6	7,385.8	12,548.8	19,191.8	33,708.1	36,131.8
9.	---	162.8	169.9[*c]	202.2	423.3	688.9	1,143.4	1,921.7	2,471.5	2,727.4
10.	1.75	1.88	1.96	2.09	2.19	2.46	2.47	2.63	3.01	2.98
11.	80	96	100	113	135	149 96	154 100	160 104	181 118	181 117
12.	89	100	100	106	121	119 97	122 100	119 97	118 97	119 97

[a] There were a number of changes in the definition of manufacturing industries through the years that affect historical comparability. See the Glossary of Terms for these changes. The changes have not appreciably affected the comparability of the historical data except for the figures on the number of establishments.

[b] Data for central administrative offices and auxiliaries included for the first time for other states but this information was not collected in Alaska and Hawaii in 1954. See the Glossary of Terms.

[c] Item 9 (1958) includes expenditures for plants under construction but not in operation prior to 1958, the data represents expenditures at operating manufacturing establishments only. See Glossary of Terms.

[d] The Census Data for 1972, 1977, 1983 and 1987 are from manufacturing. Data for 1989 are estimates based on a representative sample of establishments canvassed annually and may differ from results of a complete canvass of all establishments.

GENERAL MANUFACTURING STATISTICS, 1899-1989[89,91]						
HAWAII[*a,e]						
Item No.		1899	1909	1919	1929	1939
1.	Total establishments[90,*a]	222	500	496	---	474
2.	With 20 employees or more[90]	---	---	---	---	---
3.	All employees, number (1,000)	4.4	7.6	11.7	---	19.5
4.	Payroll ($1,000,000)	2.0	2.8	8.7	---	15.3
5.	Production workers, total (number) (1,000)	3.7	5.9	10.0	---	17.0
6.	Man hours (1,000,000)	---	---	---	---	---
7.	Wages ($1,000,000)	1.5	2.1	6.6	---	11.5
8.	Value added by manufacture ($1,000,000)	11.1	21.6	51.9	---	58.4
9.	Capital expenditures, new ($1,000,000)	---	---	---	---	---
10.	Percent of U.S. Employment	.09	.11	.12	---	.14
11.	Index of employment change (1958 = 100)	18	32	42	---	82
12.	U.S. index of employment change (1958 = 100)	30	44	61	---	59

GENERAL MANUFACTURING STATISTICS, 1899-1989[89,91] (Cont.)										
HAWAII*[a]										
Item No.	1947	1954	1958	1963	1967	1972	1977	1982	1987	1989*[d]
1.	---	520	618*[e]	672	697	773	949	966	1,020	---
2.	---	137	179	203*[e]	215	238	231	237	223	---
3.	---	24.4*[b]	23.9	25.1	25.4	24.8	25.0	23.6	22.2	20.5
4.	---	77.1*[b]	82.2	109.0	139.6	191.1	276.8	360.3	440.2	432.6
5.	---	19.5	17.8	18.7	19.0	17.7	17.4	16.0	15.2	13.0
6.	---	36.1	31.9	33.2	35.9	33.1	31.3	29.9	28.8	25.2
7.	---	50.8	51.8	67.5	86.9	113.7	160.5	217.5	254.2	244.2
8.	---	140.3	164.9	261.1	326.2	410.0	785.5	1,119.6	1,405.3	1,609.8
9.	---	11.7	17.2*[c]	15.4	26.0	46.7	44.4	89.4	102.0	98.4
10.	---	.15	.15	.15	.13	.13	.13	.12	.12	.11
11.	---	102	100	105	106	99	100	94	89	82
12.	---	100	100	106	121	97	100	97	97	97

[a] There were a number of changes in the definition of manufacturing industries through the years that affect historical comparability. See the Glossary of Terms for these changes. The changes have not appreciably affected the comparability of the historical data except for the figures on the number of establishments.

[b] Data for central administrative offices and auxiliaries included for the first time for other states but this information was not collected in Alaska and Hawaii in 1954. See the Glossary of Terms.

[c] Item 9 (1958) includes expenditures for plants under construction but not in operation prior to 1958, the data represents expenditures at operating manufacturing establishments only. See Glossary of Terms.

[d] The Census Data for 1972, 1977, 1983 and 1987 are from manufacturing. Data for 1989 are estimates based on a representative sample of establishments canvassed annually and may differ from results of a complete canvass of all establishments.

[e] Data for central administrative offices and auxiliaries included for the first time. See the Glossary of Terms.

GENERAL MANUFACTURING STATISTICS, 1899-1989[89,91]						
IDAHO[*a]						
Item No.		1899	1909	1919	1929	1939
1.	Total establishments[90,*a]	287	725	803	562	498
2.	With 20 employees or more[90]	---	---	---	---	---
3.	All employees, number (1,000)	1.6	9.1	15.0	17.0	11.7
4.	Payroll ($1,000,000)	.9	6.5	20.6	25.5	14.7
5.	Production workers, total (number) (1,000)	1.6	8.2	13.6	15.6	9.9
6.	Man hours (1,000,000)	---	---	---	---	---
7.	Wages ($1,000,000)	.8	5.5	18.0	22.5	11.5
8.	Value added by manufacture ($1,000,000)	1.6	12.5	35.7	44.5	29.8
9.	Capital expenditures, new ($1,000,000)	---	---	---	---	---
10.	Percent of U.S. Employment	.03	.13	.15	.18	.12
11.	Index of employment change (1958 = 100)	6	33	54	62	42
12.	U.S. index of employment change (1958 = 100)	30	44	61	60	59

GENERAL MANUFACTURING STATISTICS, 1899-1989[89,91] (Cont.)										
IDAHO[*a]										
Item No.	1947	1954	1958	1963	1967	1972	1977	1982	1987	1989[*d]
1.	664	981	1,065[*b]	1,103	1,131	1,190	1,495	1,404	1,496	---
2.	173	204	244	254[*b]	303	350	379	354	372	---
3.	16.9	24.2[*b]	27.6	30.5	37.1	43.0	51.6	47.6	52.9	58.1
4.	45.7	94.2[*b]	128.1	162.6	219.9	339.9	625.2	864.8	1,148.5	1,385.7
5.	14.6	20.1	22.1	24.1	29.0	34.3	39.8	34.0	38.3	43.3
6.	31.4	39.3	43.0	48.5	56.9	66.0	76.5	62.6	72.4	80.8
7.	37.9	73.2	96.5	116.6	157.0	244.6	431.9	545.2	698.3	869.7
8.	109.7	188.6	255.8	366.4	503.4	820.8	1,430.0	2,076.5	3,057.0	4,156.3
9.	11.4	19.2	19.2[*c]	28.4	57.7	74.9	158.7	147.3	234.8	341.9
10.	.12	.15	.17	.18	.19	.23	.26	.25	.28	.31
11.	61	88	100	111	134	156 83	187 100	172 92	192 103	211 113
12.	89	100	100	106	121	119 97	122 100	119 97	118 97	119 97

[a] There were a number of changes in the definition of manufacturing industries through the years that affect historical comparability. See the Glossary of Terms for these changes. The changes have not appreciably affected the comparability of the historical data except for the figures on the number of establishments.

[b] Data for central administrative offices and auxiliaries included for the first time for other states but this information was not collected in Alaska and Hawaii in 1954. See the Glossary of Terms.

[c] Item 9 (1958) includes expenditures for plants under construction but not in operation prior to 1958, the data represents expenditures at operating manufacturing establishments only. See Glossary of Terms.

[d] The Census Data for 1972, 1977, 1983 and 1987 are from manufacturing. Data for 1989 are estimates based on a representative sample of establishments canvassed annually and may differ from results of a complete canvass of all establishments.

GENERAL MANUFACTURING STATISTICS, 1899-1989[89,91]						
ILLINOIS[*a]						
Item No.		1899	1909	1919	1929	1939
1.	Total establishments[90,*a]	14,374	18,026	17,808	15,333	11,983
2.	With 20 employees or more[90]	---	---	---	---	---
3.	All employees, number (1,000)	373.8	543.7	785.9	827.5	752.7
4.	Payroll ($1,000,000)	199.7	364.8	1,071.0	1,393.6	1,107.6
5.	Production workers, total (number) (1,000)	332.9	465.8	650.0	691.6	591.0
6.	Man hours (1,000,000)	---	---	---	---	---
7.	Wages ($1,000,000)	159.1	273.3	797.1	1,024.9	742.5
8.	Value added by manufacture ($1,000,000)	439.4	758.4	1,929.1	2,930.0	2,187.2
9.	Capital expenditures, new ($1,000,000)	---	---	---	---	---
10.	Percent of U.S. Employment	7.71	7.75	8.00	7.65	8.68
11.	Index of employment change (1958 = 100)	32	46	67	70	63
12.	U.S. index of employment change (1958 = 100)	30	44	61	60	59

GENERAL MANUFACTURING STATISTICS, 1899-1989[89,91] (Cont.)										
ILLINOIS[*a]										
Item No.	1947	1954	1958	1963	1967	1972	1977	1982	1987	1989[*d]
1.	15,993	17,628	18,468[*b]	18,593	18,536	18,617	19,517	18,618	18,373	---
2.	---	6,377	6,586	6,974[*b]	7,477	7,345	7,441	7,102	7,169	---
3.	1,186.1	1,222.4[*b]	1,189.9	1,211.2	1,397.3	1,306.1	1,286.2	1,068.7	989.6	1,033.4
4.	3,589.4	5,420.9[*b]	6,224.8	7,560.6	10,013.9	12,801.1	18,740.8	22,680.9	26,234.7	29,915.7
5.	955.1	903.0	835.2	855.9	995.1	901.0	857.8	669.6	609.3	638.8
6.	---	1,787.7	1,631.8	1,717.0	1,978.8	1,780.3	1,676.7	1,256.4	1,227.5	1,295.4
7.	2,628.6	3,518.6	3,833.5	4,655.4	6,180.0	7,614.9	10,756.5	11,931.4	13,401.4	14,942.1
8.	6,683.1	9,663.8	11,664.1	14,641.5	20,016.5	25,848.9	40,279.1	47,704.6	63,350.1	70,015.7
9.	---	551.7	730.7[*c]	775.6	1,493.4	1,564.1	2,661.5	3,372.3	4,425.8	5,454.7
10.	5.27	7.59	7.42	7.14	7.23	6.86	6.56	5.60	5.22	5.43
11.	100	103	100	102	117	110 102	108 100	90 83	83 77	87 80
12.	89	100	100	106	121	119 97	122 100	119 97	118 97	119 97

[a] There were a number of changes in the definition of manufacturing industries through the years that affect historical comparability. See the Glossary of Terms for these changes. The changes have not appreciably affected the comparability of the historical data except for the figures on the number of establishments.

[b] Data for central administrative offices and auxiliaries included for the first time for other states but this information was not collected in Alaska and Hawaii in 1954. See the Glossary of Terms.

[c] Item 9 (1958) includes expenditures for plants under construction but not in operation prior to 1958, the data represents expenditures at operating manufacturing establishments only. See Glossary of Terms.

[d] The Census Data for 1972, 1977, 1983 and 1987 are from manufacturing. Data for 1989 are estimates based on a representative sample of establishments canvassed annually and may differ from results of a complete canvass of all establishments.

GENERAL MANUFACTURING STATISTICS, 1899-1989[89,91]						
INDIANA[*a]						
Item No.		1899	1909	1919	1929	1939
1.	Total establishments[90,*a]	7,128	7,969	7,558	5,091	4,192
2.	With 20 employees or more[90]	---	---	---	---	---
3.	All employees, number (1,000)	149.5	210.6	332.4	359.9	337.9
4.	Payroll ($1,000,000)	69.3	121.8	400.9	534.2	474.1
5.	Production workers, total (number) (1,000)	139.0	187.0	276.7	314.7	275.3
6.	Man hours (1,000,000)	---	---	---	---	---
7.	Wages ($1,000,000)	59.3	95.5	316.0	418.8	342.7
8.	Value added by manufacture ($1,000,000)	141.9	244.7	721.7	1,136.5	964.7
9.	Capital expenditures, new ($1,000,000)	---	---	---	---	---
10.	Percent of U.S. Employment	3.08	3.00	3.38	3.73	3.55
11.	Index of employment change (1958 = 100)	27	38	60	65	61
12.	U.S. index of employment change (1958 = 100)	30	44	61	60	59

GENERAL MANUFACTURING STATISTICS, 1899-1989[89,91] (Cont.)

INDIANA[*a]

Item No.	1947	1954	1958	1963	1967	1972	1977	1982	1987	1989[*d]
1.	5,403	6,355	6,612[*b]	6,860	6,920	7,354	8,061	7,960	8,631	---
2.	---	2,344	2,444	2,547[*b]	2,917	3,049	3,229	3,184	3,609	---
3.	548.3	588.4[*b]	551.0	609.8	710.2	703.9	705.9	585.1	602.0	626.6
4.	1,582.8	2,533.4[*b]	2,874.7	3,794.3	5,023.2	6,881.5	10,438.9	12,559.3	15,756.5	17,431.8
5.	457.5	458.9	407.5	463.1	543.6	526.1	521.9	406.0	426.7	448.0
6.	---	904.1	796.0	937.2	1,078.1	1,041.7	1,024.8	759.1	858.9	895.9
7.	1,232.2	1,798.8	1,912.8	2,622.1	3,453.5	4,640.8	7,046.5	7,821.4	9,874.1	10,915.7
8.	2,970.0	4,632.0	5,502.1	7,726.9	10,308.0	14,111.6	22,717.6	25,747.0	39,278.8	44,963.4
9.	---	301.5	515.3[*c]	555.2	1,004.4	907.3	2,078.0	2,232.7	3,363.9	4,004.2
10.	3.83	3.65	3.44	3.60	3.68	3.70	3.60	3.06	3.18	3.29
11.	99	106	100	111	129	128 100	128 100	106 83	109 85	114 89
12.	89	100	100	106	121	119 97	122 100	119 97	118 97	119 97

[a] There were a number of changes in the definition of manufacturing industries through the years that affect historical comparability. See the Glossary of Terms for these changes. The changes have not appreciably affected the comparability of the historical data except for the figures on the number of establishments.

[b] Data for central administrative offices and auxiliaries included for the first time for other states but this information was not collected in Alaska and Hawaii in 1954. See the Glossary of Terms.

[c] Item 9 (1958) includes expenditures for plants under construction but not in operation prior to 1958, the data represents expenditures at operating manufacturing establishments only. See Glossary of Terms.

[d] The Census Data for 1972, 1977, 1983 and 1987 are from manufacturing. Data for 1989 are estimates based on a representative sample of establishments canvassed annually and may differ from results of a complete canvass of all establishments.

GENERAL MANUFACTURING STATISTICS, 1899-1989[89,91]						
IOWA[*a]						
Item No.		1899	1909	1919	1929	1939
1.	Total establishments[90,*a]	4,828	5,528	5,104	3,317	2,541
2.	With 20 employees or more[90]	---	---	---	---	---
3.	All employees, number (1,000)	49.6	73.0	98.5	97.4	88.1
4.	Payroll ($1,000,000)	22.3	43.5	122.2	137.2	114.1
5.	Production workers, total (number) (1,000)	44.4	61.6	79.2	81.7	64.8
6.	Man hours (1,000,000)	---	---	---	---	---
7.	Wages ($1,000,000)	18.0	32.5	88.4	102.3	72.9
8.	Value added by manufacture ($1,000,000)	47.1	88.5	221.8	323.8	243.4
9.	Capital expenditures, new ($1,000,000)	---	---	---	---	---
10.	Percent of U.S. Employment	1.02	1.04	1.00	1.01	.92
11.	Index of employment change (1958 = 100)	30	44	59	59	53
12.	U.S. index of employment change (1958 = 100)	30	44	61	60	59

GENERAL MANUFACTURING STATISTICS, 1899-1989[89,91] (Cont.)										
IOWA*[a]										
Item No.	1947	1954	1958	1963	1967	1972	1977	1982	1987	1989*[d]
1.	2,963	3,320	3,596*[b]	3,496	3,388	3,387	3,783	3,598	3,566	---
2.	---	881	945	982*[b]	1,092	1,170	1,245	1,223	1,258	---
3.	140.4	163.7*[b]	166.1	178.2	210.1	215.5	240.3	212.8	206.1	225.3
4.	372.3	648.4*[b]	812.5	1,046.7	1,434.6	2,038.8	3,382.5	4,403.2	4,971.1	5,764.3
5.	112.5	122.8	120.7	126.9	154.0	157.0	170.6	140.0	140.1	155.7
6.	---	248.7	241.0	256.4	310.0	311.2	331.7	259.2	277.5	310.0
7.	275.4	443.6	537.7	687.0	946.1	1,355.0	2,191.3	2,648.8	3,043.4	3,517.4
8.	671.0	1,236.0	1,684.3	2,287.0	3,250.9	4,757.7	8,684.4	12,077.9	14,469.0	18,029.1
9.	---	73.4	103.2*[c]	127.0	230.7	329.4	677.8	688.6	834.2	1,109.0
10.	.98	1.02	1.04	1.05	1.09	1.13	1.23	1.11	1.09	1.18
11.	85	99	100	107	126	130 90	145 100	128 89	124 86	136 94
12.	89	100	100	106	121	119 97	122 100	119 97	118 97	119 97

[a] There were a number of changes in the definition of manufacturing industries through the years that affect historical comparability. See the Glossary of Terms for these changes. The changes have not appreciably affected the comparability of the historical data except for the figures on the number of establishments.

[b] Data for central administrative offices and auxiliaries included for the first time for other states but this information was not collected in Alaska and Hawaii in 1954. See the Glossary of Terms.

[c] Item 9 (1958) includes expenditures for plants under construction but not in operation prior to 1958, the data represents expenditures at operating manufacturing establishments only. See Glossary of Terms.

[d] The Census Data for 1972, 1977, 1983 and 1987 are from manufacturing. Data for 1989 are estimates based on a representative sample of establishments canvassed annually and may differ from results of a complete canvass of all establishments.

GENERAL MANUFACTURING STATISTICS, 1899-1989[89,91]						
KANSAS[*a]						
Item No.		1899	1909	1919	1929	1939
1.	Total establishments[90,*a]	2,299	3,435	3,149	1,916	1,418
2.	With 20 employees or more[90]	---	---	---	---	---
3.	All employees, number (1,000)	30.7	51.1	72.5	57.3	42.6
4.	Payroll ($1,000,000)	15.9	33.3	93.6	85.2	56.4
5.	Production workers, total (number) (1,000)	27.1	44.2	60.2	47.4	30.9
6.	Man hours (1,000,000)	---	---	---	---	---
7.	Wages ($1,000,000)	12.8	25.9	71.8	63.3	36.1
8.	Value added by manufacture ($1,000,000)	33.3	66.2	161.6	205.4	117.4
9.	Capital expenditures, new ($1,000,000)	---	---	---	---	---
10.	Percent of U.S. Employment	.63	.73	.74	.59	.45
11.	Index of employment change (1958 = 100)	26	43	61	48	36
12.	U.S. index of employment change (1958 = 100)	30	44	61	60	59

GENERAL MANUFACTURING STATISTICS, 1899-1989[89,91] (Cont.)										
KANSAS*[a]										
Item No.	1947	1954	1958	1963	1967	1972	1977	1982	1987	1989*[d]
1.	1,946	2,139	2,309*[b]	2,475	2,551	2,839	3,270	3,235	3,269	---
2.	---	572	643	696*[b]	812	957	1,037	1,103	1,137	---
3.	74.6	131.4*[b]	118.8	114.3	143.8	137.0	168.1	170.6	189.1	188.7
4.	204.8	560.5*[b]	590.8	684.4	964.8	1,181.1	2,114.8	3,322.8	4,597.2	4,798.6
5.	59.4	98.2	86.6	84.6	106.5	101.3	121.6	112.8	120.7	124.0
6.	---	203.1	173.9	176.9	218.1	202.5	241.5	217.9	245.3	248.5
7.	151.3	400.6	403.7	463.2	655.4	782.8	1,370.8	1,957.8	2,608.5	2,763.4
8.	461.1	2,049.3	1,171.0	1,461.6	2,112.4	2,915.4	5,337.8	8,436.5	12,908.8	12,660.8
9.	---	53.0	99.0*[c]	106.3	155.9	199.2	345.4	613.3	1,011.2	783.8
10.	.52	.82	.74	.67	.74	.71	.85	.89	1.00	.99
11.	63	111	100	96	121	115 81	141 100	144 101	159 112	159 112
12.	89	100	100	106	121	119 97	122 100	119 97	118 97	119 97

[a] There were a number of changes in the definition of manufacturing industries through the years that affect historical comparability. See the Glossary of Terms for these changes. The changes have not appreciably affected the comparability of the historical data except for the figures on the number of establishments.

[b] Data for central administrative offices and auxiliaries included for the first time for other states but this information was not collected in Alaska and Hawaii in 1954. See the Glossary of Terms.

[c] Item 9 (1958) includes expenditures for plants under construction but not in operation prior to 1958, the data represents expenditures at operating manufacturing establishments only. See Glossary of Terms.

[d] The Census Data for 1972, 1977, 1983 and 1987 are from manufacturing. Data for 1989 are estimates based on a representative sample of establishments canvassed annually and may differ from results of a complete canvass of all establishments.

GENERAL MANUFACTURING STATISTICS, 1899-1989[89,91]						
KENTUCKY[*a]						
Item No.		1899	1909	1919	1929	1939
1.	Total establishments[90,*a]	3,648	4,776	3,767	2,246	1,582
2.	With 20 employees or more[90]	---	---	---	---	---
3.	All employees, number (1,000)	56.1	74.0	79.3	88.6	76.5
4.	Payroll ($1,000,000)	22.6	37.5	85.8	113.6	89.0
5.	Production workers, total (number) (1,000)	51.7	65.4	68.7	77.8	62.5
6.	Man hours (1,000,000)	---	---	---	---	---
7.	Wages ($1,000,000)	18.5	27.8	66.3	88.6	61.6
8.	Value added by manufacture ($1,000,000)	59.1	112.0	158.5	236.1	186.5
9.	Capital expenditures, new ($1,000,000)	---	---	---	---	---
10.	Percent of U.S. Employment	1.16	1.06	.81	.92	.82
11.	Index of employment change (1958 = 100)	35	46	49	55	47
12.	U.S. index of employment change (1958 = 100)	30	44	61	60	59

GENERAL MANUFACTURING STATISTICS, 1899-1989[89,91] (Cont.)										
KENTUCKY[*a]										
Item No.	1947	1954	1958	1963	1967	1972	1977	1982	1987	1989[*d]
1.	2,245	2,651	2,903[*b]	2,946	2,994	3,167	3,548	3,502	3,688	---
2.	---	851	927	1,025[*b]	1,135	1,259	1,318	1,354	1,511	---
3.	129.6	151.1[*b]	162.2	180.5	224.6	258.7	277.5	246.6	251.6	270.4
4.	304.8	553.2[*b]	721.4	959.0	1,351.9	2,160.0	3,452.2	4,638.8	5,865.2	6,638.4
5.	110.6	119.2	124.7	140.5	175.6	200.4	209.0	173.8	184.8	200.3
6.	---	233.7	241.7	280.4	344.5	392.9	399.5	319.7	356.2	388.2
7.	236.1	383.9	491.8	657.4	926.7	1,479.8	2,302.5	2,874.0	3,752.3	4,163.7
8.	743.3	1,236.2	1,769.3	2,548.5	3,636.0	5,682.1	9,545.7	11,819.7	18,091.7	22,049.4
9.	---	124.0	112.5[*c]	223.6	338.3	380.0	715.9	996.8	1,746.0	1,861.5
10.	.91	.94	1.01	1.06	1.16	1.36	1.42	1.29	1.33	1.42
11.	80	93	100	111	138	159 93	171 100	152 89	155 91	167 97
12.	89	100	100	106	121	119 97	122 100	119 97	118 97	119 97

[a] There were a number of changes in the definition of manufacturing industries through the years that affect historical comparability. See the Glossary of Terms for these changes. The changes have not appreciably affected the comparability of the historical data except for the figures on the number of establishments.

[b] Data for central administrative offices and auxiliaries included for the first time for other states but this information was not collected in Alaska and Hawaii in 1954. See the Glossary of Terms.

[c] Item 9 (1958) includes expenditures for plants under construction but not in operation prior to 1958, the data represents expenditures at operating manufacturing establishments only. See Glossary of Terms.

[d] The Census Data for 1972, 1977, 1983 and 1987 are from manufacturing. Data for 1989 are estimates based on a representative sample of establishments canvassed annually and may differ from results of a complete canvass of all establishments.

GENERAL MANUFACTURING STATISTICS, 1899-1989[89,91]						
LOUISIANA[*a]						
Item No.		1899	1909	1919	1929	1939
1.	Total establishments[90,*a]	1,826	2,516	2,489	1,989	1,779
2.	With 20 employees or more[90]	---	---	---	---	---
3.	All employees, number (1,000)	44.5	84.2	109.8	97.6	87.8
4.	Payroll ($1,000,000)	17.7	42.4	116.7	108.0	85.3
5.	Production workers, total (number) (1,000)	40.9	76.2	97.7	87.3	70.5
6.	Man hours (1,000,000)	---	---	---	---	---
7.	Wages ($1,000,000)	14.7	33.4	93.9	83.7	54.5
8.	Value added by manufacture ($1,000,000)	36.0	89.1	243.9	246.5	198.5
9.	Capital expenditures, new ($1,000,000)	---	---	---	---	---
10.	Percent of U.S. Employment	0.92	1.20	1.21	1.01	.92
11.	Index of employment change (1958 = 100)	32	62	80	71	64
12.	U.S. index of employment change (1958 = 100)	30	44	61	60	59

GENERAL MANUFACTURING STATISTICS, 1899-1989[89,91] (Cont.)										
LOUISIANA[*a]										
Item No.	1947	1954	1958	1963	1967	1972	1977	1982	1987	1989[*d]
1.	2,388	3,020	3,156[*b]	3,222	3,639	3,651	4,276	4,107	3,806	---
2.	949	897	935	954[*b]	1,016	1,133	1,236	1,335	1,104	---
3.	132.5	145.2[*b]	136.9	139.5	164.5	179.4	194.8	202.0	161.4	166.5
4.	309.9	533.9[*b]	621.4	769.4	1,084.4	1,601.4	2,682.7	4,304.1	4,175.9	4,502.6
5.	111.6	114.4	103.5	104.7	120.8	134.3	145.2	142.4	110.8	118.3
6.	231.4	232.0	205.7	215.4	250.6	274.6	292.0	281.0	224.9	246.7
7.	229.7	375.7	426.3	526.2	712.2	1,072.1	1,798.9	2,730.6	2,587.8	2,847.6
8.	694.1	1,181.6	1,429.6	1,915.6	2,790.3	4,273.4	9,418.3	11,754.6	16,425.8	21,171.8
9.	97.2	174.4	173.4[*c]	210.8	741.4	568.2	2,072.8	2,561.9	1,419.8	2,168.8
10.	.93	.90	.85	.82	.85	.94	.99	1.06	.85	.87
11.	97	106	100	102	120	131 92	142 100	148 104	118 83	122 85
12.	89	100	100	106	121	119 97	122 100	119 97	118 97	119 97

[a] There were a number of changes in the definition of manufacturing industries through the years that affect historical comparability. See the Glossary of Terms for these changes. The changes have not appreciably affected the comparability of the historical data except for the figures on the number of establishments.

[b] Data for central administrative offices and auxiliaries included for the first time for other states but this information was not collected in Alaska and Hawaii in 1954. See the Glossary of Terms.

[c] Item 9 (1958) includes expenditures for plants under construction but not in operation prior to 1958, the data represents expenditures at operating manufacturing establishments only. See Glossary of Terms.

[d] The Census Data for 1972, 1977, 1983 and 1987 are from manufacturing. Data for 1989 are estimates based on a representative sample of establishments canvassed annually and may differ from results of a complete canvass of all establishments.

GENERAL MANUFACTURING STATISTICS, 1899-1989[89,91]						
MAINE[*a]						
Item No.		1899	1909	1919	1929	1939
1.	Total establishments[90,*a]	2,878	3,546	2,834	1,568	1,118
2.	With 20 employees or more[90]	---	---	---	---	---
3.	All employees, number (1,000)	73.0	84.8	96.1	76.8	82.2
4.	Payroll ($1,000,000)	28.8	43.4	111.2	90.3	83.5
5.	Production workers, total (number) (1,000)	69.9	80.0	88.3	70.2	74.0
6.	Man hours (1,000,000)	---	---	---	---	---
7.	Wages ($1,000,000)	25.7	37.6	93.8	74.2	67.3
8.	Value added by manufacture ($1,000,000)	51.7	78.9	201.4	174.4	150.6
9.	Capital expenditures, new ($1,000,000)	---	---	---	---	---
10.	Percent of U.S. Employment	1.51	1.21	.98	.80	.86
11.	Index of employment change (1958 = 100)	74	86	98	78	84
12.	U.S. index of employment change (1958 = 100)	30	44	61	60	59

GENERAL MANUFACTURING STATISTICS, 1899-1989[89,91] (Cont.)										
MAINE*[a]										
Item No.	1947	1954	1958	1963	1967	1972	1977	1982	1987	1989*[d]
1.	1,633	3,015	2,755*[b]	2,535	2,385	2,075	2,157	2,009	2,167	---
2.	---	627	579	594*[b]	615	590	595	616	600	---
3.	100.1	104.5*[b]	98.3	99.9	110.8	100.0	102.8	110.2	101.6	106.4
4.	233.9	325.0*[b]	377.2	438.6	577.2	699.4	1077.6	1,774.9	2,192.1	2,480.2
5.	90.3	91.1	83.7	84.1	93.6	82.6	84.2	86.4	77.4	79.3
6.	---	180.7	166.2	170.1	186.6	162.2	163.6	165.8	151.3	159.3
7.	199.1	260.0	285.2	335.1	437.3	512.9	781.0	1,236.8	1,457.0	1,621.2
8.	429.5	565.3	628.3	785.7	1,069.5	1,383.4	2,343.0	4,037.8	5,270.6	6,152.8
9.	---	58.9	44.3*[c]	62.5	98.8	138.9	222.9	510.3	539.4	954.9
10.	.70	.64	.61	.59	.57	.53	.52	.58	.54	.56
11.	102	106	100	102	113	102 97	105 100	112 107	103 99	108 104
12.	89	100	100	106	121	119 97	122 100	119 97	118 97	119 97

[a] There were a number of changes in the definition of manufacturing industries through the years that affect historical comparability. See the Glossary of Terms for these changes. The changes have not appreciably affected the comparability of the historical data except for the figures on the number of establishments.

[b] Data for central administrative offices and auxiliaries included for the first time for other states but this information was not collected in Alaska and Hawaii in 1954. See the Glossary of Terms.

[c] Item 9 (1958) includes expenditures for plants under construction but not in operation prior to 1958, the data represents expenditures at operating manufacturing establishments only. See Glossary of Terms.

[d] The Census Data for 1972, 1977, 1983 and 1987 are from manufacturing. Data for 1989 are estimates based on a representative sample of establishments canvassed annually and may differ from results of a complete canvass of all establishments.

GENERAL MANUFACTURING STATISTICS, 1899-1989[89,91]						
MARYLAND[*a]						
Item No.		1899	1909	1919	1929	1939
1.	Total establishments[90,*a]	3,886	4,837	4,725	3,231	2,712
2.	With 20 employees or more[90]	---	---	---	---	---
3.	All employees, number (1,000)	100.9	120.1	159.4	150.9	166.1
4.	Payroll ($1,000,000)	39.3	59.1	188.2	195.0	209.2
5.	Production workers, total (number) (1,000)	94.2	107.9	139.2	131.1	140.9
6.	Man hours (1,000,000)	---	---	---	---	---
7.	Wages ($1,000,000)	32.4	45.4	146.6	148.8	155.9
8.	Value added by manufacture ($1,000,000)	81.7	116.6	322.1	422.1	420.6
9.	Capital expenditures, new ($1,000,000)	---	---	---	---	---
10.	Percent of U.S. Employment	2.08	1.71	1.62	1.56	1.74
11.	Index of employment change (1958 = 100)	39	46	62	58	64
12.	U.S. index of employment change (1958 = 100)	30	44	61	60	59

GENERAL MANUFACTURING STATISTICS, 1899-1989[89,91] (Cont.)										
MARYLAND*[a]										
Item No.	1947	1954	1958	1963	1967	1972	1977	1982	1987	1989*[d]
1.	2,826	3,253	3,435*[b]	3,519	3,401	3,579	3,937	3,883	4,250	---
2.	---	1,279	1,334	1,394*[b]	1,463	1,437	1,351	1,382	1,476	---
3.	228.7	255.4*[b]	259.1	263.7	287.6	255.6	243.2	234.4	230.4	226.2
4.	612.3	1,002.0*[b]	1,257.4	1,549.8	1,956.0	2,386.3	3,419.5	4,859.3	5,955.7	6,400.7
5.	188.7	195.9	190.5	188.9	205.4	175.7	162.9	145.9	139.6	134.5
6.	---	384.2	368.5	375.9	405.6	345.7	311.6	270.6	273.5	267.0
7.	458.3	675.1	813.3	960.5	1,208.5	1,427.8	1,976.0	2,550.8	2,994.3	3,146.4
8.	1,139.2	1,888.6	2,394.4	3,017.2	3,781.3	4,706.9	7,115.6	10,133.8	14,020.0	15,892.0
9.	---	93.9	128.1*[c]	176.3	251.6	310.2	513.8	718.1	875.2	1,230.2
10.	1.60	1.59	1.62	1.55	1.49	1.34	1.24	1.23	1.22	1.19
11.	88	99	100	102	111	99 105	94 100	90 96	89 95	87 93
12.	89	100	100	106	121	119 97	122 100	119 97	118 97	119 97

[a] There were a number of changes in the definition of manufacturing industries through the years that affect historical comparability. See the Glossary of Terms for these changes. The changes have not appreciably affected the comparability of the historical data except for the figures on the number of establishments.

[b] Data for central administrative offices and auxiliaries included for the first time for other states but this information was not collected in Alaska and Hawaii in 1954. See the Glossary of Terms.

[c] Item 9 (1958) includes expenditures for plants under construction but not in operation prior to 1958, the data represents expenditures at operating manufacturing establishments only. See Glossary of Terms.

[d] The Census Data for 1972, 1977, 1983 and 1987 are from manufacturing. Data for 1989 are estimates based on a representative sample of establishments canvassed annually and may differ from results of a complete canvass of all establishments.

GENERAL MANUFACTURING STATISTICS, 1899-1989[89,91]						
MASSACHUSETTS[*a]						
Item No.		1899	1909	1919	1929	1939
1.	Total establishments[90,*a]	10,929	11,684	11,627	9,872	8,444
2.	With 20 employees or more[90]	---	---	---	---	---
3.	All employees, number (1,000)	463.5	633.2	801.3	639.2	549.6
4.	Payroll ($1,000,000)	224.8	364.5	947.8	910.1	702.5
5.	Production workers, total (number) (1,000)	438.2	584.6	712.3	557.5	458.4
6.	Man hours (1,000,000)	---	---	---	---	---
7.	Wages ($1,000,000)	195.3	301.2	764.6	694.8	498.2
8.	Value added by manufacture ($1,000,000)	409.0	659.8	1,746.5	1,710.7	1,181.5
9.	Capital expenditures, new ($1,000,000)	---	---	---	---	---
10.	Percent of U.S. Employment	9.56	9.03	8.15	6.62	5.77
11.	Index of employment change (1958 = 100)	68	93	118	94	81
12.	U.S. index of employment change (1958 = 100)	30	44	61	60	59

GENERAL MANUFACTURING STATISTICS, 1899-1989[89,91] (Cont.)										
MASSACHUSETTS[*a]										
Item No.	1947	1954	1958	1963	1967	1972	1977	1982	1987	1989[*d]
1.	10,509	11,205	11,565[*b]	11,311	10,963	10,770	11,133	11,017	11,023	---
2.	---	4,229	4,377	4,351[*b]	4,471	4,471	4,054	4,290	4,196	---
3.	718.1	685.4[*b]	680.6	674.0	713.6	618.9	613.4	643.4	591.3	561.5
4.	1,920.7	2,575.6[*b]	3,070.8	3,712.4	4,646.3	5,486.0	7,818.8	12,353.1	15,211.3	16,318.7
5.	601.4	536.5	498.1	480.7	507.9	416.0	407.9	397.0	348.3	324.3
6.	---	1,047.4	968.7	948.3	999.0	812.1	791.9	765.2	690.5	641.9
7.	1,463.1	1,769.1	1,932.0	2,234.6	2,755.3	3,027.0	4,199.2	6,000.6	7,018.9	7,315.5
8.	3,356.3	4,356.5	5,128.5	6,403.8	8,715.0	10,677.5	16,348.6	25,967.5	35,769.7	37,133.4
9.	---	180.7	228.5[*c]	273.0	493.7	537.5	952.8	1,667.3	2,169.0	2,022.0
10.	5.02	4.25	4.25	3.97	3.69	3.25	3.13	3.36	3.12	2.95
11.	106	101	100	99	105	91 101	90 100	95 105	87 96	83 92
12.	89	100	100	106	121	119 97	122 100	119 97	118 97	119 97

[a] There were a number of changes in the definition of manufacturing industries through the years that affect historical comparability. See the Glossary of Terms for these changes. The changes have not appreciably affected the comparability of the historical data except for the figures on the number of establishments.

[b] Data for central administrative offices and auxiliaries included for the first time for other states but this information was not collected in Alaska and Hawaii in 1954. See the Glossary of Terms.

[c] Item 9 (1958) includes expenditures for plants under construction but not in operation prior to 1958, the data represents expenditures at operating manufacturing establishments only. See Glossary of Terms.

[d] The Census Data for 1972, 1977, 1983 and 1987 are from manufacturing. Data for 1989 are estimates based on a representative sample of establishments canvassed annually and may differ from results of a complete canvass of all establishments.

GENERAL MANUFACTURING STATISTICS, 1899-1989[89,91]						
MICHIGAN[*a]						
Item No.		1899	1909	1919	1929	1939
1.	Total establishments[90,*a]	7,310	9,159	8,046	6,686	5,961
2.	With 20 employees or more[90]	---	---	---	---	---
3.	All employees, number (1,000)	169.2	262.1	541.2	599.2	618.7
4.	Payroll ($1,000,000)	74.9	153.8	787.2	1,041.8	1,025.0
5.	Production workers, total (number) (1,000)	155.8	231.5	470.3	530.0	520.2
6.	Man hours (1,000,000)	---	---	---	---	---
7.	Wages ($1,000,000)	62.5	119.0	638.4	840.5	788.0
8.	Value added by manufacture ($1,000,000)	143.7	316.5	1,544.6	2,067.3	1,794.0
9.	Capital expenditures, new ($1,000,000)	---	---	---	---	---
10.	Percent of U.S. Employment	3.49	3.74	5.50	6.20	6.49
11.	Index of employment change (1958 = 100)	19	30	61	68	70
12.	U.S. index of employment change (1958 = 100)	30	44	61	60	59

GENERAL MANUFACTURING STATISTICS, 1899-1989[89,91] (Cont.)										
MICHIGAN*[a]										
Item No.	1947	1954	1958	1963	1967	1972	1977	1982	1987	1989*[d]
1.	9,891	12,711	13,596*[b]	14,220	14,340	14,461	15,627	15,158	15,996	---
2.	---	4,001	3,990	4,537*[b]	5,157	5,019	5,380	5,010	5,736	---
3.	975.5	1,056.0*[b]	880.0	961.1	1,134.1	1,076.2	1,115.9	883.9	980.1	929.7
4.	3,097.3	5,248.9*[b]	5,161.2	6,950.7	9,357.2	12,745.1	20,054.0	22,223.0	30,627.8	31,437.3
5.	823.3	809.3	608.9	690.8	816.7	768.1	789.4	563.6	635.5	616.0
6.	---	1,650.3	1,204.1	1,473.9	1,669.2	1,582.6	1,626.3	1,090.5	1,300.7	1,275.6
7.	2,444.6	3,661.0	3,184.8	4,521.0	6,008.0	8,094.7	12,720.6	12,504.9	17,393.0	18,365.4
8.	5,200.1	8,707.2	8,363.6	13,090.3	17,241.6	23,375.7	37,566.0	39,118.1	60,258.6	66,131.0
9.	---	870.5	465.3*[c]	761.8	1,360.2	2,071.4	3,739.2	3,503.0	4,793.5	5,938.7
10.	6.82	6.56	5.49	5.67	5.87	5.66	5.69	4.62	5.17	4.88
11.	111	120	100	109	129	122 96	127 100	100 79	111 88	106 83
12.	89	100	100	106	121	119 97	122 100	119 97	118 97	119 97

[a] There were a number of changes in the definition of manufacturing industries through the years that affect historical comparability. See the Glossary of Terms for these changes. The changes have not appreciably affected the comparability of the historical data except for the figures on the number of establishments.

[b] Data for central administrative offices and auxiliaries included for the first time for other states but this information was not collected in Alaska and Hawaii in 1954. See the Glossary of Terms.

[c] Item 9 (1958) includes expenditures for plants under construction but not in operation prior to 1958, the data represents expenditures at operating manufacturing establishments only. See Glossary of Terms.

[d] The Census Data for 1972, 1977, 1983 and 1987 are from manufacturing. Data for 1989 are estimates based on a representative sample of establishments canvassed annually and may differ from results of a complete canvass of all establishments.

GENERAL MANUFACTURING STATISTICS, 1899-1989[89,91]						
MINNESOTA[*a]						
Item No.		1899	1909	1919	1929	1939
1.	Total establishments[90,*a]	4,096	5,561	5,633	4,315	3,735
2.	With 20 employees or more[90]	---	---	---	---	---
3.	All employees, number (1,000)	71.2	99.0	140.4	124.2	102.2
4.	Payroll ($1,000,000)	35.1	62.9	169.8	180.1	143.4
5.	Production workers, total (number) (1,000)	64.6	84.8	113.8	103.4	78.0
6.	Man hours (1,000,000)	---	---	---	---	---
7.	Wages ($1,000,000)	29.0	47.5	124.8	132.4	95.3
8.	Value added by manufacture ($1,000,000)	73.4	127.8	327.9	405.0	306.8
9.	Capital expenditures, new ($1,000,000)	---	---	---	---	---
10.	Percent of U.S. Employment	1.47	1.41	1.43	1.28	1.07
11.	Index of employment change (1958 = 100)	32	45	64	56	46
12.	U.S. index of employment change (1958 = 100)	30	44	61	60	59

GENERAL MANUFACTURING STATISTICS, 1899-1989[89,91] (Cont.)										
MINNESOTA*[a]										
Item No.	1947	1954	1958	1963	1967	1972	1977	1982	1987	1989*[d]
1.	4,563	5,027	5,380*[b]	5,500	5,409	5,698	6,637	6,775	7,110	---
2.	---	1,316	1,433	1,587*[b]	1,778	1,930	2,126	2,214	2,416	---
3.	181.5	208.5*[b]	220.8	245.9	299.8	302.2	331.7	350.0	374.2	391.4
4.	508.4	865.3*[b]	1,094.8	1,478.6	2,106.5	2,889.0	4,693.0	7,422.9	10,141.7	11,440.7
5.	145.0	151.1	149.6	165.6	198.8	196.1	211.1	200.6	214.9	223.5
6.	---	305.3	293.9	331.6	398.7	382.8	403.8	376.2	428.0	438.0
7.	358.6	560.5	654.9	865.4	1,177.6	1,555.1	2,413.1	3,428.4	4,512.7	4,899.1
8.	1,021.3	1,594.5	2,050.4	2,806.1	4,080.2	5,523.8	9,605.2	15,366.9	23,151.9	25,221.7
9.	---	82.2	108.5*[c]	159.1	231.3	305.5	576.4	1,193.0	1,765.5	2,013.9
10.	1.27	1.29	1.38	1.45	1.55	1.59	1.69	1.83	1.97	2.06
11.	80	94	100	111	136	137 91	150 100	159 106	169 113	177 118
12.	89	100	100	106	121	119 97	122 100	119 97	118 97	119 97

[a] There were a number of changes in the definition of manufacturing industries through the years that affect historical comparability. See the Glossary of Terms for these changes. The changes have not appreciably affected the comparability of the historical data except for the figures on the number of establishments.

[b] Data for central administrative offices and auxiliaries included for the first time for other states but this information was not collected in Alaska and Hawaii in 1954. See the Glossary of Terms.

[c] Item 9 (1958) includes expenditures for plants under construction but not in operation prior to 1958, the data represents expenditures at operating manufacturing establishments only. See Glossary of Terms.

[d] The Census Data for 1972, 1977, 1983 and 1987 are from manufacturing. Data for 1989 are estimates based on a representative sample of establishments canvassed annually and may differ from results of a complete canvass of all establishments.

GENERAL MANUFACTURING STATISTICS, 1899-1989[89,91]						
MISSISSIPPI[*a,e]						
Item No.		1899	1909	1919	1929	1939
1.	Total establishments[90,*a]	1,294	2,598	2,379	1,911	1,235
2.	With 20 employees or more[90]	---	---	---	---	---
3.	All employees, number (1,000)	28.1	53.8	61.5	56.3	52.1
4.	Payroll ($1,000,000)	9.0	22.4	59.0	51.4	36.5
5.	Production workers, total (number) (1,000)	26.8	50.4	57.4	52.1	45.9
6.	Man hours (1,000,000)	---	---	---	---	---
7.	Wages ($1,000,000)	7.9	18.8	51.0	42.2	27.1
8.	Value added by manufacture ($1,000,000)	17.2	43.6	100.6	107.3	72.7
9.	Capital expenditures, new ($1,000,000)	---	---	---	---	---
10.	Percent of U.S. Employment	.58	.77	.62	.58	.55
11.	Index of employment change (1958 = 100)	26	50	57	52	48
12.	U.S. index of employment change (1958 = 100)	30	44	61	60	59

GENERAL MANUFACTURING STATISTICS, 1899-1989[89,91] (Cont.)										
MISSISSIPPI*[a]										
Item No.	1947	1954	1958	1963	1967	1972	1977	1982	1987	1989*[d]
1.	1,985	2,252	2,433*[b]	2,384	2,761	2,727	3,289	3,126	3,312	---
2.	---	665	743	848*[b]	925	1,066	1,147	1,223	1,243	---
3.	77.4	90.9*[b]	108.5	128.5	160.4	200.4	219.4	201.7	218.9	226.4
4.	139.0	238.7*[b]	354.4	486.2	764.0	1,302.4	2,061.5	2,880.8	3,827.3	4,224.0
5.	70.3	79.8	92.5	108.5	133.8	166.9	177.9	158.2	171.4	181.4
6.	---	156.9	178.7	214.5	269.7	332.0	348.1	299.2	337.4	359.2
7.	116.2	188.8	280.8	367.9	560.9	958.6	1,477.3	1,977.6	2,620.6	2,930.8
8.	302.3	467.6	642.2	1,017.0	1,635.3	2,824.7	5,619.3	7,824.9	10,502.6	12,159.2
9.	---	37.0	67.7*[c]	131.2	276.2	235.9	470.8	1,154.3	647.7	1,409.9
10.	.54	.56	.68	.76	.83	1.05	1.12	1.05	1.16	1.19
11.	71	84	100	118	148	185 91	202 100	186 92	110 100	112 103
12.	89	100	100	106	121	119 97[e]	122 100	119 97	118 97	119 97

[a] There were a number of changes in the definition of manufacturing industries through the years that affect historical comparability. See the Glossary of Terms for these changes. The changes have not appreciably affected the comparability of the historical data except for the figures on the number of establishments.

[b] Data for central administrative offices and auxiliaries included for the first time for other states but this information was not collected in Alaska and Hawaii in 1954. See the Glossary of Terms.

[c] Item 9 (1958) includes expenditures for plants under construction but not in operation prior to 1958, the data represents expenditures at operating manufacturing establishments only. See Glossary of Terms.

[d] The Census Data for 1972, 1977, 1983 and 1987 are from manufacturing. Data for 1989 are estimates based on a representative sample of establishments canvassed annually and may differ from results of a complete canvass of all establishments.

[e] Percentage computed by compiler from data herein is different from percentages given in source. The above percentage is the percentage computed by compiler.

GENERAL MANUFACTURING STATISTICS, 1899-1989[89,91]						
MISSOURI[*a,e]						
Item No.		1899	1909	1919	1929	1939
1.	Total establishments[90,*a]	6,853	8,375	8,715	5,765	4,487
2.	With 20 employees or more[90]	---	---	---	---	---
3.	All employees, number (1,000)	120.2	177.5	235.8	240.6	220.3
4.	Payroll ($1,000,000)	60.0	109.8	273.7	332.3	280.7
5.	Production workers, total (number) (1,000)	107.7	153.0	193.8	202.9	176.0
6.	Man hours (1,000,000)	---	---	---	---	---
7.	Wages ($1,000,000)	46.7	80.8	194.9	240.4	187.5
8.	Value added by manufacture ($1,000,000)	132.1	219.7	534.6	777.5	581.8
9.	Capital expenditures, new ($1,000,000)	---	---	---	---	---
10.	Percent of U.S. Employment	2.48	2.53	2.40	2.49	2.31
11.	Index of employment change (1958 = 100)	32	47	62	63	58
12.	U.S. index of employment change (1958 = 100)	30	44	61	60	59

GENERAL MANUFACTURING STATISTICS, 1899-1989[89,91] (Cont.)										
MISSOURI*[a]										
Item No.	1947	1954	1958	1963	1967	1972	1977	1982	1987	1989*[d]
1.	5,721	6,198	6,588*[b]	6,540	6,545	6,732	7,355	7,069	7,314	---
2.	---	2,179	2,215	2,325*[b]	2,457	2,470	2,430	2,467	2,585	---
3.	327.1	381.9*[b]	380.5	391.4	452.2	434.3	433.3	405.9	418.8	426.0
4.	826.2	1,496.7*[b]	1,771.1	2,235.2	3,048.9	3,897.3	5,709.1	8,013.2	10,390.0	11,348.6
5.	269.4	285.4	271.5	276.2	320.9	299.8	299.1	256.4	264.5	270.1
6.	---	552.7	519.3	547.8	631.3	583.8	572.4	477.2	519.0	528.8
7.	606.8	977.3	1,088.7	1,361.7	1,851.7	2,305.4	3,408.5	4,198.9	5,401.6	5,750.7
8.	1,620.9	2,727.3	3,250.8	4,296.0	5,895.0	8,169.0	13,087.0	18,333.8	25,916.7	31,951.3
9.	---	124.4	185.9*[c]	211.1	346.8	395.9	780.9	1,339.8	1,620.1	1,601.3
10.	2.29	2.38	2.37	2.31	2.34	2.28	2.21	2.12	2.21	2.24
11.	86	100*[e]	100	103	119	114 100	114 100	107 94	110 97	112 98
12.	89	100	100	106	121	119 97	122 100	119 97	118 97	119 97

[a] There were a number of changes in the definition of manufacturing industries through the years that affect historical comparability. See the Glossary of Terms for these changes. The changes have not appreciably affected the comparability of the historical data except for the figures on the number of establishments.

[b] Data for central administrative offices and auxiliaries included for the first time for other states but this information was not collected in Alaska and Hawaii in 1954. See the Glossary of Terms.

[c] Item 9 (1958) includes expenditures for plants under construction but not in operation prior to 1958, the data represents expenditures at operating manufacturing establishments only. See Glossary of Terms.

[d] The Census Data for 1972, 1977, 1983 and 1987 are from manufacturing. Data for 1989 are estimates based on a representative sample of establishments canvassed annually and may differ from results of a complete canvass of all establishments.

[e] Percentage computed by compiler from data herein is different from percentages given in source. The above percentage is the percentage computed by compiler.

GENERAL MANUFACTURING STATISTICS, 1899-1989[89,91]						
MONTANA[*a,e]						
Item No.		1899	1909	1919	1929	1939
1.	Total establishments[90,*a]	395	677	1,235	589	552
2.	With 20 employees or more[90]	---	---	---	---	---
3.	All employees, number (1,000)	10.4	13.0	18.9	17.1	11.9
4.	Payroll ($1,000,000)	8.2	13.0	28.6	29.5	17.3
5.	Production workers, total (number) (1,000)	9.9	11.7	16.6	14.9	8.8
6.	Man hours (1,000,000)	---	---	---	---	---
7.	Wages ($1,000,000)	7.4	10.9	24.0	24.2	11.7
8.	Value added by manufacture ($1,000,000)	22.4	24.1	43.1	61.2	38.8
9.	Capital expenditures, new ($1,000,000)	---	---	---	---	---
10.	Percent of U.S. Employment	.21	.19	.19	.18	.12
11.	Index of employment change (1958 = 100)	56	71	103	93	59
12.	U.S. index of employment change (1958 = 100)	31	45	63	62	59

GENERAL MANUFACTURING STATISTICS, 1899-1989[89,91] (Cont.)										
MONTANA*[a]										
Item No.	1947	1954	1958	1963	1967	1972	1977	1982	1987	1989*[d]
1.	650	868	929*[b]	976	923	943	1,168	1,090	1,240	---
2.	---	172	174	188*[b]	191	206	202	176	184	---
3.	15.8	18.5*[b]	20.3	20.2	20.4	21.4	23.5	20.2	20.1	20.7
4.	42.8	72.1*[b]	94.8	109.2	129.5	184.6	311.8	379.1	425.8	465.3
5.	13.4	14.7	15.8	16.0	16.1	17.1	18.4	14.6	14.8	14.7
6.	---	27.8	30.2	31.7	32.1	33.6	35.9	27.0	28.8	30.9
7.	34.8	54.1	70.4	82.8	96.4	137.7	236.0	265.0	296.2	334.3
8.	90.8	141.2	191.2	236.2	311.6	462.5	802.2	713.5	1,112.0	1,377.1
9.	---	20.6	19.9*[c]	38.6	68.9	75.8	97.8	74.6	97.0	119.6
10.	.11	.11	.13	.12	.11	.11	.12	.11	.11	.11
11.	78	91*[e]	100	100	100	105 91	116 100	100 86	99 86	102 88
12.	89	100	100	106	121	119 97	122 100	119 97	118 97	119 97

[a] There were a number of changes in the definition of manufacturing industries through the years that affect historical comparability. See the Glossary of Terms for these changes. The changes have not appreciably affected the comparability of the historical data except for the figures on the number of establishments.

[b] Data for central administrative offices and auxiliaries included for the first time for other states but this information was not collected in Alaska and Hawaii in 1954. See the Glossary of Terms.

[c] Item 9 (1958) includes expenditures for plants under construction but not in operation prior to 1958, the data represents expenditures at operating manufacturing establishments only. See Glossary of Terms.

[d] The Census Data for 1972, 1977, 1983 and 1987 are from manufacturing. Data for 1989 are estimates based on a representative sample of establishments canvassed annually and may differ from results of a complete canvass of all establishments.

[e] Percentage computed by compiler from data herein is different from percentages given in source. The above percentage is the percentage computed by compiler.

GENERAL MANUFACTURING STATISTICS, 1899-1989[89,91]						
NEBRASKA[*a]						
Item No.		1899	1909	1919	1929	1939
1.	Total establishments[90,*a]	1,695	2,500	2,385	1,491	1,093
2.	With 20 employees or more[90]	---	---	---	---	---
3.	All employees, number (1,000)	21.0	29.4	44.9	34.8	26.2
4.	Payroll ($1,000,000)	11.0	19.4	60.1	51.3	34.1
5.	Production workers, total (number) (1,000)	18.7	24.3	35.4	28.2	18.4
6.	Man hours (1,000,000)	---	---	---	---	---
7.	Wages ($1,000,000)	8.8	13.9	44.5	36.9	20.2
8.	Value added by manufacture ($1,000,000)	34.3	47.9	112.6	120.0	68.1
9.	Capital expenditures, new ($1,000,000)	---	---	---	---	---
10.	Percent of U.S. Employment	.43	.42	.46	.36	.27
11.	Index of employment change (1958 = 100)	36	50	77	59	45
12.	U.S. index of employment change (1958 = 100)	30	44	61	60	59

GENERAL MANUFACTURING STATISTICS, 1899-1989[89,91] (Cont.)

NEBRASKA[*a]

Item No.	1947	1954	1958	1963	1967	1972	1977	1982	1987	1989[*d]
1.	1,341	1,423	1,553[*b]	1,611	1,672	1,723	1,965	1,928	1,872	---
2.	---	378	412	474[*b]	525	597	626	633	631	---
3.	47.0	59.4[*b]	58.6	64.9	77.0	84.9	87.7	91.1	90.7	93.8
4.	119.9	223.5[*b]	265.2	348.0	475.9	704.2	1,075.4	1,624.4	1,937.6	2,120.2
5.	37.3	43.4	42.9	47.0	58.4	63.2	62.8	64.4	64.2	67.6
6.	---	90.4	87.0	96.7	119.2	127.6	124.0	124.3	128.8	135.2
7.	87.4	150.7	174.2	228.5	325.0	469.2	680.9	1,014.8	1,211.9	1,341.0
8.	260.6	394.2	536.3	746.6	1,150.0	1,733.4	2,867.1	4,444.5	5,819.2	6,530.9
9.	---	36.4	49.9[*c]	46.1	71.4	102.3	175.1	245.3	317.9	388.0
10.	.33	.37	.37	.38	.40	.45	.45	.48	.48	.49
11.	80	101	100	111	131	145 97	150 100	155 104	155 103	160 107
12.	89	100	100	106	121	119 97	122 100	119 97	118 97	119 97

[a] There were a number of changes in the definition of manufacturing industries through the years that affect historical comparability. See the Glossary of Terms for these changes. The changes have not appreciably affected the comparability of the historical data except for the figures on the number of establishments.

[b] Data for central administrative offices and auxiliaries included for the first time for other states but this information was not collected in Alaska and Hawaii in 1954. See the Glossary of Terms.

[c] Item 9 (1958) includes expenditures for plants under construction but not in operation prior to 1958, the data represents expenditures at operating manufacturing establishments only. See Glossary of Terms.

[d] The Census Data for 1972, 1977, 1983 and 1987 are from manufacturing. Data for 1989 are estimates based on a representative sample of establishments canvassed annually and may differ from results of a complete canvass of all establishments.

GENERAL MANUFACTURING STATISTICS, 1899-1989[89,91]						
NEVADA[*a]						
Item No.		1899	1909	1919	1929	1939
1.	Total establishments[90,*a]	99	177	149	123	94
2.	With 20 employees or more[90]	---	---	---	---	---
3.	All employees, number (1,000)	.5	2.5	3.4	2.6	1.5
4.	Payroll ($1,000,000)	.4	2.4	4.8	4.4	2.4
5.	Production workers, total (number) (1,000)	.5	2.3	3.1	2.2	1.0
6.	Man hours (1,000,000)	---	---	---	---	---
7.	Wages ($1,000,000)	.4	2.0	4.2	3.6	1.6
8.	Value added by manufacture ($1,000,000)	.6	3.5	6.2	8.1	11.5
9.	Capital expenditures, new ($1,000,000)	---	---	---	---	---
10.	Percent of U.S. Employment	.01	.04	.03	.03	.02
11.	Index of employment change (1958 = 100)	11	50	67	51	29
12.	U.S. index of employment change (1958 = 100)	30	44	61	60	59

GENERAL MANUFACTURING STATISTICS, 1899-1989[89,91] (Cont.)										
NEVADA*[a]										
Item No.	1947	1954	1958	1963	1967	1972	1977	1982	1987	1989*[d]
1.	126	177	207*[b]	283	330	447	729	851	974	---
2.	33	42	45	73*[b]	74	104	147	177	240	---
3.	2.7	5.7*[b]	5.0	6.8	7.0	10.0	15.0	20.4	23.7	23.4
4.	8.4	25.3*[b]	27.1	42.2	49.6	91.7	191.6	356.2	521.4	544.5
5.	2.1	4.4	3.7	4.8	4.8	6.9	10.0	13.1	15.8	15.9
6.	4.7	9.1	7.4	9.5	9.3	13.5	19.3	24.8	30.9	31.5
7.	6.4	18.5	18.9	28.4	31.2	57.2	113.4	209.7	299.6	321.4
8.	17.3	62.7	67.6	106.3	133.8	207.7	495.2	862.6	1,279.3	1,365.0
9.	3.0	4.9	5.2*[c]	8.7	15.4	23.5	46.4	80.3	114.0	102.0
10.	.02	.03	.03	.04	.04	.05	.08	.11	.13	.12
11.	53	114	100	136	140	200 66	300 100	408 136	474 158	468 156
12.	89	100	100	106	121	119 97	122 100	119 97	118 97	119 97

[a] There were a number of changes in the definition of manufacturing industries through the years that affect historical comparability. See the Glossary of Terms for these changes. The changes have not appreciably affected the comparability of the historical data except for the figures on the number of establishments.

[b] Data for central administrative offices and auxiliaries included for the first time for other states but this information was not collected in Alaska and Hawaii in 1954. See the Glossary of Terms.

[c] Item 9 (1958) includes expenditures for plants under construction but not in operation prior to 1958, the data represents expenditures at operating manufacturing establishments only. See Glossary of Terms.

[d] The Census Data for 1972, 1977, 1983 and 1987 are from manufacturing. Data for 1989 are estimates based on a representative sample of establishments canvassed annually and may differ from results of a complete canvass of all establishments.

GENERAL MANUFACTURING STATISTICS, 1899-1989[89,91]						
NEW HAMPSHIRE[*a]						
Item No.		1899	1909	1919	1929	1939
1.	Total establishments[90,*a]	1,771	1,961	1,451	1,075	772
2.	With 20 employees or more[90]	---	---	---	---	---
3.	All employees, number (1,000)	69.7	82.2	88.7	71.2	61.2
4.	Payroll ($1,000,000)	28.0	40.4	92.3	85.3	65.2
5.	Production workers, total (number) (1,000)	67.6	78.7	82.9	65.5	55.4
6.	Man hours (1,000,000)	---	---	---	---	---
7.	Wages ($1,000,000)	25.9	36.2	79.1	70.5	52.4
8.	Value added by manufacture ($1,000,000)	47.4	66.4	167.3	147.1	104.2
9.	Capital expenditures, new ($1,000,000)	---	---	---	---	---
10.	Percent of U.S. Employment	1.44	1.17	.90	.74	.64
11.	Index of employment change (1958 = 100)	88	103	112	90	77
12.	U.S. index of employment change (1958 = 100)	30	44	61	60	59

GENERAL MANUFACTURING STATISTICS, 1899-1989[89,91] (Cont.)										
NEW HAMPSHIRE*[a]										
Item No.	1947	1954	1958	1963	1967	1972	1977	1982	1987	1989*[d]
1.	1,124	1,609	1,457*[b]	1,509	1,481	1,434	1,825	1,981	2,336	---
2.	478	497	494	546*[b]	566	566	623	721	739	---
3.	74.8	77.3*[b]	79.5	84.1	94.9	89.7	95.3	107.4	107.9	97.8
4.	177.5	246.7*[b]	297.1	378.9	512.6	663.2	1,029.0	1,792.0	2,508.7	2,591.1
5.	66.4	66.0	65.6	68.6	76.6	67.7	72.0	75.3	71.5	62.6
6.	136.1	128.5	128.1	135.1	151.0	131.4	138.0	144.9	141.6	124.2
7.	145.3	190.8	221.1	271.8	364.3	414.0	645.3	1,054.9	1,426.8	1,387.9
8.	306.9	408.8	490.7	636.1	931.9	1,278.6	2,174.7	4,004.0	8,188.6	5,771.9
9.	24.0	18.5	24.4*[c]	30.3	75.6	99.1	162.0	246.2	339.8	398.3
10.	.52	.49	.50	.50	.49	.47	.49	.56	.57	.51
11.	94	97	100	106	119	113 94	120 100	135 113	136 113	123 103
12.	89	100	100	106	121	119 97	122 100	119 97	118 97	119 97

[a] There were a number of changes in the definition of manufacturing industries through the years that affect historical comparability. See the Glossary of Terms for these changes. The changes have not appreciably affected the comparability of the historical data except for the figures on the number of establishments.

[b] Data for central administrative offices and auxiliaries included for the first time for other states but this information was not collected in Alaska and Hawaii in 1954. See the Glossary of Terms.

[c] Item 9 (1958) includes expenditures for plants under construction but not in operation prior to 1958, the data represents expenditures at operating manufacturing establishments only. See Glossary of Terms.

[d] The Census Data for 1972, 1977, 1983 and 1987 are from manufacturing. Data for 1989 are estimates based on a representative sample of establishments canvassed annually and may differ from results of a complete canvass of all establishments.

GENERAL MANUFACTURING STATISTICS, 1899-1989[89,91]						
NEW JERSEY[*a]						
Item No.		1899	1909	1919	1929	1939
1.	Total establishments[90,*a]	6,415	8,817	10,564	8,388	7,438
2.	With 20 employees or more[90]	---	---	---	---	---
3.	All employees, number (1,000)	229.3	363.1	590.9	516.6	531.1
4.	Payroll ($1,000,000)	114.2	218.0	769.3	808.9	753.9
5.	Production workers, total (number) (1,000)	214.0	326.2	507.1	442.3	431.6
6.	Man hours (1,000,000)	---	---	---	---	---
7.	Wages ($1,000,000)	95.2	169.7	598.5	610.6	519.1
8.	Value added by manufacture ($1,000,000)	218.3	425.5	1,397.8	1,771.4	1,518.2
9.	Capital expenditures, new ($1,000,000)	---	---	---	---	---
10.	Percent of U.S. Employment	4.73	5.17	6.00	5.34	5.57
11.	Index of employment change (1958 = 100)	29	46	74	65	67
12.	U.S. index of employment change (1958 = 100)	30	44	61	60	59

GENERAL MANUFACTURING STATISTICS, 1899-1989[89,91] (Cont.)										
NEW JERSEY*[a]										
Item No.	1947	1954	1958	1963	1967	1972	1977	1982	1987	1989*[d]
1.	10,765	13,183	14,219*[b]	15,208	14,740	13,790	15,696	15,126	14,437	---
2.	---	4,748	4,994	5,528*[b]	5,903	5,918	5,775	5,756	5,463	---
3.	739.0	812.4*[b]	795.0	829.2	881.3	836.1	778.3	754.0	690.8	657.9
4.	2,216.9	3,507.1*[b]	4,066.5	5,121.3	6,325.4	8,107.2	10,924.2	15,845.0	18,549.9	20,368.0
5.	602.3	605.1	564.2	573.8	603.7	546.6	489.6	440.4	394.4	360.2
6.	---	1,187.7	1,100.0	1,145.4	1,203.7	1,070.9	955.8	842.7	780.9	720.2
7.	1,645.5	2,280.1	2,508.1	3,021.0	3,617.8	4,353.7	5,561.7	7,206.7	8,389.3	8,152.3
8.	4,186.1	6,331.7	7,499.5	9,957.3	12,738.2	16,408.9	22,852.8	31,656.0	42,526.6	45,064.7
9.	---	359.8	449.7*[c]	525.0	824.3	940.1	1,376.3	2,061.3	2,312.5	2,636.0
10.	5.17	5.04	4.96	4.89	4.56	4.39	3.97	3.94	3.65	3.46
11.	93	102	100	104	111	105 107	98 100	95 97	87 89	83 85
12.	89	100	100	106	121	119 97	122 100	119 97	118 97	119 97

[a] There were a number of changes in the definition of manufacturing industries through the years that affect historical comparability. See the Glossary of Terms for these changes. The changes have not appreciably affected the comparability of the historical data except for the figures on the number of establishments.

[b] Data for central administrative offices and auxiliaries included for the first time for other states but this information was not collected in Alaska and Hawaii in 1954. See the Glossary of Terms.

[c] Item 9 (1958) includes expenditures for plants under construction but not in operation prior to 1958, the data represents expenditures at operating manufacturing establishments only. See Glossary of Terms.

[d] The Census Data for 1972, 1977, 1983 and 1987 are from manufacturing. Data for 1989 are estimates based on a representative sample of establishments canvassed annually and may differ from results of a complete canvass of all establishments.

GENERAL MANUFACTURING STATISTICS, 1899-1989[89,91]						
NEW MEXICO[*a,e]						
Item No.		1899	1909	1919	1929	1939
1.	Total establishments[90,*a]	174	313	387	250	262
2.	With 20 employees or more[90]	---	---	---	---	---
3.	All employees, number (1,000)	2.6	4.5	6.3	5.1	4.1
4.	Payroll ($1,000,000)	1.3	3.0	7.7	6.8	4.2
5.	Production workers, total (number) (1,000)	2.5	4.1	5.7	4.5	3.2
6.	Man hours (1,000,000)	---	---	---	---	---
7.	Wages ($1,000,000)	1.2	2.6	6.7	5.6	2.9
8.	Value added by manufacture ($1,000,000)	2.1	4.6	10.1	11.3	8.6
9.	Capital expenditures, new ($1,000,000)	---	---	---	---	---
10.	Percent of U.S. Employment	.05	.06	.06	.05	.04
11.	Index of employment change (1958 = 100)	19	33	46	37	30
12.	U.S. index of employment change (1958 = 100)	30	44	61	60	59

GENERAL MANUFACTURING STATISTICS, 1899-1989[89,91] (Cont.)										
NEW MEXICO*[a]										
Item No.	1947	1954	1958	1963	1967	1972	1977	1982	1987	1989*[d]
1.	431	593	668*[b]	742	749	926	1,323	1,223	1,322	---
2.	---	101*[b]	153	169*[b]	169	277	258	299	283	---
3.	6.7	9.7*[b]	13.7	15.3	16.9	23.6	29.0	33.0	34.7	38.8
4.	15.0	32.9	59.4	82.1	98.6	157.2	296.9	521.2	713.3	822.2
5.	5.5	7.1	9.8	10.2	11.3	17.2	20.9	22.2	23.7	26.9
6.	---	14.2	19.2	20.7	22.3	32.9	39.5	41.8	47.3	51.5
7.	11.4	22.2	38.0	47.2	55.6	96.0	183.8	296.6	432.5	495.5
8.	32.1	65.7	107.6	149.6	204.5	358.0	733.5	1,397.7	1,652.9	2,113.3
9.	---	6.6	24.5*[c]	10.4	10.6	30.8	75.0	120.8	196.4	196.8
10.	.05	.06	.09	.09	.09	.12	.15	.17	.18	.20
11.	49	70	100	112	123	172 81	212 100	241 114	253 120	283 134
12.	89	100	100	106	121	119 97	122 100	119 97	118 97	119 97

[a] There were a number of changes in the definition of manufacturing industries through the years that affect historical comparability. See the Glossary of Terms for these changes. The changes have not appreciably affected the comparability of the historical data except for the figures on the number of establishments.

[b] Data for central administrative offices and auxiliaries included for the first time for other states but this information was not collected in Alaska and Hawaii in 1954. See the Glossary of Terms.

[c] Item 9 (1958) includes expenditures for plants under construction but not in operation prior to 1958, the data represents expenditures at operating manufacturing establishments only. See Glossary of Terms.

[d] The Census Data for 1972, 1977, 1983 and 1987 are from manufacturing. Data for 1989 are estimates based on a representative sample of establishments canvassed annually and may differ from results of a complete canvass of all establishments.

GENERAL MANUFACTURING STATISTICS, 1899-1989[89,91]						
NEW YORK[*a]						
Item No.		1899	1909	1919	1929	1939
1.	Total establishments[90,*a]	35,957	44,935	48,331	39,395	32,672
2.	With 20 employees or more[90]	---	---	---	---	---
3.	All employees, number (1,000)	794.9	1,155.7	1,467.4	1,331.4	1,211.0
4.	Payroll ($1,000,000)	414.1	743.3	1,961.4	2,294.9	1,749.7
5.	Production workers, total (number) (1,000)	726.9	1,004.0	1,221.9	1,106.0	949.4
6.	Man hours (1,000,000)	---	---	---	---	---
7.	Wages ($1,000,000)	337.3	557.2	1,450.1	1,650.4	1,151.8
8.	Value added by manufacture ($1,000,000)	853.5	1,512.6	3,908.9	4,973.9	3,313.6
9.	Capital expenditures, new ($1,000,000)	---	---	---	---	---
10.	Percent of U.S. Employment	16.39	16.48	14.92	13.78	12.71
11.	Index of employment change (1958 = 100)	41	60	77	70	63
12.	U.S. index of employment change (1958 = 100)	30	44	61	60	59

GENERAL MANUFACTURING STATISTICS, 1899-1989[89,91] (Cont.)										
NEW YORK*a										
Item No.	1947	1954	1958	1963	1967	1972	1977	1982	1987	1989*d
1.	47,782	50,402	49,441*b	47,041	42,911	41,684	36,578	32,651	29,607	---
2.	---	15,156	15,000	15,022*b	14,730	14,353	11,425	10,670	9,488	---
3.	1,773.1	2,000.7*b	1,915.9	1,853.0	1,929.2	1,679.3	1,509.9	1,418.8	1,278.7	1,207.5
4.	5,277.7	8,444.2*b	9,627.7	11,289.7	13,851.5	16,222.0	20,876.1	29,156.0	33,915.8	35,548.0
5.	1,425.0	1,470.1	1,303.1	1,247.8	1,284.5	1,076.2	958.1	836.3	723.3	693.6
6.	---	2,842.6	2,487.1	2,431.3	2,509.8	2,068.2	1,827.5	1,613.0	1,403.5	1,363.7
7.	3,821.5	5,231.9	5,423.6	6,163.5	7,334.7	8,174.3	10,418.8	13,269.9	14,408.2	14,808.4
8.	9,655.9	14,140.5	15,892.6	19,539.3	25,246.7	30,403.5	44,289.8	62,906.6	80,033.3	85,480.2
9.	---	572.1	792.2*c	783.4	1,310.3	1,506.0	2,530.2	4,267.1	4,296.5	5,405.0
10.	12.40	12.42	11.96	10.92	9.98	8.83	7.70	7.43	6.75	6.34
11.	93	104	100	97	101	88 111	79 100	74 94	67 85	63 80
12.	89	100	100	106	121	119 97	122 100	119 97	118 97	119 97

[a] There were a number of changes in the definition of manufacturing industries through the years that affect historical comparability. See the Glossary of Terms for these changes. The changes have not appreciably affected the comparability of the historical data except for the figures on the number of establishments.

[b] Data for central administrative offices and auxiliaries included for the first time for other states but this information was not collected in Alaska and Hawaii in 1954. See the Glossary of Terms.

[c] Item 9 (1958) includes expenditures for plants under construction but not in operation prior to 1958, the data represents expenditures at operating manufacturing establishments only. See Glossary of Terms.

[d] The Census Data for 1972, 1977, 1983 and 1987 are from manufacturing. Data for 1989 are estimates based on a representative sample of establishments canvassed annually and may differ from results of a complete canvass of all establishments.

GENERAL MANUFACTURING STATISTICS, 1899-1989[89,91]						
NORTH CAROLINA[*a]						
Item No.		1899	1909	1919	1929	1939
1.	Total establishments[90,*a]	3,465	4,931	5,690	3,797	3,158
2.	With 20 employees or more[90]	---	---	---	---	---
3.	All employees, number (1,000)	75.2	128.0	167.8	226.4	293.3
4.	Payroll ($1,000,000)	16.4	41.3	148.4	198.8	245.9
5.	Production workers, total (number) (1,000)	72.3	121.5	156.4	209.8	269.2
6.	Man hours (1,000,000)	---	---	---	---	---
7.	Wages ($1,000,000)	14.1	34.4	125.0	160.9	198.5
8.	Value added by manufacture ($1,000,000)	40.4	94.8	413.7	693.0	544.1
9.	Capital expenditures, new ($1,000,000)	---	---	---	---	---
10.	Percent of U.S. Employment	1.55	1.83	1.70	2.34	3.08
11.	Index of employment change (1958 = 100)	16	28	36	49	63
12.	U.S. index of employment change (1958 = 100)	30	44	61	60	59

GENERAL MANUFACTURING STATISTICS, 1899-1989[89,91] (Cont.)										
NORTH CAROLINA[*a]										
Item No.	1947	1954	1958	1963	1967	1972	1977	1982	1987	1989[*d]
1.	5,321	6,645	7,352[*b]	7,784	8,266	8,632	9,954	10,133	10,982	---
2.	---	2,369	2,628	2,946[*b]	3,379	3,794	4,005	4,378	4,757	---
3.	381.4	434.9[*b]	461.5	530.6	643.3	743.7	765.3	798.6	842.4	836.3
4.	758.8	1,185.6[*b]	1,486.7	2,092.1	3,066.1	4,929.1	7,518.5	11,717.1	16,293.4	17,876.1
5.	350.2	380.1	391.7	444.4	537.8	604.0	611.3	604.9	637.3	633.5
6.	---	719.4	747.4	890.2	1,070.2	1,211.0	1,186.5	1,116.0	1,258.8	1,248.3
7.	641.9	915.7	1,109.7	1,527.5	2,210.1	3,427.3	5,086.3	7,297.3	10,293.0	10,842.3
8.	1,646.0	2,210.5	3,077.9	4,566.5	6,606.5	11,014.5	18,230.6	28,492.2	47,007.4	56,417.6
9.	---	129.6	191.3[*c]	314.4	664.6	986.8	1,345.3	2,583.8	2,958.7	3,396.8
10.	2.67	2.70	2.88	3.13	3.33	3.91	3.91	4.18	4.45	4.39
11.	83	93	100	115	139	161 97	166 100	173 104	183 110	181 109
12.	89	100	100	106	121	119 97	122 100	119 97	118 97	119 97

[a] There were a number of changes in the definition of manufacturing industries through the years that affect historical comparability. See the Glossary of Terms for these changes. The changes have not appreciably affected the comparability of the historical data except for the figures on the number of establishments.

[b] Data for central administrative offices and auxiliaries included for the first time for other states but this information was not collected in Alaska and Hawaii in 1954. See the Glossary of Terms.

[c] Item 9 (1958) includes expenditures for plants under construction but not in operation prior to 1958, the data represents expenditures at operating manufacturing establishments only. See Glossary of Terms.

[d] The Census Data for 1972, 1977, 1983 and 1987 are from manufacturing. Data for 1989 are estimates based on a representative sample of establishments canvassed annually and may differ from results of a complete canvass of all establishments.

GENERAL MANUFACTURING STATISTICS, 1899-1989[89,91]						
NORTH DAKOTA[*a]						
Item No.		1899	1909	1919	1929	1939
1.	Total establishments[90,*a]	337	752	755	373	342
2.	With 20 employees or more[90]	---	---	---	---	---
3.	All employees, number (1,000)	1.5	3.4	5.0	5.0	4.1
4.	Payroll ($1,000,000)	0.8	2.4	6.4	7.8	5.0
5.	Production workers, total (number) (1,000)	1.4	2.8	4.2	4.0	2.6
6.	Man hours (1,000,000)	---	---	---	---	---
7.	Wages ($1,000,000)	0.7	1.8	5.0	5.7	2.7
8.	Value added by manufacture ($1,000,000)	2.1	5.5	12.2	15.6	11.0
9.	Capital expenditures, new ($1,000,000)	---	---	---	---	---
10.	Percent of U.S. Employment	0.03	0.05	0.05	0.05	0.04
11.	Index of employment change (1958 = 100)	24	54	79	79	64
12.	U.S. index of employment change (1958 = 100)	30	44	61	60	59

GENERAL MANUFACTURING STATISTICS, 1899-1989[89,91] (Cont.)

NORTH DAKOTA*[a]

Item No.	1947	1954	1958	1963	1967	1972	1977	1982	1987	1989*[d]
1.	361	367	405*[b]	459	454	482	571	587	626	---
2.	---	65	79	78*[b]	92	117	145	142	138	---
3.	5.2	5.6*[b]	6.3	6.5	7.5	10.2	13.8	14.8	15.4	15.2
4.	12.3	19.2*[b]	26.3	31.5	41.6	78.6	162.3	245.6	310.4	335.6
5.	3.8	3.9	4.4	4.5	5.2	7.1	9.2	9.7	10.4	9.8
6.	---	8.3	8.8	9.1	10.7	14.4	17.7	18.0	20.4	19.7
7.	8.5	12.5	17.0	19.8	26.1	47.7	97.2	141.2	180.1	185.2
8.	29.4	35.0	62.6	72.4	112.8	200.7	473.3	652.1	979.0	1,042.0
9.	---	16.2	9.1*[c]	8.1	6.3	13.3	53.0	101.1	47.0	87.7
10.	.04	.03	.04	.04	.04	.05	.07	.08	.08	.08
11.	82	89	100	103	119	162 74	219 100	235 107	244 112	241 110
12.	89	100	100	106	121	119 97	122 100	119 97	118 97	119 97

[a] There were a number of changes in the definition of manufacturing industries through the years that affect historical comparability. See the Glossary of Terms for these changes. The changes have not appreciably affected the comparability of the historical data except for the figures on the number of establishments.

[b] Data for central administrative offices and auxiliaries included for the first time for other states but this information was not collected in Alaska and Hawaii in 1954. See the Glossary of Terms.

[c] Item 9 (1958) includes expenditures for plants under construction but not in operation prior to 1958, the data represents expenditures at operating manufacturing establishments only. See Glossary of Terms.

[d] The Census Data for 1972, 1977, 1983 and 1987 are from manufacturing. Data for 1989 are estimates based on a representative sample of establishments canvassed annually and may differ from results of a complete canvass of all establishments.

GENERAL MANUFACTURING STATISTICS, 1899-1989[89,91]						
OHIO[*a]						
Item No.		1899	1909	1919	1929	1939
1.	Total establishments[90,*a]	13,868	15,138	15,585	11,855	9,543
2.	With 20 employees or more[90]	---	---	---	---	---
3.	All employees, number (1,000)	336.2	508.3	867.3	853.4	731.7
4.	Payroll ($1,000,000)	164.6	317.6	1,214.6	1,404.2	1,120.8
5.	Production workers, total (number) (1,000)	308.1	446.9	728.3	741.1	595.5
6.	Man hours (1,000,000)	---	---	---	---	---
7.	Wages ($1,000,000)	136.4	245.5	941.3	1,102.2	809.4
8.	Value added by manufacture ($1,000,000)	339.4	613.7	2,182.6	2,889.8	2,116.4
9.	Capital expenditures, new ($1,000,000)	---	---	---	---	---
10.	Percent of U.S. Employment	6.93	7.25	8.82	8.83	7.68
11.	Index of employment change (1958 = 100)	28	42	72	71	61
12.	U.S. index of employment change (1958 = 100)	30	44	61	60	59

GENERAL MANUFACTURING STATISTICS, 1899-1989[89,91] (Cont.)										
OHIO[*a]										
Item No.	1947	1954	1958	1963	1967	1972	1977	1982	1987	1989[*d]
1.	12,302	14,550	15,203[*b]	15,484	15,428	16,390	17,354	16,960	17,514	---
2.	---	5,479	5,534	5,800[*b]	6,285	6,487	6,728	6,515	6,854	---
3.	1,194.3	1,292.2[*b]	1,201.0	1,239.8	1,397.0	1,346.3	1,331.2	1,102.0	1,100.2	1,100.2
4.	3,559.5	5,821.0[*b]	6,522.5	8,125.4	10,523.1	13,810.0	20,356.0	24,740.1	30,765.2	32,755.2
5.	988.1	985.7	856.5	885.7	998.1	940.0	924.4	694.9	713.4	726.4
6.	---	1,946.8	1,658.5	1,799.7	2,014.5	1,887.8	1,838.5	1,326.3	1,447.9	1,476.1
7.	2,727.0	4,015.3	4,170.2	5,257.2	6,745.4	8,717.0	12,907.5	13,816.3	17,490.4	18,811.4
8.	6,358.0	10,154.4	11,472.5	15,506.1	20,435.4	27,171.0	43,054.7	49,640.9	71,707.4	79,244.4
9.	---	760.9	795.8[*c]	847.8	1,694.1	1,695.4	2,790.7	4,216.3	4,742.2	5,637.3
10.	8.36	8.02	7.50	7.31	7.23	7.08	6.79	5.77	5.81	5.78
11.	99	108	100	103	116	112 101	111 100	92 83	92 83	92 83
12.	89	100	100	106	121	119 97	122 100	119 97	118 97	119 97

[a] There were a number of changes in the definition of manufacturing industries through the years that affect historical comparability. See the Glossary of Terms for these changes. The changes have not appreciably affected the comparability of the historical data except for the figures on the number of establishments.

[b] Data for central administrative offices and auxiliaries included for the first time for other states but this information was not collected in Alaska and Hawaii in 1954. See the Glossary of Terms.

[c] Item 9 (1958) includes expenditures for plants under construction but not in operation prior to 1958, the data represents expenditures at operating manufacturing establishments only. See Glossary of Terms.

[d] The Census Data for 1972, 1977, 1983 and 1987 are from manufacturing. Data for 1989 are estimates based on a representative sample of establishments canvassed annually and may differ from results of a complete canvass of all establishments.

GENERAL MANUFACTURING STATISTICS, 1899-1989[89,91]						
OKLAHOMA[*a]						
Item No.		1899	1909	1919	1929	1939
1.	Total establishments[90,*a]	495	2,310	2,316	1,658	1,530
2.	With 20 employees or more[90]	---	---	---	---	---
3.	All employees, number (1,000)	2.7	15.3	35.4	38.6	37.6
4.	Payroll ($1,000,000)	1.1	9.3	46.2	57.6	47.2
5.	Production workers, total (number) (1,000)	2.4	13.1	29.0	31.7	27.6
6.	Man hours (1,000,000)	---	---	---	---	---
7.	Wages ($1,000,000)	0.9	7.2	34.4	41.3	30.0
8.	Value added by manufacture ($1,000,000)	2.7	19.5	87.6	149.4	101.8
9.	Capital expenditures, new ($1,000,000)	---	---	---	---	---
10.	Percent of U.S. Employment	.05	.22	.36	.40	.40
11.	Index of employment change (1958 = 100)	2	16	38	42	41
12.	U.S. index of employment change (1958 = 100)	30	44	61	60	59

GENERAL MANUFACTURING STATISTICS, 1899-1989[89,91] (Cont.)										
OKLAHOMA*[a]										
Item No.	1947	1954	1958	1963	1967	1972	1977	1982	1987	1989*[d]
1.	1,740	2,131	2,409*[b]	2,575	2,611	3,042	3,818	4,168	3,742	---
2.	---	524	572	648*[b]	745	897	1,067	1,248	1,020	---
3.	55.4	89.3*[b]	91.6	97.7	117.7	142.7	164.4	196.9	151.2	162.1
4.	143.6	363.6*[b]	446.4	551.7	764.2	1,187.9	2,050.9	4,009.9	3,629.3	4,276.0
5.	44.3	60.6	59.7	64.2	78.7	95.7	110.4	121.4	104.8	106.7
6.	---	122.5	118.4	130.1	157.8	186.1	214.3	233.6	207.0	216.7
7.	105.3	212.2	248.5	295.0	423.0	659.0	1,164.3	2,065.1	2,195.6	2,368.4
8.	341.1	580.6	72.5	978.8	1,346.2	2,270.1	4,662.3	8,143.0	9,856.9	12,898.7
9.	---	51.7	61.9*[c]	63.6	80.9	223.8	485.8	841.3	538.4	747.3
10.	.39	.55	.57	.58	.61	.75	.84	1.03	.80	.85
11.	61	97	100	107	128	156 87	179 100	215 120	165 92	177 99
12.	89	100	100	106	121	119 97	122 100	119 97	118 97	119 97

[a] There were a number of changes in the definition of manufacturing industries through the years that affect historical comparability. See the Glossary of Terms for these changes. The changes have not appreciably affected the comparability of the historical data except for the figures on the number of establishments.

[b] Data for central administrative offices and auxiliaries included for the first time for other states but this information was not collected in Alaska and Hawaii in 1954. See the Glossary of Terms.

[c] Item 9 (1958) includes expenditures for plants under construction but not in operation prior to 1958, the data represents expenditures at operating manufacturing establishments only. See Glossary of Terms.

[d] The Census Data for 1972, 1977, 1983 and 1987 are from manufacturing. Data for 1989 are estimates based on a representative sample of establishments canvassed annually and may differ from results of a complete canvass of all establishments.

GENERAL MANUFACTURING STATISTICS, 1899-1989[89,91]						
OREGON[*a]						
Item No.		1899	1909	1919	1929	1939
1.	Total establishments[90,*a]	1,406	2,246	2,478	2,463	1,903
2.	With 20 employees or more[90]	---	---	---	---	---
3.	All employees, number (1,000)	15.6	32.2	64.6	73.9	67.2
4.	Payroll ($1,000,000)	8.0	23.9	93.9	106.2	87.9
5.	Production workers, total (number) (1,000)	14.5	28.8	57.8	65.5	57.5
6.	Man hours (1,000,000)	---	---	---	---	---
7.	Wages ($1,000,000)	6.8	19.9	80.1	86.8	69.6
8.	Value added by manufacture ($1,000,000)	15.8	42.5	158.8	206.5	156.7
9.	Capital expenditures, new ($1,000,000)	---	---	---	---	---
10.	Percent of U.S. Employment	0.32	0.46	0.66	0.76	0.71
11.	Index of employment change (1958 = 100)	12	24	48	55	50
12.	U.S. index of employment change (1958 = 100)	30	44	61	60	59

GENERAL MANUFACTURING STATISTICS, 1899-1989[89,91] (Cont.)										
OREGON*[a]										
Item No.	1947	1954	1958	1963	1967	1972	1977	1982	1987	1989*[d]
1.	3,075	5,870	5,072*[b]	4,881	4,437	4,670	5,716	5,659	6,355	---
2.	970	1,189	1,151	1,225*[b]	1,275	1,461	1,580	1,443	1,648	---
3.	105.6	135.3*[b]	134.0	145.2	163.1	178.6	202.4	185.1	202.9	217.7
4.	317.8	566.7*[b]	648.6	819.6	1,082.5	1,627.3	2,760.0	3,783.2	4,767.2	5,509.9
5.	92.4	114.5	110.2	117.6	131.2	141.5	155.1	129.6	144.3	153.6
6.	182.2	214.7	209.4	226.4	254.8	271.3	291.6	237.9	280.0	303.6
7.	265.8	447.7	499.8	617.1	798.2	1,170.0	1,901.7	2,333.7	2,948.6	3,300.6
8.	675.0	1,037.5	1,222.2	1,574.8	2,060.5	3,489.9	6,138.0	7,973.0	11,610.3	13,939.8
9.	61.7	67.8	123.3*[c]	132.0	234.2	267.3	574.5	644.0	735.4	1,112.6
10.	0.74	0.84	0.84	0.86	0.84	.94	1.03	.97	1.07	1.14
11.	79	101	100	108	122	133 88	151 100	138 91	151 100	162 108
12.	89	100	100	106	121	119 97	122 100	119 97	118 97	119 97

[a] There were a number of changes in the definition of manufacturing industries through the years that affect historical comparability. See the Glossary of Terms for these changes. The changes have not appreciably affected the comparability of the historical data except for the figures on the number of establishments.

[b] Data for central administrative offices and auxiliaries included for the first time for other states but this information was not collected in Alaska and Hawaii in 1954. See the Glossary of Terms.

[c] Item 9 (1958) includes expenditures for plants under construction but not in operation prior to 1958, the data represents expenditures at operating manufacturing establishments only. See Glossary of Terms.

[d] The Census Data for 1972, 1977, 1983 and 1987 are from manufacturing. Data for 1989 are estimates based on a representative sample of establishments canvassed annually and may differ from results of a complete canvass of all establishments.

GENERAL MANUFACTURING STATISTICS, 1899-1989[89,91]						
PENNSYLVANIA[*a]						
Item No.		1899	1909	1919	1929	1939
1.	Total establishments[90,*a]	23,462	27,563	26,614	16,947	13,116
2.	With 20 employees or more[90]	---	---	---	---	---
3.	All employees, number (1,000)	707.9	972.4	1,290.2	1,154.9	1,015.8
4.	Payroll ($1,000,000)	343.0	566.5	1,732.9	1,749.3	1,356.2
5.	Production workers, total (number) (1,000)	664.0	877.5	1,130.6	1,014.0	853.4
6.	Man hours (1,000,000)	---	---	---	---	---
7.	Wages ($1,000,000)	296.9	455.6	1,399.2	1,379.4	997.6
8.	Value added by manufacture ($1,000,000)	691.6	1,044.2	3,093.0	3,430.6	2,476.9
9.	Capital expenditures, new ($1,000,000)	---	---	---	---	---
10.	Percent of U.S. Employment	14.60	13.87	13.12	11.96	10.66
11.	Index of employment change (1958 = 100)	50	69	92	82	72
12.	U.S. index of employment change (1958 = 100)	30	44	61	60	59

GENERAL MANUFACTURING STATISTICS, 1899-1989[89,91] (Cont.)										
PENNSYLVANIA[*a]										
Item No.	1947	1954	1958	1963	1967	1972	1977	1982	1987	1989[*d]
1.	16,794	18,795	19,337[*b]	19,459	18,771	18,398	18,735	17,666	17,854	---
2.	---	7,631	7,735	7,981[*b]	8,369	8,070	7,704	7,497	7,228	---
3.	1,441.7	1,471.1[*b]	1,402.0	1,392.9	1,549.5	1,417.5	1,329.2	1,180.0	1,037.5	1,038.4
4.	3,925.2	5,903.9[*b]	6,776.1	8,008.6	10,349.7	12,794.1	18,042.7	23,314.5	25,301.6	27,345.1
5.	1,221.4	1,137.2	1,034.2	1,028.0	1,136.2	1,015.0	934.1	772.2	681.9	683.1
6.	---	2,187.0	1,960.6	2,002.1	2,211.3	1,953.9	1,781.6	1,435.9	1,330.1	1,380.6
7.	3,057.6	4,012.9	4,353.7	5,110.7	6,488.7	7,885.7	10,948.8	12,855.6	13,731.1	14,650.6
8.	6,926.1	9,930.5	11,422.6	14,043.6	19,276.8	23,518.5	36,016.9	44,824.1	57,605.2	62,713.5
9.	---	619.1	816.3[*c]	777.4	1,633.4	1,479.3	2,297.4	3,390.9	3,440.5	4,214.0
10.	10.09	9.14	8.75	8.21	8.02	7.45	6.78	6.17	5.47	5.45
11.	103	105	100	99	111	101 107	95 100	84 89	74 78	74 78
12.	89	100	100	106	121	119 97	122 100	119 97	118 97	119 97

[a] There were a number of changes in the definition of manufacturing industries through the years that affect historical comparability. See the Glossary of Terms for these changes. The changes have not appreciably affected the comparability of the historical data except for the figures on the number of establishments.

[b] Data for central administrative offices and auxiliaries included for the first time for other states but this information was not collected in Alaska and Hawaii in 1954. See the Glossary of Terms.

[c] Item 9 (1958) includes expenditures for plants under construction but not in operation prior to 1958, the data represents expenditures at operating manufacturing establishments only. See Glossary of Terms.

[d] The Census Data for 1972, 1977, 1983 and 1987 are from manufacturing. Data for 1989 are estimates based on a representative sample of establishments canvassed annually and may differ from results of a complete canvass of all establishments.

GENERAL MANUFACTURING STATISTICS, 1899-1989[89,91]						
RHODE ISLAND[*a]						
Item No.		1899	1909	1919	1929	1939
1.	Total establishments[90,*a]	1,678	1,951	2,367	1,701	1,399
2.	With 20 employees or more[90]	---	---	---	---	---
3.	All employees, number (1,000)	92.2	120.9	153.5	140.1	122.7
4.	Payroll ($1,000,000)	41.3	65.8	168.1	182.9	141.3
5.	Production workers, total (number) (1,000)	88.2	113.5	139.3	126.1	106.1
6.	Man hours (1,000,000)	---	---	---	---	---
7.	Wages ($1,000,000)	36.0	55.2	137.1	144.2	105.2
8.	Value added by manufacture ($1,000,000)	77.6	122.2	330.6	324.1	237.7
9.	Capital expenditures, new ($1,000,000)	---	---	---	---	---
10.	Percent of U.S. Employment	1.90	1.72	1.56	1.45	1.29
11.	Index of employment change (1958 = 100)	81	106	134	122	107
12.	U.S. index of employment change (1958 = 100)	30	44	61	60	59

GENERAL MANUFACTURING STATISTICS, 1899-1989[89,91] (Cont.)										
RHODE ISLAND[*a]										
Item No.	1947	1954	1958	1963	1967	1972	1977	1982	1987	1989[*d]
1.	2,213	2,635	2,737[*b]	2,710	2,703	2,756	3,107	2,855	2,878	---
2.	---	867	907	868[*b]	922	904	945	940	898	---
3.	147.4	125.0[*b]	114.5	113.9	122.3	118.1	125.0	113.8	112.0	104.0
4.	375.7	431.9[*b]	453.1	533.4	700.4	888.2	1,326.5	1,759.5	2,292.0	2,324.7
5.	128.6	103.8	91.4	90.0	96.6	91.4	94.7	82.6	76.3	69.5
6.	---	204.4	175.9	177.2	188.5	174.2	177.5	157.4	149.4	138.1
7.	298.5	314.5	314.3	365.3	466.9	565.9	825.2	1,051.9	1,252.3	1,228.3
8.	658.9	697.3	756.2	958.6	1,350.9	1,764.4	2,736.6	3,792.7	4,787.5	5,131.2
9.	---	27.7	29.8[*c]	43.1	74.8	100.5	145.6	183.8	276.4	223.0
10.	1.03	.77	.71	.67	.63	.62	.64	.60	.59	.55
11.	129	108	100	99	107	103 94	109 100	99 91	98 90	91 83
12.	89	100	100	106	121	119 97	122 100	119 97	118 97	119 97

[a] There were a number of changes in the definition of manufacturing industries through the years that affect historical comparability. See the Glossary of Terms for these changes. The changes have not appreciably affected the comparability of the historical data except for the figures on the number of establishments.

[b] Data for central administrative offices and auxiliaries included for the first time for other states but this information was not collected in Alaska and Hawaii in 1954. See the Glossary of Terms.

[c] Item 9 (1958) includes expenditures for plants under construction but not in operation prior to 1958, the data represents expenditures at operating manufacturing establishments only. See Glossary of Terms.

[d] The Census Data for 1972, 1977, 1983 and 1987 are from manufacturing. Data for 1989 are estimates based on a representative sample of establishments canvassed annually and may differ from results of a complete canvass of all establishments.

GENERAL MANUFACTURING STATISTICS, 1899-1989[89,91]						
SOUTH CAROLINA[*a]						
Item No.		1899	1909	1919	1929	1939
1.	Total establishments[90,*a]	1,369	1,854	1,821	1,659	1,300
2.	With 20 employees or more[90]	---	---	---	---	---
3.	All employees, number (1,000)	48.4	76.3	84.0	113.9	136.1
4.	Payroll ($1,000,000)	10.4	24.1	72.3	86.0	103.2
5.	Production workers, total (number) (1,000)	47.0	73.0	78.9	108.8	126.4
6.	Man hours (1,000,000)	---	---	---	---	---
7.	Wages ($1,000,000)	9.1	20.4	61.9	73.2	86.3
8.	Value added by manufacture ($1,000,000)	22.9	46.8	152.3	159.4	169.3
9.	Capital expenditures, new ($1,000,000)	---	---	---	---	---
10.	Percent of U.S. Employment	1.00	1.09	0.85	1.18	1.43
11.	Index of employment change (1958 = 100)	21	34	37	50	60
12.	U.S. index of employment change (1958 = 100)	30	44	61	60	59

GENERAL MANUFACTURING STATISTICS, 1899-1989[89,91] (Cont.)

SOUTH CAROLINA*[a]

Item No.	1947	1954	1958	1963	1967	1972	1977	1982	1987	1989*[d]
1.	2,135	2,720	2,911*[b]	3,057	3,465	3,719	4,229	4,206	4,541	---
2.	---	834	939	1,076*[b]	1,251	1,441	1,560	1,723	1,890	---
3.	188.8	219.9*[b]	225.5	261.6	304.3	345.1	374.2	367.5	365.8	370.7
4.	377.1	634.8*[b]	732.1	1,049.3	1,502.2	2,344.5	3,804.9	5,539.5	7,323.9	8,032.1
5.	175.9	190.1	193.9	221.9	253.8	282.7	299.8	279.4	279.6	280.9
6.	---	378.9	381.5	455.3	523.0	581.6	594.0	522.2	566.2	566.2
7.	330.7	487.0	565.0	797.2	1,106.6	1,679.4	2,640.3	3,576.4	4,742.2	5,129.2
8.	793.9	1,040.9	1,360.1	2,111.1	3,030.3	4,965.6	8,186.1	12,218.7	19,111.9	21,464.8
9.	---	59.6	75.6*[c]	179.8	416.6	506.8	788.6	1,503.0	1,586.0	2,177.3
10.	1.32	1.37	1.41	1.54	1.57	1.81	1.91	1.92	1.93	1.95
11.	84	98	100	116	135	153 92	166 100	163 98	162 98	164 99
12.	89	100	100	106	121	119 97	122 100	119 97	118 97	119 97

[a] There were a number of changes in the definition of manufacturing industries through the years that affect historical comparability. See the Glossary of Terms for these changes. The changes have not appreciably affected the comparability of the historical data except for the figures on the number of establishments.

[b] Data for central administrative offices and auxiliaries included for the first time for other states but this information was not collected in Alaska and Hawaii in 1954. See the Glossary of Terms.

[c] Item 9 (1958) includes expenditures for plants under construction but not in operation prior to 1958, the data represents expenditures at operating manufacturing establishments only. See Glossary of Terms.

[d] The Census Data for 1972, 1977, 1983 and 1987 are from manufacturing. Data for 1989 are estimates based on a representative sample of establishments canvassed annually and may differ from results of a complete canvass of all establishments.

GENERAL MANUFACTURING STATISTICS, 1899-1989[89,91]						
SOUTH DAKOTA[*a]						
Item No.		1899	1909	1919	1929	1939
1.	Total establishments[90,*a]	624	1,020	1,054	615	450
2.	With 20 employees or more[90]	---	---	---	---	---
3.	All employees, number (1,000)	2.5	4.3	6.8	7.8	7.3
4.	Payroll ($1,000,000)	1.3	2.9	8.8	10.7	9.0
5.	Production workers, total (number) (1,000)	2.2	3.6	5.6	6.5	5.4
6.	Man hours (1,000,000)	---	---	---	---	---
7.	Wages ($1,000,000)	1.1	2.3	6.8	8.1	5.9
8.	Value added by manufacture ($1,000,000)	3.0	6.4	17.1	22.7	19.6
9.	Capital expenditures, new ($1,000,000)	---	---	---	---	---
10.	Percent of U.S. Employment	0.05	0.06	0.07	0.08	0.08
11.	Index of employment change (1958 = 100)	19	33	53	60	57
12.	U.S. index of employment change (1958 = 100)	30	44	61	60	59

GENERAL MANUFACTURING STATISTICS, 1899-1989[89,91] (Cont.)										
SOUTH DAKOTA*[a]										
Item No.	1947	1954	1958	1963	1967	1972	1977	1982	1987	1989*[d]
1.	494	546	575*[b]	586	604	606	740	748	761	---
2.	87	92	109	115*[b]	137	171	195	205	228	---
3.	10.3	11.5*[b]	12.9	13.2	15.5	17.4	22.5	24.5	27.5	28.8
4.	25.8	41.1*[b]	54.8	70.0	92.5	134.5	251.4	397.9	497.9	543.8
5.	8.1	8.4	9.6	9.6	11.3	12.9	16.7	17.5	19.9	21.1
6.	17.7	18.0	18.6	19.9	22.4	25.1	32.0	32.6	38.8	41.9
7.	19.2	28.0	37.5	48.0	61.7	89.4	169.1	261.9	312.6	346.5
8.	51.4	77.7	114.3	140.0	171.3	284.5	611.6	1,100.2	1,476.1	1,604.7
9.	3.4	3.4	5.2*[c]	7.3	8.2	20.1	36.7	62.3	79.3	81.2
10.	.07	.07	.08	.08	.08	.09	.11	.13	.15	.15
11.	80	89	100	102	120	135 77	174 100	190 109	213 122	223 128
12.	89	100	100	106	121	119 97	122 100	119 97	118 97	119 97

[a] There were a number of changes in the definition of manufacturing industries through the years that affect historical comparability. See the Glossary of Terms for these changes. The changes have not appreciably affected the comparability of the historical data except for the figures on the number of establishments.

[b] Data for central administrative offices and auxiliaries included for the first time for other states but this information was not collected in Alaska and Hawaii in 1954. See the Glossary of Terms.

[c] Item 9 (1958) includes expenditures for plants under construction but not in operation prior to 1958, the data represents expenditures at operating manufacturing establishments only. See Glossary of Terms.

[d] The Census Data for 1972, 1977, 1983 and 1987 are from manufacturing. Data for 1989 are estimates based on a representative sample of establishments canvassed annually and may differ from results of a complete canvass of all establishments.

GENERAL MANUFACTURING STATISTICS, 1899-1989[89,91]						
TENNESSEE[*a]						
Item No.		1899	1909	1919	1929	1939
1.	Total establishments[90,*a]	3,116	4,609	4,426	2,855	2,225
2.	With 20 employees or more[90]	---	---	---	---	---
3.	All employees, number (1,000)	49.3	82.3	107.7	142.0	152.2
4.	Payroll ($1,000,000)	17.8	37.4	105.9	149.1	149.5
5.	Production workers, total (number) (1,000)	46.0	73.8	94.6	128.4	131.0
6.	Man hours (1,000,000)	---	---	---	---	---
7.	Wages ($1,000,000)	14.7	28.3	80.7	115.9	108.8
8.	Value added by manufacture ($1,000,000)	38.2	76.2	210.2	322.9	318.4
9.	Capital expenditures, new ($1,000,000)	---	---	---	---	---
10.	Percent of U.S. Employment	1.02	1.17	1.10	1.47	1.60
11.	Index of employment change (1958 = 100)	17	29	38	50	54
12.	U.S. index of employment change (1958 = 100)	30	44	61	60	59

GENERAL MANUFACTURING STATISTICS, 1899-1989[89,91] (Cont.)										
TENNESSEE[*a]										
Item No.	1947	1954	1958	1963	1967	1972	1977	1982	1987	1989[*d]
1.	3,345	4,058	4,508[*b]	4,787	5,040	5,647	6,487	6,417	6,868	---
2.	---	1,366	1,516	1,809[*b]	2,022	2,291	2,477	2,617	2,799	---
3.	222.3	267.5[*b]	279.3	334.3	418.0	467.4	489.8	461.6	484.9	499.6
4.	475.0	882.6[*b]	1,077.0	1,505.2	2,190.0	3,351.7	5,218.7	7,377.7	9,869.2	10,971.5
5.	193.2	214.0	220.8	267.0	333.6	367.0	375.7	337.5	359.2	371.6
6.	---	418.4	426.6	530.2	654.7	725.3	720.3	629.8	707.4	734.7
7.	371.6	612.5	739.5	1,040.7	1,512.2	2,295.1	3,481.2	4,602.9	6,282.6	6,882.1
8.	961.4	1,678.8	2,207.1	3,299.3	4,921.1	7,662.0	12,663.4	17,822.9	27,049.7	30,648.8
9.	---	152.7	209.7[*c]	244.9	412.4	540.0	961.1	2,061.5	1,904.7	2,777.0
10.	1.56	1.66	1.74	1.97	2.16	2.46	2.50	2.41	2.56	2.62
11.	79	95	100	120	150	167 95	175 100	165 94	174 99	179 102
12.	89	100	100	106	121	119 97	122 100	119 97	118 97	119 97

[a] There were a number of changes in the definition of manufacturing industries through the years that affect historical comparability. See the Glossary of Terms for these changes. The changes have not appreciably affected the comparability of the historical data except for the figures on the number of establishments.

[b] Data for central administrative offices and auxiliaries included for the first time for other states but this information was not collected in Alaska and Hawaii in 1954. See the Glossary of Terms.

[c] Item 9 (1958) includes expenditures for plants under construction but not in operation prior to 1958, the data represents expenditures at operating manufacturing establishments only. See Glossary of Terms.

[d] The Census Data for 1972, 1977, 1983 and 1987 are from manufacturing. Data for 1989 are estimates based on a representative sample of establishments canvassed annually and may differ from results of a complete canvass of all establishments.

GENERAL MANUFACTURING STATISTICS, 1899-1989[89,91]						
TEXAS[*a]						
Item No.		1899	1909	1919	1929	1939
1.	Total establishments[90,*a]	3,107	4,588	5,390	5,198	5,085
2.	With 20 employees or more[90]	---	---	---	---	---
3.	All employees, number (1,000)	41.5	80.1	124.1	156.1	164.0
4.	Payroll ($1,000,000)	19.8	48.8	146.2	201.7	196.7
5.	Production workers, total (number) (1,000)	38.6	70.2	106.3	134.5	125.1
6.	Man hours (1,000,000)	---	---	---	---	---
7.	Wages ($1,000,000)	16.9	37.9	114.9	151.8	126.4
8.	Value added by manufacture ($1,000,000)	38.5	94.7	295.7	460.3	448.5
9.	Capital expenditures, new ($1,000,000)	---	---	---	---	---
10.	Percent of U.S. Employment	0.85	1.14	1.26	1.62	1.72
11.	Index of employment change (1958 = 100)	9	17	26	33	34
12.	U.S. index of employment change (1958 = 100)	30	44	61	60	59

GENERAL MANUFACTURING STATISTICS, 1899-1989[89,91] (Cont.)										
TEXAS*[a]										
Item No.	1947	1954	1958	1963	1967	1972	1977	1982	1987	1989*[d]
1.	7,129	8,890	10,505*[b]	11,581	12,722	14,422	18,107	20,288	20,367	---
2.	---	2,612	3,088	3,478*[b]	4,039	4,790	5,644	7,006	6,184	---
3.	297.1	417.2*[b]	477.6	513.8	657.5	736.1	886.4	1,058.5	914.0	932.0
4.	755.4	1,659.3*[b]	2,284.9	2,890.5	4,340.4	6,344.6	11,653.1	21,434.9	23,240.9	25,684.2
5.	242.0	313.9	343.1	361.4	466.4	516.6	600.7	669.5	560.8	572.8
6.	---	639.6	683.1	741.4	958.5	1,030.5	1,190.1	1,306.0	1,125.2	1,154.1
7.	558.4	1,109.1	1,453.9	1,744.0	2,617.0	3,763.3	6,626.4	11,232.8	11,443.9	12,348.8
8.	1,727.5	3,501.7	5,045.2	7,119.5	10,922.4	15,228.0	33,080.9	53,357.8	63,899.1	79,394.7
9.	---	452.2	611.1*[c]	567.3	1,408.8	1,345.7	5,194.7	8,193.2	4,548.0	7,573.3
10.	2.08	2.59	2.98	3.03	3.40	3.87	4.52	5.54	4.82	4.89
11.	62	87	100	108	138	154 83	186 100	222 119	191 103	195 105
12.	89	100	100	106	121	119 97	122 100	119 97	118 97	119 97

[a] There were a number of changes in the definition of manufacturing industries through the years that affect historical comparability. See the Glossary of Terms for these changes. The changes have not appreciably affected the comparability of the historical data except for the figures on the number of establishments.

[b] Data for central administrative offices and auxiliaries included for the first time for other states but this information was not collected in Alaska and Hawaii in 1954. See the Glossary of Terms.

[c] Item 9 (1958) includes expenditures for plants under construction but not in operation prior to 1958, the data represents expenditures at operating manufacturing establishments only. See Glossary of Terms.

[d] The Census Data for 1972, 1977, 1983 and 1987 are from manufacturing. Data for 1989 are estimates based on a representative sample of establishments canvassed annually and may differ from results of a complete canvass of all establishments.

GENERAL MANUFACTURING STATISTICS, 1899-1989[89,91]						
UTAH[*a]						
Item No.		1899	1909	1919	1929	1939
1.	Total establishments[90,*a]	575	749	1,035	651	549
2.	With 20 employees or more[90]	---	---	---	---	---
3.	All employees, number (1,000)	6.0	13.4	21.5	18.5	15.5
4.	Payroll ($1,000,000)	3.3	10.4	26.5	26.1	19.0
5.	Production workers, total (number) (1,000)	5.4	11.8	18.4	15.6	11.5
6.	Man hours (1,000,000)	---	---	---	---	---
7.	Wages ($1,000,000)	2.8	8.4	20.9	19.7	11.9
8.	Value added by manufacture ($1,000,000)	6.5	20.7	45.8	56.7	43.3
9.	Capital expenditures, new ($1,000,000)	---	---	---	---	---
10.	Percent of U.S. Employment	0.12	0.19	0.22	0.19	0.16
11.	Index of employment change (1958 = 100)	16	37	58	50	42
12.	U.S. index of employment change (1958 = 100)	30	44	61	60	59

GENERAL MANUFACTURING STATISTICS, 1899-1989[89,91] (Cont.)										
UTAH[*a]										
Item No.	1947	1954	1958	1963	1967	1972	1977	1982	1987	1989[*d]
1.	771	852	1,000[*b]	1,110	1,124	1,358	1,748	1,962	2,088	---
2.	---	234	296	336[*b]	353	430	494	579	617	---
3.	24.5	29.9[*b]	37.6	53.5	47.0	56.6	70.2	83.2	88.8	96.0
4.	63.8	120.6[*b]	185.9	328.2	314.9	486.2	867.2	1,538.8	2,073.1	2,331.9
5.	20.0	22.6	26.7	33.4	31.7	38.8	48.8	54.2	54.8	60.6
6.	---	44.8	52.1	67.0	62.3	73.7	92.3	103.0	107.6	119.1
7.	48.0	82.4	120.8	182.0	182.7	286.9	522.3	837.0	1,002.3	1,173.0
8.	128.3	276.3	417.4	710.6	777.9	1,068.7	1,974.0	3,455.1	4,882.9	5,488.9
9.	---	23.4	31.3[*c]	29.6	59.2	67.9	393.6	327.6	403.5	441.3
10.	0.17	0.19	0.23	0.32	0.24	.30	.36	.43	.47	.50
11.	67	81	100	142	125	151 81	187 100	221 119	236 126	255 137
12.	89	100	100	106	121	119 97	122 100	119 97	118 97	119 97

[a] There were a number of changes in the definition of manufacturing industries through the years that affect historical comparability. See the Glossary of Terms for these changes. The changes have not appreciably affected the comparability of the historical data except for the figures on the number of establishments.

[b] Data for central administrative offices and auxiliaries included for the first time for other states but this information was not collected in Alaska and Hawaii in 1954. See the Glossary of Terms.

[c] Item 9 (1958) includes expenditures for plants under construction but not in operation prior to 1958, the data represents expenditures at operating manufacturing establishments only. See Glossary of Terms.

[d] The Census Data for 1972, 1977, 1983 and 1987 are from manufacturing. Data for 1989 are estimates based on a representative sample of establishments canvassed annually and may differ from results of a complete canvass of all establishments.

GENERAL MANUFACTURING STATISTICS, 1899-1989[89,91]						
VERMONT[*a]						
Item No.		1899	1909	1919	1929	1939
1.	Total establishments[90,*a]	1,938	1,958	1,702	927	659
2.	With 20 employees or more[90]	---	---	---	---	---
3.	All employees, number (1,000)	29.9	36.5	36.7	30.5	24.1
4.	Payroll ($1,000,000)	13.0	20.1	41.1	41.9	27.4
5.	Production workers, total (number) (1,000)	28.2	33.8	33.2	27.4	20.5
6.	Man hours (1,000,000)	---	---	---	---	---
7.	Wages ($1,000,000)	11.4	17.3	33.8	33.8	19.9
8.	Value added by manufacture ($1,000,000)	25.1	33.5	71.8	77.3	49.7
9.	Capital expenditures, new ($1,000,000)	---	---	---	---	---
10.	Percent of U.S. Employment	.62	.52	.37	.32	.25
11.	Index of employment change (1958 = 100)	92	112	113	94	74
12.	U.S. index of employment change (1958 = 100)	30	44	61	60	59

GENERAL MANUFACTURING STATISTICS, 1899-1989[89,91] (Cont.)										
VERMONT[*a]										
Item No.	1947	1954	1958	1963	1967	1972	1977	1982	1987	1989[*d]
1.	831	1,071	1,040[*b]	977	925	860	1,030	1,104	1,263	---
2.	---	296	277	267[*b]	281	274	298	310	332	---
3.	34.9	36.1[*b]	32.5	33.7	42.5	36.9	41.5	46.8	48.5	46.6
4.	83.1	123.6[*b]	132.5	167.9	259.1	311.4	498.0	862.7	1,140.0	1,202.8
5.	30.3	29.9	25.4	25.7	31.3	26.1	28.7	30.0	30.6	30.5
6.	---	59.3	50.3	52.4	64.6	52.2	55.9	56.2	58.3	58.9
7.	66.4	93.0	92.1	113.4	162.4	176.3	270.1	433.8	551.6	606.5
8.	149.7	223.0	235.9	309.3	515.0	576.0	1,050.1	2,036.8	2,543.1	3,034.4
9.	---	8.9	11.6[*c]	15.7	35.1	36.8	93.0	270.9	334.4	437.2
10.	.24	.22	.20	.20	.22	.19	.21	.24	.26	.24
11.	107	111	100	104	131	114 89	122 100	113 113	117 117	123 112
12.	89	100	100	106	121	119 97	122 100	119 97	118 97	119 97

[a] There were a number of changes in the definition of manufacturing industries through the years that affect historical comparability. See the Glossary of Terms for these changes. The changes have not appreciably affected the comparability of the historical data except for the figures on the number of establishments.

[b] Data for central administrative offices and auxiliaries included for the first time for other states but this information was not collected in Alaska and Hawaii in 1954. See the Glossary of Terms.

[c] Item 9 (1958) includes expenditures for plants under construction but not in operation prior to 1958, the data represents expenditures at operating manufacturing establishments only. See Glossary of Terms.

[d] The Census Data for 1972, 1977, 1983 and 1987 are from manufacturing. Data for 1989 are estimates based on a representative sample of establishments canvassed annually and may differ from results of a complete canvass of all establishments.

GENERAL MANUFACTURING STATISTICS, 1899-1989[89,91]						
VIRGINIA[*a]						
Item No.		1899	1909	1919	1929	1939
1.	Total establishments[90,*a]	3,186	5,867	5,487	3,287	2,494
2.	With 20 employees or more[90]	---	---	---	---	---
3.	All employees, number (1,000)	70.1	114.2	132.8	131.6	150.2
4.	Payroll ($1,000,000)	23.9	47.3	145.4	147.4	150.7
5.	Production workers, total (number) (1,000)	66.2	105.7	119.0	120.3	132.1
6.	Man hours (1,000,000)	---	---	---	---	---
7.	Wages ($1,000,000)	20.3	38.2	119.6	118.1	113.8
8.	Value added by manufacture ($1,000,000)	49.3	94.2	271.1	380.1	376.3
9.	Capital expenditures, new ($1,000,000)	---	---	---	---	---
10.	Percent of U.S. Employment	1.44	1.63	1.35	1.36	1.58
11.	Index of employment change (1958 = 100)	27	44	51	51	58
12.	U.S. index of employment change (1958 = 100)	30	44	61	60	59

GENERAL MANUFACTURING STATISTICS, 1899-1989[89,91] (Cont.)										
VIRGINIA[*a]										
Item No.	1947	1954	1958	1963	1967	1972	1977	1982	1987	1989[*d]
1.	3,643	4,398	4,472[*b]	4,543	4,938	4,837	5,519	5,568	6,136	---
2.	---	1,290	1,381	1,573[*b]	1,620	1,768	1,879	2,036	2,228	---
3.	216.5	242.8[*b]	258.1	302.1	339.8	375.4	395.2	391.1	429.2	424.9
4.	483.6	776.8[*b]	986.5	1,432.0	1,905.1	2,826.0	4,442.4	6,649.0	9,740.1	10,407.8
5.	189.9	202.7	204.4	239.6	268.2	293.2	302.0	287.4	305.3	305.1
6.	---	394.7	397.6	480.2	535.0	582.9	581.8	541.1	600.3	601.0
7.	384.3	576.8	686.8	992.1	1,296.1	1,902.1	2,916.8	4,191.7	5,728.2	6,094.1
8.	1,050.6	1,629.0	2,122.7	3,046.2	4,067.7	6,177.5	10,882.0	17,255.6	26,857.3	30,439.1
9.	---	109.9	146.5[*c]	231.8	347.0	585.8	953.0	1,522.9	1,542.7	1,986.7
10.	1.51	1.51	1.61	1.78	1.76	1.97	2.02	2.04	2.26	2.23
11.	84	94	100	117	132	145 95	153 100	152 99	166 109	165 108
12.	89	100	100	106	121	119 97	122 100	119 97	118 97	119 97

[a] There were a number of changes in the definition of manufacturing industries through the years that affect historical comparability. See the Glossary of Terms for these changes. The changes have not appreciably affected the comparability of the historical data except for the figures on the number of establishments.

[b] Data for central administrative offices and auxiliaries included for the first time for other states but this information was not collected in Alaska and Hawaii in 1954. See the Glossary of Terms.

[c] Item 9 (1958) includes expenditures for plants under construction but not in operation prior to 1958, the data represents expenditures at operating manufacturing establishments only. See Glossary of Terms.

[d] The Census Data for 1972, 1977, 1983 and 1987 are from manufacturing. Data for 1989 are estimates based on a representative sample of establishments canvassed annually and may differ from results of a complete canvass of all establishments.

GENERAL MANUFACTURING STATISTICS, 1899-1989[89,91]						
WASHINGTON[*a]						
Item No.		1899	1909	1919	1929	1939
1.	Total establishments[90,*a]	1,929	3,674	4,356	3,672	2,858
2.	With 20 employees or more[90]	---	---	---	---	---
3.	All employees, number (1,000)	33.6	76.9	144.3	128.7	99.1
4.	Payroll ($1,000,000)	19.1	59.6	222.5	196.6	142.6
5.	Production workers, total (number) (1,000)	31.5	69.1	131.2	114.8	82.3
6.	Man hours (1,000,000)	---	---	---	---	---
7.	Wages ($1,000,000)	17.1	49.8	192.5	160.7	108.2
8.	Value added by manufacture ($1,000,000)	32.6	102.9	361.9	367.1	367.7
9.	Capital expenditures, new ($1,000,000)	---	---	---	---	---
10.	Percent of U.S. Employment	0.69	1.10	1.47	1.33	1.04
11.	Index of employment change (1958 = 100)	16	36	67	60	46
12.	U.S. index of employment change (1958 = 100)	30	44	61	60	59

GENERAL MANUFACTURING STATISTICS, 1899-1989[89,91] (Cont.)										
WASHINGTON[*a]										
Item No.	1947	1954	1958	1963	1967	1972	1977	1982	1987	1989[*d]
1.	3,409	4,929	5,065[*b]	5,250	5,014	5,345	6,723	6,788	7,636	---
2.	---	1,152	1,157	1,233[*b]	1,375	1,463	1,712	1,707	1,953	---
3.	144.3	194.1[*b]	215.0	224.4	270.7	226.0	265.0	291.4	309.7	361.6
4.	437.8	854.1[*b]	1,173.3	1,479.1	2,119.0	2,308.4	4,054.3	6,680.6	8,841.6	10,983.5
5.	123.4	148.8	157.3	152.2	177.1	159.8	180.7	177.6	184.2	208.0
6.	---	280.8	305.8	297.3	344.6	303.3	338.2	327.0	353.5	395.1
7.	354.4	594.7	761.4	881.4	1,179.8	1,410.9	2,385.0	3,624.3	4,262.0	4,791.3
8.	874.0	1,549.1	2,166.6	2,884.9	3,764.2	4,721.4	8,955.0	12,595.5	19,016.1	23,338.0
9.	---	147.1	160.4[*c]	143.4	464.7	353.7	850.0	1,074.3	1,244.8	2,264.6
10.	1.01	1.21	1.34	1.32	1.40	1.19	1.35	1.53	1.63	1.90
11.	67	90	100	104	126	105 85	123 100	136 110	144 117	168 136
12.	89	100	100	106	121	119 97	122 100	119 97	118 97	119 97

[a] There were a number of changes in the definition of manufacturing industries through the years that affect historical comparability. See the Glossary of Terms for these changes. The changes have not appreciably affected the comparability of the historical data except for the figures on the number of establishments.

[b] Data for central administrative offices and auxiliaries included for the first time for other states but this information was not collected in Alaska and Hawaii in 1954. See the Glossary of Terms.

[c] Item 9 (1958) includes expenditures for plants under construction but not in operation prior to 1958, the data represents expenditures at operating manufacturing establishments only. See Glossary of Terms.

[d] The Census Data for 1972, 1977, 1983 and 1987 are from manufacturing. Data for 1989 are estimates based on a representative sample of establishments canvassed annually and may differ from results of a complete canvass of all establishments.

GENERAL MANUFACTURING STATISTICS, 1899-1989[89,91]						
WEST VIRGINIA[*a]						
Item No.		1899	1909	1919	1929	1939
1.	Total establishments[90,*a]	1,824	2,586	2,627	1,488	1,094
2.	With 20 employees or more[90]	---	---	---	---	---
3.	All employees, number (1,000)	34.8	68.9	90.7	93.6	87.7
4.	Payroll ($1,000,000)	14.5	38.7	118.9	136.3	113.7
5.	Production workers, total (number) (1,000)	33.1	63.9	82.6	85.3	74.4
6.	Man hours (1,000,000)	---	---	---	---	---
7.	Wages ($1,000,000)	12.6	33.0	101.3	115.3	87.8
8.	Value added by manufacture ($1,000,000)	29.8	69.1	199.6	251.6	213.3
9.	Capital expenditures, new ($1,000,000)	---	---	---	---	---
10.	Percent of U.S. Employment	0.72	0.98	0.92	0.97	0.92
11.	Index of employment change (1958 = 100)	30	59	78	81	76
12.	U.S. index of employment change (1958 = 100)	30	44	61	60	59

GENERAL MANUFACTURING STATISTICS, 1899-1989[89,91] (Cont.)										
WEST VIRGINIA*[a]										
Item No.	1947	1954	1958	1963	1967	1972	1977	1982	1987	1989*[d]
1.	1,602	2,027	1,916*[b]	1,832	1,844	1,733	1,857	1,662	1,620	---
2.	558	517	519	528*[b]	563	606	583	559	486	---
3.	127.4	122.4*[b]	116.2	117.0	124.0	120.8	117.0	95.8	83.8	83.2
4.	337.9	494.9*[b]	573.8	700.1	831.6	1,097.6	1,620.5	2,007.0	2,107.6	2,256.8
5.	109.0	97.3	90.4	90.2	96.7	92.7	89.2	65.2	58.8	59.0
6.	215.6	185.7	173.1	179.8	189.9	181.8	170.9	121.5	115.4	117.3
7.	268.5	354.7	411.0	491.3	587.3	765.4	1,124.3	1,233.0	1,312.3	1,442.1
8.	663.9	988.2	1,268.8	1,886.4	2,169.5	2,646.7	3,880.2	4,049.2	5,404.4	6,672.7
9.	82.3	98.9	171.9*[c]	173.0	269.0	216.0	402.3	393.7	434.8	522.4
10.	.89	.76	.73	.69	.64	.63	.60	.50	.44	.44
11.	110	105	100	101	107	104 103	101 100	82 82	72 72	72 71
12.	89	100	100	106	121	119 97	122 100	119 97	118 97	119 97

[a] There were a number of changes in the definition of manufacturing industries through the years that affect historical comparability. See the Glossary of Terms for these changes. The changes have not appreciably affected the comparability of the historical data except for the figures on the number of establishments.

[b] Data for central administrative offices and auxiliaries included for the first time for other states but this information was not collected in Alaska and Hawaii in 1954. See the Glossary of Terms.

[c] Item 9 (1958) includes expenditures for plants under construction but not in operation prior to 1958, the data represents expenditures at operating manufacturing establishments only. See Glossary of Terms.

[d] The Census Data for 1972, 1977, 1983 and 1987 are from manufacturing. Data for 1989 are estimates based on a representative sample of establishments canvassed annually and may differ from results of a complete canvass of all establishments.

GENERAL MANUFACTURING STATISTICS, 1899-1989[89,91]						
WISCONSIN[*a]						
Item No.		1899	1909	1919	1929	1939
1.	Total establishments[90,*a]	7,841	9,721	9,720	7,431	6,334
2.	With 20 employees or more[90]	---	---	---	---	---
3.	All employees, number (1,000)	148.0	204.9	308.0	309.4	251.8
4.	Payroll ($1,000,000)	66.2	119.6	375.7	467.5	364.6
5.	Production workers, total (number) (1,000)	137.5	182.6	262.2	264.7	198.6
6.	Man hours (1,000,000)	---	---	---	---	---
7.	Wages ($1,000,000)	55.7	93.9	288.7	352.5	249.9
8.	Value added by manufacture ($1,000,000)	141.1	243.9	715.8	949.8	682.0
9.	Capital expenditures, new ($1,000,000)	---	---	---	---	---
10.	Percent of U.S. Employment	3.05	2.92	3.13	3.20	2.64
11.	Index of employment change (1958 = 100)	34	47	70	70	57
12.	U.S. index of employment change (1958 = 100)	30	44	61	60	59

GENERAL MANUFACTURING STATISTICS, 1899-1989[89,91] (Cont.)										
WISCONSIN*[a]										
Item No.	1947	1954	1958	1963	1967	1972	1977	1982	1987	1989*[d]
1.	6,980	7,702	7,890*[b]	7,937	7,838	7,845	8,678	8,682	9,161	---
2.	---	2,294	2,331	2,467*[b]	2,727	2,861	3,163	3,197	3,460	---
3.	418.7	439.2*[b]	439.4	461.8	512.2	500.5	535.0	496.7	514.0	541.6
4.	1,190.8	1,869.1*[b]	2,208.9	2,781.1	3,577.8	4,722.3	7,317.8	10,197.1	12,763.4	14,210.9
5.	343.9	332.3	320.0	338.5	374.5	360.5	381.0	328.7	349.9	370.6
6.	---	669.3	634.1	687.8	754.8	720.5	745.4	621.0	693.6	739.7
7.	908.2	1,268.6	1,440.4	1,827.4	2,332.8	2,062.7	4,697.1	5,990.3	7,615.5	8,318.4
8.	2,263.0	3,334.0	3,959.5	5,363.2	7,014.1	9,443.3	16,606.0	22,545.6	31,653.0	36,431.8
9.	---	169.4	203.7*[c]	280.7	506.6	535.3	1,184.4	1,547.2	2,027.4	2,433.5
10.	2.93	2.73	2.74	2.72	2.65	2.63	2.73	2.60	2.71	2.84
11.	95	100	100	105	117	114 94	122 100	113 93	117 96	123 101
12.	89	100	100	106	121	119 97	122 100	119 97	118 97	119 97

[a] There were a number of changes in the definition of manufacturing industries through the years that affect historical comparability. See the Glossary of Terms for these changes. The changes have not appreciably affected the comparability of the historical data except for the figures on the number of establishments.

[b] Data for central administrative offices and auxiliaries included for the first time for other states but this information was not collected in Alaska and Hawaii in 1954. See the Glossary of Terms.

[c] Item 9 (1958) includes expenditures for plants under construction but not in operation prior to 1958, the data represents expenditures at operating manufacturing establishments only. See Glossary of Terms.

[d] The Census Data for 1972, 1977, 1983 and 1987 are from manufacturing. Data for 1989 are estimates based on a representative sample of establishments canvassed annually and may differ from results of a complete canvass of all establishments.

GENERAL MANUFACTURING STATISTICS, 1899-1989[89,91]						
WYOMING[*a]						
Item No.		1899	1909	1919	1929	1939
1.	Total establishments[90,*a]	139	268	437	248	300
2.	With 20 employees or more[90]	---	---	---	---	---
3.	All employees, number (1,000)	2.1	3.1	7.1	7.2	4.4
4.	Payroll ($1,000,000)	1.3	2.4	12.2	12.5	6.6
5.	Production workers, total (number) (1,000)	2.1	2.9	6.3	6.3	3.4
6.	Man hours (1,000,000)	---	---	---	---	---
7.	Wages ($1,000,000)	1.2	2.1	10.6	10.3	4.6
8.	Value added by manufacture ($1,000,000)	1.9	3.6	38.1	33.6	15.3
9.	Capital expenditures, new ($1,000,000)	---	---	---	---	---
10.	Percent of U.S. Employment	0.04	0.04	0.07	0.07	0.05
11.	Index of employment change (1958 = 100)	33	49	110	111	68
12.	U.S. index of employment change (1958 = 100)	30	44	61	60	59

GENERAL MANUFACTURING STATISTICS, 1899-1989[89,91] (Cont.)										
WYOMING*[a]										
Item No.	1947	1954	1958	1963	1967	1972	1977	1982	1987	1989*[d]
1.	256	328	330*[b]	342	331	377	505	511	501	---
2.	55	49	57	69*[b]	65	78	102	115	81	---
3.	5.6	6.3*[b]	6.4	6.8	5.9	7.0	8.5	9.9	7.7	8.9
4.	16.7	26.9*[b]	31.6	38.0	37.1	56.9	110.9	183.3	179.7	205.2
5.	4.3	4.6	4.7	4.6	4.2	5.1	6.2	6.6	5.4	6.2
6.	8.9	9.2	9.1	9.1	8.1	10.1	12.1	13.2	10.7	12.4
7.	12.3	18.8	22.2	24.7	23.4	39.2	73.9	115.3	118.6	132.5
8.	35.0	51.4	62.6	81.7	86.2	143.9	380.8	407.7	492.8	745.1
9.	10.2	6.9	7.0*[c]	14.0	7.6	23.4	36.2	49.8	65.3	68.5
10.	0.04	0.04	0.04	0.04	0.03	.04	.04	.05	.04	.05
11.	87	97	100	106	92	109 82	133 100	155 116	120 91	139 105
12.	89	100	100	106	121	119 97	122 100	119 97	118 97	119 97

[a] There were a number of changes in the definition of manufacturing industries through the years that affect historical comparability. See the Glossary of Terms for these changes. The changes have not appreciably affected the comparability of the historical data except for the figures on the number of establishments.

[b] Data for central administrative offices and auxiliaries included for the first time for other states but this information was not collected in Alaska and Hawaii in 1954. See the Glossary of Terms.

[c] Item 9 (1958) includes expenditures for plants under construction but not in operation prior to 1958, the data represents expenditures at operating manufacturing establishments only. See Glossary of Terms.

[d] The Census Data for 1972, 1977, 1983 and 1987 are from manufacturing. Data for 1989 are estimates based on a representative sample of establishments canvassed annually and may differ from results of a complete canvass of all establishments.

GENERAL MANUFACTURING STATISTICS, 1899-1989[89,91]						
UNITED STATES[*a,e]						
Item No.		1899	1909	1919	1929	1939
1.	Total establishments[90,*a]	204,754	264,810	270,231	206,663	173,802
2.	With 20 employees or more[90]	---	---	---	---	---
3.	All employees, number (1,000)	4,850.0	7,012.1	9,836.8	9,659.7	9,527.3
4.	Payroll ($1,000,000)	2,258.7	4,105.5	12,426.9	14,284.3	12,706.1
5.	Production workers, total (number) (1,000)	4,501.9	6,261.7	8,464.9	8,369.7	7,808.2
6.	Man hours (1,000,000)	---	---	---	---	---
7.	Wages ($1,000,000)	1,892.6	3,205.2	9,664.0	10,884.9	8,997.5
8.	Value added by manufacture ($1,000,000)	4,647.0	8,160.1	23,841.6	30,591.4	24,487.3
9.	Capital expenditures, new ($1,000,000)	---	---	---	---	---
10.	Percent of U.S. Employment	100.0	100.0	100.0	100.0	100.0
11.	Index of employment change (1958 = 100)	30	44	61	60	59
12.	U.S. index of employment change (1958 = 100)	30	44	61	60	59

GENERAL MANUFACTURING STATISTICS, 1899-1989[89,91] (Cont.)										
UNITED STATES[*a,e]										
Item No.	1947	1954	1958	1963	1967	1972	1977	1982	1987	1989[*d]
1.	240,807	286,814	303,303[*b]	311,931	311,140	320,710	359,928	358,061	368,817	---
2.	---	90,470	95,310	102,291[*b]	110,256	114,195	118,699	123,163	126,162	---
3.	14,294.0	16,098.7[*b]	16,025.2	16,958.4	19,323.2	19,028.7	19,590.1	19,094.1	18,950.3	19,040.8
4.	39,695.6	65,866.6[*b]	78,348.9	99,898.8	99,898.8	174,205.5	264,013.1	379,626.5	475,650.5	519,292.0
5.	11,917.9	12,372.0	11,665.4	12,232.1	13,955.3	13,527.9	13,691.0	12,400.6	12,242.7	12,341.5
6.	24,316.5	24,334.1	22,671.4	24,510.3	27,837.6	26,699.2	26,686.7	23,538.3	24,300.6	24,662.2
7.	30,244.0	44,590.5	49,573.8	62,090.8	81,393.6	105,501.8	157,163.7	204,787.2	251,432.2	269,331.4
8.	74,290.5	117,032.3	141,532.2	192,082.9	261,983.8	353,994.0	585,165.6	824,117.7	1,165,746.7	1,308,103.3
9.	5,998.1	8,200.7	9,543.5[*c]	11,380.0	21,503.0	24,077.7	47,459.0	74,561.5	78,647.7	97,186.7
10.	100.0	100.0	100.0	100.0	100.0	100.0	100.0	100.0	100.0	100.0
11.	89	100	100	106	121	119 97	122 100	119 97	118 97	118 97
12.	89	100	100	106	121	119 97	122 100	119 97	118 97	119 97

[a] There were a number of changes in the definition of manufacturing industries through the years that affect historical comparability. See the Glossary of Terms for these changes. The changes have not appreciably affected the comparability of the historical data except for the figures on the number of establishments.

[b] Data for central administrative offices and auxiliaries included for the first time for other states but this information was not collected in Alaska and Hawaii in 1954. See the Glossary of Terms.

[c] Item 9 (1958) includes expenditures for plants under construction but not in operation prior to 1958, the data represents expenditures at operating manufacturing establishments only. See Glossary of Terms.

[d] The Census Data for 1972, 1977, 1983 and 1987 are from manufacturing. Data for 1989 are estimates based on a representative sample of establishments canvassed annually and may differ from results of a complete canvass of all establishments.

[e] The United States' totals were taken from the source noted in the endnotes. They may not match the sum of the state totals. For example, the 1967 Census of Manufacturing notes that "the totals at the U.S. and states level were derived from separate tabulations based on industry rather than state detail. The sum of the state detail does not add to the United States total because of 1) independent rounding, and 2) independent corrections to the industry and state tabulation."

Population of Cities Having 100,000 Inhabitants or More in 1990, 1790–1990

POPULATION OF CITIES HAVING 100,000 INHABITANTS OR MORE IN 1990, 1790-1990[92,93,94,95]

CITY AND STATE	1990	1980	1970	1960	1950	1940	1930	1920	1910	1900
1. Abilene, TX	106,654	98,315	---	---	---	---	---	---	---	---
2. Akron, OH	223,019	237,177	275,425	290,351	274,605	244,791	255,040	208,435	69,067	42,728
3. Albany, NY	101,082	101,727	115,781	129,726	134,995	130,577	127,412	113,344	100,253	94,151
4. Albuquerque, NM	384,736	332,920	243,751	201,189	96,815	35,449	26,570	15,157	11,020	6,238
5. Alexandria, VA	111,183	103,217	110,938	91,023	61,787	33,523	24,149	18,060	15,329	14,528
6. Allentown, PA	105,090	103,758	109,527	108,347	106,756	96,904	92,563	73,502	51,913	35,416
7. Amarillo, TX	157,615	149,230	127,010	137,969	74,246	51,686	43,132	15,494	9,957	1,442
8. Anaheim, CA	266,406	219,494	166,701	104,184	14,556	11,031	10,995	5,526	2,628	1,456
9. Anchorage, AK	226,338	174,431	---	---	----	---	---	---	---	---
10. Ann Arbor, MI	109,592	107,969	---	---	----	---	---	---	---	---
11. Arlington, TX	261,721	160,113	---	---	----	---	---	---	---	---
12. Atlanta, GA	394,017	425,022	496,973	487,455	331,314	302,288	270,366	200,616	154,839	89,872
13. Aurora, CO	222,103	158,588	---	---	----	---	---	---	---	---
14. Austin, TX	465,622	345,890	251,808	186,545	132,459	87,930	53,120	34,876	29,860	22,258
15. Bakersfield, CA	174,820	105,611	---	---	----	---	---	---	---	---
16. Baltimore, MD	736,014	786,741	905,759	939,024	949,708	859,100	804,874	733,826	558,485	508,957
17. Baton Rouge, LA	219,531	220,394	165,963	152,419	125,629	34,719	30,729	21,782	14,897	11,269
18. Beaumont, TX	114,323	118,102	115,919	119,175	94,014	59,061	57,732	40,422	20,640	9,427
19. Berkeley, CA	102,724	103,328	116,716	111,268	113,805	85,547	82,109	56,036	40,434	13,214
20. Birmingham, AL	265,968	284,413	300,910	340,887	326,037	267,583	259,678	178,806	132,685	38,415

POPULATION OF CITIES HAVING 100,000 INHABITANTS OR MORE IN 1990, 1790-1990[53,54] (Cont.)

CITY AND STATE	1890	1880	1870	1860	1850	1840	1830	1820	1810	1800	1790
1.	---	---	---	---	---	---	---	---	---	---	---
2.	27,601	16,512	10,006	3,477	3,266	---	---	---	---	---	---
3.	94,923	90,758	69,422	62,367	50,763	33,721	24,209	12,630	10,762	5,289	3,498
4.	3,785	---	---	---	---	---	---	---	---	---	---
5.	14,339	13,659	13,570	12,652	8,734	8,459	8,241	8,218	7,227	4,971	2,749
6.	25,228	18,063	13,884	8,025	3,779	2,493	1,544	---	---	---	---
7.	482	---	---	---	---	---	---	---	---	---	---
8.	1,273	833	881	---	---	---	---	---	---	---	---
9.	---	---	---	---	---	---	---	---	---	---	---
10.	---	---	---	---	---	---	---	---	---	---	---
11.	---	---	---	---	---	---	---	---	---	---	---
12.	65,533	37,409	21,789	9,554	2,572	---	---	---	---	---	---
13.	---	---	---	---	---	---	---	---	---	---	---
14.	14,575	11,013	4,428	3,494	629	---	---	---	---	---	---
15.	---	---	---	---	---	---	---	---	---	---	---
16.	434,439	332,313	267,354	212,418	169,054	102,313	80,620	62,738	46,555	26,514	13,503
17.	10,478	7,197	6,498	5,428	3,905	2,269	---	---	---	---	---
18.	3,296	---	---	---	---	---	---	---	---	---	---
19.	5,101	---	---	---	---	---	---	---	---	---	---
20.	26,178	3,086	---	---	---	---	---	---	---	---	---

POPULATION OF CITIES HAVING 100,000 INHABITANTS OR MORE IN 1990, 1790-1990[92,93,94,95]

CITY AND STATE	1990	1980	1970	1960	1950	1940	1930	1920	1910	1900
21. Boise, ID	125,738	102,249	---	---	---	---	---	---	---	---
22. Boston, MA[*j,k]	574,283	562,994	641,071	697,197	801,444	770,816	781,188	748,060	670,585	560,892
23. Bridgeport, CT	141,686	142,546	156,542	156,748	158,709	147,121	146,716	143,555	102,054	70,996
24. Buffalo, NY	328,123	357,870	462,768	532,759	580,132	575,901	573,076	506,775	423,715	352,387
25. Cedar Rapids, IA	108,751	110,243	110,642	92,035	72,296	62,120	56,097	45,566	32,811	25,656
26. Charlotte, NC	395,934	315,474	241,178	201,564	134,042	100,899	82,675	46,338	34,014	18,091
27. Chattanooga, TN	152,466	169,514	119,082	130,009	131,041	128,163	119,798	57,895	44,604	30,154
28. Chesapeake, VA	151,976	114,486	---	---	---	---	---	---	---	---
29. Chicago, IL	2,783,726	3,005,072	3,366,957	3,550,404	3,620,962	3,396,808	3,376,438	2,701,705	2,185,283	1,698,575
30. Chula Vista, CA	135,163	83,927	---	---	---	---	---	---	---	---
31. Cincinnati, OH	364,040	385,409	452,524	502,550	503,998	455,610	451,160	401,247	363,591	325,902
32. Cleveland, OH	505,616	573,822	750,903	876,050	914,808	878,336	900,429	796,841	560,663	381,768
33. Colorado Springs, CO	281,140	215,105	135,060	70,194	45,472	36,789	33,237	30,105	29,078	21,085
34. Columbia, SC[*n]	94,029	100,792	113,542	97,433	86,914	62,396	51,581	37,524	26,319	21,108
35. Columbus, GA	179,278[*m]	170,108	154,168	116,779	79,611	53,280	43,131	31,125	20,554	17,614
36. Columbus, OH	632,910	565,021	539,677	471,316	375,901	306,087	290,564	237,031	181,511	125,560
37. Concord, CA	111,348	103,763	---	---	---	---	---	---	---	---
38. Corpus Christi, TX	257,453	232,134	204,525	167,690	108,287	57,301	27,741	10,522	8,222	4,703
39. Dallas, TX	1,006,877	904,599	844,401	679,684	434,462	294,734	260,475	158,976	92,104	42,638

POPULATION OF CITIES HAVING 100,000 INHABITANTS OR MORE IN 1990, 1790-1990[53,54] (Cont.)

CITY AND STATE	1890	1880	1870	1860	1850	1840	1830	1820	1810	1800	1790
21.	---	---	---	---	---	---	---	---	---	---	---
22.	448,477	362,839	250,526	177,840	136,881	93,383	61,392	43,298	33,787	24,937	18,320
23.	48,866	27,643	18,969	12,106	6,080	3,294	---	---	---	---	---
24.	255,664	155,134	117,714	81,129	42,261	18,213	8,668	2,095	1,508	---	---
25.	18,030	10,104	5,940	1,830	---	---	---	---	---	---	---
26.	11,557	7,094	4,473	2,265	1,065	---	---	---	---	---	---
27.	29,100	12,892	6,093	---	---	---	---	---	---	---	---
28.	---	---	---	---	---	---	---	---	---	---	---
29.	1,099,850	503,185	298,977	112,172	29,963	4,470	---	---	---	---	---
30.	---	---	---	---	---	---	---	---	---	---	---
31.	296,908	255,139	216,239	161,044	115,435	46,338	24,831	9,642	2,540	---	---
32.	261,353	160,146	92,829	43,417	17,034	6,071	1,076	606	---	---	---
33.	11,140	4,226	---	---	---	---	---	---	---	---	---
34.	15,353	10,036	9,298	8,052	6,060	4,340	3,310	---	---	---	---
35.	17,303	10,123	7,401	9,621	5,942	3,114	---	---	---	---	---
36.	88,150	51,647	31,274	18,554	17,882	6,048	2,435	---	---	---	---
37.	---	---	---	---	---	---	---	---	---	---	---
38.	4,387	3,257	2,140	175	---	---	---	---	---	---	---
39.	38,067	10,358	---	---	---	---	---	---	---	---	---

POPULATION OF CITIES HAVING 100,000 INHABITANTS OR MORE IN 1990, 1790-1990[92,93,94,95]

CITY AND STATE	1990	1980	1970	1960	1950	1940	1930	1920	1910	1900
40. Davenport, IA[*n]	95,333	103,264	98,469	88,981	74,549	66,089	60,751	56,727	43,028	35,254
41. Dayton, OH	182,044	193,536	243,601	262,332	243,872	210,718	200,982	152,559	116,577	85,333
42. Denver, CO	467,610	492,686	514,678	493,887	415,786	322,412	287,861	256,491	213,381	133,859
43. Des Moines, IA	193,187	191,003	200,587	208,982	177,965	159,819	142,559	126,468	86,368	62,139
44. Detroit, MI	1,027,974	1,203,368	1,511,482	1,670,144	1,849,568	1,623,452	1,568,662	993,678	465,766	285,704
45. Durham, NC	136,611	101,149	95,438	78,302	71,311	60,195	52,037	21,719	18,241	6,679
46. El Monte, CA	106,209	79,494	---	---	---	---	---	---	---	---
47. El Paso, TX	515,342	425,259	322,261	276,687	130,485	96,810	102,421	77,560	39,279	15,906
48. Elizabeth, NJ	110,002	106,201	112,654	107,698	112,817	109,912	114,589	95,783	73,409	52,130
49. Erie, PA	108,718	119,123	129,231	138,440	130,803	116,955	115,967	93,372	66,525	52,733
50. Escondido, CA	108,635	64,355	---	---	---	---	---	---	---	---
51. Eugene, OR	112,669	105,664	---	---	---	---	---	---	---	---
52. Evansville, IN	126,272	130,496	138,764	141,543	128,636	97,062	102,249	85,264	69,647	59,007
53. Flint, MI	140,761	159,611	193,317	196,940	163,143	151,543	156,492	91,599	38,550	13,103
54. Fort Lauderdale, FL	149,377	153,279	139,590	83,648	36,328	17,996	8,666	2,065	---	---
55. Fort Wayne, IN	173,072	172,391	177,671	161,776	133,607	118,410	114,946	86,549	63,933	45,115
56. Fort Worth, TX	447,619	385,164	393,476	356,268	278,778	177,662	163,447	106,482	73,312	26,688
57. Fremont, CA	173,339	131,945	100,869	43,790	---	---	---	---	---	---
58. Fresno, CA	354,202	217,491	165,972	133,929	91,669	60,685	52,513	45,086	24,892	12,470
59. Fullerton, CA	114,144	102,246	---	---	---	---	---	---	---	---

POPULATION OF CITIES HAVING 100,000 INHABITANTS OR MORE IN 1990, 1790-1990[53,54] (Cont.)

CITY AND STATE	1890	1880	1870	1860	1850	1840	1830	1820	1810	1800	1790
40.	---	---	---	---	---	---	---	---	---	---	---
41.	61,220	38,678	30,473	20,081	10,977	6,067	2,950	1,000	383	---	---
42.	106,713	35,629	4,759	4,749	---	---	---	---	---	---	---
43.	50,093	22,408	12,035	3,965	---	---	---	---	---	---	---
44.	205,876	116,340	79,577	45,619	21,019	9,102	2,222	1,422	---	---	---
45.	---	---	---	---	---	---	---	---	---	---	---
46.	---	---	---	---	---	---	---	---	---	---	---
47.	10,338	736	---	---	---	---	---	---	---	---	---
48.	37,764	28,229	20,832	11,567	5,583	4,184	3,455	3,515	2,977	---	---
49.	40,634	27,737	19,646	9,419	5,858	3,412	1,465	635	394	81	---
50.	---	---	---	---	---	---	---	---	---	---	---
51.	---	---	---	---	---	---	---	---	---	---	---
52.	50,756	29,280	21,830	11,484	3,235	---	---	---	---	---	---
53.	9,803	8,409	5,386	2,950	---	---	---	---	---	---	---
54.	---	---	---	---	---	---	---	---	---	---	---
55.	35,393	26,880	17,718	9,121[*o]	4,282	---	---	---	---	---	---
56.	23,076	6,663	---	---	---	---	---	---	---	---	---
57.	---	---	---	---	---	---	---	---	---	---	---
58.	10,818	1,112	---	---	---	---	---	---	---	---	---
59.	---	---	---	---	---	---	---	---	---	---	---

POPULATION OF CITIES HAVING 100,000 INHABITANTS OR MORE IN 1990, 1790-1990[92,93,94,95]

CITY AND STATE	1990	1980	1970	1960	1950	1940	1930	1920	1910	1900
60. Garden Grove, CA	143,050	123,307	122,524	84,238	---	---	---	---	---	---
61. Garland, TX	180,650	138,857	---	---	---	---	---	---	---	---
62. Gary, IN	116,646	151,968	175,415	178,320	133,911	111,719	100,426	55,378	16,802	---
63. Glendale, AR	148,134	97,172	---	---	---	---	---	---	---	---
64. Glendale, CA	180,038	139,060	132,752	119,442	95,702	82,582	62,736	13,536	2,746	---
65. Grand Rapids, MI	189,126	181,843	197,649	177,313	176,515	164,292	168,592	137,634	112,571	87,565
66. Greensboro, NC	183,521	155,642	144,076	119,574	74,389	59,319	53,569	19,861	15,895	10,035
67. Hampton, VA	133,793	122,617	120,779	89,258	5,966	5,898	6,382	6,138	5,505	2,764
68. Hartford, CT	139,739	136,392	158,017	162,178	177,397	166,267	164,072	138,036	98,915	79,850
69. Hayward, CA	111,498	93,585	---	---	---	---	---	---	---	---
70. Hialeah, FL	188,004	145,254	102,297	66,972	19,676	3,958	2,600	---	---	---
71. Hollywood, FL	121,697	121,323	106,873	35,237	14,351	6,239	2,869	---	---	---
72. Honolulu, HI[*r]	365,272	365,048	324,871	294,194	248,034	179,326	137,582	83,327	52,183	39,306
73. Houston, TX	1,630,553	1,595,138	1,232,802	938,219	596,163	384,514	292,352	138,276	78,800	44,633
74. Huntington Beach, CA	181,519	170,505	115,960	11,492	5,237	3,738	3,690	---	---	---
75. Huntsville, AL	159,789	142,513	137,802	72,365	16,437	13,050	11,554	8,018	7,611	8,068
76. Independence, MO	112,301	111,797	111,662	62,328	36,963	16,066	15,296	11,686	9,859	6,974
77. Indianapolis, IN	741,952[*m]	711,539	744,624	476,258	427,173	386,972	364,161	314,194	233,650	169,164
78. Inglewood, CA	109,602	94,162	---	---	---	---	---	---	---	---
79. Irvine, CA	110,330	62,134	---	---	---	---	---	---	---	---

POPULATION OF CITIES HAVING 100,000 INHABITANTS OR MORE IN 1990, 1790-1990[53,54] (Cont.)

CITY AND STATE	1890	1880	1870	1860	1850	1840	1830	1820	1810	1800	1790
60.	---	---	---	---	---	---	---	---	---	---	---
61.	---	---	---	---	---	---	---	---	---	---	---
62.	---	---	---	---	---	---	---	---	---	---	---
63.	---	---	---	---	---	---	---	---	---	---	---
64.	---	---	---	---	---	---	---	---	---	---	---
65.	60,278	32,016	16,507	8,085	2,686	---	---	---	---	---	---
66.	3,317	2,105	497	---	---	---	---	---	---	---	---
67.	2,513	---	---	---	---	---	---	---	---	---	---
68.	53,230	42,015	37,180	26,917	13,555	9,468	7,074	4,726	3,955	3,523*°	2,683*°
69.	---	---	---	---	---	---	---	---	---	---	---
70.	---	---	---	---	---	---	---	---	---	---	---
71.	---	---	---	---	---	---	---	---	---	---	---
72.	22,907	---	---	---	---	---	---	---	---	---	---
73.	27,557	16,513	9,382	4,845	2,396	---	---	---	---	---	---
74.	---	---	---	---	---	---	---	---	---	---	---
75.	7,995	4,977	4,907	3,634	---	---	---	---	---	---	---
76.	6,380	3,146	3,184	3,164	---	---	---	---	---	---	---
77.	105,436	75,056	48,244	18,611	8,091	2,692	---	---	---	---	---
78.	---	---	---	---	---	---	---	---	---	---	---
79.	---	---	---	---	---	---	---	---	---	---	---

POPULATION OF CITIES HAVING 100,000 INHABITANTS OR MORE IN 1990, 1790-1990[92,93,94,95]

CITY AND STATE	1990	1980	1970	1960	1950	1940	1930	1920	1910	1900
80. Irving, TX	155,037	109,943	---	---	---	---	---	---	---	---
81. Jackson, MS	196,637	202,895	153,968	144,422	98,271	62,107	48,282	22,817	21,262	7,816
82. Jacksonville, FL	672,971[*m]	571,003	528,865	201,030	204,517	173,065	129,549	91,558	57,699	28,429
83. Jersey City, NJ	228,537	223,532	260,545	276,101	299,017	301,173	316,715	298,103	267,779	206,433
84. Kansas City, KS	149,767	161,148	168,213	121,901	129,553	121,458	121,857	101,177	82,331	51,418
85. Kansas City, MO	435,146	448,028	507,087	475,539	456,622	399,178	399,746	324,410	248,381	163,752
86. Knoxville, TN	165,121	175,045	174,587	111,827	124,769	111,580	105,802	77,818	36,346	32,637
87. Lakewood, CO	126,481	113,808	---	---	---	---	---	---	---	---
88. Lansing, MI	127,321	130,414	131,546	107,807	92,129	78,753	78,397	57,327	31,229	16,485
89. Laredo, TX	122,899	91,449	69,024	60,678	51,910	39,274	32,618	22,710	14,855	13,429
90. Las Vegas, NV	258,295	164,674	125,787	64,405	24,624	8,422	5,165	2,304	---	---
91. Lexington-Fayette, KY	225,366	204,165	108,137	62,810	55,534	49,304	45,736	41,534	35,099	26,369
92. Lincoln, NE	191,972	171,932	149,518	128,521	98,884	81,984	75,933	54,948	43,973	40,169
93. Little Rock, AR	175,795	159,159	132,483	107,813	102,213	88,039	81,679	65,142	45,941	38,307
94. Livonia, MI	100,850	104,814	110,109	66,702	17,534	---	---	---	---	---
95. Long Beach, CA	429,433	361,498	358,633	344,168	250,767	164,271	142,032	55,393	17,809	2,252
96. Los Angeles, CA	3,485,398	2,968,528	2,816,061	2,479,015	1,970,358	1,504,277	1,238,048	576,673	319,198	102,479
97. Louisville, KY	269,063	298,694	361,472	390,639	369,129	319,077	307,745	234,891	223,928	204,731
98. Lowell, MA	103,439	92,418	94,239	92,107	97,249	101,389	100,234	112,759	106,294	94,969
99. Lubbock, TX	186,206	174,361	149,101	128,691	71,747	31,853	20,520	4,051	1,938	---

POPULATION OF CITIES HAVING 100,000 INHABITANTS OR MORE IN 1990, 1790-1990[53,54] (Cont.)

CITY AND STATE	1890	1880	1870	1860	1850	1840	1830	1820	1810	1800	1790
80.	---	---	---	---	---	---	---	---	---	---	---
81.	5,920	5,204	4,234	3,191	1,881*p	---	---	---	---	---	---
82.	17,201	7,650	6,912	2,118	1,045	---	---	---	---	---	---
83.	163,003	120,722	82,546	29,226	6,856	3,072	---	---	---	---	---
84.	38,316	3,200	---	---	---	---	---	---	---	---	---
85.	132,716	55,785	32,260	4,418	---	---	---	---	---	---	---
86.	22,535	9,693	8,682	*r	2,076	---	---	---	---	---	---
87.	---	---	---	---	---	---	---	---	---	---	---
88.	13,102	8,319	5,241	3,074	---	---	---	---	---	---	---
89.	---	---	---	---	---	---	---	---	---	---	---
90.	---	---	---	---	---	---	---	---	---	---	---
91.	21,567	16,656	14,801	9,321	8,159*o	6,997	6,026	5,279	4,326	1,795	834
92.	55,154	13,003	---	---	---	---	---	---	---	---	---
93.	25,874	13,138	12,380	3,727	2,167	---	---	---	---	---	---
94.	---	---	---	---	---	---	---	---	---	---	---
95.	564	---	---	---	---	---	---	---	---	---	---
96.	50,395	11,183	5,728	4,385	1,610	---	---	---	---	---	---
97.	161,129	123,758	100,753	68,033	43,194	21,210	10,341	4,012	1,357	359	200
98.	---	---	---	---	---	---	---	---	---	---	---
99.	---	---	---	---	---	---	---	---	---	---	---

POPULATION OF CITIES HAVING 100,000 INHABITANTS OR MORE IN 1990, 1790-1990[92,93,94,95]										
CITY AND STATE	1990	1980	1970	1960	1950	1940	1930	1920	1910	1900
100. Macon, GA	106,612	116,896	122,423	69,764	70,252	57,865	53,829	52,995	40,665	23,272
101. Madison, WI	191,262	170,616	173,258	126,708	96,056	67,447	57,899	38,378	25,531	19,164
102. Memphis, TN	610,337	646,174	623,530	497,524	396,000	292,942	253,143	162,351	131,105	102,320
103. Mesa, AZ	288,091	152,404	---	---	---	---	---	---	---	---
104. Mesquite, TX	101,484	67,053	---	---	---	---	---	---	---	---
105. Miami, FL	358,548	346,681	334,859	291,688	249,276	172,172	110,637	29,571	5,471	1,681
106. Milwaukee, WI	628,088	636,297	717,099	741,324	637,392	587,472	578,249	457,147	373,857	285,315
107. Minneapolis, MN	368,383	370,951	434,400	482,872	521,718	492,370	464,356	380,582	301,408	202,718
108. Mobile, AL	196,278	200,452	190,026	194,856	129,009	78,720	68,202	60,777	51,521	38,469
109. Modesto, CA	164,730	106,963	---	---	---	---	---	---	---	---
110. Montgomery, AL	187,106	177,857	133,386	134,393	106,525	78,084	66,079	43,464	38,136	30,346
111. Moreno Valley, CA	118,779	---	---	---	---	---	---	---	---	---
112. Nashville-Davidson, TN[*g]	510,784[*m]	477,811	448,003[*g]	170,874	174,307	167,402	153,866	118,342	110,364	80,865
113. New Haven, CT	130,474	126,089	137,707	152,048	164,443	160,605	162,655	162,537	133,605	108,027
114. New Orleans, LA	496,938	557,927	593,471	627,525	570,445	494,537	458,762	387,219	339,075	287,104
115. New York, NY[*a,b]	7,322,564	7,071,639	7,894,862	7,781,984	7,891,957	7,454,995	6,930,446	5,620,048	4,766,883	3,437,202[*b]
116. Newark, NJ	275,221	329,248	382,417	405,220	438,776	429,760	442,337	414,524	347,469	246,070
117. Newport News, VA	170,045	144,903	138,177	113,662	42,358	37,067	34,417	35,596	20,205	19,635
118. Norfolk, VA	261,229	266,979	307,951	304,869	213,513	144,332	129,710	115,777	67,452	46,624
119. Oakland, CA	372,242	339,337	361,561	367,548	384,575	302,163	284,063	216,261	150,174	66,960

POPULATION OF CITIES HAVING 100,000 INHABITANTS OR MORE IN 1990, 1790-1990[53,54] (Cont.)

CITY AND STATE	1890	1880	1870	1860	1850	1840	1830	1820	1810	1800	1790
100.	22,746	12,749	10,810	8,247	5,720	3,927	---	---	---	---	---
101.	13,426	10,324	9,176	6,611	1,525	---	---	---	---	---	---
102.	64,495	33,592	40,226	22,623	8,841	---	---	---	---	---	---
103.	---	---	---	---	---	---	---	---	---	---	---
104.	---	---	---	---	---	---	---	---	---	---	---
105.	---	---	---	---	---	---	---	---	---	---	---
106.	204,468	115,587	71,440	45,246	20,061	1,712	---	---	---	---	---
107.	164,738	46,887	13,066	2,564	---	---	---	---	---	---	---
108.	31,076	29,132	32,034	29,258	20,515	12,672	3,194	---	---	---	---
109.	---	---	---	---	---	---	---	---	---	---	---
110.	21,883	16,713	10,588	8,843	8,728	2,179	---	---	---	---	---
111.	---	---	---	---	---	---	---	---	---	---	---
112.	76,168	43,350	25,865	16,988	10,165	6,929	5,566	*r	*r	345	---
113.	96,045	62,882	50,840	39,267	20,345	12,960	10,180	7,147	5,772	4,049	4,487
114.	242,039	216,090	191,418	168,675	116,375	102,193	46,082	27,176	17,242	---	---
115.	2,507,414	1,911,698	1,478,103	1,174,779	696,115	391,114	242,278	152,056	119,734	79,216	49,401
116.	181,830	136,508	105,059	71,941	38,894	17,290	10,953*q	---	---	---	---
117.	4,449	---	---	---	---	---	---	---	---	---	---
118.	34,871	21,966	19,229	14,620	14,326	10,920	9,814	8,478	9,193	6,926	2,959
119.	48,683	34,555	10,500	1,543	---	---	---	---	---	---	---

POPULATION OF CITIES HAVING 100,000 INHABITANTS OR MORE IN 1990, 1790-1990[92,93,94,95]

CITY AND STATE	1990	1980	1970	1960	1950	1940	1930	1920	1910	1900
120. Oceanside, CA	128,398	76,698	---	---	---	---	---	---	---	---
121. Oklahoma City, OK	444,719	404,014	366,481	324,253	243,504	204,424	185,389	91,295	64,205	10,037
122. Omaha, NE	335,795	313,939	347,328	301,598	251,117	223,844	214,006	191,601[*k]	124,096	102,555
123. Ontario, CA	133,179	88,820	---	---	---	---	---	---	---	---
124. Orange, CA	110,658	91,450	---	---	---	---	---	---	---	---
125. Orlando, FL	164,693	128,291	99,006	88,135	52,367	36,736	27,330	9,282	3,894	2,481
126. Overland Park, KS	111,790	81,784	---	---	---	---	---	---	---	---
127. Oxnard, CA	142,216	108,195	---	---	---	---	---	---	---	---
128. Pasadena, CA	131,591	118,072	113,327	116,407	104,577	81,864	76,086	45,354	30,291	9,117
129. Pasadena, TX	119,363	112,560	---	---	---	---	---	---	---	---
130. Paterson, NJ	140,891	137,970	144,824	143,663	139,336	139,656	138,513	135,875	125,600	105,171
131. Peoria, IL	113,504	124,160	126,963	103,162	111,856	105,087	104,969	76,121	66,950	56,100
132. Philadelphia, PA[*d]	1,585,577	1,688,210	1,948,609	2,002,512	2,071,605	1,931,334	1,950,961	1,823,779	1,549,008	1,293,697
133. Phoenix, AZ	983,403	789,704	581,562	439,170	106,818	65,414	48,118	29,053	11,134	5,544
134. Pittsburgh, PA	369,879	423,959	520,117	604,332	676,806	671,659	669,817	588,343	533,905[*h]	321,616
135. Plano, TX	128,713	72,331	---	---	---	---	---	---	---	---
136. Pomona, CA	131,723	92,742	---	---	---	---	---	---	---	---
137. Portland, OR	437,319	368,148	382,619	372,676	373,628	305,394	301,815	258,288	207,214	90,426
138. Portsmouth, VA	103,907	104,577	110,963	114,773	80,039	50,745	45,704	54,387	33,190	17,427
139. Providence, RI	160,728	156,804	179,213	207,498	248,674	253,504	252,981	237,595	224,326	175,597

POPULATION OF CITIES HAVING 100,000 INHABITANTS OR MORE IN 1990, 1790-1990[53,54] (Cont.)

CITY AND STATE	1890	1880	1870	1860	1850	1840	1830	1820	1810	1800	1790
120.	---	---	---	---	---	---	---	---	---	---	---
121.	4,151	---	---	---	---	---	---	---	---	---	---
122.	140,452	30,518	16,083	1,883	---	---	---	---	---	---	---
123.	---	---	---	---	---	---	---	---	---	---	---
124.	---	---	---	---	---	---	---	---	---	---	---
125.	---	---	---	---	---	---	---	---	---	---	---
126.	---	---	---	---	---	---	---	---	---	---	---
127.	---	---	---	---	---	---	---	---	---	---	---
128.	4,882	---	---	---	---	---	---	---	---	---	---
129.	---	---	---	---	---	---	---	---	---	---	---
130.	78,347	51,031	33,579	19,586	11,334[*q]	7,596[*q]	---	---	---	---	---
131.	41,024	29,259	22,849	14,045	5,095	1,467	---	---	---	---	---
132.	1,046,964	847,170	647,022	565,529	121,376	93,665	80,462	63,802	53,722	41,220	28,522
133.	3,152	---	---	---	---	---	---	---	---	---	---
134.	238,617	156,389	86,076	49,221	46,601	21,115	12,568	7,248	4,768	1,565	---
135.	---	---	---	---	---	---	---	---	---	---	---
136.	---	---	---	---	---	---	---	---	---	---	---
137.	46,385	17,577	8,293	2,874	---	---	---	---	---	---	---
138.	13,268	11,390	10,590	9,496	8,626	6,477	---	---	---	---	---
139.	132,146	104,857	68,904	50,666	41,513	23,171	16,833	11,767	10,071	7,614	6,380

POPULATION OF CITIES HAVING 100,000 INHABITANTS OR MORE IN 1990, 1790-1990[92,93,94,95]

CITY AND STATE	1990	1980	1970	1960	1950	1940	1930	1920	1910	1900
140. Pueblo, CO[*n]	98,640	101,686	97,774	91,181	63,685	52,162	50,096	43,050	41,747[*l]	28,157
141. Raleigh, NC	207,951	150,255	121,577	93,931	65,679	46,897	37,379	24,418	19,218	13,643
142. Rancho Cucamonga, CA	101,409	55,250	---	---	---	---	---	---	---	---
143. Reno, NV	133,850	100,756	---	---	---	---	---	---	---	---
144. Richmond, VA	203,056	219,214	249,621	219,958	230,310	193,042	182,929	171,667	127,628	85,050
145. Riverside, CA	226,505	170,591	140,089	84,332	46,764	34,696	29,696	19,341	15,212	7,973
146. Roanoke, VA[*n]	96,397	100,220	92,115	97,110	91,921	69,287	69,206	50,842	34,874	21,495
147. Rochester, NY	231,636	241,741	296,233	318,611	332,488	324,975	328,132	295,750	218,149	162,608
148. Rockford, IL	139,426	139,712	147,370	126,706	92,927	84,637	85,864	65,651	45,401	31,051
149. Sacramento, CA	369,365	275,741	254,413	191,667	137,572	105,958	93,750	65,908	44,696	29,282
150. Salem, OR	107,786	89,091	---	---	---	---	---	---	---	---
151. Salinas, CA	108,777	80,479	---	---	---	---	---	---	---	---
152. Salt Lake City, UT	159,936	163,034	175,885	189,454	182,121	149,934	140,267	118,110	92,777	53,531
153. San Antonio, TX	935,933	785,940	654,153	587,718	408,442	253,854	231,542	161,379	96,614	53,321
154. San Bernardino, CA	164,164	118,794	104,251	91,922	63,058	43,646	37,481	18,721	12,779	6,150
155. San Diego, CA	1,110,549	875,538	696,769	573,224	334,387	203,341	147,995	74,361	39,578	17,700
156. San Francisco, CA	723,959	678,974	715,674	740,316	775,357	634,536	634,394	506,676	416,912	342,782
157. San Jose, CA	782,248	629,400	445,779	204,196	95,280	68,457	57,651	39,642	28,946	21,500
158. Santa Ana, CA	293,742	204,023	156,601	100,350	45,533	31,921	30,322	15,485	8,429	4,933
159. Santa Clarita, CA	110,642	---	---	---	---	---	---	---	---	---

POPULATION OF CITIES HAVING 100,000 INHABITANTS OR MORE IN 1990, 1790-1990[53,54] (Cont.)

CITY AND STATE	1890	1880	1870	1860	1850	1840	1830	1820	1810	1800	1790
140.	---	---	---	---	---	---	---	---	---	---	---
141.	12,678	9,265	7,790	4,780	4,518	2,244	1,700	2,674	*f	669	---
142.	---	---	---	---	---	---	---	---	---	---	---
143.	---	---	---	---	---	---	---	---	---	---	---
144.	81,388	63,600	51,038	37,910	27,570	20,153	16,060	12,067	9,735	5,737	3,761
145.	4,683	---	---	---	---	---	---	---	---	---	---
146.	---	---	---	---	---	---	---	---	---	---	---
147.	133,896	89,366	62,386	48,204	36,403	20,191	9,207	---	---	---	---
148.	23,564	13,129	11,049	6,979	---	---	---	---	---	---	---
149.	26,386	21,420	16,283	13,785	6,820	---	---	---	---	---	---
150.	---	---	---	---	---	---	---	---	---	---	---
151.	---	---	---	---	---	---	---	---	---	---	---
152.	44,843	20,768	12,854	8,236	---	---	---	---	---	---	---
153.	37,673	20,550	12,256	8,235	3,488	---	---	---	---	---	---
154.	4,012	1,673	---	---	---	---	---	---	---	---	---
155.	16,159	2,637	2,300	731	---	---	---	---	---	---	---
156.	298,997	233,959	149,473	56,802	34,776*e	---	---	---	---	---	---
157.	18,060	12,567	9,089	---	---	---	---	---	---	---	---
158.	3,628	---	---	---	---	---	---	---	---	---	---
159.	---	---	---	---	---	---	---	---	---	---	---

POPULATION OF CITIES HAVING 100,000 INHABITANTS OR MORE IN 1990, 1790-1990[92,93,94,95]

CITY AND STATE	1990	1980	1970	1960	1950	1940	1930	1920	1910	1900
160. Santa Rosa, CA	113,313	82,658	---	---	---	---	---	---	---	---
161. Savannah, GA	137,560	141,654	118,349	149,245	119,638	95,996	85,024	83,252	65,064	54,244
162. Scottsdale, AZ	130,069	88,622	---	---	---	---	---	---	---	---
163. Seattle, WA	516,259	493,846	530,831	557,087	467,591	368,302	365,583	315,312	237,194	80,671
164. Shreveport, LA	198,525	206,989	182,064	164,372	127,206	98,167	76,655	43,874	28,015	16,013
165. Simi Valley, CA	100,217	77,500	---	---	---	---	---	---	---	---
166. Sioux Falls, SD	100,814	81,343	72,488	65,466	52,696	40,832	33,362	25,202	14,094	---
167. South Bond, IN	105,511	109,727	125,580	132,445	115,911	101,268	104,193	70,983	53,684	35,999
168. Spokane, WA	177,196	171,300	170,516	181,608	161,721	122,001	115,514	104,437	104,402	36,848
169. Springfield, IL	105,227	100,054	91,753	83,271	81,628	75,503	71,864	59,183	51,678	34,159
170. Springfield, MA	156,983	152,319	163,905	174,463	162,399	149,554	149,900	129,614	88,926	62,059
171. Springfield, MO	140,494	133,116	120,096	95,865	66,731	61,238	57,527	39,631	35,201	23,267
172. St. Louis, MO	396,685	452,801	622,236	750,026	856,796	816,048	821,960	772,897	687,029	575,238
173. St. Paul, MN	272,235	270,230	309,980	313,411	311,349	287,736	271,606	234,698	214,744	163,065
174. St. Petersburg, FL	238,629	238,647	216,232	181,298	96,738	60,812	40,425	14,237	4,127	1,575
175. Stamford, CT	108,056	102,466	108,798	92,713	74,293	47,938	46,346	35,096	25,138	15,997
176. Sterling Heights, MI	117,810	108,999	---	---	---	---	---	---	---	---
177. Stockton, CA	210,943	148,283	107,644	86,321	70,853	54,714	47,963	40,296	23,253	17,506
178. Sunnyvale, CA	117,229	106,618	---	---	---	---	---	---	---	---
179. Syracuse, NY	163,860	170,105	197,208	216,038	220,583	205,967	209,326	171,717	137,249	108,374

POPULATION OF CITIES HAVING 100,000 INHABITANTS OR MORE IN 1990, 1790-1990[53,54] (Cont.)

CITY AND STATE	1890	1880	1870	1860	1850	1840	1830	1820	1810	1800	1790
160.	---	---	---	---	---	---	---	---	---	---	---
161.	43,189	30,709	28,235	22,292	15,312	11,214	7,303	7,523	5,215	5,146	---
162.	---	---	---	---	---	---	---	---	---	---	---
163.	42,837	3,533	1,107	---	---	---	---	---	---	---	---
164.	11,979	8,009	4,607	2,190	1,728	---	---	---	---	---	---
165.	---	---	---	---	---	---	---	---	---	---	---
166.	---	---	---	---	---	---	---	---	---	---	---
167.	21,819	13,280	7,206	3,832	1,652	---	---	---	---	---	---
168.	19,922	---	---	---	---	---	---	---	---	---	---
169.	---	---	---	---	---	---	---	---	---	---	---
170.	44,179	33,340	26,703	15,199	11,766	10,985	6,784	3,914	2,767	2,312	1,574
171.	21,850	6,522	5,555	*r	415	---	---	---	---	---	---
172.	451,770	350,518	310,864	160,773	77,860	16,469	4,977	---	---	---	---
173.	133,156	41,473	20,030	10,401	1,112	---	---	---	---	---	---
174.	273	---	---	---	---	---	---	---	---	---	---
175.	10,396[*o]	2,540	---	---	---	---	---	---	---	---	---
176.	---	---	---	---	---	---	---	---	---	---	---
177.	14,424	10,282	10,066	3,679	---	---	---	---	---	---	---
178.	---	---	---	---	---	---	---	---	---	---	---
179.	88,143	51,792	43,051	28,119	22,271	---	---	---	---	---	---

POPULATION OF CITIES HAVING 100,000 INHABITANTS OR MORE IN 1990, 1790-1990[92,93,94,95]

CITY AND STATE	1990	1980	1970	1960	1950	1940	1930	1920	1910	1900
180. Tacoma, WA	176,664	158,501	154,581	147,979	143,673	109,408	106,817	96,965	83,743	37,714
181. Tallahassee, FL	124,773	81,548	---	---	---	---	---	---	---	---
182. Tampa, FL	280,015	271,577	277,767	274,970	124,681	108,391	101,161	51,608	37,782	15,839
183. Tempe, AZ	141,865	106,919	---	---	---	---	---	---	---	---
184. Thousand Oaks, CA	104,352	77,072	---	---	---	---	---	---	---	---
185. Toledo, OH	332,943	354,635	383,818	318,003	303,616	282,349	290,718	243,164	168,497	131,822
186. Topeka, KS	119,883	118,690	125,011	119,484	78,791	67,833	64,120	50,022	43,684	33,608
187. Torrance, CA	133,107	129,881	134,584	100,991	22,241	9,950	7,271	---	---	---
188. Tucson, AZ	405,390	330,537	262,933	212,892	45,454	35,752	32,506	20,292	13,193	7,531
189. Tulsa, OK	367,302	360,919	331,638	261,685	182,740	142,157	141,258	72,075	18,182	1,390
190. Vallejo, CA	109,199	80,303	---	---	---	---	---	---	---	---
191. Virginia Beach, VA	393,069	262,199	172,106	8,091	5,390	2,600	1,719	846	320	---
192. Waco, TX	103,590	101,261	95,326	97,808	84,706	55,982	52,848	38,500	26,425	20,686
193. Warren, MI	144,864	161,134	179,260	89,246	727	582	515	326	297	350
194. Washington, DC[*c]	606,900	638,432	756,510	763,956	802,178	663,091	486,869	437,571	331,069	278,718[*c]
195. Waterbury, CT	108,961	103,266	108,033	107,130	104,477	99,314	99,902	91,715	73,141	45,859
196. Wichita, KS	304,011	279,838	276,554	254,698	168,279	114,966	111,110	72,217	52,450	24,671
197. Winston-Salem, NC	143,485	131,885	132,913	111,135	87,811	79,815	75,274	48,395[*i]	22,700[*i]	13,650[*i]
198. Worcester, MA	169,759	161,799	176,572	186,587	203,486	193,694	195,311	179,754	145,986	118,421
199. Yonkers, NY	188,082	195,351	204,297	190,634	152,798	142,598	134,646	100,176	79,803	47,931
200. Youngstown, OH[*n]	95,706	115,436	140,909	166,689	168,330	167,720	170,002	132,358	79,066	44,885

POPULATION OF CITIES HAVING 100,000 INHABITANTS OR MORE IN 1990, 1790-1990[53,54] (Cont.)

CITY AND STATE	1890	1880	1870	1860	1850	1840	1830	1820	1810	1800	1790
180.	36,006	---	---	---	---	---	---	---	---	---	---
181.	---	---	---	---	---	---	---	--	---	---	---
182.	5,532	720	796	---	---	---	---	---	---	---	---
183.	---	---	---	---	---	---	---	---	---	---	---
184.	---	---	---	---	---	---	---	---	---	---	---
185.	81,434	50,137	31,584	13,768	3,829	1,222	---	---	---	---	---
186.	31,007	15,452	5,790	759	---	---	---	---	---	---	---
187.	---	---	---	---	---	---	---	---	---	---	---
188.	5,150	7,007	3,224[*q]	---	---	---	---	---	---	---	---
189.	---	---	---	---	---	---	---	---	---	---	---
190.	---	---	---	--	--	---	---	---	---	---	---
191.	---	---	---	---	---	---	---	---	---	---	---
192.	---	---	---	---	---	---	---	---	---	---	---
193.	---	---	---	---	---	---	---	---	---	---	---
194.	188,932	147,293	109,199	61,122	40,001	23,364	18,826	13,247	8,208	3,210[*q]	---
195.	28,646	17,806	10,826	10,004	---	---	---	---	---	---	---
196.	23,853	4,911	---	---	---	---	---	---	---	---	---
197.	10,729	4,149	443	---	---	---	---	---	---	---	---
198.	84,655	58,291	41,105	24,960	17,049	7,497	4,173	2,962	2,577	2,411	2,095
199.	32,033	18,892	12,733	8,218[*o]	---	---	---	---	---	---	---
200.	33,220	15,435	8,075	2,759	---	---	---	---	---	---	---

NOTES

[a] Population shown for years prior to 1900 is for New York and its boroughs as constituted under the act of consolidation in 1898.

[b] Brooklyn and other territory consolidated with New York in 1898.

[c] City has been considered coextensive with the District of Columbia since 1895.

[d] Spring Garden, Northern Liberties, Kensington, Southwark, and Moyamensing annexed by Philadelphia, in 1854.

[e] Figure is that given in State census of 1852. 1850 returns for San Francisco were destroyed by fire.

[f] Not returned separately.

[g] Figure for 1970 is for the Metropolitan government of Nashville and Davidson County; figures for previous years are for Nashville city.

[h] Allegheny annexed by Pittsburgh in 1907. Combined population, 1900 451,512.

[i] Winston city and Salem town consolidated as Winston-Salem city between 1910 and 1920. Figures for 1910, 1900, 1890, and 1880 represent combined population of Winston and Salem; population given for 1870 is that of Winston alone.

[j] Roxbury annexed by Boston in 1867.

[k] Charlestown annexed by Boston in 1874.

[l] Connected figure; exclusive of population (2,648) of certain territory outside city limits. (Pueblo, CO.)

[m] Consolidated city.

[n] Cities which had a population of 100,000 or more in 1970 or 1980 but not in 1990.

[o] Estimated.

[p] Returns incomplete; slave population not counted.

[q] Population prior to incorporation.

[r] Data represent the census designated place as delineated by state and local authorities.

Other census designated places in 1990 and their 1970 - 1990 populations are: (refer to note r)[96]

Census Designated Place	1970	1980	1990
Arlington, VA.	174,000	153,000	171,000
Citrus Heights, CA.	22,000	86,000	107,000
Metarie, LA.	136,000	164,000	149,000
Paradise, NY.	24,000	85,000	125,000

States of the United States: Admission Dates and 1990 Land Area

STATES OF THE UNITED STATES: ADMISSION DATES AND 1990 LAND AREA[a]

STATE	YEAR OF ADMISSION TO STATEHOOD	TOTAL AREA RANK	TOTAL AREA SQUARE MILES	LAND AREA[b] SQUARE MILES
Alabama	1819	30	52,423	50,750
Alaska	1959	1	656,424	570,374
Arizona	1912	6	114,006	113,642
Arkansas	1836	29	53,182	52,075
California	1850	3	163,707	155,973
Colorado	1876	8	104,100	103,730
Connecticut	1788[c]	48	5,544	4,845
Delaware	1787[c]	49	2,489	1,955
Florida	1845	22	65,758	53,997
Georgia	1788[c]	24	59,441	57,919
Hawaii	1959	43	10,932	6,423
Idaho	1890	14	83,574	82,751
Illinois	1818	25	57,918	55,593

STATES OF THE UNITED STATES: ADMISSION DATES AND 1990 LAND AREA[a] (CONT.)

STATE	YEAR OF ADMISSION TO STATEHOOD	TOTAL AREA RANK	TOTAL AREA SQUARE MILES	LAND AREA[b] SQUARE MILES
Indiana	1816	38	36,420	35,870
Iowa	1846	26	56,276	55,875
Kansas	1861	15	82,282	81,823
Kentucky	1792	37	40,411	39,732
Louisiana	1812	31	51,843	43,566
Maine	1820	39	35,387	30,865
Maryland	1788[c]	42	12,407	9,775
Massachusetts	1788[c]	44	10,555	7,838
Michigan	1837	11	96,810	56,809
Minnesota	1858	12	86,943	79,617
Mississippi	1817	32	48,434	46,914
Missouri	1821	21	69,709	68,898
Montana	1889	4	147,046	145,556
Nebraska	1867	16	77,358	76,878

STATES OF THE UNITED STATES: ADMISSION DATES AND 1990 LAND AREA[a] (CONT.)

STATE	YEAR OF ADMISSION TO STATEHOOD	TOTAL AREA RANK	TOTAL AREA SQUARE MILES	LAND AREA[b] SQUARE MILES
Nevada	1864	7	110,567	109,80
New Hampshire	1788[c]	46	9,351	8,968
New Jersey	1787[c]	47	8,722	7,419
New Mexico	1912	5	121,598	121,365
New York	1788[c]	27	54,475	47,224
North Carolina	1789[c]	28	53,821	48,718
North Dakota	1889	19	70,704	68,994
Ohio	1803	34	44,828	40,953
Oklahoma	1907	20	69,903	68,679
Oregon	1859	9	98,386	96,003
Pennsylvania	1787[c]	33	46,058	44,820
Rhode Island	1790[c]	50	1,545	1,045
South Carolina	1788[c]	40	32,007	30,111

STATES OF THE UNITED STATES: ADMISSION DATES AND 1990 LAND AREA[a] (CONT.)

STATE	YEAR OF ADMISSION TO STATEHOOD	TOTAL AREA RANK	TOTAL AREA SQUARE MILES	LAND AREA[b] SQUARE MILES
South Dakota	1889	17	77,121	75,898
Tennessee	1796	36	42,146	41,220
Texas	1845	2	268,601	261,914
Utah	1896	13	84,904	82,168
Vermont	1791	45	9,615	9,249
Virginia	1788[c]	35	42,769	39,598
Washington	1889	18	71,303	66,582
West Virginia	1863	41	24,231	24,087
Wisconsin	1848	23	65,503	54,314
Wyoming	1890	10	97,818	97,105

[a] U.S. Bureau of the Census, unpublished date reprinted in Statistical Abstract of the United States, 1991, 201.

[b] HSUS 70, 38. Dry land and land temporarily or partially covered by water, such as marshland, swamps, etc.; streams and canals under one-eighth statute mile wide; and lakes, reservoirs, and ponds under 40 acres.

[c] Year of ratification of Constitution; one of the original 13 States.

Glossary of Terms

Introduction

"The Problem of Historical Statistics" is a subdivision of the introduction to Historical Statistics of the United States, Colonial Times to 1970 (HSUS 70) (Washington, D.C.: GPO, 1975), Part I, xii. The concluding paragraph is:

> Impediments to the use of historical statistics,...include the initial difficulty of determining whether the data in fact exist, of identifying the document in which the data may be found, of constructing time series where the data may not be arranged in suitable form, and of identifying and interpreting changes in concept and coverage. Definitions employed in published historical tables, moreover, may have to be sought in separate publications if, indeed, they have been published at all.

The candidness of the last few words is instructive. Historically many items in the census have not been adequately defined. Many general descriptions were no doubt deliberately vague because the nature of the collection or processing dictated at least this type of qualification, e.g. personnel conducting the census interpreted the census questions (and type of answers sought) differently which weakened the cumulative data. As the above quote concludes, in some cases needed definitions apparently were never published.

Historical Statistics of the States of the United States (HSSUS 93), an initial effort at compiling state-level data for the entire federal census-taking period, focused on data with less definition problems. The attempt to collect and present useable 1790-1990 statistics with maximum value for specific years and comparable for as many years as possible is a major reason for the selection of the data that is included and the omission of data that is not included. Of course the prime reason for omitting categories a contemporary user of the census may deem logical is because the data was not available in the 19th century. A large part of the Population section begins in 1790, Agriculture in 1850, and Manufacturing in 1899 (and a 1850-1890 table is included for statistics generally comparable for that period).

Perhaps an amazing qualifying statement to a casual user of historical data in the census but understandable to more in-depth users is the final paragraph of the introduction to HSUS 70 under the subtitle "Statistical Reliability and Responsibility":

> The contents of this volume were obtained from a large number of sources. All data from either censuses and surveys or based on estimates or administrative records are subject to error arising from a number of sources: Sampling variability (for statistics based on samples), reporting errors in the data for individual units, incomplete coverage, nonresponse, imputation, and processing error. The Bureau of the Census cannot accept responsibility for the accuracy or the limitations of data presented here, other than for those which it collects. Every attempt has been made, within the limits of time and available personnel, to verify and correctly identify the material. Final responsibility for selection of the material, and for its accurate and proper presentation, rests with the Bureau of the Census, even though carried out with the cooperation of many individuals and agencies who devoted much time and energy in providing data and descriptions of series for this publication.

In the same vein the compiler of HSSUS 93 recognizes that the selections and omissions of data herein, the determination of accuracy and workable comparability (within certain limitations), and the total presentation is the responsibility of the compiler. One final note: the user of historical statistics from the census must be cautious, but at the same time, he knows there is no better systematic source of information for the subjects and dates covered. Except as noted in the source notes, the following pages of the Glossary were excerpted verbatim from the source cited.

POPULATION

History[1]

The principal source of population data is the Decennial Census of Population, a house-by-house enumeration made by the Bureau of the Census. In accordance with a Constitutional provision for a decennial canvass of the population, the first census enumeration was made in 1790. The primary reason for the Census of Population, as set forth in the Constitution, is to provide a basis for the apportionment of Members of the House of Representatives among the several States. Until 1902, the census organization was temporary. It was assembled before each decennial census and disbanded after the work was finished. In 1902, the Bureau of the Census was established as permanent agency of the Government, charged with responsibility for the decennial census and for compiling statistics on other subjects as needed.

In accordance with census practice dating back to 1790, each person is counted as an inhabitant of his usual place of residence or usual place of abode, that is, the place where he lives and sleeps most of the time. This place is not necessarily the same as his legal residence, voting residence, or domicile, although, in the vast majority of cases, the use of these different bases of classification would produce identical results. Indians living in Indian Territory or on reservations were not included in the population count until 1890, and in earlier censuses large tracts of unorganized and sparsely settled territory were not covered by enumerators. Alaska and Hawaii were territories through 1950 and were first included in the United States in the 1960 census. Many tables show two sets of 1960 data, one for the conterminous United States and one for the United States including Alaska and Hawaii.

Through 1930, the data presented are based on complete counts. Many of the data shown from subsequent censuses are based on sample tabulations (ranging from 3 1/3 percent to 25 percent), as indicated in footnotes to the tables.

Exact agreement is not to be expected among the various samples, nor between them and the complete census count, but the sample data may be used with confidence where large numbers are involved, and may be assumed to indicate patterns and relationships where small numbers are involved. Detailed statements regarding the sampling errors are given in the original sources.

The Bureau of the Census has always been concerned about the degree of completeness of enumeration in the decennial censuses, although public interest in census coverage and statistical techniques for estimating coverage were quite limited prior to 1950. Discussions of coverage in earlier censuses were limited mostly to qualitative statements.

While the earlier census no doubt were characterized by under-enumeration, the amounts generally are difficult to determine. One technique is the comparison of rates of change with respect to consistency and reasonableness. On this basis, it is believed that figures for the South show unreasonably low rates of increase for the decade 1860-1870 and abnormally high rates of increase for 1870-1880. The differences are so great that it appears evident that the enumeration of 1870 in this area was seriously incomplete, undoubtedly as a result of the unsettled conditions of the Reconstruction period. For the portion of the United States outside the South, the rate of increase for 1860-1870 was about the same as for 1870-1880. Therefore, the number initially enumerated in 1870 for the South was revised upward. For a detailed discussion of the adjustment, see U.S. Census of Population: 1890, vol.I, pp. xi-xii.

Race[2]

The concept of race as used by the Census Bureau reflects self-identification; it does not denote any clear-cut scientific definition of biological stock. The data for race represent self-classification by people according to the race with which they most closely identify. Furthermore, it is recognized that the categories of the race item include both racial and national origin or socio-cultural groups.

During direct interviews conducted by enumerators, if a person could not provide a single response to the race question, he or she was asked to select, based on self-identification, the group which best described his or her racial identity. If a person could not provide a single race response, the race of the mother was used. If a single race response could not be provided for the person's mother, the first race reported by the person was used. In all cases where occupied housing units, household, or families are classified by race, the race of the householder was used.

The racial classification used by the Census Bureau generally adheres to the guidelines in Federal Statistical Directive No. 15, issued by the Office of Management and Budget, which provides standards on ethnic and racial categories for statistical reporting to be used by all Federal agencies. The racial categories used in the 1990 census data products are provided below.

White - Includes persons who indicated their race as "White" or reported entries such as Canadian, German, Italian, Lebanese, Near Easterner, Arab, or Polish.

Black - Includes persons who indicated their race as "Black or Negro" or reported entries such as African American, Afro-American, Black Puerto Rican, Jamaican, Nigerian, West Indian, or Haitian.

Historical comparability:[3] Questions on "race or "color" have been asked in each census since 1790. In 1970, when persons with parents of different races were in doubt as to their classification, the race of the father was used. In 1980, the race of the mother was used for persons who could not provide a single response. The 1970 category "Negro or Black" has been retitled "Black or Negro."

Urban and Rural[4]

The Census Bureau defines "urban" for the 1990 census as comprising all territory, population, and housing units in urbanized areas and in places of 2,500 or more persons outside urbanized areas. More specifically, "urban" consists of territory, persons, and housing units in:

1. Places of 2,500 or more persons incorporated as cities, villages, boroughs (except in Alaska and New York), and towns (except in the six New England States, New York, and Wisconsin), but excluding the rural portions of "extended cities."

2. Census designated places of 2,500 or more persons.

3. Other territory, incorporated or unincorporated, included in urbanized areas.

Territory, population, and housing units not classified as urban constitute "rural." In the 100-percent data products, "rural" is divided into "places of less than 2,500" and "not in places." The "not in places" category comprises "rural" outside incorporated and census designated places and the rural portions of extended cities. In many data products, the term "other rural" is used; "other rural" is a residual category specific to the classification of the rural in each data product.

In the sample data products, rural population and housing units are subdivided into "rural farm" and "rural nonfarm." "Rural farm" comprises all rural households and housing units on farms (places from which $1,000 or more of agricultural products were sold in 1989); "rural nonfarm" comprises the remaining rural.

The urban and rural classification cuts across the other hierarchies; for example, there is generally both urban and rural territory within both metropolitan and nonmetropolitan areas.

In censuses prior to 1950, "urban" comprised all territory, persons, and housing units in incorporated places of 2,500 or more persons, and in areas (usually minor civil divisions) classified as urban under special rules relating to population size and density. The definition of urban that restricted itself to incorporated places having 2,500 or more persons excluded many large, densely settled areas merely because they were not incorporated. Prior to the 1950 census, the Census Bureau attempted to avoid some of the more obvious omissions by classifying selected areas as "urban under special rules." Even with these rules, however, many large, closely built-up areas were excluded from the urban category.

To improve its measure of urban territory, population, and housing units, the Census Bureau adopted the concept of the urbanized area and delineated boundaries for unincorporated places (now, census designated places) for the 1950 census. Urban was defined as territory, persons, and housing units in urbanized areas and, outside urbanized areas, in all places, incorporate or unincorporated, that had 2,500 or more persons. With the following three exceptions, the 1950 census definition of urban has continued substantially unchanged. First, in the 1960 census (but not in the 1970, 1980, or 1990 censuses), certain towns in the New England States, townships in New Jersey and Pennsylvania, and Arlington County, Virginia, were designated as urban. However, most of these "special rule" areas would have been classified as urban anyway because they were included in an urbanized area or in an unincorporated place of 2,500 or more persons. Second, "extended cities" were identified for the 1970, 1980, and 1990 censuses. Extended cities primarily affect the figures for urban and rural territory (area), but have very little effect on the urban and rural population and housing units at the national and State levels--although for some individual counties and urbanized areas, the effects have been more evident. Third, changes since the 1970 census in the criteria for defining urbanized areas have permitted these areas to be defined around smaller centers.

Documentation of the urbanized area and extended city criteria is available from the Chief, Geography Division, U.S. Bureau of the Census, Washington, DC 20233.

AGRICULTURE

History[5]

Beginning 1840, a census of agriculture has been taken every 10 years and, beginning 1925, a mid-decade census of agriculture has also been taken. Census information was obtained by a personal canvass of individual farms until 1969, when for the first time the Census Bureau shifted to a questionnaire mailed to persons or organization associated with agricultural operations in the Nation to be completed by them and returned by mail.

The first census was limited in scope. It included such items as an inventory of the principal classes of domestic animals, the production of work, the value of poultry, the value of dairy products, and the production of principal crops. The number of farms and the acreage and value of farmland were first included in 1850 and information on farm tenure was first obtained in 1880. A detailed classification of farmland according to use was first obtained in 1925; in earlier censuses, farmland was classified only as improved land, woodland, and other unimproved land. For brief discussions of the comparability of various agriculture data, census to census, see Bureau of The Census, U.S. Census of Agriculture: 1969, Vol. II, Chapter 1-2.

For each decade from 1840 through 1900, the census of agriculture was taken as of June 1. The five decennial censuses since then have been taken as of April 15, 1910; January 1, 1920; April 1, 1930, 1940, and 1950. The 1925, 1935, and 1945 quinquennial censuses of agriculture were taken as of January 1; the 1954, 1959, and 1964 censuses were taken during October and November. For the 1969 census the report forms were mailed to farm operators in the last week of December, 1969. The reports covered production and sales for the 1969 calendar year, with livestock inventories as of December 31, 1969. For 1969, data for farms with less than $2,500 are based on a 50-percent sample of these farms.

The 1987 Census of Agriculture was the 23d taken by the U.S. Department of Commerce, Bureau of the Census. From 1954 to 1974, a census of agriculture was taken for the years ending in 4 and 9. In 1976, Congress authorized the census of agriculture to be taken for 1978 and 1982 to adjust the data reference year so that it coincided with the economic censuses covering manufacturing, mining, construction, retail trade, wholesale trade, service industries, and selected transportation activities. This adjustment in timing established the agriculture census on a 5-year cycle collecting data for years ending in 2 and 7.[6]

Farm

Since 1850, when minimum criteria defining a farm for census purposes first were established, the farm definition has been changed nine times. The current definition, first used for the 1974 census, is any place from which $1,000 or more of agricultural products were produced and sold or normally would have been sold during the census year.[7]

For the 1959, 1964, and 1969 censuses, census farms comprised places on which agricultural operations were conducted at any time under the control or supervision of one person, a partnership, or a manager. Places of less than 10 acres were counted as farms if the estimated sales of agricultural products for the year amounted to $150 or more. Places of less than 3 acres were counted as farms if the estimated sales of agricultural products for the year amounted or normally would amount to at least $250. Places of 10 or more acres were counted as farms if the estimated sales of agricultural products for the year amounted or normally would amount to at least $50.[8]

For the 1954 Census of Agriculture, places of 3 or more acres were counted as farms if the annual value of agricultural products for sale or home use (exclusive of home-garden products) amounted to $150 or more. Places of less than 3 acres were counted as farms only if the annual value of sales of agricultural products amounted to $150 or more. Places for which the value of agricultural products for 1954 was less than these minimums because of crop failure or other unusual conditions and places operated for the first time in 1954 were counted as farms if normally they could be expected to produce these minimum quantities of agricultural products.

If a place had croppers or other tenants, the land assigned each one was considered a separate farm, even though the landlord handled the entire holding as one operating unit in respect to supervision, equipment, rotation practice, purchase of supplies, or sale of products. Land retained by the landlord and worked by him with the help of his family and/or hired labor was likewise considered a farm.

For the 1950 Census of Agriculture, the definition of a farm was the same as for 1954. For the 1945 and earlier censuses, the definition of a farm was somewhat more inclusive. For 1925-1945, farms included (1) places of 3 or more acres on which there were agricultural operations and (2) places of less than 3 acres if the agricultural products for home use or for sale were valued at $250 or more. The only reports excluded from the 1925-1940 tabulations were those taken in error and those with very limited agricultural production, such as only a small home garden, a few fruit trees, a very small flock of chickens, etc. In 1945, reports for places of 3 acres or more with limited agricultural operations were retained only if (1) there were 3 or more acres of cropland and pasture or (2) the value of products in 1944 amounted to $150 or more.

The definition of a farm in the 1910 and 1920 censuses was similar to that used from 1925 to 1940 but was even more inclusive. In those years, farms of less than 3 acres with products valued at less than $250 were to be included provided they required the continuous services of at least one person. In 1900, there were no acreage or production limits. Market, truck, and fruit gardens, orchards, nurseries, cranberry marshes, greenhouses, and city dairies were to be included provided the entire time of at least one person was devoted to their care. For 1870, 1880, and 1890, no tract of less then 3 acres was to be reported as a farm unless $500 worth of produce was sold from it during the year. For 1860, no definition was given the enumerators. For 1850, no acreage qualification was given, but there was a lower limit of $100 for value of products.[9]

Comparability of Data

Data on acreages and inventories for 1987 and 1982 are generally comparable. Dollar figures shown for expenses and agricultural product sales are expressed in current dollars and have not been adjusted for inflation or deflation. In general, data for censuses since 1974 are not fully comparable with data for 1969 and earlier censuses due to changes in the farm definition.

The 1978 U.S., region, and State data shown in the 1978 Census of Agriculture publications included data for farms on the mail list plus estimates from an area sample for farms not on the mail list. For comparability, the 1978 data in the 1987 publications include only farms on the mail list.[10]

Land-Use Classifications, 1850-1920

From 1850 to 1920 all land in farms was classified as "improved" and "unimproved." In general, improved land included land in crops; land in pasture that had been cleared or tilled; land lying fallow; land in orchards, nurseries, vineyards, and gardens; and land occupied by buildings.

Cropland harvested for 1879 to 1919 was obtained by adding the acreages of the individual crops harvested for these censuses.[11]

Cropland Harvested, 1929-1969

The 1969 definition included land from which crops were harvested; land from which hay (including wild hay) was cut; and land in small fruits, orchards, vineyards, nurseries, and greenhouses. Land from which two crops or more were harvested was counted only once in the land-use section. However, in the crop sections, each crop was counted as acres of the specific crop harvested.[12]

Table 4 of Vol. II, Chapter 2, page 11 of the 1969 Census of Agriculture, listed cropland harvested as being comparable for the 1929-1969 years but not with earlier (1879-1919) years. Post-1969 definitions are similar although sometimes listed as "Harvested Cropland".[13]

Farm Values

Value of land and buildings--Respondents were asked to report their estimate of the current market value of land and buildings owned, rented or leased from others, and rented or leased to others. Market value refers to the value the land and buildings would sell for under current market conditions. If the value of land and buildings was not reported, it was estimated using the average value of land and buildings from a similar farm in the same geographic area.[14]

The value of land and buildings has been obtained for each census since 1850. The values shown for 1945 and prior censuses represent totals obtained by adding the value of land and buildings for all farms...Specific instructions for reporting the amount for which the land and buildings would sell were first given for the 1900 census. Prior to that time, the inquiries asked for "cash value" or merely "value," without further specifications.[15]

Value of livestock and poultry on farms

1987 Explanation--Data for the value of livestock and poultry on farms were obtained by multiplying the inventory of each major age and sex group by State average prices. The State average prices for cattle, hogs, sheep, Angora goats, hens and pullets of laying age, and turkeys were obtained primarily from data published by the National Agricultural Statistics Service, USDA. Prices applied to other livestock and poultry were census-derived averages based primarily on reported value of sales in the census.[16]

The 1954 Census of Agriculture contains explanations of the "Value of Livestock and Livestock Products" for the 1850-1954 years. The value was reported in one lump sum for the 1850-1890 years after which more specific listings were enumerated. Values of inventories began in 1900 and were based on state-unit prices in 1935 and 1954, and county-unit prices in 1925, 1930, 1940, 1945, and 1950. Separate values of sales were available for most livestock subdivisions for 1950 and 1954.[17]

Livestock, 1870-1970

HSUS 70[18] notes that "livestock" covered all cattle, hogs and pigs, and stock sheep for the 1870-1970 years.

Farms Operated by Owners

The 1880 Census began the "cultivated" by owner category and it was repeated in 1890. The 1900-1954 censuses broke it down into three categories; full owners, part owners, and managers.[19]

Owners are farm operators who own all or part of the land they operate. **Full owners** own all the land they operate. An owner who also rents land from others was classed as a full owner if he subrented to others all the land he rented from others, retaining and operating only land owned. **Managers** operate farms for others and are paid a wage or salary for their services.[20]

MANUFACTURING

Introduction

The manufacturing census traces its beginnings to the 1810 Decennial Census, when questions on manufacturing were included with those for population. Coverage was expanded for 1840 and subsequent censuses. In 1902, Congress established a permanent Census Bureau and directed that a census of manufactures be taken every 5 years. The 1905 manufactures census was the first time a census was taken apart from the regular every-10-year population census.[21] The census was suspended during World War II, but was resumed for 1947. Legislation enacted in 1948 provided for a census of manufactures every 5 years, with annual sample surveys authorized for interim years. The 1954 census was the first to be taken as a result of this legislation. Subsequently, the census intervals were revised and censuses were taken in 1958, 1963, 1967, 1972, 1977, 1982, and 1987.

There have been changes in scope from one census of manufactures to another. For "factories and hand and neighborhood industries," data for 1849-1899 are for all establishments with products valued at $500 or more. For "factories, excluding hand and neighborhood industries," data for 1899-1919 are for establishments reporting value of shipments of $500 or more; for 1921-1939, for establishments reporting value of shipments of $500 or more; for 1921-1939, for establishments reporting value of shipments of $5,000 or more, while data beginning 1947 are for establishments employing one or more persons at any time during the census years. These changes in the minimum size limit have not appreciably affected the historical comparability of the census figures except for data on number of establishments.

There have also been a number of changes in the definition of manufacturing industries. Among the more important were changes in the treatment of "railroad repair shops" and "manufactured gas." These industries are included in the figures for 1899-1933, but excluded for 1935-1970. When the change results in the omission of an entire industry for which separate tabulations are available during each census, the adjustments are usually carried back through the previous censuses. Beginning 1954, the figures cover the logging camps and contractors industry, which was not included within the scope of the 1947 census; and establishments engaged in the processing and distribution of fluid milk, which were not included in the figures for earlier census years. Beginning 1958, the figures cover establishments classified in the ready-mixed concrete industry, and establishments classified in the miscellaneous machinery industry that were engaged exclusively or almost exclusively in machine shop repair work. Data for such establishments are excluded for 1939 to 1957 but included for 1929 and earlier years.

For a discussion of changes between 1929 and 1958, see U.S. Bureau of the Census, *Census Working Paper*, No. 9, 1959, by Harold T. Goldstein. There have been no major changes since 1958.[22]

1850-1890 Manufacturing

Manufacturing Establishments: The Censuses of 1850 to 1920 use the term "manufacturing establishment" to designate factories or plants whose products were valued at $500 or more.[23]

Capital: The form of the inquiry regarding capital, at all censuses from 1850 to and including 1880, was so vague and general in its character that it cannot be assumed that any true proportion exists between the statistics on this subject as elicited prior to 1890.[24] The censuses from 1890 through 1920 contain data on capital which was compiled on the basis of more specific instructions; however, its value is limited to comparisons of very general conditions.[25] At the census of 1880, the question on capital read: "Capital (real and personal) invested in the business." At the Census of 1890, live capital, i.e., cash on hand, bills receivable, unsettled ledger accounts, raw materials, stock in process of manufacture, finished products on hand, and other sundries, was for the first time included as a separate and distinct item of capital, and the capital invested in realty was divided between land, buildings, and machinery. The form of inquiry in 1890 and 1900 was so similar that comparison may safely be made.[26]

Average number of Wage Earners: At the censuses of 1850, 1860, and 1870, the inquiries regarding employees called for "average number of hands employed." The inquiries of 1880 were similar. In the Census of 1890 the average number of persons employed during the entire year was called for; and the average number was computed for the actual time the establishments were reported as being in operation. at the census of 1900 the greatest and least numbers of employees were reported, and also the average number employed during each month of the year. The average number of wage earners (men, women, and children) employed during the entire year was computed in the Census office by using 12, the number of calendar months, as a divisor into the total of the average numbers reported for each month. This difference in the method of ascertaining the average number of wage-earners during the entire year has resulted in a variation in the average number as between these two censuses, and should be considered in making comparisons.

The schedules for 1890 included in the wage-earning class "overseers and foremen or superintendents (not general superintendents or managers)," while the census of 1900 separated from the wage-earning class such salaried employees as general superintendents, clerks, and salesmen. Therefore this item varies in exactness.[27]

Manufacturing: The Census of 1900 and earlier censuses included establishments engaged in the neighborhood, household, and hand industries. The number of establishments canvassed was therefore relatively far greater at these earlier censuses than at the censuses following 1900, but as the establishments in the neighborhood, household, and hand industries are for the most part small, the other criteria show less change. For comparative purposes the statistics for 1899 (but not 1900) have been revised by the Bureau of the Census so as to exclude these neighborhood, household, and hand industries. The censuses of 1909 and 1910 and later years were confined to manufacturing establishments conducted under what is known as the factory system, exclusive of the so-called neighborhood, household, and hand industries.[28]

General Statistics for Manufacturing Establishments, 1899-1989

Number of establishments. The reporting units in each census have been establishments rather than legal entities or companies. Conceptually, an establishment is a geographically isolated manufacturing unit maintaining independent bookkeeping records, regardless of its managerial or financial affiliations. An establishment may be a single plant or, a group of closely located plants operated by a single company without separate records for each. The establishment is also the basic unit of industrial classification, being assigned to an industry on the basis of its reported product of chief total value. Establishments owned and operated by the Federal government are excluded from census coverage.[29]

Persons Engaged in Manufacturing. The figures for 1939-1970 exclude personnel reported by manufacturing establishments as in distribution and in construction work (the 1939 and subsequent censuses required separate reporting for such employees). Therefore, the employee figures for earlier years probably are not strictly comparable with those for 1939-1970. It is not known how many of the wage earners and the salaried employees reported in previous censuses were engaged in distribution and construction, and how many were engaged in manufacturing. The figures for nonproduction employees are derived by subtracting the figures for production workers from those for all employees shown in the source. For nonproduction employees, series P4, the figures for 1939 and earlier years refer to one payroll period, usually in October; for 1947, to an average of 12 monthly figures; for 1949 to 1954, to an average for the payroll period ended nearest the 12th of March, May, August, and November; and for 1955 to 1970, to the payroll period ended nearest the 12th of March. For production workers, series P 5, the figures for 1947 and earlier years represent the average of 12 monthly figures; for 1949 to 1970, they are based on employment for the payroll period ended nearest the 12th of March, May, August, and November.

Employees comprise all full-time and part-time employees on the payrolls of operating establishments who worked or received pay for any part of the pay period specified on the report form. Officers of corporations are included as employees; proprietors and partners of unincorporated firms are, however, excluded from the total. In recent censuses, employment at separate administrative offices and auxiliary units is excluded from this category.

There has not been a consistent treatment of employees in central administrative offices. The latter are defined as offices which operate one or more manufacturing plants located in a city or cities other than that in which the administrative office is located. For the censuses of 1909-1923, data on employees in such offices were collected on a separate "administrative schedule" and were tabulated and included with those for salaried employees (and, therefore, with all employees) of the manufacturing plants. Thereafter, these data were collected and tabulated for the censuses of 1925, 1929, and 1937. Beginning 1954, separate data on employment in administrative offices and auxiliary establishments were compiled in census years and are shown in census of manufactures publications. The figures for nonproduction employees for 1925 and 1929 include employees in central administrative offices. To make the 1937 figure for nonproduction employees more comparable to the figures for 1929 and earlier years (except 1927), 130,854 employees in central administrative offices should be added to the 1937 figure (*1937 Census of Manufactures*, p. 1652), and to make the 1954 figure more comparable to the figures for 1929 and earlier years (except 1927), 474,256 employees in administrative and auxiliary units should be added to the 1954 figure (*U.S. Census of Manufactures: 1954*, vol. II, part 1, p. 2).

Collection of data on proprietors and partners was discontinued after the 1963 census.

Production workers are defined as workers (up through the working foreman level) engaged in fabricating, processing, assembling, inspection, receiving, storage, handling, packing, warehousing, shipping (but not delivering), maintenance, repair, janitorial, watchman services, product development, auxiliary production for plants' own use (e.g., power plant), recordkeeping, and other services closely associated with these production operations at the establishment covered by the report. Supervisory employees above the working foreman level are excluded from this category.

Decennial estimates of wage earners (production and related workers) excluding hand and neighborhood industries have been prepared for 1869-1899 by John W. Kendrick and Maude Pech for the National Bureau of Economic Research. The following is the estimated number of wage earners for each of these years; 1869, 1,803,000; 1879, 2,454,000; 1889, 3,562,000; 1899, 4,496,000. This estimate for 1899 differs from the official Census bureau estimate by only one-tenth of one percent. For details of estimating procedure, see John W. Kendrick, *Productivity Trends in the United States*, National Bureau of Economic Research, New York, 1961, appendix D.[30]

Man-hours, production workers. This series covers all plant man-hours of production and related workers. It represents all man-hours worked or paid for except hours paid for vacations, holidays, or sick leave and includes actual overtime hours. Where employees elected to work during vacation periods, only the actual hours they worked were reported. The man-hour figures issued by the Census Bureau differ from those published by the Bureau of Labor Statistics which cover all hours paid for, whether or not worked.[31]

Payroll. These figures include gross earnings paid in the calendar year to all employees on the payroll of operating manufacturing establishments. They include all forms of compensation such as salaries, wages, commissions, dismissal pay, all bonuses, vacation and sick leave pay, and compensation in kind, prior to such deductions as employees' Social Security contributions, withholding taxes, group insurance, union dues, and savings bonds. Salaries of officers of these establishments are included for corporations; payments to proprietors and partners are excluded for unincorporated concerns. Also excluded are payments to members of Armed Forces and pensionsers carried on the active payrolls of manufacturing establishments. Employers' Social Security contributions or other nonlabor costs such as pension plans, group insurance, and workmen's compensation are also excluded.[32]

Value added by manufacture. The standard formula for calculating value added by manufacture since 1958 differs from the one used for 1954 and earlier years. Prior to 1958, the value added of an establishment was calculated by subtracting the cost of materials, supplies, containers, fuels, purchased electric energy, and contract work from the value of shipments for products manufactured plus miscellaneous receipts for services rendered. This is known as unadjusted value added. Beginning 1958, the measure of value added has been adjusted for each establishment in two respects. Value added now includes: (1) Value added by merchandising, i.e., the difference between the sales value and cost of merchandise sold without further manufacture, processing or assembly; and (2) an adjustment for the net change in finished goods and work-in-process inventories between the beginning and end of the year. The resulting figure is the adjusted value added. This procedure avoids the duplication in the "value of shipments" figures which results from the use of products of some establishments as materials by other.[33]

Capital expenditures, new. Manufacturers were asked to report expenditures made during the year for permanent additions and major alterations to their plants, as well as for new machinery and equipment purchases that were chargeable to fixed-asset accounts of manufacturing establishments and were of a type for which depreciation accounts are ordinarily maintained. Excluded are costs of maintenance and repairs charges as current operating expense, new facilities and equipment leased from other companies, new facilities owned by the Federal Government but operated under contract by private companies, and plant and equipment furnished to manufactures by communities and organizations. Beginning 1951, the figures include expenditures for plants under construction and not yet in operation. (In the series by major groups, however, such expenditures are included beginning only in 1958.)[34]

Special treatment of very small establishments--Beginning with the 1967 census, an effort was made to relieve the very small establishments from the necessity of filing a census report. Approximately 155,000 small single-establishment manufacturing firms identified as having up to 20 employees (cutoff varied by industry) benefited from this procedure for 1987. Limited data on payrolls, sales, and industry classificaiton from the administrative records of the Social Security Administration (SSA) and the Internal Revenue Service (IRS) were made available to the Census Bureau. (These special arrangements safeguarded the confidentiality of both tax and census records.) Estimates of data for these small establishments were developed using industry averages in conjunction with the administrative information. The effect on industry aggregates is slight in most industries; for manufacturing as a whole, these small administrative records account for only 2.2 percent of the value added. Detailed product and materials data for these small establishments were not estimated: the entire value of product shipments and cost of materials was inputed to a "not specified by kind" (n.s.k.) category. Nevertheless, the total establishment counts in most industries should be viewed as approximations rather than precise measurements. The counts for establishments with 20 employees or more are far more reliable than the total number of establishments.[35]

---

[1] Historical Statistics of the United States: Colonial Times to 1970 (Washington, D.C.: GPO, 1975), Part I.

[2] Ibid., B-11.

[3] Bureau of the Census, Users' Guide, Part B, Glossary, 1980 Census of Population and Housing, (Washington, D.C.: GPO, November, 1982), 39.

[4] Bureau of the Census, 1990 Census of Population and Housing: Summary Population and Housing Characteristics United States (Washington, D.C.: GPO, March, 1992), A-11, A-12.

[5] HSUS 70, Part I, 449.

[6] Bureau of the Census, 1987 Census of Agriculture, Volume I, Part 51, (Washington, D.C.: GPO, November 1989), vii.

[7] Ibid.

[8] HSUS 70, Part I, 449.

[9] Ibid., See Census of Agriculture: 1959 Volume II, General Report Statistics by Subjects, xxvi-xxvii On "Minimum Criteria for Census Farm of 3 or more Acres: Census of 1850 to 1959."

[10] 1987 Census of Agriculture, Volume 1, Part 51, viii.

[11] Bureau of the Census, Census of Agriculture, 1969, Volume II, General Report, Chapter 2, Farms, 10.

[12] Ibid., 8.

[13] 1987 Census of Agriculture, Volume I, Part 51, Appendix A, A-4 paraphrased.

[14] Ibid., A-3.

[15] 1969 Census of Agriculture, Volume XI, Chapter 2, 13.

[16] 1987 Census of Agriculture, Volume I, Part 51, Appendix A, A-8.

[17] Bureau of the Census, Census of Agriculture: 1954, Volume II, General Report, Statistics By Subject (Washington, D.C.: GPO, 1956), Table 3, 436-439 paraphrased.

[18] Part I, 451.

[19] U.S. Census of Agriculture: 1954, Volume II, 943 paraphrased. Table 1 gives the U.S. totals for 1880-1890 and the 1900-1954 subdivisions.

[20] Ibid.

[21] Bureau of the Census, 1987 Census of Manufacturing Subject Series, General Summary (Washingtion, D.C.: GPO, March, 1991), v-vi.

[22] HSUS 70, Part II, 652-653.

[23] Bureau of the Census. Census of Manufactures: 1963, Volume I, 5-9.

[24] Bureau of the Census. Twelfth Census of the United States: 1900, Volume VIII, Part. II, viii.
[25] Bureau of the Census. Fourteenth Census of the United States: 1920, Volume IX, 17.
[26] Bureau of the Census. Twelfth Census of the United States: 1900, Volume VIII, Part.II, viii.
[27] Ibid.
[28] Bureau of the Census. Thirteenth Census of the United States: 1910, Volume VIII, 19.
[29] HSUS 70, 653-654.
[30] Ibid.
[31] Ibid.
[32] Ibid.
[33] Ibid.
[34] Ibid.
[35] 1987 Census of Manufacturing: General Summary, xiii-xiv.

Endnotes

1. U.S. Bureau of the Census. *U.S. Census of Population: 1970*, Volume I, Part 1, Sec. 1, pp. 48-49.
2. U.S. Bureau of the Census. *U.S. Census of Population: 1970*, Volume I, Part 1, pp. 1-50.
3. U.S. Bureau of the Census. *Twelfth Census of the U.S.: 1900*, Volume I, Part 1, pp. 4-5.
4. U.S. Bureau of the Census. *U.S. Census of Population: 1970*, Volume I, Part 1, pp. 1-51.
5. U.S. Bureau of the Census. *U.S. Census of Population: 1970*, Volume I, Part 1, pp. 1-52.
6. U.S. Bureau of the Census. *Statistical Abstract of the U.S.: 1940*, p. 6.
7. U.S. Bureau of the Census. *U.S. Census of Population: 1970*, Volume I, Part 1, pp. 1-53.
8. U.S. Bureau of the Census. *Negro Population 1790-1915* (1918), pp. 44-45.
9. U.S. Bureau of the Census. *Statistical Abstract of the U.S.: 1942*, pp. 12-13.
10. U.S. Bureau of the Census. *Statistical Abstract of the U.S.: 1972*, p. 28.
11. U.S. Bureau of the Census. *Twelfth Census of the U.S.: 1900, Special Reports of the Census Office, Supplementary Analysis*, pp. 242-246.
12. U.S. Bureau of the Census. *Abstract of the Fourteenth Census of the U.S.: 1920*, p. 105.
13. U.S. Bureau of the Census. *Abstract of the Fifteenth Census of the U.S.: 1930*, p. 89.
14. U.S. Bureau of the Census. *Fifteenth Census of the U.S.: 1930*, Volume 11, Population, p. 38.
15. U.S. Bureau of the Census. *Statistical Abstract of the U.S.: 1972*, p. 28.
16. U.S. Bureau of the Census. *A Century of Population Growth in the U.S. 1790-1900*, p. 133.
17. U.S. Bureau of the Census. *U.S. Census of the Population: 1970*, Volume I, Part 1, Sec. 1, pp. 62-71.
18. U.S. Bureau of the Census. *U.S. Census of Agriculture: 1959*, Volume II, *General Report, Statistics by Subject*, pp. 53-64.
19. U.S. Bureau of the Census. *U.S. Census of Agriculture: 1969*, Volume II, *General Report*, pp. 21-27, 64.
20. U.S. Bureau of the Census. *Abstract of the Fourteenth Census of the U.S.: 1920*, pp. 590-599.
21. U.S. Bureau of the Census. *Twelfth Census of the U.S. Taken in the Year 1900, Agriculture*, Part 1, pp. 688-689.
22. U.S. Bureau of the Census. *Abstract of the Fourteenth Census of the U.S.: 1920*, p. 630.
23. U.S. Bureau of the Census. *Statistical Abstract of the U.S.: 1940*, pp. 644-645.
24. U.S. Bureau of the Census. *Statistical Abstract of the U.S.: 1941*, pp. 682-683.
25. U.S. Bureau of the Census. *Statistical Abstract of the U.S.: 1960*, p. 628.
26. U.S. Bureau of the Census. *Statistical Abstract of the U.S.: 1962*, p. 619.
27. U.S. Bureau of the Census. *1969 Census of Agriculture*, Volume II, *General Report*, pp. 23-24.
28. U.S. Bureau of the Census. *Twelfth Census of the U.S. Taken in the Year 1900, Agriculture*, Part 1, pp. 700-701, Part II, pp. 700-701.
29. U.S. Bureau of the Census. *Abstract of the Fourteenth Census of the U.S.: 1920*, pp. 752-753, 860.
30. U.S. Bureau of the Census. *U.S. Census of Agriculture: 1959*, Volume II, *General Report, Statistics by Subject*, pp. 497, 829, 835.
31. U.S. Bureau of the Census. *U.S. Census of Agriculture: 1945*, Volume II, *General Report, Statistics by Subject*, pp. 466-467, 474-475, 496.
32. U.S. Bureau of the Census. *Statistical Abstract of the U.S.: 1952*, p. 621.
33. U.S. Bureau of the Census. *U.S. Census of Agriculture: 1909 and 1910*, pp. 591, 592, 601, 641.
34. U.S. Bureau of the Census. *Sixteenth Census of the U.S. 1940, Agriculture*, Volume III, pp. 780-781.
35. U.S. Bureau of the Census. *U.S. Census of Agriculture: 1959, Volume II, General Report, Statistics by Subjects*, pp. 722-723, 740-741.
36. U.S. Department of Agriculture. *Agricultural Statistics 1972*, pp. 2-4, 36, 44-45, 76, 125, 162-163, 320, 359, 398-399, 506-509, 564-565.
37. U.S. Bureau of the Census. *Twelfth Census of the U.S. Taken in the Year 1900*, Volume VI, *Agriculture*, Part 2, pp. 80-81.
38. U.S. Bureau of the Census. *U.S. Census of Agriculture: 1959*, Volume II, *General Report, Statistics by Subject*, pp. 706-707.
39. U.S. Bureau of the Census. *Statistical Abstract of the U.S.: 1961*, p. 658.
40. U.S. Bureau of the Census. *U.S. Census of Agriculture: 1930*, p. 770.
41. U.S. Bureau of the Census. *U.S. Census of Agriculture: 1959, General Report, Statistics by Subjects*, pp. 770-771.
42. U.S. Bureau of the Census. *Eleventh Census of the U.S. Taken in the Year 1890, Agriculture*, pp. 95-98.
43. U.S. Bureau of the Census. *U.S. Census of Agriculture: 1959*, Volume II, *General Report, Statistics by Subject*, pp. 792-793.
44. U.S. Bureau of the Census. *Fourteenth Census of the U.S. 1920*, Volume V, *Agriculture*, pp. 794-795, 818.
45. U.S. Bureau of the Census. *Twelfth Census of the U.S. Taken in the Year 1900*, Volume VIII, Part 2, pp. 982-989.
46. U.S. Bureau of the Census. *U.S. Census of Population: 1970*, Table 10, pp. 51.
47. U.S. Bureau of the Census. *U.S. Census of Population: 1970*, Table 11, pp. 52.
48. U.S. Bureau of the Census. *U.S. Census of Population: 1970*, Table 12, pp. 53.
49. U.S. Bureau of the Census. *U.S. Census of Population: 1970*, Table 18, pp. 64.
50. U.S. Bureau of the Census. *U.S. Census of Population: 1980*, pp. 10.
51. U.S. Bureau of the Census. *U.S. Census of Population: 1980*, pp. 11.
52. U.S. Bureau of the Census. *U.S. Census of Population: 1980*, pp. 12.
53. U.S. Bureau of the Census. *U.S. Census of Population: 1980*, pp. 6.
54. U.S. Bureau of the Census. *U.S. Census of Population: 1980*, pp. 20.
55. U.S. Bureau of the Census. *U.S. Census of Population: 1980*, pp. 8.
56. U.S. Bureau of the Census. *U.S. Census of Population: 1980*, Table 12.
57. U.S. Bureau of the Census. *U.S. Census of Population: 1980*, Table 13.
58. *1990 U.S. Department of Commerce News*, Table 2.
59. *1990 U.S. Department of Commerce News*, Table 5.
60. *1990 U.S. Department of Commerce News*, Table 4.
61. *1990 U.S. Department of Commerce News*, Table 6.
62. *1990 U.S. Department of Commerce News*, Table 7.
63. U.S. Bureau of the Census. *U.S. Census of Population and Housing: 1990.* Table 8.
64. U.S. Bureau of the Census. *U.S. Census of Agriculture: 1969*, Volume II, Chapter 2, pp. 24.
65. U.S. Bureau of the Census. *U.S. Census of Agriculture: 1969*, Volume II, Chapter 2, pp. 98-101.

66. U.S. Bureau of the Census. *Statistical Abstract of the U.S.: 1972*, pp. 589.
67. U.S. Bureau of the Census. *Statistical Abstract of the U.S.: 1972*, pp. 613.
68. U.S. Bureau of the Census. *U.S. Census of Agriculture: 1974*, Volume I, Part 51, Table 1, pp. 11-2.
69. U.S. Department of Agriculture. *Agricultural Statistics 1974*, Table 3.
70. U.S. Department of Agriculture. *Agricultural Statistics 1974*, pp. 36.
71. U.S. Department of Agriculture. *Agricultural Statistics 1974*, pp. 45.
72. U.S. Department of Agriculture. *Agricultural Statistics 1974*, Table 190.
73. U.S. Bureau of the Census. *U.S. Census of Agriculture: 1982*, Volume I, Part 51, pp. 134-140.
74. U.S. Bureau of the Census. *U.S. Census of Agriculture: 1987*, Volume I, Part 51, Table 15, pp. 264-270.
75. U.S. Bureau of the Census. *U.S. Census of Agriculture: 1987*, Volume I, Part 51, pp.271-277.
76. U.S. Bureau of the Census. *U.S. Census of Agriculture: 1987*, Volume I, Part 51, pp. 144-150, Table 2, pp. 158-164.
77. U.S. Bureau of the Census. *U.S. Census of Agriculture: 1987*, Volume I, Part 51, pp. 218-225.
78. U.S. Bureau of the Census. *Statistical Abstract of the U.S.: 1990*, pp. 639.
79. U.S. Bureau of the Census. *Statistical Abstract of the U.S.: 1990*, pp. 645.
80. U.S. Department of Agriculture. *Agricultural Statistics 1991*, pp. 41.
81. U.S. Bureau of the Census. *Statistical Abstract of the U.S.: 1991*. pp. 646.
82. U.S. Department of Agriculture. *Agricultural Statistics 1991*, pp. 355.
83. U.S. Department of Agriculture. *Agricultural Statistics 1991*, pp. 63, 393.
84. U.S. Department of Agriculture. *Agricultural Statistics 1991*, pp. 5.
85. U.S. Department of Agriculture. *Agricultural Statistics 1991*, pp. 33.
86. U.S. Department of Agriculture. *Agricultural Statistics 1991*, pp. 41.
87. U.S. Department of Agriculture. *Agricultural Statistics 1991*, pp. 123.
88. U.S. Department of Agriculture. *Agricultural Statistics 1991*, pp. 234.
89. U.S. Bureau of the Census. *1967 Census of Manufactures*, Volume I, *Summary and Subject Statistics*, pp. 62-80.
90. U.S. Bureau of the Census. *1987 Census of Manufactures*, Table 3.
91. U.S. Bureau of the Census. *1989 Annual Survey of Manufactures*, Table 1.
92. U.S. Bureau of the Census. *Statistical Abstract of the U.S.: 1960*, Table 14, pp. 18-21.
93. U.S. Bureau of the Census. *U.S. Census of Population: 1970*, Table 28, pp. 1-116 through 120.
94. U.S. Bureau of the Census. *U.S. Census of Population: 1980*, Table 4 and U.S. Bureau of the Census. *U.S. Census of Population and Housing: 1990*, Table 2.
95. U.S. Bureau of the Census. *1990 U.S. Census of Population, News Brief prior to July 15, 1991.*
96. U.S. Bureau of the Census. *Statistical Abstract of the United States: 1992*, Table 38, pp. 35-37.

About the Compiler

DONALD B. DODD is Professor of History at Auburn University at Montgomery and is the author of several books, including *State and Local Government Administration* (1985).